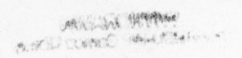

A History of Psychoanalysis

A History of Psychoanalysis

Reuben Fine

Columbia University Press · New York · 1979

Library of Congress Cataloging in Publication Data
Fine, Reuben, 1914–
    A history of psychoanalysis.

    Bibliography: p.
    1. Psychoanalysis—History. I. Title.
[DNLM: 1. Psychoanalysis—History. WM11.1 F495h]
BF173.F494   150'.19'509   78-31425
ISBN 0-231-04208-6

Columbia University Press
New York and Guildford, Surrey

To my grandchildren

in the hope that they will find a better-analyzed world

Preface

From the accidental treatment of a young hysterical girl in 1880, psychoanalysis has moved on to become a profound theory of psychotherapy, a comprehensive system of psychology, a philosophy of living, and in all areas one of the major intellectual forces of the twentieth century. This book describes how such dramatic changes came about.

No science owes as much to one man as psychoanalysis does to Freud. Accordingly his legacy is traced in considerable detail. His self-analysis is here accorded more importance in his development than is usual. There is an enormous shift in his ideas from the work of the early 1890s, which was more or less a continuation of nineteenth-century psychiatry, to the great systematization of the early 1900s, which marks the beginning of psychoanalysis and the formation of a new system of psychology.

Chapters 4 and 5 describe the growth of psychoanalytic organizations. From the four physicians who gathered in the Wednesday circle at Freud's home in 1902, the movement has grown to an international association of more than 4000 members, with thousands of other analysts unaffiliated with the official society.

In reviewing this organizational history, it would be a serious mistake to ignore the numerous splits and dissensions that have been the hallmark of psychoanalysis almost from its beginnings. Even as this is being written, a chair of psychoanalysis has been established at the Hebrew University in Jerusalem, and twelve leading analysts in Washington have resigned from their local society because they could no longer tolerate the "bad" education that had been occurring. Such is the story of psychoanalysis throughout—growth on the one hand, fratricide on the other.

The psychological and social factors at play in the splits have been given careful attention. Any history that did not offer some explanation of the constant friction in psychoanalysis would be remiss. Some of the reasons for the splits have been described in the journals, but most of the time undeclared motives have to be inferred from the actions of the participants.

Much of the book is underlain by two main theses: first, that psychoanalysis represents a comprehensive psychology which is the foundation for a unified science of man, and second, that the many ideas put forth by numerous gifted theoreticians and clinicians can be integrated into this one unified science.

Although numerous groups of psychologists have presented themselves to the public as different "schools" with varying points of view, such a presentation is highly misleading. It is my contention, documented throughout, that there is only one science, and that the emphasis on schools has been pursued primarily for personal rather than intellectual reasons. Ideas must be judged on their merit rather than on the basis of who espouses them.

In order to integrate the enormous literature of psychoanalysis, I have used the following approach. First the position of Freud in an area is given, then the alterations, contradictions, and corrections from this beginning have been described. Many persons have said the same thing in different words. It is often quite important to realize that the language may be different, yet the ideas remain the same. We have grown accustomed to old ideas presented in new dress, and must also realize that new ideas have often been rejected merely because they were put in unfamiliar terms. It is chiefly the attempt to lead up to a unified science of man that brings greater clarity, and this attempt has guided my efforts throughout the book.

In the course of gathering historical material, I have received useful communications, many of them unpublished, from all over the world. I wish to thank all the persons who have been kind enough to send information about their country or local institute. The following persons and institutes have been especially helpful. From Europe: Dr. Adam Limentani, London; Dr. Pedro Luzes, Lisbon; Dr. Daniel Limenet, Liège; Dr. Wolfgang Loch, Tübingen; Dr. Janos Paal, Frankfurt am Main; Dr. Gerhardt Maetze, Berlin; Dr. Wilhelm Solem-Rodelheim, Vienna; Dr. F. Meerwein, Zurich; also the International Psychoanalytic Association, the British Psychoanalytic Association,

the Berlin Psychoanalytic Institute, and the Deutsche Psychoana-
lytische Gesellschaft. From Canada: Dr. James Naiman, Montreal;
Dr. W. C. M. Scott, Toronto. From the United States: Dr. Sanford
Gifford, Boston; Dr. Gordon Derner, Garden City, N.Y.; Dr. Gerard
Chrzanowski, Dr. Arthur Feiner, Dr. Bernard Kalinkowitz, Dr.
Leonard Shengold, and Dr. Rose Spiegel, New York; Dr. A.
d'Amore, Washington, D.C.; Dr. George Kriegman, Richmond,
Va.; Dr. Edward J. Schiff, Cleveland; Dr. George Pollock, Chicago;
Dr. Alex H. Kaplan, St. Louis; also the American Psychoanalytic
Association and the American Academy of Psychoanalysis. From
Latin America: Dr. G. Sanchez Medina and Dr. Luis Yamin, Bogotá;
Dr. F. Aberastury and Dr. Jaime Sapilka, Buenos Aires. From Asia:
Dr. H. Ghosal and Dr. T. C. Sinha of Calcutta.

I also wish to express my gratitude to the editors at Columbia
University Press, Mr. Joe Ingram and Mrs. Maria Caliandro, for their
friendly and useful criticism.

Reuben Fine

New York
January 1979

Contents

Contents

A History of Psychoanalysis

Chapter One
The Need for Historical Perspective

As its first century of existence draws to a close, psychoanalysis is generally regarded as one of the most significant intellectual developments of the twentieth century. But this science, which emphasizes history and the historical method so strongly, has yet to have its own history accurately portrayed. Some general works in the field, such as Bromberg (1954) and more recently Ehrenwald (1976), discuss the broad history of psychotherapy. And there are a number of partisan tracts, such as Clara Thompson's *Psychoanalysis: Its Evolution and Development* (1950), which are completely one-sided and hopelessly inaccurate. Another work, by Dieter Wyss (1966), is written from a highly biased Jungian viewpoint.

Freud's own history, written in 1914, is of course invaluable, but it is relevant only for the earliest period of psychoanalysis, and then only as source material, not as a final statement. For example, even there Freud omits any extended discussion of his self-analysis, one of the epochal events in human history.

Perusal of the psychoanalytic literature reveals a paradox. Serious articles generally begin with a review of the literature, yet upon closer scrutiny it often turns out that these reviews are limited to certain sections of the literature: everything else is "irrelevant." Today this applies particularly to the two sides of the largest and longest split in the history of psychoanalysis, that between the "culturalists" and the "Freudians." Because of this split, in which neither side makes any real effort to understand the other, the wildest statements may be seen. A culturalist may proclaim that there is no Freudian literature on adolescence. Conversely, the Freudians, who in recent years have engaged in an extensive discussion of the self-image and the self-concept, never mention the pioneering work of Sullivan in this area, even though Sullivan was a bona fide member of the American Psychoanalytic Association throughout his lifetime. Many other instances could be quoted.

In *The Idea of History* (1946) the noted scholar R. G. Collingwood observed that in earlier times two types of historical writing predominated: theocratic and mythical. In theocratic history there is a glorification of some god, to whom all good is traced. Mythical history is a concoction in accordance with human wishes. While such an assessment may seem somewhat harsh, much of the historical writing about psychoanalysis still falls into these two categories. There is a constant recurrence of charismatic figures, each of whom is virtually deified by his or her followers. Instead of dealing dispassionately with issues, scholars hide behind a "point of view," which stops them from presenting their data to the public. Even though there are people alive today who knew the founder of the science, and many others who have lived through the historical events described, mythological stories are found much too frequently.

It is a common, though wholly incorrect, practice to divide psychoanalysis into different "schools," each of which is supposed to have different theories and different techniques. Yet closer examination all too often reveals that these differences are figments of the imagination or, when they do exist, are maintained with a ferocious tenacity by their partisans that does not yield to any rational discussion. Freud once commented that whole decades can go by in psychoanalytic research and the most obvious facts are still overlooked. The field is difficult; the partisan battles only make it worse.

Even as this is written, a report comes in of still another battle arising within the supposedly unified American Psychoanalytic Association.[1] A split has occurred within the ranks of the Los Angeles Psychoanalytic Institute, with the customary threats of lawsuits, accusations of intimidation and stifling of scientific progress, favoritism because of theoretical views, all similar to what has been heard time and again in the past. Even more surprising, the special committee headed by Dr. Joan Fleming frankly stated that "of much more concern was the *unrelenting hostility and distrust among various groups and individuals, whatever their theoretical orientation*" (italics added).[2] And in 1978 the *Journal of the American Psychoanalytic Association* (pp. 429–33) carried a report that 12 training and supervisory analysts of the Washington Psychoanalytic Institute had decided to leave the faculty of that institute and form one of their own, because, they said, "they have spent years attempting to abolish bad psychoanalytic teaching and example and now believe these efforts are futile."

The historian must attempt to clarify why psychoanalysis has been bedeviled by these innumerable inner conflicts, so similar in many ways to the inner conflicts that psychoanalysts find in their patients. It is essential to have a clear view of the mainstream of psychoanalytic development, from Freud onward, and to fit the various historical facts into this mainstream. Such a task requires a painstaking search of the available records. Yet once it is properly done a new synthesis emerges that clarifies the past and provides an adequate basis for further progress in the future.

The synthesis offered here is that psychoanalysis embodies first a vision of what mankind is, second a vision of what mankind can become, and third a conceptual framework within which psychological observations can be placed. According to this view, psychoanalysis is to be seen as a systematic approach to psychology, not a separate science in its own right. In this systematic approach, it touches on many separate fields, including psychiatry, sociology, anthropology, and biology. To trace all the developments in each of these fields would be confusing and superfluous; instead the emphasis will be on material that is central to the major synthesis presented.

Chapter Two

The Precursors of Psychoanalysis

The precursors of psychoanalysis may be sought, first, in certain general ideas that formed the basis of all of Western thought for several thousand years and, second, in certain specific discoveries that were made in the nineteenth century.

In general the humanistic background of Western thought was continued and preserved in psychoanalysis. It can be traced as far back as the Greek philosophers. Two of the wise sayings of the ancients, "All things in moderation" and "Know thyself," became almost verbatim precepts of psychoanalysis. They were given a more precise psychological meaning for the first time by means of a psychoanalytic approach.

Psychoanalysis has always had a broad philosophical viewpoint relying more heavily on the great works of literature and philosophy of Western thought than on the specific texts of psychology and psychiatry. Among the authors whom Freud liked, none was quoted more often than Shakespeare. Freud's psychological insights led to a renewed valuation of the insights of poets and philosophers of past centuries.

Among the more specific influences which led to the development of psychoanalysis, four in particular can be mentioned.
CHARLES DARWIN AND THE DEVELOPMENT OF BIOLOGY. The theory of evolution was the greatest scientific discovery of the nineteenth century. It laid a hold on the minds of all thinkers and scientists concerned with mankind, changing their approach once and for all. Freud in particular was more influenced by Darwin than by any other scientists of the era. Many of the major assumptions and ideas of psychoanalysis are taken over directly from evolutionary theory,

e.g., development, the process of change, and the concepts of fixation and regression.

ASSOCIATION PSYCHOLOGY. The development of the psychological idea of association, which goes far back in recorded history, was particularly prominent during the eighteenth and nineteenth centuries. Such thinkers as George Berkeley, David Hume, David Hartley, and Thomas Reid in England, and Johann Friedrich Herbart and the anthropological school of his day in Germany (with such scholars as Wilhelm von Humboldt), provided the first broad framework in which mental functioning could be understood. The crucial discovery of free association came directly out of this school.

THE GROWTH OF NEUROLOGY. It was in the nineteenth century that neurology reached its first peak as a branch of medical science. Among the leading pioneers was the Frenchman Jean Charcot, whom Freud revered as one of his greatest teachers. By the time Freud began to work in the 1880s the main outlines of the central nervous system were fairly well understood.

NINETEENTH-CENTURY PSYCHIATRY. As Ellenberger has shown in *The Discovery of the Unconscious* (1970), toward the latter part of the nineteenth century a new dynamic psychiatry was developed which had the following main characteristics:

1. Hypnotism was adopted as the main approach to the unconscious.

2. Particular attention was devoted to certain critical illnesses (sometimes called magnetic diseases)—spontaneous somnambulism, lethargy, catalepsy, multiple personality, and hysteria.

3. A new view of the human mind evolved. It was based on the quality of the conscious and unconscious psyche. Later it was modified to the form of a cluster of subpersonalities underlying the conscious personality.

4. New theories concerning the pathogenesis of nervous illnesses, based at first on the concept of an unknown fluid, were soon replaced by the concept of mental energy.

5. Psychotherapy relied mostly on the use of hypnotism and suggestion, with special attention given to the rapport between the patient and the magnetizer, later called the hypnotist.

However, it must be emphasized that the new dynamic psychiatry of the nineteenth century was developed almost entirely outside the major centers of official psychiatry. In a number of cases the new ideas in France, Germany, and the United States were fought bitterly by the academic establishment; hypnotism, for example, was considered one step removed from quackery. The heritage of this bitter battle between the new approach and the old was continued with Freud.

The Cultural Background

Technical links cannot explain the emergence of psychoanalytic thought from the past; far more important is the social and intellectual climate of the second half of the nineteenth century, which was eventually transformed by Freud into what W. H. Auden called a "whole new climate of opinion." In 1880, the date at which Josef Breuer treated Anna O., and which Freud used as the starting point of psychoanalysis, Europe was outwardly the master of the world. The imperialist powers were supreme everywhere except in the United States, the major bastion of democracy at that time. Astounding technological improvements seemed to occur daily. Few doubted that European supremacy would remain undisturbed for centuries to come. The sun never set on the British empire, and the other European imperialisms were not far behind.

Yet underneath, as historians now note with increasing frequency (e.g., Gay and Webb, 1973), there were many indications of impending disaster.[1] In the *Communist Manifesto* (1848) Marx had claimed that the specter of communism haunted Europe; although his claim was exaggerated, socialist ideals increasingly began to replace traditional capitalist and religious values. Discontent was found everywhere in Europe, but migration was still available as a way out. Between 1820 and 1930 some 62 million people left Europe; 18 million of these emigrated to the United States between 1861 and 1920. While no large-scale conflagration had occurred since the defeat of Napoleon in 1815, smaller wars occurred all the time: the Crimean War in 1854 (which cost half a million deaths)[2] and the Franco-Prussian War in 1870 were the largest. But the threat of a violent confrontation was always in the air. Gay and Webb remark that the early years of the twentieth century were marked by what can only be called moral schizophrenia:[3] in no age were the linked causes of peace and international cooperation more zealously pursued and in no age were war and conflict more passionately praised or more coolly planned for.

In this schizophrenic atmosphere, intellectuals became severe critics of society and were sharply at odds with prevailing values. Ibsen and Strindberg castigated the moral hypocrisy of the family. Flaubert made his hatred for the bourgeoisie into a program. Zola wrote devastating realistic novels. The Impressionists set off a similar upheaval in art. Walter Pater in England preached "art for art's sake," spawning a coterie of "decadents" who urged the most decisive separation of art from life. Even music, with Wagner, Stravinsky, Schoenberg, and others, underwent radical changes. When Freud began his work, modern art and the modern world were steeped in violence and change.

The Sciences in 1880

At one point or another, psychoanalysis has made contact with psychiatry, psychology, sociology, biology, anthropology, economics, literature, and a host of other scientific and humanistic areas. Actually the past can only be properly understood in terms of the future; Jakob Burckhardt once commented that history is a record of what one age finds of interest in another. Accordingly it is important to review the state of the sciences in 1880, especially those, like psychiatry and psychology, which have been most closely related to psychoanalysis.

Psychiatry

It is customary to state that the first great synthesis of modern psychiatry came with Emil Kraepelin (1856–1926). His first modest *Compendium* of 400 pages was published in 1883; eventually it evolved into the imposing ninth edition of two volumes totaling 2425 pages, which appeared in 1927, a year after his death.[4] These texts became the major source of what has since been called Kraepelinian psychiatry, which emphasized sharp diagnostic categories, especially dementia praecox (later renamed schizophrenia by Eugen Bleuler), presumed organic causation (though, at the time, with no evidence) and a feeling of therapeutic hopelessness. Furthermore, the Kraepelinian system was limited to the most severely disturbed, what today would be called the "back ward" patients.

A closer look at the historical picture reveals that Kraepelin merely was partially redressing the massacres and tortures that the mentally ill had been subjected to through the centuries, quite often at the hands of the church. As for this theoretical "system," Drabkin (1954) has shown by careful study of available texts that it was mainly a recapitulation of the classical Greek position, without the leavening effect of Greek humanism.

The Greeks (and their Roman followers) held that mental disease is essentially physiological, that there is a predisposition on the part of certain individuals to mental disease, as to other diseases, and that such predisposition is a matter of bodily constitution and temperament. This theory does not minimize the importance of psychic factors in provoking an attack of mental illness but holds that the psychic cause such as fear or anxiety, just like an external physical cause such as a wound, merely provokes the physiological process that constitutes the disease.[5] And the theory seeks to explain how this action is brought about and why, in terms of constitutional makeup, different individuals react to these psychic influences. With their recognition of the effect of psychic influences, the Greeks were actually ahead of Kraepelin.

Even more surprising is the Greek understanding of what we would call psychosomatic illness. A sense of the inseparability of the psychic and the somatic life grows out of basic human experience, and ancient literature, medical and nonmedical, has many examples of the somatic effects of emotional changes and the emotional effects of somatic changes. Bodily changes brought about by joy, love, anger, fright, grief, and so on, as well as emotional and mental changes wrought by drugs, poison, wine, by brain injuries, or by other forms of disease or deformity, can all be well documented from ancient texts.[6] The general thought lies behind Plato's often quoted words: "The great error of our day in the treatment of human beings is that some physicians separate treatment of soul from treatment of body."[7]

As Entralgo (1970) has documented, the Greeks also developed a rather sophisticated form of psychotherapy, which was not surpassed until Freud developed his ideas. Entralgo shows that the Sophists were therapists as well as teachers (the usual emphasis) and that they were often closely allied with the medical treatment of emotional disturbance. Their theory centered around the force of persuasion.

In the soul of the ancient Greeks, the pleasure of persuading by speaking must have been an emotion religiously and psychologically connected with sexual pleasure; Peitho is the goddess of both amorous seduction and persuasive speech.[8] Gorgias, the first prominent Sophist, elaborated the theory of persuasion extensively. The word, he thought, "is a powerful sovereign, for with a very tiny and completely invisible body it performs the most divine works. *It has in fact the power to take away fear, banish pain, inspire happiness and increase compassion''* (italics added).[9]

A number of Sophists applied this theory of persuasion to the treatment of mental and emotional disturbance. Antiphon[10] held that there is a technique for eliminating pain from life; moreover he practiced that technique by informing himself of the causes of the affliction and speaking to the patient accordingly. The thought and the word of the curative rhetorician set in order and rationalized the psychic and physical life of the sufferer. Outside Corinth, near the agora, he arranged a place with a sign, in which he announced himself as able to treat the grief-stricken by means of discourses; evidently numerous other Sophist-physicians also treated depression by verbal psychotherapy.

As is known, Freud was steeped in the study of antiquity, especially the Greeks. He may well have been influenced by his reading of the Sophists and recognized that the conventional image in the histories of philosophy,[11] describing them as one step above charlatans, is entirely wrong. In his paper "On Psychical Treatment" (1905) he refers to the "magic of words" in a manner reminiscent of the quoted passage from Gorgias.[12] In any case, it is clear that the Greek understanding of persuasion and psychotherapy was far superior to that demonstrated by Kraepelin and his followers.

In the light of what has happened since the nineteenth century, it is worth inquiring how and why psychiatry assumed such a medical orientation at that time. As Ilza Veith (1965) has shown, there was quite a struggle in the century before Freud. On the psychological side was Baron Ernst von Feuchtersleben (1806–1849), in whose book on *The Principles of Medical Psychology* (1845) the terms "psychosis" and "psychiatric" were introduced in their modern sense.[13] Feuchtersleben took his medical degree at the University of Vienna in 1833 and subsequently became a member of its faculty and ultimately its dean.

Feuchtersleben's awareness of mental activity and its derangements was a measurable advance in medical psychology (the usual term for psychiatry). He even urged the study of dreams, "not because it is to be considered a spiritual divination, but because as the *unconscious language* [of the mind], it often very clearly shows . . . the state of the patient though he himself is not aware of this."[14]

Feuchtersleben had the most extravagant admiration for philosophy, especially for Immanuel Kant (1724–1804), who claimed the traditional hegemony of the philosopher over matters dealing with the soul and all other factors relating to mind and emotions. Kant adjudged himself an authority on mental disturbances, and he went so far as to propose his own classification of mental diseases, as his contemporaries in other countries had done. He postulated that the various aberrations could be equated with stages of civilization. Thus primitive people were free from the danger of mental disease, whereas the growing complexities of civilization posed increasing threats to personal freedom and hence to psychological balance;[15] this erroneous idea may have had some influence on Freud.

The only disagreement Feuchtersleben had with Kant was his insistence that the physician should be included in the study of psychology and psychiatry. Freud does not mention Feuchtersleben in his works, but in *The Interpretation of Dreams*[16] he does refer briefly to Kant, whom he quotes as having said (1764): "The madman is a waking dreamer."

The somatic side of the discussion was led by Feuchtersleben's contemporary Wilhelm Griesinger (1817–1868), whose book *Mental Pathology and Therapeutics* was also published in 1845. Griesinger is responsible for the famous slogan: "Mental diseases are brain diseases."[17] In accordance with this precept, he banished all discussion of psychology and philosophy, concentrating exclusively on organic brain pathology.

In psychiatry proper the somatic approach won the day, and Kraepelin could be considered Griesinger's most illustrious disciple. As a result, psychiatry and psychoanalysis developed independently of one another until World War II, although most psychoanalysts were trained physicians (the residency in psychiatry had not yet appeared as a standard requirement). Even today in many countries they remain independent of one another.

In spite of the advances in biological psychiatry, in the United States after World War II psychoanalysis became the leading point of view in psychiatric residency training. After a survey of psychiatric residences, Strassman et al. (1976) wrote:

Our study makes clear that psychoanalytic theory and concepts have a firm central position in the teaching and training of residents in psychiatry. In fact, what analysts teach is so much a part of residency training that it is no longer identified as "psychoanalytic," but, rather, as "dynamic"—and the sum and substance of psychiatry proper.[18]

In any case we may note that in 1880 psychiatry was a nihilistic medical discipline that offered no real understanding of mental illness and no real techniques for treating the mentally ill. If the situation has changed radically in the past century, most of the credit for this change must go to psychoanalysis.

Psychology

Since psychology covers a much broader field than psychiatry, it is much harder to pin down precise dates and trends. Nevertheless, it can be said that in 1880 psychology was predominantly sensory-physiological and that it was beginning to turn to the experimental method as its prime tool of research. Wilhelm Wundt (1832–1920) probably expressed most comprehensively the scientific forces that were remaking psychology at that time.[19] Much of the psychology of the mid-nineteenth century was incorporated within experimental physiology. Wundt published his monumental *Principles of Physiological Psychology* in 1873–1874, stressing a psychology investigated by physiological methods. For him, a genuinely psychological experiment involved an objectively knowable and preferably measurable stimulus, applied under stated conditions, and resulting in a response likewise objectively known and measured. Thus, insensibly, the emphasis shifted from the problem (mankind) to the method (experiment). In this shift, which has dominated academic psychology ever since, few noticed, as Ludwig Wittgenstein later observed, that problem and method often pass one another by (Fine, 1969).

Here, too, experimental psychology and psychoanalysis developed at the same time and along independent lines. Since the psychoanalysts refused to experiment, they were considered outside the pale of "scientific" psychology. Since the experimentalists refused to deal with major human concerns, the psychoanalysts had little interest in them. A true rapprochement is not in sight even today. In the election pleas for the presidency of the American Psychological Association in 1977, Richard Thompson wrote: "A major crisis is developing at present in the American Psychological Association. Academic-research psychologists in all areas of psychology are abandoning the American Psychological Association in growing numbers."[20]

A trend running counter to experimentalism in American psychology, prior to the advent of modern clinical psychology, was the thought of William James. Murphy (1972) comments that just as Wundt was the systematic psychologist par excellence, James might be called the unsystematic psychologist par excellence. He had wide-ranging interests, including philosophy, religion, evolution, and art. His major work, *The Principles of Psychology,* was published in 1890, though the contract for it had been signed in 1878.[21] He was thus active at the same time as Wundt and the experimentalists.

Like the psychoanalysts, James was more interested in the problem than in the method. Hence his book deals with such basic human experiences as habit, feelings, the self, consciousness, will, and religion. *The Varieties of Religious Experience* (1902) is still as fresh as ever and is perhaps his most enduring contribution. It is not surprising that when James heard Freud's lectures at Clark University in 1909, he remarked to Ernest Jones: "The future of psychology belongs to your work."[22]

In spite of William James, the emphasis on experimentation remained the dominant voice in American psychology until the advent of clinical psychology after World War II. Unlike academic colleagues who could avoid the deepest human concerns by sticking to their "methods," the clinicians came face to face with these concerns, whether they wanted to or not. As clinical psychology grew, its major weapon became psychoanalysis, and psychoanalytic ideas gradually began to assume increasing importance. In 1976 it was estimated that 37 percent of the members of the American Psychological Association were clinicians of one kind or another,[23] and for the first time in their history the psychologists elected a practicing clinician as president (Theodore Blau).

To recapitulate, in 1880 psychology, like psychiatry, stood on the threshold of vast growth. It was still an infant science. Its development proceeded *pari passu* with that of psychoanalysis.

Sociology

In 1880 sociology scarcely existed in the modern sense. The term "sociology" was coined in 1837 by Auguste Comte (1798–1857) to delineate an all-inclusive social science, a synthesis of all knowledge about humanity. General theories about the nature of society have been put forth from time immemorial, with no consensus reached.

A variety of thinkers have had varying degrees of influence on the course which sociology has taken. In America the dominant trend has been toward empirical research in a delimited number of fields, but there is still no generally accepted classification of the fields within sociology.[24] A typical text divides the discussion into four main areas: the discipline of sociology; social organization; group behavior; social processes (Rankin and Lowry, 1969). Which areas will be chosen for closer study seems rather arbitrary (Boas, 1908), again showing that historical accidents play a considerable role in determining the shape of any modern social science.

From the very beginning, psychoanalysis expressed a keen interest in the social milieu that led to mental illness. Two world wars, with their catastrophic destructiveness and the Holocaust experience, have led to a considerable increase in this interest. Consequently psychoanalysts from Freud onward have made observations about the structure of the society that modern man has created. Many profound thinkers—Max Weber, Talcott Parsons, Erich Fromm, and numerous others—have made serious attempts to bridge the gap between the individual and society. As a result, for many people a fruitful interaction has taken place between psychoanalysis and sociology (Wallerstein and Smelser, 1969); others, however, have stressed the antagonism between the two fields.

In any case, even had he wished to do so, in 1880 there was no solid body of sociological knowledge on which Freud could draw. As with the other social sciences, the two disciplines have developed independently, within the same time period.

Anthropology

Anthropology is an older field than sociology; literally it means the "science of man," and such a science has been the source of extensive speculation from the time of the Greeks. In practice, it received its major impetus from the attempt to answer the question of the differences between "primitive" and "civilized" peoples.

After Darwin had proposed his theory of evolution, it was taken up by anthropologists as the first great organizing principle which enabled them to understand the history of human growth from the primitive to the civilized. This theory dominated from 1860 to 1890 (Tax, 1964) and was thus the prevailing intellectual doctrine in 1880.

The evolutionists tended to view the development of mankind as a growth upward from barbarism and savagery; the term "savage," still used by Malinowski in the 1920s, has completely disappeared, especially since the savagery of the twentieth century has reached depths never before seen or even suspected. This view of evolutionary growth and progress was rather naively taken over by Freud.

In their emphasis on progress, the evolutionists of the latter part of the nineteenth century did not hesitate to express contempt for primitive peoples. Tylor, whose work *Primitive Culture* (1871) remained a classic for some time, devoted much attention to traits that are "worn out, worthless, or even bad with downright harmful folly."[25]

Before the development of modern, sophisticated fieldwork, the raw material of anthropology was the accounts given by a host of untrained observers, such as missionaries, travelers, and traders. These obviously could have been highly unreliable. Franz Boas (1858–1942), whose systematic fieldwork with the Indians of northwest America began in 1888 and continued through many years, is widely regarded as the father of modern anthropology. Since that time no serious statement can be made in anthropology without reference to field research carried out by trained anthropologists.

It is interesting that Boas and Freud are almost exact contemporaries, yet the two men very rarely mentioned one another. The reason is not far to seek. Boas was primarily a collector of facts unilluminated by any psychological theory; Freud had the theories but had to rely on others for the facts. On varying grounds, many later anthropologists have criticized Boas's fact-gathering;[26] similarly the major criticism of Freud stems from the point where he wanders too far from his clinical observations (G. Klein, 1976).

In the post-Freudian developments, anthropology and psychoanalysis have been intimately connected in many ways (Kardiner and Preble, 1965). Many people have done outstanding work in both fields; prominent among these are Geza Roheim, Abram Kardiner, Erich Fromm (studies of a Mexican village), Erik Erikson, George Devereux, and L. Bryce Boyer. As will be seen, it was Freud who unwittingly disproved the evolutionary theory of human culture, demonstrating what most scholars would agree to today, that human psychology is the same everywhere, so that from a larger point of view anthropology and psychology merge into one broader discipline.

History

The writing of history naturally goes back to ancient times. Yet, as Gay and Cavanaugh (1972) observe, history is easier to write than to define. Even today, historians continue to disagree not only on how to do what they are doing but on what it is they are doing.

In the first place, history must portray facts accurately. The attainment of such accuracy matured in the nineteenth century, which experienced a revolution in this respect.[27] It required the perfection of the machinery of research through the more precise contributions of a host of auxiliary sciences. By 1880 such accuracy had reached a stage (assuming the sources to be available) not much different from what it is today.

Nevertheless, as every schoolchild knows, history is more than a mere record of the past. It has to have some perspective on why human beings behave the way they do. Probably because this perspective was lacking in his day, Freud showed little interest in modern European history and confined himself largely to classical antiquity, which formed the backbone of education at that time.

In the intervening century two major changes have occurred. First of all, beginning in the latter part of the nineteenth century, the Marxist emphasis on economic causation began to gain momentum; by the twentieth century no sensible history could be written without close attention to the economic factor, though how it should be interpreted remained open to differing opinions.

The second change, which is still going on, is the introduction of the psychological factor. The notion that a pope or a ruler could be psychotic, or that European civilization suffered from a "moral schizophrenia," would have been unthinkable to a professional historian even a generation ago. Yet once introduced, the idea seems clear enough. Human beings make history, so their psychology must be an essential part of such history. In this view all of history is essentially psychohistory, in which the scholarly reconstruction of past facts is illuminated by an understanding of the motives in the lives of the participants. It is in that sense that psychoanalysis can be said to have penetrated all historical writing. This development, however, has only taken place gradually over the past century (Fine, 1977).

Economics

Economics is preeminently a discipline of the twentieth century, although its roots too go as far back as recorded history. Even the term came into vogue only in this century, replacing the older phrase "political economy."[28] After the era of the classical economists and Marx, the major developments which dominate the scene today are all of relatively recent origin.

Although economists have exerted themselves to find "immutable" laws of human behavior in the economic realm, all these theories are just as much psychological as objective, as Heilbroner (1967) has shown. In more recent years, after the Keynesian revolution (Keynes, 1935) and the maturation of tools of psychological research, many economists have been more outspoken in their advocacy of the psychodynamic point of view (Galbraith, 1976; Weisskopf, 1955, 1971). In 1880, when Freud began, all of this was still in the distant future.

Biology, Medicine, and Physiology

Singer[29] has emphasized that the whole outlook on the nature of living things underwent a complete and profound change in the period of about 1860–1880, the formative years of Freud's education. He ascribes this change to the following causes:

1. The discovery of the essential identity in the mode of reproduction of animals and plants.
2. The discovery of the essential identity in the living substance

of animals and of plants, and the emergence of the concept of protoplasm.

3. The examination of the methods of nutrition and respiration, and the realization that these too are fundamentally the same for all living things.

4. The view of the balance of life and of organic nature as one huge mechanism came to the fore.

5. The reduction of all living processes to terms of the cell.

6. An evolutionary view of life that revolutionized biological thought. Thus there arose the tendency to examine the manner of life and habits of living things, involving also their relations to other forms of living things.

7. The conviction that so far as scientific experience extends, all living things are derived from living things and are not generated from nonliving things.

Of subsequent developments in biology, the most important for psychoanalysis was the discovery of genetics (Mayr, 1970), which is usually dated from Mendel's work in 1866 (rediscovered in 1900). Mendel's work was unknown to Darwin, and of course to the young Freud. The Lamarckian doctrine of the inheritance of acquired characteristics, which has been emphatically rejected by modern genetics, still held sway at that time. It is interesting that in 1939, when Freud knew all about the rejection of Lamarckism by biologists, he still clung to the theory,[30] showing that even a great man finds it very difficult to get past the teachings of his youth.

It is also worth noting that medicine in the nineteenth century was in the midst of a tremendous arc of progress in the conquest of disease. All the fundamental scientific discoveries had already been made, and their application to human illness proceeded apace, with new discoveries appearing almost every day. It is not surprising that in such an atmosphere Freud began by regarding hysteria as an illness which he could conquer by the same methods that others had used to conquer other illnesses.

Recapitulation

The major background factors to be considered in the evolution of psychoanalysis are the indirect ones of the general intellectual and social climate of that day. Taking 1880 arbitrarily as a jumping-off date, we have seen that the political world existed in a state of moral schizophrenia, which was soon to erupt into a series of violent catastrophes. In the intellectual world, psychiatry had not yet caught up with the humane and enlightened attitude of the Greeks, psychology was virtually confined to the experimental investigation of sensory modalities, sociology and anthropology relied mainly on armchair speculation, history had perfected the means of recovering the facts of the past but lacked a meaningful vantage point from which to interpret them, while economics was concealing its psychological speculation behind so-called iron laws of work and history. The biological sciences had just completed their major revolution, establishing the scientific position that prevails today; the major theoretical change since then has been the rediscovery of genetics. Medicine had conquered many diseases, and was to conquer many more in the ensuing century.

These were the essentials of the background scene which led to Freud's epochal discoveries.

Chapter Three
The Legacy of Freud

1886–1895: The Exploration of Neurosis

Sigmund Freud was born on May 6, 1856 in Pribor, now in Czechoslovakia. For a while the street on which he was born was renamed Ulice Freudova (Freud Street) in his honor. When he was 3 years old his family moved to Vienna, where he remained until 1938, when the Nazi persecutions forced him to flee to England, one year before his death. Undaunted by his persecution, when he crossed from France to England he dreamed that he was landing at Pevensey, the place where William the Conqueror had disembarked in 1066.[1]

Outwardly there is relatively little to relate about Freud's life. He was always a very bright student and from an early age seemed destined for an academic or intellectual career. He studied at the University of Vienna, eventually doing research from 1876 to 1881 under the famous physiologist Ernst Brücke. Because the financial prospects in research were so poor, in 1881 he took his M.D. degree. In 1885 he received a traveling grant to go to Paris for several months to study with Jean Charcot, the most famous neurologist of that day.

After his return to Vienna in 1886, he set himself up in private practice as a neurologist. That same year he married Martha Bernays, with whom he had six children. The youngest, Anna, became one of the world's leading figures in psychoanalysis.

In 1885 he had been appointed Privatdocent (roughly, lecturer) in neuropathology at the University of Vienna. Some 20 years later he was made a Professor Extraordinarius (associate professor), and in 1920 he became a full professor. All these honors came to him as a result of his work in neurology. His psychoanalytic labors never received any official recognition from the university.

In 1923 he developed a cancer of the jaw, which after many operations and much suffering ultimately proved fatal in 1939.

Such is the outline of his life. The reader who looks for more excitement in Freud's biography will find none. His epic lay in his great intellectual adventure, the development of psychoanalysis.

Freud's work can be divided into four major periods:

1. The exploration of neurosis, from the inception of practice (1886) until the *Studies on Hysteria* (1895).

2. Self-analysis, 1895–1899.

3. Id psychology, in which the first system of psychoanalytic psychology was elaborated, roughly 1900–1914.

4. Finally, ego psychology, involving a considerable extension and elaboration of the earlier ideas, lasting from 1914 until 1939.

Exploring Neurosis

For the first ten years of his professional career, Freud practiced in much the same way as other neurologists of his day. The two major illnesses he saw were hysteria, which had been known from time immemorial, and neurasthenia, first described by the American psychiatrist Beard in 1869.[2] While he treated the usual run of neurological conditions, his practice centered increasingly on what would be called today the psychogenic disorders.

Freud exemplified the cultured physician of his day, having wide interests in literature, art, and theater, an extensive knowledge of languages (embracing all the major European tongues), and a genteel way of living never touched by a breath of scandal. The transition from this way of life to the discovery of psychoanalysis is a remarkable story.

To begin with, Freud was inordinately ambitious. His wish to be a great man has been concealed by the fact that he became such a great man; nevertheless, through the years of struggle a hope for some great discovery together with a fear of failure because the discovery continued to elude him are prominent features of his personality, brought out in his posthumously discovered letters to his Berlin friend, the ear-nose-and-throat specialist Wilhelm Fliess. Typical is a letter to Fliess on November 14, 1897: "It was on November 12,

1897. The sun was in the eastern quarter; Mercury and Venus were in conjunction. . . . I gave birth to a new piece of knowledge."[3] Then again he would come back to thoughts such as those described in a letter to his fiancée; "I am no genius, and I no longer understand how I could have wished to be one."[4]

Through these early years he kept on looking for some cure for the illnesses he was treating, since the medical science of that day really had neither theory nor remedy to offer him that were of any value. He began, of course, by adopting what was common practice at that time. It was assumed that the neuroses were due to some unknown organic factor, since biology and medicine were so far ahead of any psychosocial understanding; in fact, psychology smacked of a return to the charlatanry of the Middle Ages.

The therapeutic arsenal of that day was confined to two major remedies: electrotherapy and hypnotism. Electrotherapy was different from the electric shock later introduced by Cerletti; it involved a series of faradic shocks, enough to startle the patient but not enough to cause any serious upheaval or convulsion. With his sense of total honesty, Freud soon realized that electrotherapy was a waste of time. In his *Autobiography,* in 1925, he wrote

My knowledge of electrotherapy was derived from W. Erb's textbook, which provided detailed instructions for the treatment of all the symptoms of nervous diseases. Unluckily I was soon driven to see that following these instructions was of no help whatever and that what I had taken for an epitome of exact observations was merely the construction of fantasy. The realization that the work of the greatest name in German neuropathology had no more relation to reality than some Egyptian dream book, such as is sold in cheap bookshops, was painful, but it helped to rid me of another shred of the innocent faith in authority from which I was not yet freed. So I put my electrical apparatus aside.[5]

The only method of treatment that remained at Freud's disposal was hypnotism. In 1889 he made a special trip to Nancy, France, to visit Hippolyte Bernheim, then probably the leading expert on the subject, whose book Freud had translated into German. Freud practiced hypnotism for a number of years, until he finally discarded it in 1896 and replaced it entirely by the psychoanalytic method. He had to invent an entirely new technique for studying and treating the neuroses.

Freud's first major discovery was that the key to neurosis lies in psychology. This can be stated in many different ways. Through an understanding of psychopathology we reach normal psychology, through psychology we can explain the manifestations of neurosis as well as normal behavior. While he realized that there must be some physiological basis for his psychological descriptions, usually he insisted that the physiology be put to one side until more was discovered, so that the phenomena he described had to be understood in purely psychological terms.

In the letters to Fliess, his preoccupation with setting up a new system of psychology comes out again and again. In one he wrote on May 25, 1895, he says:

My tyrant is psychology; it has always been my distant, beckoning goal and now, since I have hit on the neuroses, it has come so much nearer. I am plagued with two ambitions: to see how the theory of mental functioning takes shape if quantitative considerations, a sort of economics of nerve-force, are introduced into it; and secondly, to extract from psychopathology what may be of benefit to normal psychology. Actually a satisfactory theory of neuropsychotic disturbances is impossible if it cannot be brought into association with clear assumptions about normal mental processes.[6]

Or in the letter of April 2, 1896:

When I was young, the only thing I ever longed for was philosophical knowledge, and now that I am going over from medicine to psychology I am in the process of attaining it. I have become a therapist against my will; I am convinced that granted certain conditions in the person, I can definitely cure hysteria and obsessional neurosis.[7]

Then in a more despairing moment he confessed (October 23, 1898): "How can I ever hope to gain an insight into the whole of mental activity, which was once something I proudly looked forward to?"[8]

As he well knew, the shift to psychology signified a sharp break with the past. Where were the physicochemical forces that his teachers had taught him were at the root of all mental life? What was the bodily basis of all the conflicts, traumas, and defenses that he kept seeing?

True to his traditions, he attempted a grand physiological theory according to which psychology would be put on a firm neurological basis. He sent a draft of it to Fliess, referring to it as a "Psychology for Neurologists;" later it was known simply as the "Project." For a while he was wildly enthusiastic, then he cooled down and discarded the "Project." It was never published in his lifetime.[9]

Freud's physiology was not particularly novel (Amacher, 1965). From Brücke he took over the idea that there was only one type of excitation in the nervous system, and that this involved electrical activity. The mechanism of transmission was such that it led to nervous processes in terms of a quantity of excitation originating at a certain place in the nervous system and moving along the nerves to collect in a larger place in the channel. The function of the nervous system was to get rid of excitation; later he was to formulate this as the "Nirvana principle." The modern idea that stimulation is as important a function of the nervous system as quiescence was unknown at that time. The recognition of sensory deprivation came only after World War II.

From Theodor Meynert, whom he considered the greatest brain anatomist of the day, Freud took over in 1895 the idea that a single functional energy, though as inexplicable as all physiological forces, is inherent in the brain cell, and that is sensitiveness. Excitation was assumed to vary quantitatively, and these quantitative variations could account for all the known phenomena. Later Freud was to formulate this first as psychic energy, and subsequently as the libido theory.

Meynert accepted association psychology fully; accordingly he viewed the mind as a passive spectator to the reception and combination of sense perceptions. In so doing he tended to eliminate psychological faculties, and therefore when Freud dared to assert the existence of such faculties on an unknown physiological basis, he was defying his masters.

Meynert also accepted a concept of a primary ego, formed by experiences in the discharge of impinging excitation, calling this the "nucleus of the individuality." He stressed the avoidance of pain as a determining motive; accordingly Freud talked of the "unpleasure principle" (*Unlust Prinzip*), not moving on to the pleasure principle as such until 1911. Meynert's division of nervous processes into subcortical and cortical was later reformulated by Freud as two processes, primary (subcortical) and secondary (cortical), though without the physiological assumptions inherent in Meynert's ideas.

Sigmund Exner (1846–1926), another of Freud's teachers, stressed the significance of instincts, which he defined as the "association between an idea and an emotion center" (similar to Freud's later definition of an instinct as being on the border between the somatic and the psychic). He even discussed the determinants of sexual behavior at some length. His views on instinct were not particularly different from those of other theorists of his day (Fletcher, 1966).

These antecedents of Freud's views should be kept in mind in everything that follows. Much has been made of Freud's biological bias, but it has been overlooked that his biology and neurology were not original at all; it was his psychology that was revolutionary.

The main novel element in the 1890s was that the key to neurosis lies in psychology. However, Freud could not yet make this theory complete, so he always allowed for some unknown physiological or constitutional factor. At one point he even hypothesized that a large number of his hysterical patients came from syphilitic fathers, a comment that he let stand as late as the 1920s,[10] although he called attention to other errors that he had discarded. It was always difficult for Freud to admit that he had abandoned some previous position.

In the 1890s he divided the neuroses into the *actual neuroses* and the *psychoneuroses*. The actual neuroses, comprising neurasthenia and anxiety neurosis, were due, he believed, to actual sexual frustration which in some unknown way released toxins into the system. Since they were caused by direct physiological factors, their cure had to be physiological, that is, an alteration of the sexual practices leading up to them. Freud postulated that neurasthenia was caused by excessive masturbation, anxiety neurosis by undischarged stimulation, especially coitus interruptus. The psychoneuroses were hysteria and obsessional neurosis. He thought both were caused by sexual trauma in childhood: hysteria by passive seduction, obsessional neurosis by active seduction. Hence hysteria is more common in women; obsessional neurosis more common in men. All these divisions and constructions soon became obsolete, yet Freud did not clearly indicate this change; therefore many, even today, confuse his pre-analytic views of the 1890s with analysis proper, which should be dated from *The Interpretation of Dreams* in 1900.

In psychotherapy Freud utilized and expanded two tools which Breuer had used before him: abreaction and making the unconscious conscious, or insight. Abreaction means the release of emotion which had been repressed at the time of the traumatic experience. This led Freud to lay primary stress on the discharge phenomenon and the striving for discharge.

Freud's output before 1900 was meager. In the Standard Edition it occupies only one volume, of which the major portion is devoted to *Studies on Hysteria* (1895).

In terms of the future course of psychoanalysis, the most significant paper of that period was "The Defense Neuropsychoses" (1894). Here Freud introduced the idea, ever since fundamental, that *all neurosis involves a defense against unbearable ideas*. In one sense much of the history of psychoanalysis can be viewed as an elaboration and clarification of this formula.

Initially his attention was directed to the unbearable ideas, which he then equated with sexuality. Here too his views underwent a number of changes through the years. It is useful to summarize the major changes that occurred.

1. In the beginning (1886–1900), Freud had a simple theory of the sexual causation of neurosis. Sexual difficulties cause neurosis; neurosis, in turn, is always caused by sexual difficulties.

2. Around 1900, he began to abandon this simple, direct sexual theory and turned to the investigation of infantile sexuality.

3. At the same time the concept of sexuality was broadened, and the term *psychosexual* came into use. The broadening involved, first, an extension of sexuality to all physical pleasure and, second, its extension to affection, love, and all the tender emotions. This was crystallized in the *Three Essays on Sexuality* (1905).

4. The newer concepts of sexuality led to a newer concept of neurosis, which Freud referred to as the libido theory, although this term has several meanings. The direct sexual theory of neurosis was abandoned, except for the one instance of actual neurosis. Instead, a view was put forth in which the individual's character structure is related in fairly definable ways to his instinctual drives and their life history. This theory dates mainly from 1905–1915.

5. In 1914, in the paper on "Narcissism," he revised the libido theory further with the assumption that the ego was libidinally charged or cathected.

6. In 1920, he postulated the existence of two fundamental instincts, instead of one: sexuality and aggression or, to use his own terms, Eros and Thanatos, or the life and death instincts.

7. In 1923 he proposed a new theory of the mind called ego psychology, which has been the dominant theory ever since. The instincts interact with the ego functions to form the total personality

structure. The defense against unbearable ideas is now reformulated as the conflict between the ego and the id.

The defense processes received very little attention until much later in the history of psychoanalysis; the term "defense" was soon replaced by "repression" and was not reintroduced until 1926.

1895–1899: Self-Analysis

The new publications from Freud's pen in the period from the *Studies on Hysteria* in 1895 to *The Interpretation of Dreams* in 1900 were primarily reformulations of positions already established. What he was preoccupied with, as is now known from biographical and autobiographical data, was his self-analysis. It was this analysis of himself that brought about the decisive change from neurology to psychology and created a whole new field, psychoanalysis.

It is scarcely possible to overestimate the role that Freud's self-analysis played in the history of the science. It established the precedent for the training analysis, still the most essential part of the preparation of any psychoanalyst. It showed that the difference between the neurotic and the normal person is a quantitative one of degree, not a qualitative one of kind. Freud had always had an inkling that this was so. In 1882 he had written to his fiancée: "I always find it uncanny when I can't understand someone in terms of myself." [11] Now he was to prove his hunch.

Appreciation of the role that self-analysis played in Freud's development has come only gradually and late. He made few allusions to it in his published writings, and in these he attached no real importance to what he had done. After his death some scattered references to autobiographical data were brought to light and commented on. Then his letters to Fliess were found and published in 1950.

Wilhelm Fliess was a physician in Berlin who was a close friend of Freud's from 1887 to 1902. The two often met to discuss scientific matters and engaged in a lively correspondence. Fliess kept Freud's letters. After Fliess's death, his widow sold them to a Berlin bookdealer named Stahl. During the Nazi regime Stahl fled to France, where he offered the letters to Marie Bonaparte, a descendant of Napoleon and a leading French psychoanalyst. She immediately bought them and, though Freud advised her to throw them away, she kept them and eventually had them published.

In these letters Freud reveals as nowhere else the tremendous inner struggles that accompanied the birth and early origins of psychoanalysis. He also bared innumerable details of his life in *The Interpretation of Dreams* and in the later *Psychopathology of Everyday Life* (1901). *The Interpretation of Dreams* in particular may be seen as a new kind of autobiography, in which the inner life is exposed as no one had ever exposed it before (Burr, 1909).

To coordinate the many aspects of Freud's life and work requires a great amount of careful research. This task has recently been performed by the French analyst Didier Anzieu (1975). Anzieu has rearranged all of Freud's dreams in chronological order and correlated them with memories and known facts of Freud's life to give a coherent picture of Freud's intellectual and emotional development from 1895 to 1902—a truly grand undertaking for which the scholarly world can be grateful. The following account relies heavily on Anzieu.

In 1895, when his intensive self-analysis began, Freud was 39 years old. He was a successful neurologist, happily married, the father of five children, with a sixth on the way; his daughter Anna was born on December 3, 1895. To all outward appearances he was a happy man. His time was devoted to his practice, his family, and his friends. He read widely in many fields and was a man of considerable cultural attainments in addition to his medical specialty.

Inwardly, however, he was full of moods and fears. He was frequently depressed; he formed violent hatreds; he was afraid to travel, at times even afraid to cross the street. He had somatic symptoms and alternated between diagnoses of stomach trouble and heart trouble. His dependence on Fliess clearly was not based on purely objective considerations.

Nevertheless, all Freud's inner fears and conflicts were scarcely different from those of other men in his community. He was what is called in modern parlance a "normal-neurotic," and no compelling reason can be given for his analysis. Like so many others before and since, he might have shrugged off his problems by saying, "That's life," or given himself some esoteric medical diagnosis, or "taken up a hobby." Instead he entered on an intellectual adventure which opened a whole new world, the inner life of mankind. This new world now seems familiar enough to us, and so many others have followed in Freud's footsteps, that we have lost sight of the revolutionary character of his undertaking. Freud's self-analysis, however, must rank as one of the great discoveries of all time. It is on a par with Darwin's theory of evolution and Einstein's principle of relativity.

Much as an analysis today begins with what later turn out to be trivial symptoms, Freud began with the wish to explore two ideas: free association, and the hypothesis that a dream is the fulfillment of a wish of the previous day (the day residue). The dream of Irma's injection on July 24, 1895—Irma was a patient of his—revealed to him that dreams have meaning and showed how this meaning could be extracted from them. (This dream has since been called the "dream specimen" of psychoanalysis; see Erikson, 1954.) This dream and its interpretation mark the beginning of his self-analysis. Freud was well aware of the magnitude of his discovery and soon afterward jokingly suggested in a letter to Fliess[12] that a tablet be placed on the house in which the meaning occurred to him, with the inscription:

ON JULY 24, 1895
THE SECRET OF THE DREAM
WAS REVEALED TO DR. SIGMUND FREUD

The interpretation of this dream showed Freud that he could apply the method of free association to himself. In so doing he also made a serendipitous observation: there are unconscious wishes in the dream. The structure of the dream is similar to that of the neurotic symptom in that both are symbolic. This discovery came about in the course of the dream itself, thus offering a new illustration of the creative power of dreams. Finally the particular dream, which is one of guilt and expiation, contains a new personal insight: Freud is haunted by feelings of guilt toward his patients, his colleagues, his family, and his friends.

Apart from all this, the dream set loose a process in Freud which was to continue throughout his entire life and work. Sooner or later psychoanalysis touches on every human concern. It was no longer a matter of scientific research; it became an intense human experience.

The year 1895–1896 was the one in which this transformation occurred. Freud finished his previous work. He resigned himself to the loss of Breuer, who was frightened by Freud's sexual theories, and moved closer to Fliess, whom he looked on as an expert in biology and the chemistry of the sexual processes, and from whom he hoped to receive the enlightenment he needed on these subjects.

The death of his father in September 1896 created an upheaval from which it took him three years to recover. His dreams became more importunate and more precise. It was as though they embodied a dialogue that gave voice to his inner conflicts. A son necessarily experiences violent hostility toward his father, even the most beloved of fathers. This hostility Freud had denied and forgotten, and it was reawakened in him by his father's death. He was experiencing the "return of the repressed" that was to occupy such a central role in all his later thinking. The hostility explains the feelings of guilt that had been apparent since the dream of Irma's injection. Freud recognized his hostility and analyzed each of its forms: jealousy, rivalry, ambition, resentment. Gradually he freed himself from their inevitable corollaries of shame, remorse, impotence, inhibition, and the wish to fail.

Much of this became clear to him in a time of trouble, during the summer of 1897. He could no longer work intellectually. His theories had collapsed; his practice was shrinking; he felt incapable of finishing the analyses he was engaged in; the difficulties of his patients aroused enormous personal repercussions. He again began to feel threatened by doubts about the future. He was even paralyzed in his correspondence with Fliess, toward whom he was beginning to experience the same ambivalence that analysis had revealed toward his father. The crisis was accompanied by an exacerbation of all his weak points: fear of cardiac illness and of approaching death, fear of railroad trips, and depression to the point where he feared he was suffering from a neurosis.

Under this tension, his self-analysis turned toward his memories of childhood. In the course of his interpretations of dreams, childhood memories cropped up with increasing frequency and helped to convince him that the unconscious wish in the dream stems from childhood as well as from the previous day. His personal experience made him certain that the unconscious of the adult is in large measure made up of the child that slumbers within the adult. A child is driven by his own desires and impulses, which lead him to create imaginary satisfactions in a rich fantasy life; later an adult is no longer able to distinguish between fantasy and reality.

These two key areas of fantasy and of childhood were clarified in a period of intensive self-analysis at the end of September and the beginning of October, 1897, which followed the summer crisis. He reconstructed the libidinal emotions of his childhood—the incestuous wishes for his mother, sadism toward his niece Pauline, who was the same age as he (she was the child of his half-brother), shame and fear of punishment by his nurse—and the corresponding aggressive feelings—jealousy of his father, the wish to murder his younger brother Alexander, fierce competition with Pauline's brother John (who was a year older than he). The two sides of his nature he combined in his theory of the Oedipus complex.

The following period, from the fall of 1897 to the summer of 1898, saw the application ("working through") of these insights to his neurosis, his friendships, and his profession. His cardiac anxieties and fear of traveling disappeared. His dependence on Fliess changed into competition. He discarded hypnosis altogether and henceforth in his practice relied on dreams, free association, and childhood memories. The wish to write a book on dreams became stronger. Brücke and Charcot ceased to be his models; instead he identified with Goethe. Like Goethe, he was beginning to extend his findings to the entire range of human activity.

Freud's inner life in the spring and summer of 1898 was marked by anal material: excremental dreams, reading of Rabelais and Zola, digestive difficulties, coarseness of images and memories. He was reliving the time of his toilet training.

For a while Freud's interest in his own dreams diminished. He had already made his most significant discoveries and was eager to publish a book on the topic. A necessary review of the previous literature bored him but gave him the satisfaction of reconfirming that nothing of any consequence had ever been said on the subject. He began to think of his next book, *The Psychopathology of Everyday Life*.

Nevertheless, there were relapses. The fall of 1898 saw a new crisis: a return of his inner suffering, and intellectual paralysis. From this depression a dream rescued him. He thought of all his vanished friends, and all the rivals on whom he had wished death.

But there was another side to his depression: his relation to his mother and the oral stage. A further dream makes clear the ambiguity of the mother-image which he had re-experienced in his wife: giver of life and nourishment but also instrument of implacable death, inviting love and pleasure but forbidding or punishing them at the same time.

After these dreams he could reconstruct the stages of his love life: his attachment to his niece Pauline, his first adolescent love-dream, his first erotic fantasies, his love-marriage and resentment toward his wife because of his difficulties in the relationship.

His difficulties were resolved by refinding the father-image, the serene authority who had ruled so happily in his childhood, and the mother-image who gave him that sublime self-confidence which he always ascribed to the love which a mother gives to her first-born and son.

Finally, surmounting his inner conflicts, he turned back to work. In the first nine months of 1899 he finished the manuscript of *The Interpretation of Dreams*. From then to the end of his life, with minor interruptions, he found his place in life as a calm and serene father. For the most part his symptoms disappeared, although he occasionally showed signs of depression and somatic difficulties throughout his life. In his personal life he found much happiness with his family. The break with Fliess finally came in 1900, although Freud tried to maintain the relationship for another two years. Henceforth Freud had disciples, but no longer any need for close friends. His fear of traveling was overcome. In 1901 he was able to visit Rome, which he had previously felt compelled to avoid. And in his work he was able to lay the foundations for the new science of psychoanalysis.

Although his immediate conflicts subsided ("his analysis was terminated"), in one sense self-analysis continued to the end of Freud's life. He told Ernest Jones at one time that he devoted the last half-hour of every day to this purpose.[13]

The effect of Freud's self-analysis on the further development of his views and the science in general was momentous. Two immediate consequences can be highlighted here.

First of all, Freud had reached his most important discoveries only through self-exploration. What had begun as a kind of intellectual game became a bitter internal struggle lasting five years and in one sense continuing all his life. Since it was only after this struggle on his part that the meaning of his findings became clear to him, he made the same demand on others. In 1910 he stated:

Now that a considerable number of people are practising psychoanalysis and exchanging their observations with one another, we have noticed that no psychoanalyst goes further than his own complexes and internal resistances permit; and we consequently require that he shall begin his activity with a self-analysis and continually carry it deeper while he is making his observations on his patients. Anyone who fails to produce results in a self-analysis of this kind may at once give up any idea of being able to treat patients by analysis.[14]

However, the demand goes further than the practitioner. Experience has shown that an intellectual grasp of the doctrines of psychoanalysis is extraordinarily difficult, because these doctrines involve such a drastic change in a person's ways of thinking. The emotional heat generated by Freud is so great that many of the writers who have examined his views have not even been able to quote them accurately. This fact has led to the suggestion that all workers in the social sciences should have some analysis. It is quite possible, however, that with the spread of public knowledge of psychoanalysis this difficulty will diminish.

A second consequence of Freud's self-analysis was the realization that the difference between the neurotic and the normal is one of degree rather than of kind. The neurotic is a person with troubles, not someone who is suffering from some obscure medical illness. As Sullivan once put it with laconic eloquence: "We are all much more simply human than otherwise."[15]

Without detracting from the magnificence of Freud's achievement, it is necessary to examine his self-analysis critically. The effect of Freud's personality on the historical development of psychoanalysis can of course hardly be exaggerated, and it was the self-analysis which produced the mature man.

In spite of his success, Freud had doubted that he could analyze himself. In November 1897 he had written to Fleiss: "My self-analysis is still interrupted and I have realized the reason. I can only analyze myself with the help of knowledge obtained objectively (like an outsider). Genuine self-analysis is impossible, otherwise there would be no illness."[16] And in 1936 he wrote: "In self-analysis the danger of incompleteness is particularly great. One is too easily satisfied with a part explanation, behind which resistance can easily keep back something that may perhaps be more important."[17] Nevertheless, for a long time Freud was modest enough to believe that any-

body could do what he had done. As late as 1914, he was still willing
to accept self-analysis as adequate for analytic training.[18]

Experience soon dashed the hope that everybody's self-analysis
could flow even as smoothly as Freud's, which had been rather
rocky. It quickly became apparent how seriously countertransferences
came to interfere in analytic practice. After World War I the conviction grew that the only way to overcome these countertransferences
was through a personal analysis by a more experienced analyst. Since
roughly 1930, personal analysis has become an absolute requirement
of every training institute. Where at first it was held that anybody
could do what Freud had done, it was finally concluded that nobody
could.

In retrospect, certain gaps and biases can be pointed out in
Freud's self-analysis. By and large, Freud tended to stress his personal experience too much. The death of his father had precipitated
his own great inner turmoil, and accordingly he wrote that the death
of a man's father is "the most important event, the most incisive loss
of a man's life."[19] But what if, unlike Freud, a man lost his mother
first or a child or a beloved grandparent, or retained his parents but
had his home uprooted?

More serious are Freud's predominant emphasis on male psychology and his astounding confessions of ignorance about women.
His writings are replete with protestations of how little is known
about women. As late as 1932 in an essay on "The Psychology of
Women" he wrote: "Throughout the ages the problem of women has
puzzled people of every kind. . . . You too will have pondered over
this question insofar as you are men; from the women among you that
is not to be expected, for you are the riddle yourselves."[20]

Here are some other representative statements from earlier writings. In the 1923 paper on the phallic phase he wrote: "Unfortunately
we can describe this state of things only as it affects the male child;
the corresponding processes in the little girl are not known to us."[21]
In the *Three Essays* in 1905 he wrote: "The significance of the factor
of sexual overvaluation can be best studied in men, for their erotic
life alone has become accessible to research. That of women . . . is
still veiled in an impenetrable obscurity."[22]

Thus, just as *The Interpretation of Dreams* was based largely
on his own dreams, the theoretical description of infantile sexuality
leaned most heavily on his understanding of his own development.

Not without reason did he once comment that much that is of general occurrence and clearly true can be overlooked by psychoanalysts in spite of decades of unremitting observation.[23]

In his self-analysis Freud made a host of fundamental discoveries: the unconscious, the Oedipus complex, the anal stage, infantile sexuality, and how to interpret dreams, free associations, transferences, and resistances. This is assuredly a tremendous contribution for any person to make. Yet he omitted a number of others. He knew little about the oral stage, particularly the infant's hostility toward the mother, and maternal rejection of the infant. These features of human development have become subjects of interest and exploration only since about 1940.

As surprising as Freud's masculine bias and professed ignorance of the psychology of women is his failure to examine more critically his relationships to his own children. In his self-analysis he was interested in his functioning as a child; how he behaved as a parent was apparently of no concern to him. His own conflicts with his parents he ascribed to a biological factor, namely his instinctual impulses. In a sense his biological orientation was rooted partly in his desire to exonerate his parents, particularly his mother. His main concern was to uncover his own instinctual development; how his parents handled these instincts was a secondary matter. Although the role of parents in the formation of the Oedipus complex and of the child's personality in general is readily implicit in psychoanalytic theory, it took a long time before Freud dealt with this in more detail (Hart, 1948).

No doubt it was this neglect of the parental aspect which stopped Freud from undertaking the analysis of young children, although if they were old enough to talk about their sexual fantasies (10 and upward) he did treat them.[24] A natural opening with younger children came with little Hans, then 5 years old. Hans was a boy who developed a fear of horses that prevented him from going out on the street. Freud could have analyzed the child but chose instead to work through the father. It remained for his daughter Anna and her colleague Melanie Klein to go on to systematize the direct treatment of children.

The particular problems that Freud was grappling with had little relationship to the society in which he found himself. Accordingly, for a long time he tended to ignore the milieu and concentrate on the personal-individual features of the neurosis. This too was a gap that was filled in later.

Freud's self-analysis was conducted by means of dreams, free association, and childhood memories. In all three of these he was astoundingly gifted. Modestly he assumed that others would be equally gifted; if they did not produce the material quickly, he ascribed this to resistance. But subsequent history has shown that many people find it difficult to recall dreams or to free associate or to remember their childhood, despite the most intensive analysis of resistances. There has been a tendency to call those who could do to any degree what Freud did "analyzable" and those who could not "unanalyzable." This is one of the many factors that has led to the controversies about analyzability.

Thus in more than one sense Freud's self-analysis is the matrix from which the whole science grew. It was here that he had the great insights which form the basis of psychoanalysis. And it was here that he left the broad gaps which he and other workers in the field later filled in.

1900–1914: Id Psychology

When the International Psychoanalytical Association was founded in 1910, its goals were to: "foster and further the science of psychoanalysis founded by Freud, both as a pure discipline of psychology and in its application to medicine and the mental sciences." [25]

The "pure discipline of psychology" which Freud had in mind, and which may be called the first psychoanalytic system, rested on three bases: the unconscious, the libido theory, and transference and resistance as the basis of therapy. It can be called a system because these three are intimately connected. The libidinal impulses are repressed into the unconscious, thus avoiding anxiety. Because unconscious forces predominate, simple rational therapy does not work; instead the therapist has to work out the transference (feelings about the therapist) and the resistances to becoming aware of libidinal or other forbidden impulses.

Nothing available at that time in psychiatry, psychology, or any allied discipline could remotely compare with the profundity and breadth of Freud's theory. In this sense he can be said to have created a new vision of what mankind is. Through therapy he was to create a new vision of what mankind might become. And the conceptual framework in which he clothed his ideas was indispensable to these goals.

Although all the ideas contained in this system were known to Freud in one way or another before 1900, the new approach can justifiably be called an entirely new system of psychology. This has been obscured by several factors. First of all Freud found it very difficult to admit that he had given up any position that he had reached by hard work. For example, in the meetings of the Vienna Psychoanalytic Society, Stekel rightly pointed out in 1910 that Freud's views about neurasthenia had changed radically and that "there is no longer any [neurasthenia] to see."[26] Freud somewhat indignantly replied that "regarding Freud's view about neurasthenia, it has changed much less than is generally believed, and he still adheres to the essentials of his former standpoint. . . . Freud is quite prepared to assume that psychic processes are added on to purely physiological ones."[27] These "physiological" processes have been pushed to one side because they could not be found, and the psychology has persisted, as Freud emphasized in many places. The concept of neurasthenia has virtually disappeared from the literature. In the first edition of Grinstein's *Index of Psychoanalytic Writings,* published in 1960, there were 46 references to neurasthenia in the subject index; in the third edition (1971) there were only 5, none of them significant. Historically, Stekel was more correct about Freud's views than Freud himself.

Second, Freud, with his conflicts about father figures, gave some of his predecessors too much credit for what they had done. In the early days he repeatedly cited Breuer as the founder of psychoanalysis because of the older man's cathartic treatment of Anna O. in 1880–1882, thus emphasizing the 1895 book *Studies on Hysteria,* which should be regarded as a pre-analytic publication. Likewise he expressed too much gratitude to Fliess, whose absurd views on numbers and rhythms he shared for a while. Freud's indignant resignation from the editorial board of the *Wiener klinische Rundschau* in 1898 because that journal had printed a scathing review of Fliess's book was a sign of good schoolboy camaraderie, not scientific judgment.[28] Again, in retrospect the reviewer was justified, not Freud, since Fliess's book was sheer balderdash; except for the concept of bisexuality, which others had expressed as well, Fliess had nothing to offer.

Third, Freud's proverbial pessimism and self-doubt led him to question the value of his theories for a long time. It was only late in his life that worldwide recognition reached him; prior to that he was afraid that he would be forgotten, his ideas to be resuscitated only after his death.[29]

These personal characteristics, which enter into all of Freud's writings, have obscured for many the radical change that occurred in him between the 1890s and the first id period, 1900–1914. It is important to realize that the first psychoanalytic system presented a radically new view of psychology, which has since been incorporated into virtually the whole of psychological thought.

Freud's thinking in this period is contained in his writings, although in a number of cases additions were made afterward. The two major works were *The Interpretation of Dreams* in 1900 and *The Three Essays on Sexuality* in 1905.

The Unconscious

In all of Freud's published summaries of psychoanalysis, the unconscious played a primary role. He frequently referred to psychoanalysis as "psychology of the depths" or "psychology of the unconscious." To the end of his life he never tired of presenting new illustrations of the power of the unconscious in mental life.

By the "unconscious," Freud meant unconscious mental processes. The unconscious is not anatomically located, it is not a reified object. It is a concept that unifies a series of clinical observations, any of which can be repeated by anyone who cares to do so.

The theory, though still essentially unchanged today, never really satisfied Freud. In 1915 he wrote:

Study of the derivatives of the unconscious will completely disappoint our expectations of a schematically clear-cut distinction between the two psychical systems. This will no doubt give rise to dissatisfaction with our results and will probably be used to cast doubts on the value of the way in which we have divided up the psychical processes. Our answer is, however, that we have no other aim but that of translating into theory the results of observation, and we deny that there is any obligation on us to achieve at our first attempt a well-rounded theory which will commend itself by its simplicity. We shall defend the complications of our theory so long as we find that they meet the results of observation, and we shall not abandon our expectations of being led in the end by these very complications to the discovery of a state of affairs which, while simple in itself, can account for all the complications of reality.[30]

The theory of the unconscious stems from numerous sources, but its major explication is found in connection with dreams, which he called the royal road to the unconscious. Chapter 7, "The Psychology of the Dream Processes," of *The Interpretation of Dreams* contains the heart of his theory and can be summarized here. In this chapter Freud asks: In the light of what has been uncovered of the nature of dreams, what kind of mental structure can we postulate to account for the phenomena? Emphasis is placed on the ability of the theory to account for the observations, an ability that shifts it from the sphere of speculation to that of science.

After some brief preliminary remarks pointing to the complexity of the task, the chapter is divided into six sections:
1. THE FORGETTING OF DREAMS. How does one know whether dreams are accurately remembered or not? As with memory in general, one does not know. But experience shows that the extent of forgetting is overestimated. The principle that psychic events are determined makes it certain that what is remembered is meaningful, provided one knows how to extract the meaning from it.

In analysis, forgetting serves the purpose of resistance. Similarly in dreams, to explain forgetting one refers to the power of the censorship.

In view of the censorship and the resistance to which it points, the question arises: How is a dream possible at all? The answer is that the state of sleep reduces the power of censorship.
2. REGRESSION. The most striking psychological characteristic of the dream is that a thought is objectified. Two features stand out: thought is represented as an immediate situation with the "perhaps" omitted; and thought is transformed into visual images and speech. In respect to the first point, dreams and daydreams are similar; in respect to the second, they are not.

Fechner had suggested that dreams take place in a different psychic locality; this view, which Freud adopts, has nothing anatomical about it. In general, psychic processes advance from the perceptual to the motor end; this is the familiar *reflex arc concept*. A system in front of the apparatus receives perceptual stimuli but retains no trace of them and thus has no memory, while behind it lies a second system which transforms momentary excitations into permanent traces. Further considerations of this kind led Freud to describe the division of the mind into conscious, preconscious, and unconscious, as in the accompanying diagram.

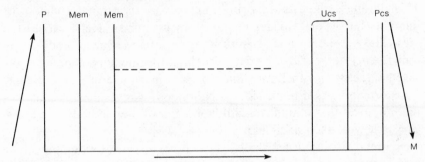

IN *THE INTERPRETATION OF DREAMS* FREUD USES THIS DIAGRAM OF THE DIVISION OF THE MIND INTO CONSCIOUS (*CS*), PRECONSCIOUS (*PCS*), AND UNCONSCIOUS (*UCS*). AT LEFT IS THE PERCEPTUAL END (*P*) WITH MEMORIES (*MEM*), AND AT RIGHT IS THE MOTOR OR ACTION END (*M*).

In the diagram, the left side is the perceptual end, the right side the motor end. The diagram is to be read as follows: Percepts lead to memories or permanent traces, which are unconscious. The unconscious is accessible to consciousness only through the preconscious; the unconscious cannot become conscious directly. The path from the preconscious in the diagram is the road to consciousness, which must fulfill certain conditions. The perceptual end is, of course, also conscious.

Within this structure Freud then asks: Where is the impetus to the construction of dreams to be found? The answer is: in the *unconscious*. In dreams the excitation moves in a backward direction. Instead of going from percept to motor activity, it goes from motor activity to the sensory end and finally results in a perception. This backward movement is "regressive." It is *regression* because in a dream an idea is turned back into the sensory image from which it was originally derived.

What modification makes possible in the dream a regression that cannot occur in the waking state? The first explanation is that during the waking state there is a current from the perceptual end to the motor end, in the progressive direction. This current stops during sleep and hence facilitates the reverse, or regressive, direction.

But the foregoing does not explain pathological regression in waking states—hallucinations and visions. These turn out to be linked with repressed memories which break through in such states. This finding suggests that in dreams too the transformation of thoughts into visual images results from memories. Hence arises the view that the dream is a substitute for an infantile scene modified by transference to recent material. The infantile memory cannot be revived directly and therefore must be satisfied to return as a dream. Thus dreaming is a regression to childhood, a revival of the instinctual impulses that dominated childhood and of the methods of expression that were then available.

Freud distinguishes three types of regression: topographical, in terms of the three systems, conscious, preconscious, unconscious; temporal, going back in time to older structures; and formal, where archaic methods of expression and representation take the place of the more ordinary ones.

3. WISH-FULFILLMENT. It has already been shown that recent and indifferent material can appear in a dream. But such material is secondary. A wish that is represented in a dream must be an infantile one. It comes from the unconscious.

The unconscious cannot enter consciousness directly, but establishes connections with ideas that already belong to the preconscious. This is an example of *transference*. As used here, "transference" is related to but not the same as the "transference" observed in the analytic relationship. The most recent and indifferent elements are objects of this transference; furthermore, they are more likely to stand out because they have less to fear from the censorship.

Why does the unconscious offer nothing but a wish? In earliest childhood, wishing ended in hallucinating the gratification, and thinking was nothing but a substitute for the hallucinatory wish. Then it becomes almost redundant to say that a dream is wish-fulfillment, since only a wish can impel the psychic apparatus to activity.

Dreaming is thus a piece of mental life that has been superseded. No matter what wishes come up, one need feel no concern—it is only a dream and therefore now harmless. If the wishes break through the censorship in waking life, what results is a psychosis. This led Freud to say later that in his dream the normal person becomes psychotic every night.

Psychoanalysis has shown that all neurotic symptoms are to be regarded as fulfillments of unconscious wishes. From this the value of dreams for an understanding of neurosis and the close tie between dreams and neurosis becomes evident.

4. AROUSAL BY DREAMS; THE FUNCTION OF DREAMS; ANXIETY DREAMS. Releases of pleasure and unpleasure automatically regulate the course of emotionally intense material; this was called the *economic* factor in the metapsychological scheme. Every dream has some arousing effect; at the same time, dreams serve to get rid of the disturbance of sleep. An unconscious wish can either be left to itself and discharged in movement, or it can be influenced by the preconscious and be bound by it instead of being discharged. The second process is the one that occurs in dreams. Thus the dream is a safety valve, or the guardian of sleep.

Anxiety in dreams is no different from anxiety in general. Anxiety dreams, too, contain a hidden gratification.

5. THE PRIMARY AND SECONDARY PROCESSES; REPRESSION. The dream work, involving extensive departures from rational thought, is a perplexing problem. To explain this and kindred phenomena, Freud postulated two basic processes, the primary and the secondary. The primary process is that which operates in the unconscious; it makes use of condensation and displacement; it easily shifts cathexes (emotionally intense material); it tolerates contradictions; it does not recognize negation; and in general it allows free mobility of cathexes. It seeks free discharge. It aims at perceptual identity. It is present from birth. The secondary process, by contrast, is a person's rational self. It seeks to inhibit rather than discharge. It can permit an idea to come to consciousness only if it can inhibit the unpleasure proceeding from it. It establishes thought identity. It is not present at birth, but develops only later.

The contrast between primary- and secondary-process thinking explains the phenomena of neurosis. Hence it can be said that the psychic mechanism employed by the neuroses is already present in the normal structure of the mental apparatus.

6. THE UNCONSCIOUS AND CONSCIOUSNESS; PSYCHIC REAL-

ITY. Theodor Lipps, one of the leading German psychologists of the 1890s, had said that the unconscious is *the* problem of psychology. With this, of course, Freud was in fullest agreement: ''The unconscious is the true psychical reality; *in its innermost nature it is as much unknown to us as the reality of the external world, and it is as incompletely represented by the data of consciousness as is the external world by the communication of our sense organs.*'' [31]

There are two kinds of unconscious. The one is inadmissible to consciousness (the true unconscious); the other is admissible (the preconscious). From this point of view Freud describes consciousness as a sense organ for the perception of psychical qualities.

There is a close connection between censorship and consciousness. The hypercathexis or excessive concentration leads to the thought processes, which are a new kind of regulation of unpleasure and constitute the superiority of people over animals.

Freud's theory of the dream was worked out with such thoroughness and attention to detail that it remains essentially unaltered today. (The same is not true for his other theories of this period.) The alternative to Freud is to state that dreams are cognitive reconstructions or meaningless aberrations. Neither of these positions is tenable.

Perhaps the major alteration which should be made in Freud's theory is his assumption of a preconscious. The division into three kinds of consciousness goes back to the three kinds of neuroses of the ''Project'' (1895). However, since for Freud the unconscious is the result of repression stemming from anxiety, the difference between the preconscious and the unconscious can only be one of degree. Hence the sharp dividing line which Freud attempted to draw can be ignored (Arlow and Brenner, 1964).

Manifestations of the Unconscious

Once he had developed the idea of the unconscious, Freud began to expand his observations in many directions. In his early days he had worked extensively with hypnosis, which could demonstrate the existence of unconscious motives experimentally (as in posthypnotic suggestion and posthypnotic amnesia), even though he had decided that hypnosis was therapeutically worthless. In spite of this abandonment, he remained convinced that it could illuminate the nature of mental life. In 1905, in a nontechnical paper, "On Psychical Treatment," he wrote:

The curative power of hypnotic suggestion is something real and it needs no exaggerated recommendation. On the other hand, it is not surprising that physicians, to whom hypnotic mental treatment promised so much more than it could give, are indefatigable in their search for other procedures, which would make possible a deeper, or at least a less unpredictable, influence on a patient's mind. It may safely be anticipated that systematic modern mental treatment, which is a quite recent revival of ancient therapeutic methods, will provide physicians with far more powerful weapons for the fight against illness. A deeper insight into the processes of mental life, the beginnings of which are based precisely on hypnotic experience, will point out the ways and means to this end.[32]

After hypnosis came dreams, which we have already discussed. Next Freud applied the concept of the unconscious in more detail to neurosis. In psychotherapy, free associations were seen as an avenue to the unconscious. These phenomena were still confined primarily to therapeutic or clinical situations. A complete break with therapy came when he turned his attention to two entirely novel subjects: parapraxes (now usually referred to as Freudian slips) and jokes. In 1901 he wrote *The Psychopathology of Everyday Life,* in which he described the various slips of the tongue, errors of omission and commission, symptomatic actions, failures to carry out actions, and a host of other minor and major slips and mistakes. Freud's thesis was that any slip has to be taken seriously. If it is, the need for gratification and wish-fulfillment, which is the basis of all mental life, appears clearly.

In 1905 he published his book on *Jokes and Their Relation to the Unconscious.* Here he demonstrated a wide-ranging similarity between the techniques used in jokes and those used in slips and dreams, again pointing to a basic conceptual tool for understanding mental life. In jokes, too, the individual is in the grip of psychic conflicts which need discharge, and the joke serves as a discharge phenomenon.

At about the time that he wrote on jokes, Freud also began to investigate the matter of artistic production. As early as 1904 he wrote a paper on "Psychopathic Characters on the Stage," which embodies many of the essential ideas in the psychoanalytic interpretation of art. In the theatrical performance, both the performer and the audience find some gratification for their neurotic needs. The needs which are gratified are unconscious in nature; were they to become conscious, the attraction of the artistic performance for both the performer and the audience would be lost.

And so the horizons continued to broaden. In 1907 Freud wrote a paper about obsessional acts and religious practices, in which he called attention to the close similarity between the two. He showed that religion, too, is motivated by unconscious forces.

By this time he had begun to have some followers, and several of them, particularly Otto Rank and Hanns Sachs, did essential work in the application of psychoanalysis to mythology and the social sciences. In 1913 Freud published his classic application of psychoanalytic thinking to other societies, *Totem and Taboo*. Here he demonstrated that the unconscious processes found in one form of society are not really dissimilar from those found in others. The psychic unity of mankind is the basic thesis of this seminal masterpiece.

Still later, some of his followers applied the theory of the unconscious not merely to slips in behavior but also to ordinary everyday behavior, such as the way a person walks, talks, and dresses. They were able to show that everything has or can have an unconscious aspect to it.

Thus among the aspects of human living in which manifestations of the unconscious can be found are hypnosis, neurotic symptoms, free associations, daydreams, dreams, slips of everyday life, jokes, art, religion, mythology, other societies, and behavior in general. In other words, the unconscious may be applicable to every area of human existence. A new domain, the area of psychic reality, is opened to scientific investigation. Through the exploration of psychic reality, psychoanalysis lays an indispensable basis for a general psychology. This was what justified Freud's claim that he had opened up a whole new world for mankind, the inner world of psychic reality.

Psychosexual Development

The second cornerstone of the first psychoanalytic system is psychosexuality, which Freud also came to refer to as the libido theory. By "libido" he meant a quantitatively variable force that can serve as a measure of processes and transformations occurring in the field of

sexual excitation. In practice, libido is equated with the broad meaning of sexuality.

The first presentation of the libido theory came in 1905 in *Three
Essays on Sexuality*. After that it changed, through the work of Freud
and others, more than any other of his views of that period. Accordingly the "libido theory" consists of a number of different hypotheses that stem from different periods in Freud's development. Today
there is broad agreement on certain points, but there remains wide
disagreement on many others, leading to a considerable amount of
controversy in the current literature.

As formulated by Freud in this period, the libido theory consisted of six main hypotheses: 1. There is a developmental process
consisting of various libidinal stages. 2. Libido is the major source of
psychic energy. 3. Object choice (interpersonal relations) results from
the transformations of libido. 4. The libidinal drives can be gratified,
repressed, handled by a reaction formation, or sublimated. For most
instinctual needs, sublimation is the normal human adjustment. 5.
Character structure is built on the modes in which the biologically determined instincts are handled. 6. Neurosis is a fixation on, or a
regression to, some phase of infantile sexuality. Furthermore, the earlier the fixation or the deeper the regression, the greater the psychopathology.

The Psychosexual Stages

In the 1890s Freud had pursued a rather simplistic view; that neurosis
results from the frustration of genital sexual desire. He eventually
came to see that this was inadequate. The sexual instinct, he realized,
had a long history. In the earlier period he had already started the
search for the traumas in childhood that lead to hysteria or obsessional neurosis. As time went on he came to see more and more that
no single trauma could be held responsible for the complexity of the
clinical picture; rather, there was a biologically determined course of
sexual development which could be used as a basis for further understanding.

The naive assumption generally held at that time, by professional and lay people alike, had been that the sexual instinct comes
into existence full-blown at puberty. Freud rephrased this to state that
at puberty the aim and the object go together.

The aim of the sexual instinct is the discharge of tension or of the sexual products. The object is the person (or substitute) who is sought out to gratify this discharge. The ordinary view can be rephrased to the effect that the average person assumes that the sexual drive consists of the wish to have sexual intercourse with a person of the opposite sex, and that this wish arises only with the maturation of the sexual organs.

Clinical experience, however, contradicted this common-sense view. Particularly significant was the connection between neurosis, perversion, and childhood. This connection was described by Freud in two formulas: the neurosis is the negative of the perversion; and the child is polymorphous perverse.

By the first formula Freud meant that the neurotic does in fantasy what the pervert (read today: person with acting-out disorder) does in actuality. Thus sexual perversions are found in which a man defecates or urinates on a woman, or beats her or is beaten by her. Or the man may be homosexual and choose only men as love objects. Or again he may derive his main sexual pleasure from articles of clothing or other inanimate objects, known as fetishes. All these are found as unconscious wishes in the fantasies of neurotics.

By the second formula, that the child is polymorphous perverse, Freud meant that all the activities that are carried out by the pervert and fantasied by the neurotic are normal to the child at some state in childhood. The concepts of the unconscious and of infantile sexuality and the hypothesis of a close tie between the two have great explanatory value.

Thus it becomes apparent that the aim and the object are not always as close as popular opinion believes. This separation into aim and object Freud utilized as a basis for further investigation. The development of each can be traced separately.

In the course of this investigation Freud extended the concept of sexuality in two directions. On the one hand it was broadened to include all bodily pleasure; on the other it was extended to cover feelings of tenderness and affection as well as the desire for genital contact. For both of these extensions there is ample ground in common observation and in clinical experience. For example, ordinary language uses the word "love" in many different senses: I love my wife; I love to smoke; I love music; I love America; I love my alma mater, etc.

Freud then divided the human sex life into three periods: infantile sexuality (roughtly up to age 5), the latency period, and puberty. Infantile sexuality is further subdivided into the oral, anal, and phallic stages, culminating in the Oedipus complex, somewhere between the ages of 3 and 5. Before the Oedipus stage, the aim of the sexual instinct is not tied to an object; the model for gratification is masturbation rather than intercourse with another human being. Freud did, however, recognize some so-called partial instincts in this period: sadism, voyeurism, and exhibitionism, that is, the impulses to cruelty, looking, and showing oneself, which are regularly tied to other people or objects.

Infantile sexuality culminates in the Oedipus complex, the wish to have sexual relations with the parent of the opposite sex, and the corresponding antagonistic wishes toward the parent of the same sex. Freud saw the Oedipus complex as the source of all personality structure, whether neurotic or normal. By his analysis of the Oedipal situation, Freud was the first to show how crucial the family constellation is for the formation of personality.

The latency period, which roughly covers the elementary-school age, Freud saw as a biologically determined stage, in which the manifestations of sexuality are either absent or reduced to a minimum.

This historical development was now made the basis for an understanding of the development at puberty. At this time in the normal person there must be a union of the sexual and tender feelings toward a person of the opposite sex; in other words, object love is reached. The object whom individuals choose at puberty, that is, the person whom one wants to marry or marries, is a repetition of the object that had become important at the time of the Oedipus stage. Or to put it in simpler language, a person tries to find a mate who is like his parent of the opposite sex.

Thus the normal course of the development of the sexual aim is from the oral stage, when the infant derives his main pleasure from sucking at the breast, to that of genital primacy, when the major gratification is sexual intercourse.

A particularly crucial aspect of psychosexual development was the subject of love, a topic which preoccupied Freud a great deal and to which he came back repeatedly. In a footnote added in 1915 to the *Three Essays on Sexuality,* he wrote: "The innumerable peculiarities of the erotic life of human beings as well as the compulsive character of the process of falling in love itself are quite unintelligible except by reference back to childhood and as being residual effects of childhood.''[33]

Throughout his works Freud was concerned with correlating his clinical observations of love with these "residual effects of childhood." The most important instance in actual practice was that of transference love, in which the patient, unconsciously and compulsively, recapitulates with the analyst the profound feelings of love and hate he felt toward his parents when he was a child. This transference love differs only in degree from ordinary love.[34] Freud saw love as essentially a fixation on the parents. Its irrationality, its compulsiveness, its frequently self-damaging aspects were to be understood in terms of the disturbances in the child's relationship with the parents.

Two essays, one written in 1910, the other in 1912, take up two aspects of neurotic love behavior in the man. One is the need on the man's part to fall in love with some sexually promiscuous woman, often a prostitute, and to bend his every effort to rescue her. In spite of his great love, he is constantly tormented by terrible feelings of jealousy. The woman in such cases is the mother, transformed through the eyes of the little boy.

The second essay deals with the most prevalent form of degradation in the sphere of love. Here the man sets as a precondition for sexual satisfaction the debasement of the woman. She belongs to an inferior race (compare the white man with the black woman in the southern United States), is inadequate, or is "bad" merely because she has intercourse. The spread of Freud's teachings has done much to obliterate this distinction between the "good" and the "bad" woman, but one must bear in mind how common this split was in Freud's day and how common it still is in many parts of the world. This culturally determined taboo on sexual gratification again derives from the image of the "good" mother who would not engage in a "dirty" activity such as sex. As Freud points out, the consequences of this sharp split between "good" and "bad" women can only be psychic impotence in men and frigidity in women.

It is not to be concluded from these and similar essays, however, that Freud considered love to be inherently neurotic. As a clinician he was confronted with the infantile forms of love, such as the need to rescue a prostitute, or the need to degrade the woman, or love as a kind of hypnotic trance, and to these he devoted most of his attention. But he was also well aware of the constructive character of love, as, for example, in his famous statement that the normal person is the one who can work and love.

Freud discussed love at many other points in his writings. He traced the relationship between narcissism and love and held that by and large men love according to the anaclitic type of object choice (sexual overestimation of the woman), while women love according to the narcissistic type (they wish to be loved). In these various positions his own puzzlement about women seems to have colored his vision unduly and led him to rely too heavily on his self-analysis; for instance, he makes the strange remark that perhaps the only unambivalent love in the world is that of a mother for her son.[35]

With the theory of sexual causation of neurosis, and that of the development of sexuality in general, Freud emerged upon the broader scene of social criticism. As long as neurologists believed the myth that mental illness was merely a variety of brain pathology, the significance for civilization in general of neurology and psychiatry was small. But if sex is a source of disturbance in neurotics and actually in all people, as Freud soon came to realize, then the whole structure of society is at stake, for modern society prescribes, even today, a rigid code of sexual abstinence. The vaunted morality of the great nations, said Freud in effect, is a pack of lies and produces a world of neurotics.

When the theoretical position that sexual restrictions and disturbances lead to neurosis had been established, it seemed inevitable that Freud should turn his attention to the kind of society that prescribed such a harmful code. Privately he left no doubt of where he stood. Yet publicly he was reluctant to take a stand. Political action in any form was foreign to his nature; one consequence of this weakness was the inadequate structure of organized psychoanalysis.

In the matter of sexuality another curious change occurred. Since his views led to the clear need for social reform, which frightened him, he began to change his views. As a consequence of cultural development, he argued,

we may perhaps be forced to become reconciled to the idea that it is quite impossible to adjust the claims of the sexual instinct to the demands of civilization; that in consequence of its cultural development renunciation and suffering, as well as the danger of extinction in the remotest future, cannot be avoided by the human race.[36]

Libido and Psychic Energy

Libido is the major source of psychic energy. The sexual instincts provide the major though not the sole drive for the functioning of the individual. Freud also allowed for the ego-instincts, or drives, which are nonsexual in nature. But in both practice and theory the emphasis in this period was on the sexual drives.

The concept of psychic energy has probably occasioned more controversy than any other of Freud's basic ideas. It stems from the old argument among the hypnotists[37] as to whether the cause of magnetic (or hypnotic) influence was a mental influence or an actual fluid; Freud's concept combines both these possibilities—it was never entirely clear whether psychic energy was physical or psychological. Although many attempts have been made to do so, it cannot be equated in any way with physical energy (Theobald, 1966). Yet despite its ambiguities, it has been held tenaciously by many subsequent analysts. The later controversies are discussed in chapter 15.

Object Choice

Object choice results from the transformation of libido. Objects are required by the individual to satisfy libidinal needs. This topic was not in the forefront of Freud's thought in this period, and so his early position can only be seen as a first approximation.

Defense Mechanisms

The libidinal drives can be gratified, repressed, handled by a reaction formation, or sublimated. Inasmuch as they are biological givens, they must be handled somehow. In this early period the major emphasis was on repression and sublimation, the socially acceptable transformation of the instinct. The full theory of defenses came later.

Character Structure

Character structure is built on the ways in which biologically determined instincts are handled. This proposition was added in 1908 in the paper on "Character and Anal Erotism," in which Freud wrote: "We can at any rate lay down a formula for the way in which character in its final shape is formed out of the constituent instincts: the permanent character traits are either unchanged prolongations of the original instincts, or sublimations of those instincts, or reaction-formations against them."[38]

In Freud's own work the only character type delineated with any thoroughness was the anal character. He described the traits of orderliness, parsimony, and obstinacy as typical of the anal character and traced their development to the conflicts surrounding the child's early bowel training. Later the connection between anal erotism and obsessional neurosis was brought out (1913).

Descriptions of the anal character and obsessional neurosis dominated the analytic literature before World War I. For example, Ferenczi described one type of homosexual as an obsessional neurotic.[39] To a considerable extent this overemphasis on anality was due to the fact that the stages of libidinal development were still only partially known, and that in particular almost nothing was known about the oral stage. As late as 1924 Abraham could write that "a retrograde transformation of character . . . in the main comes to a stop at the anal stage."[40]

When further clinical experience and information about libidinal development became available, the understanding of character structure broadened considerably. Wilhelm Reich's book *Character Analysis* (1933) was a milestone in this area. However, Reich was much too schematic; as the insights of ego psychology grew, his work became less important. Today this aspect of psychoanalysis is still in a state of considerable flux (see chapter 12).

Neurosis and Infantile Sexuality

"Neurosis is a fixation on, or a regression to, some phase of infantile sexuality." This proposition, first enunciated in the latter part of the *Three Essays* in 1905, has become the kernel of all modern theories of neurosis and psychosis; differences appear only with regard to detail, not the general idea. The corollary is that the earlier the fixation or the deeper the regression, the greater the psychopathology. The elaboration of these two propositions leads to a resolution of the problem of the classical neuroses—hysteria and obsessional neuroses. It still leaves many questions unanswered in the broader area of psychosis and character neurosis.

The classical neuroses, hysteria and obsessional neurosis, may be approached in terms of idea and affect, or emotion. In hysteria ideas are repressed, while affects overwhelm the individual (usually a woman). In obsessional neurosis, ideation is clear but affect is blocked (usually a man). Patients suffering from these neuroses form transferences to the analyst. By the analysis of these transferences and their concomitant resistances, the symptoms can be traced back to their source in infantile sexuality and eventually dissipated. The analytic treatment of these two classical neuroses was a great therapeutic victory for Freud.

Transference and Resistance

The third cornerstone of id psychology is transference and its allied resistance. In fact, Freud characterized psychoanalysis in terms of these two. In 1914 he wrote:

It may thus be said that the theory of psychoanalysis is an attempt to account for two striking an unexpected facts of observation which emerge whenever an attempt is made to trace the symptoms of a neurotic back to their sources in his past life: the facts of transference and resistance. Any line of investigation which recognizes these two facts and takes them as the starting point of its work may call itself psychoanalysis, though it arrives at results other than my own.[41]

Unfortunately Freud never gave a systematic account of these two phenomena. In all his writings not a single paper is devoted exclusively to resistance in the psychoanalytic process. From 1910 onward, when he began to have a number of followers and noticed that some of them did not grasp what he was teaching, he began to write a series of papers on technique, stressing transference particularly. Even these papers, however, are rather sketchy and scarcely satisfactory for the purpose. Nevertheless, all analysts since Freud have been unanimous in the belief that the observations of transference and resistance are the most profound ever made about psychotherapy, and that they help to explain at one stroke the whole gamut of baffling phenomena which occur in the process of trying to help another human being.

"Transference" may be described as the observation that patients in therapy do not submit to a dispassionate consideration of their difficulties but instead soon enter into an intense relationship with the therapist. As could be predicted from theory, this relationship centers primarily around the two aspects of the Oedipus complex, the sexual attraction for the parent of the opposite sex and the antagonism toward the parent of the same sex. The individual finds it extremely difficult to recognize his or her unconscious emotional drives and so represses them. In the psychoanalytic treatment process this repression becomes a resistance, a refusal (unconscious, of course) to see the real nature of the ties to the therapist, the instinctual drives which motivate the individual, and the ties to other people.

Again the interconnectedness of the three cornerstones of id psychology becomes apparent. The unconscious deals mostly with the remains of infantile sexuality; conversely, infantile sexuality is unacceptable to the individual and is repressed into the unconscious. The total process causes persons to be driven by a mass of irrational urges which they can neither fathom nor adequately control. Under the impulse of these urges they come as patients into analytic treatment; there they resist the uncovering of their wishes in the same way that they oppose their recognition in real life. Consequently rational therapy must necessarily fail because it does not take into consideration the nature of the illness. To succeed, the therapist must apply the principles of transference and resistance.

For the student and the lay person, the doctrines of transference and resistance are the hardest of all the Freudian theories to grasp. Yet they are the most fundamental to the theory and practice of psychotherapy. There is no easy way of bridging this gap. Even today there always remains a highly personal element in psychoanalysis which makes it more of an art than an exact science.

1914–1939: Ego Psychology

It is one mark of the progress made in the past 60 years that the first psychoanalytic system is scarcely recognized as psychoanalysis by the modern generation. In its essentials it has been absorbed into the mainstream of all of psychology and psychiatry, and by application, all the social sciences. Arguments exist about detail, not about the basic structure. There are of course die-hards who will deny the validity of any proposition dealing with the inner life, but increasingly they appear to be in the minority. Auden was certainly justified in his famous remark that Freud created a whole new climate of opinion.

Yet Freud himself was eternally dissatisfied. He had always had in mind a complete system of psychology that would explain the whole of mental functioning. In 1915 he began a book variously titled *Introduction to Metapsychology, Introductory Essays on Meta- psychology,* and *A General Review of the Transference Neuroses.* By "metapsychology" he meant a comprehensive description of mental processes along psychoanalytic lines. Unfortunately, only 5 of the 12 projected essays in this book were ever published; the other 7 were destroyed by Freud, for unknown reasons.[42]

One element in his system had always disturbed him—the lack of an adequate physiological base. No psychology could be complete without such a base; hence he was always discontent with his achievements. Other factors contributed as well. Up to 1914 his work had been almost entirely confined to the neuroses. The psychoses could not yield to the standard psychoanalytic treatment he had de- vised, though he always expressed the hope that someday modifica- tions would be discovered which would make it possible for them to be treated (which has actually happened). In 1911 he published his study of the Schreber case, the first time anyone had ever penetrated so deeply into the mental life of a psychotic. But Schreber was a paranoiac who had written a book about himself; he was not one of Freud's patients (Niederland, 1974). Therefore many doubts re- mained. Freud hoped that the study of the ego would prove as fruitful for the understanding and therapy of the psychoses as the study of the id had proved for the neuroses.

Second, he was still elaborating his basic formula that neurosis involves a defense against unbearable ideas. The nature of the un- bearable sexual ideas had been quite thoroughly explored; the nature of the defensive processes had lagged behind. Various formulas de- scribing this defensive process appeared at different times. In the early 1900s it was put in terms of repression. In 1911 he saw the op- position as that between the pleasure principle and the reality princi- ple. In the second decade he began to explore the countercathexes. And finally in 1923 in *The Ego and the Id* he put forward the version that has remained standard ever since: the ego versus the id. Ego psy- chology may be dated from 1914, with the paper on "Narcissism," or from 1923; in either case it is a natural outgrowth of the concept of defense first formulated in 1894. Since 1923 all of psychoanalysis has been ego psychology.

Third, as his therapeutic experience grew, Freud was forced to pay more attention to character structure. As he wrote in 1915:

When a doctor carries out the psychoanalytic treatment of a neurotic, his interest is by no means directed in the first instance to the patient's character. He would much rather know what the symptoms mean, what instinctual impulses are concealed behind them and are satisfied by them, and what course was followed by the mysterious path that has led from the instinctual wishes to the symptoms. But the technique which he is obliged to follow soon compels him to direct his immediate curiosity towards other objectives. He observes that his investigation is threatened by resistances set up against him by the patient, and these resistances he may justly count as part of the latter's character. This now acquires the first claim on his interest.[43]

Eventually character was to be equated with ego structure or total personality structure (Alexander, 1927).

Fourth, there was the catastrophic impact of World War I. Except for relatively minor skirmishes, Europe had known peace for almost a hundred years, since Napoleon's defeat at Waterloo in 1815. The fury of the onslaught, the barbarism displayed by the participants, the unprecedented slaughter, the disappearance of the active monarchies in its wake, all made a profound impression on every cultured European. Faced with such a massive social upheaval, Freud felt that he had to refine his theoretical conceptualizations to explain more adequately what had happened.

And finally there was the personal factor, which always weighed heavily with Freud. With the growth of the psychoanalytic movement, he was subject to severe criticism from many directions; in addition, a number of his adherents defected. Most painful were the loss of Alfred Adler in 1911, whom he had appointed head of the Vienna group, and Carl Jung in 1913, whom he had appointed head of the International. In his writings after World War I, time and again there are passages, sometimes seemingly interjected out of nowhere, in which he takes up the cudgels against either Adler or Jung. And then there was the ongoing correspondence with the American neurologist James Putnam, for whom he had the highest regard. Putnam had consistently criticized Freud for not paying sufficient attention to the moral needs of the patient.

From 1914 Freud struggled with a new synthesis, which finally saw its present form as the tripartite structure of id, ego, and superego in *The Ego and the Id* in 1923. The id is the reservoir of instinctual impulses, the ego is that part of the personality that deals with reality, and the superego is the unconscious conscience, the heir of the parents.

Freud was not a man who engaged in argument or responded to criticism. In his entire life there is only one reply to an attack, an early paper in answer to Leopold Löwenfeld's criticism of his concept of anxiety neurosis. Yet careful perusal of his work shows that he considered his opponents' commentaries very carefully. When they seemed to make sense, he absorbed them into his system, meanwhile avoiding any arguments. Thus he had successively incorporated the neurology of his teachers, the cathartic therapy of Breuer, the hypnosis of Bernheim, the classification of hysteria as a disease by Charcot, and Fliess's notion of bisexuality, emerging with a system much superior to what had been offered to him.

A similar process occurred with the tripartite structure. In the id he absorbed the concept of George Groddeck, who had taught that we are lived by unknown and unknowable forces, the Adlerian notion of an aggressive drive, Jung's extension of sexuality to a more all-inclusive kind of instinctual urge, and even the wholesale slaughter of the war. The ego was inherent in his earlier system; indeed it is inherent in the language, since the German word for ego is *Ich,* the ordinary word for "I." Here he also incorporated Adler's constant references to ego forces at the Vienna Psychoanalytic Society meetings. With the superego he was able to reply to Putnam's objection that psychoanalysis omitted the higher strivings of mankind. And yet the final synthesis stands as a brilliant systematization that still remains the most fruitful basis for human psychology.

Unlike the first psychoanalytic system, which was published in final form, omitting the process which led up to the conclusions, ego psychology, or the second psychoanalytic system, saw the light in a series of publications from Freud's pen between 1914 and 1926, with a final important paper in 1937. Some of his ideas, as in *Beyond the Pleasure Principle* (1920), were offered with great hesitation; others, such as the paper on narcissism (1914), were superseded by later works, thus losing a place in the organic whole of Freud's thought. His views have to be teased out from many sources. The works that have stood the test of time best are *The Ego and the Id* (1923), in which the tripartite structure was first clearly formulated; *The Problem of Anxiety* (1962), in which he clarified the concept of defense mechanisms; and "Analysis Terminable and Interminable" (1937), in which he summed up a lifetime of experience with psychoanalysis and psychotherapy. The material of the later period can best be ordered in terms of the id, the ego, the superego, and his philosophical position.

The Id

The id is the reservoir of the instinctual impulses. In this conception, three major changes occurred: the shift to a dual instinct theory, the switch to the second theory of anxiety, and the beginnings of an exploration of the oral stage.

The Dual Instinct Theory

In all respects but one the instinct theory proposed by Freud in 1905 was identical with that held by other theorists of the day (Fletcher, 1966). The difference lay in Freud's emphatic insistence that all the other instincts could be derived from one basic instinctual drive— sexuality, or libido, as he later called it. Yet his theory of the instincts never pleased him entirely. He referred to it as "our mythology" and kept revising it in various ways.

Finally he offered a new revision in *Beyond the Pleasure Principle* in 1920, which staggered the analytic world. Here he proposed that there are two major kinds of instinct: Eros, or life, and Thanatos, or death. The death instinct manifests itself in the form of destructive wishes, first toward oneself (primary masochism) and later toward other people and the outside world.

From 1910 to 1920 Freud's attention had been directed increasingly to the problems of guilt and hatred. The war forced him to consider why mankind periodically regressed to wholesale massacres that would never be tolerated in peacetime (at least it was thought so at that time).

Even within the libido theory the significance of the sadistic drives dawned on Freud rather late. The anal-sadistic stage and the connection which he drew between the anal-sadistic fixation and the obsessional neurosis were not included in the first description of libidinal development in 1905, but were added in 1913.

In 1915, when he came to systematize his whole approach, sadism remained a puzzle. Originally he had seen sadism as a component instinct of sexuality, but upon more careful consideration he found this view unacceptable. In 1915 he stated: "The case of love and hate acquires a special interest from the circumstance that it refuses to be fitted into our scheme of the instincts." [44]

If love and hate cannot be fitted into the scheme of the instincts, whence does hatred arise? In the obsessional neurosis there is a regression from love to hate, and the ambivalence between love and hate plays a particularly significant role in the symptomatology and character formation. Freud argued that the attitudes of love and hate cannot be made use of for the relations of instincts to their objects, but are reserved for the relations of the total ego to objects. Thus he concluded that the true origins of the relationship of hate are derived from the ego's struggle to maintain and preserve itself, not from sex.

Freud's change of position in 1917 to the view that sadism is associated with the ego instincts stands in marked contrast to his earlier position on the question of aggression. The concept of an aggressive impulse had first been proposed by Adler in 1908, at which time it was emphatically rejected by Freud, who castigated it as a "cheerless" view of the world. [45] Soon he was to propose something far more cheerless than anything Adler had envisaged.

At the same time, clinically the problem of masochism became more important. In *Mourning and Melancholia* (1917) for the first time he took up seriously the problem of depression and its metapsychology. He recognized that depression is intimately linked with punishment. In neurotic or psychotic depression, this punishment derives from an internalized object, or introject, while in mourning it derives from the loss of an external object. In *A Child Is Being Beaten* (1919) he considered at length some clinical observations on beating fantasies in childhood. He argued that the memory of being beaten or of other children being beaten derived ultimately from the incestuous wish to be loved by one's father; in the fantasy, love was turned into a beating.

With these views he still remained within the pleasure principle. His shift to the death instinct the following year was therefore all the more disconcerting. And in fact his assumption of a death instinct is the one view that has been emphatically repudiated by his followers. In a review of the literature up to 1957, Jones found that of the 50 or so papers devoted to the topic since Freud's original publication, during the first decade only half supported Freud's theory, during the second decade only a third, and during the last decade none at all.[46]

Although the death instinct has been almost universally rejected, the dual instinct theory has been preserved through the conceptualization of sexual and aggressive instincts. However, the situation remains far from clarification even today (see chapter 8).

The Second Theory of Anxiety

From the very beginning, Freud saw anxiety as being at the heart of neurosis; "unbearable" ideas obviously are anxiety-producing ideas. Originally his theory was that anxiety is dammed-up libido, that is, libido which, unable to find expression in the normal sexual manifestations, then turns into fear or anxiety. The "toxicological" theory was seen as a purely physiological process: he assumed that in some as yet undiscovered way the sexual excitation was "transformed" into anxiety.

In the 1890s he proposed the theory of the "actual-neurosis"—the neurosis that results from real sexual frustration, which is then transformed into some physiological disturbance. For such patients, the only cure is a change in their sexual regimen.

As with so many of his early theories, although he rejected these two in practice, he did not do so either in his published writings or in his discussions of theory. As late as 1910, when pressed by Federn, Stekel, and other members of the Vienna Psychoanalytic Society (Nunberg and Federn, 1962–1975), he reaffirmed his old position even though it was clearly not consistent with his later views. He even stated in 1910 that he had not subjected a "sufficient" number of cases of actual-neurosis to strict examination during the "past fifteen years" (i.e., since 1895), yet he still clung to the idea.[47] Part of the reason for holding onto the theory of actual-neurosis is that he felt too uncomfortable without a physiological basis for his theories.

Eventually, however, the weight of the evidence was overwhelming and led him to conclude that anxiety is in the ego, not in the id. Fear is fundamentally, as Darwin had already pointed out, a biological response to danger. Anxiety differs from fear only in that here the danger is not real; it is a threat to the individual for subjective reasons. Furthermore, Freud could now see that the instinctual impulse is not immediately transformed into anxiety, since the same anxiety can arise from different impulses.

All of this was pulled together in the second theory of anxiety. *Anxiety,* he now held, *is a signal given by the ego that danger threatens* (*Problem of Anxiety,* 1926). The nature of this danger can then be explored. He saw it as originally *separation anxiety,* fear of separation from the mother. The prototype of this separation anxiety is the birth situation with the actual separation from the mother. In this respect Freud saw some merit in the birth trauma theory of Rank, but he discarded the extreme exaggeration of that theory.

Later forms of anxiety repeat the fear of separation in other ways. Punishment is a threat because of the loss of the parental love. Castration involves separation from the penis. Later dangers can all be viewed as variations on this threat of separation.

The second theory of anxiety also required a change in the conceptualization of the defensive process. Previously repression had been the only defense considered, after the earliest papers. In the toxicological period, his interpretation was that repression led to anxiety by a biochemical process. Now the reverse was seen to be the case: anxiety leads to repression. But anxiety can also be handled in other ways. Hence the road was open for an examination of the entire defensive process.

The second theory of anxiety carried such an overwhelming sense of conviction that it has not been seriously challenged. It has become one of the bases of all psychoanalytic and psychological theory.

The Oral Stage

This revised theory of anxiety led Freud back for the first time to the oral stage, the relationship between mother and child before the father enters the picture. It is remarkable that Freud, despite his insistent emphasis on the significance of the infantile factor, recognized the importance of the oral stage only at a relatively late period in his work. For most of his life he seems to have held the idea that nothing could really go wrong between a mother and child and that, accordingly, neurotic difficulties must begin later.

The first year of life always remained something of a mystery to Freud. Since Freud's was in some respects a personal system, an explanation for this situation might be found in the facts of his own life. In his self-analysis he recognized that this process had been set off by the death of his father. Freud's mother, on the other hand, lived to an extremely old age. When she died, he was already in his seventies. He remained a dutiful son all his life, and he never analyzed his conflicts with his mother, although he did do so in others (e.g., in Leonardo da Vinci, in 1910).[48]

Once the new theory of anxiety was propounded and the significance of the oral stage recognized, a new era in psychoanalytic thinking began. It reached its full swing only after World War II, and in many respects it is still continuing. The exploration of the oral stage has brought about widespread changes in both theory and technique (see chapter 6).

The Ego

The ego is that part of the psychic apparatus that deals with reality. It is the secondary process, whereas the id is the primary process.

At birth, ego and id are undifferentiated. Gradually, as the individual develops, an ego emerges. The first point at which an ego can be said to exist is when bodily sensations are perceived; hence Freud states that the ego is first and foremost a body ego.

The ego is the part of the id that has been modified by the direct influence of the external world acting through the system of perception-consciousness. By its control of perception and consciousness, the ego wards off anxiety-provoking situations.

Against the dangers threatening from the external world, the ego is in a good position to defend itself; if necessary, it can take flight. But this is not possible with regard to internal dangers (instinctual impulses). Freud saw this greater susceptibility to internal dangers as one source of neurosis.

The ego depends on a neutral displaceable *energy,* which is desexualized Eros. This displaceable energy or desexualized libido could also be described as sublimated energy. Here Freud arrives at a version of sublimation somewhat different from his earlier view of finding a socially acceptable means for gratifying forbidden impulses.

For him the ego was a composite of a number of defense mechanisms, such as sublimation, reaction formation, regression, repression, isolation, and undoing (*Problem of Anxiety,* 1926). The concept of repression was replaced by that of defense; repression was now seen as one of many defense mechanisms. The different neuroses were characterized by different defenses: e.g., hysteria used primarily repression, while obsessional neurosis used regression and reaction formation. In 1936, in *The Ego and the Mechanisms of Defense,* Anna Freud described the various defense mechanisms in greater detail and clarified their role in the functioning of the personality.

Freud's concept of personality structure now centered around the ego. The various components of the ego may vary in many different ways, from normal to psychotic. In 1937 he wrote:

Every normal person, in fact, is only normal on the average. His ego approximates to that of the psychotic in some part or other and to a greater or lesser extent; and the degree of its remoteness from one end of the series, and of its proximity to the other will furnish us with a provisional measure of what we have so indefinitely termed an "alteration of the ego."[49]

These modifications or variations of the ego may be either hereditary or acquired. Every individual has certain characteristic ways of relating to the world, and these are a mixture of inborn structures and environmental influences.

Finally, an ego can be regarded as strong or weak. The capacity of the ego to handle reality, both internal and external, is the measure of its strength.

While Freud laid the basis for modern ego psychology, his views have undergone considerable expansion and modification. These are considered in chapter 11.

The Ego and Therapy

The formulation of the ego concept necessarily led to wide-ranging alterations in the whole concept of psychoanalysis and psychoanalytic therapy. Freud considered them at length in his memorable 1937 paper, "Analysis Terminable and Interminable." For an understanding of that paper, it is useful to sketch briefly the historical development of his views on therapy.

Originally Freud began with the *cathartic method,* which he had learned from Breuer. In this method the patient is hypnotized and taken back to the *traumatic situation* that set off the neurosis. This trauma was seen as resulting in a *strangulation of affect* that had to be *abreacted* (released) in the therapeutic situation. Once the affect was abreacted, the patient was cured. The formula here was: *Make the unconscious conscious.*

Once he had moved to the first psychoanalytic system, in the 1900s, this approach was seen as much too simplistic and was discarded as therapeutically inadequate. Now the basis of therapy became *transference and resistance.* The patient was no longer hypnotized; his full conscious cooperation was essential. Instead he was asked to lie on a couch and *free associate.* Because of the transference, nobody was willing to make associations completely freely; hence attention was drawn to the resistances. Intellectual understanding, which had been the dominant motif in the early years of the century, proved to be of no avail. Instead, the patient had to work through the resistances. This was the position Freud reached in 1914, when he wrote: "This working-through of the resistances may in practice turn out to be an arduous task for the subject of the analysis and a trial of patience for the analyst. Nevertheless, it is a part of the work which effects the greatest changes in the patient and which distinguishes analytic treatment from any kind of treatment by suggestion."[50]

Once the tripartite structure was formulated, in the 1920s, and the neurotic structure was defined in terms of the ego (neurosis was seen as a conflict between the ego and the id), the ego had to be included in the theory of therapy. Then the formula became: *Where the id was, the ego shall be.* That is, the patient had to replace compulsive, id-driven behavior by rational considerations under ego control.

After World War I, Freud conducted very few therapeutic analyses; his work was confined largely to training foreign physicians, mainly from America and England. Nevertheless he kept in touch with developments, and summed up his lifetime thoughts in the 1937 paper. This paper centers around the question: When can an analysis be said to be terminated?

Freud holds that the results of an analysis depend on three main factors: the relative importance of the traumatic element, the relative strength of the instincts, and the modifications of the ego in the defensive conflict. It is only in the first instance that a simple outcome in psychoanalysis can be anticipated, one that involves the strengthening of the ego and the replacement of an inadequate childhood decision by a larger correct solution. In the other two instances quantitative factors play a major role, and the question of when an analysis is terminated is a thorny one indeed. By and large the goal is to produce the best possible conditions for the functioning of the ego. Freud writes:

Our aim will not be to rub off every peculiarity of human character for the sake of a schematic normality, nor yet to demand that the person who has been "thoroughly analyzed" shall feel no passions and develop no internal conflicts. The business of the analysis is to secure the best possible psychological conditions for the functions of the ego; with that it has discharged its task.[51]

It may be useful to review the different theoretical conceptualizations that led Freud to change his image of termination and analysis through the years. Seven different discoveries can be specified that led to correspondingly different demands on the analysis and different views of what analyzability is. These are the importance or existence of: dreams, childhood memories, infantile sexuality, transference, resistance, working through, and ego structure.

DREAMS. As soon as Freud discovered the paramount significance of dreams, a new and essentially indeterminate element was introduced into the process of psychoanalysis. For the patient could be completely free from symptoms and yet have dreams which pointed to a variety of underlying problems. This interest in dreams paved the way for character analysis of culturally normal individuals, which is the rule rather than the exception today.

CHILDHOOD MEMORIES. In the cathartic period Freud held that the release of one specific memory could unravel and cure the whole neurotic structure (the movies still hold this image). To a certain extent he retained this view when he switched to psychoanalysis. He felt that amnesias should be lifted, especially from the vital childhood period of ages 2 to 4 (which had been his main personal concern). But eventually he came to feel that memories and reconstructions were of equal value. Hence the mere recovery of memories does not cure the neurosis, and this criterion had to be abandoned.

INFANTILE SEXUALITY. Next Freud turned his attention to the sexual material of early childhood which the neurotic had repressed, particularly the Oedipus complex. The demand was made that the patient should overcome his Oedipal fixations. This process is a quantitative rather than a qualitative one, however, and obviously can lead to many different outcomes.

TRANSFERENCE. Soon Freud realized that, regardless of intellectual understanding, the overcoming of the transference was the decisive factor. In 1912 he wrote: "finally every conflict has to be fought out in the sphere of transference." [52]

RESISTANCE. Resistance is so closely allied to transference that the two can always be considered together. It may be noted that the positive transference in the male (to a male analyst) and the negative transference in the female (as in Freud's case of Dora) were only worked out by analysts after Freud.

WORKING THROUGH. The principle of working through meant that the repetition of interpretations over a period of time was indispensable. Patients cannot be expected to get better as a result of one interpretation. In more conventional psychological terms, this working through could be called learning. It has turned out to be by far the most important technical aspect of psychotherapy, yet the hardest to convey to the student. The point at which patients have learned enough about themselves is not something that can be specified with precision.

EGO STRUCTURE. The particular ways in which the ego must be reconstructed to allow one to say that an analysis has been properly terminated have engaged the attention of analysts ever since the 1937 paper. It can scarcely be said that there is any agreement in the field, even among members of the same group (Hamburg et al., 1967; Langs, 1976; Pfeffer, 1963a,b). A lively controversy in this area persists (see chapter 18).

The Superego

The superego is the wholly novel aspect of ego psychology; it had no exact parallels in the id period. Through this concept Freud approached the topic of interpersonal relations, expanded the psychological meaning of the family structure, and further clarified the meaning of the Oedipus complex.

Among both the general public and professionals, the image of Freud has long been that of the instinct theorist. To some extent this image was furthered by Freud's own hope that some day a "scientific" biology would explain his psychological findings. In part the image stems from the fact that historically the unbearable ideas in the basic formula were considered before the defensive processes.

Yet Freud, as we have seen, was always keenly aware of the

central role of human relationships. Beginning with the paper on narcissism in 1914, he began to consider the question more systematically. There he postulated the existence of an ego-ideal, which the person uses as a standard by which to measure his actual performance. He also referred to the self-image, self-regard, and other aspects of the self which he had previously ignored. In *Mourning and Melancholia* (1917) he clarified how depression can come about through the introjection, or internalization, of a harsh critic. In *Group Psychology and the Analysis of the Ego* (1921) he stressed the central role of the leader in the group and showed that cohesiveness in groups derives from the fact that the members have a common ego-ideal, or superego.

The initial differentiation between the ego-ideal and the superego was dropped in 1923 when he began to use the term "superego" more consistently.

Just as the ego is differentiated out of the id, so the superego is differentiated out of the ego. The superego is the heir of the Oedipus complex and arises out of the internalization of the parental images after the Oedipus has been overcome. Freud defines it as follows:

The broad general outcome of the sexual phase dominated by the Oedipus complex may, therefore, be taken to be the forming of a precipitate in the ego, consisting of these two identifications in some way united with each other. This modification of the ego retains its special position; it confronts the other contents of the ego as an ego ideal or superego.[53]

This definition requires an elaboration of the notion of identification, a topic which Freud considered many times in these years. The earliest identification precedes object cathexis; it is the wish of the child to be like the father (perhaps, Freud says, like the parents: but, as has been noted, he tended to neglect the conflicts with the mother in the early years). In early childhood, before, during, and after the Oedipal phase, the child tries to form interpersonal relations or object cathexes. Frequently the child is frustrated in the endeavor. Then *the object cathexes regress to identifications;* e.g., frustrated in his wish to be like the father, the child falls back on the wish to be the father. This formula had originally been discovered in connection with depression, but Freud now came to see the process as one of much greater frequency, and not confined to that illness.

Study of these early identifications led to an important revision of the concept of the Oedipal phase. From that point onward, he states that it is essential to speak of the complete Oedipus complex, involving both sides of the ambivalent conflict toward both parents:

one gets an impression that the simple Oedipus complex is by no means its commonest form, but rather represents a simplification or schematization which, to be sure, is often enough justified for practical purposes. Closer study usually discloses the more complete Oedipus complex, which is two-fold, positive and negative, and is due to the bisexuality originally present in children: that is to say, a boy has not merely an ambivalent attitude towards his father and an affectionate object-choice towards his mother, but at the same time he also behaves like a girl and displays an affectionate feminine attitude to his father and a corresponding jealousy towards his mother.[54]

A curious feature of Freud's theory of the superego, one which has been relegated to the background over time, is that the superego retains the character of the father.[55] Today it would be seen more generally as deriving from both parents. The superego is closely allied to the id. Guilt, which is superego punishment, results particularly from the projection of hostile impulses to the parents; in fact, Freud held, the superego is frequently harsher than the parents.

The superego is one of Freud's most brilliant conceptualizations. He began its use; enormous extensions of the concept have occurred since then (see chapter 16).

Freud's Expansion to Philosophy

Even though psychoanalysis had always had far-reaching social implications, for most of his life Freud remained tied to the workbench of technique. He did not want to philosophize or to expand his views until the scientific system was complete. Perhaps because he had finally completed his system with the superego concept, or perhaps because he was getting old, he did turn to philosophical considerations in his last years. These have been given too little attention in the literature.

Sometime after World War I he began to see that psychoanalysis had a much broader range than he had originally envisioned, and that it could conceivably play a much more significant role in human history than the narrow technical one of treating neuroses (he always remained convinced, incorrectly, that psychoanalysis was therapeutically inapplicable to the psychoses). In contradictory fashion, he would at one point refer to these expansions of psychoanalysis as "speculation," then at another point as seemingly established truth. Thus in his *Autobiography* (1925) he wrote:

I should not like to create an impression that during this last period of my work I have turned my back upon patient observation and have abandoned myself entirely to speculation. . . . Even when I have moved away from observation, I have carefully avoided any contact with philosophy proper. This avoidance has been greatly facilitated by constitutional incapacity.[56]

Yet at the same time he confidently asserted that psychoanalysis was a system of psychology: "The field of application of psychoanalysis is as broad as that of psychology, to which it adds an enlargement of powerful consequence."[57]

Even more revolutionary was the book on *The Question of Lay Analysis* (1926). Here for the first time he took up the question of preliminary qualifications for admission to analytic training, insisting that it should not be confined to physicians. In order to justify that position, he had to show that psychoanalysis is an essential part of psychology:

we do not consider it at all desirable for psychoanalysis to be swallowed up by medicine and to find its last resting place in a textbook of psychiatry under the heading of "methods of treatment," alongside of the procedures such as hypnotic suggestion, autosuggestion, and persuasion, which, born from our ignorance, have to thank the laziness and cowardice of mankind for their short-lived effects. It deserves a better fate and, it may be hoped, will meet with one. As a "depth-psychology," a theory of the mental unconscious, it can become indispensable to all the sciences which are concerned with the evolution of human civilization and its major institutions such as art, religion and the social order. It has already, in my opinion, afforded those sciences considerable help in solving their problems. But these are only small contributions compared with what might be achieved if historians of civilization, psychologists of religion, philologists and so on would agree themselves to handle the new instrument of research which is at their service. The use of analysis for the treatment of the neuroses is only one of its applications; the future will perhaps show that it is not the most important one. In any case it would be wrong to sacrifice all the other applications to this single one, just because it touches on the circle of medical interests.[58]

In *The Question of Lay Analysis*, Freud also considered the unique and unexpected difficulty in applying psychoanalysis to the mental (we would say today, social) sciences. All too often, perhaps as a rule, the scholars in these sciences fail to grasp what psychoanalysis is saying. The explanation he offered is that their personal resistances stand in the way. Accordingly the only way that they can learn psychoanalysis is by themselves undergoing an analysis.

This considerably expands the patient population for analysis. Who then is to perform the analyses? He called for a new profession. In 1928 he wrote to Oskar Pfister: "I do not know if you have detected the secret link between the *Lay Analysis* and the *Future of an Illusion*. In the former I wish to protect analysis from the doctors and in the latter from the priests. I should like to hand it over to a profession which does not yet exist, a profession of *lay* curers of souls who need not be doctors and should not be priests." [59]

In the earlier book, on lay analysis, for the first time he envisioned the possibility of psychoanalysis as virtually a panacea:

Our civilization imposes an almost intolerable pressure on us and it calls for a corrective. Is it too fantastic to expect that psychoanalysis in spite of its difficulties may be destined to the task of preparing mankind for such a corrective? Perhaps once more an American may hit on the idea of spending a little money to get the "social workers" of his country trained analytically and to turn them into a band of helpers for combatting the neuroses of civilization. [60]

In 1930 Freud published *Civilization and Its Discontents,* his most widely publicized philosophical tract. Unfortunately it does not show Freud at his best. Full of somewhat superficial observations, some of them little more than clichés, it offers a number of contradictory theses rather than really summing up a lifetime devoted to psychoanalytic research. Nonetheless certain points are outstanding. Best known is his assertion that civilization is inimical to instinctual gratification. [61] This goes together with his pessimistic denial that happiness is an attainable goal:

The program of becoming happy, which the pleasure principle imposes on us, cannot be fulfilled; yet we must not—indeed, we cannot—give up our efforts to bring it nearer to fulfillment by some means or other. . . . Happiness, in the reduced sense in which we recognize it as possible, is a problem of the economics of the individual's libido. There is no golden rule which applies to everyone: every man must find out for himself in what particular fashion he can be saved. [62]

Yet, though he maintains that "there are difficulties attaching to the nature of civilization which will not yield to any attempt at reform,'' [63] he still holds the view that psychotherapy can help to alleviate the miserable conditions that do exist:

If the development of civilization has such a far-reaching similarity to the development of the individual . . . may we not be justified in reaching the diagnosis that under the influence of cultural urges, some civilizations, or some epochs of civilization—possibly the whole of mankind—have become "neurotic"? . . . As regards the therapeutic application of our knowledge, what would be the use of the most correct analysis of social neuroses, since no one possesses authority to impose such a therapy upon the group? But in spite of all these difficulties, we may expect that one day someone will venture to embark upon a pathology of cultural communities.[64]

In Lecture 34 of the *New Introductory Lectures on Psychoanalysis* (1932), he ventures a number of opinions that have received scant attention.[65] He considers education, law, crime, therapy, even the hormonal treatment of psychosis. Yet the wider meaning of psychoanalysis is still considered an ''application.'' He writes: ''I feel a strong temptation to conduct you through all the applications of psychoanalysis to the mental sciences. . . . But I must renounce the idea: it would once more carry us outside the framework of these lectures.'' [66] But then he goes on to suggest the possibility of universal analysis:

The recognition that most of our children pass through a neurotic phase in the course of their development carries with it the germ of a hygienic challenge. The question may be raised whether it would not be expedient to come to a child's help with an analysis even if he shows no signs of a disturbance, as a measure for safeguarding his health, just as today we inoculate healthy children against diphtheria without waiting to see if they fall ill of it. . . . *Prophylaxis such as this against neurotic illness, which would probably be very effective, also presupposes a quite other constitution of society* (italics added).[67]

As in earlier periods, Freud shrank from issuing too blunt a challenge to society. In the following years, from 1933 to 1939, the optimistic mood of 1925–1932 is no longer in evidence; once more he returns primarily to technical problems. Yet it is clear that inherent in his thought is a philosophical system, that he did hold that psychoanalysis is a general psychology or at least lays the basis for one, that psychology must be incorporated into all the social sciences, and that he placed his faith for the amelioration of the human lot in a universal analysis which would be offered by lay curers of souls.

Implicitly, then, Freud's philosophy represents a step beyond all preexisting philosophies in that it rests on a sound psychological basis. His psychology goes beyond all other psychologies in that it embraces a philosophical position, namely the desirability and efficacy of psychotherapy. And the image of cultural change brought about by universal analysis stands for a unique kind of social reform. However, it remained for others to develop the full implication of these positions.

Chapter Four

Organizational Vicissitudes

The history of psychoanalysis lends itself naturally to three main historical divisions. In the first period, from the beginnings to World War I, the field was almost entirely dominated by Freud. In the period between the two world wars (1918–1939) a host of lesser-known personalities appeared, many of whom extended Freud's ideas, while others offered different and at times opposing views. Finally, in the period since World War II, the major thrust has been toward organization within the societies and consolidation of theoretical positions within the science.

From the Beginnings to World War I

Freud's epochal early work received little attention in the professional world. It took eight years to sell the 600 copies which formed the first edition of *The Interpretation of Dreams*;[1] several years elapsed without the sale of a single copy. When Freud offered his first public lectures on dreams at the University of Vienna in 1900, only three persons attended, one of them the son of a close personal friend.[2]

Later Freud spoke of his 10 years of splendid isolation. Which 10 years he meant is not clear, but it did take a long time for his ideas to get across. Understandably, he welcomed every new adherent to the "cause," as he came to call it, with open arms.[3]

The Mainstream of Psychoanalysis

It is well known that there have been innumerable splits and dissensions within the psychoanalytic fold. Sandor Ferenczi once sarcastically commented that the history of psychoanalysis can be divided into three periods: the heroic age, the time of guerrilla warfare, and the setting up of organizations. Although many dates overlap, this rough division does describe much of what has happened. Nevertheless one can speak of a *mainstream psychoanalytic tradition,* or *mainstream psychoanalysis,* which despite all attacks and propaganda to the contrary has consistently grown and dominated the thought of the leading scholars in the field. While it would be a serious mistake to discount the disagreements in the field, it is an equally serious mistake to ignore the considerable body of doctrine on which most analysts agree. This doctrine begins with Freud but expands, alters, and enlarges his views in many different ways. It may be said that Freud laid a solid foundation upon which the building is still being constructed. The foundation, like Einstein's relativity and Darwin's evolution, is so solid that it probably will never change, but the building can be altered in many ways.

The Vienna Psychoanalytic Society

Apart from the biographies and autobiographies of numerous psychoanalytic pioneers (Alexander et al., 1966) and the monumental biography by Ernest Jones (1953–1957), the events of the early years have been preserved in the minutes of the Vienna Psychoanalytic Society, which were edited, translated, and published by Hermann Nunberg and Ernst Federn (son of Paul Federn) in four volumes, between 1962 and 1975. These minutes begin with the year 1906 and continue until 1915. In that period Otto Rank was the official, salaried secretary of the Society, entrusted with the task of recording its meetings. He recorded the essence of the discussion, not every word that was said.

The meetings began in 1902 with Freud and four other persons—Alfred Adler, Wilhelm Stekel, Max Kahane, and Rudolf Reitler—all physicians practicing psychoanalytic psychotherapy as Freud had described it at that time; in addition Stekel had at one time been Freud's patient. However, one must realize that before about 1930 a personal analysis was not required of prospective analysts. Hence they practiced psychoanalytic therapy with "autodidactic veracity," as one of my correspondents put it, which means that it is hard to know what they actually did with their patients. The meetings were held in Freud's apartment on Wednesday evenings; hence they were known as the Wednesday Evening meetings. In 1910, the meetings were moved from Freud's apartment to the Doktoren Collegium (the College of Physicians).[4] Until 1908, everyone who attended the meetings was required to participate in the discussions; from then on, participation was voluntary.[5]

The Wednesday group was highly heterogeneous, attracting members from all walks of life. Of the 22 persons whose biographies are listed in the first volume of minutes, only 10 were practicing psychotherapists at that time. Other members were David Bach, music critic of the Vienna *Arbeiter Zeitung;* Hugo Heller, a publisher; Otto Rank, a student and Freud's secretary; Maximilian Steiner, a specialist in venereal diseases; Oskar Rie, Freud's pediatrician, and the like. The Society in a sense already foreshadowed the emergence of psychoanalysis from a narrow medical specialty to a broad-spectrum psychology and philosophy of great cultural significance.

The meetings were never well attended. At the first one recorded, on October 3, 1906, there were 17 persons present; frequently the group was much smaller, e.g., on November 28, 1906 only 7 persons were there besides Freud. Still, the Society served as a spawning ground for many who were later famous in the psychoanalytic movement: Paul Federn, Eduard Hitschmann, Alfred Adler, Hermann Nunberg, Otto Fenichel, Max Eitingon, Carl Jung, Ernest Jones, and many others.

Topics discussed at the meetings ranged very widely, the only unifying thread being that all were illuminated by a psychoanalytic point of view. In 1906, on November 7 Adler read a paper on the organic basis of neurosis; on November 21 Philipp Frey discussed the megalomania of the normal person. In 1907, Alfred Meisl read a paper on hunger and love; Rudolf Reitler discussed a novel by Wedekind, entitled *Spring's Awakening;* on February 20 Freud discussed the book by Moebius on *The Hopelessness of All Psychology;* on April 17 David Bach spoke about Jean Paul, the writer; on May 15 there was a discussion of Fritz Wittels's book on female physicians.

Opposition to Freud was still intense at that time. When Rudolf von Urbanschitsch, son of an eminent professor of otolaryngology at the University of Vienna, and owner-director of the fashionable Cottage Sanitarium, joined Freud in 1909 and supported him in publications, the financial existence of his sanitarium was threatened. For a while he was forced to withdraw.[6]

Most interest in these minutes attaches, of course, to Freud's comments, which were made at every meeting and which can be used as a supplement to his published views. In this way further glimpses are offered of the way in which his published material finally emerged.

The discussion and comments by other members show how right Nunberg is when he states in his introduction that for the others Freud was an unattainable ego ideal. The dated character of the discussions is also obvious from a meeting such as that on April 14, 1910, where the question arose as to whether women should be admitted to the meetings. Freud said he would see it as a gross inconsistency if women were excluded on principle. Sadger declared himself opposed; Adler was in favor of admitting women physicians and women seriously interested in the subject. In the secret ballot, of the 11 members present, 3 were opposed in principle to the admission of women, obliging the president (Adler) "to proceed with extreme caution on this point."[7]

Much scientifically worthless material is to be found in the minutes. On April 7, 1909, Rank read a paper on the psychology of lying, which he attributed primarily to the need to conceal masturbation. Freud was seriously critical;[8] he said the paper contained gross methodological errors and involved an unwarranted kind of scientific work, and stated that he did not wish the paper to be submitted for publication. At the meeting on November 11, 1908, Federn stated that the most serious cases of male hysteria occur in meat-eating families.[9] Such absurdities, which could not even get into print today, are perhaps more comprehensible in the light of Freud's comment at the previous meeting, that "hysteria surely has its own metabolism."[10]

In 1914 Freud said about the Vienna Group that

there were only two inauspicious circumstances which at last estranged me inwardly from the group. I could not succeed in establishing among its members the friendly relations that ought to obtain between men who are all engaged upon the same difficult work; nor was I able to stifle the disputes about priority for which there were so many opportunities under these conditions of work in common.[11]

International Recognition

In *The History of the Psychoanalytic Movement* (1914) Freud paints his own picture of the development of psychoanalysis outside the confines of Vienna.[12] He says that in 1907 the situation changed at once and "contrary to all expectation."[13] In January 1907 Dr. Max Eitingon, the first member of the Zurich clinic to pay attention to Freud, came to Vienna. Eitingon remained a significant and loyal adherent of Freud till his death. Also, correspondence with Jung had begun with a letter from Freud to Jung on April 11, 1906, to which Jung replied 6 months later.[14]

More international recognition began to flow in. In 1907 Karl Abraham came; he was then at Burghölzli, was later the intellectual founder of the Berlin Institute, and next to Freud had the keenest mind in the early history of the movement. In 1908 Jones came from London, and Ferenczi from Budapest. In 1910 Hanns Sachs joined the circle, and that year Jones proclaimed Freud to be the Darwin of the mind.[15] In 1909 Freud was invited to give his first public lectures on psychoanalysis, at Clark University in the United States, an honor which his own University of Vienna, where he was a professor, had refused him. Before then an international meeting had been held at Salzburg, Austria, with 42 persons present, of whom half were or became practicing analysts.[16] In 1910 the International Psychoanalytical Association was founded. Thereafter growth continued regularly all over the world.

In the founding of the International Psychoanalytic Association in 1910 Freud made a great blunder by appointing Jung president, a move which he described as "in fact not very wise."[17] In explanation Freud wrote: "I was no longer young: I saw that there was a long road ahead, and I felt oppressed by the thought that the duty of being a leader should fall to me so late in life."[18]

Freud's abdication of the leadership which belonged to him by right did great damage to the international psychoanalytic movement, from which it took time to recover, although the damage can also be exaggerated, as it so often has been. As on so many occasions in his professional life, when it would have been appropriate to take practical action, Freud withdrew. Evidently he felt much more secure in his theories and books, even in his psychoanalytic work; perhaps, in the Jewish Talmudic tradition, he preferred to leave the practical tasks of the world to others.

In addition to Freud's works, periodicals and journals were started in order to provide a forum for the views of Freud and other analysts. The *Zentralblatt für Aerztliche Psychoanalyse,* edited by Adler and Stekel, became the official organ of the International. When Adler and Stekel both defected, Freud started a new international journal, the *Internationale Zeitschrift für Aerztliche Psychoanalyse* in 1913, which continued until World War II. In 1920 Jones founded the English-language periodical *International Journal of Psychoanalysis,* which has been published uninterruptedly ever since.

The early history of the International Psychoanalytical Association was disturbed by the resignations of several important members. Adler left in 1911, Jung in 1913; both took with them a number of their colleagues. Nevertheless the majority of the analysts in the society stayed with Freud. After Jung's resignation, Abraham took over and guided it through murky waters until its later emergence after World War I. Since then it has grown continuously, though quite slowly, and exists today in essentially the same form as it did when it was founded in 1910.

The growth of the International is paradigmatic for the growth of all psychoanalytic societies. First a charismatic figure comes along, in this case Freud, who has some startling new ideas which gather adherents. They band together and form a society. The further development of the society is then strictly regulated from within. Once the organization is formed, there is expansion but no fundamental change. The merits and demerits of this system are evaluated at the conclusion of this chapter.

Early Splits and Dissensions

From the very beginning of psychoanalysis, schisms and dissensions within its ranks have been notorious. No sooner had Freud recognized the importance of sexuality than Breuer broke off with him. The founding of an International Psychoanalytical Association in 1910 was bitterly opposed by the Vienna group, its original members.[19] When Abraham Brill formed the New York Psychoanalytic

Society in 1911, Jones, then in Toronto, immediately formed the American Psychoanalytic Association in opposition to him.[20] In his presidential address to the American Psychoanalytic Association in 1974, Burness Moore made various pessimistic statements about the organization (Moore, 1976), such as that "schisms in psychoanalysis have been particularly damaging to our status."[21] The same issue of the *Journal of the American Psychoanalytic Association* (May, 1976) carried news of another impending split, with a fierce struggle going on in Los Angeles.[22]

The historian must offer some rational explanation of these innumerable splits and divisions, which are paralleled perhaps only in the history of religion. The analogy is by no means inappropriate, for psychoanalysis has also been dominated by a long series of charismatic figures, like the religious sects. When the works of these charismatic figures are carefully perused, they often make little or no sense, as for instance the balderdash of Wilhelm Reich's "orgonomy."

"Charisma" is a sociological term popularized by Max Weber (Bendix, 1960). It can be defined as "magic power as a unique and hence transient attribute of an individual." What has to be understood is why the history of psychoanalysis is filled with charismatic figures.

First of all, there is the enormous difficulty involved in understanding the ideas of psychoanalysis. Most of the early leaders in the field were not psychoanalyzed and their grasp of psychoanalytic principles was often poor. Neither Jung nor Adler, as will be seen, grasped the bases of the first psychoanalytic system, involving the unconscious, psychosexual development, and transference-resistance.

Second, psychoanalytic theory has always been associated with therapy. Deviations in therapeutic procedures have immediate practical consequences. Hence every group has had to limit the degree of flexibility allowed its members. In addition, competition for patients has often been concealed behind wordy (and meaningless) theoretical disputes.

Third, the division into schools has prevented a rational discussion of ideas. If someone is challenged, he can escape into the statement that he is now a "member of another school," thereby immediately ending the discussion. This is usually accompanied by a misrepresentation of the views of other schools, as is particularly noticeable in the anti-Freudian literature.

Fourth, poor therapy offering the patient immediate gratification is often more attractive than good therapy, which insists on waiting longer for a more lasting and worthwhile result. Hence adherents of "quick," "revolutionary" therapy (as in today's "primal revolution") can always be found.

Fifth, there is the all-too-human element of a personal battle. Freud retained his need for a beloved friend and a hated enemy until late in life; the result was that Jung became for a while the beloved friend while Adler was stigmatized as the hated enemy (Fine, 1975b). This split between the "good guy" and the "bad guy" has been perpetuated in many later battles. Nor can it be denied that the simple wish to conquer has played a powerful role. Jung, for example, did not hesitate to take over the editorship of the *Zentralblatt für Psychotherapie* after it had become state-regulated by the Nazis in 1933, to gratify his desire to take revenge on Freud and replace him as the center of the world psychotherapeutic movement.

Finally, there is the lack of official status of psychoanalysis, which has led to a problem unique to the field. Psychoanalysis is the heart of psychiatry, psychology, and social work, yet the budding analyst must first get a degree in one of these fields before admission to a psychoanalytic training institute. This results in a severe dilemma: if someone has had a personal analysis, why should he study medicine (or psychology, or social work)? And if he has a medical degree (or Ph.D. or M.S.W.), why should he be analyzed? The dilemma has never been satisfactorily resolved; it is still at the heart of many of the acrimonious disputes in the field.

Alfred Adler (1870–1937)

Adler was born in Vienna in 1870, obtained his medical degree in 1895, and worked as a general practitioner, especially interested in the problems of the working class, for many years. In 1902 he was one of the first four to come to Freud; evidently through his contacts with Freud he began to specialize more and more as a psychiatrist (*Nervenarzt*) from 1909 onward, although he maintained his contacts with general medicine for some time thereafter.

In 1910 Freud appointed him president of the Vienna Society and, with Stekel, editor of the major psychoanalytic journal, the *Zentralblatt für Psychoanalyse*. His emphasis leaned increasingly toward what we would call today ego psychology (for which Freud gave him full credit), although, as Freud rightly pointed out, he kept inventing new names for old ideas, such as masculine protest for repression, or psychic hermaphroditism for bisexuality.

Whereas Jung actively rebelled against Freud, for a long time Adler did not see himself as opposed to his teacher. Thus what he says in the meeting of the Vienna Society on February 8, 1911, seems quite justified: "In conclusion, the speaker emphasizes that it was not his aim to devalue Freud's conception of the neurosis and its mechanisms, but merely to obey the practical and theoretical necessity of placing it on a broader basis and giving weight to a developmental standpoint that he believes Freud has already left behind him."[23]

However, Freud at that time was by no means as serene as his biographers would picture him. Somehow Adler became the hated enemy, and we note in the minutes of the meetings Freud's continued attacks on the younger man. The posthumously published letters to Jung also show that he was determined, all through 1911, to get rid of Adler, whom he referred to amazingly as a "paranoiac."[24] The notes to the meeting of February 22, 1911 finally announced that at the following committee meeting Adler would resign as chairman of the society, while Stekel would resign as deputy chairman. Still, both remained in the journal and continued to come to meetings. Freud's animosity persisted. In a letter to Jung on March 14, 1911, he wrote:

The palace revolution in Vienna has had little effect on the *Zentralblatt*. Naturally I am only waiting for an occasion to throw them both out, but they know it and are being very cautious and conciliatory, so there is nothing I can do for the present. Of course I am watching them more closely, but they put up with it. In my heart I am through with them. *None of these Viennese will ever amount to anything; the only one with a future is little Rank, who is both intelligent and decent* (italics added).[25]

At the following meeting, when the resignations of Adler and Stekel were announced, Freud took over the chair. In spite of that, an amendment was voted stating that the views of Adler and Freud were not incompatible, in the opinion of the Society; Nunberg calls this "rather puzzling," overlooking the deep agitation that Freud was obviously manifesting.[26] Finally, at the meeting on October 11, 1911, Freud announced that Adler and three others had resigned.

Adler then oganized a Society for Free Psychoanalytic Investigation, soon renamed the Society for Individual Psychology.[27] Thereafter Adler continued his work uninterruptedly and vigorously until the end of his life, in 1937. He wrote extensively, toured widely and exerted a particularly strong influence on educators.

Adler's views represented an embryonic ego psychology. However, since he had never been psychoanalyzed, it remained at a superficial level, where the depths of the unconscious and the transference problem in therapy remained unknown. As usual, Adler's followers have made all kinds of absurd claims for priority for Adler, ignoring the actual historical course of events. For example, Ansbacher and Ansbacher (1956) accuse Freud of "taking sex too literally,"[28] quite oblivious of the shift from the direct sexuality of the 1890s to the psychosexual theories of the 1900s. Adler's superficiality (which persists today) has made his views especially palatable in school situations, where counselors fear to plumb the depths of the soul too boldly.

Unfortunately, in their acrimonious desire to beat out the old man, both Adler and Jung produced a caricature of Freud's thinking, which has been taken over by many of their followers and has sown the deepest confusion in the field. Adler says, for instance, that Freud claimed "from the first that dreams are fulfillments of infantile sexual wishes."[29] Then Adler tells us that he profited from Freud's mistakes concerning dreams, leading him to appreciate "the unity of the personality,"[30] as though Freud were unaware of this unity. Numerous other instances could be found.

There is no longer any justification for calling the Adlerian system a separate "school." Its major tenets are all, in more elaborate form, at the core of psychoanalytic psychology today. Adler should be given full credit (as Freud did give in the *History of the Psychoanalytic Movement*) for contributing to the general rethinking of early psychoanalysis that led to ego psychology.

Carl Gustav Jung (1875–1961)

An entirely different picture emerges from a reconsideration of the historical data on Jung, the Swiss psychiatrist. Born in Switzerland, he lived there all of his life, except for many trips abroad. His father was a Protestant chaplain, which helps to explain his lifelong interest in religion. He obtained his medical degree in 1899, and shortly thereafter went to work as a psychiatrist in the famous hospital at Burghölzli, which was headed by Bleuler.

Even before he met Freud, Jung had done some respectable work in the field. He devised the word-association test, variations of which have become a standard projective technique. In 1906 he published the *Psychology of Dementia Praecox,* in which he made an early psychological approach to the illness, though he always maintained a theory of toxic physiological causation. However, he did not pursue this work to its logical conclusion.

In 1906 he received a letter from Freud, who thanked him for the copy of *Diagnostic Association Experiments,* which, the older man said, he had already acquired. Then began a correspondence and friendship that lasted seven years, until the break in 1913.

Since the publication of the Freud–Jung letters in 1974, a more balanced picture of the relationship between the two men has emerged (Fine, 1975b). Freud felt lonely, isolated, insecure, unsure of his radical new ideas, unsupported by any first-rate minds. He thought he detected in Jung a way out of his conflicts.

On the whole it is clear that the correspondence meant much more to Freud than to Jung. He waited breathlessly for each letter, replied almost as soon as they came, and poured a tremendous amount of his inner life into them. This was much less true for Jung, who delayed frequently, generally began by apologizing for the overwork which had led to the delay and said much less about himself and his inner life. As one goes through the letters, the sudden break announced by Jung at the end of 1912 comes as almost a complete surprise.

What was Freud looking for in Jung? In 1906 he still felt terribly isolated. Some of this isolation he ascribed to his Jewishness, and Jung was a gentile; some he ascribed to his separateness from psychiatry, and Jung was a hospital-affiliated psychiatrist. Yet above all his longing had a particularly personal flavor. Had he reflected on it, as he had done with Fliess, Freud might have again concluded that the affair with Jung was another piece of the "unanalyzed homosexual transference." The warm expressions of endearment, the fainting episodes, the constant search for signs of love, the constant fear of abandonment (as Fliess had abandoned him) appear over and over.

Hence the son–father relationship to Fliess reappears here as the father–son relationship to Jung. It is not long before Jung is hailed in so many words as "my dear son and successor," the crown prince, the Joshua who will fulfill the destiny marked out by Moses, the leader of the next generation, the genius among his students, and so on. All along, these terms were based more on Freud's desires for a son than on anything that Jung had said or contributed.

In his letters Jung dutifully hailed the old man's achievements. But, he complains over and over, "I do not understand." These repeated remarks have to be taken seriously; like Adler, he did not really grasp the three cornerstones of the first psychoanalytic system.

It was one of Freud's characteristics that he never replied publicly to any of the innumerable critics who poured so much abuse on him during his lifetime. Yet it is abundantly clear from the letters that he was thoroughly incensed at what was being written about him. The terms in which he refers to his opponents are quite extreme. Some of them are referred to as "feeble-minded." Emil Braatz is an example of "affective imbecility," Albert Moll is a "brute," not really a physician but a "pettifogging lawyer"; he urges Jung to "stem the interminable flow of Isidore Sadger's 'rubbish' " (and Sadger was one of his loyal Viennese followers). Evidently Freud needed Jung as an outlet for his hatreds.

That the father–son relationship embodies ambivalences on both sides, no one knew better than Freud. And so it was inevitable that a rivalry with Jung would ensue. Apart from the personal questions, it was undoubtedly this competition, in which Freud won out, that embittered Jung, who on three separate occasions missed a chance to make a fundamental contribution to the field. Thus the difference between hysteria and schizophrenia was first apparent to Jung around 1907, but it was Abraham who published the first paper on it, in 1908.

More important was the material about psychosis and mythology. It was Jung who first called Freud's attention to Schreber's *Memoirs,* but he did not properly fathom its significance. When Freud published his elegant interpretation of Schreber's psychosis, the first time that anyone had ever really penetrated the dynamics of psychosis, it must have come like a bolt from the blue to the younger man. All he could say to Freud was: You are a hard man to have as a rival.

Apparently Jung then turned to mythology, which both men

agreed needed clarification. If the anthropologists do not do it, Freud said, we will have to do it ourselves. And so he did. *Totem and Taboo,* published in 1912–1913, for the first time provided a solid psychological foundation for anthropology.

Jung's jealousy on this score is well documented in the letters. His own work along these lines, *The Transformations of the Libido,* was published in the psychoanalytic journals while he was still a member of the Society. But his colleagues ignored it; compared to Freud's work, it lacked any real significance. Jung had already begun his descent into the obscurantist mysticism that later led him to astrology and flying saucers, the absurdity of which was obvious to all but his most ardent followers. Thus as early as May 8, 1911, he wrote to Freud:

Occultism is another field we shall have to conquer—with the aid of the libido theory, it seems to me. At the moment I am looking into astrology, which seems indispensable for a proper understanding of mythology. There are strange and wondrous things in these lands of darkness. Please don't worry about my wanderings in these infinitudes. I shall return laden with rich booty for our knowledge of the human psyche.[31]

At that time Ferenczi was also interested in the occult. Freud wrote to him: "It is a dangerous expedition and I cannot accompany you."[32]

After *Totem and Taboo,* the father–son rivalry was complete. Once more the father had knocked out one of his son's teeth, once more he had proved to him that he was not yet on a par with the old man.

It was undoubtedly these blows which led Jung to the break. For, unlike his hatred of Adler, Freud still loved Jung as a son, heir, and follower; a pure transference love, we would say today, yet still a love. He was not pressing Jung to leave; on the contrary, Freud incurred the enmity of other analysts by promoting Jung too strongly. The posthumously discovered fact that he took Jung's letters with him to London in 1938 shows how much libido was still attached to the younger man.

Jung broke with Freud in 1913, even though he did not resign as president of the International until 1914 (again a rather shabby way of treating his colleagues, since he remained an inactive president for a year). Then he seems to have gone into a long period of self-analysis, isolating himself from his previous contacts (Ellenberger, 1970).

From this he emerged with a wholly new set of theories, which were eventually to characterize a "Jungian" school. In 1948 a C. G. Jung Institute was founded in Zurich, which offered a three-year training program in Jungian psychoanalysis. Various such institutes exist all over the world, but what they teach is so strictly confined to Jung that it cannot be called analysis in the ordinary sense of the word.

Jung remained embittered about the break with Freud, as all his letters and subsequent writings show, even though he had engineered it himself. In later years, when the Nazis came to power Jung allowed himself some enlargement of an earlier anti-Semitism; he co-operated with the Nazis until about 1940, apparently in the hope that he could found an international union of psychotherapists which would take the place of Freudian psychoanalysis. The numerous overtures he made to psychiatrists all over Europe[33] show that this was not a mere accommodation, as his followers claimed, but a serious effort to get rid of Freud once and for all. His refusal before 1940 to condemn the Nazis is confirmed in the record. For example, in 1937 his only objection to Alfred Rosenberg's *Der Mythus des 20 Jahrhunderts,* the bible of Nazi "theory," is that Rosenberg errs in stating that the Jews despise mysticism![34] In 1934 he had spoken of an Aryan and a Jewish psychotherapy, in the German (then Nazi) journal of psychotherapy where he had taken over the editorship from Kretschmer.[35] Werner Kemper, a Berlin analyst who stayed there all through the war years, relates[36] that Matthias Göring (a relative of the notorious Nazi leader), a psychiatrist who was nominally in charge of the Berlin analytic group, ordered them to create a national-socialist (Nazi) oriented "German mental healing" (*Deutschen Seelenheilkunde*) by incorporation of the Jungian doctrines, thereby replacing the "Jewish-Marxist" corrupted psychology of Freud and Adler. While Jung may not have known of Göring's intentions (which is unlikely, since he edited the journal under Göring's direction), it is nonetheless highly significant that the Nazis considered his psychology to be thoroughly compatible with their views.

It is rather difficult to extract from Jung's voluminous writings a clear picture of his doctrines. Dieter Wyss (1966), who is sympathetic to him, has emphasized the following as central:

1. Jung is primarily concerned with self-knowledge, not with sick people. "Become the person you are" may be seen as the basis

of his philosophy, or what he called the principle of individuation.

2. The libido he saw as psychic energy, subject to self-regulation and compensation. Thus there is a constant imbalance in the mind which a person strives to correct. In the unconscious he distinguished the collective from the personal unconscious.

3. Individuation involves a constructive relationship to the collective psyche. Every man has an anima, the feminine aspect of the male psyche, while every woman has her animus, the masculine aspect of the female psyche. By working out the ''shadow'' (aspects of personal experience that have been repressed), one achieves self-realization.

4. There are archetypal human experiences. These are expressed in manifold symbols. (Actually the careful study of symbols is probably Jung's most enduring contribution.) The psyche has four basic functions—thinking, feeling, sensation and intuition—and two basic attitudes—extraversion and introversion. (The four basic functions represent a reversion to faculty psychology; the two basic attitudes have become widely popular but, as Jung himself showed in *Psychological Types,* 1923, represent another version of the typology which has existed throughout Western history.)

5. The goal of therapy is individuation.

Jung's theoretical position, as he clarified it from the 1920s onward, derives from many sources. His emphasis on psyche is taken over from Freud, but he pushed it to extremes including discussions of mysticism, astrology, occultism, alchemy, religion, and the lore of the East. Brett (1965) comments that much of his later work is ''so mysterious as to be almost undiscussable.''[37] The collective unconscious is the inherited capacity of the human mind; the archetypes are the universal human experiences.

While his language is unusual and often obscure, considered more closely his system has little merit. He should really be classified as a religious philosopher instead of as a psychoanalyst, since he discarded the major tenets of psychoanalysis rather early. Thus in a letter to Dorothee Hoch, on May 28, 1952, he writes:

I share your opinion entirely that man lives wholly when, and only when, he is related to God, ... In my practice I often had to give elementary school lessons in the history of religion in order to eliminate, for a start, the disgust and nausea people felt for religious matters who had dealt all their lives only with confession-mongers and preachers.[38]

Unlike the case with Adler, Jung cannot be said to have exerted any real influence on the history of psychoanalysis. In fact, had it not been for Freud, Jung would long since have been relegated to the limbo of history, like many of the mystics and alchemists for whom he had so much admiration. Paradoxically, his memory lives on mainly because of his diatribes against Freud.

The Notion of "Schools" of Psychoanalysis

Careful objective discussion of different positions has never been a hallmark of the analytic literature. The reason is primarily that dissident thinkers have preferred to present themselves as adherents of a new "school." This position stems originally from Adler and Jung. Unfortunately, Freud went along with them, preferring to forget them as men of different views rather than to refute their ideas.

The result of this kind of thinking has been that whenever anything out of the way is presented in analysis, the originator avoids serious criticism by saying that he represents a different "school." Such an attitude must be emphatically rejected, since it makes the unification of a scientific psychology, which is the goal of psychoanalytic research, utterly impossible. If a thinker has something to contribute, it can be incorporated into the science. If he has nothing to say, his views should be discarded. Hence the notion of schools should be rejected.

The Committee

The early defections of Adler, Jung, and Stekel (who later returned) were all highly distressing to Freud and damaging to the growth of psychoanalysis. In 1912 Ernest Jones[39] conceived the idea of forming a committee of persons who would remain loyal to Freud throughout. Freud was enthusiastic about the idea, and wrote to Jones:

What took hold of my imagination immediately is your idea of a secret council composed of the best and most trustworthy among our men to take care of the further development of psychoanalysis and defend the cause against personalities and accidents when I am no more. . . . . I know there is a boyish and perhaps romantic element too in this conception, but perhaps it could be adapted to meet the necessities of reality. . . . . I daresay it would make living and dying easier for me if I knew of such an association to watch over my creation.[40]

Apart from Jones (1879–1958), the other members were Karl Abraham (1877–1925), Sandor Ferenczi (1873–1933), Hanns Sachs (1881–1947), Otto Rank (1885–1939), and, from 1919 onward, Max Eitingon (1881–1943). On May 25, 1913, Freud celebrated the event by presenting each member with an antique Greek intaglio from his collection, which was then mounted in a gold ring.

Precisely what role the committee did play in the history of psychoanalysis is hard to know. Its formation is indicative of the deep feelings of despair that must have gone through Freud in those days when he thought of the future of psychoanalysis.

Between Two Wars: 1918–1939

During World War I all organized psychoanalytic activity came to a standstill. Before the outbreak of hostilities, psychoanalysis had always had a pitifully small group of followers. In the Vienna Psychoanalytic Society the roll of members for 1911–1912 was 34,[41] and no other country could even approach a group of that size. Freud's fear that the science would disappear, especially after the defections of Jung and Adler, seemed to be well-founded.

Once peace was restored, psychoanalytic work could resume, yet at first there seemed to be few signs that it would flourish. At the annual meeting of the American Psychoanalytic Society, held in New York on June 4, 1920, only 10 persons attended. The president, Abraham Brill, said he had heard that some of the members thought it advisable to discontinue the society because it had outlived its usefulness. Instead of the official organization it was suggested that yearly informal gatherings be instituted, at which those interested could present papers on psychoanalysis.[42] The motion did not carry.

However, the war had set off a tremendous upsurge in interest in psychoanalysis. Unlike the academic psychologies, here was a psychology that did have something to say about the breakthrough of mankind's most primitive and irrational urges, which had just caused such havoc in the civilized world. The great public interest was bound to be reflected sooner or later in organizational growth.

The first postwar meeting of the International Psychoanalytical Association was held in The Hague, in Holland, in 1920, with Ferenczi as president. At this meeting Jones was elected the next president. There were 62 members present,[43] of whom only 2 came from America, 7 from Austria, 15 from England, 11 from Germany, 16 from Holland, 3 from Hungary, 1 from Poland, and 7 from Switzerland.

Opposition was still intense, and the organization had to be tightened up in many ways. Oberndorf (1953) relates that during this period he mentioned in a lecture that the sight of the genitals of an exhibitionist who suddenly exposed himself was a factor in the development of a hysterical eye symptom in a young woman. Two women students immediately submitted a formal complaint to the dean's office, which agreed emphatically with their point of view and chastised Oberndorf for his "bizarre" interpretation.[44]

The training regulations of the International were not firmly established until the Bad Homburg congress in 1925;[45] they lasted until 1938, when the American group declared its independence of the International.[46] Thus even between the two wars the affairs of psychoanalysis ran none too smoothly.

Many ups and downs must be reported from this period. In 1918 Ferenczi was appointed the first university professor of psychoanalysis in Budapest by the new Communist government; when that was overthrown shortly thereafter, he had to withdraw.[47] At the same time Roheim was appointed professor of anthropology in Budapest; he too had to leave.[48] It was already becoming clear that politics would play a role in the history of psychoanalysis.

Overall, the most significant shift between the two wars was the move to America by many distinguished psychoanalysts for whom Hitler and the constant threat of war made life impossible on the Continent. In 1926 the International Psychoanalytic Association numbered 294 members, of whom 58 were American, 47 Viennese, 56 British, and 38 Swiss (including, surprisingly, Jean Piaget).[49] By 1938 the total number had grown to 556, but the proportions had changed radically.[50] There were then 184 members in the American Association, and 92 in the British (including associate members); the Americans, although still few in absolute numbers, had already become the dominant group. The American Psychoanalytic Association at that time had six constituent societies, of which the one in New York, with 77 members, was the largest.

At the 1938 meeting in Paris, Ernest Jones, as president, read a communication from the president and secretary of the American Psychoanalytic Association, which altered the entire structure of the International. The Americans demanded that the International Association should cease to exist as an administrative body and should resolve itself into a congress for scientific purposes only. They described the International Training Committee as a "paper institution," and resolved that they would no longer cooperate with it in any way. They further specified that the status of membership-at-large should not apply to individuals residing and practicing in the United States. The International appointed a committee to deal with these proposals, but the advent of the war made cooperation impossible. After the war, when the American Psychoanalytic Association had become more numerous than the rest of the world combined, the proposals were adopted in toto.[51]

Psychoanalytic Training

Hardly had the International Psychoanalytical Association been reestablished after World War I than it faced the thorny problem of training. Still reeling from the defections of Jung and Adler, and shortly thereafter Rank and perhaps Ferenczi and Reich, the organization experienced much apprehension about its own future and the future of the science. Prior to the war, training had been a haphazard process; in fact, most of the pioneer analysts had not had even a minimal personal analysis. As late as 1914 Freud had expressed the feeling that if a person were sufficiently "normal," examination of his dreams was sufficient to prepare him for the profession.[52] As noted, Freud's initial feeling that any intelligent person could analyze himself soon changed to the conviction that no one could do it properly.

Thus three questions arose after the war: What are the essential aspects of psychoanalytic training? Who should be in charge of the training, and how is it to be conducted? What should the preliminary requirements be for admission to training?

The Training System

After the war new societies were founded in all the democratic countries: in Switzerland in 1919 (replacing the Jungian Society); in Dresden, Leipzig, and Munich in 1921; in Kazan in 1923; the Berlin Clinic in 1920; the Vienna Clinic in 1922; the Italian Society in 1932, and so on.[53] Because of the many students, a systematic course of instruction had to be devised.

EITINGON AND THE BERLIN PSYCHOANALYTIC INSTITUTE. As so often in the history of psychoanalysis, the training system that is now almost universally the standard resulted from the efforts of one person in one situation. The person was Max Eitingon, and the situation was Berlin of the Weimar Republic.

That Eitingon should have been the one to set the standards for psychoanalytic training is surprising. Freud was still alive and active in 1920, surrounded by a host of brilliant students in Vienna. Yet he left it to Eitingon's initiative to set up the first institute in Berlin, even sending him one of his favorite disciples, Hanns Sachs, as the first training analyst.

Eitingon was born in Russia, the son of a wealthy Jewish family (Pomer, 1966). Afflicted with a stutter, he took his medical degree but because of his emotional conflicts he never took the examination permitting him to practice; thus technically he always remained a lay analyst. Furthermore, he worshipped Freud with such biblical devotion that he never wrote a single technical paper; everything, in his opinion, had already been said by Freud, and the only task left was to disseminate his teachings (Jones, 1943).

Eitingon is usually said to have had some personal analysis with Freud (Jones, 1943), but all that it amounted to was a few casual talks in the evening, so that essentially the man who founded the system of psychoanalytic training was himself untrained. What he lacked in training, he made up in devotion and dedication. In 1920 he moved to Berlin, where he founded an analytic clinic and institute financed by his personal funds. He remained there until 1933, when the Hitlerian tyranny forced him out. He then emigrated to Palestine, where he founded the Palestine Psychoanalytic Society, which he led until his death in 1943.

The Berlin Institute of 1920–1930 has been described in several publications. The first, entitled *Zehn Jahre Berliner Psychoanalytisches Institut* (Ten years of the Berlin Psychoanalytic Institute) was originally issued by the Internationaler Psychoanalytischer Verlag in 1930; it was reissued in 1970 under the editorship of Gerhardt Maetze, on the fiftieth anniversary of the founding of the Institute. Maetze has also written a detailed history of his own (Maetze, 1976).

The horror of the Hitler period has obliterated the extraordinary cultural achievements of Germany in the Weimar period. Einstein lived there at that time, as did Max Weber and numerous other artistic and intellectual luminaries. The roster of students and faculty at the Psychoanalytic Institute reads like a who's who of psychoanalytic history: Ernst Simmel, Karl Abraham, Otto Fenichel, Karen Horney, Hanns Sachs, Franz Alexander, Sandor Rado, Siegfried Bernfeld, Gregory Zilboorg, Bertram Lewin, and William Silverberg are only a few of the illustrious names that graced its doors. It was easily the most distinguished institute of that period, even though Freud led the group in Vienna. The system of education and training devised in Berlin has persisted to this day with no essential change. It has since been called the tripartite system: personal analysis, didactic instruction, and control analysis.

THE TRAINING ANALYSIS. First and foremost was the personal analysis. It was universally agreed that the future analyst should be analyzed by a more experienced person. At first this was called a "didactic" analysis, based on the illusion, soon to be dispelled, that the "normal" person had no particular problems. Later the term didactic was dropped, and it was recognized that all analysis was therapeutic in nature. The intensity, duration, and outcome of this *training analysis,* as it soon came to be called, all varied widely. It may be assumed that since about 1930 every practicing analyst has been through a training analysis.

The training analysis, first suggested by Nunberg in 1919, was accepted by the International Training Commission in 1925, and became an official international requirement thereafter.[54] At first it was brief, but it gradually lengthened and luxuriated, as Balint (1954) put it, until we may say with Balint that "nobody has any idea how long a training analysis should or does last."[55] It is generally recognized that the controversies about the training analysis have been at the heart of all dissensions and splits within the psychoanalytic movement, and these controversies cannot be said to have been settled even today (Goodman, 1977).

When Sachs set up the first system of training analysis in Berlin, he combined two goals. One was to transmit the understanding of the unconscious which had been so laboriously accumulated by Freud and his early co-workers, and the other was to enforce absolute obedience to the theoretical position of the school. He wrote that "the future analyst must learn to see things which other people easily, willingly and permanently overlook, and must be in a position to maintain this capacity to observe, even when it is in sharpest contradiction to his own wishes and feelings. . . . As one sees, analysis requires something which corresponds to the novitiate of the church."[56]

The issue is one of education versus indoctrination. In spite of valiant attempts to overcome this conflict between education and indoctrination, it has proved to be impossible to separate the two, and there can be no doubt that today psychoanalytic education, through the training analysis, remains a form of indoctrination. Glover (1955) described it as a system of "training transferences." However desirable it may be to get around the problem, a better system has yet to be found. The dilemma may be put in this way: if the student is left free to choose whatever theoretical system he wishes, he can easily wander off into some absurdity, such as those of Jung, Reich, or Rank. If, however, he is forced to agree with the official position, he may become unnecessarily submissive. The dilemma remains acute, undoubtedly accounting for much of the acrimony within the psychoanalytic movement.

THEORETICAL INSTRUCTION. Next came instruction in the theory of psychoanalysis. This meant studying the material that had been covered in Freud's basic works, and extensions of his ideas: dreams, development, structure of the psyche, nature of neurosis and psychosis, etc. The ideal training system followed the lines laid down by Freud. In 1927 he wrote:

A scheme of training for analysts has still to be created. It must include elements from the mental sciences, from psychology, the history of civilization and sociology, as well as from anatomy, biology, and the study of evolution.

There is so much to be taught in all this that it is justifiable to omit from the curriculum anything which has no direct bearing on the practice of analysis and only serves indirectly (like any other study) as a training for the intellect and for the powers of observation. It is easy to meet this suggestion by objecting that analytic colleges of this kind do not exist and that I am merely setting up an ideal. An ideal, no doubt. But an ideal which can and must be realized. And in our training institutes, in spite of all their youthful insufficiencies, that realization has already begun.[57]

In varying measure, analytic training institutes have been inspired by Freud's ideal and have moved toward it over the years. In this area the least amount of controversy exists.

CONTROL ANALYSIS. The third innovation of the Berlin Institute was control analysis, the term which Eitingon used for supervision. As such, this met little opposition, since budding analysts were only too happy to discuss their difficulties with a more experienced person. Eitingon in fact states that control analysis developed spontaneously and without compulsion (*zwanglos*), and that the rules were set up only later, when they reflected on what they had done.[58] Therese Benedek, who was a student at the Berlin Institute, described the control as focusing almost exclusively on the technical difficulties presented by the patient; countertransference was left out. Balint (1948) was later to call this "superego training." At any rate, the problems inherent in control analysis were not appreciated at that time, nor did the system arouse any real antagonism in the students.

Society Control

Another development, less noticed though equally fateful for the history of psychoanalysis, was the shift of control of training from the individual practitioner to the analytical society. This meant that individual members were no longer free to analyze and train students, without the prior approval of the society. Those authorized to treat were known as *training analysts;* those authorized to supervise were *control analysts.* Sometimes members combined both functions; sometimes they did not.

It is difficult to determine when this society control of training became effective. Even today there is so much opposition to it, covert and overt, that it is difficult to enforce. It must have been far more difficult to enforce in the hectic atmosphere of the 1920s and 1930s.

The justification for this limitation is somewhat difficult to establish. In theory, it makes any society more homogeneous in its theoretical position, which is certainly the case. But if psychoanalysis is well understood, what is the need for such homogeneity? Presumably all the members of any society are in substantial agreement anyhow.

In practice it has meant that seemingly minor details of doctrine are established by the society, and the individual analyst is not permitted much leeway for disagreement. The result has been innumerable and unending charges of rigidity and excessive orthodoxy, which have bedeviled every institute, as well as a diminution in the number of students applying for training.[59]

A sociological explanation might be most appropriate. Psychoanalytic societies are organizations, like any other. And in all organizations there is a struggle for power. Establishment of the proper theoretical position becomes a way of asserting and maintaining power. Psychoanalytically, the Argentine analyst Leon Grinberg has suggested that as a result of his practice the analyst tends to suffer from isolation, lack of communication, and regression.[60] These may lead on occasion to intensification of persecutory anxieties, with increased reactions of rivalry, resentment, envy, or fear. All of these reactions are kept in check by the tight control exercised by the society; nevertheless, as everyone knows, the underlying disagreements are often strong.

The Berlin System as a Model

The Berlin system, devised primarily by Eitingon but with the cooperation of many outstanding analysts, became the model for all future analytic institutes. Its core of tripartite training including personal analysis, didactic courses, and control analyses, plus society control of training have remained essentially unchanged to this day. Whatever its limitations, its logic is so compelling that virtually all analytic institutes, whatever their theoretical orientation, have followed suit. And even though the terms used are different, other forms of therapy in their training approaches have sooner or later fallen into the same mold.

Preliminary Requirements for Training—Lay Analysis

Once the training system was established, the next question was: Who should be admitted to training? In practice this boiled down to the question of lay, or nonmedical, analysis.

In 1926 Freud published *The Question of Lay Analysis,* in which he strongly urged the admission of otherwise qualified lay persons to the training institutes. He also wrote to Eitingon that in his opinion the opposition to lay analysis was "the last mask of the resistance against psychoanalysis, and the most dangerous of all." [61]

By then the topic had assumed such importance that an international symposium was arranged, the proceedings of which were published in the *International Journal of Psychoanalysis* in 1927. Twenty-four of the world's leading psychoanalysts participated. The strongest objections to lay analysis were voiced by the Americans Abraham Brill and Smith Ely Jelliffe: for the most part their European colleagues did not share the Americans' reservations. Nunberg[62] stressed the cultural significance of analysis most strongly when he said: "It is therefore more necessary that all physicians should undergo psychoanalytical training before they so much as approach the sick than that non-medical analysts should first study medicine." Among the societies the strongest position against lay analysis was taken by New York, the strongest favoring it by the Hungarians.

The vehemence of the American opposition to lay analysis is hard to understand, especially since it was accompanied by deliberately false statements about the American legal situation, which the Europeans surprisingly swallowed. In 1926 Oberndorf referred to "the strictness of the American law against quack treatment, as well as certain unfortunate experiences in connection with American candidates for membership"; [63] neither of these remarks has any ascertainable basis in fact. If anything, the American laws against quackery have always been much looser than the European, and as for undesirable experiences with nonphysician candidates, the medical opposition to psychoanalysis has always been much stronger than any other factor. Thus in his own book, *A History of Psychoanalysis in America* (1953), Oberndorf wrote: "To most of the neurologists of higher rank in these departments psychoanalysis remained a hazy, somewhat disreputable subject." [64]

Oberndorf's extraordinary piece of hokum was repeated, amazingly enough, in 1934 by a large number of prominent American analysts, including Lewin, Menninger, and Alexander,[65] who mysteriously referred to "obsolete legal enactments" and "most severe and vigorous action on the part of the authorities." Again the Europeans failed to penetrate the American fog.

Theoretically, the greatest legal need has always been to prevent untrained persons, including physicians, from practising analysis. But the respect for the physician has prevented any interference with his activities. The only recorded instance where physicians were required to have training in order to practice analysis was in Norway in 1938 (Schjelderup, 1939), when a royal decree required physicians to get special authorization from the king before using psychoanalytic methods.[66]

Eitingon, as chairman of the International Training Commission, finally proposed two resolutions that were eventually adopted. While medical training was recommended, it was determined that each branch society was free to determine independently its conditions of admission to training. In practice, this meant that the training of lay analysts was officially outlawed in the United States but permitted in all other countries. However, the American prohibition was not more successful than that other American attempt at prohibition, generally called the "noble experiment." The further story of training and lay analysis is continued in the next chapter.

The Psychoanalytic Movement

As the wounds of the war began to heal, a new spirit of optimism became noticeable, especially in the years from 1925 to 1933; at that point, Hitler put an end to it. In this period psychoanalysts, much surer of their ground than before, tried to extend the range of their doctrines. The term "psychoanalytic movement" was born, referring to the hope that psychoanalysis, through its therapeutic and educational efforts, might make a significant contribution to the welfare of the world.

It has already been noted that from these years stem some of the most optimistic of Freud's postwar publications, such as *The Question of Lay Analysis* (1926), *The Future of an Illusion* (1927), and

The New Introductory Lectures (1932). Others were active along related lines. Storfer, a journalist in the Vienna group, edited a journal called *Die psychoanalytische Bewegung* (The psychoanalytic movement); it was an official publication of the Psychoanalytic Publishing House and existed from 1929 to 1933.[67] Hitschmann also served as an editor. Thomä (1969) has stressed the degree to which psychoanalysis had penetrated German thought and culture in the pre-Hitler period.

Heinrich Meng (1887–   ), a German-born analyst, devoted his considerable energy in these years to the advancement of mental hygiene through psychoanalytic ideas. He founded a publishing house which issued *The Popular Book on Psychoanalysis,* with his analyst Paul Federn as co-editor, in 1924. Together with others he founded the *Journal of Psychoanalytic Education,* which was designed to influence psychology and education. Then he started the Institute for Psychoanalysis at the University of Frankfurt, with Karl Landauer; the institute was one of the bases for the distinguished series of publications that came out of that city.[68]

In England, Ernest Jones carried on innumerable activities, as analyst, president of the British and International Societies, and prolific author. His published works did much to expand the understanding of psychoanalysis in both professional and lay circles. He was the first to realize that the incorporation of psychoanalysis into American psychiatry had really created an entirely new profession.[69] In an address at the opening of the Psychiatric Institute in Columbia University, New York, in 1929, he said that in a very important respect the profession of psychiatry does not exist in any other country in the world. This change, he said, had come about in the past 20 years. He saw the shift to a dynamic psychiatry, as we would put it today, as an expression of the American social conscience. While it was still primarily medical, he predicted that someday psychology too would benefit from it (thereby anticipating the post–World War II growth of clinical psychology). He wrote:

It may sound paradoxical, but I venture to predict that in a not far distant future psychopathology, particularly of the psychoneuroses, will constitute the standard study of psychology, the basis from which the student will proceed later to the more obscure and difficult study of the so-called normal, and moreover I should not be altogether surprised if America achieved this consummation before any other country.[70]

Once Hitler came to power in 1933, the efforts of European analysts had perforce to be directed toward saving their lives. From then until the outbreak of the war in 1939 there was a continual exodus of analysts from the Continent to England and the United States, changing the entire nature of the analytic picture, especially after Freud's death in 1939.

One historically significant feature of the analytic experience after World War I is the development in Russia. A sizable Russian group was formed before the war, and continued after the Revolution. Notices of their activities were published regularly in the *International Journal of Psychoanalysis* until 1928; thereafter all news from them ceased. Ever since then, the attitude of official communism toward psychoanalysis has been completely condemnatory; for years, psychoanalysis was spoken of as "the last stand of capitalism." Thus from 1930 onward, psychoanalysis and psychoanalytic psychology were limited to the democratic countries, hated by extremists of both the Right and the Left. This fact has been insufficiently appreciated in the evaluation of the cultural role of psychoanalysis (see chapter 19).

The Expansion of Psychoanalytic Thought

Apart from the general development of national and international organizations, the period between the two wars is notable for the very considerable expansion of psychoanalytic thought in a number of directions. These centered in the main around other than the classical neuroses on which Freud had concentrated.

Children

The first analyst who treated children on any extended scale was the Viennese Hermine von Hug-Hellmuth (1871–1924), who published her first child case, the analysis of the dream of a 5½-year-old boy, in 1912. In 1921 she published a summary of her therapeutic experiences with children in the *International Journal of Psychoanalysis*. She espoused no set method, leaving it to the situation and her ingenuity to decide what to do. In this paper she stated that analysis is not possible before the seventh or eighth year, that it lasts several months (!), and recommended that it be carried on in the child's home. Hug-Hellmuth was mysteriously murdered by her nephew in 1924; with equal mystery she left a will expressly forbidding any account of her life and work, even psychoanalytical publications.[71]

MELANIE KLEIN (1882–1960). An entirely new thrust in the treatment of children was provided by Melanie Klein with her technique of play therapy, as a result of which she could treat infants as young as age 2.

Apart from her work with children, Klein was the first to explore in depth the psychic processes of the pre-Oedipal stage (Segal, 1973), where she made a host of contributions. In England, to which she emigrated in 1926, she was sponsored by Ernest Jones. Perhaps as a result of his enthusiasm, a strong group of followers gathered around her. After World War II, the British society was divided into three groups: Kleinians, Freudians (Anna Freud was there as well), and eclectics (Glover, 1966). Although many of her followers saw her as the head of a school, she insisted that she was merely continuing in Freud's footsteps.

ANNA FREUD (1895–). In her approach to children, Anna Freud stayed closer to the work of her father and Hug-Hellmuth. Her emphasis was on the need for educational measures because, unlike Melanie Klein, she denied that children could form transferences in the same way as adults.

Anna Freud published her first book on the treatment of children in 1927; it was translated into English in 1928. Melanie Klein, after a number of papers, published a book in 1932 (Klein, 1949). These two pioneers may fairly be said to have initiated the psychoanalytic treatment of children. Child analysis later became a significant specialty within the field.

Psychotics

In his 1914 paper on narcissism, Freud had divided the treatment population into those with transference neuroses and those with narcissistic neuroses, characterizing the latter as patients who were unable to form a transference and were therefore untreatable. Freud was not a hospital psychiatrist, however, and had no experience with psychotics. When psychiatrists came along who were working with psychotics and applied the principles of psychoanalysis to them, it soon became apparent that Freud's stricture was too severe.

Various isolated reports of the treatment of psychotics had always appeared in the analytic journals. Jung should be given credit for having been one of the first to try his hand, though with little success.

The first to present the results of large-scale psychoanalysis of psychotics was Harry Stack Sullivan (1892–1949). Writing at a time when the attitude toward the therapeutic amelioration of psychotics, including all the leading analysts from Freud on down, was one of almost total hopelessness, Sullivan (1931b) reported on the "more or less elaborate investigation" [72] of 250 young male schizophrenics seen at Shepard and Enoch Pratt Hospital near Baltimore. Of these, he chose 100 of the first 155 serial admissions for more careful statistical study relating onset to outcome. In these 100, the onset was insidious in 22, acute in 78. He reported that 48, or somewhat over 61 percent, of those with acute onset showed marked improvement; "in a considerable number, the change has amounted to a recovery from the mental disorder." [73] These figures would be remarkable even today; they are nothing short of phenomenal for the 1920s; it should be remembered that the period covered in Sullivan's paper was 1924–1931. While Sullivan gave little detail, the patients were all treated by what today would be called modified psychoanalytic therapy, or an ego-psychological approach, in contrast to classical psychoanalysis, or id-dominated therapy, which was still the prevalent mode at that time.

In his later years Sullivan became the spokesman for a new "interpersonal" approach, which was erroneously differentiated from psychoanalysis. Furthermore, after his death many of his followers almost deified him, while the more orthodox analytic community excoriated him unmercifully (Jacobson, 1955). Both of these extremes are erroneous and overlook Sullivan's close identification with psychoanalysis and his significant contributions to theory. These contributions are primarily two: that schizophrenia is treatable, and that the self system is an important and hitherto overlooked aspect of the personality.

Sullivan was closely identified with the American Psychoanalytic Association for many years. He joined in 1924 (Noble and Burnham, 1969) and was elected to the Executive Council in 1929. In 1932 he headed the committee that drafted the new constitution. In 1930 he and Ernest Hadley formed the Washington–Baltimore Psychoanalytic Society, one of the constituent members of the American when it was reorganized as a federation of societies in 1932. In 1933 he, Brill, and Oberndorf were the prime movers in the formation of a section of psychoanalysis within the American Psychiatric Association, against the bitterest opposition from the more orthodox psychiatrists. Subsequently he lost interest in the organizational activities of the American Psychoanalytic, devoting himself to his lectures and to the development of his own Washington Psychoanalytic Institute.[74] However, he remained a member of the American Psychoanalytic Association until his death in 1949.[75] As Mary Julian White comments, the fact that Sullivan was talking about a dynamic form of ego psychology (which has since become the dominant trend) has not been recognized because of his peculiar terminology.[76] This peculiar language may in turn be ascribed to his deficiency in formal schooling, as Chapman's recent biography reveals (1976). It appears that Sullivan never graduated from college and that the medical school he attended was a diploma mill.

Somewhat later than Sullivan, but with considerable overlap in time, Melanie Klein in England was also pioneering in the analytic treatment of psychotics. Unlike Sullivan, she approached them with classical methods, analyzing the transference and resistances. Her work with psychotics is perhaps best summarized in the book of her most brilliant student, Herbert Rosenfeld, *Psychotic States* (1965).

The work of Sullivan, Klein, and others forced a recasting of psychoanalytic theory to encompass the most severe disturbances known to us. The continuum theory, which Freud had always favored but never elaborated, was given reinforced impetus by these therapeutic experiences. Ernest Jones put it most clearly in 1929 in an address delivered at the opening of the Psychiatric Institute in New York:

All mental morbidity is, therefore, a state of schizophrenia, although Professor Bleuler has proposed to reserve this term for the most striking of its forms. What we meet with clinically as mental disorder represents the endless variety of the ways in which the threatened ego struggles for its self-preservation. In the nature of things, therefore, our conception of it can be cast only in terms of active dynamic strivings.[77]

Even though the demonstration that schizophrenics can be helped by psychoanalytic means goes back to the 1920s, the lag in the transmission of ideas is so long that even today one often hears that "psychotics cannot be analyzed."[78] It is clear that political controversies within the field have often led to a denial of therapeutic realities.

Normals

The realization that psychoanalysis applies to all human beings, and not just neurotics, had been with Freud from the earliest days. Yet its full implementation came only gradually. In the period between the two world wars psychoanalysis was, as Eitingon once put it, still a "pariah" and it had to fight hard for its right to exist. Nevertheless there was increasing recognition in the 1920s and 1930s that psychoanalysis was indeed a general psychology, offering a form of salvation for all, and not merely a specialized technical device. Freud had broached this position in his later works, yet he never made it entirely clear.

During this period many prominent analysts repeatedly raised the question of the applicability of psychoanalysis to broader human problems. Jones (1931) pointed out that when character problems occupied the center of the stage, as they did more and more at that time, broader philosophical problems of what is "normality" become important.

The name of the new journal of the International, started in 1929, *Die psychoanalytische Bewegung* (The psychoanalytic movement), reveals the true intent of the publication: psychoanalysis was really to regard itself as a social movement designed to change the world situation. A succinct statement to this effect had been made as early as 1921 by the Dutch analyst August Staercke: "The old-style psychiatrist is a servant of the censorship, an instrument of society, he treats the 'out-casts.' The analyst, who has here and there to some slight extent pushed aside the barrier of the censorship in himself, should use society itself as an instrument for social progress; he must serve society without reference to the censorship."[79]

Although Freud had argued that psychoanalysis subscribed to no specific Weltanschauung, or world view, and indeed had no need of one other than that derived from science, others disagreed with him. Hartmann (1933) in a notable paper on "Psychoanalysis and Weltanschauung," criticized Freud for using "Weltanschauung" in too narrow a sense. He held that the question cannot be answered for all time; each generation must answer it for itself. Nevertheless psychoanalysis can and should be decisive for mankind's realization of ethical and educational goals. Thus there was broad agreement with the proposition that psychoanalysis had all of mankind as its patient.[80]

Unfortunately, publication of *Die psychoanalytische Bewegung* had to be suspended in 1933, along with so many other worthwhile cultural causes, because of the ascendancy of the Hitlerian barbarism. OTTO RANK (1884–1939). In retrospect, the man who foresaw the universal applicability of psychoanalysis more clearly than any other was Otto Rank. Unfortunately his therapeutic innovations beginning with the 1920s have little merit, and thus obscure his real contribution. He insisted that neurosis was dis-ease, not disease, thus that it was a problem in living experienced by large numbers of people, not an illness in the technical sense. For Rank, the core of this problem lay in the repression of creativity, and it was to the elucidation of the problem of creativity that he devoted his masterpiece, *Art and the Artist: Creative Urge and Personality Development* (1932). Rank saw the creative type as the forerunner of a new kind of man:

The artistic individual has lived in art creation instead of actual life. . . . the creative type who can renounce this protection by art and can devote his whole creative force to life and the formation of life will be the first representative of the new human type, and in return for this renunciation will enjoy, in personality-creation and expression, a greater happiness.[81]

The Lower Classes, and the Rise of Clinics

Prior to World War I, psychoanalysis had largely been a luxury of those who could afford to take off considerable time from their work and devote themselves almost entirely to the experience of psychoanalysis. In 1919 Freud had already predicted that sooner or later the state would have to pay attention to the mental health needs of the indigent, just as it was already paying attention to their physical needs.

Spurred by this statement, a number of prominent analysts sponsored the formation of low-cost clinics. Again first and in a sense foremost was Eitingon, with the Berlin Clinic and Institute, the work of which has been described in the greatest detail. One of the striking features of this clinic was the intensive analytic work and training that were conducted. Various attempts to shorten the analytic hour, or to shorten the time required, proved abortive and were discontinued.[82] In 1928 Eitingon also reported that of the approximately 400 members then in the International Psychoanalytic Association, 66 had been trained at the Berlin Institute.[83]

Shortly thereafter Jones followed with a clinic in London, and Franz Alexander with one in Chicago. Jones (1936b) and Alexander (1937) published reports on their work. Once these pioneers had shown that low-cost therapy in a clinic was feasible, similar clinics appeared everywhere.

Psychosomatic Patients, and Medicine in General

Although psychoanalysis began with a considerable group of patients, hysterics, who produced somatic symptoms, it took some time before the full applicability of psychoanalysis to medicine was realized. Hysterics simulate somatic symptoms but do not alter their body structure. An entirely different problem is posed by patients whose tissues are actually affected by the emotional disturbances. For these the term "organ neurosis" was adopted, later to be changed to "psychosomatic disorders."

FRANZ ALEXANDER (1891–1964). The work of numerous investigators was already available for summary in the pioneering handbook of Flanders Dunbar on *Emotions and Bodily Changes* (1935). But Franz Alexander did the first long-term research on the major psychosomatic disorders and did it so well that the significance of psychiatry and psychoanalysis for medicine could never again be ignored.

In 1930 Alexander visited the United States and stayed to work in Chicago, where he occupied the first university chair for psychoanalysis. He started the Chicago Institute for Psychoanalysis, whose director he remained for 25 years. In the 1930s he gathered around him a brilliant team of researchers, who explored in depth a number of the major psychosomatic entities. In 1939, together with others, he founded the journal *Psychosomatic Medicine*. While he was a tireless and prolific worker in many fields, it is in psychosomatic medicine that Alexander made his most enduring contributions. Even if these have been superseded by more sophisticated and refined conceptualizations (see chapter 8), he remains the pioneer who opened the path to a virtually unexplored world.

Other Cultures

One of the recurrent criticisms of psychoanalysis in the early days was that its doctrines applied only to Viennese (or at best, Western) neurotics. Nevertheless, Freud's book *Totem and Taboo* (1913) made it obvious to far-sighted anthropologists that here was a psychology which could be useful to them. When the war ended, a number of fieldworkers emerged who made free use of psychoanalytic concepts; most prominent among them were Margaret Mead and Bronislaw Malinowski. In 1924 Ernest Jones gave a notable address (Jones, 1924; Fortes, 1977) on psychoanalysis and anthropology to the Royal Anthropological Institute in London, which helped to open new vistas on the applicability of psychoanalysis to anthropology.

GEZA ROHEIM (1891–1953). The first fully-trained psychoanalyst who did fieldwork in a primitive community was Geza Roheim. Roheim was the only child of a prosperous bourgeois family in Budapest. Interested in folk tales from an early age, he decided to take a doctorate in anthropology. No such degree existed in Hungary, so he went to Germany; even there he had to take his degree in geography (Labarre, 1966). In 1915 and 1916 he was analyzed by Ferenczi. For the next 12 years he practiced psychoanalysis in Budapest.

Then in 1928 came a great opportunity. Marie Bonaparte donated enough money to finance a 2–3-year expedition among primitive tribes. For the next several years Roheim spent his time in Central Australia and Normanby Island, off New Guinea; he also studied the Somali people. His work was justifiably considered so important by the editors of the *International Journal of Psychoanalysis* that they devoted a special double number to his report (January–April, 1932). Roheim was still working in an extremely id-oriented framework; for example, at the conclusion he wrote: "We see, then that the sexual practices of a people are indeed prototypical and that from their posture in coitus their whole psychic attitude may be inferred."[84] Nevertheless Roheim's report is of great historical importance. He showed in effect that both the theories and the therapeutic techniques of psychoanalysis were applicable to the most primitive of peoples, but that in order to do so proper attention must be paid to their fantasy lives, just as is the case with Westerners. Although he did no more fieldwork, Roheim's interest in anthropology continued, and was finally summed up in *Psychoanalysis and Anthropology* (1950).

ABRAM KARDINER (1892–   ). Another pioneer whose work began in the 1930s was the New York analyst Abram Kardiner. After analysis with Freud in Vienna in 1921–1922 (Kardiner, 1977), he returned to New York to practice analysis. In 1933 he organized a seminar on Freud's sociological writings at the New York Psychoanalytic Society. Within three years he had a class of 100, chiefly anthropologists. Among his students were Cora du Bois, Ralph Linton, and James West, all of whom did distinguished work in anthropology.[85] Shortly thereafter the seminar moved to the department of anthropology at Columbia University.

Unlike Roheim, whose originality lay in his fieldwork, Kardiner's contribution was in organizing psychoanalytically the fieldwork of others. He was the first to offer a comprehensive integration of psychoanalysis and anthropology in terms of ego psychology. This was presented in his two major books, *The Individual and his Society* (1939) and the *Psychological Frontiers of Society* (1945).

After the pioneering work of Roheim and Kardiner, the integration of psychoanalysis and anthropology proceeded apace. The field is still in a state of flux. It is more fully reviewed in chapter 17.

Other Groups

The 1920s and 1930s also saw further pioneering applications of psychoanalysis in many directions. August Aichhorn (1878–1949) undertook the treatment of delinquents and criminals in Vienna. Wulf Sachs in 1937 published the analysis of a South African medicine man, John Chavafambira (Loveland, 1947). Ernst Simmel (1882–1947) pioneered in the treatment of drug addicts and in the development of the hospital care of patients using psychoanalytic principles. Heinrich Meng (1887–   ) devoted himself to the application of psychoanalysis to mental hygiene. Hans Zulliger (1893–   ) applied psychoanalysis to education.[86]

All of these efforts, now viewed as routine, met with considerable opposition when they started. Thus Hitschmann relates (1932) that when the Vienna group petitioned for permission to open a low-cost clinic, the petition was referred to Julius von Wagner-Jauregg; after a long delay, he recommended rejection. Wagner-Jauregg was an eminent traditional psychiatrist who had received the Nobel Prize for his discovery of the malaria treatment for general paresis (paralysis), the last stage of syphilis. But he had no use for psychoanalysis. Finally the clinic was opened in 1922; 6 months later the municipal authorities suddenly ordered it closed. Lay persons and medical students were not permitted to do treatment; furthermore, the clinic was forbidden to make any charges for its services. Despite all these obstacles it went on.[87]

Similarly Oberndorf recounts[88] that in 1927 when the New York Psychoanalytic Society, represented by himself, Brill, and Jelliffe, petitioned the State Board of Charities to start a treatment center, they were turned down because they were not attached to an established hospital or medical school.

Thus while psychoanalysis made great strides between the two world wars, neither the established professions nor the official authorities knew much of what was taking place.

Marxism and Psychoanalysis

Prior to 1930 a number of well-known analysts, still inspired by the liberal promises of the October Revolution in Russia, attempted a combination or synthesis of psychoanalysis and Marxism. Some of the persons in this group were Siegfried Bernfeld, Wilhelm Reich, Otto Fenichel, Erich Fromm, and the sociologist Max Horkheimer.[89] These analysts did not admit the dichotomy between the individual and society which seemed to be inherent in Freud's thought. They attempted to integrate psychoanalysis into Marxism, but with little success. There was even for a short time a "Marxist opposition" in the International Psychoanalytic Association under the leadership of Wilhelm Reich and Otto Fenichel, but it soon collapsed. In 1934 Reich was expelled from the International;[90] Fenichel altered his views. In the meantime the vituperously destructive attacks on psychoanalysts by orthodox Communists destroyed whatever possibility of cooperation might have existed.

Wilhelm Reich (1897–1957) is one of the most bizarre figures in the history of psychoanalysis. Up to 1933 he was one of the leading figures in the field, and he headed the seminar for psychoanalytic therapy at the Vienna Psychoanalytic Institute from 1924 to 1930 (Briehl, 1966). His book *Character Analysis* (1933) made a significant contribution to the understanding of character structure.

Reich went to extremes, however, in his attempt to combine Freud and Marxism. When Reich called the death instinct a "product of the capitalistic system,"[91] he was merely countering one absurdity with another; Freud and other analysts were outraged and were concerned about the influence he might have on the science. However, Reich was equally critical of what was going on in Russia (I. Reich, 1969). He then left psychoanalysis and went on to what he called "orgonomy," a concoction of blatant absurdities for which he nonetheless found some followers. In later years he saw "orgone energy" as the antidote to nuclear energy and envisioned himself as one of the saviors of mankind whom the FBI was protecting because of his knowledge of secrets. He was convicted of fraud regarding the "orgone box," and his obvious paranoia led to his eventual incarceration in a federal prison (which he could easily have avoided). He died there in 1957. Sterba (1953), who had been a student of Reich's, tied Reich's overemphasis on resistances to his own suspiciousness and denial of real love, thus implying that the paranoia which broke out in full force in the later years was present in embryo earlier. In any case, Reich's later work has no scientific value.

The various attempts to create a Freudo-Marxism, which originally stemmed from Reich, have died out, especially since official communism still remains violently antagonistic to any analytic ideas. In France, surprisingly, there have occasionally been attempts to revive the Freudo-Marxist ideas, but with little success (Barande and Barande, 1975). Of contemporary psychoanalysts, Erich Fromm is one of the few who see some merit in Marx's ideas, but not in the official Communist governments (*The Sane Society,* 1955).

The American Revolution

As long as Freud was alive, the center of the psychoanalytic world had to be where he lived; Vienna until 1938, then London for the next year and a half. But the storm clouds over Europe forced an increasing number of analysts to emigrate, and most of them went to the United States.

Before the emigration of the 1930s the American group had been neither particularly strong nor particularly influential in the international movement. Brill, Freud's first English translator, had the curious notion that Freud's system was virtually complete in 1907.[92] Oberndorf has called the decade 1920–1930 "stormy years in psychoanalysis" in the United States.[93] The course of psychoanalysis, he says, had not been running smoothly. Every new book by Freud brought forth extended argument and controversy before it was fully digested.

Then European leaders began to come here. Sandor Rado went to the New York Psychoanalytic Society in 1931, Hanns Sachs to Boston, Franz Alexander and Karen Horney to Chicago, Robert Waelder to Philadelphia, Ernst Simmel and Otto Fenichel to Los Angeles, later Heinz Hartmann, Ernst Kris, Herman Nunberg, and Rudolf Loewenstein to New York, and so on. American psychoanalysis, which had not even required a didactic analysis before 1929,[94] became increasingly conscious of organization and training.

However, the rebellion against European domination, which reached a high point by the end of the 1930s, remains hard to explain. After all, the major luminaries of the psychoanalytic world were still either in Europe or with extensive European training and connections. Some have suggested that it was simply an Oedipal revolt: having been trained to obey their masters in Europe, once they reached America they turned against the father-figures.

Whatever the dynamics, opposition was expressed against the training rules which permitted an analyst trained in one country to move freely to another. It is not clear from an examination of conditions prevailing at that time why the Americans were so opposed to new blood, especially since training in psychoanalysis had already become uniform according to the model of the Berlin Institute. It has been suggested that the American resistance was against lay analysis, but that too requires some explanation.

The International Training Commission had been set up with American agreement in 1925, and had functioned as the official regulating body ever since. Suddenly in 1936 at the Marienbad Congress, Rado, representing the American group, demanded its complete abolition. His resolution read as follows:

We are opposed to an I.T.C. in its present form, as well as to any reorganization which would retain it as a legislative or administrative body. We suggest that the I.T.C. should be replaced by an *entirely informal* International Training Conference, to be open for instructors and various officers and committee members of our Institutes and Societies, convening at the occasion of

Congresses under the Chairmanship and Secretaryship of the President and General Secretary of the International Psycho-Analytic Association; that is, without having special officers of its own. There should be no voting, no representation, nothing of that kind.[95]

Although Rado's motion was unanimously rejected, the American group nevertheless put it into effect without consulting the international body. Two years later, in 1938, no American representatives appeared at the meeting in Paris.[96] The war then intervened, stopping all organized international activity. When peace was restored the Americans, who had more analysts than the entire rest of the world, had their way, retaining complete independence from the International. No change in this situation has occurred since. Thus the Americans in 1938 unilaterally transformed the International from a regulatory body into an administrative one.

The Literature of Psychoanalysis

The inter-war period saw the disappearance of many of the old journals and the appearance of many new ones. With the onset of the war all the German-language journals vanished, never to be revived in the same form. *The International Journal of Psychoanalysis* was founded by Ernest Jones in 1920, and has continued uninterrupted publication. *The Psychoanalytic Quarterly* was founded by Dorian Feigenbaum, Bertram Lewin, Franklin Williams, and Gregory Zilboorg in 1932, with the rather curious statement:

This Quarterly will be devoted to theoretical, clinical and applied psychoanalysis. It has been established to fill the need for a strictly psychoanalytic organ in America, where, although Freudian analysis has been received more favorably than in any other country, it nevertheless is exposed to the danger of misrepresentation and dilution with ideas foreign to it, both in respect to theory and method.[97]

A *Bulletin of the American Psychoanalytic Association* was started in 1937 (Oberndorf, 1953), to be replaced by the present *Journal of the American Psychoanalytic Association* in 1953. *Psychiatry* was initiated by Harry Stack Sullivan in 1938 as a forum for his views and those of analysts in agreement with him.

Among the books published, the most notable was Otto Fenichel's *Psychoanalytic Theory of Neurosis,* in 1934, with a revised and enlarged edition in 1945. Fenichel's book may justly be said to summarize all major psychoanalytic knowledge to that date.

Developments in Allied Fields

In psychiatry the period from 1918 to 1939 was characterized chiefly by experimentation with organic methods, especially the shock therapies, all of which appeared in the 1930s. Nevertheless, even with shock the mentally ill remained housed in large, poorly kept hospitals and, in accordance with the tenets of Kraepelinian psychiatry, their prognosis was virtually hopeless. This situation began to change only when psychoanalytic ideas started to filter in, and then only very gradually.

In psychology the academic community became enamored of behaviorism, both in the American variety and in the application of Pavlov's ideas about conditioning. As a result, it set itself determinedly against psychoanalysis, which was castigated mercilessly as an unscientific kind of hokum, even though many prominent psychologists underwent personal psychoanalysis (American Psychological Association, 1953). The only dynamic element in the psychology of that day was the Gestalt view, but that was limited to some propositions about the cognitive functions. Gestaltists too, such as Kurt Lewin, had little use for psychoanalysis.

Thus almost everywhere psychoanalysis was forced to develop outside the bounds of the established medical schools and universities. Analysts banded together in independent institutes, and the hallmark of an analyst was that he belonged to a certain institute, which had a consistent philosophy and a consistent method of training. This official kind of exclusion was to have a fateful effect on the further course of psychoanalysis.

Summary Comments

Organized psychoanalytic activity virtually stopped during World War II. Paradoxically the only national European group which continued was the Berlin Society, under a different name, which apparently was allowed to exist because of the high incidence of mental breakdowns in the Nazi officialdom.[98] Nevertheless the achievements of the years 1919–1939 were enormous and laid the foundations for the revival and flowering of psychoanalysis from 1945 onward.

The International Psychoanalytical Association was revived in 1919; its prime mover in the years before World War II was Ernest Jones. Toward the end of the period the Americans seceded and have been independent ever since. However, the rules of the International Training Commission, first set up in 1925, have been universally adopted. They follow the model of the Berlin Psychoanalytic Institute, first organized by Eitingon in 1920. The training system involves the tripartite structure involving personal analysis, didactic courses, and control analyses. To these must be added society control of training. Although the training system is universally used, considerable controversy about each of its component parts has always existed and continues to exist, even today.

Many pioneers extended Freud's work in a number of directions: Melanie Klein and Anna Freud with children, Sullivan and Klein with psychotics, Rank, Jung, and others with normal persons, Alexander with psychosomatic disorders, Roheim and Kardiner with other cultures, while a variety of individuals pioneered many other applications.

A period of flirtation with Marxism by some analysts soon came to an end. Wilhelm Reich may be seen as the extreme analytic deviation to the left, Jung as the extreme to the right; both have since been completely rejected by the main body of psychoanalysts, which remains tied to the democratic humanistic traditions of Western culture.

In spite of continued professional growth and seeming organizational unity, splits and dissensions were to be found everywhere. The most important in this period was the secession from the New York Psychoanalytic Institute of Karen Horney, William Silverberg, and Clara Thompson in 1941. These three became part of the culturalist group which in later years was to offer the most formidable alternatives to classical Freudian psychoanalysis.

Chapter Five

Organizational Vicissitudes
Since World War II

Just before World War II broke out, the International Psychoanalytic Association had about 560 members, of whom some 30 percent were in the United States (Jones, 1939). According to its 1977 roster, the International numbers somewhat over 4,000 members, with more than half in the United States. Although this is not a spectacular growth in sheer numbers (far less than the increases recorded by the major mental health professions), the qualitative changes are significant. In these four decades psychoanalytic psychology or the dynamic point of view introduced by Freud became, if not the dominant view, at least one of the most important viewpoints in psychiatry, psychology, and all the social sciences.

As a result of these far-reaching changes, it is much harder to delimit the field in the postwar period than before. Psychiatry, dynamic psychiatry, clinical psychology, psychology, psychotherapist, and psychoanalyst have all become virtually interchangeable designations in the mind of the lay person, and large numbers of professionals as well are baffled by the many terms and controversies in the field. A committee of the American Psychoanalytic Association labored for six and a half years shortly after the war, trying to arrive at a definition of psychoanalysis acceptable to the members of the Association, and could not reach a consensus (Cushing, 1952). On the other hand a recent study of psychiatric practice (Marmor, 1975) simply lumped psychoanalysts and psychiatrists together, failing to make any distinction in their training, philosophy, or practice. Henry et al. (1971) coined the term "the fifth profession" to describe psychotherapists, and showed that while there were four different training systems for psychotherapy—psychiatry, psychoanalysis, psychology, and social work—members of each group triumph over the manifest goals of their particular training system and become with time increasingly like their colleague psychotherapists in other training systems.

Henry and associates fail to state that the basic model for psychotherapy has become the psychoanalytic one. Yet within this model, all kinds and degrees of training are currently included, so that the background of any psychotherapist other than a traditionally trained psychoanalyst is largely unclear.

Intellectually, psychoanalysis has affected every science that deals with mankind. Yet what is psychoanalytic and what is not has become thoroughly obscured. In a classic paper, Kris, Herma, and Shor (1943) showed that whenever a psychoanalytic idea was incorporated into the mainstream of psychology, it was then labeled "psychology," while if it was not incorporated it was labeled "psychoanalysis." As a result, the student and professional get the completely erroneous impression that psychoanalysis somehow stands outside the tenets of the accepted behavioral disciplines.

The International Psychoanalytic Association

When the war ended, the International Psychoanalytic Association (still headed by Ernest Jones, who had been president since 1934) began to resume its normal operations. Acceptance of the independence of the American Association was made official (Jones, 1949). For all other countries of the world, the regulations of the International were mandatory. It should again be recalled that in all essential respects the training and membership requirements of the International and American Associations are identical, except that since 1938 nonmedical or lay analysts have been barred from membership in the American but accepted everywhere else in the world. (This situation is now changing, as will be detailed below.)

The first postwar meeting was held in Zurich, Switzerland, in 1949. Jones, presiding, reported that he could not give the precise number of members of the International but that it was slightly less than 800, of whom more than half were in the United States.[1] He then went on to describe the rebuilding of national societies in a number of European and non-European countries, as well as new societies in the process of formation. Jones also reported on the negotiations with the Americans about the prewar proposals for their independence. Although he did not actually say so, and it is not incorporated in the statutes,[2] the independence of the American Association in all regulatory bodies was recognized de facto and has remained ever since.

The postwar reconstruction of psychoanalytic organizations has proceeded everywhere along similar lines. Founding members have either been previous members of some recognized component group of the International, or trained in one of the component groups. They then set themselves up as training analysts and adopt the usual training regulations. The tripartite system of training, including society control, has become universal.

With this system, and in the absence of any large-scale international conflicts, the rebuilding and expansion of the psychoanalytic world have proceeded smoothly. As of 1977 the International comprised 1 regional association, the American; 2 other North American associations, in Canada and Mexico; 9 South American associations, 4 of which were in Brazil; 14 European associations, 2 of which were in France; 3 Asian societies; 1 Australian; 3 study groups, 2 in Europe and 1 in Argentina; and some direct and associate members. A systematic basis for growth all over the world is thus assured. It is noteworthy that no groups exist in Communist countries, the postwar societies in some of the East European countries having quickly disappeared.

The Rise of Regional Associations

Following the reestablishment of the older national societies and the establishment of new ones, the next logical step was the formation of larger regional bodies. The most important of these in the postwar period has been the European Psychoanalytical Federation, the statutes of which were officially approved by the International at the meeting in Rome in 1969.[3] Other regional associations that have held meetings from time to time have been the Latin American, Pan-American, Romance-language, German-speaking, and Scandinavian groups. None of these, unlike the European group, have formalized their activities into an official federation.

Child Analysis

The most controversial issue facing the International since the war has been the proposal to make child analysis an official part of training, originally made by the Dutch group at the Copenhagen meeting in 1967. The proposal was fully discussed at the next meeting, in Rome in 1969.[4]

The plan offered by the Dutch provided that the training in child analysis should run parallel to and follow in all its features, sequences, and general setting the pattern of the existing psychoanalytic training for the treatment of adult patients, with which it is, to some extent, interlinked. The conditions for admission, the criteria for selection and evaluation, the educational standards determining the training program in general and curriculum in particular, as well as the general level of instruction, are equivalent. The ultimate responsibility for both courses was to rest with the Training Committee of the Dutch Psychoanalytical Society.

Thus the Dutch plan offered its trainees the same possibilities and rights as now exist for those trained for the psychoanalytic treatment of adults. Ultimately this means that if the training is successful, they may, on the recommendation of the Training Committee, be proposed for election to the Society and hence the International Psychoanalytical Association.

The Dutch plan presented the first significant break with the system originally set up by Eitingon at Berlin in 1920, the major difference being that the patients treated would be children rather than adults. Considerable caution was expressed by different members of the International about the plan. Adam Limentani reported that the British group viewed the step with "some degree of concern."[5] Michael Balint called it "a very important new innovation"[6] and urged postponement of the final decision. Victor Smirnoff of France deplored the move as "a split inside of analysis."[7] Heinz Kohut made the interesting comment that "all of us . . . are not fully trained in psychoanalysis."[8]

Finally a motion was made to appoint a study commission to examine the question. As of the present, no final decision has been reached by the International on the plan. It was reported in the official proceedings, however, that by 1967 the Hampstead Child Therapy Course and Clinic, headed by Anna Freud, had qualified 68 psy-

choanalytic child therapists in a 4-year training course.[9] While the
Dutch reserved the right to require persons trained only in child analysis to take further full training in adult analysis if they wished to
treat adults, in practice this must be just as hard to enforce as the reverse, i.e., to require adult analysts to take further training before
they treat children. Thus, de facto, by the end of the 1960s another
route was opened toward analytic training. Similar problems are now
being faced by the American Psychoanalytic Association.

Whatever theoretical standards are set up, the actual nature of
training is determined just as much by the conditions prevalent in the
field as by the authoritarian rules. When the Berlin system was set
up, there was no official child analysis, so nothing had to be done.
Once child analysis had developed into a full-fledged system, it had
to be incorporated somehow into the analytic training programs, and
this created innumerable problems. Similar difficulties have arisen
with regard to the treatment of psychotics, group analysis, lay analysis, and other "specialties" within analysis: the practical realities
have often been more decisive than the official rules.

Freudian Base

In the postwar period the International has been emphatically a
Freudian group. The statutes, accepted at the Copenhagen congress in
1967 (but little changed from the previous statutes) defined psychoanalysis as follows:

The term "psychoanalysis" refers to a theory of personality structure and
function, application of this theory to other branches of knowledge, and, finally, to a specific psychotherapeutic technique. This body of knowledge is
based on and derived from the fundamental psychological discoveries of
Sigmund Freud.[10]

Many efforts were then made to define "psychoanalysis" and
"Freudian" further. Questionnaires were sent out all over the world.
At the Vienna meeting in 1971, William Gillespie, then president, reported that there were rather few replies from the United States, and
that half of the other component organizations around the world did
not reply. The replies received were so divided that no change in the
wording of the statute was recommended,[11] and it still stands.

Nevertheless, as in the United States, concern about deviant and
unorthodox views has been strong. In 1969 Joseph Sandler, then edi-

tor of the *International Journal of Psychoanalysis,* saw fit to reprint the original editorial by Ernest Jones, written 50 years earlier,[12] in which Jones had warned that there were two main forms of resistance against psychoanalysis: one was to deny its validity altogether, the other was to accept it as true, but to deprive the ideas of their real value or meaning. Jones had argued that the second type of resistance was more insidious and more dangerous than the first, and also more widespread, especially in the United States.

The International is thus in the peculiar position of demanding strict adherence to a doctrine that it can define only approximately, while all attempts to define it more precisely have failed. Nevertheless the meaning of "Freudianism" has been sufficiently clear that the bitter disputes of the 1920–1940 period have been avoided. It must also be borne in mind, however, that since the International has relinquished control over the American situation, it has no voice in the training practices of its largest and most prosperous component. This could be seen as an experiment of nature showing that once the training role is discarded, disputes within psychoanalytic societies tend to disappear.

Growth of the International and Developments in Individual Countries

From its modest beginnings in 1902, when four enthusiasts joined Freud on Wednesday evenings, the International has displayed remarkable growth. Through two disastrous wars, many revolutions, and social upheavals with the most disastrous consequences, it has maintained its organization and its unity for more than 60 years, truly a phenomenal record. A man, Freud once said, is only as strong as the ideas he represents. Surely this is convincing evidence of the profound significance for mankind of the Freudian ideas.

The pattern for the growth of psychoanalysis has been uniform throughout the world since World War II. In some countries, existing institutes and societies simply expanded. In others, new institutes and societies were formed by persons trained in other countries. By 1945 the "autodidactic" phenomenon of the earlier period had disappeared. Once the founding fathers had established an institute and society, further growth was assured. Splits and divisions were to be found everywhere, however, varying with local conditions. It is to the developments in the individual countries that we now turn.

The United States

In the United States the decisive fact has been the domination of the field by the American Psychoanalytic Association. By the mid-1950s a great increase in numbers and prestige had led it to a pinnacle of power and prestige. The emigration in the late 1930s to England and the United States meant that almost all the prominent leaders of psychoanalysis were away from Europe, most of them in the comparative safety of the United States.

In 1953 the Association founded the *Journal of the American Psychoanalytic Association,* which has become one of the foremost in the world. In the first issue Robert Knight published his presidential address to the Association in 1952, which casts some illuminating light on the achievements and conflicts of the Association.

Knight reported the numerical growth of the Association as highly satisfactory. Of the 485 members in 1952, one-third had become members since 1948, over one-half since 1942, and three-fourths since 1938. There were approximately 900 candidates in training in the approved institutes.

Three major periods in the history of the Association were delineated: a loose organization of individual members from 1911 to 1932, a federation of constituent local societies from 1932 to 1946, and the reconstituted national organization with individual membership since 1946.

Until 1938 the American Psychoanalytic Association subordinated its decisions in training to the International Training Commission of the International Psychoanalytic Association, which regulated analytic training all over the world. In that year, as noted, the Americans rebelled and set up their own standards (not essentially different from those of the International, except that nonmedical persons were not permitted as members or as students).[13] At its first postwar meeting at Zurich in 1949, the International was reorganized in conformity with the American proposals.

The major point at issue, then as now, was training. This will be considered and reconsidered at many different points, since it is still essentially unresolved, remaining the storm center of numerous controversies.

The 1946 reorganization of the American Association, which has been amended only in minor particulars, made the Association one of individual members on a national basis (instead of groups), made the societies affiliates rather than constituent member societies, permitted individual membership in several societies, removed all limitations on the number of societies or institutes in a single locality, broke the compulsory tie between society and institute to allow for any kind of institute connection, and provided for voting by individuals at a regular meeting or by mail ballot.

Knight observed that Association membership had increased by geometric progression during each decade, and confidently predicted that the membership should be 1000 in 1962, and 2000 in 1972; neither of these figures has been reached.

Geographically, analysts were concentrated in the more populous states, and even there in the larger cities. In 1952 there were 9 states in which only one analyst was practicing; in 21 states there were none at all.

Knight noted the numerical preponderance of the American analysts in the International: in 1925 it had 210 regular members, of whom 33 (16 percent) resided in the United States; in 1921 the IPA membership was 307, with 68 (22 percent) in this country; and in 1952 the IPA membership was 762, with 485 (64 percent) in the U.S. While the numbers of analysts in the United States and the world have increased considerably since then, the percentages have not altered significantly.[14]

Knight bluntly acknowledged that the major issue leading to controversy within the Association was training. As the three regular ingredients of such dissension he listed: disagreement over teaching content, usually between a conservative, orthodox position and what was considered to be a "deviant" position; complaints from those in the deviant position that they were being prevented by the orthodox group from operating with academic freedom in their pursuit of scientific truth; and personality clashes.[15] Thus the conflict between the "orthodox" and the "progressive" branches of psychoanalysis, often referred to (mistakenly) as the "Freudian" and the "culturalist," had already been born. From that time on, virtually every city has had a liberal and a conservative wing, sometimes combining the two in one institute.

Knight paid only slight attention to the question of lay analysis. He stated, erroneously, that in New York City there were two unrecognized institutes (there were at least half a dozen) training nonmedical persons. While he admitted that the regulations of the American Psychoanalytic "may have the effect of drying up the supply of research psychoanalysts," all he could offer was that "this problem needs further careful study."[16]

The close connection between psychiatry and psychoanalysis, so characteristic of the American scene and absent from the European one, was documented in his talk. In 1952, some 400, or 82 percent, of the members of the American Psychoanalytic were also members of the American Psychiatric Association, and of the candidates then in training approximately 73 percent were members of the American Psychiatric.

Since Knight concentrated on numbers, there is little qualitative evaluation in his address. One remark, however, pointing to the diminishing frequency of classical analysis, is worth quoting:

It is my impression from talking with many analytic colleagues that the "pure" psychoanalyst, one who does only classical psychoanalysis, is a much scarcer individual at present, and that many analysts would privately admit that they are treating a number of patients with modified analytic techniques, or even with psychotherapy, and have relatively few patients with whom they employ a strictly classical technique.[17]

Knight also noted a marked change in the composition of the analytic candidates. He thought that perhaps the majority of them were "normal" characters or, more precisely, had "normal character disorders."

They are not so introspective, are inclined to read only the literature that is assigned in institute courses, and wish to get through with the training requirements as rapidly as possible. Their interests are primarily clinical rather than research and theoretical. *Their motivation for being analyzed is more to get through this requirement of training rather than to overcome neurotic suffering in themselves or to explore introspectively and with curiosity their own inner selves* (italics added).[18]

Two years later Ives Hendrick, in his presidential address to the American Psychoanalytic Association in 1954, echoed the confident pronouncements of his predecessor. But, he added, one consequence of the tightened organization was an increase in power:

Our success . . . hugely magnified by our growth in numbers and by the esteem of other medical groups, has given us unsought and unexpected powers, the equivalent of powers of faculty appointment, selection of students, and the curriculum policies of universities, and the powers of accreditation of specialty groups by Boards recognized by the A.M.A.[19]

In contrast to Knight's address and to presidential addresses in more recent years. Hendrick referred to the "tattered dialectics" of the lay analysis problem. He did not consider that the growth of the organization had perpetuated Freud's eternal problem of the beloved friend and the hated enemy, with the psychiatrist now representing the beloved friend and the lay analyst the hated enemy.

Through the years psychoanalysis continued to grow in numbers and prestige. Yet there were disquieting rumbles under the surface. Lewin and Ross, in their study of psychoanalytic education (1960), found much to criticize, as discussed later. The Fact-Gathering Committee, set up to evaluate the results of psychoanalysis, ended in a complete fiasco (Hamburg et al., 1967). Despite the official taboo, lay analysis grew by leaps and bounds. In the marriage with psychiatry, it was increasingly unclear whether, as Freud had once put it, the embrace by medicine was oral-erotic or oral-cannibalistic (Marmor's 1975 report is clearly oral-cannibalistic toward psychoanalysis).

The dissatisfactions began to surface in various ways, including presidential addresses. In 1964 Gitelson argued that psychoanalysis was caught in an identity conflict with psychiatry, from which it should be separated, in that psychiatry is a therapeutic specialty of medicine, while psychoanalysis is a basic science. He urged a broader basis for selection of analysts (thus implicitly favoring lay analysis), when he wrote: *"I think the time has come for psychoanalysis to accept its identity as a separate scientific discipline* whose practitioners can be various kinds of intellectually qualified persons who are humanly qualified for the human experiment which is the analytic situation."[20]

Another note was struck by Samuel Ritvo in his presidential address in 1969.[21] Ritvo frankly stated that "the drop in the popularity of psychoanalysis is based in part on a disillusionment following an equally excessive overvaluation as a therapy in the postwar period."[22]

He deplored the subsidiary and secondary role that psychoanalysis had taken in relation to psychiatry, which had led to the "astonishing" situation that the majority of psychoanalysts only became full-fledged members of the profession when they were well past the middle of their lives. He argued that "the situation which has prevailed now for 25 years has produced deleterious effects. The psychoanalytic societies are organizations of middle-aged and old men."[23]

Some statistics released by the New York Psychoanalytic Society in 1969 were revealing. Of a total of 274 members, only 2 were below the age of 40. The largest number were 50–59 years old. The average age of the 63 faculty members was 61 years. It was only natural, commented Ritvo, that the conditions of psychoanalytic education bred resentment among the candidates and graduates and created morale problems in the American Association. His recommendation again was to permit an earlier start in psychoanalytic education. Once more he pleaded for lay analysis, stating that "we have been, and could be once again in the future, enriched by people from other backgrounds who also have the qualities for functioning in the psychoanalytic situation."[24]

The same kind of stance was taken by Burness Moore in his presidential address in 1974.[25] He argued that the "present requirements represent an effort to maintain control over standards in an illogical way."[26] More than any other profession, he stated, psychoanalysts nurture their young much too long. In many respects he saw psychoanalysis as declining, both qualitatively and quantitatively:

The preeminent position of psychoanalysis in American psychiatry no longer prevails. It was at its peak at the time of Rangell's address in 1962. Other modalities of therapy have been developed and are the vogue, even though their scientific validity and therapeutic effectiveness are, for the disorders analysts treat, no better established than that of psychoanalysis.[27]

Paradoxically, the very success of the American Psychoanalytic Association in consolidating its ranks had created a confused and confusing situation in the 1970s. Psychoanalysis had been married to psychiatry, but many urged divorce. The Association had controlled training, yet "unauthorized" training, as Moore acknowledged, had blossomed. Now it seemed more useful to try to control this unauthorized training than to ban it or be silent about it, as had been the custom in the past. Above all, the qualitative problems of training, which were brought up over and over again and had been considered and reconsidered by numerous committees, seemed insoluble. A new Committee on Psychoanalytic Education and Research had been appointed, yet whether its recommendations would have any more effect than those of the past remained an open question. Organization as such could not be the answer to the problems of psychoanalysis.

The Lewin–Ross Study

Psychoanalysis involves a continuous, unprejudiced self-scrutiny. Such self-scrutiny has also been characteristic of the analytic societies. The American Psychoanalytic Association has appointed numerous committees to review its educational program and improve the quality of its training. In 1954 it authorized an extensive survey project, utilizing several full-time analysts. Bertram Lewin, one of the leading American analysts all through his life, and Helen Ross were appointed project directors in the fall of 1956; their work formally terminated in September 1959. The results of their survey were published as *Psychoanalytic Education in the United States* (1960). Although it goes back almost 30 years, this book is still the best source of information about the details of practices and procedures within the American Psychoanalytic.

In 1972 the Committee on Psychoanalytic Education and Research (COPER) appointed a subcommittee to update, as quickly as possible, much of the information contained in the Lewin and Ross study. The committee began its work in 1972, sending out questionnaires to the 20 psychoanalytic training institutes then officially approved and to 1 training center. It took more than a year to receive a sufficient number of returns for a representative sample of institute analysts and students.

The full report of the committee was published in 1977, edited by Stanley Goodman, as *Psychoanalytic Education and Research*. The general conclusion was that "the practice of psychoanalysis, at least as it is reflected in the didactic analysis, has not changed from 1958." [28]

Inasmuch as the Lewin–Ross study was more complete, basing its conclusions on a 100 percent return and personal interviews rather than a sampling from questionnaires, their work is used here as the basis for further discussion. When appropriate, comparisons are drawn with the 1972 COPER study.

At the time of the Lewin–Ross survey there were 14 officially approved psychoanalytic institutes and 3 approved training centers. (As of the latest count, in 1976–1977, there were 33 approved affiliate societies, and 26 approved training institutes.) [29] The survey directors made 18 visits to the training institutes and centers. The time spent in each place depended on the size and complexity of the facility. Questionnaires and other personal contacts supplied the information given in the book. Their main findings can be summarized under six headings: the psychoanalytic student, selection, the training analysis, supervision, the curriculum, and advanced study.

THE PSYCHOANALYTIC STUDENT. In July 1958 there were 880 students, of whom 80 (or 9 percent) were women. (In view of the interest devoted to the promotion of feminine welfare since then, it may be noted that at that time 13 percent of the members of the American Psychoanalytic Association were women, and 27 percent of the training analysts were women. Thus the percentage of women students is surprisingly low.) The mean age of the students at admission was 31.3, while the mean age at graduation was 39.3. Therefore, even though the training course theoretically required four years, in practice it usually required double that amount (see Ritvo's remarks, quoted earlier). The authors note that ''the sense of getting older . . . is quite marked among the students.''[30]

About half of the students were board-certified psychiatrists. For most of them, psychoanalysis was thought about as early as any other specialty, was not usually discriminated from psychiatry in general, and was thus usually looked upon as a subspecialty of psychiatry.

The cost of training, while high, about $20,000 at that time, was manageable; by 1972 it was $31,000.[31] Only minor assistance was available at the institutes.

SELECTION. On a national average 38.2 percent of the applicants were accepted, with a range of 25.1 percent in San Francisco to 64.3 percent in Topeka. The wide variability from one city to another is also brought out in many other ways.

No topic is more extensively discussed than the proper selection and admission of students. Aware of their responsibility, the institutes and their staffs were dissatisfied. Every conceivable device was used in the initial selection: previous evaluation (especially of psychiatric performance), letters of recommendation, psychological tests, individual and group interviews.

In general, the institutes were wary of the more ''normal-appearing'' candidates. It was generally felt that a certain amount of neurosis was not only inevitable but also, if conquered sufficiently in the course of a personal analysis, an advantage. Certain kinds of psychopathology, such as overt homosexuality, or obvious psychopathy automatically led to rejection, but a wide leeway was allowed for other kinds of problems. Lewin and Ross emphasize that no matter what method was used, in the end the decision was made on impressionistic grounds. One person wrote: "The real conflict among us in the group still holds as to whether we are looking for mediocre or exceptional analysts. Undoubtedly personal and prejudicial elements enter into this." [32] However, once students were admitted, their chances of getting through were excellent. Only 4–6 percent of the student population was dropped. [33]

TRAINING ANALYSIS. The training analysis is the unique aspect of the analytic institute. It has no real counterpart in any other field. Of it Lewin and Ross say: "The requirement that a student be "analyzed satisfactorily" defies academic definition, is bound to rest on individual or "jury" opinion, and can be subjected to measurement as little as "true scholarship" (as distinct from official pedantry) or, for that matter, as little as love, which notoriously "n'a jamais connu la loi." [34]

Within the training analyses extraordinary differences in length and even frequency were noted from one institute to another, and sometimes even within one institute. Lewin and Ross's tabulation of the length of 918 training analyses from 1932 to 1957 showed that 62.7 percent of these analyses lasted from 300 to 700 hours. That still leaves 37.3 percent outside these figures, with 6 analyses lasting under 200 hours, and 18 lasting 1300 hours or more. [35]

Even more surprising is the consistency of differences from one city to another. From 1932 to 1957, the mean number of hours of training analyses varied from a low of 473 at the Philadelphia Society to a high of 963 at the Cleveland Training Center, just about double the Philadelphia figure. Even within Philadelphia, the Philadelphia Society had an average length of training analysis of 473, while the Philadelphia Association had a mean length of 792 hours. Since the training analysis is central to the whole process, it seems clear that institutes, even within one city, are operating on different philosophical grounds.

The same wide variability is apparent in the later COPER report. In 1971 the national mean number of hours to complete analysis was 772.6 (48.2 months). The didactic analysis took the most hours to complete at the Cleveland Institute (mean: 1386 hours) and was most quickly completed at the University of North Carolina–Duke Training Center (mean: 506.6 hours). The average number of hours per week spent in training analysis per active student was 4.2 in 1958 and 4.4 in 1971.[36]

If even the simple numerical figures show such a wide range from city to city, from institute to institute, and from analyst to analyst, the qualitative differences must be even greater. Indeed, in all the papers on the topic, as Lewin and Ross point out, none treats clinically what the length of an analysis might mean for the unconscious. They quote a poem by George Meredith:

> Ah, what a dusty answer gets the soul
> When hot for certainties in this our life![37]

In accordance with the revised standards of the American Psychoanalytic, the usual frequency for a training analysis was four sessions per week, although at various periods in the person's analysis this might be increased or reduced. Here too the qualitative factor is not considered.

SUPERVISION. The idea of control analysis was brought to this country around 1930.[38] The regulations of the American Psychoanalytic Association set 150 hours as a "barely adequate minimum," with a minimum of 50 hours for each supervised case. The frequency of one session of supervision per week was adhered to. In general, these regulations were observed, almost to the letter. About one-third as much time was spent in control analyses as in personal analysis. Again, as in personal analysis, the choice of supervising analyst and the evaluation of the supervision rest on highly subjective grounds.

THE TRAINING-SUPERVISING ANALYST. No procedure is as unique to the analytic situation, and no procedure has been fraught with so much dissension as the existence of the training-supervisory analyst. Theoretically these two functions are separate, but in practice they overlap to such an extent that they can be considered together.

Although this topic is discussed at greater length later, the Lewin–Ross findings can be summarized here. As in other areas, there was great variability among institutes. In some cities, the training load was carried by a few individuals, and in others it was distributed among many. No rule could be established for the appointment of training analysts; they were selected in much the same way as university faculty members. They were held in honor and endowed with a fantastic charisma.

Much discontent with the training analysis was expressed in the late 1950s, when the Lewin–Ross report was made, and the discontent has continued. In some groups they studied, the training analysis was so inadequate that over half of the candidates had to be reanalyzed.[39]

One significant variation in the training analysis was noted. In some institutes the student had to enter his analysis before he was permitted to take courses; in others the two were simultaneous. In some institutes the student's further progress was heavily influenced by the attitude of his training analyst toward him, obviously creating an impossible analytic situation. This led to the discussion of the "nonreporting training analyst," i.e., whether the training analyst should report to the institute or maintain absolute secrecy, as in an ordinary analysis.

THE CURRICULUM. With remarkably little change, except for attention to newer theoretical work, the Berlin curriculum has remained standard for institutes all over the world. Although the New York Institute experimented with many variations, ultimately its curriculum still conforms to that originally proposed.

ADVANCED STUDY. It has been widely recognized that the basic curriculum is not fully adequate to meet the needs of the analytic student. To remedy this defect, advanced study groups have been set up in various localities. The best established of these was Ernst Kris's in New York, which at one time had 70 advanced students. Since his death in 1957 the system has been continued with other leaders. In other localities similar study groups have been set up.

Subsequent Developments: Achievements and Conflicts

Following Lewin and Ross's report, a committee on psychoanalytic training was set up, charged with the task of continuing their work; they were appointed consultants to the committee, known as COPE (Committee on Psychoanalytic Education). The numerical growth of the American Psychoanalytic Association since that time is well documented. Undoubtedly the system has produced a large body of highly competent analysts, administrators, and educators, who have advanced the cause of psychoanalysis greatly.

Nevertheless, enormous dissatisfaction has existed and still exists. A report by the COPE committee in 1971 (Arlow, 1972) was anything but sanguine.[40] Arlow reported that by 1971 there had already been half a dozen splits within the American Psychoanalytic (not counting those outside the association), and another half dozen had been narrowly averted by "judicious outside assistance" (not further explicated).[41]

The Training Analyst

On one point at least there is agreement: the heart of the controversies is about who shall have the right to train, i.e., about the training analyst, that person unique to psychoanalytic education. Originally Freud was very casual about training analysts: he felt that anybody who knew something could analyze and train others. When Bernfeld in 1922 discussed the advisability of a didactic analysis with Freud, the latter replied: "Nonsense, go right ahead. You certainly will have difficulties. When you get into trouble we will see what we can do about it." Only a week later Freud sent him his first didactic case, an English professor who wished to study psychoanalysis and planned to stay in Vienna about one month. Alarmed, Bernfeld went back to Freud, who said: "You know more than he does. Show him as much as you can."[42]

Freud's casual attitude was questioned by his students. By 1925, when Eitington delivered the report of the International Training Commission, training analysts were already being appointed in the various institutes, although the practice had not yet become fixed.

In the course of time, more and more power was vested in the hands of a relatively small number of training analysts. In the 1971 COPE report, Joan Fleming (1972) reported the following statistics:[43] In 1945 there were 69 training analysts in institutes recognized by the American Association. In that year 61 applications for training were processed and 28 were accepted. Between 1945 and 1949, the number of applications increased to 1298, or 21 times; *490 candidates were accepted, or 17 times the 1945 figures, but the training faculty was only doubled.*

It is not surprising that with so much power concentrated in the hands of a small number of persons, innumerable conflicts have developed. Arlow (1972) has the following pertinent comments:

It is disturbing but true that most of the conflicts have originated over who shall have the right to train, that is, who shall be training analyst. The tensions emanating from the division of colleagues into two categories of analysts, intrude themselves into the organizational and scientific life of the institutes. It is an ever-present problem, and its impact is accentuated by the aura of special status which surrounds the position of training analyst, a position endowed with charismatic implications. The training analyst is regarded as possessing the psychoanalytic equivalent of omniscience. . . .

Consciously or unconsciously, the mythology of the institutes infiltrates the training program. . . . Mythologies, moreover, do not remain suspended in mid-air. They are translated into institutionalized practices. In the social situation such practices are recognized as rituals.[44]

In a later report of COPER (research had now been added to the committee), similar feelings were expressed.[45] Indeed, it is against the ritualization of psychoanalytic training that all the splits and objections have been directed. As yet no satisfactory solution has been found. Fleming,[46] as have many others, frankly recognized that the differences within the society derived more from personal quarrels than from theoretical disagreements. Thus the old political adage has been borne out in psychoanalytic societies as well: excessive concentration of power creates disaffection, hostility, and problems. One would think that psychoanalysts, with their profound knowledge of and experience with Oedipal problems, would have anticipated such dissension, but the fact is that they did not, and still do not, know what to do about it.

Recently the argument has centered about the reporting by the training analyst, because when the training analyst has the power to decide the professional future of the candidate this must necessarily affect the analysis. Arguments pro and con are raging in the journals, with no solution in sight (Calef and Weinshel, 1973; Goodman, 1977; Lifschutz, 1976; McLaughlin, 1973; Shapiro and Sachs, 1976). Obviously reporting or nonreporting will not affect the power hierarchy and the extraordinary charisma attached to the training analyst, which, as Arlow emphasized, were the never-ending causes of resentment and secession.

Freudian Base

The numerous postwar battles within the American Psychoanalytic Association all served to reinforce its stance as a Freudian organization. However, when attempts were made after the war to define Freudian psychoanalysis (or even psychoanalytic therapy) more precisely, no agreement could be reached (Cushing, 1952; Hamburg et al., 1967). Like the International, the American was thus in the position of demanding adherence to a doctrine which it could not define with adequate precision. But since, unlike the International, it maintained strict control over training, numerous disputes arose and continue to plague the society. (The statutes of the American Association do not contain the name of Freud, or the adjective Freudian.[47] By contrast, the *Bulletin of the William Alanson White Institute* in New York, the largest competitor to the American, and one that considers itself neo-Freudian on non-Freudian, pays due respect to the "significant contributions of Sigmund Freud."[48])

Growth of the American Psychoanalytic Association; Geographic Rule

The growth of the American Psychoanalytic Association, at a time when mental health activities have multiplied in so many areas, has been rather slow but steady. The slowness of this growth has been due mainly to the extreme caution observed by the leaders regarding possible deviations and secessions.

To maintain personal continuity of analytic training and still allow for the formation of new training facilities, in 1949 the geographic rule was adopted.[49] This rule stipulates that a training analyst from one city may function as a training analyst for another city by making periodic visits to the other city, or by having students make periodic visits to him (or her), still adhering to the minimal hours required for personal analysis and controls. Obviously this makes it quite difficult for training facilities to grow in out-of-the-way locales. Still, growth has taken place.

The current by-laws require a minimum of 10 active members in any one locale ("any given geographical area"[50]) for the formation of a new affiliate society, which then by taking the required steps eventually becomes a component society of the American Psychoanalytic Association. The time required for this procedure may run into many years; e.g., in 1945 not a single member of the American Psychoanalytic resided between Washington, D.C. and New Orleans. It took 30 years before the Virginia group could accumulate 10 members to become an affiliate study group, which then went on to become a component society of the American Association. A previous attempt to set up a Southeastern Psychoanalytic Society had proved abortive.[51] Even now (as of 1978–1979), Virginia is not a recognized training institute, and students from that area who wish to train must still go elsewhere.[52]

The number of graduates from institutes remains small. From 1958 to 1964 the mean annual number of graduates for all institutes was 63, compared with 76 for the years 1965 to 1971.[53] There has been an increase in the total number of students in training, but it is generally agreed that this results primarily from the opening of new institutes, not increased enrollment in the older ones.[54]

Because of the slow growth of the society, an amendment was passed in 1972 creating categories of affiliate and associate membership, which allowed the advanced students to join before they graduated.[55] The next year the treasurer reported that they had welcomed over 600 new active, affiliate and associate members.[56] This represented a sudden spurt in growth of some 40 percent in one year.

Selection of Students

The selection of students has always been on an impressionistic basis. The COPER report (Goodman, 1977) had so little to say about the question that it was omitted from the discussion.[57] Until recently, new admissions were limited to fairly young physicians, largely psychiatrists, many of them with their boards in psychiatry. Even then the acceptance rate averaged only 38 percent between 1945 and 1957.[58] More recently it has gone up to about 50 percent.[59] However, acceptance rates still vary widely from one city to another.[60] Loomie (1970) reported that four institutes accept 25 percent of the applicants, five 40 percent, eleven more than 50 percent, and three more than 70 percent.[61] With the recent relaxation of the rules, many waivers have been given, and therefore the number of nonmedical students is increasing though still very small.[62]

Various experimental approaches have been tried to improve the selection process. Best known is the work of Holt and Luborsky at the Menninger Clinic (1958), Henrietta Klein at Columbia (1965), and Pollock and associates at Chicago (1976). While all of them report improved performance with careful selection procedures, they agree that the ultimate decision must be clinical rather than statistical.

Certification: The Quest for Status

Although psychoanalysts have prided themselves, with some justification, on being at the pinnacle of power and wisdom in the mental health professions, psychoanalysis as such still has no official
recognition. Dissatisfied with this situation, the American Psychoanalytic has repeatedly, and fruitlessly, sought this recognition.
Applications to the Federal Office of Education for listing as the
sole accrediting agency for psychoanalytic education have been rejected, the latest in 1975.[63]

Disappointed in these efforts, the Association has more recently
gone over to internal certification. The present membership committee is to be replaced by a certifying board. Membership, however,
will not be essential for certification.[64] How this plan will work out
remains to be seen.

Political Maneuvering

Historically, the American group chose to ally itself with medicine
and psychiatry rather than pursue a course as an independent profession, as the European societies had preferred to do. This led to a
highly complex relationship with psychiatry: on the one hand, psychoanalysts were extremely critical of both the theories and the techniques of organic psychiatry, while on the other, they joined with
psychiatrists in political activities, including lobbying.

In search of recognition, some members at the meeting in 1958
proposed that psychoanalysis should be made a subspecialty of the
American Medical Association's Board of Psychiatry and Neurology.[65] This proposal, after vigorous debate in the component societies, was defeated by the Board of Professional Standards the following year.[66] It has never officially been revived.

An extraordinary piece of political legerdemain took place in
1972. In the preliminary discussions about coverage for national
health insurance, the American Psychiatric Association issued a position paper in which it essentially recommended exclusion of psychoanalysis and long-term psychotherapy from national health insurance
coverage. After some consultation the American Psychoanalytic came
up with the following compromise:

As a result of that meeting [with the psychiatrists] the Committee on Health Insurance concluded that a Position Statement of the American Psychoanalytic Association should *not* emphasize the special and unique features of psychoanalytic treatment, but rather the similarities and commonality of psychoanalytic treatment with the mainstream of psychiatric and medical care. It was felt that such an approach would be much more effective in offering a strong case for its coverage under national health insurance.[67]

Since only 10–30 percent of psychiatric residents apply to psychoanalytic institutes,[68] and the ratio has remained stable over many years, in effect this compromise throws away the unique features of psychoanalytic training for the benefits of health insurance.

Standards

A Board of Professional Standards has been operative in the American Association for many years. Nevertheless the basic standards have not changed in any significant respect from the Berlin system. In 1970 Loomie reported that two attempts to have revised standards accepted had failed.[69] At roughly the same time, Frosch reported an apparent decline in scientific productivity in the Association, as reflected in the quality and quantity of papers submitted to the *Journal of the American Psychoanalytic Association*.[70] Such complaints are frequently voiced, both here and abroad.[71]

Child Analysis

As in the International, an increasing interest in child analysis has been demonstrated in the American Association. Here the tendency has been to make child analysis a specialty within the broader field. However, the committee on child analysis of COPER envisaged a broader function for it, recommending that since psychoanalysis has reached a degree of maturity that not only permits but calls for a shift of emphasis within our conceptual framework, the curriculum should be revised in accordance with our current knowledge of developmental processes. Reactions to this proposal were mixed (Goodman, 1977).

Group Analysis

In the main, group psychoanalysis (and therapy) and Freudian psychoanalysis (and therapy) have proceeded independently of one another. Among group experts, Alexander Wolf is best known for his integration of group work along the principles of psychoanalysis; he calls his method psychoanalysis in groups, utilizing the principles of transference and resistance as in individual psychoanalysis (Wolf, 1949–1950). While Wolf trained a whole generation of group therapists in New York, by and large group therapy has proceeded along other lines. For a review of its history, see Rosenbaum and Snadowsky (1976).

It is of interest to note that in 1953 a questionnaire was sent to all members of the American Psychoanalytic Association to elicit their opinions on psychoanalytic group therapy.[72] About 24 percent of the membership replied. Of the respondents, 75 percent felt that the concept "psychoanalytic" may be used in group therapy: 76 percent felt that group therapy permits an analytic approach; 77 percent felt that group work revealed aspects of the individual's personality that remained hidden in individual work. The report concluded that there seemed to be growing support for members working in this field. Thus apparently the considerations militating against the incorporation of group therapy into the psychoanalytic scheme of things have been primarily political rather than scientific.

Splits and Dissensions, and Disciplinary Action

In spite of careful selection, cautious screening, and tight control of all organizational activities, splits and dissensions have abounded within the American Association. The largest split, that of the Academy of Psychoanalysis in 1956, is described below. But there have been others, and many threats have never seen the light of day.

The best publicized example of disobedience is the disaccreditation of the Detroit Psychoanalytic Institute. This group was disaccredited at the midwinter meeting of the Association in 1953.[73] Because of the confidential nature of the matter, "its details could not be divulged."[74] However, at the midwinter meeting in 1955 it was stated that there were "irreconcilable difficulties stemming from personal disagreements."[75]

Despite numerous attempts to improve the situation, problems remained in Detroit. In the minutes of the annual meeting for May 1976, almost 25 years later, it was again reported that the Detroit Psychoanalytic Society had to desist from unauthorized training or face disaffiliation.[76]

Equally surprising is the more recent furor in Los Angeles, where the possible split has been discussed openly in the *Journal* for the first time. Joan Fleming, as chairman of the ad hoc committee to investiage the situation, stated:

Unfortunately, rumors were circulated by both groups that the American Psychoanalytic Association considered the basic problem in the Los Angeles Institute to be the controversy in regard to Freudian and Kleinian points of view; this was not correct. Of much more concern was the unrelenting hostility and distrust among various groups and individuals, whatever their theoretical orientation. There was no single discernible basis for the presence of so much bad feeling.[77]

This does not sound too different from the situation in Boston 40 years earlier, as described by Henry Murray. Murray had been chairman of the education committee of the Boston Psychoanalytic Institute. He withdrew, charging that he found "an atmosphere too charged with humorless hostility . . . an assemblage of cultists, rigid in thought, armored against new ideas, and (in the case of 2–3 overly ambitious ones) ruthlessly rivalrous for power."[78]

Nevertheless the struggle for power within the American Association continued. In 1954 the association took punitive measures against William Silverberg for conducting unauthorized training with his institute attached to Flower–Fifth Avenue Hospital and Medical School in New York. Silverberg retaliated by retaining Abe Fortas (later a Supreme Court justice) of the celebrated law firm of Fortas, Arnold, and Porter, who threatened to sue the American for violation of its constitution which, he alleged, did not give it the right to prescribe training or to declare what unauthorized training is.[79] Although the Association voted to provide funds for legal action, it preferred to be pragmatic and withdrew its action against Silverberg.

The next step was, again on advice of counsel, to draw up a clause that would give the Association the right to punish members for unauthorized training. Such an amendment on discipline was approved by the Executive Council in 1956 and submitted to the membership.[80] The membership, perhaps fearful of granting the

Council excessive power, defeated the motion by a vote of 245 to 146.[81] Subsequently no strong amendment on discipline has been passed. The current by-laws merely contain a general clause that has, so far as I know, never been invoked against any particular person.

Thus the American Association appears to maintain its disciplinary hold on members more by the power to make appointments and recommendations, together with whatever binding character moral force may have, than by any clear legal enabling clause. It is difficult to sum up the situation briefly, but it is well known that many violations of the training system are tolerated, provided that they do not threaten the structure of the Association.

Literature

The growth of psychoanalytic literature has been spectacular. In the English language all the old journals have been continued. The most important new one in this period is the *Journal of the American Psychoanalytic Association,* which began in 1953. *The Psychoanalytic Study of the Child,* an annual since 1945, has become one of the most important theoretical journals. James Strachey completed his translation of Freud's works, and his standard edition, finished in 1974, is invaluable. Freud's works are now available in more complete form in English than in German. Alexander Grinstein, a Detroit analyst, began an *Index of Psychoanalytic Writings* in 1956; to date, 14 volumes have been issued. Almost every country has at one point or another started its own national journal. No compilation similar to Fenichel's (1945) has appeared; the entire literature is now far too vast to be mastered by any single individual.

The Academy of Psychoanalysis

The authoritarian structure of the American Psychoanalytic Association has fostered deep discontent. Indeed, every presidential address and every discussion of training and standards (including the Lewin–Ross survey) has presented evidence of such discontent. The most serious outcome of such dissatisfaction was the formation of the Academy of Psychoanalysis at Chicago in 1956. The account given here is taken from that by John Millet (1966), one of the founders of the Academy.

In 1941, as a result of what they felt was a lack of academic freedom, Karen Horney, Clara Thompson, William Silverberg, and others left the New York Psychoanalytic Institute and organized themselves into the Association for the Advancement of Psychoanalysis, with the American Institute of Psychoanalysis as its teaching branch. Harry Stack Sullivan and Erich Fromm gave their support to this group. However, new tensions developed in this splinter group owing to Karen Horney's resistance to having nonmedical personnel participate in the training of students. Again on grounds of lack of academic freedom, another group led by Thompson, Fromm, and Sullivan withdrew from this new association and formed the William Alanson White Institute in 1942. Several years later a group led by Silverberg, Bernard Robbins, Judd Marmor, and others likewise withdrew to form the Flower–Fifth Avenue Center of the New York Medical College, the first medical school–affiliated training institute in the country.

When World War II ended, in the central New York area there were thus three powerful splinter groups, led respectively by Clara Thompson (acting for Sullivan), Karen Horney, and William Silverberg. All of these, in their teaching and writing, stressed the crucial role of the culture in the formation of personality and neurosis. Although this was not actually a contradiction of Freud, the older societies saw it as a contradiction and vehemently opposed the position and activities of these three groups. Karen Horney had resigned from the American Psychoanalytic Association, but the others all remained members of the larger body. Soon the field seemed to be divided between the "culturalists" who had split off and the "Freudians" who had remained.

The split widened over time, perhaps more as a result of personality clashes than as a consequence of fundamental ideological differences. More prominent names joined the ranks of the culturalists: Franz Alexander in Chicago, Martin Grotjahn in Los Angeles, Nathan Ackerman and Sandor Rado in New York, to mention only a few.

In 1956 the culturalists formed their own organization, known as the Academy of Psychoanalysis. Its major journal was *Psychiatry,* which had been founded by Sullivan in 1938. In 1973 it formed its own journal, the *Journal of the American Academy of Psychoanalysis,* edited by Silvano Arieti. The Academy has also joined with like-minded groups in other countries in the *International Psycho-analytic Forum*.

Thus the field has been split into two fairly large bodies, each with its own jargon, its own training institutes, and its own literature. Neither seems especially eager to understand the viewpoint of the other, although it is generally acknowledged that Freud's thinking is basic to all workers in the field, and it could also be maintained that the neglect of the cultural factor is the most important single omission in the Freudian conceptualization.

The Academy is organized in much the same way as the American Psychoanalytic Association, although Millet emphasizes the "need for a free forum for scientific discussion to keep alive the spirit of scientific inquiry."[82] It too has its roster of training analysts, which carries with it the same kind of dissension, resentment, and eventual splitting characteristic of the older and larger organization. It too has banned lay analysis and "unauthorized training," again with similar consequences. While the system centering around the training analyst has many problems, it seems to be difficult to find a better one, so that sooner or later all analytic organizations fall into the mold originally formed by Max Eitingon in 1925.

The Fact-Gathering Committee

The American Psychoanalytic Association's continual self-scrutiny of its work led to the establishment in 1947 of a Committee on the Evaluation of Psychoanalytic Therapy (Rangell, 1954b). In over 6 years this committee was never able to arrive at a definition of psychoanalysis, psychoanalytic therapy, and transitional forms that was acceptable to a majority of its members. Incredibly, it was even forced to conclude "that a strong resistance to any investigation of this problem existed among the members of the American Psychoanalytic Association."[83]

Accordingly, the original committee was discharged and was replaced in 1952 by a Central Fact-Gathering Committee, chaired by Harry Weinstock and charged with setting up a method for pooling the data of psychoanalytic practice (Hamburg et al., 1967).

Initial enthusiasm ran high. Questionnaires were sent out to all members of the association and to all advanced students. The design was simple enough: to compare the state of the patient at the beginning of treatment with his state at the end. Nevertheless, innumerable unforeseen difficulties arose. Returns began to fall off, and the Committee was discharged in 1957. Quite unexpectedly, the Association at its business meeting in 1958 voted that *none of the accumulated material should be published.* In May, 1960, it was recommended that this action be reversed, and that the material be published.[84]

Subsequently a second committee, chaired by Ives Hendrick, reviewed the project and reported principally on the methodological difficulties encountered. Interest lapsed, until a third committee was appointed in 1961 to prepare a report that would clarify the methodological problems and derive any substantive findings that might be stimulating to psychoanalysts generally and to future investigators particularly. The report, published in 1967, was prepared by this third committee, chaired by David Hamburg.

While the report is noncommittal in its remarks, it is devastating to the illusion that conceptual unity exists among the members of the American Psychoanalytic Association. The two largest areas of unresolved difficulty were in diagnosis and in judgments of treatment outcome. The approach of the committee had been along rather conventional psychiatric lines, using accepted diagnostic categories rather than more extensive ego profiles such as those recently introduced by Bellak et al. (1973) and others. Although most of the patients who finished their analyses were regarded as "improved" (as in the earlier studies by Fenichel (1930), Jones (1936b), Alexander (1937), and others), a dynamic clarification of this "improvement" was not offered. The whole episode must be regarded as a fiasco.

Regrettably the sorry tale has been repressed by the American Psychoanalytic Association. No mention of it has been seen in subsequent issues of the journal. A new Committee on Psychoanalytic Practice, chaired by Daniel Jaffe, is currently in operation[85] but makes no reference to the work of the earlier committee.

Such repression seems highly damaging to the image of integrity and full disclosure of all suitable material relating to analytic practice. It can only be concluded that the monolithic organization of the American Association conceals enormous differences under the surface in terms of the fundamental appraisal and evaluation of all aspects of the psychoanalytic process. This is not to be taken as a slur on the American Psychoanalytic Association; I feel that it is true of all psychoanalytic societies. The major conclusion is that there is a

crying need to integrate the doctrines and treatment results of psychoanalysis and psychoanalytic therapy in a constructive fashion. Hartmann (1956) stressed that such a constructive attitude required an adequate historiography, which psychoanalysis has not yet had, and a
"freedom from myth."[86]

Lay Analysis

Within the psychoanalytic movement, the worst battles have been
fought over "lay" or "nonmedical" analysis. Inasmuch as the opposition to nonmedical analysis is almost exclusively American, its
history must be linked with that of the American scene.

Before World War I there were so few analysts that nobody, as
Freud said, seemed to care who practiced. With the growth of the
field after World War I, the establishment of institutes and the International Training Commission (1925), the question of admission to
the institutes came to the fore. Freud himself was the greatest propo-
nent of nonmedical analysis.[87] In view of the differences in opinion,
a symposium on the topic was held, and published in the *International Journal of Psychoanalysis* in 1927.

At that time the New York Psychoanalytic Society, whose authority then surpassed that of the American Association, took the
strongest stand against lay analysis, while the Hungarian Society took
the strongest stand for it. This seems paradoxical, since in 1927 the
New York Society was a fledgling organization, with no requirements
for admission other than interest in the field, while the Hungarian Society was, next to Freud's Vienna group, the oldest and most pres-
tigious one and contained such great analysts as Ferenczi, Roheim,
and Imre Hermann.

When it rebelled against the International in 1938, the American
Association passed a "Resolution against the Training of Laymen,"
which was the legal position until recent years. Unofficially, the rule
had little effect.

When World War II had ended and psychoanalytic training resumed, nonmedical persons were trained in increasing numbers by
members of the American Psychoanalytic Association. Generally this
took the form of study groups, not particularly different from the official ones of the larger organization. A few nonmedical persons were
admitted to the American Association as "special students" and

asked to sign a pledge that they would not practice. It was widely recognized, however, that this pledge would not be enforced.

In 1948 Theodor Reik started the National Psychological Association for Psychoanalysis (NPAP), an organization of lay analysts, which now has about 160 members and some 300 students. Other associations followed.

Although Hendrick (1955) had spoken of the "tattered dialectics" of the lay analysis problem, there seemed to be no real solution available. The very nature of psychoanalysis militates against such a restriction. Analytic training consists of personal analysis, courses, and supervised analyses. Personal analysis could always be secured. Supervision was generally available for the payment. There remained only the courses, which could then be given on a private basis, as had been done in the early stages of the history of psychoanalysis. Eventually persons so trained formed institutes and trained others. By 1974 Burness Moore in his presidential address said: "A piece of reality has been overlooked. We have no exclusive prerogative to Freud's heritage. Lay analysis is here to stay. It is only a question of whether our Association will play a significant role in guiding and promoting its development along lines that we believe advantageous to psychoanalysis."[88]

Beginning in the 1970s, various measures were adopted that eased the ban on lay analysis by the American Psychoanalytic Association. In 1971 an amendment was passed granting recognition to nonmedical training and supervisory analysts.[89] In 1972 an amendment was recommended (and eventually passed) stating that research graduates be permitted full membership in the association.[90]

In 1973 the Chicago Institute proposed a special Ph.D. program in psychoanalysis, which was eventually turned down but only after lively debate. The Committee on Research and Training stated at that time:

Insofar as the Chicago Proposal is designed as a pilot program to demonstrate that persons who do not meet the current minimal requirements for admission to training can be trained to conduct psychoanalysis, the experiences of the Committee on Research and Special Training can be cited to affirm that it is indeed possible to do so; thus, no further demonstration is required.[91]

In 1975, in the report of the Conference on Psychoanalytic Education and Research[92] one speaker after another emphasized the need to broaden the base of psychoanalysis by including persons from fields other than medicine. Pollock (1972b), in a COPE report, had already wondered out loud whether the profession would still be in existence a decade hence if it did not extend its membership base.[93] In 1974, when the Chicago Ph.D. proposal was turned down, Pollock expressed his disappointment and his feeling "that the Association . . . had missed an opportunity to develop vital and creative scientific leadership by opting to continue traditional ties with medicine rather than trying to establish psychoanalysis as an independent profession."[94]

Examination of the American Association's committee reports in recent years discloses an increasing number of "waivers" for training. While the 1938 resolution is still on the books, it has been modified in so many ways that it has lost much of its original meaning.

In the meantime, nonmedical groups outside the American Psychoanalytic Association have multiplied enormously. It almost seems as if the 1938 resolution signaled the beginning of lay analysis rather than its end. The formation of the NPAP by Theodor Reik in 1948 has already been noted. A number of splits from this group ensued, following the time-honored psychoanalytic custom. At present my informal count discloses at least 11 training groups in the New York City area, all operating within the broad framework of psychoanalysis. These are: the National Psychological Association for Psychoanalysis; the New York Center for Psychoanalytic Training; the New York University Post-Doctoral Program; the Adelphi University Post-Doctoral Program; the Postgraduate Center for Mental Health; the New York Society of Freudian Psychologists; the Institute for Psychoanalytic Training and Research; the Washington Square Institute; the American Institute for Psychotherapy and Psychoanalysis; the New Jersey Institute for Psychoanalytic Studies; and the Westchester Institute for Psychoanalytic Studies. While these groups operate on somewhat different lines, it is estimated that they have about 600 active members in the various societies attached to the training centers and about 2000 active students, primarily psychologists and social workers.

The organization and politics of the nonmedical societies have followed closely the procedures of the older and larger bodies. The curriculum is the same. It too centers around the training analyst, with the same resulting conflicts: who shall do the training, resentment, and eventually splitting. Still, as in the larger societies, a considerable body of competent analysts has been produced and continues to be produced. Legal status has been obtained by psychologists and social workers in the face of severe medical opposition. It seems unlikely that the growth of the nonmedical analytic movement can be halted in the foreseeable future. The Federal Office of Education has held that many organizations have the right to call themselves analysts and to train analysts.[95]

England

The distinctive feature of the British scene has been the existence of three groups since the 1930s—one led by Melanie Klein, another by Anna Freud, and a middle group uncommitted to either. Melanie Klein considered herself a strict Freudian, yet found herself unable to collaborate on a theoretical level with Anna Freud. The division into three groups hardened after the war, when Anna Freud assumed the leadership of the classical Freudians. According to Glover (1966), the Freudian and Kleinian subgroups are gradually dwindling, while the middle group has greatly increased its strength and administrative power.

Germany

Hitler had of course totally destroyed the German psychoanalytic movement. Nevertheless, the Deutsche Psychoanalytische Gesellschaft was reestablished on October 16, 1945.[96] However, it was led by Harald Schultz-Hencke, who had developed a peculiar theory of his own, and it was not recognized by the International. The Deutsche Psychoanalytische Vereinigung was established in 1950 and was recognized by the International in 1951.[97] Since then there have been splits into "liberal" and "conservative" groups, as in the United States. Family therapy under Horst Richter and Helm Stierlin has become especially popular.

A special—and surprising—feature of the German situation has been the large amount of governmental assistance in rebuilding the therapeutic groups. In October 1967 a ministerial decree permitted payment for up to 150 hours of psychoanalysis of psychoanalytically oriented therapy.[98] A similar generosity had been shown by the city of Berlin just after the war ended. Shortly afterward the Ford Foundation, by a sizable grant, subsidized the formation of a psychosomatic clinic in Heidelberg.[99] Since 1961 the Deutsche Forschungsgemeinschaft (Research Society) has been awarding stipends covering about two-thirds of the fee for training analyses. A report by Goerres et al. (cited in Thomä, 1969) led to the foundation's decision to further the course of psychotherapeutic research by giving scholarships to trainees.

Partly as a result of all this support, psychoanalysis is now flourishing in Germany. The institutes have been unable to handle the rush of applicants for training. As elsewhere, the potential number of patients seems endless.

France

The psychoanalytic movement in France has experienced more splits and dissensions than in any other country. In 1952 Daniel Lagache and Jacques Lacan resigned from the older Association Psychoanalytique de France to form a new society,[100] from which Lacan eventually withdrew to form his own École Freudienne. There are currently two French groups in the International, the French Psychoanalytical Association and the Paris Psychoanalytical Society, two others not in the International (one of which is Lacan's) and a fifth intergroup attempt, in existence since May 1968, which seeks to bridge the differences among the groups and reach some kind of unification on an adequate basis.[101] Psychoanalysis in France is less medical than in other countries, more inclined to the private sector, and more integrated into the universities. The significance of psychoanalysis for the culture may be gauged from the fact that during the Paris student uprisings of 1968 one of the demands was that all university students should be analyzed.[102]

The most colorful postwar figure on the French psychoanalytic scene is Jacques Lacan, who has had, according to Barande and Barande,[103] a stimulating effect on French psychoanalysis because of the nature of his criticism and the directions of his research. Lacan is another of the many charismatic figures in the history of psychoanalysis, worshipped by his followers, ignored by the rest of the world. Like the German Alfred Lorenzer, he centers his theory of psychoanalysis around language. Two of his main pronouncements are: the unconscious is structured like a language; and the unconscious is the discourse of the Other. Lacan also calls for a return to the pure Freud and inveighs against behaviorism, dynamic psychiatry, ego psychology, and culturalism. He sees himself as a representative of the structuralist way of thinking. Recently an American analyst has tried to make his ideas available to the English-speaking public (Leavy, 1977). Some of Lacan's ideas may turn out to have value, but on the whole he seems too confused and disorganized to be able to make any real contribution to the mainstream of psychoanalytic thought.

Latin America

The most notable feature in the Latin American societies is the great strength of the Kleinian viewpoint. This circumstance may be due to the troubled political climate of the continent, which makes it easier to delve into the mysterious intricacies of the first few years of life than to face the conflicts between the analytic concept of normality and the social structure, as is so commonly done in the United States.

Two significant figures in the history of psychoanalysis in Latin America are Angel Garma, a Spaniard trained at the Berlin Institute who moved to Argentina in 1938,[104] and Erich Fromm, who set up a group of "Fromistas" in Mexico in the mid-1950s.

Other Countries

In general, other countries have followed the American pattern, except for our emphasis on medicine. In 1972 Arlow reported that during the previous 8 years alone the Central Executive of the International had to deal with splits or threatened splits in France, Spain, Brazil, Venezuela, Colombia, and Australia.[105] Apparently the battle between the "liberals" and the "conservatives" goes on, with similar arguments, all over.

In India a psychoanalytical society was founded by Girindrashekhar Bose, an "autodidact," in 1922 in Calcutta, and it has flourished ever since. A noteworthy feature of the Indian scene is the almost complete integration of psychoanalysis into the psychology departments of various universities (Sinha, 1966).

In Japan a psychoanalytic group was formed shortly after World War I. It still exists as a member of the International but is small in numbers and influence (Kawada, 1977). According to Kawada, psychoanalytic therapy has never taken hold in Japan. He argues that the nonindividualistic culture, shaped by Japanese Buddhism, has developed an ideal of the harmonic integration of the person into the group, society, and nature which is alien to psychoanalysis.[106]

Developments in Psychiatry, Psychology, and Social Work

The most significant concurrent professional development in allied fields has been the enormous growth of the three major mental health professions—psychiatry, psychology and social work. Inasmuch as it has never received legal recognition in its own right either as a profession or as a title, psychoanalysis has had to be grafted onto these three professions, even though ideologically it represents their core. The results have been confused and confusing.

Because of the emphasis on mental health, the number of psychiatrists increased from 5,500 in 1950 to 19,532 in 1966; during this period the number of clinical psychologists rose from 3,500 to 18,430; and the number of psychiatric social workers from 3,000 to 12,100. This rapid growth has continued.[107] For example, the American Psychological Association membership directory for 1976 lists 42,028 persons, of whom a surprising 37 percent are in the clinical field.[108]

In the main the psychoanalytic training institutes have limited themselves to people with advanced degrees in one of the three major mental health professions. This has repeated the old dilemma: if the person has a degree, why should he accept analysis? And if he has been analyzed, what does he need a degree for? No adequate solution to this dilemma has ever been found, other than a fundamental reorganization of the educational process leading to a degree. The result has been the widespread syncretism predominant in the field.

Furthermore, new developments have created new professional resistances to psychotherapy. In psychiatry the use of the tranquilizing drugs since the mid-1950s has been accompanied by renewed doubts about the efficacy of psychotherapy. The same is true in psychology, which has enthusiastically embraced behavior modification since the middle of the 1960s. It is true that the analyzed professional comes back to psychoanalytic psychotherapy, but before he can get there he is often exposed to a continual antitherapeutic barrage from his teachers. In one recent study of the choices made by psychiatric residents (Strassman et al., 1976), the authors bluntly stated that even though psychoanalytic theory had become the sum and substance of psychiatry proper, psychoanalysis as a technique must now compete with such other approaches as transactional analysis, Gestalt therapy, and reality therapy, which are generally more seductive and therefore more attractive to the beginner.[109] With the huge increase in the number of paraprofessionals, we can only anticipate that the problems will become worse in the future.

The Historical Approach to Psychoanalytic Ideas

After this necessarily brief recapitulation of the main political events in the field, our attention now turns toward the history of ideas, which is even more important.

I have already indicated that an approach in terms of schools would be futile and misleading. Instead, the central conceptual framework of psychoanalysis will be systematically reviewed. In each case, a beginning can be made with Freud's position, since he touched base on virtually every important topic in psychoanalysis. From there the historical review can go on to see how his ideas were continued, transformed, corrected, or elaborated, as the case may be. Many gifted thinkers have contributed to the development of psychoanalytic thought. Some have called themselves Freudian; others have not. What counts is the idea, not the label. In the beginning almost everything in the field came from psychoanalytic practitioners. As time has gone on, more and more has come from other disciplines. It often happens that what has been said by one thinker is repeated by another in different terminology. My goal is, as far as possible, to unify all the data into one science of man.

Chapter Six

Extensions and Elaborations of the Developmental Scheme: The Oral Stage

The concept of development, with its concomitant fixation and regression, which Freud had introduced into psychopathology, cast a far-reaching light on all normal and disturbed personality manifestations. Once noted, it can never again be forgotten or overlooked.

It was in the *Three Essays on Sexuality* (1905) that Freud offered his first extensive discussion of development, this time psychosexual. Yet, unlike dreams, this was one area which he kept on amending all through his life. Strachey[1] notes that the order of publication of Freud's views on the successive early organization of the sexual instinct may be summarized as follows: auto-erotic stage, 1905 (privately described, 1899); narcissistic stage, 1911 (privately described, 1909); anal-sadistic stage, 1913; oral stage, 1915; phallic stage, 1923.

To this chronology must be added the fact that in his last years Freud gave up the idea of a rigid chronological sequence. In 1938 he wrote of the oral-anal-phallic phases: "It would be a mistake to suppose that these three phases succeed one another in a clear-cut fashion: one may appear in addition to another, they may overlap one another, they may be present alongside of one another."[2]

Accordingly it is understandable that a large number of additions to Freud's scheme have been proposed. The most important is the new knowledge of the oral stage, most of which comes from the post–World War II period, though it had its origins earlier.

Historically, it is surprising that Freud never fully appreciated the significance of the oral stage. His thinking pressed the early manifestations of neurosis back further and further; he even held onto phylogenetic theories and the Lamarckian hypothesis, long after these had been disavowed by biological science.[3]

Freud's first published case history, in 1892–1893, described the hypnotic cure of a young woman who vomited uncontrollably after the birth of her baby. Today we would automatically say that if this was psychogenic it must be a manifestation of the rejection of the baby. Yet nothing of the sort occurred to Freud at that time.

Zetzel (1966) reviewed Freud's famous case history of the Rat Man. She uncovered more than 40 references to a highly ambivalent mother–son relationship in the original clinical notes, which were found posthumously. Freud does not touch on the mother relationship at all in the case history, concentrating instead on the hostility to the father.

Although Freud had established a theoretical basis for the significance of the oral stage with his second theory of anxiety (1926), which stressed separation from the mother as the paradigm for all anxiety, only scattered references to the mother and the oral stage appeared in the analytic literature before World War II. Fenichel (1945), whose book could be seen as a codification of Freud's thought, referred to the oral stage as the "oral (more correctly the intestinal) stage of organization of the libido."[4] The paramount importance of the relationship of the infant to the mother is almost entirely ignored by him, as it had been by Freud. The scheme of development in which the oral stage was divided into oral-erotic and oral-cannibalistic (or oral-sadistic) stemmed from Abraham rather than Freud. Jones had a good point when he said that to Freud the first year of life always remained something of a mystery. Schur (1972) speculates that Freud stayed away from the oral stage because he did not want to analyze his own oral fixations, particularly the addictive cigar smoking that conceivably may have shortened his life.

Pioneering Observations

All the extensions of Freud's thinking in the 1920s and 1930s led to a heightened appreciation of the oral stage. Melanie Klein, who pushed neurosis and psychosis back to the earliest days of life, was most elaborate. She placed considerable stress on aggression. She saw the child as caught up in the paranoid-schizoid position for the first 3 months of life, then in the depressive position for the next 3 months (the precise timing varies somewhat). The anxiety led to rage which was projected to the mother, then reintrojected by the child. Rage attached to oral greed led to envy, the dominant emotion of many disturbed individuals, in contrast to gratitude. She traced the vicissitudes of this rage, envy, and projection-rejection processes through the earliest years.

Sullivan (1962) traced schizophrenia back to the relationship with a "bad" or "schizophrenogenic" mother (the term itself was coined by his disciple Frieda Fromm-Reichmann). This mother was seen as hostile, punitive, malevolent, restrictive, antisexual, clinging, and more concerned with her own welfare than with that of the child. The self-image of the child was filled with hateful feelings (self-hatred) because of the rejection by the mother.

Alexander (1946), in his studies of psychosomatic patients, emphasized the oral dependence from which these people suffered. In fact, in his therapeutic work he came to believe that this oral dependence could not be overcome, so that it became the therapist's job to teach the patient to adjust to it.

Child therapy naturally brought home the more central importance of the mother than the father, especially when preschool children were brought into treatment. In work with other cultures it soon became apparent that there were many possible variations to the mothering role, and that all of these variations had powerful consequences for the child.

Finally, a factor of some importance was the high rejection rate of draftees in the American army, and the high rate of neuropsychiatric disabilities. These were largely traced to poor mothering, which kept the young men excessively dependent. Philip Wylie at that time popularized the term "momism."

The Mother–Child Relationship

Once the importance of mothering for the young infant was realized by the profession, a flood of publications poured forth—clinical, experimental, and later in animal psychology as well. The book which many felt had sounded the clarion call for better mothering was *The*

Rights of Infants, written by the New York analyst Margaret Ribble in 1943.

Ribble reported on 8 years of research with well babies, sick babies, and mentally ill adult patients. For the first time she specified the infant's psychological needs: to feel secure, to get pleasure from his body functions, and to feel that he is a going concern in the world of human beings. She coined the term "tlc" (tender loving care), which has become part of the language, and laid great stress on the need for a warm emotional relationship between mother and child in the first year of life. In protest against the mechanization of life she wrote:

our highly impersonal civilization has insidiously damaged woman's instinctual nature and has blinded her to one of her most natural rights—that of teaching the small baby to love, by loving it consistently through the period of helpless infancy. It is for this reason that the modern woman may need help and guidance in her relationship with her baby. She needs reassurance that the handling and fondling which she gives are by no means casual expressions of sentiment but are biologically necessary for the healthy mental development of the baby.[5]

The stress on the need for mother love led to many social changes in the mother–child situation. Benjamin Spock's book *Baby and Child Care* sold in the millions and had many imitators; it translated into ordinary language the insights of psychoanalysis. Grantley Dick Read and later Lamaze pioneered in natural childbirth and rooming-in of mother and child, thus preserving the physical tie between mother and child uninterruptedly. Breast feeding, to maintain the naturalness of the relationship, was again in favor with many, and a group was eventually formed, the La Leche League, to spread the gospel to new mothers. Most recently, Ferdinand Leboyer has proposed that the newborn be given an immediate soothing massage, kept in a warm comfortable room, and given other special care to lessen the shock of birth.

Spitz's Exploration of the First Year of Life

In 1935 the psychoanalyst René Spitz began a series of observations and experiments on young infants which proved to be of far-reaching significance. At first, he says, he was a lonely figure; later many workers explored the same problems. He published his work in the annual *Psychoanalytic Study of the Child,* beginning with the first issue in 1945 and continuing for many years. His overall results were summed up in his book *The First Year of Life,* published in 1965.

Spitz's work was designed to explain the behavior of both normal and abnormal infants. It centered around the role of the libidinal object in the mental life of the infant. He distinguished three stages in the development of this libidinal object:

1. The preobjectal or objectless stage (first 3 months).
2. The stage of the precursor of the object (3 to 8 months).
3. The stage of the libidinal object power (8 months' anxiety; from 8 months onward).

An unusual aspect of Spitz's work was the use of developmental tests in the research; this marks the first union of clinical psychoanalytic and experimental methods. The tests were adapted from the Bühler–Hetzer tests of infant development, which had been standardized in Vienna around 1932. They permitted quantification of six sectors of the personality:

1. Development and maturation of perception.
2. Development and maturation of body functions.
3. Development and maturation of interpersonal relations.
4. Development and maturation of memory and imitation.
5. Development and maturation of manipulation of things.
6. Intellectual development.

The quantitative evaluation of the tests provided a series of developmental quotients. Infants were investigated in private homes, from various cultures and races, and in two institutions described as the Nursery and Foundling Homes.

In his description of development Spitz stressed that from the beginning of life it is the mother, the human partner of the child, who mediates every perception, every action, every insight, every piece of knowledge. In visual perception, when the eyes of the child follow each movement of the mother, when he succeeds in segregating and establishing a sign Gestalt within the mother's face, then, through the mother's instrumentality he has segregated a meaningful entity within the chaos of meaningless "environmental" things. Owing to the continuing affective exchanges, this entity, the mother's face, will assume for the child an ever-increasing significance. More generally, the significance of the mother's feelings about the child can hardly be overrated. During his first few months, affective perception and affects predominate in the infant's experience, practically to the exclusion of all other modes of perception. From the psychological point of view, the sensorium, the perceptive apparatus, and sensory discrimination have not yet sufficiently developed. Indeed, much of this apparatus has not even matured. Therefore, the mother's emotional attitude and her affects will serve to orient the infant's affects and confer the quality of life on the infant's experience. Manifestly there are endless variations from mother to mother.

Spitz also contributed the valuable concept of the *organizer* of the psyche. In analogy with the discovery of critical periods for learning in animals, he distinguishes critical periods in the growth of the infant away from mother. During these critical periods the currents of development are integrated with one another in the various sectors of the personality as well as with the emergent functions and capacities resulting from the processes of maturation. The outcome of this integration is a restructuring of the psychic system on a higher level of complexity.

Three such organizers are enumerated by Spitz. The first is around 2–3 months. Its indicator is the appearance of the *smiling response*. The second is the *8-month anxiety,* at which time the infant demands comfort from the mother, and only the mother. In other words, a differentiation has been established between the mother and other people. The third is the appearance of the *"No" response,* first as a gesture and then as a word. Because of numerous unpleasure experiences, the no is invested with aggressive cathexis. This makes the no suitable for expressing aggression, and this is the reason why the no is used in the defense mechanism of identification with the aggressor, and turned against the libidinal object. Once this step has been accomplished, the phase of stubbornness can begin. The "no" first appears at around 15 months of age.

After describing theoretically normal development, Spitz was able to show the vast differences between infants brought up with "good" mothering and those brought up with "bad" mothering. He emphasized that in the mother–child relation the mother is the dominant active partner. The child, at least in the beginning, is the passive recipient. This leads to the proposition that disturbances of the maternal personality will be reflected in the disorders of the child. Conversely, in infancy, damaging psychological influences are the consequence of unsatisfactory relations between mother and child. Such unsatisfactory relations are pathogenic and can be divided into two categories: improper mother–child relations, and insufficient mother–child relations. Stated differently, disturbance of object relations may be either qualitatively or quantitatively caused.

Among the "psychotoxic" attitudes of the mother he enumerated: overt primal rejection, primary anxious overpermissiveness, hostility in the guise of anxiety, oscillation between pampering and hostility, cyclical mood swings, hostility consciously compensated, partial emotional deprivation, and complete emotional deprivation.

In the realm of pathology, one of his most meaningful contributions was the concept of *anaclitic depression*. This is a depression induced by some defect in the mother, qualitative or quantitative. Its most extreme form is *marasmus,* or the wasting away disease of young infants. This was particularly prevalent in foundling homes: in one group of 91 children originally observed, 34 had died by the end of the second year.[6] This contrasts with a mortality rate of 2 deaths through intercurrent disease of 220 infants observed in another setting.[7] The major difference was in the amount of mothering the infants received: tender loving care. After the findings of Spitz and others were published in the 1940s, social agencies began to discontinue orphan asylums and to place motherless children in foster homes.

Spitz also made a number of other observations on the effects of inadequate mothering in the first year of life. He compared his findings with those of Hans Selye in animal stress and sensory deprivation, offering a comparative table.

Spitz's pioneering research is of enormous importance in the history of psychoanalysis. At least six major contributions stem from his work.

1. He showed that the direct observation of infants, if inspired by psychoanalytic hypotheses, could yield fruitful results.
2. As a result, a rapprochement between psychoanalysis and experimental psychology could be effected. For some time this has been noticeable, particularly with regard to Piaget, but it is more generally true as well.

PARALLELS BETWEEN THE GENERAL ADAPTATION SYNDROME AND THE EMOTIONAL DEPRIVATION SYNDROME[8]

General Adaptation Syndrome (Selye)	Emotional Deprivation Syndrome (Spitz)
Tension	Weepiness
Excitement	Demanding attitude
Loss of appetite	Loss of appetite, loss of weight
Resistance to evocative stimulus increases	Social sector increases
Adaptability to other agents diminishes	Arrest and regression of developmental quotient
Libido subnormal	Absence of autoerotic activity
Depression of nervous system	Withdrawal
Adaptation stops	Insomnia
Resistance ceases	Decreased motility
Arteriosclerosis of brain vessels	Regression of developmental quotient irreversible
Breakdown	Infection liability
Death	Facial rigidity
	Atypical finger movements
	Morbidity increases
	Spectacular mortality

3. He demonstrated once and for all the signal and unique role of the mother in the first year of life.

4. He established the general proposition that a good mothering experience leads to health, a bad one to illness.

5. He showed that psychic development proceeds around organizers, thus establishing the concept of a growth process involving increasingly complex hierarchical integrations at different levels of life.

6. He showed that the cognitive and affective components of the personality could be separated only for theoretical reasons. The good ego, which involves the capacity for competence in the cognitive functions, results as much from good mothering as from native endowment.

David Levy: The Overprotective Mother

Whereas Spitz's work had concentrated on the obviously harmful aspects of maternal rejection, particularly desertion and neglect, another pioneering piece of work by the New York psychoanalyst David Levy pointed up the harmfulness of overprotection, the opposite side of the coin. Levy's study was based on the perusal of more than 2,000 case records, representing more than 100 hours of contact per case, at the former Institute for Child Guidance in New York City (Levy, 1943).

He found that the child of an overprotective mother has a difficult time in social adjustment, presumably in proportion to the extent to which the relationship to the mother has permeated all others. If the picture of the infant did not change later, the result would be the fixed role of a demanding, selfish, tyrannical person anticipating constant attention, affection, and service; responding to denials of his wishes or to requirements of discipline with impatience, outbursts of temper, or assault; restless and completely at a loss in solitude when not immersed in a book; gifted in conversation and in the use of every device of charm, wheedling, coaxing, and bullying, in order to get his own way.

Full growth into the infant-monster, or egocentric psychopath, is stemmed by numerous reality experiences, but the basic problem arising out of the indulgent, overprotected background, i.e., selfish, demanding, undisciplined behavior, is revealed with monotonous regularity. The indulged, overprotected patient's problem in adjustment is to overcome the need of forcing every situation into the original pattern of his life, the need of being the beloved tyrant of an ever-responding mother.

"Bad" Mother or "Bad" Child

Once the recognition of the crucial significance of the mother was well established, a controversy arose between those who held that the mother was responsible and those who held that somehow the child was defective. The slogan of the one was "There are no bad children, only poor mothers." In the other camp the emphasis was on heredity and organic impairment.

It has already been seen that Freud built up his system only gradually, and left many gaps in the theoretical structure. One of these was the relative roles of nature and nurture. In 1905 it was still too hard for him to believe that there could be cruel or rejecting or destructive parents. In his self-analysis he had concentrated on his own instinctual development, ignoring what his parents had done—thus the bad child.

The weight of Freud's words has been so great that for many who considered themselves devout Freudians the emphasis remained on the bad child rather than on what the parents did, although Freud's writings can also be interpreted in another way—that if parents disregard the lines laid down by heredity, they will damage the child. Once the battle lines between the Freudians and the culturalists hardened after World War II, the culturalists, citing various Freudian passages, stressed the bad mother, especially in the United States, where the democratic tradition had always favored a belief in environmental amelioration.

Clearly, as in other nature–nurture controversies, there is evidence on both sides. Nevertheless, in subsequent discussions it is well to bear in mind that writers have often merely, and perhaps unconsciously, tried to remain within the original Freudian mold, or rebelled against it. Those who remained within the mold were concerned with the instinctual development of the child; those outside were more concerned with the effect of the parents or the environment. This dichotomy has even extended to therapy. In the arguments about analysis, the more Freudian analysts have stressed the role which the patient plays, culminating in concepts of untreatability of the schizophrenic and severe borderline patient, while the culturalists have stressed the role which the analyst plays, and by varying the activities of the analyst have tried to bring even the severest disturbances within the purview of analytic therapy (Langs, 1976).

Anthropological Data

At first a rather simplistic image of the connection between childhood experience and adult personality emerged. Moloney (1945) in a well-known article attributed the mental health of the Okinawans to the fact that they were nursed for almost 5 years. Gorer and Rickman (1949) tried to interpret Russian national character as an outcome of the custom of swaddling the infant for an excessively long time.

These early oversimplifications soon gave way to a more sophisticated understanding of the process of personality development, especially as the concepts of ego psychology came to be better known. Kardiner (1945) in his analysis of the Alorese was able to show that widespread maternal neglect did produce character traits of insecurity and apathy, much as in Spitz's studies, but that these had to be comprehended within a wider cultural framework. Mead and Wolfenstein (1955) provided other excellent accounts of the complex relationships between childhood training experiences and adult personality. Statistically, however, few conclusions (if any) could be reached. Whiting (1963) in a study of six cultures, presented the data without conclusions. Levine (1973) has recast the problem in methodological terms, as a comparative study of the relationship between the individual and the environment. Hsu (1971) struck a dominant note when he wrote:

We hope to convince students of psychological anthropology that it is the broader aspects of interpersonal interaction patterns in the nuclear family and not merely certain limited child-rearing practices that are crucial to human development; and to convince students of social structure that they have unnecessarily restricted the scientific fruitfulness of their efforts by ignoring psychological anthropology.[9]

In sum, while the anthropological data confirm the psychoanalytic position that the mother is of crucial importance in the development of the child, further conclusions are hard to put in acceptable quantitative terms.

The Bowlby Controversy

World War II had dislocated millions of people, leaving untold numbers of children homeless or in homes away from their biological parents. In 1948 the United Nations decided to study the needs of homeless children and entrusted the task to the British psychoanalyst John Bowlby. His report was published in the book *Maternal Care and Mental Health* (1951). The significance of this work lies in the fact that the psychoanalytic position had become official doctrine for the world at large. Bowlby held that what is essential for mental health is that the infant and young child should experience a warm, intimate, and close relationship with his mother (or permanent mother-substitute) in which both find satisfaction and enjoyment.

Less clear were the effects of maternal deprivation. Bowlby (1961) emphasized that the loss of the mother between the ages of 6 months and 3 or 4 years leads to a process of mourning highly unfavorable to future personality development. He distinguished three phases in this mourning process: *protest, despair,* and *detachment.* Denying Melanie Klein's theory that a depressive position came in the second quarter of the first year, he maintained that the responses in young children to the loss of the mother are no different from the bereavement reaction in adults. The psychological responses following bereavement are: thought and behavior still directed toward the lost object; hostility; appeals for help; despair, withdrawal, regression, and disorganization; and reorganization of behavior directed toward a new object.

Disagreement on the consequences of loss in early childhood as described by Bowlby was expressed by Anna Freud and Max Schur (1960). Both stressed that the role of the ego had been ignored or underplayed in Bowlby's formulation, and that how the child reacted to the loss of the mother depended on the strength of his ego structure.

Object Loss

Eventually the crucial role of the mother and of other people in personality development and functioning crystallized in the concept of *object loss.* In the first edition of Grinstein's *Index,* published in 1960, there is no entry for this topic; in the second edition, 1966, there is one entry; and in the third, 1971, there are 25. In the next edition there will probably be hundreds. The overwhelming significance of the loss of an important person has become an integral part of all psychoanalytic theory.

Lewin's Oral Triad: Mania and Denial

Once attention had been focused on the oral stage, its significance in various types of psychopathology moved into the foreground. One of the most penetrating analyses of a severe disturbance was the book by Bertram Lewin, *The Psychoanalysis of Elation* (1950). Lewin postulated an *oral triad* of to eat, to be eaten, and to sleep. He showed that the manic and hypomanic patient denied the wish to be eaten and to sleep, and lived in a state of constant ingestion or eating, taking in the whole world. Mania he likened to a waking dream. Denial was the major defense mechanism used.

Bergler's Oral Triad: Masochism and Revenge on the Mother

Another oral triad was described by Edmund Bergler, in connection with masochism. Bergler wrote extensively, but his views are summed up in *The Basic Neurosis: Oral Regression and Psychic Masochism* (1949). His main thesis was that psychic masochism, the "ubiquitous" mental illness, results from an oral regression in which a triad is set up: to provoke, to be rejected, and to flaunt this rejection as revenge against the mother.

Schizophrenia and the Oral Stage

By far the greatest attention has been devoted to schizophrenia. Beginning in the 1920s Sullivan had tied the schizophrenic development to bad mothering. Although he and his position were looked on as rather eccentric by many psychiatrists, his views began to carry increasing weight. The later demonstration by Spitz, Levy, and others of the damaging effects of maternal deprivation was easy to extrapolate to schizophrenia to form a consistent theory. A considerable controversy then ensued as to whether there was a qualitative difference between psychosis and neurosis, or whether they were on a continuum. In general, analysts have favored a continuum theory, although there are many exceptions.

In the Schreber case (1911) Freud had already described the paranoid's withdrawal of libido from the outside world, as had Abraham in an earlier paper (1908). Sullivan in 1926 had described this more phenomenologically as a state of panic, the end result of a long series of anxiety states, thus making the continuum more meaningful and more available operationally.[10] If the panic reached a height, it resulted in a catatonic state; there might be a readjustment by a paranoid process; or the conflict might be resolved by disintegration of social skills (hebephrenia). The continuum was demonstrated by the idea that the panic of the schizophrenic is only an extreme form of the anxiety suffered by the neurotic and is defended against in the same structural form in which the neurotic defends himself against his anxieties.

Subsequent research and experience have confirmed and enlarged these views in various ways. Since anxiety goes back ultimately to separation from the mother, if the mother is in reality neglectful or destructive or overly possessive, then a weak ego is created, from which a schizophrenic illness may develop. John Rosen (1953) emphasized that every schizophrenic he had seen had had a directly destructive mother, and he geared his treatment accordingly. His innovation of direct analysis at least opened a way to the deteriorated schizophrenic, who had been given up as untreatable by all other means.

Lidz (1973), whose research group studied a number of schizophrenic families in depth, synthesized the various significant findings of the family studies, as well as the essential clinical features of schizophrenic disorders, into a coherent theory. This evolved from the recognition that the serious disturbances of the family settings derived from the profound egocentricity of one or both parents; that the disturbances of language and thought that form the critical attribute of schizophrenic disorders are largely types of egocentric cognitive regressions; and that the parents' disturbed styles of communication, which are manifestations of their egocentricities, are essential precursors of the patient's cognitive regression, which occurs when he cannot surmount the essential developmental tasks of adolescence.

Burnham et al. (1969) described what they termed the need-fear dilemma of the schizophrenic. He has both an inordinate need and an inordinate fear of objects, which goes back to a disturbed relationship with the mother. To avoid the disaster of complete disintegration, his relationships are dominated by one of three general patterns: object clinging, object avoidance, and object redefinition.

The inability to separate properly from the mother underlies the symptoms of schizophrenia. Blatt et al. (1976) emphasize that the capacity for differentiation and separation in an interpersonal matrix and the development of the cognitive-perceptual capacity to experience, perceive, and represent events and objects as separate and distinct are all aspects of the early stages of the internalization of object relations associated with boundary-setting functions. Once basic boundary differentiations have been established between self and nonself and inside and outside, then object- and self-representations can become increasingly articulated, diverse, integrated, symbolic, and constant.

It is generally agreed that the progression from maternal mishandling to schizophrenia occurs in a number of patients, but there is disagreement on the percentage. In 1968 Bellak and Loeb stated that they were fairly certain that purely psychogenic factors (i.e., early maternal deprivation) will be demonstrated to play the primary role in the etiology and pathogenesis of about 50 percent of all schizophrenic pathology.[11]

Evidence from Animal Behavior

Unexpected support for the thesis that maternal love is essential to healthy mental development came from animal studies initiated in the 1950s, although material had also been available earlier. A classic paper by Imre Hermann[12] had pointed to the close connection between clinging and searching, a common clinical syndrome; both are related to the mother and to separation from the mother. Hermann buttressed his argument with data taken from observations of apes.

The first major piece of research with animals that linked psychopathological states with the relationship to the mother was the work of Harry Harlow with rhesus monkeys, from the 1950s onward. His conclusions are summarized in *Learning to Love* (1974).

Harlow first performed a series of experiments comparing the infant monkey's need for physical contact with his need for food, and found that the need for contact was far greater. Then he went on to examine all aspects of the monkey's life. He distinguished five kinds of affectional systems: mother–infant, infant–mother, peer–peer, heterosexual, and paternal. Obviously this classification is just as applicable to human beings. For all of these types of affectional systems, the decisive factor was a good, warm relationship between infant and mother. One of his surprising findings was that if this mother–infant relationship is unsatisfactory, the monkey will not be able to engage in normal sexual relationships later on.

A large number of studies with various animal species followed. Much of this material is summarized in Scott and Senay (1973). In general it has been found that in highly social animals, including the dog, separation from either close social relatives or familiar physical surroundings or both is followed by strong, unpleasant, and persistent emotional reactions. In animal species genetic differences are present, so that one species may react with prolonged depression to a separation, while another species may not.

This research can be summed up in the general statement that in all mammals the mother–infant bond is of primary importance. If this bond is gratified, the infant grows up healthy; if it is frustrated, the infant grows up disturbed in one of various ways. Thus the central importance of the mother–infant relationship established in people extends far down the evolutionary scale.

The Bowlby Synthesis

In 1969, Bowlby, whose professional writings had mainly been devoted to the subject of mother–child relationships, published the first volume in what was intended to be a grand synthesis of all available data on attachment and separation behavior in infancy. The first volume was on attachment; the second, on separation, appeared in 1973. The third and final one has not yet been published.

Bowlby now offers what he calls a control systems approach to attachment behavior. He points out that a child's attachment behavior is one of four classes of behavior: the child's attachment behavior; behavior of the child that is antithetic to attachment, notably exploratory behavior and play; the mother's caretaker behavior; and behavior of the mother that is antithetic to parental care. Attachment can take a number of different forms, but in all there is a dynamic equilibrium between mother and child. (Presumably if this is disturbed, trouble will ensue.) In this work Bowlby surprisingly moves quite a way from the psychoanalytic position toward a behavioristic approach.

Summary: The Transition to a General Psychology

The study of the oral phase has branched off in many directions: normal and abnormal development, the mother–child relationship, the family, schizophrenia and other forms of psychopathology, physiological factors, genetic factors, ego development, and so on. It is clear that what has emerged is a transition to a general psychology in which psychoanalysis still offers the organizing lead of the dynamic point of view but is able to incorporate and integrate findings from many different disciplines. The crucial significance of the mother to the infant in the first year of life is established beyond question. Maternal deprivation, just like any later object loss, has a variety of damaging effects; in the earliest year it may cause death or severe stunting of growth that is not remediable with current therapeutic methods. If the deprivation is not too severe, however, and remedial measures are brought to bear early enough, the child's development may still proceed satisfactorily. Since cognitive, affective, and physiological factors can scarcely be disentangled at this stage in life, study of this area is relevant to all the sciences that deal with mankind.

Winnicott: The Transitional Object

Given the crucial importance of good mothering, the next question is, How can the child succeed in growing away from the mother? Here a variety of viewpoints have become relevant in the postwar period.

In 1953 (the original paper was read in 1951 but not published for two years) the British psychoanalyst Donald Winnicott, who had come to psychoanalysis through pediatrics, described the *transitional object*. This is the first not-me possession, adopted by the infant some time between 4 months and 12 months (there are wide variations; occasionally there are infants who have none at all).

As every observant parent knows, this transitional object—a diaper, a piece of blanket, a piece of cloth, or the like—is held onto by the infant with ferocious tenacity. If it is taken away, the infant screams until it is returned. There is no difference between boys and girls.

Winnicott describes the following qualities in the transitional object:

1. The infant assumes rights over the object, which are agreed to. Nevertheless some abrogation of the infant's omnipotence is there from the start.

2. The object is affectionately cuddled as well as excitedly loved and mutilated.

3. It must never change, unless changed by the infant.

4. It must survive loving and hating.

5. Yet it must seem to the infant to give warmth, or to move, or to have texture, or to do something that seems to show it has vitality or reality of its own.

6. It comes from without, from our point of view, but not so from the point of view of the baby.

7. Its fate is gradually to be decathected, so that in the course of years it becomes not so much forgotten as relegated to limbo.

It seems clear enough that this transitional object symbolizes the mother; hence the name. It is a sign that enough ego has been developed to allow the infant to use a symbolic object instead of the mother proper.

In his paper Winnicott went on to describe a number of other transitional phenomena, such as play and artistic creation. However, while his notion of a transitional object struck an immediate responsive chord in the analytic community, his idea of transitional phenomena seemed less convincing. The description of the transitional object is one of the earliest in the chain of observations that led to the realization that growth away from the mother (and from other persons later on in life) must be gradual and must be accomplished by a variety of substitutions and symbolic maneuvers.

Busch (1974) distinguished two transitional objects, one at around 6 months of age, and the other at around 2 years. It seems reasonable to assume that the first object centers around the attachment to the mother, while the second would be more closely related to the attachment to the father. However, the essential principle is confirmed—that growth away from any important person must be gradual and must be accomplished by means of substitutions and symbolic equations.

Mahler: The Separation-Individuation Process

For more than a quarter of a century Margaret Mahler headed a research project at the Masters Children's Center in New York, investigating the detailed steps of the process by which the child frees itself from its mother and becomes a human being in its own right. Her research has been summarized in *The Psychological Birth of the Human Infant* (Mahler et al., 1975). This focused on normal development, while her earlier work, *On Human Symbiosis and the Vicissitudes of Individuation* (1968), explored infantile psychosis.

At first Mahler concentrated on the *autistic* and *symbiotic* modes of relatedness to the mother. She posited an autistic period (the same as Freud's primary narcissism) followed by a symbiotic period. She saw the core disturbance in infantile psychosis as being faulty or absent individuation, resulting from a deficiency or defect in the child's intrapsychic utilization of the mothering partner during the symbiotic phase, and his subsequent inability to internalize the representation of the mothering object for polarization. Thus she saw infantile psychosis as hereditary or organic, following Freud's early assumption of inherent failures in the child's development (the "bad child" theory), although the examples she gave almost invariably presented severely disturbed mothers.

The autistic phase gives way to the symbiotic at around 2 months. Following the symbiotic phase there is a separation-individuation process that takes several years. This process Mahler divides into four subphases. The first is differentiation and development of the body image (hatching), from 4 or 5 months to 10–12 months.

The second is practicing, from 10 or 12 months to 16 or 18 months. This in turn is divided into two phases: an early one ushered in by the infant's earliest ability to move away physically from mother by crawling, paddling, climbing, and righting itself, yet still holding on, and the practicing period proper, characterized by free, upright locomotion. This second period she calls "the love affair with the world." From time to time, however, the infant goes back to mother for "refueling."

The third phase is rapprochement. Now there is a deliberate search for, or avoidance of, intimate bodily contact. This phase gradually leads up to a *rapprochement crisis,* an idea that is one of Mahler's distinctive contributions. This crisis arises because while individuation proceeds very rapidly and the child exercises it to the limit, he also becomes more and more aware of his separateness and employs all kinds of mechanisms in order to resist and undo his actual separateness from his mother. The fact is, however, that no matter how insistently the toddler tries to coerce the mother, she and he can no longer function effectively as a dual unit. In this crossroads the crisis arises. Individual solutions of the crisis result in patternings and personality characteristics with which the child enters into the fourth subphase, the consolidation of individuation. The rapprochement crisis extends from 18 to 24 months and beyond.

The fourth phase, object constancy, involves the consolidation of individuality and the beginnings of emotional object constancy. The main task of this subphase is twofold: first, the achievement of a definite, in certain aspects lifelong, individuality and, second, the attainment of a certain degree of object constancy. This object constancy depends on the gradual internalization of a constant, positively cathected, inner image of the mother. This last phase covers roughly the third year of life. In its course a stable sense of identity is formed (self boundaries), and primitive consolidation of gender identity takes place as well.

Mahler's work has cast much light on the vicissitudes of infantile development in the first three years of life. From a theoretical point of view, her main contribution lies in the concept of the rapprochement crisis, to which she devotes a great deal of attention; the other stages were all well known before, though not in such detail. Rapprochement expresses the intense ambivalence that the child feels about separating from the mother and becoming an individual in his own right. However, at this stage other persons also begin to play a role, particularly the father (Abelin, 1975). Thus a full synthesis of all the available data is still not provided by Mahler's study, important though it is.

The concepts of the autistic and symbiotic stages, and the separation-individuation process have proved to be felicitous and have stimulated a large number of confirmatory studies in the literature. It is now generally recognized that the separation-individuation process, the paradigm for which is described in Mahler's work with the mother–child pair, goes on all through life with every later relationship.

The Modern Synthesis: Psychosocial Health

The centrality of the mother–child relationship has led to a fruitful interchange between psychoanalysis and other disciplines, in which all have benefited. Inasmuch as a good, warm relationship with the mother is essential to mental health, the earliest stages of life have a vital importance for the individual and for the culture; the principle even applies to many animal species.

Since the mother assures the mental health of the child, what assures the mental health of the mother? Clearly, she too must have a secure, warm ambience in which she has the leisure and the emotional maturity to devote herself to the infant. Thus a good family environment is necessary (Beavers, 1977).

What ensures the good family environment?—the surrounding culture, free from evidences of social unrest and disorganization and disintegration, such as war, slavery, oppression, poverty, alcoholism, drug addiction, and crime. Failure to provide an adequate milieu leads to "neurosis," more properly designated as psychosocial disturbances (Freedman and Redlich, 1966). Physiological data, where relevant and appropriate, can easily be fitted into this scheme of things; however, a complete reductionism to physiological causation is not supported by any currently available evidence.

A synthesis of this kind has been reached by many different thinkers. Well known is Erik Erikson's *scheme of psychosocial development,* in which he describes eight stages of life, from birth to death, thereby going beyond the more traditional Freudian schema of psychosexual development (Erikson, 1950), which had been superseded by then anyhow.

Among anthropologists, although Freud's *Totem and Taboo* was ritualistically dismissed as a "fairytale," its essential thesis of the psychic unity of mankind had been almost universally accepted. In 1948 Kroeber wrote.

The involved doctrine is the famous "psychic unity of man." This cannot be considered to be either a proved fact or an axiomatic principle, but is so overwhelmingly brought out by the run of total experience that the anthropologist or the sociologist feels warranted in assuming the principle of essential psychic unity as at least a sufficient approximation to truth and to employ it as a working hypothesis, or at any rate as a convenient symbol.[13]

This concept of the psychic unity of mankind, which derived primarily from dynamic psychoanalytic concepts. was further defined by Kardiner (1939) as an examination of the reciprocal relations between the individual and his culture in connection with the following: the organization of the family and character of the in-group formation, and the psychological constellations in the individual formed by them; the basic disciplines, sexual and anal, and the consequences, vicissitudes, and basic constellations in the individual derived from them; the psychobiological factors responsible for the establishment of discipline and its perpetuation, and the psychology of dependence and discipline; the various forms of mastery ontogenetically considered and the reasons for studying them, also infantile types, and training for adult pursuits generally called "economic"; the conflicts derived from the social conditions of work, subsistence conflicts, prestige conflicts, rivalry and competition; aggression, its forms, and the effects of social control; forces that hold society together, external sanctions and their internalization and superego formation; life goals and ideals of the culture.

From a technical point of view Anna Freud has provided the best description of growth from a healthy mother–child situation in her conceptualization of *developmental lines* (1965). She states that there are lines of development which can be shown to be valid for every area of the child's personality. In every instance they trace the child's gradual outgrowing of dependent, irrational, id- and object-determined attitudes to an increasing ego mastery of his internal and external world. Whatever level any child reaches in any area represents the results of interaction between drive and ego-superego development and their reaction to environmental influences, i.e., between maturation, adaptation, and structuralization.

From another angle, the careful study of the mother–child relationship in the first year of life has led to an increasing focus on the severe anxieties experienced by the infant in this period, and on the development of ego mechanisms to cope with this anxiety (Freud, 1926) as well as the growth of an autonomous ego structure resulting from an atmosphere of love and trust (Hartmann, 1939). Failures in the earliest relationship result in a weakened ego that becomes the core of all later personality disturbance.

Chapter Seven
Extensions and Elaborations of
the Developmental Scheme:
Later Stages

W hile the revised views on the oral stage are the most dramatic, leading in many respects to a radically different theory in psychoanalysis, many other changes have been introduced through the years into Freud's original developmental scheme. Only the most important changes can be noted here, but whatever aspect of psychoanalytic theory is touched permits a broadening into a comprehensive general psychology.

Erikson: the Total Life Cycle

Before moving on to the consideration of the specific phases of development, I wish to mention perhaps the most important broadening of Freud's scheme, to the total life cycle. In his concern with the first five years, Freud had tended to neglect the later stages of life. The first to point this out was Jung, who posited a principle of individuation and discussed in some detail the psychological problems of the second half of life. However, Jung's religious and mystical orientation did not appeal to his fellow analysts.

The first to offer a full view of the life cycle which made sense to the analytic community was Erik Erikson (1902–   ). His scheme centered on the sense of identity, unlike Freud's, which centered on sexuality. Erikson is a rare phenomenon in the history of psychoanalysis. Without formal degrees of any kind, he has functioned as a play therapist, psychoanalyst, anthropologist, applied psychoanalyst, and distinguished man of letters. His major theoretical writings on identity are *Identity and the Life Cycle* (1959) and *Childhood and Society* (1950). Both of these books have become indispensable in the education of every psychoanalyst, and have also had wide repercussions among social scientists.

Erikson tells us that he was led to the concept of identity through concern with other fields, especially social anthropology and comparative education. He offers no final definition, instead stating the following:

First a word about the term identity. As far as I know Freud used it only once in a more than incidental way, and then with a psychosocial connotation. It was when he tried to formulate his link to the Jewish people that he spoke of an "inner identity" which was not based on race or religion. . . . It is this identity of something in the individual's core with an essential aspect of a group's inner coherence which is under consideration here. . . .

I can attempt to make the subject matter of identity more explicit only by approaching it from a variety of angles—biographic, pathographic, and theoretical; and by letting the term identity speak for itself in a number of connotations. At one time, then, it will appear to refer to a conscious *sense of individual identity;* at another to an unconscious striving for a *continuity of personal character;* at a third, as a criterion for the silent doings of *ego synthesis;* and finally, as a maintenance of an inner solidarity with a *group's* ideals and identity. In some respects the term will appear to be colloquial and naive; in another, vaguely related to existing concepts in psychoanalysis and sociology. If, after an attempt at clarifying this relation, the term itself still retains some ambiguity, it will, so I hope, nevertheless have helped to delineate a significant problem and a necessary point of view.[1]

In line with his background, Erikson's contribution lies mainly in his delineation of the growth and crises of the healthy personality. In 1950 he proposed an outline of the life cycle in eight main stages, and the main tasks facing the individual at each stage, which has been widely adopted by students of human behavior.

According to Erikson, there are critical psychological conflicts for each stage of development. Criteria for the healthy personality all must recognize the child's cognitive and social development; hence the term "psychosocial" stages, widening Freud's concept of psychosexual stages. Erikson proceeds from such notions as Marie Jahoda's delineation of the healthy personality as one who actively masters his environment, shows a certain unity of personality, and is able to perceive the world and himself correctly. Also basic is the epigenetic principle, which states that anything that grows has a ground plan, and that out of this ground plan the parts arise, each part having its time of special ascendancy until all parts have arisen to form a functioning whole. "Personality can be said to develop according to steps predetermined in the human organism's readiness to be driven toward, to be aware of, and to interact with, a widening social radius, beginning with the dim image of a mother and ending with mankind, or at any rate that segment of mankind which 'counts' in the particular individual's life."[2]

Erikson sees his approach as bridging the theory of infantile sexuality (with no essential changes) and knowledge of the child's physical and social growth within his family and the social structure. He distinguishes both a sequence of stages and a gradual development of component parts. For each stage a crisis occurs. Each stage becomes a crisis because incipient growth and awareness in a significant part function go together with a shift in instinctual energy and yet cause specific vulnerability in that part. Thus, different capacities use different opportunities to become full-grown components of the ever-new configuration that is the growing personality.

After these general considerations Erikson describes the eight main stages of human life as follows:

1. BASIC TRUST VERSUS BASIC MISTRUST. Basic trust is an attitude toward oneself and the world derived from the experiences of the first year of life. The crisis of the oral stage during the second part of the first year seems to consist of the coincidence in time of three developments: a physiological one, a psychological one, and an environmental one. Even under favorable circumstances this stage seems to intrude into the psychic life a sense of division and a dim but universal nostalgia for a lost paradise.

Basic trust is not something acquired once and for all. What the child acquires at a given stage is a certain ratio between the positive and the negative which, if the balance is toward the positive, will help him to meet later crises with a better chance for unimpaired total development.

The firm establishment of enduring patterns for the balance of basic trust over basic mistrust is the first task of the budding personality and therefore first of all a task for maternal care.

2. AUTONOMY VERSUS SHAME AND DOUBT. The overall significance of this stage lies in the maturation of the muscle system, the

consequent ability (and doubly felt inability) to coordinate highly conflicting action patterns such as "holding on" and "letting go," and the enormous value that the still highly dependent child begins to give his autonomous will. To develop autonomy, a firmly developed and a convincingly continued stage of early trust is necessary.

The basic need of the individual for a delineation of his autonomy in the adult order of things seems to be taken care of, in turn, by the principle of "law and order."

3. INITIATIVE VERSUS GUILT. The child of 4 and 5 years is faced with the next step and the next crisis. Being firmly convinced that he is a person, he must now find out what kind of a person he is going to be. Three strong developments help at this stage, yet also serve to bring the child closer to his crisis: he learns to move around more freely and more violently and therefore establishes a wide and, so it seems to him, unlimited radius of goals, his sense of language becomes perfected to the point where he understands and can ask about many things just enough to understand them thoroughly; and both language and locomotion permit him to expand his imagination over so many things that he cannot avoid frightening himself with what he has dreamed and thought up. Nevertheless, out of all this he must emerge with a sense of unbroken initiative as a basis for a high and yet realistic sense of ambition and independence. This is also the stage of infantile sexual curiosity, genital excitability, and occasional preoccupation and overconcern with sexual matters.

It is at this stage of initiative that the great governor of initiative, namely conscience, becomes firmly established. Many adults feel that their worth as people consists entirely in what they are doing, or rather in what they are going to do next, and not in what they are as individuals. Only a combination of early prevention and alleviation of hatred and guilt in the growing being, and the consequent handling of hatred in the free collaboration of people who feel equal in worth although different in kind of function or age, permits a peaceful cultivation of initiative, a truly free sense of enterprise.

4. INDUSTRY VERSUS INFERIORITY. This fourth stage is crystallized around the conviction: "I am what I learn." The child now wants to be shown how to get busy with something and how to be busy with others.

If the first use of the thing-world is successful and guided properly, the pleasure of mastering toy things becomes associated with the mastery of the conflicts which were projected on them and with the prestige gained through such mastery. Finally, at nursery-school age playfulness reaches into the world shared with others.

All children sooner or later become dissatisfied without a sense of being useful, without a sense of being able to make things and make them well and even perfectly. This Erikson calls the sense of industry. The danger at this stage is the development of a sense of inadequacy and inferiority. Identification with strong leader-figures is important here: "Again and again I have observed in the lives of especially gifted and inspired people that one teacher, somewhere, was able to kindle the flame of hidden talent."[3]

5. IDENTITY VERSUS IDENTITY DIFFUSION. With the establishment of a good relationship to the world of skills and to those who teach and share the new skills, childhood proper comes to an end. Youth begins. The growing and developing young people, faced with the physiological revolution within them, are now primarily concerned with attempts at consolidating their social roles. The integration now taking place in the form of ego identity is the inner capital accrued from all those experiences of each successive stage, when successful identification led to a successful alignment of the individual's basic drives with his endowment and his opportunities.

The danger at this stage is identity diffusion. In general it is primarily the inability to settle on an occupational role which disturbs young people. The dynamic quality of the tempestuous adolescences lived through in patriarchal and agrarian countries (countries which face the most radical changes in political structure and in economy) explains the fact that their young people find convincing, satisfactory identities in the simple totalitarian doctrines of race, class, or nation.

Democracy in a country like America poses special problems in that it insists on self-made identities ready to grasp many chances and ready to adjust to changing necessities. Psychologically speaking, a gradually accruing ego identity is the only safeguard against the anarchy of drives as well as the autocracy of conscience.

Erikson next distinguishes the three stages of adulthood.

6. INTIMACY AND DISTANTIATION VERSUS SELF-ABSORPTION. It is only after a reasonable sense of identity has been established that real intimacy with the other sex (or, for that matter, with any other person or even oneself) is possible. The counterpart of intimacy is distantiation. Psychoanalysis has emphasized genitality as one of the chief signs of a healthy personality.

7. GENERATIVITY VERSUS STAGNATION. Generativity is primarily the interest in establishing and guiding the next generation, although there are people who, from misfortune or because of special and genuine gifts in other directions, do not apply this drive to offspring but to other forms of altruistic concern and of creativity, which may absorb their kind of parental responsibility.

8. INTEGRITY VERSUS DESPAIR AND DISGUST. Integrity involves an acceptance of the fact that one's life is one's own responsibility. It is a sense of comradeship with men and women of distant times and of different pursuits, who have created orders and objects and sayings conveying human dignity and love. The lack or loss of this accrued ego integration is signified by despair and an often unconscious fear of death: the one and only life cycle is not accepted as the ultimate of life.

The Clinical Picture of Identity Diffusion

When identity is not well established according to the preceding criteria, there are symptoms of identity diffusion. It usually makes itself manifest in early adolescence. Often only an attempt to engage in intimate fellowship and competition or in sexual intimacy fully reveals the latent weakness of identity. The clinical picture may be one of diffusion of time perspective, consisting in a sense of great urgency and yet also a loss of consideration for time as a dimension of living. Likewise there is an acute upset in the sense of workmanship. Another typical manifestation is an expression of scornful and snobbish hostility toward the roles offered as proper and desirable in one's family or immediate community (negative identity).

Having traced the modern view of the life cycle, we can now turn to the changes in emphasis in the various phases of development.

The Anal Phase

Freud's original observations on the anal phase and the anal character, which dominated the literature before World War I, have remained essentially unchanged. Yet even a cursory examination of the recent literature shows that references to the anal stage have almost disappeared. The main reason is that Freud had concentrated too heavily on the specific libidinal problem of that phase, the control of the sphincters, and underplayed or ignored many other factors that have since been extensively explored. Thus, although what Freud says about that stage remains correct, it has to be fitted into a much larger framework. This larger framework can be summed up broadly as ego psychology and interpersonal relations (also referred to by many as object relations).

Language and Communication

A child says its first words shortly before its first birthday; from then on the development of language proceeds apace. And before then many different kinds of communication occur between mother and child.

Although attempts have been made to tease out a Freudian "theory of language" from Freud's writings (Ekstein, 1965; Laffal, 1965; V. Rosen, 1977), in the main these go back to the discarded "Project" of 1895, with its theoretical neurologizing. The simple historical truth is that Freud never devoted careful systematic attention to the questions of language and communication which seem so central today. In the index to the standard edition of his works, for example, there are only a few scattered references to these topics.

In the meantime the field of linguistics has expanded tremendously. Technical publications abound, and in many universities there are even separate departments of linguistics. In part this development was touched off by explorations in the foundations of mathematics (for example, by Bertrand Russell, Ludwig Wittgenstein, and Willard Quine), which showed that linguistic analysis could resolve many of the persistent and baffling, recurrent problems of philosophy.

Many psychoanalysts have attempted to "apply" the findings of linguistics to psychoanalytic data (Edelheit, 1969; Edelson, 1972; Litowitz, 1975). Problems arise because linguistics deals with rational cognitive operations, while psychoanalytic investigation is directed more toward affective and unconscious determinants. As a result, as Wolff has pointed out (1967), the field is still in its infancy.

Particular attention has been directed to language in the clinical study of the schizophrenic, who is unable to use language in the normal manner and whose communications are difficult or impossible to penetrate. Since schizophrenia has been traced back to a disturbance in the mother–child relationship, the study of early communication processes should shed much light on the psychosis, and vice versa.

Actually, disturbed communication was investigated by Freud in his studies in hysteria. There he could show that the innumerable distortions of body, affect, and movement were all unconscious communications of some disturbing affect or trauma. The cure consisted in bringing these nonverbal communications under conscious control so that they could be discussed rationally. (Freud, of course, did not put it in this way, because the problem of communication as a theoretical issue had not yet been brought to the fore.) Likewise, obsessionals and other neurotics use nonverbal communication in similar ways. In a sense, the whole study of the many forms of the unconscious is a study of unconscious communication.

Sullivan stressed language more than Freud had.[4] The first work to make explicit the genetic roots of disturbed language was Spitz's *No and Yes* (1952). Spitz saw language as the third organizer of the psyche, tracing its origin to about 15 months of age. Prior to this early verbal communication, there are other forms which relate to the attachment and separation experiences of the infant. Bowlby listed five responses leading to attachment behavior: crying, smiling, following, clinging, and sucking. After 4 months, calling becomes important.[5] The same apparatus activity, which was at first directed toward need gratification, is transformed into a series of communications. Eventually, the crucial connection is established in the child's mind between the head-shaking gesture, the concept of refusal or negation, and the memory traces associated with the articulated sound "no."

If the mother is responsive to the child, healthy growth ensues, which as a result of ego development leads to normal language patterns. But if the mother is not responsive, a "derailment" of the dialogue ensues. Spitz's hypothesis is that the dialogue consists of a series of mutual exchanges between mother and child, a give and take of action and reaction between the two partners, which requires from each of them both active and passive responses. The dialogue acts as a vector of the baby's development, influencing its direction and stimulating it to adaptive efforts and psychic growth. The derailment of the dialogue is triggered, perhaps even caused, by the social setting. Either over- or understimulation may interfere with the healthy dialogue.

Many contributions have described the "derailment of the dialogue" in the schizophrenic adult and child. Searles (1961) stressed that the schizophrenic is, in contrast to the normal person, never sure of his communicational abilities and hence, paradoxically, always preoccupied with communication. Lidz and his co-workers (1965) traced the transmission of irrationality through the family structure. Wynne and his group (1970) at the National Institute of Mental Health described in many different empirical ways how the relatedness and communication in schizophrenic families go awry when the children are very young.

Sullivan (1944) had already pointed out that the schizophrenic uses language in a defensive manner (in Sullivan's terms: since he has given up hope of ever finding satisfaction, he always looks for security). He is constantly looking for reassurance that he will not be destroyed by the bad mother. Ekstein and Caruth (1967) make essentially the same point for schizophrenic children. They describe a developmental line of speech with stages of babbling, echoing or echolalia, delayed echolalia, self-echoing, expressing, appealing, and finally symbolic communication. The normal child moves on to communication, the schizophrenic remains fixated at the appeal stage (the cry for help).

Since the normal communicative function of language is lost to him, the schizophrenic child, later adult, engages in a variety of distorted communications or nonverbal communications. It requires much skill to sort out what is meant by them; yet with enough patience and empathy that can be done (Rosenfeld, 1965; Boyer and Giovacchini, 1967). At the same time his distorted communications reinforce his social isolation. This early transmitted irrationality and communicational disability serve as a matrix from which later, more serious disorders develop.

The psychology of language at later stages is considered in chapter 10.

Masturbation and Infantile Sexuality

It is noteworthy that the topic of infantile sexuality, which formed the bulk of every analytic journal before World War I, has a markedly lower frequency in the current literature. In the first edition of Grinstein's *Index* in 1960 there were still 47 references to infantile sexuality; in the latest, in 1971, there were only 10, none of them of any consequence.

In part this lack of interest has resulted from the shift from the id to the ego as a central focus of psychoanalytic thought and investigation. In part it reflects the feeling that Freud and his original co-workers said all there is to say on the subject. But other causes could be adduced as well. Martha Wolfenstein (1953) has shown from careful study of the United States government bulletin *Infant Care* how the official attitude toward such aspects of childhood sexuality as masturbation, thumb-sucking, weaning, bowel training, and bladder training has become steadily more permissive, clearly under the influence of psychoanalytic thought. As a result these aspects of infant development, which were once such a source of discomfort and overt neurotic reaction, have been handled more smoothly by millions of parents. Hence conflicts about infantile sexuality have been sharply reduced.

In Freud's day, masturbation was seen as a prime cause of distress in the educational process. Even Freud (1912) could not rid himself entirely of the idea that masturbation is inherently a harmful activity at any age, although eventually he exploded the notion, universal when he started, that masturbation leads to neurosis and psychosis.

In a bibliographic investigation Spitz (1952) showed that up to 1940 masturbation was treated as a disease in textbooks of pediatrics. Severe treatment was recommended, including mechanical restraints, corporal punishment in the very young, circumcision in boys "because of the moral effect of the operation"; in girls, surgery or cauterization of the clitoris, blistering the inside of the thighs, the vulva, or the clitoral area. From 1890 to 1925 at least, there had existed in the United States a peculiar medical organization called the Orificial Surgery Society, which offered training in surgery of the prepuce, clitoris, and rectum. Spitz states that "even in psychoanalytic circles one does not always realize how extremely cruel the persecution of the masturbator has been up to our days; nor is it generally known that these sadistic practices found support among authoritative physicians and that they were recommened up to [1940] in official textbooks." [6]

Several analytic symposia have clarified the current analytic attitude to masturbation (reported in the *Journal of the American Psy-*

choanalytic Association, in 1951, 1961, 1966). Francis and Marcus (1975) summarize the contemporary position as follows in their book, which has the arresting title *Masturbation from Infancy to Senescence.*[7] Longitudinal and clinical studies have shown that genital play in the first two years aids in developing the body image and establishing interpersonal relatedness, as well as assisting in the process of separation and individuation. Genital play develops into what may more correctly be called masturbation, and it is in the phallic-Oedipal period, when masturbation is phase-specific, that full genital masturbation, with the associated fantasy, is developed. In latency, when there is a relative quiescence of instinctual urges with the aid of the superego, ego ideal, and developing ego, the masturbatory act and fantasy are repressed and derivatives develop in the form of intellectual achievement, skills, play, and defensive character traits. Genital masturbation is again phase-specific in adolescence and further aids in establishing interpersonal relatedness and gradual subordination of pregenitality to genitality. Inadequate suppression of masturbation, however, can inhibit the seeking of persons outside the family circle and retard the advance to true genital heterosexuality. Disturbances preventing the adequate channeling of libidinal and aggressive energy by this particular form of instinctual activity may occur at any stage of development. Such disturbances will result in various types of symptoms and character distortions. Analysis of the masturbatory act and fantasy serves an important function in the analytic process and provides another ''royal road'' to the unconscious.

Knowledge and understanding of this complex psychophysiological phenomenon are still incomplete. Considerable work remains in the area of the relation of masturbation to psychic structure, in terms of both its formation and later disruptions. There is still a good deal of controversy about female sexuality in general and the form and function of masturbation in all phases of female development.

Motility and Body Language

Another facet of the anal phase which Freud did not consider in his theoretical structure is the development of motility and increasing command of the body. While many have since discussed this topic anecdotally and descriptively, it remains difficult to integrate into a comprehensive theoretical structure.

Wilhelm Reich was the first to call attention to the patient's *character armor* in the analytic situation, including ways of walking, talking, mannerisms, gestures, and the like. This character armor serves to crystallize the patient's defensive manuevers and therefore is extremely difficult to affect. Reich did not make any statements about the development of this armor, and his later departure from the field of analysis turned others away from his ideas. However, it is a concept that could and should be followed up.

Various other ideas, research programs, and results have been reported by a number of authors. Felix Deutsch (1951) did a careful study of the posture of the patient on the couch. He hypothesized that every person returns finally to a basic posture which expresses psychosomatic homeostasis. The experience of developing a sense of self (separate from the outside world) entails a sense of loss. Parts of one's body are first perceived as external objects and only progressively become integrated into the unity of the body, which is the basis of the ego. A folded-arms posture or a fetal position may be interpreted as an attempt to hold the "parts" of the ego together. In analysis the posture with the worst prognosis is the immobile one.

Rangell (1954) devoted a communication to a careful study of poise. He said that poise in its essence is an integrative and sometimes a defensive function of the ego, constituting a state of anticipation of and readiness for oncoming stimuli, which comes into play only in a social or interpersonal situation. The organs especially cathected for its maintenance are the perioral or mouth and nose region, the postural system, and the hand.

Mittelman (1954, 1957, 1960) has done the most careful developmental study of motility of the skeletal musculature. He discusses it in regard to motivation, pattern formation, and genetics. He discusses motility as an urge, motility and its relationship to emotions, emotional reactions evoked by motor experience, motility in relation to mastery, reality testing, integration and self-preservation, motility in relation to aggression, attack on the self, conscience and feeling of abandonment.

For many years Kestenberg has headed a study group that has devoted careful attention to the development of the young child as expressed through bodily movement. Her conceptualization (1971) centers on two distinct mechanisms of self-regulation: flow of tension and flow of shape, which she traces through the various libidinal phases. Surprisingly, a paper by Siegal (1973), a member of Kestenberg's group, on movement therapy as a psychotherapeutic tool was published in the *Journal of the American Psychoanalytic Association;*[8] motor therapy, as recommended in her paper, is contrary to both the principles and practices of psychoanalytically oriented psychotherapy. Most recently Dunkell (1977) has published an analysis of sleep positions, which he calls the "night language of the body."

All of these studies must be regarded as suggestive leads that await integration into a fully developed theoretical structure. One complication that hobbles the scrutiny of body responses is the high degree of primary and secondary autonomy that enters into the picture. Like much physiological functioning, it is either independent of affect from the very beginning (primary autonomy) or soon becomes independent (secondary autonomy). While specific individuals may be better understood in this framework, a full theory is still a long way off.

Gender Identity

The question of when boys and girls become aware of their sexual identity has always been urgent and intriguing. In the past decade this matter has been called *gender identity.*

The question preoccupied Freud considerably. The first of the *Three Essays on Sexuality* (1905) is devoted to homosexuality, which shows that the topic was important then as well. To the end of his life, however, Freud remained convinced that differentiation only begins at the phallic stage. In the *Outline of Psychoanalysis* (1938) he wrote: "With the phallic phase and in the course of it the sexuality of early childhood reaches its height and approaches its dissolution. Thereafter boys and girls have different histories."[9] Although Jones and others had objected to this position, which had been enunciated as early as 1923, Freud would not budge. Since then much empirical work has been published, and analysts have generally recognized that Freud's position was mistaken (Fliegel, 1973; Schafer, 1974).

The most extensive empirical investigation of gender identity is by Stoller, *Sex and Gender* (1968). His main conclusions are:[10] First, those aspects of sexuality that are called gender are primarily culturally determined, that is, learned postnatally. This learning process starts at birth, though only with gradually increasing ego development are its effects made manifest in the infant. This cultural process springs from the society, but a sense of it is funneled through the mother, so that what actually impinges on her infant is her own idiosyncratic version of society's attitudes. Second, while gender identity is primarily learned, there are biological forces that contribute to it.

The most extensive directly psychoanalytic observation of infants is the work by Mahler and her associates (1975). They found that girls discovered the anatomical sex differences sometime during the 16–17-month period or even earlier, but more often at 20–21 months. However, the boy's discovery of his own penis usually took place much earlier. The sensory-tactile component of this discovery may even date back into the first year of life (Roiphe and Galenson, 1972, 1973) but there is uncertainty as to its emotional impact. Around 12–14 months the upright position facilitates the visual and sensorimotor exploration of the penis. Possibly in combination with a maturational advance in zonal libidinization, this leads to greater cathexis of this exquisitely sensuous, pleasure-giving organ.

Thus it is quite clear that, contrary to Freud's view, the awareness of gender difference first occurs in the anal phase; other studies show that the parental decision about the gender of the child may occur from birth onward. These observations would fit in with behavioral studies (Maccoby and Jacklin, 1974). The interpretation of gender, and its subsequent elaboration, would depend on the total family structure, with biological factors playing a role of varying importance. This is true even where the child's sexuality is anatomically disorganized (Money and Ehrhardt, 1972).

In recent years much has been made by antianalytic authors of the ''biological'' basis of transsexualism, including homosexuality, and the ''need'' for surgical intervention to change the sex to that which is psychologically acceptable to the individual (Green and Money, 1969; Green, 1974). The arguments are usually buttressed by the bald assertion that ''psychotherapy does not work with these patients.'' In fact, Bieber's study (1962) showed that psychoanalysis is effective with a considerable percentage of homosexuals in changing them over to heterosexuality. The absurd action of the American Psychiatric Association in changing homosexuality to a ''sexual disorientation disturbance'' has been aptly characterized by Kardiner (Socarides, 1974, 1978) as part of a *social distress syndrome.*

Parental Personality

Initially Freud evinced little interest in the personality structures of the parents of his patients; his concern lay chiefly with the elucidation of the stages of libidinal development, which he conceived of as biologically (we would say today, physiologically) determined. However, gradually the focus has shifted. The major impetus came from the studies of infants, where the mother provided the main emotional nurturance. Mothers' failure to provide such nurturance led to such concepts as the rejecting mother, the depriving mother, the phallic mother, the schizophrenogenic mother, and the overprotective mother.

The mother is a more powerful figure in infancy than later on; hence her influence is bound to be greater. Spitz (1965) had already shown in his pioneering studies that with the more normal mother the child reaches genital play earlier, while the depressed mother tends to produce a child who is preoccupied with feces (thus correcting Freud's earlier notion that fecal preoccupation is a biological "given"). Sylvia Brody (1956) studied the way in which mothers feed their infants, dividing them into four types, primarily those who could sense and accommodate the needs of the infants adequately, and those who could not. Her subjects were infants 4–28 weeks of age. In her most recent work (Brody and Axelrad, 1978), she states that a warm, empathic mother in infancy is the most important single basis for healthy social, emotional, and intellectual development.

As the infant gets older, the situation becomes much more complex. Winnicott (1975) used to like to shock his audiences by saying, "There is no such thing as a baby; there is only a baby in a certain environment." Since for a long time the major part of the environment remains the mother, the emphasis shifts to what he calls the mother–infant experience of mutuality.

The Emergence of Family Dynamics

Following World War II, many theoreticians placed increasing emphasis on the family as a psychosocial system. It was recognized that the child does not exist in the abstract but in relation to what the parents do. And in turn the parents are affected by the child. The whole leads to an approach in terms of family dynamics, or a family system.

While numerous authors had already described the overall importance of the family, the first book by a psychoanalyst that clearly delineated the family as a psychological system was Ackerman's *The Psychodynamics of Family Life* (1958). Here the following points were made: personality cannot be properly understood when it is abstracted from the family matrix in which it exists. The major foci of attention, the child-rearing techniques and the emotional quality of the nurturant care provided to the child, although clearly very important, do not encompass the topic. The child's development is guided by the dynamic organization of his family, which channels his drives and directs him into proper gender and generational roles. The child must grow into and internalize the institutions and roles of the society as well as identify with persons who have themselves assimilated the culture. The child acquires characteristics through identification but also by reactions to parental figures and through finding reciprocal roles with them. His appreciation of the worth and meaning of both social roles and institutions is markedly affected by the manner in which his parents fill their roles, relate to one another, and behave in other contexts.

The concept of family dynamics carries with it the notion that identity is forced on the child by the family structure, not offered as a conscious possibility. Considerable empirical evidence, accumulated in the past quarter century, shows that differential types of family structure lead to different types of psychopathology. Studies have correlated a number of kinds of psychopathology with family structure, including schizophrenia (Lidz et al., 1965), phobias (Strean, 1967), psychosomatic disorders (Meissner, 1966), delinquency (Ferreira, 1960), addictions (Ewing et al., 1961), homosexuality (Bieber et al., 1962), depression and suicide (Goldberg and Mudd, 1968).

In continuation of the idea that psychopathology results from the family climate, several authors in the 1960s and later began to offer typologies of families. Like typologies in general, these have not been markedly successful but are suggestive. Stierlin (1972) divided families into centripetal ones, where the focus of gratification lies mainly within the family, and centrifugal ones, where the major sources of gratification are to be found outside the family. More usual is the general kind of classification offered by Beavers (1977), differentiating severely dysfunctional, mid-range, and healthy families.

A comparison of the more recent literature with the older treatments, such as Flugel (1921) on *The Psychoanalytic Study of the Family,* shows the extensive changes that have occurred in the theory. Flugel, following the early Freud, saw the family as primarily either frustrating or gratifying the child's biologically determined instinctual needs. Later this oversimplification came to be replaced by considerations of the self-image, identity formation, security, and most recently the total emotional climate of the family as the decisive force in the life pattern of the individual.

Unfortunately family analysis has been pursued mainly by family therapists (e.g., Nathan Ackerman, Salvador Minuchin, Helen Stierlin), who have tended to ignore or even jettison the hard-won insights of psychoanalysis, while the more classical analysts have tended to ignore the material from family studies. There can be no doubt that these two sources of information about people will have to be more satisfactorily brought together very soon, since each provides important insights overlooked by the other.

Ego-Psychological Considerations

In addition to filling in some of the gaps left by Freud, by far the most imporant change in the attitude to the anal phase has been the shift from id emphasis to ego-psychological considerations. This could be viewed as a broadening of Freud's drive scheme to a total psychosocial scheme of development, of which Erikson's outline of the life scheme of the individual is the most widely used example. This is discussed more fully below, after the changes in ego psychology have been described. The main point to be noted here is that the anal libidinal drives, like other libidinal drives, can only be properly understood within a broader interpersonal and familial context.

The Oedipal Phase

The structure of the Oedipus complex was so well and so thoroughly handled by Freud that no substantial change has occurred. There are only confirmations and extensions of Freud's position, and of course the broader shift to ego psychology, which places the Oedipal conflict in a different light without altering the accuracy of the initial observations.

Arguments have arisen about the universality of the Oedipus complex. Many texts have erroneously quoted Malinowski as "proving" that the Oedipus complex is not universal, in that among the Trobriand Islanders the uncle plays the role that the father does in our culture (Fine, 1973). What Malinowski actually said was:

The family is the biological grouping to which all kinship is invariably referred and which determines by rules of descent and inheritance the social status of the offspring. As can be seen, this relation never becomes irrelevant to a man and has constantly to be kept alive. Culture, then, creates a new type of bond for which there is no prototype in the animal kingdom. And as we shall see, in this very creative act, where culture steps beyond instinctive endowment and natural precedent, it also creates serious dangers for man. Two powerful temptations, the temptation of sex and that of rebellion, arise at the very moment of cultural emancipation from nature. Within the group which is responsible for the first steps in human progress there arise the two main perils of humanity: the tendency to incest and the revolt against authority.[11]

Other anthropologists, however, have questioned the universality of the Oedipus conflict. Viewed as tendencies, the two sides of the conflict, incest and rebellion, would appear to be universal. Roheim (1952) assembled the evidence available in his day. Murdock (1949) has shown that the nuclear family is a universal human grouping.[12] In the 250 cultures which he surveyed, not a single exception was found: it was either the prevailing form of the family or the basic unit from which more complex familial forms were compounded.

Even more striking is some animal evidence that has come to light. Temerlin (1975), a psychologist who brought up a chimpanzee named Lucy as his daughter, reported that when she reached the age of sexual activity she began to avoid him even though she made the most obvious sexual invitations to other men.[13] And Van Lawick–Goodall (1971) reported that in her observations of chimpanzees in their natural habitat she had never observed any sexual intercourse between mother and son. In addition, although the young chimpanzees would "play copulate" with other chimpanzees while growing up together, as soon as the females began to ovulate they would leave the group in which they had been raised and join strange groups so that they bred with unrelated males.[14]

The origin of the incest taboo remains an unresolved problem. However, Mayr (1970) states that in animal and plant species severe inbreeding leads to "inbreeding depression," manifested by loss of fertility, increased susceptibility to disease, growth anomalies, and metabolic disturbances. "Countless laboratory stocks have been lost owing to inbreeding."[15] Ember (1975) has tried to show that the dangers of inbreeding would account for the incest taboo among humans.

Granted all the features of the Oedipal phase which Freud described, the shift to ego psychology has changed the focus to the total family structure rather than the Oedipal components as such. Again this leads to such a broad area of investigation that full consideration is reserved for chapter 17, on psychoanalysis and culture.

The Latency Phase

Freud described the latency period but had little to say about it. Fenichel commented in 1945 that the question was still very much in need of research,[16] by contrast with the infantile and adolescent periods, which had been much better explored.

Sarnoff (1976) has recently published a book summarizing the literature on this phase, as well as his own experience. Following him, as well as Bornstein (1951), Blos (1962), and others, latency could be divided into three subperiods: ages 6 to 8, 8 (or 9) to 11, and 11 to puberty, each period showing different maturational characteristics.

In the classical description stemming from Freud, sexual manifestations are quiescent in this period; in particular there is a deep repression of masturbation, which then remains the great temptation and problem of the age. It was the preoccupation with masturbation and other direct libidinal manifestations that led the early analysts to neglect this period, though an additional factor was the virtual absence of child patients. (However, it is not widely known that Freud did try to analyze some younger patients; e.g., in *The Interpretation of Dreams* he mentions a 12-year-old boy and a 14-year-old boy,[17] both patients of his. In the analysis he focused on their sexual experiences.)

It is still recognized that masturbation is a conflict in this period, but the major changes in thinking that have occurred relate to the greater emphasis on ego and superego development, and to the signif-

icant interpersonal experiences through which the child passes. These
will be dealt with more fully in chapter 15 but are briefly summarized
here, together with what knowledge there is of the drive changes that
occur.

The first part of latency from *6 to 8* is characterized, as Freud
pointed out, by the passing of the Oedipus complex and the formation
of a superego. The child is still rather tied to the parents, though the
formation of a superego allows him to go to school. There is also a
first love affair at around 6, though it may vary up to 10 (Fine,
1975b), with a child of the same or similar age. This is quite intense
while it lasts, then is abandoned after a fairly short interval. The consolidation of the superego and the strengthening of ego mechanisms
remain primary concerns.

The second period from *8 to 10* (or 11) is characterized by moving out to peers and the formation of peer groups, for both boys and
girls, and by considerable endocrinological changes. (The exact ages
show considerable variability here. According to Tanner (1972), the
onset of puberty may vary by as much as four years within a normal
population.)

The bodily changes that occur at puberty are so striking that they
have obscured the bodily and hormonal changes that occur earlier.
Recent studies have shown that beginning at about age 8 there are
widespread hormonal changes in boys, and that estrogenic substances
or their precursors can be discovered in girls between 7 and 8
(Schechter et al., 1972). Kestenberg (1967) has drawn together information from biochemical and psychological sources and adapted a
chart which shows a definite shift in hormonal substances in the male
and female with advances in the internal genitalia in the female from
7 to 8 and in the external genitalia of the male between 10 and 11.
There is also a suggestion from the work of Anita Bell (1965) that
penile and testicular growth perhaps antedates these ages. The rise
toward pubertal levels of hormone starts well before; in boys it com-
mences between ages 9 and 11 (Money and Ehrhardt, 1972). Scott
(1962) has summarized the evidence for considering this time a critical period in behavioral development.

Even though the changes are much less noticeable to the child
and the adult than those which occur later at puberty proper, virtually
all societies have found themselves constrained to adopt new measures for the social regulation of children at this age. Cohen (1966)

has summarized the evidence from many cultures which shows that the great danger feared at this time is brother–sister incest, and accordingly measures have been taken to keep brother and sister apart. The two institutionalized customs are *brother–sister avoidance* and *brother–sister extrusion*. Usually it is the boy who is extruded in the latter case, and forced to live elsewhere.

From *11 to puberty* there is a homosexual period (often referred to as preadolescent homosexuality or prepubescent homosexuality) in which the strongest libidinal attachment is to a member of the same sex, usually of the same age, but not infrequently an older man or woman, a substitute parent-figure or ego-ideal. Kinsey (1948, 1953) presented extensive statistical data on the incidence of homosexuality in our society. More than half (57 percent) of the men recalled some sort of preadolescent sex play, mostly between the ages of 8 and 13, though some occurs at any age. Most of it was with boys of the same age. In girls the incidence was somewhat lower (33 percent) and did not last as long. Furthermore, only 5 percent of the girls with homosexual play continued it into their adolescence, as contrasted with 42 percent of the boys.

In interpersonal terms, Sullivan has described the significance of a *chum* at this age. This is an intense and important experience, for the relationship usually constitutes the child's first major attachment to a person of the same sex outside the family. There is a constant need to be with the chum, and an altruistic attitude develops in which the chum's welfare is as important as one's own. Sullivan (1940) maintained that persons who do not form such a chum relationship at this age are much more likely to develop a schizophrenic illness later on.

Adolescence

Adolescence was discussed at great length by Freud in the *Three Essays* (1905) and in numerous other works. It was here that he made the great discovery that led to the liberation of sexuality: the sexual wish does not spring full-blown into being at puberty but has a long developmental history, which can be traced in terms of aim and object. This material was so thoroughly worked out by Freud that it has been incorporated into all of psychology and psychiatry.

Changes in the image of the adolescent reactions have occurred primarily in the areas of ego psychology, interpersonal relations, and cultural forces. Erikson's concept of identity diffusion has already been mentioned. These changes, while extensive, do not alter the original theory in any basic way.

Stages of Adolescence

In 1962 Peter Blos, one of the leading authorities on adolescence, offered a detailed breakdown of the various growth stages in the adolescent process, which has proved to be very fruitful. Blos distinguished seven different stages.

1. THE LATENCY PERIOD, AN INTRODUCTION. The latency period furnishes the child with the equipment, in terms of ego development, which prepares him for the encounter with the drive increment of puberty. Consequently he is able to divert instinctual energy into differentiated psychic structures and into psychosocial activities, instead of having to experience it solely as an increase in sexual and aggressive tension.

2. PREADOLESCENCE. During the preadolescent phase a quantitative increase of instinctual pressure leads to an indiscriminate cathexis of all those libidinal and aggressive modes of gratification that have served the child well during the early years of his life. Neither a new love object nor a new instinctual aim can yet be discerned at this phase.

3. ADOLESCENT OBJECT CHOICE. The state of mind and body which is generally associated with adolescence (both early adolescence and adolescence proper) has a distinctly different quality from the preadolescent phase. The difference shows itself in a far richer and wider emotional life, in a turn to a more goal-directed orientation aiming at growing up, and in a relentless attempt at self-definition in answer to the question, "Who am I?" The problem of object relations moves to the foreground as a central theme, and its variations color the entire psychological development of the two subsequent phases. What differentiates this period from the phase of preadolescence is therefore the shift from a merely quantitative drive increase to the emergence of a distinctly new drive quality.

4. EARLY ADOLESCENCE. Pubertal maturation normally forces the boy out of his preadolescent defensive self-sufficiency and pregenital

drive cathexis; the girl is equally pushed toward the development of her femininity. Both boy and girl now turn more forcefully to the libidinous object outside the family; that is to say, the genuine process of separation from early object ties has begun. This process moves through various stages until, ultimately and ideally, mature object relations are established. The distinctive character of early adolescence resides in the decathexis of the incestuous love objects; as a consequence, free-floating object libido clamors for new accommodations.

5. ADOLESCENCE PROPER. The search for object relations, or conversely, the active avoidance of them, illuminates the psychological developments taking place during adolescence proper. During this phase the search for object relations assumes new aspects, different from those prevalent during the preadolescent and early adolescent phases. Heterosexual object finding, made possible by the abandonment of the narcissistic and bisexual positions, characterizes the psychological development of adolescence proper. More appropriately, we should speak of the gradual affirmation of the sex-appropriate drive moving into ascendancy and bringing increasingly conflictual anxiety to bear on the ego.

6. LATE ADOLESCENCE. Late adolescence is primarily a phase of consolidation. It involves the elaboration of: a highly idiosyncratic and stable arrangement of ego functions and interests; an extension of the conflict-free sphere of the ego (secondary autonomy); an irreversible sexual position (identity constancy), summarized as genital primacy; a relatively constant cathexis of object- and self-representation; and the stabilization of mental apparatuses that automatically safeguard the integrity of the psychic organism. Each component influences the other in terms of a feedback system until during postadolescence an equilibrium is reached within certain limits of intrinsic constancy.

7. POSTADOLESCENCE. The transition from adolescence to adulthood is marked by an intervening phase, postadolescence, which can be claimed rightfully by both and can, indeed, be viewed from either of these two stages. Such an individual is usually referred to as a young adult. The total achievement still lacks harmony. In terms of ego development and drive organization, the psychic structure has acquired a fixity that allows the postadolescent to turn to the problem of harmonizing the component parts of the personality. This integra-

tion comes about gradually. It usually occurs coincidentally with or preparatory to vocational choice. One of the foremost concerns at this age is the elaboration of safeguards that automatically protect the narcissistic balance.

Terminologically, according to Blos, what we usually and loosely refer to as adolescence is predominantly restricted to the period of instinctual reorganization. Ego-integrative processes do not cease to be operative after the adolescent storm has passed; in fact, they undergo their most essential and enduring modifications at that time.

Literature and Organization

The literature on adolescence has now become so vast that it cannot be encompassed within any simple review. The formation of a Society for Adolescent Psychiatry in New York in 1958[18] indicated that the study of adolescence had reached an independent stage. This society has sponsored an excellent series of volumes entitled *Adolescent Psychiatry*. The first was published in 1971, edited by Sherman C. Feinstein, Peter Giovacchini, and Arthur A. Miller. Volume 5 of this series, which embodies some of the best current thought on adolescence, was published in 1977.

Parenthood

Benedek (1959) was the first to call attention to parenthood as a distinct developmental phase. Since it occurs when the individual is already a mature adult (biologically speaking), it can only be understood in terms of interaction with the child. The fluctuating psychic economy is explained by the mutuality of interpersonal communication and contact. In responding to their child's behavior, parents experience not only mood changes that motivate their surface behavior but also shifts in their intrapsychic systems that arouse latent conflicts and thereby are conducive to various kinds of pathologic states. The psychoeconomic balance depends on the outcome of tensions arising from conflicts between the parents' internalized developmental experiences and their current responses to the needs and behavior of the child. This double origin of the psychology of parental behavior is universal and holds true for all the adaptations that parents have to make, concomitant with the growing autonomy of their developing children.

A panel on parenthood held by the American Psychoanalytic Association in 1974 cautioned against overgeneralization (Parens, 1975). Parens, in summary, noted that any consideration of parenthood as a phase of development would have to answer the question: To what epigenetic process or line of development does it pertain? This question draws attention to a lack of clarity in the widely used and accepted formula for the epigenetic development of the total personality. Perhaps, argued Parens, the lack of clarity results from excessive reliance on the psychosexual model for formulations of personality development. It would seem that the proper epigenetic sequence of psychosexual development phases might conclude with parenthood rather than adulthood. Although the psychosexual line of development makes a large contribution toward total personality development, he concluded, it may be fruitful to distinguish the psychosexual development line from that of total personality development and specifically from the line of development pertaining to the concept of self.

The Middle Years

Few psychoanalytic studies have been devoted to the middle years of life as such. Psychoanalytic understanding of this phase would be the same as general understanding of the adult.

A panel discussion of the American Psychoanalytic Association in 1972 devoted the most extensive attention to this phase that is to be found in the literature. An interesting innovation of this panel was the comprehensive material produced by Bernice Neugarten (professor of human development at the University of Chicago) on normal development in the middle years, another instance of the increasing cooperation between psychoanalysis and related disciplines. The panel's entire presentation centered around how the experience of separation and individuation, now seen as so crucial throughout the life cycle, operates in middle age. One panelist offered the opinion that social and political freedom was dependent on the "biological urge" toward separation-individuation that is rooted in sound object relationships and love. In our culture, such freedom offers opportunities for the expansion of abilities, the pursuit of interests, and the realization of pleasure.

Old Age

With the increase of longevity that has marked the present century, quite a few psychoanalysts have offered psychodynamic views on old age. Robert Butler (1967) has explored the psychology of experiencing the process of aging, of approaching death, of dying, and of the concomitant personal and social experiences of the last chapter of life. He puts all these together in what he calls the "life review." The life review is visualized as a normative, universal process triggered by the sense of approaching death, precipitated and reinforced by current isolating experiences, and leading to various observable effects—creative, adaptive, pathological, or a combination of these. The life review is seen as an intervening process between the sense of impending death and personality change and as a preparation for dying; the nature of its inception, course, and outcome is affected primarily by the lifelong unfolding of character.

There is abundant evidence that creative potential exists in many older people. In spite of Lehman's (1953) generalization that achievement declines with age, innumerable older people have contributed a great deal to the world's welfare. Butler expresses the hope that the life review will stimulate the uncovering and release of much creative talent.

A number of observations indicate that hopefulness, even in the face of certain death, tends to prolong life, while despair tends to hasten death. Weisman and Kastenbaum[19] studied the social and emotional circumstances surrounding the death of aged persons in an institution. They discovered that frequently an important personal loss had occurred in the weeks preceding a patient's final illness. One example given is that of a fairly hearty man who had anticipated a brief reunion with his children on Thanksgiving Day. When the holiday arrived, no one came. He waited in vain for an explanation. Although he did not complain, he did not resume his customary activities. His chronic respiratory condition worsened and shortly thereafter he died. Even in animal experiments, Curt Richter (1959) has collected experimental evidence that a feeling equivalent to hopelessness may precipitate sudden death in the Norway rat.

There has long been a tendency for overhospitalization of geriatric patients in the United States. A study by Haas (1963) reported that the aged population in mental hospitals in the United States was 32 percent, as compared with 10–13 percent in England, Scandinavia, and Switzerland, even though these European countries have 25 percent more aged in the total population than does the United States. One of many reasons given is that the American youth-oriented culture increases the sense of inadequacy and lowers the self-esteem of the older person. With the current trend toward dehospitalization, this percentage may be decreasing.

Eissler (1955) devoted a book to the topic of the psychiatrist and the dying patient; his main recommendation was that the patient should not be told the true facts. Weisman (1972) has outlined the dynamics of the final stage most clearly. He distinguishes three phases of personal response to the course of fatal illness: (1) primary recognition, (2) acceptance of established disease, and (3) final decline. Each stage presents differing degrees of denial and acceptance. Stage 1 shows denial and postponement. Stage 2 is typified by mitigation and displacement of concerns about death. Stage 3 presents problems of counter-control and cessation. Thus the dynamics of the final illness begin with denial, and then move on to the vicissitudes of how such denial is handled further.

It is quite clear that a more realistic attitude toward death, an awareness of the potential assets of the older person, a recognition of the ways in which his life style can be maintained, as well as improvements in medical care, can all contribute to make the last part of life a much more meaningful and significant experience than it has been for many in the past. Therapeutic work with older people indicates that they suffer from the same kinds of emotional problems that younger people do. Fear of death actually seems to be secondary to the more usual conflicts about being unloved or forced into a humiliating, needlessly dependent position. An attitude of hopefulness seems to be the major single quality that keeps people alive longer and makes them more productive. Thus this position stressing the central importance of hope runs as a unifying thread throughout all of contemporary psychoanalytic theory.

Concluding Remarks

The scheme of psychosexual development introduced by Freud in the *Three Essays* in 1905, though revolutionary for its time, has remained essentially unchanged. It has been absorbed as an essential part of psychology, psychiatry, and all the social sciences. Furthermore, Freud's basic correlation of growth and development with healthy personality structure, and regression-fixation with pathology, remains the cornerstone of all contemporary approaches to psychopathology.

The changes that have occurred have been additions to Freud's scheme rather than alterations in it. These additions involve primarily ego-psychological and interpersonal developments. Technically, the most extensive changes are to be found in the conceptualizations of the oral stage and the first three years of life, though enlargements and corrections are to be found all along the line.

Chronologically, three main periods may be distinguished:

1. The elaboration of drive theory, from 1905 to 1923, by which time it was virtually complete. It was given its most rounded form by Abraham in his 1924 essay, "A Short Study of the Development of the Libido."

2. The uncovering of a variety of ego mechanisms, from 1923 to 1960, which explain how the drives are molded into the personality structure. In these studies there is still little regard paid to external reality factors.

3. The more extensive study of interpersonal, familial, and cultural determinants of the life cycle, from 1960 to the present time. These studies are continuing and form the focus of virtually all contemporary work, which thus takes the earlier material on drive development and ego structure more or less for granted. Unfortunately, political and personal controversies obscure the essential unification that has already taken place. It may be anticipated that this unification will increase as time goes on.

Chapter Eight
Instinct Theory

Unlike the theory of development, Freud's conceptualization of instincts changed continuously throughout his life. It was characteristic of him that once he had expressed some point of view about instincts he would become thoroughly dissatisfied with it, soon offering some alteration. We have already seen, for example, how his theory of sexuality changed from a direct reference to genital sexuality in the 1890s to psychosexuality in the early 1900s, to the pleasure principle in the next decade, and then to aggression in the 1920s.

Here again a distinction must be drawn between the clinical and the metapsychological aspects of psychoanalysis. The clinical theory of instincts contained in the *Three Essays* in 1905 proved to be of enduring value and, as mentioned, has been incorporated into all theory. The metapsychological theory attached to the clinical observations has proved to be much less clear, much more subject to change, and much less valuable, to the point where many thinkers have urged that the metapsychological aspect be discarded entirely.

Careful scholars have always been critical of the metapsychological instinct theory. Jones relates that the 1914 paper on narcissism, which offered a radical revision of instinct theory (it is from this paper that the term "libido theory" derives), was "disturbing" and "gave a disagreeable jolt to the theory of instincts on which psychoanalysis had hitherto worked."[1]

A generation later Fenichel wrote that "at first glance one finds many contradictory presentations of the essence of the instincts both in Freud's writings and in psychoanalytic literature in general."[2] Fenichel goes on to offer a detailed criticism of Freud's views and also comes out with a theory of his own, placing everything within the pleasure principle and totally denying any validity to the concept of the death instinct.

In another generation, Max Schur (1966), attempting to straighten out the unpleasure principle, wrote that "Freud's attempts at a *general* conceptualization of the id remained somewhat vague. All of them pose many questions and leave the door open to much speculation."[3]

Jones, Fenichel, and Schur are assuredly among the keenest and staunchest supporters of Freud. If they found his instinct theory unclear, vague, or confusing, there could be only one reason: Freud's instinct theory has all of those qualities. He said so himself many times. The theory of instincts has given rise to the most acrimonious debates in the literature of psychoanalysis. The root of this acrimony is now crystal clear: the opponents have not known what they were attacking, and the defenders have been confused about what they were defending.

There are two reasons for this confusion in Freud. The first is that in the early period, after producing a brilliant clinical exposition of sexuality (1905), he tried to graft an impossible metapsychology onto it (the libido theory of 1914). The second is his assumption of a death instinct.

Fletcher (1966) has shown that in the early period Freud was, with one exception, in general accord with the instinct theorists of his day. William McDougall, the leading instinct theorist of that time, had offered the following definition in 1908:

[An instinct is] an inherited or innate psychophysical disposition which determines its possessor to perceive, and to pay attention to, objects of a certain class, to experience an emotional excitement of a particular quality upon perceiving such an object, and to act in regard to it in a particular manner, or, at least, to experience an impulse to such action.[4]

With this definition Freud would have been in agreement, with the one great exception: at that time he had reduced all instincts to sexuality, had traced the development of the aim and object in the growth of sexuality toward puberty, and had described the many psychological devices used to ward off the dangers of sexuality. Hence Freud's real contribution lay not in instinct theory but in his elucidation of sexuality; his instinct theory was, as a theory, no different from that of McDougall or any of the other early theorists.

The second change in Freud has been vastly more disturbing than the first. The theory of a death instinct is so absurd that had it not come from Freud it would have been consigned to limbo forthwith. Instead analysts puzzled dutifully over what Freud could have meant (and still puzzle over it), reluctant to admit the obvious—that Freud was mixed up. Jones does admit this and adduces a number of psychological reasons which could have led to the theory.[5] What came out in a positive sense was the shift to the study of the aggressive drive, which had been relatively neglected in the earlier period. However, because of this background, the theory of aggression has never been adequately clarified.

Before we turn to the specific psychoanalytic literature since Freud, it is important to review the relevant changes that have occurred in related fields that bear on the topic of instinct. These fields are evolutionary biology, ethology, endocrinology, medicine (psychosomatics), psychology (sensory deprivation), and anthropology (the experiments of nature).

EVOLUTIONARY BIOLOGY. The concept of evolution current in Freud's early days has been enormously modified. Mayr (1970) characterizes the shift to the modern synthesis as involving the replacement of typological thinking by population thinking—"perhaps the greatest conceptual revolution that has taken place in biology."[6] Natural selection is no longer regarded as an all-or-none process but rather as a purely statistical concept. The environment is restored to its place as one of the most important evolutionary factors, but in a drastically different role than it held in the various Lamarckian theories. The new role of the environment is to serve as principal agent of natural selection. Freud had clung tenaciously to Lamarckian theory to the very end.

There still exists wide controversy over the concept of adaptation (Stern, 1970). In genetics, the emphasis is on diversity of individuals in genetic endowment but equality of persons in terms of their inherent value (Dobzhansky, 1973). Genetic endowment is not absolutely preformed but is conditioned by the environment in which it unfolds.[7] In addition, the outstanding feature of mankind is our psychology. Dobzhansky writes that "although most species are unique, the human species is the most unique of all. Furthermore, its most outstanding unique properties are predominantly not in the morphological or physiological, but in the psychological realm."[8]

Had Freud realized that the evolutionary uniqueness of mankind lay in our psychology, he certainly would not have built up the kind of metapsychology that he did, and instead would have rested content with his own extraordinary psychological discoveries. Standard biology has lost interest in the question of instincts, instead concerning itself with the vicissitudes of genetic variation (Mayr, 1970).

ETHOLOGY. The work of Konrad Lorenz, Nikolaas Tinbergen, William Thorpe, and other ethologists, which began to be published in the 1950s, made a profound impression on psychoanalysts. The animals, in the contexts described, seemed much more human than in the traditional behavioristic experimentation of Americans, or the Pavlovian conditioning. Animal behavior confirmed the existence of elaborate innate instinctual drives, in many ways parallel to what was assumed in humans. In 1959, the centenary year of Darwin's *Origin of Species,* a symposium on psychoanalysis and ethology was held at the congress of the International Psychoanalytic Association in Copenhagen; that same year another symposium on the topic was held by the American Psychoanalytic Association.

Ostow (1960) saw ethology as valuable for psychoanalysis in four ways: it confirms the biological soundness of Freud's original assumption that motivation is internal and that the motivational impulse is displaceable; it demonstrates the primitive, archaic nature of some forms of human behavior; it demonstrates animal behavior corresponding to psychoanalytically inferred unconscious impulses in humans; it dissects out of total behavior discrete performances as integral components of instinctive mechanisms.

Kaufman (1960), an analyst who spent a year as an ethologist, stressed two conclusions stemming from animal studies: purposive psychic drives (expressed by wishes) in which goals are causes, regardless of their topographic location in the mind, represent an emergent function of the psychic apparatus which develops partly by learning during maturation of that apparatus; we need no longer postulate that the full panorama of sexuality as we know it in people is derived from an inborn biological urge or force pressing inexorably for discharge. Rather we may view the manifestations of sexuality in terms of an ontogenetic development of inborn sensorimotor patterns, achieving a maturational, hierarchical, unitary structure by progressive synthesis of components through a series of transactional experiences, in the course of which the goals and thereby the drive are acquired. The basis of the continuity and ultimate unity of libidinal drive must be sought not in some mysterious *élan vital* but rather in some characteristic physiological mechanism underlying sexual excitation.

ENDOCRINOLOGY. The hormonal basis of sexual behavior, unknown in Freud's day, has since received considerable clarification. In addition, the "stress" hormones (Mason, 1968; Selye, 1956) and reactions have become much better understood, though much remains to be learned. Certain aspects of sexuality are hormonally controlled; others are not. One discovery of great significance is that while sexuality is under hormonal control, hostility is not.

MEDICINE: PSYCHOSOMATIC FACTORS. Although much had come out before, the first large-scale investigation of psychosomatic correlations was done by Alexander and his group at the Chicago Institute for Psychoanalysis in the 1930s and 1940s, when the publications began to appear. A large number of illnesses were classed as psychosomatic; in many others, even though the organic basis was clear, psychological factors were shown to be operative. The field is now too huge to be summed up in any formula; actually it embraces all of medicine. The true outgrowth of instinct theory lies in psychosomatic medicine, i.e., the careful study of the ways in which the instinctual drives, deprived of their natural sources of gratification, affect the functioning of the body. It is noteworthy that the effect of the mind on the body has turned out to be more consistent than the effect of the body on the mind.

PSYCHOLOGY. The extreme behaviorist position that prevailed in the United States since the 1920s often led to the position that "there are no instincts." It was assumed that any person could learn anything, until experiments ran up against species-specific blocks (Breland and Breland, 1961). More recently, both nature and nurture have been recognized as factors in behavior, leaving it to empirical research to decide what role each plays in any specific pattern. The notion that learning is fundamental to human existence has attenuated the force of the early instinct theory.

Another significant development in psychology has been the discovery of *sensory deprivation*. Whereas Freud had assumed, in accordance with the neurology of his day, that the nervous system was designed to get rid of stimuli, the modern position is that the nervous system also serves the function of handling all kinds of stimuli, and that stimulation is essential to proper growth and performance. This, too, leads to a greater stress on learning and a lesser one on instinct.

ANTHROPOLOGY. The widespread study of other cultures since the 1920s has provided the "experiments of nature" with which to test the various theories of what is innate in human behavior and what is acquired. The general finding has been that sexuality and hostility are present in all cultures, but that they can be molded in many different ways by the environment.

Developments within Psychoanalysis

Because of the rapidity and striking character of developments outside the strictly clinical field of psychoanalysis, Freud's concern with the metapsychology of the instincts has not been pushed any further. His critics have castigated him as excessively biological; his followers and supporters have in the main refrained from further speculation along the lines that he initiated, instead contenting themselves with accumulating clinical data. As a result the field has remained disunited, with almost as many instinct theories extant as there have been analysts writing on the subject. Within the range of clinical observation, however, numerous valuable additions to the traditional theory have been made.

The "Culturalists" versus the "Freudians"

Beginning in the 1930s, especially with the publication of Karen Horney's book *New Ways in Psychoanalysis* (1939) and the split in the New York Psychoanalytic Institute, much ink has been spilled in the battle between culturalists and Freudians. The argument relates specifically to instinct theory; the culturalists have claimed that the Freudians have overestimated the biological factor, while the Freudians have replied that the culturalists overstress the cultural.

Inasmuch as both sides admit the existence of heredity and environment, on paper at least the question becomes one of emphasis. A reading of the literature makes it difficult to see in retrospect what all the furor has been about. For example, Kardiner, a leader of the culturalist school, wrote in 1939: "The study of psychology must begin

with the biological characteristics of man. These biological characteristics delimit the field in which psychological processes take place."[9]
In a footnote to his *Autobiography* in 1935 Freud wrote: "The period
of latency is a physiological phenomenon. It can, however, only give
rise to a complete interruption of sexual life in cultural organizations
which have made the suppression of infantile sexuality a part of their
system. This is not the case with the majority of primitive peoples."[10] It becomes clear that the two men are actually saying pretty
much the same thing.

However, it is a historical fact that the two positions repeatedly
clashed throughout the years. Perhaps the last open discussion between the two points of view took place at a panel of the American
Psychoanalytic Association in 1954, in which the participants were
Frieda Fromm-Reichmann and Franz Alexander for the culturalists,
and Leo Rangell, Edward Bibring, and Merton Gill for the Freudians.
Fromm-Reichmann stressed that both groups had shifted the center of
their therapeutic interest from the investigation of the content of the
id to the investigation of the dynamics and functioning of the ego.
Nevertheless, she insisted that classical psychoanalysts saw personality as the outcome of the vicissitudes of the psychosexual energies,
while the dynamic psychiatrists saw personality as the outcome of
early interpersonal relationships; this misconception seriously de-
tracted from the value of her arguments.

As described in chapter 5, the lines continued to harden until the
culturalists formed a society of their own, The American Academy of
Psychoanalysis. Thereafter it became a shibboleth of this group to
castigate the Freudians for being too biological, whereas the true
forces that form personality are cultural. This position totally ignores
both the early Freud and the great changes that have occurred in psychoanalytic theory, including ego psychology and the study of interpersonal relations. Thus instinct theory became a political football
rather than a serious subject for study.

Conversely, the classical analysts, in a natural reaction to bolster
their own position, have tended to underplay the role of culture in the
formation of personality and neurosis. As time has gone on, the battle
has become less important to both sides. At present there seems to be
an inevitable rapprochement of the two points of view, with the culturalists stressing sexuality and the Freudians stressing object relationships. Only the elaboration of a total psychological science can

undo the confusion and the needless wrangling that has taken place. At the same time, for the acceptance or rejection of any particular position, evidence of an objective kind must be presented, and not the arbitrary pronouncements of authorities.

The Shift to Ego Psychology

I have already noted that since 1923 all of psychoanalysis has been ego psychology. The shift from the id to the ego has not been accomplished, however, at one stroke. What is seen historically is an increasing emphasis on the ego and a decreasing stress on the id, together with the growing conviction that id manifestations as seen in the clinical picture have a defensive quality rather than an instinctual one, so that the pure id becomes as much an inference as the ego was at one time.

It should not be thought that this shift to the ego and away from the id has met with unanimous approval among analysts. The French analyst Laplanche wrote in 1974, for example:

the evident role of "sexuality in the etiology of neurosis"—the foundation of Freud's discoveries—is disputed in favor of a secondary, artificial, defensive sexualization of conflicts. These conflicts are related to the *survival* of the individual rather than to his *desire. I would like to state my distrust of the desexualization of psychoanalysis, which can be clearly seen in much of the modern theorizing* (italics added).[11]

As a result of this desexualization, which Laplanche and others deplore, another split, less publicized and less obvious on the surface, has taken place in the theoretical positions of analysts. It is between those who talk almost exclusively of the ego, and those who stress the transformations of the id. The nature and extent of this split will become clear in what follows.

Clinical versus Metapsychological Theories

If Freud's metapsychological instinct theory has not found universal acceptance but stiff resistance, this is scarcely surprising, since his whole concept of metapsychology has been under such severe attack (Klein, 1976). I have stressed here that Freud's clinical theories, not his metapsychology, provide the basis for his greatness. Nor has any subsequent metapsychology found much favor with the analytic community. Increasingly, material from other disciplines has had to be incorporated into psychoanalytic theory to make sense of the clinical observations which, however, still remain unique to psychoanalysis. As indicated, in instinct theory new information from many different fields has to be considered. Accordingly, the remainder of this chapter is organized around the subsequent development of clinical material relating to the primary instinctual drives.

Sexuality

If the whole body of Freud's writings is examined critically, his ambivalence about instinct and defense is striking. The first formula, that the *neurosis is a defense against unbearable ideas* (1894), was followed by a concentration on the unbearable ideas. At first these were seen as sexual in the direct sense, then as psychosexual, which gave the direct genital wishes a more defensive character. Once hostility was introduced in 1920 as a basic instinct, the instinctual nature of sexuality became even more obscure. On the one hand Freud could write a paper like the one on "anatomy is destiny" (1925), in which the stress is strongly on biology, and the famous letter to an American mother, in which he consoled her for the homosexuality of her son by pointing out that it was a fixation in development, not a sign of moral degeneracy: "We consider it to be a variation of the sexual function produced by a certain arrest of sexual development."[12] On the other hand he could write a book like *The Problem of Anxiety* (1926), in which virtually everything was seen as related to defensive processes and his old conception of actual neurosis was abandoned for the first time.

What has since come to be known as the analytic theory of sexual maturity was formulated most clearly by Wilhelm Reich in *The Function of the Orgasm* (1927). It was here that Reich made explicit the implicit psychoanalytic position that orgasm, including vaginal orgasm, was essential to full maturity, and that failure to achieve it was a sign of neurosis. Reich's description of the process is in all essential respects the same as that given 40 years later by Masters and Johnson (1966), who do not seem to be aware of his existence and writing.

Freud was rather dubious about Reich's theory of genitality, even though it was fully in accord with his own thinking at that time. In 1928 he wrote to Lou Andreas-Salomé: "We have here a Dr. Reich, a worthy but impetuous young man, passionately devoted to his hobby-horse, who now salutes in the genital orgasm the antidote to every neurosis. Perhaps he might learn from your analysis of K. to feel some respect for the complicated nature of the psyche."[13]

Defensive Instinctual Gratification

The first problem that arose in connection with the theory of sexuality was the appearance of the impulsive character—the person who tried to gratify every impulse that came along. Was this behavior instinctual, or was it defensive? On the one hand the person was apparently gratifying his instincts, yet on the other hand he was also obviously disturbed. A way out of this paradox was found in the concept of the "corruptible superego" (Alexander, 1927). It was hypothesized that the impulsive character, who often tried to justify his actions by reference to psychoanalytic theory, was alternating the gratification of his impulses with depressive episodes, which served as a sop to the superego: crime and punishment, or psychologically, mania and depression, or a manic-depressive cycle found to some extent in everybody.

Analysts became increasingly dubious of the amount of gratification the impulsive character did get from his acting out (a term entering into common usage in the 1950s). In an important paper Leo Spiegel (1954) moved to the next stage, in which the instinctual gratification came to be seen as purely defensive, and not gratification at all.

Spiegel argued that defensive instinctual gratification which aims at preserving the patient's narcissism at all costs can do so only by the toleration of a serious breach with inner and outer reality. The connection of painful affects with the Oedipus complex is lost through acting them out in the environment, and the need for the renunciation of Oedipal objects is thus completely obscured. The reduction of narcissism involved in the resolution of the Oedipus complex (which increases the adaptation to reality) is avoided; instead a rationalized reality ("private psychosis") is imposed on external reality. Reality testing remains quite defective, especially in sectors relating to the partial drives such as voyeurism and masochism, external reality being merely a setting for their gratification. He concluded that patients who employ instinctual gratification as a defense, although they do not belong to any specific diagnostic group, must necessarily approach borderline conditions.

Spiegel's paper raises several questions that have been slighted in the analytic literature. First of all, what determines the strength of a drive? For a long time Freud assumed it was the drive's instinctual character; as the same time he stressed the unconscious factor, as in compulsion neurosis. Over time, instinct has tended to recede into the background, while the unconscious has moved more and more into the foreground. Thus the strength of a drive has come to be connected primarily with its unconscious roots.

This leads to the second question, What then becomes of the instinctual drives, in this case, sexuality? Is all sexuality to be considered defensive? That would obviously be absurd, yet it is a position that some analysts seem to take, under the impact of the significance of the defensive process. For example, Kohut, in his recent book on *The Restoration of the Self* (1977), makes the remarkable statement that "drive experiences occur as disintegration products when the self is unsupported."[14] Others take a different approach. Since the appearance of the Masters–Johnson material, the topic has been considered in a number of different publications, which are reviewed next.

Female Sexuality

It is noteworthy that almost all the discussion of sexuality in the analytic literature centers around women, and in particular their capacity to have vaginal orgasms, and the relationship of these orgasms to psychological maturity. Reich did differentiate in men between orgastic and ejaculatory potency, but the differentiation had little impact.

Initially the question of vaginal orgasm was put primarily by adherents of the culturalist school. Karen Horney (1939) had criticized Freud's emphasis on penis envy, arguing that it was a cultural phenomenon. Others (e.g., Thompson, 1941) likewise had insisted that the role of women is primarily determined by the culture, a point which can scarcely be argued (see Schafer, 1974; Fliegel, 1973). Nevertheless, whether produced by the culture or by biologically based neurosis, female frigidity was a real problem, culturally as well as clinically. The prevailing opinion until about 1960 remained that a woman could reach vaginal orgasm in intercourse and that her orgasm was a mark of her psychological (genital) maturity. Helene Deutsch (1945) was particularly eloquent in arguing this position.

Helene Deutsch's Revised Position

In 1960, at a panel on frigidity in women held by the American Psychoanalytic Association, Helene Deutsch (1961) set forth an extensive revision of her former position. Clinical experience had shown her that many healthy, relatively normal women did not achieve vaginal orgasm, even with analysis, while many psychotic and aggressive, masculine women did experience intense vaginal orgasm.

Accordingly she had come to question whether the vagina was really created by nature for sexual function. She had come back to the conviction that the female sexual apparatus consists of two parts with a definite division of function. The clitoris is the sexual organ and the vagina primarily the organ of reproduction. The central role of the clitoris is not merely the result of masturbation but serves a biological destiny. Into it flow waves of sexual excitement that may be more or less successfully communicated to the vagina. The transition of sexual feeling from the clitoris to the vagina is a task performed largely by the active intervention of the penis. The muscular apparatus of the vagina is primarily in the service of reproduction and may or may not become involved in orgastic activity. Deutsch still subscribed to Freud's view that although frigidity is sometimes psychogenic, in other cases it is constitutionally conditioned or even partly caused by anatomical and physiological factors.

The typical function of the vagina during intercourse is passive-receptive. Its movements have the character of sucking in and relaxing, with a rhythm adjusted to that of the male partner. In the vast majority of women, if they are not emotionally disturbed, the sexual act does not culminate in a sphincterlike activity of the vagina, but is brought to a happy end in a mild, slow relaxation with simultaneous lubrication and complete gratification. Although she did not question the existence of orgastic vaginal experience in many women, she now assumed that the form here described is the typical and most feminine one.

Psychological factors, she held, accompany both spheres of vital activity, the sexual and the reproductive. Both processes share not only the apparatus but also the emotional cathexis, a duality of function which she thought bears the greatest responsibility for female frigidity. While the clitoris is the executive of castration fear, the vagina is the bearer of the deepest anxiety, of death, which is mobilized in pregnancy and accompanies all acts of motherhood.

If the more passive-receptive way of gratification for women is accepted as normal, then, she felt, frigidity is not so common as is assumed by analysts, nor is it on the increase. What have increased are demands for a form of sexual gratification not fully in harmony with the constitutional destiny of the vagina.

Taken literally, Deutsch's revised views involved a complete about-face from the traditional analytic position on vaginal orgasm. She seemed to agree with writers like Albert Ellis ("the vaginal orgasm is a myth," 1953)[15] and Kinsey ("the vaginal orgasm is a biological impossibility," 1953).[16] While other speakers on the panel, such as Benedek, agreed with her, the full implications of this reversal for psychoanalytic theory were not drawn.

Mary Sherfey and the Masters–Johnson Study

More startling to the general public was the book by Masters and Johnson, on *Human Sexual Response* (1966), reporting on their long-term study in St. Louis. Various summaries of their work had trickled through before the book was finally published. It was brought to the attention of the psychoanalytic community quite forcefully by publication of a very long article by Mary Sherfey in the *Journal of the American Psychoanalytic Association* in 1966; Sherfey's paper was later republished in book form (1972). For the historian of psychoanalysis, it is relevant to note that most of the essentials of the Masters–Johnson findings were contained in Wilhelm Reich's book, *The Function of the Orgasm* (1927), that the date of Reich's book is incorrectly given by Masters and Johnson as 1942, and that Sherfey's bibliography does not mention Reich's work.

The major point stressed by most writers is Masters and Johnson's contention that there is no difference between a clitoral and a vaginal orgasm; the nature of the orgasm is the same regardless of the erotogenic zone stimulated to produce it. Sherfey made the following further points:

1. The erotogenic potential of the clitoral glans is probably greater than that of the lower third of the vagina.

2. Under optimal arousal conditions, women's orgasmic potential may be similar to that of primates. In both, orgasms are best acheived with the high degree of pelvic vasocongestion and edema associated with estrus in the primates and the luteal phase of the menstrual cycle in women or with prolonged, effective stimulation. Under these conditions each orgasm tends to increase pelvic vasocongestion; thus the more orgasms achieved, the more that can be achieved. Orgasmic experiences may continue until physical exhaustion intervenes.

3. In these primates and in women an inordinate cyclic sexual capacity has thus evolved, leading to the paradoxical state of sexual insatiability in the presence of the utmost sexual satiation.

4. The rise of modern civilization, while resulting from many causes, was contingent on the suppression of the inordinate cyclic sexual drive of women.

Sherfey did not feel that her data required extensive emendations of psychoanalytic theory. Innate bisexuality, the rigid dichotomy between masculine and feminine sexual behavior, and derivative concepts of the clitoral-vaginal transfer theory will have to go, but otherwise, she wrote, "It is my strong conviction that these fundamental biological findings will, in fact, strengthen psychoanalytic theory and practice in the area of female sexuality." [17]

Several years later the *Journal of the American Psychoanalytic Association* devoted an entire issue to discussions of Sherfey's paper (July, 1968). In general the contributors felt that there was no essential incompatibility with psychoanalytic theory, that the Masters–Johnson data supplement rather than refute the psychoanalytic position. This hardly seems accurate since, as subsequent papers show, the older theory of genital primacy has had to be abandoned.

Moore[18] stressed the fundamental significance of the psychic factor, saying that psychic rather than physical satisfaction seems to determine the preference of most women for vaginally induced orgasm, despite the fact that clitorally induced orgasms may be more intense. Then he suggested "that cathexis of coitus and the achievement of intrapsychic change sufficient to improve significantly the object relationship be substituted for preconceptions about the desirable intensity and localization of orgastic experience as the criteria for improvement in cases of frigidity treated by psychoanalysis."[19]

Following the heavy concentration in the few years after Sherfey's paper, only sporadic comments have appeared more recently. These portray a variety of viewpoints, and thus one can no longer maintain that there is a unitary psychoanalytic position on sexuality, except in the general sense that pleasure is good if it does not interfere with healthy ego functioning. Lichtenstein has suggested that sexuality is the earliest and most basic way available in which the growing human personality can experience an affirmation of the reality of its existence.[20]

Ross frankly and pessimistically stated: "As for those mature persons whose sex life is not very satisfactory . . . I do not see what we have yet to offer by way of explanation in psychoanalytic terms at the present time."[21] On the other hand, Sarlin argued that the level of psychosexual development of the mother in every culture determines the characterological patterns of both men and women of the next generation.

In another symposium, Hornick (1975) surprisingly put in a plea for sexual celibacy in the adolescent.[22] Contrariwise in the same symposium Adelson (1975) advocated authentic feminine orgastic response, involving a consideration of the female sexual act and its climax as a totality, as something genuine and nonmanipulative, and as a response within the woman to another person.

Sex Therapy

In the wake of the Masters–Johnson report and their subsequent work *Human Sexual Inadequacy* (1970), with their startling claims of extraordinary cures and improvement in sexual dysfunction, sex clinics came into being all over the country, following the Masters–Johnson model. A seemingly new profession was created, that of the sex therapist, whose therapy is limited to the treatment of sexual dysfunction (as defined by the patient). For the most part these therapists are opposed to psychoanalysis and psychotherapy, but some, like Helen Kaplan (1974), attempt to combine the two.

Officially the attitude of the analytic community toward these sex therapists has been one of silence. Unofficially it has been condemnatory, as it has been toward behavior therapy in general. Psychoanalytic theory would hold that the substitution of physiological manipulation for psychic restructuring is bound to be inadequate in the long run.

Concluding Remarks

One may still ask how the contemporary attitude of psychoanalysis is to be defined after Deutsch's change of view, the Masters–Johnson report, and the rapid growth of nonanalytic sex therapy. In general, a healthy ego structure remains the basic desideratum. Such health includes the mature management of aggression and satisfactory interpersonal (object) relationships. Once that is established, sexual gratification remains a highly desirable goal.

With regard to the question of orgasm, the available data do not really demolish the classical theory, as many have pointed out. The difference between clitoral and vaginal orgasm is a psychological one, not a physical one. Hence the developmental transfer from the clitoris to the vagina involves the psychological maturation of the woman from masturbation to gratification with a man. Paradoxically Masters and Johnson have shown for certain that women can experience vaginal orgasm in intercourse; what is left in doubt is whether this capacity can be equated with psychological maturity (genital primacy). Nor does it detract from the value of the orgasm that the same physiological sensations can be experienced clitorally; the situation in the man is exactly parallel, since the pleasure of ejaculation is the same whether he has intercourse or masturbates. Yet no one would dream of saying that the man should prefer masturbation to intercourse.

In 1898 Freud wrote that it would take our civilization 100 years to come to terms with the claims of our sexuality.[23] The somewhat devious pathways followed by psychoanalytic theory and related disciplines may yet bear out his prediction.

Aggression

The whole question of aggression was left in a highly unsatisfactory state by Freud. Although his first approach to the death instinct in

1920 was highly tentative, and he referred to it as "speculation," eventually he became convinced of its soundness. Yet he fully recognized the gaps in the whole theory. In a letter to Marie Bonaparte in 1937 he wrote: "I will try to answer your question [about aggression]. The whole topic has not yet been treated carefully and what I had to say about it in earlier writings was so premature and casual as hardly to deserve consideration."[24]

The rejection of the death instinct hypothesis was followed by a dual instinct theory (Hartman, 1949), which failed, however, to solve many of the problems involved. In the past few years analysts have repeatedly stressed the tentative character of our knowledge of aggression. In 1973 Arlow wrote: "Even within psychoanalysis, we know much less about the development of aggressive patterns, their influence on ego formation and the evolution of the sense of self than we do about the comparable influences of sexual drives."[25]

In 1971 the meeting of the International Psychoanalytical Association, held appropriately in Vienna, was devoted to the topic of aggression. A number of different viewpoints were expressed, emphasizing the absence of a universally accepted analytic theory of aggression. Some speakers even reverted to the death instinct hypothesis (Garma, 1971). The most reasoned summary of the situation at that time was given by Brenner, who made the following points:[26]

1. Psychological evidence seems to be an acceptable basis for the concept of aggression as an instinctual drive. Supporting evidence from other branches of biology, though it would be welcome, is not essential, nor is it available at present.

2. No source of aggression can be specified, other than a psychological one. Aggression cannot, at present, be related to any physiological phenomenon other than brain functioning.

3. There is no evidence at present to support the view that the aggressive drive is a measure of the demand of bodily processes on mental functioning.

4. Aggression and libido bear similar relations to the pleasure principle. In general, discharge is associated with pleasure; lack of discharge, with unpleasure.

5. The respective roles of the two drives are likewise similar with regard to physical conflict.

6. The aim of aggression is not uniformly the destruction of the

cathected object. On the contrary, the aim is variable and is intimately related to experience and to ego functions.

7. In general, the relationship between ego functions and the
drives is an extremely complex and close one.

8. It seems impossible to decide at present between the theory
of drive fusion and that of drive differentiation.

If the theory of aggression beyond this point is still little explored, many aspects of its functioning are much better understood
today than in Freud's time. It could be said, in fact, that the chief virtue of Freud's shift of instinct theory was to focus on the aggressive
aspects of human behavior, which had previously been largely ignored. Even when Adler had proposed the existence of an aggressive
impulse in 1908,[27] Freud and his other co-workers viewed it as another expression of libido, criticizing Adler for confounding sadism
and aggression. Aggression, they felt, was present in every libidinal
drive. Since Freud was so exclusively focused on sexuality at that
time, he did not appreciate the value of Adler's suggestion. Later he
did incorporate it into his thinking and did direct the attention of the
analytic world to the ubiquitous influences of aggression. Accordingly, the subsequent analytic literature can best be summarized in
terms of the various rubrics under which the investigations have been
concentrated.

Clinical Observations

As late as 1945 Fenichel wrote: "It seems rather as if aggressiveness
were originally no instinctual aim of its own, characterizing one category of instincts in contradistinction to others, but rather a mode in
which instinctual aims sometimes are striven for, in response to frustrations or even spontaneously."[28] In his work Fenichel, like the
early Freud, paid relatively little attention to aggression, hostility,
hatred, or their derivatives. Following World War II, the emphasis
shifted markedly.

Among the earlier writers Melanie Klein (1948a) was the first to
highlight the great significance of hostile fantasies, especially in the
young infant but in the adult neurotic and psychotic as well. She
postulated a much earlier appearance of the superego than had Freud,
and attributed to it very savage characteristics, oral, urethral, and

anal. In her theory of child development she held that anxiety is due more to the operation of aggression than of libido, and that it is primarily against aggression and anxiety that defenses are erected. Among these defenses denial, splitting, projection, and introjection are active before repression is organized. She saw the child, under the spur of anxiety, constantly trying to split its objects and feelings, trying to retain good objects and good feelings, while expelling bad objects and bad feelings. She described a variety of hostile fantasies in the infant which had escaped the notice of other theoreticians and investigators, such as the desire to "scoop out" the mother's body, or of biting, tearing, and destroying the objects inside the mother's body. Her ideas were rejected for a long time as too fanciful, especially in American circles. In more recent years, with careful exploration of the first year of life, it has been recognized that she made many astute observations, and many of her ideas have been incorporated into the thinking of other writers. Although she clung to the theory of the death instinct, her clinical material is highly valuable.

Before World War II, Wilhelm Reich (1933) also placed tremendous emphasis on hostility but only in the analytic situation, viewing every transference as negative. His ideas had considerable influence on technique, but little on theory.

Following World War II the shift in emphasis to aggression and hostility began. Almost every journal brought some article offering a reformulation of traditional material in terms of aggression. For example, in the *International Journal of Psychoanalysis,* in 1948 Sacha Nacht[29] published a paper on "Clinical Manifestations of Aggression and Their Role in Psychoanalytic Treatment," in which he said:

Although for centuries now men have been told to love one another, they usually live in a state of mutual hatred, discord and destruction, enthusiastically following 'anti-', rather than 'pro-' movements, whatever their aim. That this should be so despite society's attempts to subdue aggression is not astonishing when one considers that life itself exacts a hostile reaction right at the very start. . . . Apparently for many, the weight of emphasis in psychoanalytic work has been on the first emotion (love) in its widest sense. . . .

However, it has seemed to me that those whom we are called upon to observe find greater difficulty in mastering the conflicts set up by aggressive tendencies than those of other origins. The condition necessary for lack of sexual satisfaction to have pathological effects seems to me to lie in the degree of aggresssion. . . . Observation of both men and animals . . .

shows clearly enough that the disposition towards aggressive reaction in all
live matter is due to the constant tendency to eliminate that excitement or
tension which would disturb the settled equilibrium of the organism.[30]

Nacht then proceeded to enumerate the standard instances of clinical
difficulties and to explain them in terms of aggression rather than sexuality.

In 1949 Winnicott published a paper on ''Hate in the Countertransference,''[31] in which he expressed the conviction that analysis
of psychotics becomes impossible unless the analyst's own hate is extremely well sorted-out and conscious.

In 1950 Hoffer wrote a paper on ''Oral Aggressiveness and Ego
Development.''[32] His main point was that there is a pain barrier, in
operation from birth, which deflects the destructive instinct from the
baby's own body and self, and which becomes reinforced from the
third month onward by the gradual development of a self that regu-
lates and spreads instinctual tensions, aggressive and erotic alike.
This double protection against self-destructiveness explains the intensity of aggressiveness turned against the outer world and the subsequent increase of narcissistic feelings if this form of mastery is successful.

In 1951 Milton Wexler published a significant paper on ''The
Structural Problem in Schizophrenia.''[33] His main thesis was that
with the schizophrenic patient it is often necessary for the analyst to
be harsh and punitive rather than kind and loving because after a certain point only hostility is acceptable to these patients.

In 1952 Michael Balint[34] published a paper on ''Love and
Hate.'' His main novel thesis was that hate is the last remnant, the
denial of, and the defense against, the primitive object love (or the
dependent archaic love).

In 1953 Angel Garma, an Argentine analyst, published a paper
on ''The Internalized Mother as Harmful Food in Peptic Ulcer Patients.''[35] Garma took issue with Alexander's hypothesis of the longing for mother as the root of peptic ulcer, arguing instead for a theory
of a digestively aggressive internalized mother in an individual with
an oral digestive regression. His emphasis on the terrifying, cruel,
and frustrating internalized mother or maternal breast has been
echoed in the descriptions of many other regressed states.

In 1954 Robert Bak published a paper on ''The Schizophrenic

Defense against Aggression.''[36] He saw the ego's inability to neutralize the aggressive drives as the core of the ego disorder.

Further research led to the general opinion that a surplus of aggression is at the root of all the more serious emotional disturbances, including schizophrenia, addiction, psychosomatic disorders and, lately, even all the classical neuroses. However, analysts have not reached a consensus on a clear theoretical exposition of the nature of aggression.

The Two Theories of Psychoanalysis

There have arisen through the years two theories within psychoanalysis, one stressing sexuality and the other stressing aggression. At the present time competent theoreticians frankly admit that there is no good way of deciding between the rival claims of the two theories. Evidence has to be sought not only from clinical psychoanalysis but also from biology, anthropology, history, ethology, child psychology, psychiatry, and other sciences dealing with mankind. In general two basic explanations of aggression exist: one deriving it from frustration (the so-called frustration-aggression hypothesis), the other seeing it as a biologically given instinct (the dual instinct hypothesis). Purely physiological causes of aggression have also been postulated, as well as simple social learning. Material from the analytic literature on these various theories can be briefly summarized.

The Frustration-Aggression Hypothesis

The frustration-aggression hypothesis was most clearly formulated by Dollard and Miller (1939), in collaboration with a number of other investigators. They made it clear that this hypothesis lies at the root of Freud's earlier (pre-1920) thinking on aggression, and they pulled together a lot of material from his works and many other sources to buttress their hypothesis. Their formulation was that aggression is always a consequence of frustration[37] and that the occurrence of aggressive behavior always presupposes the existence of frustration and, contrariwise, that the existence of frustration always leads to some form of aggression.

One advantage of this theory is that it fits in neatly with the clinical procedures encouraged in psychoanalysis. Thus if a patient produces some anger or other form of aggression, the analyst would routinely look for the source of frustration. A drawback of the theory is the apparent presence of states of rage, especially in early infancy, which seem to have nothing to do with frustration, and the fact that many forms of anger would appear to result from identification with the parents (social learning) rather than frustration as such.

The Dual Instinct Theory

After the collapse of the death instinct theory, a way out of the resultant dilemma was suggested by the hypothesis of dual instincts, sexuality and aggression, without referring the latter to the death instinct at all. This position was put forth most cogently by Hartmann, Kris, and Loewenstein in their paper, "Notes on the Theory of Aggression" (1949). Here they attempted to compare the four characteristics of a drive enumerated by Freud in 1915—impetus, source, aim, and object—with regard to sexuality and aggression. These authors were not particularly successful in their endeavor, partially because Freud's concept of instinct is full of unresolvable contradictions. Thus with regard to aim they were already in a quandary, stating:

It seems that at the present stage in the development of psychoanalytic hypotheses the question as to the specific aims of the aggressive drive cannot be answered; nor is a definite answer essential. However, it seems possible to distinguish between degrees of discharge of aggressive tension. The aims of aggression could then be classified according to the degree of discharge they allow for and according to the means utilized in discharge.[38]

Nevertheless, the dual instinct theory has been adopted by many writers, most of whom appear to be blissfully unaware of the numerous theoretical problems attached to such a theory. Certainly, as instincts, aggression and sexuality behave in entirely different ways.

Neutralization of Aggression

Perhaps Hartmann's most enduring contribution in this area is his concept of the neutralization of aggression. By neutralization he meant the change of both libidinal and aggressive energy away from the instinctual and toward a noninstinctual mode.[39] The developmental task with aggression is then to neutralize the drive, thereby providing neutralized energy with which the ego can work. Thus neutralization is tied up with the concept of psychic energy.

The most significant application of this doctrine lies in the area of schizophrenia, where Hartmann maintains that there is a failure of neutralization, and in the area of psychosomatic disorders, where there is a rupture of the neutralized barrier (Schur, 1965). Writers employing these concepts now speak of libidinal, aggressive, and neutralized energies (Jacobson, 1964). However, this whole type of metapsychology has been regarded, and justifiably so, as extremely cumbersome by others, and can be replaced by a simpler system (Klein, 1976; Fine, 1975b).

With regard to the dual instinct theory proper, the main criticism leveled at it is that if aggression is an instinct, it is of an entirely different order from sexuality. Thus merely to postulate two instincts, without clarifying what is meant by an aggressive instinct, begs the question. Ultimately the dual instinct theory fails to satisfy the requirements of psychological science because it oversimplifies the situation.

The Somatic Factor

After a certain point it becomes increasingly difficult to separate psychoanalytic material from that contributed by other disciplines. Once more the investigation of hostility (aggression, rage) shows that psychoanalytic thought provides the impetus to far-reaching investigations but that the ultimate conclusions derive from a host of other disciplines, leading to a unified psychological science in which psychoanalysis provides the dynamic basis but not the full-bodied elaboration. One of the most startling findings with regard to hostility is that while extensive research has not been able to show any precise physiological basis for it, what has been demonstrated is that: a large number of persons live in a state of chronic repressed resentment all their lives; this state is accompanied by rage, anxiety, depression, and all the other "negative" emotions (Rado, 1969); and, most significant, such a state of inner stress and conflict can and often does lead to a variety of somatic illnesses, including ultimately death.

Walter Cannon, a physiologist, had already shown in the early part of the century that the bodily changes in pain, hunger, fear, and rage were extensive and could be correlated with the normal physiological responses to danger experienced by animals, as Darwin had hypothesized (Cannon, 1929). Following Cannon, the term "fight–flight syndrome" became popular, since the affects of fear and rage produce very similar bodily reactions and always seem to accompany one another. At that time Freud still limited his instinct theory to sexuality, still held the now-outdated theory of actual neurosis, and was still ignoring the numerous bodily consequences of internal conflict. What psychoanalysts from the 1920s onward contributed to the understanding of the psychosomatic equation was the recognition that conflict is much more widespread than had been thought, that it always involves hostility and anxiety (which are dynamically often interchangeable with one another), and that unconscious hostility, anxiety, and their concomitant emotional results are in the long run far more important that the conscious ones to which Cannon had limited himself.

In the 1920s and 1930s the confluence of these two approaches, the psychoanalytic and the physiological, produced a host of valuable clinical and theoretical papers. It is noteworthy that as long as Freud was focused on sexuality, the somatic manifestations investigated were limited to hysterical conversion reactions, which are comparatively less important in the total psychosomatic framework. Only when the focus shifted to hostility could the deeper psychosomatic consequences be brought to the fore.

The first compendium of research on psychosomatic relationships was by Flanders Dunbar, *Emotions and Bodily Changes,* (1935). In that period Alexander and his co-workers at the Chicago Institute of Psychoanalysis were undertaking their detailed psychoanalytic and psychophysiological investigations into seven psychosomatic illnesses: peptic ulcers, bronchial asthma, rheumatoid arthritis, ulcerative colitis, essential hypertension, neurodermatitis and thyrotoxicosis (Alexander, 1950).

Reiser (1975) divides the history of psychosomatic research into two major periods: 1940 to 1960, and 1960 to the present. In the earlier period, meticulous and detailed joint clinical studies by internists and psychiatrists (e.g., Engel, 1955; Mirsky, 1950; Lidz, 1950; Sperling, 1946; Weiss, 1957; Wolff, 1947) demonstrated beyond a doubt that many medical diseases first became clinically manifest during periods of psychosocial crisis and that the course of disease could be profoundly influenced by psychological factors. It then became common to state that 70–80 percent of the practice of the average physician was concerned with psychogenic illnesses.

The central theoretical issue of that period was specificity. Do specific psychological factors constitute necessary and/or sufficient factors in determining the patient's choice of organ system and disease? The major theoreticians of that day—Dunbar, Wolff, and Alexander—all agreed that some correlation could be found between personality type and illness. Alexander was most precise. He drew a fundamental distinction between conversion hysteria and "visceral neurosis" (now more commonly referred to as psychosomatic illness) in 1939 (Alexander, 1950). He hypothesized that whereas in conversion hysteria the symptom formation acts to resolve unconscious conflict, in the visceral neuroses the basic conflict remains unresolved; he postulated that the chronic affect associated with unresolved conflict, even though repressed or suppressed, would nonetheless be accompanied by its appropriate physiological concomitants. The physiological changes accompanying the chronic emotions associated with unresolved conflict were the physiological changes that would give rise, first, to altered function in a particular organ system and, if long enough sustained, to alterations in structure and to disease. Thus for each of the seven diseases that he and his group studied, a formulation of specific conflict was derived from the clinical data produced in the course of psychoanalytic treatment or investigation.

Alexander agreed that the significant psychological influences, such as anxiety, repressed hostile and sexual impulses, frustrated or dependent cravings, inferiority and guilt feelings, are present in all psychosomatic disorders. Nevertheless, he said, "It is not the presence of any one or more of these psychological factors that is specific but the presence of the dynamic configuration in which they appear."[40] For instance, in peptic ulcers he stressed the frustration of dependent desires originally oral in character, frequently overcompensated by increased activity and ambition. In ulcerative colitis he noted particularly the frustrated tendency to carry out an obligation, and a frustrated ambition to accomplish something which requires the concentrated expenditure of energy.[41] In allergy he saw the nuclear psychodynamic factor as an excessive unresolved dependency on the mother.[42] In essential hypertension he emphasized chronic inhibited aggressive impulses which are always associated with anxiety.[43] In thyrotoxicosis he found a threat to security in early infancy or child-hood, frequently related to pronounced fears of death, to which most of the patients had been exposed early in their lives.[44]

Investigations after Alexander's work have generally found that he had too narrow a focus (Reiser, 1975). Even the distinction of psychosomatic from other disorders is rapidly losing its meaning and utility, since there has developed an appreciation that understanding states of health and disease requires a much fuller understanding of biological, psychological, and social parameters. Thus the literature, especially in the past 10 years, has placed great stress on object loss; it has been shown that bereavement, object loss, and the associated reactive affective states may have profound reverberations in the physical sphere, even affecting the capacity to sustain life itself. States of "helplessness" and "hopelessness" together with the con-comitant wish to give up are particularly dangerous to the individual. In this connection Selye's work on the endocrinology and biology of stress in animals, and his demonstration of the GAS (general adapta-tion syndrome) as the base of many diseases, is particularly relevant (Selye, 1956). Engel (1967) has postulated a fundamental biological stress or danger response of "conservation withdrawal" in addition to the more familiar fight–flight syndrome.

All of this somatic material renders much of the psychoanalytic controversy about hostility (see Fromm, 1973) trivial or irrelevant. What counts is not so much where hostility comes from as what it does to the individual once it appears. The fuller implications of this finding for instinct theory are drawn below.

Aggression and Sexuality

The dual instinct theory again brings to the fore the question of the relationship of the two classes of instinct. Here Freud's second theory, of the death instinct, was accompanied by a supplementary theory of the fusion and defusion of instinct. He argued[45] that the erotic instincts and the death instincts would be present in living beings in regular mixtures or fusions, but "defusions" would also be liable to occur. Later this theory was extended in a pseudobiological manner. He wrote:

On this view, a special physiological process (of anabolism or catabolism) would be associated with each of the two classes of instincts; both kinds of

instinct would be active in every particle of living substance, though in un-
equal proportions, so that some one substance might be the principal representative of Eros.

The hypothesis throws no light whatever upon the manner in which the
two classes of instinct are fused, blended, and alloyed with each other; but
that this takes place regularly and very extensively is an assumption indispensable to our conception.[46]

This position of Freud's, which confuses physiology with psychology and makes assumptions completely at variance with established knowledge, has further confused the theory of aggression.
Some writers, like Melanie Klein, take over Freud's position uncritically; others, like Fenichel and Schur, reject it in its entirety.

Ethological Data

In the ongoing arguments about the instinctual character of aggression, data have been sought from every conceivable source. In the
postwar period one of the most intriguing and useful new fields has
been ethology. Ethologists, operating more in the Darwinian tradition
than American behavioral psychologists, have in general tried to reestablish the existence of instincts, in a manner which seems very close
to the psychoanalytic position. With regard to aggression, the most
vocal member of the ethological school has been Konrad Lorenz,
who published a book on the topic in 1963. Lorenz's argument
briefly is that there is an instinctual aggression in all animals above a
certain evolutionary level, that this aggression involves an instinctual
system that generates its own sources of aggressive energy independently of external stimulation; this fighting urge builds up until released by an appropriate releasing stimulus. The property of being
self-generating rather than reactive to external conditions accounts for
its danger and its unmodifiability. Aggression serves a number of
positive functions, which have been modified and utilized in the
evolutionary process. Mankind, Lorenz claims, is endowed with the
same fighting instinct as the lower animals, but it is poorly controlled
because we lack inborn inhibitions against severely injuring and crippling our fellow human beings.

Lorenz's rather naive conceptualization of the aggressive instinct
has been challenged by other researchers (Bandura, 1973; Montagu,
1976). In particular it has been argued that the generalization from

animals to humans is unjustifiable. Whatever the situation might be in the animal kingdom, it does not shed much light on the human dilemma.

Hamburg (1973) has made the most sophisticated attempt to combine the findings from animal experimentation and human clinical findings. In "An Evolutionary and Developmental Approach to Human Aggressiveness," he argues that aggressive patterns common to a variety of primate species, such as chimpanzees, gorillas, and baboons, seem to be similar in some respects to those found in man. Present evidence permits at least an approximation of the conditions under which aggressive patterns are likely to occur: [47]

1. In daily dominance transactions.
2. In redirection of aggression downward in the dominance hierarchy.
3. In the protection of infants, most often by females.
4. When sought-after resources, such as food or sexually receptive females, are in short supply.
5. When meeting unfamiliar animals.
6. In defending against predators.
7. In the killing and eating of young animals of other species.
8. When terminating severe disputes among subordinate animals.
9. In the exploration of strange or dangerous areas.
10. When long-term changes in dominance status occur, especially among males.
11. When an animal has a painful injury.
12. When there is a crowding of strangers in the presence of valued resources.

Anthropological Data

In order to understand the problems involved in human aggression, since the 1920s psychoanalysts have also turned to the mounting body of anthropological data, the "experiments of nature." In general, it has been shown that whereas aggression exists in all human societies, its intensity and manifestations vary widely. Montagu (1974) has assembled evidence that many peoples of different kinds are almost completely unaggressive. Fine (1975b) has proposed a division of cultures into love cultures and hate cultures; love cultures are those in which the predominant mode of human interaction is love, while hate cultures are those in which the predominant mode of human interaction is hatred. In this sense Western civilization is and has been for at least 2,500 years a hate culture.

Montagu (1976) has devoted a book to disproving Lorenz's thesis that man is inherently a killer. He shows, on the basis of the available evidence, that no specific human behavior is genetically determined and that aggressive behavior is but one type of human behavior, all of which must be explained by psychological science. Essentially this is the social learning theory of aggression, which rests more on the frustration-aggression view than on anything else (Bandura, 1973).

Physiological Data

It is a basic assumption in all psychological science that a physiological explanation must be ruled out before a psychological one is attempted. In aggression, various physiological theories have been put forth from time to time: chromosomal, hormonal, and brain-damage theories have been the most prominent. In general it can be said that while in isolated cases physiological damage may increase the propensity to aggression, actual aggression (whether fantasied or in the form of violence) seems to result mainly from psychological factors (Bandura, 1973; Whalen, 1974). After reviewing all the neurological evidence, Plotnik concluded that "neurological evidence for innate (unlearned) aggressive circuitry is lacking in lower as well as in higher species."[48] Although some (e.g., Mark and Ervin, 1970) have made wide-reaching claims about the underlying brain causes of aggression, such as lesions in the amygdala, careful sifting of the evidence does not support these claims. The fact that improved surgical techniques have led to the performance of more than 500 surgical procedures on the amygdala in human patients (Valenstein, 1973) proves only that surgeons may rush in where careful theoreticians fear to tread. After reviewing all the material—clinical, theoretical, and experimental—Valenstein concludes:

most of the present upsurge in violence can be related to a rejection of previously accepted values and social roles and to the existence of large groups of people who feel that they have no vested interest in the stability of the society in which they live. It may not be easy to find or to implement the changes that are necessary, but *there is a great danger in accepting the delusion that biological solutions are available for these social problems* (italics added).[49]

Thus the evidence from other disciplines tends to support the psychoanalytic position that aggression is a psychologically determined drive that can only be properly understood in the light of the total ego structure.

The Aggression of Large Groups

Even though war and its disastrous consequences have been one of mankind's worst scourges from time immemorial, very little attention has been devoted by psychoanalysts to the aggression of large groups. The German analyst Alexander Mitscherlich, deeply affected by the barbarous character of his countrymen in World War II, has written extensively on this topic (1971).

Mitscherlich rightly argues that the task of understanding social violence cannot be undertaken by the analyst alone. He must allow empirical sociological research to inform him of the degree and significance of certain factors in the formation of intrapsychic conflict. Warfare, with its rational objectives and its unconscious motivations, cannot be comprehended as a collective activity if the functions of the institutions of society are left out of account. It is through them that not only the rational aims and regulatory tasks but also the aggressive needs of a leadership group can be transmitted to the whole population. This is a supra-individual process that has its beginnings in individual needs. Furthermore, these institutions can topple the individual's whole constellation of values. What in peacetime would be considered the behavior of a severely disturbed, violent criminal becomes, when political or economic interests are being pursued by means of war, a virtue—and, what is more, one that earns visible reward (Eissler, 1960). Mitscherlich concludes:

One might gain the impression that while in the past two decades the metapsychological positions of psychoanalysis have been refined, they have also to some degree become ossified. In opening our theory to the questions and answers of the related sciences, we might be able to counteract this. But that is not a problem of aggression, rather it is one of engagement, of libido.[50]

Concluding Comments on Aggression

The historical development of the psychoanalytic theory of aggression has led in two contradictory directions, one clinical, the other metapsychological. From the clinical point of view, attention has shifted from sexual to aggressive behavior, with an enormous benefit in terms of both theoretical understanding and clinical effectiveness. All of the major psychopathological disturbances have been shown to involve a surplus of aggression over sexuality, with an attendant weakness of the ego that prevents the adequate handling of aggression. Although aggression has not been found to have any single physiological basis or source, it has far-reaching somatic consequences. This information has led to elaboration of the psychosomatic approach and psychosomatic medicine. The vicissitudes of the management of aggression, the defensive stances adopted, intercalations with sexuality, and the effects on ego and superego have all been carefully studied. A class of patients whose primary affect is anger or rage has been described as borderline, or, alternatively, narcissistic, and has increasingly attracted the attention of clinicians.

On the theoretical side, however, little progress has been made. Freud's death instinct theory produced a metapsychological chaos from which psychoanalysis has not yet recovered. Replacement of the death instinct hypothesis by the dual instinct theory offers little improvement because of the numerous difficulties attached to the concept of a "hostile instinct." Brenner's position, that aggression is a psychological drive which must be understood psychologically rather than biologically, probably accords best with the available evidence.

Psychic Energy

Attached to Freud's first instinct theory was the concept of psychic energy. This concept, rather contradictory in Freud's writings and difficult to define at best, has led to some of the most acrimonious argumentation in the psychoanalytic literature. It is most useful to approach the question historically.

Freud first introduced the concept of psychic energy in "The Project for a Scientific Psychology" in 1895; it was never published but did form the basis for much of his later metapsychology. There he wrote:

The intention is to furnish a psychology that shall be a natural science: that is, to represent psychical processes as quantitatively determinate states of specifiable material particles, thus making those processes perspicuous and free from contradiction. Two principal ideas are involved: 1) What distinguishes activity from rest is to be regarded as Q, subject to the general laws of motion. 2) The neurones are to be taken as the material particles.[51]

The concept of a quantitatively varying energy of the nervous system is an old one, antedating Freud. In addition to standard physiological reasoning, it can also be traced back to Mesmer, who could not decide whether the effects of his magnetic therapy were due to a kind of "magnetic fluid" flowing from the therapist to the subject (Mesmer actually used real magnets at a time when the nature of magnetism was not understood by physics) or whether it was due to some psychic influence. The dispute about whether "magnetic energy" was physical or psychical persisted throughout the nineteenth century, down to Freud's day, when the term "magnetism" had long since been replaced by "hypnotism."

Strachey has shown that the term "quantity" used by Freud in the "Project" suffers from the same ambiguity; does he mean something physical or something psychic? Even Freud's wording is ambiguous. Sometimes he uses the symbol Q and sometimes $Q\epsilon$.[52]

The uncertainty about whether psychic energy is psychic or physical remains all through Freud's work. In his final summation, in *The Outline of Psychoanalysis* in 1938, he wrote:

Here we have approached the still shrouded secret of the nature of the psychical. We assume, as other natural sciences have led us to expect, that in mental life some kind of energy is at work; but we have nothing to go upon which will enable us to come nearer to a knowledge of it by analogies with other forms of energy. We seem to recognize that nervous or psychic energy occurs in two forms, one freely mobile and another, by comparison, bound; we speak of cathexes and hypercathexes of psychical material, and even venture to suppose that a hypercathexis brings about a kind of synthesis of different processes—a synthesis in the course of which free energy is transformed into bound energy. Further than this we have not advanced.[53]

A comparison of these two passages reveals their remarkable similiarity, indicating that Freud, despite his epoch-making discoveries, was still bothered by the fact that he had not been able to uncover any physical basis for his psychological discoveries.

A further insight into Freud's dilemma is provided by an examination of his instinct theory, which, as mentioned, agrees with the instinct theory prevalent in his day (e.g., McDougall) in all essentials except the emphasis on sexuality. That theory postulated a series of instincts that provide the energy for the psychic apparatus; this energy is then transformed into the various affects. Freud says, for example, in his paper on repression:

The *quantitative* factor of the instinctual representative has three possible vicissitudes, as we can see from a cursory survey of the observations made by psychoanalysis: either the instinct is altogether suppressed, so that no trace of it is found, or it appears as an affect which is in some way or other qualitatively colored, or it is changed into anxiety. The two latter possibilities set us the task of taking into account, as a further instinctual vicissitude, the *transformation* into *affects,* and especially into *anxiety,* of the psychical energies of *instincts.*[54]

With such a background it is not surprising that the whole assumption of a psychic energy has been confronted with an energetic attack. Kardiner et al., (1959) rejected it in its entirety. Holt (1962) in a careful examination of the concepts of free and bound energy, on which Freud had placed so much weight, was able to distinguish more than a dozen different ways in which Freud had used the term "binding" and its opposites, "freedom" and "mobility of cathexis," thus requiring an overhauling of the entire theory.

In 1962 (Modell, 1963) a panel of the American Psychoanalytic Association engaged in a discussion on psychic energy, seeking to determine what the essential components of the theory are, what the concept attempts to explain, and whether we agree that some theory of psychic energy is essential. Among the panelists, Robert Waelder summarized the objections to the theory as being its vagueness, the dubious assumption of the transformation of one kind of energy into another, and the fact that it cannot be measured. Mortimer Ostow was the only one who defended the use of the concept, primarily because it explains what happens in drug therapy, but David Beres questioned whether he was using the term "energy" in the same sense. The most vigorous objection came from Lawrence Kubie, who argued that Freud's use of the concept was tied up with an outmoded image of the nervous system. Our conception of the nervous system is that of a communication machine, which receives and transmits signals, scans, paces, orders, codifies problems, and solves problems like a computer. This model, Kubie urged, makes possible a wholly different approach, as a result of which we can and must dispense with the wholly misleading concept of psychic energy.

Numerous attempts have been made to justify the continued use of the concept by reference to clinical data or to material from related sciences (e.g., Grinker and McLean, 1940; Nelson, 1967). In the most extensive review of the subject, Applegarth (1971) argues that we have been attempting to extend the quantitative point of view far beyond what it is able to carry. She urges that some assumption of forces at work in the mental apparatus must be made, but that Freud's views must be considerably modified to bring them into consonance with current neurophysiological knowledge. She develops the following conclusions: [55]

1. Grave theoretical complexities are produced by our attempt to derive almost all the energies of the ego and superego from instinctual sources, and a case can be made for considering each system to have its own inherent energies.

2. The hypothesis of separate types of instinctual energy, sexual and aggressive, conflicts with our understanding of neurophysiology and is similar to old ideas of separate energies for different sensations.

3. Difficulties arising from the idea of discharge of energy in consummation of instinctual drive and cessation of instinctual activity upon consummation can be better understood as resulting from terminating stimuli.

4. Neutralization, fusion, and binding all involve the idea of a change in the quality of the energy itself, an idea that is not compatible with what we know of neurophysiology and that can be superseded by explanations in the form of changes in the directing structures.

5. The process of structure formation is the central question for psychoanalytic theory and is not understood at present. The idea has been advanced that energies are transformed into structure, a process which is difficult to understand neurophysiologically, although some possible corresponding physiological correlates can be observed.

6. There is reason for not casting our theory in terms that are incompatible with neurophysiology, as we must eventually achieve some closure with it.

Anxiety

The situation with the theory of anxiety is entirely different from that with hostility. Here Freud's second theory, first enunciated in 1926 in *Inhibitions, Symptoms and Anxiety,* has been virtually universally accepted, has encountered no real rival, and has been elaborated in a variety of directions.

Freud's second theory is that anxiety is a danger signal emitted by the ego. The original danger is separation from the mother, and all later dangers involve either new separations or memories of older separations. Thus there are three factors involved in the revised theory: the ego, separation, and danger.

The crucial importance of the ego is highlighted by the reversal of his first theory of anxiety. There, since anxiety was seen as transformed libido, repression led to anxiety; now, since anxiety is an ego danger signal, anxiety leads to repression. A further contribution of the 1926 book was to reestablish the old concept of defense, so that attention shifted to more careful study of the various modes of defense against anxiety, regardless of its original nature. Hence modern ego psychology (see chapter 11) is in a very real sense an outgrowth of the revised theory of anxiety.

The significance of separation as a source of anxiety has become increasingly apparent, especially in the light of the catastrophic social developments in World War II and later, which led to wholesale separations of children from parents on a scale scarcely ever seen before. In technical terms, it has most often been formulated in Mahler's paradigm of separation-individuation, the question then being how separation from the mother is effected to the point of ultimate independence from her. Again, the emphasis has been on the ego mechanisms involved rather than on the nature of the anxiety.

The third factor, that of danger, has also been dominated by ego-psychological considerations. Many dangers threaten the individual apart from separation, but the initial one, which produces an overwhelming sense of helplessness and despair, is that of separation from the mother. If this danger is not properly mastered, a weakness of the ego results that dominates all later life experiences.

Hence it may be said that whereas the early period of psychoanalysis was dominated by the study of castration anxiety and the id, the later period has been dominated by the study of separation anxiety and the ego. In addition, the extraordinary somatic consequences of stress, first demonstrated by Selye (1956) on animals in the 1930s, have directed attention to the physiological aspects of anxiety and deflected attention from speculation about its ultimate nature. As expected, the somatic consequences of anxiety are closely related to those of hostility, from which they are often indistinguishable (Mason, 1975).

Much of the literature since Freud's 1926 book has been devoted to scrapping or reinterpreting some of the older material based on the earlier theory of anxiety. Thus the entity of actual neurosis, an essential part of the toxicological theory, has virtually disappeared (Brenner, 1956). The transformation of libido into anxiety, and the reverse, have been reinterpreted in dynamic terms; thus a fear remains a disguised wish, and vice versa (Compton, 1972). Helplessness and traumatic shock remain part of the phenomenon (Rangell, 1968).

Although there are no real rivals to Freud's separation theory within psychoanalysis (Bowlby, 1973), behavioristic psychology has tended to cling to a more superficial conditioning theory, frequently denying the deeper nature of anxiety. In so doing, behaviorists are necessarily forced to dispense with the entire structure of psychodynamic thinking, which seems absurd though it is urged often enough.

One significant theoretical question remains: Why should anxiety not be considered an instinct, like sexuality and aggression? Such a position has been proposed by a number of authors (Brunswick, 1954; Fine, 1975b; Rangell, 1968; Schur, 1966). This would fit in with the more common-sense proposition that the basic human drives are fear, anger, and sex. It is fully in accordance with psychoanalytic theory and would assuredly serve to correct the imbalance caused by Freud's almost fanatical dualism (Jones, 1953–1957).

Summary Comments on Instinct Theory

Freud's initial position on instinct was taken from the instinct theory prevalent in his day, which, following Darwin, ascribed the major impetus in human behavior to instinctual drive. The one momentous change introduced by Freud was a focus on sexuality as the only physiological instinct. (Freud always paid lip service to the ego instincts but did not take them seriously.)

When Freud shifted to the life and death instincts in 1920, vast changes were required to make his theory fully consistent. His notion of a death instinct was confused and confusing, as was his notion of an instinct as a return to an inorganic form of matter. The conflicting frameworks he offered led to vagueness, contradictions, and ambiguities in the psychoanalytic theory of instincts, from which psychoanalysis has not yet recovered. The result is that today it is meaningless to speak of the "psychoanalytic theory of instinct."

What has emerged instead is a host of clinical observations that have proved immensely fruitful and illuminating. Freud's clinical observations on sexuality have been incorporated almost in their entirety into all psychological systems. The theory of hostility has led to a much deeper understanding of all the more regressive forms of psychopathology, from schizophrenia to drug addiction. The demonstration of the somatic consequences of aggression has also opened up an entirely new field, psychosomatic medicine. In one sense it could be said that one of the most significant outcomes of Freudian instinct theory is an entirely novel approach to medicine. By contrast, the effect on biology, which he hoped his instinct theory would have, has been nil. Reiser has in fact suggested that the term "psychosomatic" has outlived its usefulness, and that we must now specify both the psychic and the somatic aspects of every human phenomenon.

The almost total victory of Freud's second theory of anxiety in all psychoanalytic circles has been surprising. The lack of speculation has allowed both clinicians and theoreticians to shift their attention to the manifestations of the ego.

Freud's insistence on the "tyranny of the drives" was always accompanied by an equally firm insistence on the fundamental importance of psychic reality. Both of these factors are accorded full weight in contemporary ego psychology.

Chapter Nine

The Unconscious:
The Fantasy Life of Mankind

One of the most important contributions of psychoanalysis to psychology is the revelation of the significance of the fantasy life of mankind and its connection with unconscious processes. No other theoretical approach to psychology or psychiatry has taken more than superficial notice of fantasy. This is one reason why the psychoanalytic approach in a certain sense turns out to be the most scientific of all, since the first duty of science is to deal with the observable phenomena, and fantasy is definitely an observable phenomenon. By now all the significant fantasy productions of mankind, from the dream to the nature of history, have come under psychoanalytic scrutiny. Often this is referred to as the "inner world" of mankind. It is indeed a new world, this inner world, which only poets and philosophers had glimpsed before Freud.

The Theory of the Unconscious

While some theory of the unconscious had always existed, it was Freud in *The Interpretation of Dreams* (1900) who first proposed a clear and explicit theory that makes sense of the psychological observations. This has already been sketched: the unconscious can be divided into the *descriptive* and the *dynamic* unconscious (Freud, "The Unconscious," 1915). The descriptive unconscious consists of those aspects of cognition which are not within immediate awareness. More important for psychoanalytic theory is the dynamic unconscious, which consists of material repressed because it arouses anxiety (Freud, "The Defense Neuro-Psychoses," 1894; *The Interpretation of Dreams,* 1900; *The Ego and the Id,* 1923). Because of this repressive process, the core of the personality comes to consist of anxiety and the defenses against anxiety (Freud, *The Problem of Anxiety,* 1926; A. Freud, *The Ego and the Mechanisms of Defense,* 1936).

Jung and Adler took a different view of the unconscious, partly, it would seem, because they did not grasp fully what Freud was trying to say. Adler virtually ignored the unconscious in its entirety. Jung went to the opposite extreme, positing a kind of autonomy for the unconscious, an idea which other analysts have rejected. To understand the course of psychoanalytic history it is worth looking at Jung's ideas in a little more detail.

For Jung the unconscious was divided into the *personal* and the *collective.* The personal was approximately the same as what Freud called the unconscious. More profound significance was attached to the collective unconscious. About it he wrote:

there is another class of contents of definitely unknown origin, or at all events of an origin which cannot be ascribed to individual peculiarity, and that is their mythological character. It is as if they belong to a pattern not peculiar to any particular mind or person, but rather to a pattern peculiar to *mankind in general.* . . .

These collective patterns I have called *archetypes,* using an expression of St. Augustine's. . . . I am perfectly well aware that I can give you only the barest outline of this particular question of the collective unconscious. . . .

Because I speak of a collective unconscious, I have been accused of obscurantism. There is nothing mystical about the collective unconscious. It is just a new branch of science, and it is really common sense to admit the existence of unconscious collective processes. . . .

The deepest we can reach in our exploration of the unconscious mind is the layer where man is no longer a distinct individual, but where his mind widens out and merges into the mind of mankind—not the conscious mind, but the unconscious mind of mankind, where we are all the same.[1]

Although he never used those terms, Freud was drawn in some measure to Jung's idea of an inherited group of psychic ideas. However, he always placed the main stress on the dynamic unconscious, and his followers all eventually abandoned the idea of phylogenesis in favor of seeing the unconscious as the precipitate of personal experience. The fact that unconscious symbols are found in the same or similar form in many cultures, a fact verified over and over by anthropological research, can be explained more economically by the inevitable developmental stages in human existence, determined by our biological makeup. Archetypes can thus be understood more efficiently as typical life experiences faced by people in all cultures. The arguments pro and con Freud or Jung went on for some time in the 1920s and 1930s (e.g., Jung was invited in 1935 to lecture at the Tavistock Clinic[2] in London) but have since died down in favor of Freud's theory of the dynamic unconscious, now essentially the only one in the field (Bychowski, 1964, Glover, 1956).

While the physiological basis of consciousness and unconsciousness still remains a source of speculation, worth mentioning here is Sperry's work on the split-brain phenomenon and commissurotomy, which has led him to view mental phenomena as causal determinants in brain function, in what he calls an emergent theory (Globus et al., 1976; Sperry, 1977).

Manifestations of the Unconscious

Inasmuch as the unconscious combination of anxiety and defense forms the core of the personality, the unconscious enters into virtually everything that the person does. But it is more prominent in some aspects of functioning than others. It becomes most prominent in the wide variety of fantasy productions that characterize the human being. Of these, dreams are still the most important for theoretical understanding. But considerable knowledge has also accumulated about daydreams, altered states of consciousness, language, communication, symbolism, jokes, fantasizing, art, creativity, mythology, folklore, and other areas of human functioning. It now even appears that some of these unconscious productions may exist in some of the higher primates as well, thereby lessening the gap between human beings and our nearest evolutionary neighbors.

The Dream: Developments after Freud

The aspect of the unconscious that Freud explored first and most thoroughly was the dream. His basic theory, first carefully expounded in *The Interpretation of Dreams* (1900), still stands almost unchallenged; no alternative has ever been proposed which need be taken seriously. The only alternative, if it can be called that, is the behaviorist position that ignores the dream entirely.

The Freudian theory of the dream has been described in detail earlier. Although he revised the book many times, the major theoretical change was the addition of the superego mechanism, which allows for a much more elegant explanation of anxiety and punishment dreams than had been possible in 1900. Thus in 1930 he added a footnote: "Since psychoanalysis has divided the personality into an ego and a superego, it has become easy to recognize in these punishment dreams fulfillments of the wishes of the superego."[3]

Nevertheless, in rather confusing fashion he allowed his earlier explanations of anxiety dreams to stand side by side with his later ones. He left standing: "The essential characteristic of punishment dreams would thus be that in their case the dream-constructing wish is not an unconscious wish but a punitive one reacting against it and belonging to the ego, though at the same time an unconscious (that is to say, preconscious) one."[4] Then in a footnote after the last word he added (1930): "This would be the appropriate point for a reference to the 'superego,' one of the later findings of psychoanalysis."[5]

The concept of the *censor,* so prominent in the first edition of the book in 1900, was also replaced by ego and superego considerations, which in his later theory guard the access to consciousness. Thus the full theory should have been rewritten to state that a dream represents the distorted gratification of a wish, which is permitted to come into consciousness by the ego and then frequently punished by the superego; quite often (in many people, as a rule) the superego punishment, either before or afterward, is the condition for allowing the wish to appear in consciousness (Alexander, 1927). As before, this becomes a general principle of personality functioning.

The REM Studies

The most striking development since Freud has been in the rapid eye movement (REM) studies. In 1953 Aserinsky and Kleitman (1953, 1955a,b) found that there were regularly recurring periods of sleep that were physiologically different from the rest, showing a characteristic EEG pattern together with bursts of bilaterally synchronous, conjugate, rapid vertical and horizontal eye movements, and that this physiological pattern was highly correlated with the sleeper's recall of dreams. Following these initial reports, the EEG–REM monitoring technique was further developed and applied to a variety of problems (Dement, 1955, 1958, 1960; Dement and Wolpert, 1958; Fisher, 1965; Fisher et al., 1970; Hartmann, 1970, 1973). Charles Fisher, a psychoanalyst, initiated a series of studies at Mt. Sinai Hospital in New York, utilizing the REM technique together with various other, more traditional psychological techniques (Fisher, 1956, 1957, 1959, 1965; Fisher et al., 1970). By now a very large literature has developed. The most recent summaries are by Fisher (1965) and Hartmann (1970, 1973). Considerable research is still going on all over the world, and a substantial body of well-established knowledge has already accumulated. Generally the opinion is expressed that whereas this knowledge has done little to change the basic interpretation of dreaming and the dream offered by Freud, it is interesting and useful in its own right. The information can be summarized from various standard sources.

The Dream–Sleep Cycle

The sleep cycle is divided into REM and NREM (non–rapid eye movement) periods. REM periods occur only during stage I sleep (sleep can be divided into four stages that exhibit different patterns of brain waves, measured with an electroencephalograph, or EEG), and they are associated with significant changes in other physiological variables. An EEG graph shows a regular alternation of REM and NREM sleep. One cycle, composed of REM plus NREM sleep, lasts about 90–100 minutes. The number of cycles in an average 7- or 8-hour night varies from three to six, but in the majority of instances four cycles occur (Fisher, 1965). The REMs vary in duration from a few minutes to over an hour, the mean being about 20 minutes (Dement and Kleitman, 1957).

One of the most striking findings has been the large amount of dreaming universally present. Normal young adults spend from one-fifth to one-fourth of their sleep in dreaming. The mean percentage over a series of nights tends to be quite consistent, a low figure on one night being followed by a higher one on the next night. There do not appear to be any significant sex differences (Fisher, 1965), but there are significant differences with age, the amount of REM time being greatest in infancy and diminishing as the person grows older, going from 50 percent for the newborn to 13 percent for a 100-year-old patriarch (Fisher, 1965). While there are large individual differences, the sleep of any one person shows considerable consistency from night to night.

Recallers and Nonrecallers

Since the REM studies show that dreaming is virtually universal, the absence of dream reports in the majority of persons requires some explanation. Goodenough (1967) found that nonrecallers of dreams showed the same cyclic variations in REMs and had the same number of dream periods and NREMs as recallers. Antrobus et al. (1964) found that nonrecallers had the usual number of dreams (an average of four) but that these periods were shorter, i.e., the nonrecallers showed a 22 percent decrease in total dream time. It has been suggested that nonrecallers dream less and recall their dreams less often because of a generally repressive orientation toward inner experience. Lewis (in Witkin and Lewis, 1967) found that nonrecallers showed considerable anxiety when awakened during REM periods and asked to report their dreams.

It is a common observation that persons in analysis or analytic therapy will dream far more often than before. Hall and Castle (1961) also found that they could elicit dreams from average college students by questioning. Thus part of the explanation for nondreaming must lie in the lack of interest in dreams shown by the surrounding environment.

The Dream–Sleep Cycle in Animals

In 1958 Dement found that the EEG of sleeping cats showed two distinct alternating phases, similar to NREM and REM sleep in humans. After that initial report, a large number of studies showed that there is an analogous cycle in all mammalian and primate forms investigated—the cat, rabbit, dog, rat, sheep, monkey, and chimpanzee (Fisher, 1965). While not strictly germane to psychoanalysis, this shows that Freud's work on dreams was indeed of fundamental biological importance, as he had hoped. With many other recent reports, it tends to lessen the gap between human beings and other mammals.

Dream Deprivation

In 1960 Dement reported on his experiments in "dream deprivation," in which he awakened subjects as soon as a REM pattern appeared during sleep, thereby depriving them of the chance to dream.
His results indicate that the dream is an indispensable part of human
experience: if subjects are prevented from dreaming on one or more
nights, they make up for it on subsequent nights. These results have
been confirmed in a number of investigations (Dement and Fisher,
1963; Fisher and Dement, 1963; Hoedemaker et al., 1963; Snyder,
1966), although not in others. Disturbances found to result from
dream deprivation were: moderate degrees of tension and anxiety,
with a major anxiety attack in one subject; a brief period of depersonalization in one subject; disturbances in motor coordination; memory disturbances; difficulty in concentration; an increased startle reaction in one subject; development of irritability and hostility;
disturbances in time sense in several subjects.

Analyzing the dream fragments of the dream-deprived subjects,
Fisher (1965) hypothesized that unconscious wishes and conflicts
revolving around activity-passivity, masculinity-femininity, and
heterosexuality-homosexuality were activated by the experimental situation and the transference relationship to the experimenter. There
was some evidence that at deeper levels conflicts around oral-recep-
tive and oral-sadistic drives related to maternal figures and the nursing situation were aroused. Latent homosexual conflicts and pregnancy wishes in the female subjects, and oral sexual wishes in both
male and female subjects, appeared to play a predominant role. There
was some indication that dream deprivation was experienced as a sort
of weaning or food deprivation at the hands of a bad, rejecting maternal figure, and oral-sadistic wishes directed against this depriving figure were present in the latent content of the dreams.

Sleep Deprivation

While people obviously differ in the amount of sleep needed, and
their reactions to lack of sleep, prolonged sleep deprivation is invariably destructive to the psyche. Totalitarian torture methods have used
this knowledge to the full (Lifton, 1969).

Many analytic authors have surmised that psychosis is the acting out of a dream (Freud, 1900; Lewin, 1950; Sullivan, 1940). West et al. (1962) noted that after 100 to 120 hours of sleep deprivation, gross psychotic manifestations become progressive. Hallucinatory experiences become prolonged and vivid, reality testing breaks down, ideas of reference and gross delusional thinking of a paranoid variety become increasingly prominent. The total impression is that of a progressive disorganization of ego structure. A desire for oral activity and sensation develops, and caloric intake may increase if not controlled. Even during the first 100 hours of sleep deprivation, Morris et al. (1960) and Williams et al. (1962) were able to demonstrate significant changes in the perceptual sphere, cognitive changes, and temporal disorientation.

In an attempt to integrate biochemical and psychodynamic findings Hartmann (1973) hypothesized that sleep, especially D-sleep (dream sleep), is needed in larger quantities after days of stress, worry, or intense new learning, especially if the learning itself is somewhat stressful. D-sleep may thus have a role in consolidating learning or memory, but there is a strong hint that stress is important and that more D is needed when there have been emotionally involving changes during the day. In other words, those who require more sleep are not so much persons who have learned a lot of new facts during the day, but persons who have disrupted their usual ways of doing things, who have, often stressfully, reprogrammed themselves during their waking hours. Thus sleep and D-sleep may have a role in consolidating or reconnecting these important alterations made during the day. Thinking of psychodynamic concepts in somewhat too literal a sense, Hartmann argues, one can almost see psychic structures, when they are tried out in new ways (at times of stress), rubbing against each other and producing friction and then requiring restoration by sleep; while these same mechanisms, when they are functioning smoothly, can handle a great deal of input without requiring much sleep for restoration.

Effect of Drugs

It has been found that some drugs suppress REM sleep, while others facilitate its appearance (Fisher, 1965). These observations have clinical importance, but have not yet been integrated into theory.

REM, NREM, and Sleep Disturbances

One of the more significant discoveries of the REM investigations is that sleep disturbances seem to arise more often out of NREM sleep than out of REM sleep. In their study of nightmares, Fisher et al. (1970) found that awakenings with anxiety occur during all stages of sleep, but the most severe type of nightmare (*pavor nocturnus,* or night terror) of children arises out of the deepest stages of nondreaming sleep, stage IV; the more severe posttraumatic nightmares are evidently of this type also. Although initiated out of stage IV sleep, this type of severe nightmare is in some sense a "disorder of arousal." It is characterized by: a sudden, cataclysmic breakthrough of uncontrolled anxiety; a sudden soul scream of blood-curdling intensity, or cry for help; the passing into an arousal reaction—the subject is dissociated, confused, unresponsive, hallucinating; a waking EEG pattern, but the subject not being fully alert; the subject frequently being propelled out of bed and moving through the house as though in flight; intense activity of the autonomic nervous system, the heart rate doubling or nearly tripling in 15–30 seconds and respiratory rate and amplitude increasing; difficulty in retrieving content and rapid onset of amnesia for the attack.

Fisher argues that the stage IV nightmare does not serve to master anxiety but rather represents a massive failure of the ego to control it. He agrees with Freud that the posttraumatic nightmare is some sort of exception to the wish-fulfilling theory of dreams, but does not believe that it operates beyond the pleasure principle, under the domination of the repetition compulsion, nor that it supports the theory of the death instinct. He suggests that the stage IV nightmare is not a dream at all in the ordinary sense, but a relatively rare symptom, a pathological formation of NREM sleep. The REM anxiety dream, on the other hand, is a normal phenomenon, present from infancy throughout life. Thus REM-sleep and the dream–sleep cycle may be said to be controlling devices for the regulation of the nervous system. While not directly confirmatory, these data on the whole lend support to Freud's theory of the dream.

The Dynamics of the Nightmare

In 1912 Ernest Jones published an analytic-historical study of nightmares which is easily integrated with the more recent work of Fisher
et al. (1970). The whole theory provides an explanation in psychological terms of what can only be described as the mass psychoses of
several centuries. It is quite possible that the accusations against
witches were projections of the nightmares of the clergy. The main
elements of the witch theory of the Middle Ages were the beliefs in
sorcery, lewd intercourse with incubi, transformations of human
beings into animals, and night journeys with demons and witches.
During the Middle Ages and later, belief in these superstitions tended
to assume epidemic proportions and then gave rise to frightful suffering and an outbreak of persecutory mania almost without parallel. In
the unconscious material, Jones pointed out, two features are especially prominent: incestuous wishes and infantile forms of sexuality.

The superstitions themselves may psychologically be designated
as phobias, the latent content of which represents repressed incestuous wishes. In the intensity of the dread accompanying them they
are surpassed by no other experience than that of the nightmare and
allied anxiety dreams. Many of their features contain a symbolism
highly characteristic of anxiety dreams. The central content of the
material is composed of repressed incestuous wishes relating to coitus. It is probable that actual dream experiences were of considerable
importance in making elaboration of the wishes possible.

Influences in the Formation of Dreams

A variety of studies have attempted to examine what goes into the
formation of dreams. Fisher, in a series of papers (1953, 1957,
1959), explored the effects of suggestion, transference, and subliminal perception. He found that suggestion could lead to the formation of what he called an "experimental dream," which depends on
the existence of a certain ego control of the dreaming function. It is
also possible to have the control of this function taken over by another individual. The incorporation of subliminal perceptions and of
day residues going as far back as 72 hours was demonstrated. Comparing analytic patients with controls, he found that patients respond
not only to the content of the dream suggestion but also the signifi-

cant experience of being given the suggestion by an experimenter. Fisher showed that suggestions are accepted or rejected in relation to the degree of anxiety or gratification activated by certain incorporative or expulsive fantasies, e.g., the suggestion is accepted when it is equated unconsciously with the oral incorporation of a "good" substance, and rejected when it takes on the meaning of a "bad" substance. The same impulse dynamics are involved in the suggestive process in analytic patients and in normal subjects in nontherapeutic relationships.

Several investigations have examined the nature of dreaming under hypnosis (Brenman and Gill, 1947, 1961). Moss (1967), reviewing the data, concluded that the hypnotic stimulation of dreams and their hypnotically induced interpretation result in clinically valuable projective material. Irrespective of the nature of the hypnotic dream or the truthfulness of the interpretation of symbolic productions generally, these methods may have real therapeutic utility. However, Moss could not equate the hypnotic dream with the ordinary night dream on the basis of EEG findings.

Typical Dreams

In *The Interpretation of Dreams* Freud listed a number of typical or symbolic dreams in which associations were secondary or inconsequential. He divided them in two classes: those which really always have the same meaning and those which do not.[6] Among those which always have the same meaning he listed examination dreams, dreams with a dental stimulus, dreams of flying or floating in the air, dreams of falling, passing through narrow streets, walking through whole suites of rooms, being pursued by wild animals, and dreams of being threatened by knives, daggers, lances. This whole topic leads into the question of symbolism, which is treated later.

Subsequent authors have proposed other typical dreams. Feldman (1943) cited the dream of finding money; Bonaparte (1947) reported a lion hunter's anxiety dreams, similar to an examination dream. Loewenstein (1949) described a posttraumatic dream. Miller (1948) described mirror dreams and catastrophe dreams. Gross (1949) wrote on the sense of time in dreams.

The Isakower Phenomenon and the Dream Screen

Several authors have attempted to describe and interpret the typical sensations of an individual upon falling asleep. Isakower (1938) portrayed the sense of giddiness, dizziness, and loss of support upon falling asleep. Lewin (1946) described the dream screen, which he equated with the breast. Genetically, he argued, Isakower phenomena, dream and blank screens are in essence the same thing: they reproduce some of the impressions that the infant has at the breast.

Dreams during Analysis

Since psychoanalysis stimulates an interest in dreams far beyond that ordinarily experienced in life, it is only natural to pay special attention to the kinds of dreams that are peculiar to the analytic situation. Most striking are those dreams in which the analyst appears undisguised. Rapaport (1959) had, following Gitelson, warned against the early appearance of such dreams as indicating a poor prognosis. Harris (1962) proposed that such dreams indicate that the patient has sensed something from the analyst which gives some hope that the analyst may become or wish to become the need-fulfilling object.

Rosenbaum (1965) published the most extensive study on the subject, including some statistical data. He found that such dreams, in which the analyst appears undisguised, occur with some frequency among the dreams of analytic patients (9.3 percent of the dreams investigated) and occur in some 91 percent of analytic patients in the course of a completed analysis. He did not find that such dreams had any prognostic value, or that they were associated with an intense transference or countertransference. He interpreted them symbolically as pointing to the face–breast equation, and therefore indicative of conflicts in the early oral stage of development. He concluded that "the chief significance of this type of dream is the analyst's awareness of it as a distinct occurrence of special significance. Should such special attention be aroused, then the analyst might well consider his reaction to this type of dream as a signal to search within himself as well as within his patient." [7]

Feldman (1945) reported a typical dream in which the analyst appears with a number of others in his office while the patient is there. This he saw as a disguised wish to be alone with the analyst.

The folklore of psychoanalysis has often held that the first dream may contain the kernal of the neurotic conflict. Saul (1940) held that the first 10 or 14 dreams may yield a satisfactory formulation of the patient's dyynamics.

Freud's Dreams

In view of Freud's heavy reliance on his own dreams in *The Interpretation of Dreams,* there have been many reviews and elaborations of his work. Perhaps most important is Grinstein's book (1968), in which he provides a wealth of personal and historical material to make Freud's dream more intelligible. Anzieu (1975) has combined the dreams with other material to recreate vividly Freud's self-analysis. Erikson (1954) subjected the dream of Irma's injection, which he rebaptized "the specimen dream of psychoanalysis," to intensive scrutiny; among other points he showed how Freud omitted all references to his own sexuality. Grigg (1973) showed the significance of the nursemaid in Freud's dreams, tracing it back to his earliest experiences with a Catholic maid who was very threatening to him.

Normative Data

Calvin Hall has provided a wealth of normative data on dreams obtained from college students and other "normal" components of the culture (1963, 1966). He has also published a variety of schemes for classifying the material in dreams. None of this has found wide acceptance, since practitioners usually prefer the deeper dynamic approach provided by Freud.

Anthropological Data

Dreaming is a universal phenomenon. Once the significance of psychoanalysis for anthropology was recognized after World War I, fieldworkers began to collect dreams from a wide variety of primitive groups; historical material also appeared (the dreams discussed in the Bible are well known). Although cultural differences are of course present, analysts have been able to interpret the dreams of primitive peoples in much the same way that dreams are interpreted in our culture (Roheim, 1952b; Devereux, 1951).

However, primitive groups themselves generally take an entirely different attitude toward dreams. Devereux (1951) lists the characteristics of the primitive attitude to dreams as follows:

1. There is a tendency to define the manifest content of the dream as a genuine and partly extrapsychic event, which occurs not merely on a supernatural plane but also on the level of objective reality.

2. There is a tendency to feel morally and otherwise responsible for dreamed behavior. For example, Dawson (in Kiev, 1964) relates that among the Temme a number of mothers who had lost their children dreamt that they had given their babies to be ritually eaten by the witch cult. This was called "I dream a witch." The native doctor would elicit the dream, force the woman to confess, after which she was "cleansed" and could resume her activities.

3. The form, style, and pattern of dreams are rather consistently influenced by cultural expectations and predilections.

4. The manifest content of the dream is considered of primary importance.

Thus the primitive attitude to dreams may fairly be said to have been the prevailing view until Freud came along (Hill, 1967; Woods and Greenhouse, 1974).

Some primitive groups have used dreams in an almost Freudian manner. Wallace has described the dream cult of the Iroquois (in Opler, 1959), in which the significance of repressed wishes in dreams was recognized. Kilton Stewart (1953–1954) reported on a group in Malaya where, in the morning, the family would sit around and discuss the dreams of the previous night in a fairly insightful manner, apparently aware of many of the mechanisms described in contemporary dream theory. These are rare exceptions, however; almost all primitive groups use dreams in a magical manner, if they use them at all.

Reformulations and Popularizations

A large number of reformulations and popularizations of Freud's seminal work have been issued; often the reader is unaware that the writer is merely rephrasing Freud. Among the better known works of this genre are Altman (1969), Bonime (1962), Fromm (1951), Gutheil (1960), and Sharpe (1937).

Theoretical and Clinical Perspectives

A variety of reports in the literature expand on Freud's basic dream theory, at times offering somewhat novel perspectives. Although the underlying theory has not been amended in any really significant way, a number of additional points made by other authors are worth recording.

The Use of Dreams in Analysis

Inasmuch as the discovery of the meaning of dreams by Freud is intimately tied up with the discovery of the process of psychoanalysis, and psychoanalysts are still the principal students of the dream, their experiences serve as an empirical test of the validity and usefulness of the basic theory.

In the main, analysts have agreed with Freud. Blum (1976) in a symposium on the changing use of dreams in psychoanalytic practice stated: "Within the framework of psychoanalytic psychology, Freud's masterful conceptions and insights into the dream have been so rich and relatively complete that new additions to dream theory have been very limited. During the rapid growth of our entire science, the dream has remained a most solid and fundamental keystone."[8]

Blum considered the adaptation of dream analysis to the changes brought about by ego psychology. He emphasized the dream as a clinical communication, of greater or lesser importance, but nevertheless a communication. The royal road to treatment is no longer the dream, as was once the case, but the analysis of the transference, in which the dream plays a varying role. He saw the capacity to recall and report dreams as an ego achievement, and expressed the opinion that a patient who never dreams probably cannot be analyzed.

Other analysts have also stressed the communicative value of the dream (Arlow and Brenner, 1964; Kanzer, 1955). Brenner in particular has recently urged that dreams should not be accorded the special place that they previously had, arguing that many dreams are intelligible with no or few associations, and that the urge to communicate is more important than what is actually communicated (Brenner, 1976). Perhaps this position could be put more economically by pointing out that with increasing sophistication many patients today have an understanding of dreams which was unknown in previous eras, so that the analyst must perforce direct their attention to less explored areas of the personality.

The Termination Dream

It is only natural that considerable analytic folklore has grown up around dreams. One widely held belief is the existence of the "termination" dream, supposedly the dream that signals the satisfactory end of an analysis. Oremland (1973) reported three cases in which a dream occurred during the termination phase with the following specific characteristics: it occurred in relationship to a termination event; it portrayed the presenting or a major symptom with significant modification; and it represented the analyst undisguised and in intimate relationship with the symptom. He suggested that in these cases the dream demonstrates to varying degrees the alteration which the analysis has brought about in both the symptom and the transference. However, in the light of the basic significance of wish-fulfillment in all dreams, other analysts have questioned the existence of termination dreams (Blum 1976). Sharpe (1937) noted that the dreams of analyzed people tended to display the id impulses in less disguised form than those of the unanalyzed; however, this would still fit into the wish-fulfillment theory.

The First Dream

Some have urged that the first dream in analysis reveals the undisguised neurotic structure. Blum (1976) refers to this as an "analytic myth," claiming instead that initial dreams are often difficult to understand at the time they are reported but can be used to delineate and interpret early transference resistance.

The Dreaming Experience

Khan (1976) called attention to the nature of the subject's experience in dreaming, proposing a distinction between the dreaming experience and the meanings of the remembered dream text. This notion is added to his earlier concepts of the "good" dream (Khan, 1962) and the dream space (Khan, 1972). Khan's view is that in his dreaming experience the person can actualize aspects of the self that perhaps never become overtly available to his introspection or his dreams. And yet the experience enriches his life and its lack can impoverish his experience of others, himself, and his sleep. Khan's position is an interesting addition to Dement's hypothesis of dream deprivation.

The Manifest Content of the Dream

Freud's contribution lay in the discovery of the latent content behind the manifest one in the dream, a latent content that could be reached only by the associations of the dreamer. This discovery shifted attention from the manifest to the latent content, but, as he himself had occasion to observe,[9] the pendulum swung too far and manifest content was virtually ignored by many analysts. A number of contributions have made attempts to redress the balance.

Erikson (1954), in a superb reanalysis of Freud's dream of Irma's injection, offered an outline for the analysis of a dream's manifest content. As long ago as 1925 Alexander showed that many dreams occur in pairs or series and called attention to the interconnectedness of dreams of the same night. Alexander and Wilson (1935) performed an extensive quantitative analysis of the dreams of psychosomatic patients, showing that the basic vectors of these patients appeared on the surface in dreams in not too disguised a form.

Richardson and Moore (1963), as part of the Kris Study Group of the New York Psychoanalytic Institute, analyzed the dreams of 25 schizophrenics, using 25 nonschizophrenic patients as controls. To their surprise, they found that the manifest content did not differentiate the two groups. The only major difference lay in a certain sense of bizarreness, strangeness, or incomprehensibility in the dreams of the schizophrenics, but this occurred in only a small percentage of their dreams and might easily have been added in the secondary revision (the process of putting the dream images together in coherent form). A number of other studies have failed to demonstrate clear-cut differences between the dreams of schizophrenics and nonschizophrenics (Boss, 1938; Frosch, 1976; Kant, 1952; Noble, 1950–51; Trapp and Lyons, 1936). This would tend to confirm Freud's position that the dream is a "normal psychosis," to which every individual regresses during the night.

At a panel discussion of the question in 1965 by the American Psychoanalytic Association (reported in Babcock, 1966), the participants generally agreed that much dynamic information could be deduced from the manifest content of the dream but that no diagnostic significance could be placed on it (also Brenner, 1976). Kligerman (Panel, 1966) showed how the manifest content of the dreams of Charles Dickens made sense, given the known facts of his life. Nevertheless, it was stressed, to extract the full meaning of a dream, associations must be used and latent content uncovered.

Cognitive Factors

Once it had been shown that everyone has a dream–sleep cycle and that everybody dreams four to eight times a night, some doubt was cast on Freud's assumptions that the dream is the guardian of sleep and that all dreams necessarily embody wish-fulfillment. If dreaming is such a regularly recurring phenomenon, it was argued, cognitive factors must play more of a role than had originally been thought.

This hypothesis has indeed been borne out in a number of studies. Wolpert (1972) demonstrated the existence of a dream recall factor depending on four concepts of classical faculty psychology: the laws of consolidation, stimulus characteristics, decay, and awakening characteristics. He argued that such laws indicate that the prerequisites for the psychological act of dream recall include biologically given limitations. Witkin and Lewis (1967) have also marshaled the evidence for the effect of presleep experience on dreams. Breger et al. (1971) have shown how severe stress may be directly reflected in dream experience. From another angle, Piaget proposed that dreams also obey the laws of accommodation and assimilation that prevail in other cognitive structures.[10]

Thus in a sense Freud's classical theory must be modified to allow for the working of more cognitive factors. However, this does not alter the total view of human functioning as reflecting a high degree of conflict and wish-fulfillment.

Alternative Theories

No real alternatives to Freud's theory have held their ground for any period of time. Jung's assumption of a predictive value for dreams is simply incorrect (Jung, *Abstracts of Writings,* 1976).

Likewise the notion of the "telepathic" dream (Ullman, in Masserman, 1966) must be discarded, along with the notion of telepathy in general, as devoid of any convincing objective evidence.

Roheim's suggestion of the progressive and regressive tendencies in dreams (Roheim, 1950) can easily be integrated into Freud's general theory.

Daydreaming and Fantasizing

The recognition that our mental life revolves around pleasurable fantasies, which was originally derived from the study of dreams, was soon extended to all areas of psychic functioning. Varendonck (1921) was the first to establish the undisguised nature of erotic and aggressive fantasies in the daydream. Later Singer (1975) elaborated on his essential theses. The demonstration that much of the mental life of mankind revolves around basic ungratified and often ungratifiable wishes remains one of the major contributions of psychoanalysis to psychology. The further application of this principle to all mental functioning is now a basic postulate of all psychology.

Symbolism

That people think in symbols is obvious. Differences arise only over the meaning of the symbols. Christianity, which makes wide use of symbols (as do other religions), insists that the believer must attach a certain meaning to them and rejects any "deeper" interpretation. It was in such an atmosphere that psychoanalysis came upon the scene.

Since symbols appear in such profusion in dreams, it was to be expected that Freud would consider them in detail. Yet it was not until the second edition of *The Interpretation of Dreams* (1909), after Stekel had called his attention to the matter, that Freud included a long section on symbolism.

Because of their concern with sexuality, the earlier analysts engaged in extensive investigations of the unconscious meanings of a wide variety of symbols. This work was carried out so thoroughly, by Freud, Rank, Jones, Abraham, Ferenczi, and other analytic pioneers, that little revision has taken place. As with dreams, there are some attempts to reinterpret symbols in ego-psychological terms, but they remain unconvincing. Again as with dreams, the exploration of symbolic language is another solid achievement of the early analysts. What has followed has been largely an expansion of their insights.

The best account of the classical theory of symbolism, which has also been referred to as the Jones–Ferenczi theory (although it does not differ from Freud in any essential) is in a 1916 paper by Jones on "The Theory of Symbolism." It is simplest to begin with a summary of his account.

Symbolism, according to Jones, is a form of indirect representation that is adopted because direct representation would arouse too much anxiety. All symbolism betokens a relative incapacity for either apprehension or presentation, primarily the former; this may be either affective or intellectual in origin, the affective factor being more important. As a result of this incapacity the mind reverts to a simpler type of mental process, and the greater the incapacity the more primitive is the type of mental process reverted to. Hence in the most usual forms the symbol is of the kind of mental process that costs the least effort—it is sensorial, usually visual; visual because in retrospect most perceptual memories become converted into visual forms, this conversion in turn being partly due to the ease of visual representation. For the same reason symbolism is always concrete, since concrete mental processes are both easier and more primitive than any other. Most forms of symbolism may therefore be described as the automatic substitution of a concrete idea, characteristically in the form of its sensory image, for another idea that is more or less difficult of access, that may be hidden or unconscious, and that has one or more attributes in common with the symbolizing idea.

The essential difficulty that goes with all forms of symbolism is in the adequate apprehending (and therefore also in the conveying) of feeling. This is doubtless to be ascribed to the innumerable inhibitions of feeling that are operative throughout the mind.

The basic feature in all forms of symbolism Jones calls identification; we would call it similarity today, inasmuch as "identification" has acquired an entirely different meaning in psychoanalysis.

Two main reasons can be adduced for the reliance on similarity: it is easier, and therefore more pleasant, to note the features of a new idea that resemble those of an older and more familiar one. Furthermore, the mind tends to notice especially those features that interest it because of their resemblance to previous experiences of interest. In the second place, the appreciation of resemblances facilitates the assimilation of new experiences by referring the unknown to the already known.

Affective inhibition can be of the most varied degrees, and on this variation depends the multiplicity of the processes that are grouped under the name of "symbolism." When the inhibition is at its maximum, we have symbolism in its most typical form. The distinctions between this and other forms of indirect pictorial representation are qualitative as well as quantitative.

In this direct, strict sense the two major characteristics of symbolism are that the process is completely unconscious and that the affect attached to the symbolized idea has not, insofar as the symbolism is concerned, been proved capable of sublimation. In both these respects symbolism differs from all other forms of indirect representation.

The typical attributes of true symbolism are: representation of unconscious material; constant meaning, or very limited scope for variation in meaning; nondependence on individual factors only; an evolutionary basis; linguistic connections between the symbol and the idea symbolized; phylogenetic parallels with the symbolism as found in the individual existing in myths, cults, religions, etc.

The number of ideas that can be symbolized is quite small—fewer than a hundred—in comparison with the endless number of symbols. All the ideas relate to the physical self, members of the immediate family, or the phenomena of birth, love, and death. They typically, and perhaps always, arise as the result of regression from a higher level of meaning to a more primitive one; the actual and "real" meaning of an idea is temporarily lost, and the idea or image is used to represent and carry the meaning of a more primitive one with which it was once symbolically equivalent. When the meaning of a symbol is disclosed, the conscious attitude is characteristically one of surprise, incredulity, and often repugnance.

In the main, Jones's theory has been used and applied by several generations of analysts, has clarified clinical material, and has shed much light on data from all the human sciences, including folklore, religion, anthropology, and psychiatry. Differences have arisen with regard to details, not with regard to the overall theory. Subsequent work, has, with some exceptions, largely concerned itself with elucidating the specific meanings of a large number of symbols in all human fantasy productions. Even evidence for the evolutionary origin of some symbolic actions has been offered (Guthrie, 1970).

The symbol, as Jones points out, arises out of simile and metaphor in ordinary language. In therapeutic work the interpretation of symbols is often profitably carried out by asking the patient to think of what the symbol might mean in ordinary language, and extend it from there.

Within this framework the question immediately arises whether symbols might not be used to stand for more abstract ideas. Silberer, and later Jung, were proponents of this position, with which Freud eventually agreed. Thus the range of symbolic expression is broadened considerably.

Freud's treatment of symbolism came primarily in the later editions of *The Interpretation of Dreams* (after 1909). He argues that the meaning of symbols is general, not absolute, and may vary from one person to another. Nevertheless, certain common symbols can be pointed to. For instance, an emperor or empress, or any high authority figure, may stand for the parents. Sexual symbols are found everywhere, long hard objects standing for the penis, soft receptacles for the vagina. Castration is often symbolized by baldness, hair-cutting, falling out of teeth, and decapitation.

It is not essential to the psychoanalytic theory that symbols should have the same meaning for all people at all times. It is sufficient that they should have similar meanings for many people, but it is also in accordance with the theory that many persons have individual symbols whose meaning can only be elicited by associations or life-history reconstruction.

Within the mainstream of psychoanalytic thought, Jung's chief contribution lies in the abundant material he collected and presented on symbolization (Jung, 1912, 1964). For universal symbols he coined the term "archetypes." The number of archetypes is large. Among the most important are the shadow, which stands for the dependency of the child on the parents; the anima, the idealized woman that the man desires; and the animus, the masculine ideal of the woman.

However, Jung's theoretical explication of the symbol goes beyond what is ordinarily meant by that term. For him the living symbol represents an essential unconscious factor. The more widely this factor operates, the more generally valid is the symbol, for in every soul it evokes a resonance. Examples of specifically religious symbols which have wide resonance are the Heavenly child, Christ, as a symbol of the self, symbols of transformation in the ritual of the mass, the eastern symbolism of the golden flower, the Buddhist symbol of the wheel (always changing yet always the same), the mandala as the symbol of wholeness. The search for wholeness, or an integration of the personality, he designated as the process of individuation. This is the first discussion in the analytic literature of the concept of self and identity, which was later to play such an important role in psychoanalytic theory (see chapter 15).

Nonanalytic authors have also written extensively on symbolism, but without the depth contributed by psychoanalysis. The Christian exegesis of symbols seems virtually endless and is based on a denial of unconscious meaning. Werner and Kaplan (1963) attempted to combine the theory of symbolism with ordinary cognitive psychology, characterizing their approach as "organismic-developmental." They conclude that symbols are essential to intellectual functioning, but they omit the deeper meanings. The anthropological literature remains highly varied. Some anthropologists, such as Harris (1968), do not mention symbolism at all (it is not listed in his index). Others, like Turner (1967), describe the symbols of primitive peoples in an oversimplified manner. Still others, like Roheim (1952b) and Kluckhohn (discussed below), have succeeded in applying psychoanalytic concepts to a wide range of anthropological material.

In recent years some authors have attempted a more complex integration of the earlier theory of symbolism into contemporary ego psychology. Donadeo (in Segel, 1961), reporting for the Kris Study Group on Symbolism, tried to broaden the field, considering symbol formation as an ego function, perhaps autonomous. They propose a "broad" view of symbolism (as contrasted to the earlier "narrow" view) in which the symbol should be considered the result of a hierarchy of functions, developing concomitantly with the ego. Pinchas Noy (1969) similarly proposed a revision of the psychoanalytic theory of the primary process, arguing that primary processes are not "inferior" to secondary, but that they almost never disappear from conscious thought process and that all the primary processes continue to develop and change in integration with all mental functions. Both of these positions make valid points about the development of symbolism and its usage in the total ego structure, but these were implied in the earlier positions and do not appear to call for a new theory. The clarification of symbolism remains one of the solid achievements of Freud and his immediate co-workers.

Some Typical Work on Symbolism

The material on symbolism can be found in profusion in the works of the early analysts, especially before World War I, when the new insights were first applied in fields ranging from clinical psychoanalysis to religion and mythology. Typically Freud's proposition of the similarity of the mental processes in the dreamer, the child, the primitive, and the schizophrenic was used to integrate material from many sources. Basic to this literature is Freud's book *Totem and Taboo* (1913), where he shows that the two main taboos of the Oedipal conflict, sexual desire for the mother and hatred of the father (in the boy), are universally found, and that the mental processes of all human groups shows certain essential similarities. In more recent years this position has been vigorously attacked by structuralists, who have argued that each element in any culture can only be understood in relation to the other elements in that culture. While this position has some merit, it ignores the vast mass of data showing similar processes and similar reactions among the most varied peoples and at the most varied periods in history.

Once he had accepted the idea, Freud described a large number of symbols. The Index of Symbols in volume 24 of the standard edition runs to five pages, ranging from animals to doors falling, to Medusa's head to Zeppelins. The writings of Abraham, Ferenczi, Jones, Rank, Sachs, and others of that period are replete with comments on symbols. Ferenczi (1926) had articles on the bridge, the Don Juan legend, the shoe, bed linen, the kite, Medusa's head, the fan, vermin, and the sunbath. Jones (*Essays in Applied Psychoanalysis,* 1951) devoted a good deal of attention to the rituals of Christianity, showing, for example, how the infantile reaction to the discovery of intercourse between the parents is often one of denial, which is reflected in the myth of the virgin birth. The Christian trinity represents a variation of the trinity of many religions of that period which included the father, the mother, and the child; in Christianity the Holy Ghost replaced the mother, pointing to the desexualization characteristic of Christianity.[11]

The literature on symbolism is by now so large that not even a summary can be attempted. A few of the more important works on symbolism may be mentioned. Vangaard pulled together a wide variety of contemporary and historical materials on the symbolic significance of the penis in his book *Phallos* (1972). Bettelheim (1954) attempted a reinterpretation of many puberty rites as pointing to male envy.

Kluckhohn (1959) presents a number of mythological themes that are universal. One of these is witchcraft. The following themes seem to appear always and everywhere:

1. Were-animals that move about at night with miraculous speed, gathering in witches' sabbaths to work evil magic.
2. The notion that illness, emaciation, and eventual death can result from introducing by magical means some sort of noxious substance into the body of the victim.
3. A connection between incest and witchcraft.

Other themes which are almost universal (according to Kluckhohn) are floods, slaying of monsters, incest, sibling rivalry, castration (including symbolic), and androgynous deities.

Oedipal myths are part of a broader pattern, named by Rank (1909) the myth of the birth of the hero. This has also been described by Raglan (1956) and Campbell (1949). Rank abstracted the following pattern in 34 myths from the Mediterranean basin and western Asia:

The hero is the child of most distinguished parents; usually the son of a king. His origin is preceded by difficulties, such as continence, or prolonged barrenness, or secret intercourse of the parents, due to external prohibitions or obstacles. During the pregnancy, or antedating the same, there is a prophecy in the form of a dream or oracle, cautioning against his birth, and usually threatening danger to the father, or his representative. As a rule he is surrendered to the water, in a box. He is then saved by animals, or lowly people (shepherds) and is suckled by a female animal, or by a humble woman. After he is grown up, he finds his distinguished parents in a highly versatile fashion; takes his revenge on his father, on the one hand, and is acknowledged on the other, and finally achieves rank and honors.[12]

Devereux (1955) compared abortion practices as described in a wide variety of ethnographic groups from Murdock's Human Relations Area Files at Yale University. He felt that his data yielded universally valid conclusions, and offered the thesis that

were anthropologists to draw up a complete list of all known types of cultural behavior, this list would overlap, point by point, with a similarly complete list of impulses, wishes, fantasies, etc. obtained by psychoanalysts in a clinical setting, thus demonstrating, by identical means and simultaneously the psychic unity of mankind and the validity of psychoanalytic interpretations of culture, both of which have hitherto been validated only empirically.[13]

Chapter Ten

The Unconscious:
Creativity, Language, and Communication

Art and Creativity

Once the significance of dreams in human life was established, and the techniques for interpreting them were worked out, Freud realized that he had a major key to all of human experience. Soon he turned his attention to creative endeavor and art, referring to all artistic and creative endeavor, regardless of the medium.[1] However, in the early years, before World War I, Freud was primarily concerned with seeking evidence for his theories, then ridiculed by most of his professional colleagues. Accordingly he approached the artist with a rather narrow vision, which only expanded slowly as time went on. Again, though Freud gave the impetus, most of the significant psychoanalytic contributions to art and creativity have come from other analysts.

Historically the artist has been considered either a genius or a madman. One of Freud's main contributions was to bring him back to earth, and show him as a human being. To do this Freud had to demonstrate that the mechanisms at work in the creative artist are not essentially different from those in other people. Hence for a long time his concern was with the impulses contained in the artistic production, together with the devices used by the artist to distort or conceal those impulses.

As early as 1897, in a letter to Fliess, he wrote that the mechanisms of creative writing (*Dichtung*) is the same as that of hysterical fantasies. "So Shakespeare was right in his juxtaposition of poetry and madness [fine frenzy]."[2]

Once he had hit upon the idea of the Oedipus complex, he saw that it was displayed in many of the great works of literature. In the editions of *The Interpretation of Dreams* after 1914, he added several paragraphs, on *Hamlet,* with its themes of father murder and mother incest. While he stressed the existence of these themes in Shakespeare's work, he did not really try to oversimplify the interpretation. He wrote:

just as all neurotic symptoms, and, for that matter, dreams, are capable of being "over-interpreted" and indeed need to be, if they are to be fully understood, so all genuinely creative writings are the product of more than a single motive and more than a single impulse in the poet's mind, and are open to more than a single interpretation. In what I have written I have only attempted to interpret the deepest layer of impulses in the mind of the creative writer.[3]

Freud's first full-length discussion of the subject of artistic production came in a paper on "Psychopathic Characters on the Stage," which was written in 1904 and presented to Dr. Max Graf, although it was never published during Freud's lifetime.[4] Here he made many of the important points that have since become the foundations of the psychoanalytic theory of art.

Drama, says Freud, is a way of opening up sources of pleasure or enjoyment in our emotional life, much of which is otherwise inaccessible. Being present at a play does for adults what play does for children. The playwright and actor enable adults to do this by allowing them to *identify* themselves with a hero.

Since drama is so often concerned with suffering, the spectator's enjoyment derives from a double illusion: first, because it is someone other than himself who is acting and suffering on the stage, and second, because it is, after all, only a game which can threaten no damage to his personal security. However, the conflicts depicted on the stage must be within the realm of experience of the spectator. Hence, if the stage suffering becomes too intense, the spectator must be highly neurotic to enjoy it. Thus there is an interplay between the writer and the audience, just as there is in jokes. Freud concludes: "In general, it may perhaps be said that the neurotic instability of the public and the dramatist's skill in avoiding resistances and offering fore-pleasures can alone determine the limits set upon the employment of abnormal characters on the stage."[5]

In 1907 Freud published a paper on a novel by the German writer Wilhelm Jensen. The question Freud took up was whether a dream in a novel can be interpreted in the same way as a dream in a live person; and he concluded that it could be, under certain circumstances.

Then in 1908 came his most important theoretical paper up to that time on the creative process, "Creative Writers and Daydreaming." [6] Here he took up the question of fantasies, and of how the creative writer produces his effects. Fantasies, he argued, are a substitute for the play of childhood; after a certain point the child, instead of playing, fantasizes. Fantasy is inherently unhealthy: "We may lay it down that a happy person never fantasizes, only an unsatisfied one." [7] The fantasies center around two main sets of wishes: erotic and ambitious.

In his further discussion he emphasized the dangerous character of fantasies: "If fantasies become over-luxuriant and over-powerful, the conditions are laid for an onset of neurosis or psychosis. Fantasies, moreover, are the immediate mental precursors of the distressing symptoms complained of by our patients. Here a broad by-path branches off into pathology." [8]

The creative writer deals with wishes and wish fulfillments; in this respect he is similar to all other mortals, and his fantasies deal with similar universal themes. "A piece of creative writing, like a daydream, is a continuation of and a substitute for what was once the play of childhood." [9] However, the writer softens the character of his egoistic (we would say today, narcissistic) daydreams by altering and disguising his wishes. This allows the spectator to enjoy the artistic effort by the same mechanism which applies in jokes: art has the character of forepleasure, and our actual enjoyment of an imaginative work depends upon a liberation of tensions.

Freud's first long study of the personality of a major artist was on Leonardo da Vinci in 1910. This book, the first full-length study of a great artist along psychoanalytic lines, set the stage for a whole genre of literature, at first called pathography (pathological biography), later psychological biography, and eventually simply psychohistory. In the introduction Freud felt constrained to apologize for studying a great man: "It [psychoanalysis] cannot help finding worthy of understanding everything that can be recognized in those illustrious models, and it believes there is no one so great as to be disgraced by being subject to the laws which govern both normal and pathological activity with equal cogency.''[10]

Freud's study was guided by his desire to explain two facets of Leonardo's life, the inhibitions in his sexual life and in his artistic activity. He was able to trace both of these to the circumstances of Leonardo's childhood.[11] Born illegitimate, Leonardo was brought up by his mother until he was 5, when he was taken over by his father, never to see his mother again. True to his mother, he never had a sex life. In his artistic work he sought his lost mother; his constant hesitation was brought about by the realization that he could seek her but never find her. Freud explicitly denied that his pathography included an explanation of Leonardo's genius: ''Since artistic talent and capacity are intimately connected with sublimation we must admit that the nature of the artistic function is also inaccessible to us along psychoanalytic lines.''[12]

Two other questions tackled by Freud in his writings of this period were the meaning of symbolic materials in works of art and the interpretation of a work of art. In ''The Theme of the Three Caskets'' (1913) he takes up a theme of Shakespeare's *Merchant of Venice,* in which Portia is bound at her father's bidding to take as her husband only that one of her suitors who chooses the right casket from among those before him: gold, silver, and lead. The right one turns out to be lead. The caskets stand for three women; the lead symbolizes dumbness or death, which by a transformation becomes the Goddess of Love, the fairest, best, and most desirable and lovable of women.

In ''The Moses of Michelangelo'' (1914) Freud for the first time studied a piece of sculpture exhaustively. His goal was to explain Michelangelo's intention in creating the statue; he concluded that Michelangelo ''has added something new and more than human to the figure of Moses; so that the giant frame with its tremendous physical power becomes only a concrete expression of the highest mental achievement that is possible in a man, that of struggling successfully against an inward passion for the sake of a cause to which he has devoted himself.''[13] There can be little doubt that Freud had a strong personal identification with Moses, to whom he devoted an inordinate amount of time and the most speculative of his works (*Moses and Monotheism,* 1938).

While Freud made many other comments on artists and artistic productions in his writings, he never elaborated any systematic theory of art. Spector is quite justified in his remark that Freud, despite his many insights, seems to intrude some of his own problems into the discussion of art;[14] for example, he could not understand modern abstract art, so he avoided any comments on it. Similarly, Freud was not musical, so he ignored music.

The first consistent account of the psychoanalytic approach to art came with the work of Hanns Sachs and Otto Rank. They edited the new periodical *Imago,* founded by Freud in 1911, which still continues today as *The American Imago*. In 1913 Rank and Sachs published a monograph on *The Significance of Psychoanalysis for the Social Sciences* [*Geisteswissenschaften*]. Various other papers and books established them as the two leading psychoanalytic authorities on art and what came to be known as applied psychoanalysis. In *The Creative Unconscious* (1942) Sachs put together his most important essays on the topic. Rank summarized his views in *Art and the Artist* (1932). These two books sum up the early Freudian approach to art, with each author adding some of his own ideas.

The artist, Sachs wrote, is closer to his id than the average person. Always attuned to a new inspiration, the artist becomes more narcissistic. Inherently it is a form of healthy narcissism, but it may be distorted. However, the narcissism is transferred to his work, and he shares it with an audience rather than focusing it on himself. Once the narcissism is transferred to his work a number of possibilities arise:

1. There could be an acceptance of impulse all the way around. This is the image of the Renaissance man—a hearty individual capable of enjoying life to the full. Rank saw this kind of man as normal, in contrast to the conforming average and the will-crippled neurotic.

2. The artist may remain stuck in his narcissism. He has intimate contact with a small portion of reality, but outside of that sphere he is not different from the ordinary inhibited person.

3. Because of the opportunity for narcissistic gratification, many people are attracted to art as an avenue of release for their narcissism. They may have little or no talent for art, or little or no interest in it. They play artist in order to be Bohemian, rather than being Bohemian because this is indispensable for their art.

4. Frequently this process fails because the artist is dealing with dangerous material. The impulses come out too strongly, and he becomes more interested in gratifying them than in doing his work. The gratification of the impulses without a brake carries all the dangers of psychosis, suicide, and self-destructive activity that it does in persons who are not artists. This is one reason why pathology is so common among artists—they are playing too close to the fire.

5. Then again the narcissism may become so severe that it takes the place of art. In that event, the artist no longer has the buffer of his artistic production—he becomes directly interested in displaying himself. Such an increase in narcissism likewise leads to a greater or lesser degree of pathology.

6. The narcissistic release may be temporarily frightening, so that artistic productivity comes to a halt. This causes the *creative block,* the most frequently observed symptom among artists. It brings them to analysis more often than does anything else. It is readily understood from an analysis of the circumstances.

7. The narcissistic absorption may become so fatiguing that the artist gives up his art in order to return to ordinary living. This is not so much creative block as creative fatigue. Sometimes the retreat is permanent; more often it is temporary. It is the narcissistic absorption which accounts for the ''loneliness'' of the artist (Niederland, 1976).

The Role of the Ego

By the time of the First World War it was well established that the instinctual impulses found in neurotics were universally present in all people. The artist had merely found a means of expressing forbidden impulses in a socially approved manner. Thus the artist was neither madman nor genius, as had previously been supposed. But what manner of man was he? Or, in the more technical terms of psychoanalysis, his id was the same as that of other people, but what was his ego like? It was to this question that psychoanalytic research began to direct itself from the 1920s onward, especially after Freud had formulated the theory of ego psychology in 1923.

Freud himself remained ambivalent about the psychology of the artist. On the one hand he maintained that healthy persons do not fantasize, which made the artist per se neurotic. On the other, he argued that psychoanalysis cannot explain genius. Thus he remained stuck in the old dilemma: is the artist a madman or a genius? Freud's mature summation of his position can be found in his *Introductory Lectures* (1916–1917), where he writes:

there is a path that leads back from fantasy to reality—the path, that is, of art. An artist is once more in rudiments an introvert, not far removed from neurosis. He is oppressed by excessively powerful instinctual needs. He desires to win honor, power, wealth, fame and the love of women; but he lacks the means for achieving these satisfactions. Consequently, like any other unsatisfied man, he turns away from reality and transfers all his interest, and his libido too, to the wishful constructions of his life of fantasy, whence the path might lead to neurosis. . . .

For those who are not artists the yield of pleasure to be derived from the sources of fantasy is very limited. . . . A man who is a true artist has more at his disposal. In the first place, he understands how to work over his daydreams in such a way as to make them lose what is too personal about them and repels strangers, and to make it possible for others to share in the enjoyment of them. He understands, too, how to tone them down so that they do not easily betray their origin from proscribed sources. Furthermore, he possesses the mysterious power of shaping some particular material until it has become a faithful image of his fantasy; and he knows, moreover, how to link so large a yield of pleasure to this representation of his unconscious fantasy that, for the time being at least, repressions are outweighed and lifted by it. If he is able to accomplish all this, he makes it possible for other people once more to derive consolation and alleviation from their own sources of pleasure in their unconscious which have become inaccessible to them; he earns their gratitude and admiration and he has thus achieved *through* his fantasy what originally he had achieved only *in* his fantasy—honor, power and the love of women.

Paul Federn: Healthy versus Pathological Narcissism

The first psychoanalytic approach to the ego of the artist came in terms of his narcissism. What accounts for the difference between a narcissistic regression into psychosis and the narcissistic capacity to execute a fine piece of art? A significant contribution to this problem was offered by Paul Federn in 1929 with the first of his papers on healthy and pathological narcissism. The importance of this paper has been obscured because of its connection with Federn's idiosyncratic theory of the ego (discussed later); it should really be read without reference to his metapsychological propositions. His main conclusions in his own terms are as follows: [15]

1. Healthy narcissism is employed as countercathexis to the object strivings and for their support (for example, hope, ambition), but

not as their substitute. The more narcissism functions as a substitute, the more pathological it becomes.[16]

2. The ego boundaries are resistant in normal narcissism; the ego is sufficiently stable due to the adequate narcissistic counter-cathexes.

3. The affects are resolved without sentimentality, though without intensity—that is, without renewed investment of narcissism.

4. The level of the forepleasure satisfaction resulting from the narcissistic cathexes is not too high; whereas the level of such fore-pleasure inherent in the permanent ego feeling is in general as high as possible.

5. The satisfaction in conscious and unconscious narcissistic fantasies is conditional on real object libidinal discharges, although the converse conditionality is not lacking. In pathological narcissism the latter predominates [i.e., object libido depends on narcissistic fantasies].

6. The contents of conscious and unconscious narcissistic fantasies are more in accord with reality, less infantile, and cathected by fewer perverse infantile sexual components.

7. Point 6 is further confirmed by the fact that the promise magically established in these fantasies becomes more grandiose and more impossible in the same measure as the contributory narcissistic attitude deviates from normality.

Federn's views were taken over by many other analytic authors, often in different language. A clearer exposition, though with the same essential ideas, is found in the paper by Erich Fromm on "Self-ishness and Self-Love" (1939). Fromm puts it this way: love of others and love of ourselves are not alternatives. On the contrary, an attitude of love toward oneself will be found in all those who are capable of loving others. Love, in principle, is indivisible as far as the connection between objects and one's own self is concerned. Genuine love is an expression of productiveness and implies care, re-spect, responsibility, and knowledge. It is not an "affect" in the sense of being affected by somebody, but an active striving for the growth and happiness of the loved person, rooted in one's own ca-pacity to love.

Rank: The Creative Individual as Superior

Another significant contribution came from Otto Rank, who stressed
the creative element in the human personality as something superior
rather than a neurotic sublimation, as Freud tended to think. Rank
published his views in a number of works. He approached the problem in terms of a triad of impulse–fear–will, especially the latter. The
normal (i.e., culturally average) individual is the one who bends his
own will to conform to the majority. The neurotic is "broken on the
wheel of fate"; he gives up activity because of neurotic inhibitions.
Only the creative individual is able to assert his will independently
and to rise above the conventional norms.

Rank did not glorify the artist as such, but rather the creative individual, whose expressions varied with the cultural conditions in
which he found himself. His goal, he said, was to reveal the human
creative impulse, broadly and genetically, and then to arrive at an understanding of its specifically artistic manifestations through their cultural development and spiritual significance. It is thus necessary to
consider all the expression-forms of human culture, however various,
first in relation to their origins in the creative impulse, and thereafter
in respect of their reciprocal action. In fact, Rank argued, the creative
artist is still seeking in art a refuge which it would be better to give
up and return to real life. Once he does that, he becomes the new
man whom psychoanalysis is seeking to create.

Ella Sharpe: Similarities between Art and Science

The numerous discussions of creativity soon led to the question:
What is the difference between the artist and the scientist? Obviously
great genius and outstanding creativity can be found in both. Ella
Sharpe, a British analyst, offered one widely accepted answer. She
argued that similar mechanisms are at work in both, but that neither
has achieved genital primacy. She stressed the role of introjection and
projection in both, and linked creative achievement with the mastery
of aggression much more consistently than had hitherto been done.

The artist, she argued, by producing a work of art which ex-
hibits the characteristics of harmony and design, is identifying himself with this good experience which means physical and psychical
life. He thereby restores the rhythm of his aggressive impulses.

On the other hand, the scientist finds out facts based on bodily experience, allied with observation of events in his external environment, and experiences of pleasure and pain. The need to know, to investigate, is heightened by aggressive fantasy. The projection is made more massive because of fear of the responsibility for injury to the mother. Knowledge of reality is a bulwark against fantasy, but the fact of conflict with reality, the actual power to find out causes and laws, is based not on aggression per se but on a fundamental experience of psychical and physical reality, namely, rhythmic order. This triumphs over aggression and in fantasy preserves the good image.

Melanie Klein: Art as Reparation to the Injured Mother

In 1925 Melanie Klein published the first of many pioneering studies of artistic expression, in which she attempted to show that creativity stems from the desire to make reparation to the mother for the injuries that the child has done to her psychologically. This theme of injury and reparation for Klein lies at the root of artistic creation. Thus she also showed that in the analysis of children, when the representation of destructive wishes is succeeded by an expression of reactive tendencies, we constantly find that drawing and painting are used as means to restore people. This anxiety about reparation and guilt is one of the main incentives to achievement. Hanna Segal (in M. Klein, 1953) put it as follows:

The memory of the good situation, where the infant's ego contained the whole loved object, and the realization that it has been lost through his own attacks, gives rise to an intense feeling of loss and guilt, and to the wish to restore and recreate the lost loved object outside and within the ego. This wish to restore and recreate is the basis of later sublimation and creativity.[17]

Rickman (1940) equated "ugly" with destroyed, the incomplete object. Beauty, an undisturbed rhythm in a composed whole, seems to correspond to the state in which our inner world is at peace. However, both beauty and ugliness must be present for a full esthetic experience.

A number of studies of artists and works of art have shown the relevance of this theory of guilt and reparation. Levey (1938) showed how a patient of his used poetry as a defense against her anxieties, and how her poems reflected the vicissitudes of the transference. Joan

Riviere (1955) offered numerous examples of the unconscious fantasy of an inner world reflected in examples from literature; the treatment of this inner world by the author touches the heart of the creative process. Bunker (1953) showed how a writer pushed this further by making the bad mother the persecuting object who would not permit him to publish his poetry. Bergler (1949) showed that such a masochistic orientation is the core conflict of many artists.

Melanie Klein: Projective Identification as an Artistic Device

Identification has always been known as one of the major mechanisms in artistic production and enjoyment; Freud directed attention to it in his earliest paper on the topic in 1904. In 1946 Melanie Klein added the allied mechanism of *projective identification* for the process during the paranoid-schizoid position in which parts of the ego are split off and projected to the outside world. For artistic production she illustrated the thesis by the analysis of a novel by the French writer Julian Green. The essence of the story is that the hero, Fabian, acquires the magic power to change himself into other people by making a compact with the Devil, who teaches him a secret formula by which the change can be effected. The split-off part of Fabian submerges in varying degrees in his objects and loses the memories and characteristics appertaining to the original Fabian.

Immortality, Mourning, and Artistic Creativity

Many writers have commented on the artist's search for immortality, which arises from the mourning for a lost one and the fear of death. Pollock has devoted a long series of papers to this topic. In one paper he discussed the role of music in mourning and memorialization (1975b), and in another he showed how mourning influenced the musical creativity of Gustav Mahler (1975c).

Shakespeare had given a beautiful expression to this wish in the famous sonnet 55.[18]

> Not marble nor the gilded monuments
> Of princes shall outlive this powerful rhyme. . . .
> So, till the judgment that yourself arise,
> You live in this and dwell in lovers' eyes.

As many have pointed out (see Peters, 1961), art recreates, unites, restores, and retains lost objects. The artist can decathect that which is lost and then recathect the newly created object. Perhaps the ultimate aim of art is to conquer death or the fear of death and so achieve immortality. Indeed, this is a fairly conscious and widespread motive among artists themselves, who often speak of "great," "immortal," "eternal" works of art and are constantly harassed by the fear that their work will be forgotten. Pollock points out that before there can be a new creation there must be a mourning process for the old, whether for the lost object, the lost ideal, or the lost creation.

Ernst Kris: Regression in the Service of the Ego

In 1936 Ernst Kris published a widely hailed paper in which he proposed that the difference between the artist and the neurotic is that the artist can execute a regression in the service of the ego while the neurotic cannot, he merely regresses. Subsequently this conceptualization has been applied in many different frameworks.

However, Kris's thesis rests on the assumption that awareness of impulse is somehow necessarily "regressive," ignoring the fact that much of neurotic inhibition arises from the failure to recognize impulse. Bush (1969) has offered the most incisive critique of Kris's position. For a fuller discussion, see chapter 11.

Phyllis Greenacre: The Childhood of the Artist

In 1957 Greenacre published a paper on the childhood of the artist in which she hypothesized that the potentially gifted infant possesses a conspicuously greater than average sensitivity to sensory stimulation, which might mean both an intensification of the experience and also a widening of it to include not only the primary object that is focused on but more peripheral objects that are related in some degree or fashion to the primary one in their ability to arouse somewhat similar sensory responses. She attempted to tie this heightened ability to libidinal phase development, though she stated that she herself remained largely convinced that genius is a "gift of the Gods" and is already laid down at birth.

Her paper was largely theoretical in nature, however, deriving more from metapsychological reasoning than actual case study.

While many artists are known to have severe privation in childhood, others have not. The one fact that seems well established[19] is that conspicuous talent in later life rests on some ability which matures early. While Mozart is almost unparalleled, the average competent musician has been active at playing or even composing from early in childhood; the same is true of other fields (Fine, 1967). Perhaps the major conclusion to be drawn from the significance of work is that talent without lifelong devotion to hard work at it is wasted. The sculptor Chaim Gross commented that he customarily devotes 5 to 10 hours a day to his painting, and observed that most of his competent colleagues do likewise (Fried et al., 1964).

Psychological studies (Oden, 1968) have shown that great ability in any field in adulthood is preceded by great ability, in childhood, of a general nature. Terman found that many eminent scientists had also been gifted artists as children but had given up art to devote themselves to science. This casts considerable doubt on the opinion expressed by many analysts that artists in general have had seriously disturbed childhood experiences. Many specific instances could be found, and have been pointed to in the literature, but it has never been shown that the artist per se is more disturbed than his nonartist peers. The idea seems to be, in fact, a continuation into analysis of the old notion that the artist is either a madman or a genius.

The Release of Creativity in Psychoanalysis

In the clinical field, the contact between creativity and psychoanalysis has moved in two different though related dimensions. First of all, many creative individuals have come to psychoanalysis to overcome inhibitions in their work, creative blocks. Second, many hitherto uncreative individuals have found a new creative release and ability in themselves as a consequence of their psychoanalysis.

In 1964 Fried et al. published a study of the therapeutic results in six creative personalities treated at the Postgraduate Center in New York. The widespread fear among artists that psychoanalysis would blunt or destroy their creative abilities turned out to be completely unfounded. Quite the contrary: the researchers found that both with regard to quantity of output and constructiveness and appropriateness of the work patterns there was positive development. In many areas, notable and decisive improvements occurred.

With regard to the other question, the release of creativity in the average analytic patient, clear-cut data are harder to obtain. Nevertheless it is part of every analyst's experience to have patients who were formerly severely crippled or inhibited overcome these inhibitions and blossom in many directions. Sometimes the growth is in the area of what is technically called creativity, i.e., achievement in one of the arts. But more often it involves a release of spontaneity or *inner creativity* (Fine, 1975b). If neurosis is viewed as stereotypy and repetitiousness, then it becomes clear that overcoming these blocks, releasing variety and spontaneity, becomes to a greater or lesser extent a goal of every analytic treatment. The degree to which it will succeed is naturally variable.

The release of inner creativity is tied to another vitally significant phenomenon, the shift in the patient population after World War II, especially in America. This is discussed in more detail in chapter 19. Here it suffices to point out that a large number of seemingly well-functioning persons have been convinced by the teachings of psychoanalysis that their lives have become dull, uncreative, rigid, repetitious, and frustrating and have come to psychoanalysts to find "fresh air" (as one patient put it). It had been noticed long ago (Eitingon, 1928) that the patient population that went to psychoanalysts changed dramatically after World War I. Part of the ideological basis for this shift lay in the recognition that the individual's creative living tends to be stifled by the conditions of our culture, to which psychoanalysis provides an indispensable corrective. Thus the patient population has gradually shifted from primarily being "sick" in the conventional sense to being "uncreative" in the analytic sense.

The Contribution of Projective Techniques

The projective techniques, which became part of the standard equipment of the clinical psychologist after 1945, threw a fresh light on the problem of creativity. Essentially the projectives involve a request of the subject to release his creativity, under the conditions imposed by the test. Some are directly similar to the usual artistic forms, such as the Draw-a-Person Test, in which the subject is asked to draw a person, or the Thematic Apperception Test, in which the subject is asked to make up a story; others are indirect, such as the Rorschach, involving creative perception, or the Kahn Test of Symbol Arrangement, involving use of symbols. By now a great amount of data is available which shows conclusively that there is an enormous body of untapped artistic potential in the general population. The conclusion is inescapable that every human being has some creative potential; why some bring it out, while others do not (or only in disguised form) becomes a subject for a social-psychological analysis.

Every Man as Artist: The Empirical Approach

From all of these facets of the study of art and creativity there has emerged an empirical approach that shies away from the easy generalities of the past. For a creative achievement both id and ego are needed, *creative thrust* and *creative mastery* (Schneider, 1950). The artist is not necessarily either a madman nor a genius. He is a person with a varying amount of talent whose life circumstances have made it possible for him to express this talent in some manner which makes sense to his fellow men. Only a few artists manage to create the "magic synthesis" (Arieti, 1976); the vast majority are competent craftsmen who produce works of varying degrees of excellence.

It is not to be anticipated that any particular set of childhood circumstances per se will lead to the formation of an artist; social, economic, and cognitive-psychological factors play just as much of a role (Egbert, 1970). Consequently, while all of the above-mentioned factors may play a role in the work of some artists, it is not possible to generalize. Rothenberg has stressed this empirical approach to creativity (Rothenberg, 1969), which fits in very well with our knowledge of ego structure (Rothenberg and Hausman, 1976).

In a panel on creativity held by the International Psychoanalytical Association (Grinberg, 1972), Bernard Meyer expressed this modern point of view well:

It would seem unlikely that so universal an activity . . . that is begun so early in the course of each individual life could possess a single mental significance. It would appear more plausible to view the creative impulse as comparable to a biological function, like breathing or parturition, which under certain circumstances may become the vehicle for a host of psychological meanings and consequently to wide fluctuations of functioning.[20]

Studies of Artists

The first study of a great artist was Freud's book on Leonardo da Vinci in 1910. Since then innumerable essays have appeared on a wide variety of famous painters, writers, sculptors, and other creative individuals, as well as their creative productions. While there is no longer any theoretical yield from this material, the fascination inherent in "dissecting" a great personality remains so strong that there is no stop to the rush of publications.

De Levita (in Grinberg, 1972) has divided psychoanalytic writing on art into four stages of development:

1. A work of art is used to illustrate psychic mechanisms, e.g., Freud's "Gradiva" (1907), in which he took up the question of whether a dream in a novel can be interpreted in the same way as a dream in real life.

2. The establishment of connections between biographical data of the artist and elements of his work, e.g. Freud's study of Leonardo. Shakespeare has been the subject of tens of studies, perhaps hundreds (Holland, 1966).

3. The next question approached is the distinction between artistic production and other psychic phenomena. An example is Selma Fraiberg's study of Kafka.

4. Finally, there is the outline of artistic activity as a process.

Besides the *American Imago,* a number of other journals have been devoted to art and creativity, including *Literature and Psychology* and, in recent years, *The Psychoanalytic Review.* Even a bare summary of the available literature on the topic would fill a volume. Apart from the works cited above, Phillips collected a number of excellent papers in *Art and Psychoanalysis* (1957). A good theoretical discussion of the whole topic is found in J. J. Spector's book *The Aesthetics of Freud* (1972).

The Introject: The First Three Years of Life

Although Freud had always spoken of the inner world, or psychic reality, the recognition that much happened in the first three years of life only dawned gradually on the analytic world. A first tentative step was taken by Freud in his 1911 paper, when he described the transition from the pleasure principle to the reality principle. Two years later Ferenczi (1913, in *Collected Papers,* 1916) followed this up with a paper on "Stages in the Development of a Sense of Reality," where he delineated omnipotence, hallucinatory wish-fulfillment, magic, and symbolism as preliminary to command of reality; these were all psychic processes operative in the very young infant, even before the anal stage. Freud (1914) then offered his rather puzzling formulations on narcissism. Particularly dubious was the idea of a primary narcissism at the beginning of life; e.g., by equating sleep and narcissism (1917), Freud was confusing a physiological with a psychological state.

After the paper on narcissism, Freud made a number of attempts to unravel the early years. These culminated in the concept of an internalized object, or superego, derived from the parents, which resolved the conflicts of the Oedipal stage.

Since the superego does not crystallize until five or six years of age (Gould, 1972), the question then arose as to what happened earlier. Was there an introject, formed at younger years, that was a forerunner to the superego?

In the 1920s and 1930s, with the advent of child analysis and analytic treatment of psychotics, many analysts began to suspect that much happened before the Oedipal period which had simply been overlooked by Freud. The exploration of this period, roughly the first three years of life, then opened up a whole new area of investigation. Inasmuch as the psychic events of this period have to be reconstructed from adult and child analysis, and inferred from direct observation, the investigation has proved to be exceedingly difficult though indispensable.

Full credit must go to Melanie Klein for being the first to explore in detail this period of life. Without attempting to clarify the numerous ambiguities, from 1921 onward she began to put forward the notion of an internalized good object, or good breast. At first she saw this as developing at about six months of age, later she pushed it back virtually to the beginning of life. In her final important work, in 1957, she said:

I have repeatedly put forward the hypothesis that the primal good object, the mother's breast, forms the core of the ego and vitally contributes to its growth, and have often described how the infant feels that he concretely internalizes the breast and the milk it gives. Also there is in his mind already some definite connection between the breast and other parts and aspects of the mother. . . . If this primal object, which is introjected, takes root in the ego with relative security, the basis for a satisfactory development is laid.[21]

However, tied as she was to the preposterous theory of the death instinct, Melanie Klein never made clear that the good object is actually an incorporation of the good mother. She wrote (1957):

The struggle between life and death instincts and the ensuing threat of annihilation of the self and of the object by destructive impulses are fundamental factors in the infant's initial relation to his mother. For his desires imply that the breast, and soon the mother, should do away with these destructive impulses and the pain of persecutory anxiety.[22]

The years 1920–1940 saw considerable discussion of this question of early introjection. The introject was variously called an internal object, a primitive internalized object (or object relationship), and parental imago. Sullivan (1940) described early experience in terms of the good-me, bad-me, and not-me, all deriving from the reflected appraisals of the parents. Thereafter the question was systematically discussed by a wide variety of theoreticians, centering around two major questions: What can be said about the early introjects, and do they derive from the parents or are they innate?

To see how far understanding of this period has progressed, reference may first be made to a paper by Fuchs (1937), "On Introjection," which gives an accurate image of the state of theory at that time. Fuchs defines the main terms as follows.[23]

Primary identification. The whole world is taken as part of the ego. This, according to Freud, is the earliest object relationship. It is at the basis of primary projection and introjection, forerunner of symbol-formation, all of which are at the root of ego- [superego] formation. It is not always kept clearly apart from [secondary] identification, which can only take place if the ego already exists.

It would be more correct to speak of the early stage of complete indistinctness of ego and outside world and to consider the gradual differentiation into ego and external world. This would render the term unnecessary.

Secondary identification [identification]. The inclusion of characteristics of a foreign being into the ego. There is a great variety of different forms of identification, not sufficiently known or kept apart.

Introjection. An instinctive incorporation into the mind.

This term is still often used vaguely for any inclusion into the mind, according to the original conception [of Ferenczi]. More and more, however, it is used to designate the instinctive nature of such an intake which was, phylogenetically speaking at any rate, a real eating up.

Appersonization.[24] Adoption of part of the emotions, experiences, and actions of another person.

Projection. A person's own unconscious tendencies are ascribed to other persons, often after transformation, especially into the opposite. Again, the great variety of forms of projection must be considered.

Ejection. Corresponding to introjection, the instinctive act of transplanting into the external world; for instance, anal or oral elimination on a mental plane.

The Inner or Representational World

A more elegant formulation than Melanie Klein's was that of Sandler and Rosenblatt (1962), who attempted to conceptualize their material as the *representational world*. They regarded this as a central one in psychoanalysis, the child's subjective world, a world which is only gradually differentiated in the course of development as a consequence of processes of biological and psychological adaptation. It includes Freud's internal world (1938) and Hartmann's inner world (1939) and is related to the concepts of the child's world described by Piaget (1973) and Werner (1940) as well as to the work of Head (1926) and Schilder (1935) on the body schema or image.

Critique of Melanie Klein

Into the 1970s the ideas of Melanie Klein found only a limited audience, and almost none in the United States, on the grounds that her descriptions of the early mental life of the infant were too "fanciful." Kernberg (1969), for example, listed the following as an ego-psychological critique of the Kleinian position: the theories of an inborn death instinct and of an inborn sexual knowledge are incorrect; structural considerations are neglected; terminology is ambiguous; there is excessive focus on primitive conflicts and mechanisms; character analysis is neglected in favor of early deep interpretations; de-

fense mechanisms are neglected in favor of the content of unconscious fantasies.

Margaret Mahler: Object Constancy and Separation–Individuation

Dissatisfied with Melanie Klein's chronology, analysts and other pe-
diatric researchers turned their attention in the 1950s and later to the
actual investigation of the attainment of object constancy by the
child, i.e., when the mother is introjected and becomes a good internal object (or bad internal object, as the case may be). In her earlier
book Mahler used 3 years as the approximate time when the child
achieves object constancy, but in her later book (1975) she gives this
age as appropriate only in "ideal cases."[25] It is of course true that
the full achievement of object constancy goes on over a period of
years, so that wide individual variations are to be expected.

The Real Mother as the Source of the Introject

The establishment of the actual mother as the source of security and
the internalization of a good object, in the works of Spitz, Ribble,
Sullivan, Bowlby, Winnicott, and many others (see chapter 6) could
be said to have been the work of the two decades from 1940 to 1960.
By then, when the World Health Organization commissioned Bowlby
to describe the characteristics of the good mother, the evidence
seemed incontrovertible. Nevertheless, relics of the old emphasis on
"innate badness of the child" still persisted and persist today.[26]

The Self-Image and Self–Object Differentiation

By the 1950s it had become apparent that the establishment of an internal object carries with it the establishment of a self-image, so that
an adequate self–other or self–object differentiation becomes possible.

By the early 1960s the concepts of self- and object-representations, their development and differentiation, had been reviewed many
times, and the field was ripe for some integrative studies. Sullivan
himself, though he had many of the essential ideas, did not develop
them further, nor did any of his immediate followers. Jacobson

(1964) described the following infantile stages in the process of energic and structural differentiation: [27]

1. The primal (embryonal) condition of diffuse dispersion of undifferentiated drive energy in the unstructured "primal" psychophysiological self.

2. With birth, growing cathexis of the perception and memory systems, of the motor apparatus, and of the pregenital erogenous zones.

3a. The stage of beginning structural differentiation and ego formation.

3b. When the child learns to walk and talk and acquires urinary and bowel control, a more organized stage sets in. Object- and self-awareness grows, perception and organization of memory traces expand.

4. Infantile sexuality reaches its climax: fusion and neutralization of sexual and aggressive drives has set in.

5. Drive neutralization is greatly enhanced by superego formation; the latency period begins.

Schmale (1972) put it as follows: gradually there is a recognition that both gratification and nongratification may come from objects as the result of accepting both need and gratification as a part of object representations. This is the beginning of what is usually referred to as the ambivalently held object or object relationship. This stage involves a partial acceptance of needs as coming from the self and an acceptance of the intermittent quality and varying quantities of gratification for the needs.

Along with this acceptance of both frustration and gratification from relationship activity is the further biological capacity to differentiate more realistically between object-gratification and self-gratification. This in turn leads to the further differentiation of psychic-need-gratification into representations of object and self in the mental apparatus. The mother-object's handling of the child's ambivalence will greatly influence how quickly and to what degree this differentiation occurs. This period of self-differentiation probably extends from about 16 to 36 months and encompasses the anal period of libidinal development.

Schafer (1968) made explicit the "immortality" of the object. As evidence for this psychic immortality he cited: the nature of primary-process ideation; the history of object representation in relation to self representation; and the systemic change that may be brought about by identification. Schafer further distinguished three possible fates (not mutually exclusive) for the immortal psychic object: establishment as introjects or other primary-process presences; transformation into identifications which, to a degree, may take on the character of impersonalized systemic regulations; or preservation as an object, with the characteristic of being external to the subjective self.

Even though once again precise definitions have proved to be elusive (Koff, 1961; Meissner, 1974), the literature has increasingly been concerned with these early identifications or introjects, the self–object differentiation and early interpersonal relations (object relations). Volkan (1976) surveyed the literature on what he called primitive internalized object relations, viewing such relations as especially important in schizophrenic, borderline, and narcissistic personalities. For him, internalized object relations may be considered primitive when cathectic processes that involve object- and self-representations are reflected in introjective–projective relatedness, when primitive splitting supported by denial rather than repression is the dominant defense (while the presence of primitive splitting indicates failure to achieve a tolerance of ambivalence) and when reality testing is not adequate.

Kohut (1977) has moved off in a somewhat different direction with his emphasis on the relatively novel category of narcissistic personality disorder. For him there are two separate lines of development, one for narcissism and the other for object relations. His position here shows a certain similarity to Jung's doctrine of inborn introversion–extraversion, and differs from that of other contemporary analysts. Kohut posits a period in childhood when a grandiose self-image is normal. He groups the disorders of the self into five categories (1977): psychoses, borderline states, schizoid and paranoid personalities (these three, he claims, are in principle not analyzable), narcissistic personality disorders, and narcissistic behavior disorders. Kohut however does not attempt a more precise delineation of when the self–object differentiation takes place, or of how it takes place.

Most systematic is Kernberg (1976), who outlines a general theory of: the origin of the basic "units" (self-image, object-image, affect disposition) of internalized object relations; the development of four basic stages in their differentiation and integration; the relationship between failure in these developments and the crystallization of various types of psychopathology; and the implications of this sequence of phases for general structural developments of the psychic apparatus.

The five stages he enumerates are: normal "autism," or primary undifferentiated stage—the first month of life; normal "symbiosis," or stage of the primary, undifferentiated self–object representations—from second month to sixth or eighth month; differentiation of self- from object-representations—from sixth or eighth month to completion between the eighteenth and thirty-sixth month; integration of self-representations and object-representations and development of higher level intrapsychic object-relations-derived structure—from latter part of third year through Oedipal period; consolidation of supergo and ego integration—beginning with the completion of the integration of all the levels of supergo. "An integrated self, a stable world of integrated, internalized object-representations, and a realistic self-knowledge reinforce one another."[28]

In the same book (1976) Kernberg also offers a systematization of psychopathology on the basis of the above levels of development. He distinguishes three broad levels. At the lowest, splitting predominates as the defense mechanism; at the intermediate level, repression; and at the highest level is the ideal person described above. The lower levels are defined primarily by the kinds of disturbances in internalized object relations.

Summary and Critique

The exploration of the inner world of the first three years of life has led, especially in conjunction with direct infant observation, to enormous insights into the early psychic life. Instead of an emphasis on drives, the stress has shifted to object relations, or interpersonal relations, and pathology has been viewed primarily in these terms rather than in terms of the drives. This marks an important step forward in both theory and practice. However, even though so much significance is attached to the early environment, the characteristics of the environment tend to be neglected by most of the authors cited in this section; Kernberg's strictures (1969) on Melanie Klein's theory can be applied with equal force to his own present theory. On the other hand, people who deal with the environment—family theorists, sociologists, and the like—generally tend to neglect the internal factors. Thus a gap has been created which will undoubtedly be filled in the near future.

Language and Communication

The English poet Francis Thompson wrote:

> We speak a language taught we know not how
> And what it is that from us flows
> The listener better than the utterer knows.
> *The Hound of Heaven*

This could easily be taken as a text for the psychoanalytic theory of language and communication. As indicated earlier, Freud, although he made a number of comments on the topic, did not pay systematic attention to the question of language. Accordingly it has been pursued more intensively since his death.

Once the significance of dreams was recognized, it immediately became clear that since people do not communicate their dreams, much of vital importance that goes on between people remains unverbalized. As the patient population of psychoanalysis began to shift toward the more normal groups (see chapter 19), theoreticians increasingly realized that even the most normal individual suffers from a variety of problems in communication.[29]

The Symptom (Classical) Neuroses

Freud had already discovered that the classical symptoms of neurosis are unconscious forms of communication. In hysteria the patient speaks in symptom language, which is made possible by the fact that the listener does not understand the meaning of the symptom. Thus, for example, the typical scene of the Victorian lady who fainted in the drawing room and was promptly given smelling salts, has disappeared today because everybody would know that she was just trying to get attention and rush out to call the nearest psychiatrist. The woman's arc-de-cercle position is never seen today because it is obviously a sexual presentation. In obsessional neurosis, idea and affect are isolated from one another; they have to be disentangled to get to what is being communicated. It is generally held today that mixed neuroses (or ''character'' neuroses) are the rule in clinical practice. In these the study of communication becomes part of the study of the total ego structure.

Rose Spiegel (1959) proposed a five-fold classification of manipulative communication: grossly destructive, authoritarian, disjunctive, pseudocommunicative, and noncommunicative. This can be useful in understanding all kinds of material.

Information, Systems Theory, and Communication

Spurred on by the development of the mathematical theories of information processing and systems structure, many psychologists undertook a more intensive study of the whole process of communication. Foremost among the contributions on the topic are three books by Jurgen Ruesch: *Communication: The Social Matrix of Psychiatry* (with Gregory Bateson, 1951), *Disturbed Communication* (1957), and *Therapeutic Communication* (1961).

In his paper ''Values, Communication and Culture'' (in Ruesch and Bateson, 1951), Ruesch established the basic conceptual framework of the theory. This framework involves: delineation of the universe; the social situation; interpersonal communications; intrapersonal communication; mass communication; communication apparatus; limitations of communication; function of communication; effect of communication; interference and communication; adjustment; disturbances of communication; psychiatric therapy (aims at improving the communication system of the patient); nature of psychotherapy; the psychiatrist's value system; the psychiatrist and culture change; distorted communication and marginal status of the patients; mental hygiene, ''The psychiatrist's work is aimed at helping the patient to acquire a communication system which is similar to that of the core group.''[30]

In *Disturbed Communication* (1957), Ruesch offered a guide to the clinical observation of communicative behavior. This guide centers around six foci: systems of communication; functions of communication; language and codification; content and information; meta-communication; and correction, feedback, and reply. In *Therapeutic Communication* (1961) he distinguished a number of therapeutic attitudes which make for improved communication, e.g., a discriminating permissiveness, bringing up the unmentionable, expectant readiness, cathartic listening, understanding the language of the patient, and unconditional responsiveness. I am reminded of the nineteenth-century observation that most people have a "burdensome secret" which they are dying to tell to somebody, and which, when told, brings great relief (Ellenberger, 1970).

Most attention has been devoted to the peculiarities of communication in schizophrenia, where indeed they are most obvious. As early as his book on *Aphasia* (1891), Freud had distinguished between "word" and "thing" functions, a distinction which he carried over into his analytic work. In the essay on "The Unconscious" (1915), he made this more explicit: "In schizophrenia *words* are subjected to the same process as that which makes the dream-images out of latent dream-thoughts—to what we have called the primary psychical process."[31]

In "The Schreber Case" (1911) Freud himself disentangled many of the bizarre locutions of Schreber, a judge who had become paranoid and written his memoirs. Subsequently innumerable psychoanalytic (and other) authors have systematically tried to unravel the complexities and confusions of schizophrenic language. The differences in emphases over time reflect the growing shift from id psychology to ego psychology. The core observation today is that in the schizophrenic family there is a transmission of irrationality (see chapters 6 and 13).

Linguistics and Psychoanalysis

The development of linguistics as a quasi-independent discipline has occurred only recently. As with other areas of cognitive psychology, the contribution of psychoanalysis to the basic theory has been small, inasmuch as language is an autonomous ego function. What psychoanalysis has contributed, from the very beginning, is an understanding of the id interferences with ego functioning (Freud, 1901).

Ekstein (1965) distinguishes six stages in the psychoanalytic conceptualizations of language evolvement:

1. The early Freudian model of 1895, developed in the context of neurophysiological considerations, attributed the emergence of

speech to the early helplessness of the infant. This has been a useful first framework.

2. In the early 1900s the origin of language was speculatively related to various psychosexual factors.

3. In the 1920s, writers, utilizing reconstructions from the analyses of adults and children, stressed the pre-Oedipal mother–child relationship and the importance of "primitive love talk" in terms of needs to be met by the mother tongue.

4. From the 1950s onward the dominance of ego psychology has become increasingly manifest, together with the adaptive point of view and notions of differentiation of psychic functions. Molecular considerations of speech mechanics and often too-literal assumptions about the origin of speech elements gave way to more sophisticated models relating the origin of speech to the development of ego functions (Edelheit, 1969).

5. Since the 1960s the stress has been on direct observation of infants under both empirical and experimental conditions (Emde et al., 1976). In this stage there has been a growing willingness to collaborate with other behavioral scientists.

6. All along, the language in schizophrenia and related disorders has been studied, particularly as these disorders occur in childhood. Increasingly sophisticated theories have appeared with the growing knowledge of ego psychology, from Spitz's work on the origins of dialogue (*Yes and No,* 1959) onward.

Among the most interesting interactions of psychoanalysis and linguistics is the work of Victor Rosen, who headed a special study group on the topic at the New York Psychoanalytic Institute for many years, beginning in the 1960s (Rosen, 1977). Samuel Atkin, in the introduction to Rosen's book, divides Rosen's research into four categories: the application of linguistics to special problems of ego psychology; developmental psychology, in which he attempted to demonstrate the interactive and correlated development of the language faculty and the psychological phases of personality development; information that psychoanalysis and psycholinguistics share with each other; and a critique of psychoanalysis and psycholinguistics as sciences and the conceptualization of a theoretical model that fitted them both in the same field. The rules of language enter into the operation of the ego functions, superego development, social rules, and the relationship of language and thought. Rosen (1977) also published an examination of disorders of communication in psychoanalysis, distinguishing paraverbal, paramimetic, simile, and continguity disorders.

In spite of the progress made, this whole area is still almost virgin territory.

Nonverbal Communication

Although it seems intuitively obvious that the body can be and is used by everybody for varied communications, it has been exceedingly difficult to translate this everyday knowledge into any scientific theory. Freud's early studies on hysteria and other neuroses did establish the communicative meaning of many nonverbal actions, but no general principles resulted, except perhaps that verbal communication is at a higher genetic level than nonverbal.

One of the most significant contributions in this area was made by Wilhelm Reich (1933) with his notion of *body armor* or *character armor*. Reich thought that the hardening of the ego, expressed in typical bodily constellations, takes place essentially on the basis of three processes: identification with frustrating reality, specifically, with the main person who represents this reality; turning against oneself the aggression which was mobilized against the frustrating persons and which caused anxiety; formation by the ego of reactive attitudes toward the sexual impulses and use of the energies of these reactive attitudes in warding off these impulses.

Many other writers have described various aspects of body communication. Sandor Feldman (1959) extended some of Freud's observations on parapraxes (Freudian slips) (see also chapter 7).

In spite of these and other suggestive papers, the whole area of nonverbal communication is still in its infancy. The nonanalytic field on the topic likewise remains speculative (Birdwhistell, 1970).

Jokes and Humor

Jokes and humor in general are important expressions of fantasy. Freud's book on jokes (1905) is still the classic treatment of the subject; other contributions have largely been elaborations of his theses.

Freud makes it quite plain that the joke is a form of communication:

The generally recognized experience that no one can be content with having made a joke for himself alone. . . . . I myself cannot laugh at a joke that has occurred to me, that I have made, in spite of the unmistakable enjoyment that the joke gives me. It is possible that my need to communicate the joke to someone else is in some way connected with the laughter produced by it, which is denied to me but is manifest in the other person.[32]

The pleasurable effect of jokes, according to Freud, depends on two factors: a *special technique* and the *tendency* of the joke. In a joke with a play on words the commonest technique is condensation. Other mechanisms similar to those seen in dreams are also found. As to the aim of jokes, the harmless ones merely offer an expenditure of pleasure; the tendentious ones, however, derive from the release of sexual and aggressive wishes. In a subsequent paper, on "Humor" (1927) written after the structural system had been formulated, Freud attributes some of the pleasure derived to the mitigation of the severity of the superego, thus again making the joke an exercise in communication. Freud actually maintains that as a rule *three* persons are involved in a joke: the teller, the listener, and a third person who is the subject of the joke; thus the joke is truly a social-interpersonal process.[33]

A few later studies supplement Freud's work. Wolfenstein (1954) traced the development of children's humor, showing the developmental changes in the attitude toward jokes. Grotjahn (1957) considered the humorist as a personality type. Murdock (1949) summarized the evidence on joking relationships in other societies, showing that in general such a joking relationship is permitted only between relatives standing in a potential sexual relationship with one another. Israel Zwerling (1955) and Joseph Richman (unpublished data) have shown how diagnostic conclusions can be drawn from the jokes that patients tell.

Summary Comments on Fantasy Life

With his work on fantasy, Freud opened up a whole new world of investigation, and a whole new approach to psychology. This has culminated in the recognition of the development of an inner or representational world which is decisive for the way in which the individual thinks and behaves. Increasingly, psychoanalysis has become concerned with this inner world and has explored it in every area of human endeavor. The emphasis on fantasy, both conscious and unconscious, is one of the most distinctive features of psychoanalytic psychology.

Chapter Eleven

Ego Psychology: An Overview, and Defense Processes

The switch from id psychology to ego psychology took place gradually, over a period of many years. Freud first began the systematic consideration of the ego in the paper on narcissism (1914). There followed a series of papers and books culminating in *The Ego and the Id* (1923), where he first proposed the tripartite division of the psychic apparatus into id, ego, and superego. This tripartite, or structural, theory proved to be so convincing that it has maintained itself ever since. Hence, properly speaking, since 1923 all of psychoanalysis has been ego psychology.

In another sense, however, the ego was always part of psychoanalytic theory. The German word for ego, *das Ich,* is the same as the ordinary word for *I,* whereas English employs the Latin term. Thus ego considerations were always present in Freud's thought. It was merely that for historical reasons the study of the id took precedence in the period from 1900 to 1914.

Yet even in this period some analysts spoke more extensively of the ego, particularly Adler. In his *History of the Psychoanalytic Movement* (1914), Freud gave Adler credit for his contributions to ego psychology, though he tempered this credit by pointing to Adler's relative neglect of the id. Freud's peculiar animosity toward Adler (the "hated enemy") was mentioned in chapter 4. It is only fair to correct the historical error and give Adler credit for being one of the pioneers of ego psychology. If his formulations lacked the precision which they would have today, that is also true for everybody else writing at that time, including Freud.

The ego is defined as that part of the personality which deals

with reality, both inner and outer. Freud left the definition rather
loose. In *The Ego and The Id* he wrote:

It is easy to see that the ego is that part of the id which has been modified by
the direct influence of the external world through the medium of the
Pcpt.-Cs. [perception-consciousness]; in a sense it is an extension of the
surface differentiation. Moreover, the ego seeks to bring the influence of the
external world to bear upon the id and its tendencies, and endeavors to
substitute the reality principle for the pleasure principle which reigns unre-
strictedly in the id. For the ego, perception plays the part which in the id
falls to instinct. The ego represents what may be called reason and common
sense, in contrast to the id, which contains the passions. All this falls into
line with popular distinctions which we are all familiar with; at the same
time, however, it is only to be regarded as holding good on the average or
"ideally."[1]

In this definition or, more precisely, description, Freud laid the
basis for all future discussion, based on the *functions of the ego*.
These ego functions have come to include: the defense mechanisms,
the affects, ego strength and ego weakness; perception and other cognitive functions (learning, thinking, memory); and management of
reality. These latter were elaborated by Hartmann (1939) and his
co-workers in their work on ego autonomy. Many aspects of the ego
have also been dealt with by other disciplines, thus offering an avenue of interdisciplinary elaboration with physiology and the social
sciences. It is in this way that the further development of ego
psychology has paved the way for psychoanalysis to become a general psychology (see chapter 19).

The discussion of the history of ego psychology can best proceed by discussing its various functions separately. (The rather widespread references to a "school of ego psychology" or to the "ego
psychologists" rest upon a misconception of the history of psychoanalysis [Gedo, 1975].)

The Defense Mechanisms

The concept of defense, which dominated Freud's writings in the
1890s, was the first great discovery of psychoanalysis and remains
one of its principal contributions. It was first enunciated in the 1894
paper on "The Defense Neuropsychoses," which proposed the explanation that the neurotic (and psychotic, then scarcely distinguished

from one another) defends himself against unbearable ideas. Freud described three methods of defense in three forms of illness, and then went on to suggest a metapsychological explanation for the defensive process:

I should like to dwell for a moment on the working hypothesis which I have made use of in this exposition of the neuroses of defense. I refer to the concept that in mental functions something is to be distinguished—a quota of affect or sum of excitation—which possesses all the characteristics of a quantity (though we have no means of measuring it), which is capable of increase, diminution, displacement and discharge, and which is spread over the memory-traces of ideas somewhat as an electric charge is spread over the surface of a body.[2]

It is upon the three basic ideas in this paper that the theory of the defense mechanisms has been built up—the methods of defense (later referred to as the mechanisms of defense), the correlation of defense(s) with illness, and the metapsychological explanation.

More preoccupied with other questions, Freud then dropped the idea of defense, limiting himself to repression. Adler did elaborate on what he called the "guiding fictions," which are variations of the defense mechanisms, though he did not perceive the deep anxieties that lay behind these fictions. Then in 1926 Freud took up where he had left off in 1894 and returned to the concept of defense, listing various defense mechanisms (of which repression was only one) and trying to correlate defense with illness. Thus he saw repression as characteristic of hysteria, regression and reaction formation as characteristic of obsessional neurosis, and avoidance in phobia. As to the metapsychological clarification, in this book (1926) he refrained from speculation, stating only that "after tens of years of psychoanalytic labors we are as much in the dark about this problem [whence neurosis comes] as we were at the start."[3]

The next step came with the publication of Anna Freud's classic, *The Ego and the Mechanisms of Defense* in 1936. Here she pointed out that the "odium of analytic unorthodoxy" (read: Adler) no longer attached to the study of the ego, and she defined the task of analysis as one of acquiring the fullest possible knowledge of all three parts (id, ego, and superego) and of learning what are their relations to one another and to the outside world. She went on to list the nine defense mechanisms which Freud had already described in various works (regression, repression, reaction-formation, isolation, undoing, projection, introjection, turning against the self, and reversal), to which she added a tenth; sublimation, or the displacement of instinctual aims. As for technique, she said: "It is the task of the practising analyst to discover how far these methods prove effective in the processes of ego-resistance and symptom-formation which he has the opportunity of observing in individuals." [4]

Anna Freud did not attempt to correlate defense with illness (beyond what her father had already done), nor did she attempt any metapsychological explanations. She did call attention, however, to four other defense mechanisms: denial (in fantasy, and in word or act), restriction of the ego, identification with the aggressor, and a form of altruism (in adolescence).

A survey of other literature discloses the usual inconsistencies and differences among various authors. With regard to the list of defense mechanisms, wide variations exist. Fenichel (chapter 9) adds denial to Anna Freud's list, but omits turning against the self, reversal, identification, ego restriction, and altruism. He also differentiates between the defenses against anxiety and the defenses against other affects, which other authors do not do.

Horney popularized a wide variety of other ego mechanisms, such as the neurotic need for affection, the quest for power, prestige, and possession, and neurotic competitiveness (1937), guilt feelings (1939), moving toward, against, and away from people, and externalization (1945), the search for glory, neurotic pride, the appeal of mastery, and the appeal of love (1950). Sullivan (1940) described 10 developmental syndromes: psychopathy, self-absorption, incorrigibility, negativism, stammering, being driven by ambition, asocialism, inadequacy, homosexuality, and chronic adolescence. Laughlin (1969) added others, such as idealization, compensation, fantasy, and the "King David" reaction.

The most extensive list was drawn up by Bibring and her associates (1961) at the Boston Psychoanalytic Institute, in connection with a study of pregnant women. They divided defenses into basic, or first order, and complex, or second order. They ended up with no fewer than 39 defenses, of which 24 were first order, and 15 second order. Their list seems to include everything, including somatization, detachment, magical thinking, even clowning, falling ill, and whistling in the dark.

Still others have published papers describing weeping, laughing, and adolescent giggling as defenses. Grand (1973) saw masochism as a double exposure defense, as had Menaker (1953). Modell (1975) has depicted narcissism as a defense against affect. Kohut (1971) speaks of vertical splits (disavowal or denial) and horizontal splits (repression).

The extension of the defense concept has in fact become so broad that little theoretical content remains beyond Freud's initial observation. It almost seems as if anything can be used as a defense against something else. In fact, Laplanche and Pontalis (1973) argue that the extension of the concept has placed the whole idea in doubt:

Inevitably, the blanket use of the concept of the defense mechanism raises a number of problems. When operations as diverse as, say, rationalization, which brings complex intellectual mechanisms into play, and turning against the self, which is a "vicissitude" of the instinctual aim, are attributed to a single function, . . . it may well be asked whether the concept in question is a really operational one.[5]

Despite the misgivings of these and other authors, and the enormous variations in the defense mechanisms listed, the concept itself, which provides a dynamic underpinning for the personality structure, seems to retain its great usefulness and even explanatory power as contrasted with more static images of the personality. If it has not been possible, as originally thought, to restrict defenses to a few basic devices, that should be taken as an indication that defense may be as broad as personality itself.

Within this variability, nevertheless, it has been possible to focus on certain kinds of defensive operations. Among the defenses known to Freud that have received considerable attention are sublimation, introjection–projection, regression, and denial. Among those scarcely mentioned by him that have received much attention are acting-out, neutralization, splitting, and identification (including the formation of the self-image). Some additional comments about each of these are in order.

Sublimation

For a long time, sublimation was regarded as the main normal solution to the conflicts surrounding the instincts. Freud defined it in the *Three Essays* (1905) as follows:

[Sublimation] enables excessively strong excitations arising from particular sources of sexuality to find an outlet and use in other fields, so that a not inconsiderable increase in psychical efficiency results from a disposition which is in itself perilous. Here we have one of the origins of artistic activity; and according to the completeness of the sublimation, a characterological analysis of a highly gifted individual, and in particular of one with an artistic disposition, may reveal a mixture, in every proportion, of efficiency, perversion and neurosis. A sub-species of sublimation is to be found in suppression by reaction-formation, which, as we have seen, begins during a child's period of latency and continues in favorable cases throughout his whole life.[6]

Thus for him the essence of sublimation was its social desirability. While this tie-in with the social structure seemed appropriate in 1905, it came under increasing criticism after World War I, when intellectuals were appalled by the brutality of the existing regimes (Bernfeld, 1922, 1931). Fenichel (1945) later took a somewhat different tack, reflecting these criticisms. He saw sublimation as characterized by inhibition of aim, desexualization, a complete absorption of an instinct into its sequelae, and an alteration within the ego. Nevertheless the reliance on social approval, even though combined with instinctual discharge, remained a stumbling block.

As time went on, the whole notion of normality with its relation to the social structure moved along different lines, so that less reliance was placed on sublimation as the normal outlet. In 1962 Kubie offered an incisive critique of the whole conceptual structure. He pointed out that sublimation has been used to imply: the resolution through philanthropic behavior of a constellation of unconscious processes that can induce homosexual behavior; the resolution by socially valuable behavior of polymorphous perverse trends (in Freud's original and naive sense) and also of libidinal thrusts and proddings from hypothetically overinvested erotogenic zones; the diversion into socially valuable channels of a stream of hypothetical and, as we now know, nonexistent psychic "energies" that derive from a constellation of unconscious processes, which would otherwise have produced socially destructive or at the least useless patterns of neurotic symptoms; any patterns of consistent behavior which arise from such sources yet are socially desirable; the substitution of a noninstinctual drive for an instinctual goal, with the implication that the instinctual drive itself is thereby attenuated. Kubie argued that as analysts we are passing through a transition during which we cling to the concept as a verbal short-cut while rejecting its essence. He urged that it be dropped in its entirety. In fact, as one surveys the literature, the concept of sublimation has almost disappeared.

Hacker (1972), while admitting the cogency of the arguments of Kubie, Bernfeld, and others, has suggested that sublimation might still be retained in another sense. He argues for an expanded principle of mature functioning beyond the reality principle, based on the original premise of sublimation, which would also include the potentially constructive uses of aggression for motivation, for novel structures, and for rational action that involves changing others (alloplastic action) simultaneous with action that involves changing oneself (autoplastic action). He confronts the function and possibilities of such a reality principle of the future with the conventional reality principle that commands adjustment or resignation rather than change or improvement.

However, except for isolated papers such as Hacker's, Freud's original notion that sublimation is the normal defense has been virtually abandoned by analytic theory. In its place has come a much more sophisticated discussion of what constitutes normal behavior (see chapter 19).

Introjection and Projection

Although Ferenczi coined the term introjection in 1909 (in *Collected Papers,* 1916) and Freud wrote two classic papers on projection ("The Schreber Case," 1911; "Jealousy," 1922), the significance of introjection and projection in the earliest period of mental life was not fully appreciated until Melanie Klein described them in great detail (1934 and later, in Klein, 1948). She argued that the development of the infant is governed by the mechanisms of introjection and projection. From the beginning the ego introjects objects as being "good" and "bad," for both of which the mother's breast is the prototype— for good objects when the child obtains it, for bad ones when it fails him or her. In Klein's view it is because the baby projects its own aggression onto these objects that it feels them to be "bad," and not only in that they frustrate its desires; the child conceives of them as actually being dangerous—in short, as possibly encompassing its destruction by all the means that sadism can devise.

At first Klein's description of such complex internal events in the mind of an infant was strongly rejected, especially by American psychoanalysts (Bornstein, 1945; Glover, 1945; Kernberg, 1969; Zetzel, 1956). In more recent years due credit has been given to her for her pioneering work in early object relations (Mahler, 1968; Schafer, 1968; Sperling, 1974; Stoller, 1968; Volkan, 1976). The sequence that she first described, of introjection–projection–reintrojection, is now firmly established as a basic dynamic of infancy, although arguments about its timing continue (Axelrad and Brody, 1970).[7]

An important variation of projection first described by Melanie Klein is *projective identification*. In this maneuver, parts of the self and internal objects are split off and projected onto the external object, which then becomes possessed by, controlled, and identified with the projected parts. Projective identification has manifold aims. It may be directed toward the bad object to gain control of the source of danger. Bad parts of the self may be projected in order to get rid of them as well as to attack and destroy the object, good parts may be projected to avoid separation or to keep them safe from bad things inside or to improve the external object through a kind of primitive projective reparation. Projective identification starts when the paranoid-schizoid position is first established in relation to the breast, but it persists and very often becomes intensified when the mother is perceived as a whole object and the whole of her body is entered by projective identification.[8]

Regression

With Freud's overwhelming emphasis on the developmental processes, the defenses of *regression* and its complementary *fixation* necessarily played a large part in his thinking. As early as 1897, in a letter to Fliess he had enunciated the principle (ever since fundamental to psychoanalytic thinking) that the choice of neurosis varies with the depth of the regression, or, as he put it then, with the chronological placing of the wave of development.[9]

In the theoretical section, chapter 7, of the *Interpretation of Dreams,* he distinguished three types of regression: topical (or topographic), in the sense of the systems of conscious, preconscious, and unconscious; temporal, as a regression to older psychic formations; and formal, when primitive modes of expression and representation take the place of the customary modes. In the case of the Rat Man

(1909), Freud saw regression as a specific characteristic of the obsessional neurosis, describing a regression from acting to thinking, as well as a regression from object-love to autoeroticism.

In the *Introductory Lectures* (1916–1917) Freud summed up his thinking about regression as follows:

in the case of every particular trend . . . some particular portions of it have stayed behind at earlier stages of its development, even though other portions may have reached their final goal. . . . We propose to describe the lagging behind as a fixation, that is, of the instinct.

The second danger in a development by stages of this sort lies in the fact that the portions which have proceeded further may also easily return retrogressively to one of these earlier stages—what we describe as a *regression.* The trend will find itself led into a regression of this kind if the exercise of its function—that is, the attainment of its satisfaction—is met, in its later or more highly developed form, by powerful external obstacles. It is plausible to suppose that fixation and regression are not independent of each other. The stronger the fixations on the path of development, the more readily will the function evade external difficulties by regressing to the fixations—the more incapable, therefore, does the developed function turn out to be of resisting external obstacles in its course. Consider that, if a people which is in movement has left strong detachments behind at the stopping-places on its migration, it is likely that the more advanced parties will be inclined to retreat to these stopping-places if they have been defeated or have come up against a superior enemy. But they will also be in the greater danger of being defeated the more of their number they have left behind on their migration.

It is important for your understanding of the neuroses that you should not leave this relation between fixation and regression out of sight. . . .

After what you have learned of the development of the libidinal function, you will be prepared to hear that there are regressions of two sorts: a return to the objects first cathected by the libido, which, as we know, are of an incestuous nature, and a return of the sexual organization as a whole to earlier stages. Both sorts are found in the transference neuroses and play a great part in their mechanism. In particular, a return to the first incestuous objects of the libido is a feature that is found in neurotics with positively fatiguing regularity.[10]

Ten years later, in *The Problem of Anxiety* (1926), Freud offered a further metapsychological explanation of regression in terms of his dual instinct theory, seeing it as a " 'defusion of instinct' in a detachment of the erotic components which, with the onset of the genital stage, had joined the destructive cathexes belonging to the sadistic phase."[11]

In 1964, Arlow and Brenner summed up the ego-psychological view of regression as follows: [12]

1. We have reviewed the history of the development of the concept of regression and we have observed how the meaning of this term was expanded steadily to explain different types of phenomena. We have described five different ways in which the term regression has been used: genetic, systemic, instinctual, phylogenetic and biogenetic. We have considered the different uses of the concept regression within the framework of the structural theory and have concluded that regression in the phylogenetic and biogenetic sense is of limited use scientifically and that the concept of systemic regression is inconsistent with the structural theory.

2. Regression is defined as the reemergence of modes of mental functioning characteristic of earlier phases of psychic development.

3. The process of regression may affect all the three portions of the psychic apparatus, the ego, the id, and the superego. Regression is a general tendency of mental life. Drive regression and ego regression may be independent variables. Drive regression by itself does not determine the ego regression.

4. Regression affects the functioning of the constituent parts of the psychic apparatus in a selective fashion. Regression is not global.

5. Regressions are usually transient and reversible. Pathology is not determined by the depth of the regression but rather by its irreversible nature, by the conflicts which it engenders, and by its interference with the process of adaptation.

6. Primitive modes of mental functioning exist side by side with more mature forms. What is observed in regressive phenomena is a shift in dominance of function. In regressive phenomena the primitive aspects of function which had been controlled and held in abeyance come to the fore.

It is clear that apart from cleaning up certain aspects of Freudian theory, such as his liking for biogenetic and phylogenetic explanations (which have since been dropped from psychoanalytic theory), the ego-psychological approach to regression does not go much beyond Freud, if at all. Some of Arlow and Brenner's propositions are of dubious validity, such as the statement that regressions are usually transient and reversible, or that drive regression and ego regression may be independent of one another.

The topic of regression has assumed particular importance among the defense mechanisms because of the greatly increased interest attached to borderline and psychotic conditions. In this respect Freud's earlier view that regression is characteristic of the obsessional neurosis is certainly outmoded from the viewpoint of ego psychology. This question, as well as others related to technique, is considered more fully in chapters 13 and 18.

Regression in the Service of the Ego

In 1936 Ernst Kris, in a paper on caricature, first described the defense of regression in the service of the ego, which immediately found a responsive echo in the psychoanalytic literature:

in dreams, the ego abandons its supremacy and the primary process obtains control, whereas in wit and in caricature the process remains in the service of the ego. This formulation alone suffices to show that the problem involved is a more general one: the contrast between an ego overwhelmed by a regression and a "regression in the service of the ego" . . . covers a vast and imposing range of mental experience. . . . It seems that the ego finds its supremacy curtailed whenever it is overwhelmed by affects, irrespective of whether an excess of affect or its own weakness is to be held responsible for the process. But the opposite case, where the ego enrolls the primary process in its service and makes use of it for its purposes, is also of the widest significance.[13]

Later Kris elaborated his idea further, in *Psychoanalytic Explorations in Art* (1952), in the section on preconscious mental processes.[14] Thus originally the idea was confined to the creative process and was found useful in explaining the regression of the artist, who then can come back to the normal world, and the psychotic, who cannot.

In 1954 Bellak expanded the concept further by conceptualizing the degree of ego participation on a continuum from daydreams, fantasies, phenomena of falling asleep, and preconscious fantasies to free association and projective techniques. In 1958 (quoted in Bellak et al., 1973), he redefined it in the following terms:

[there is] a brief, oscillating, relative reduction of certain adaptive functions of the ego in the service of [i.e. for the facilitation of] other, specifically the "synthetic" ego functions. What happens is that cognitive selective, adaptive functions are decreased; this weakens the sharply defined boundaries of figure and ground, of logical, temporal, spatial and other relations, and permits them to reorder themselves into new configurations with new boundaries, under the scrutiny of the again sharply functioning adaptive forces. . . . Our main concern above was to stop speaking of "the ego" as an entity and to speak of different ego functions at different levels of efficiency at the same time.[15]

Bellak also saw one metapsychological basis of free association in the therapeutic process as being regression in the service of the ego (1961).

Roy Schafer (1958) enumerated six conditions in the personality that favor regression in the service of the ego: a well-developed set of affect signals; a secure sense of self and/or a well-defined ego identity; a relative mastery of early traumas; mild rather than severe superego pressures; a history of sufficient trust and mutuality in interpersonal relations; and cultural meaningfulness accruing from the results of the process.

A wide body of literature has dealt with various aspects of the conceptualization (Geleerd, 1964; Joffe and Sandler, 1968; Kubie, 1958; Pine and Holt, 1960; Schafer, 1968; Schnier, 1951; Waelder, 1960; Wangh, 1957; Weissman, 1961, 1968, 1969; Wild, 1965). Its greatest elaboration is found in a book of Bellak et al. (1973), who view adaptive regression in the service of the ego as one of the 12 main ego functions and have measured it in people who are normal, neurotic, or schizophrenic. A related approach is that of Balint in *The Basic Fault* (1968); he distinguishes a benign from a malignant regression in the therapeutic process, seeing the latter as the characteristic problem of psychosis.

The most cogent criticism of the concept has come from Marshall Bush (1969), who feels that the role of regression in creative thinking has been overemphasized in psychoanalytic discourse. He argues that a developmentally primitive aspect of thinking which becomes elaborated into a highly adaptive and stable feature of reality testing and reality thinking enters into the creative act not as a regression in the service of the ego, but as a special secondary-process cognitive facility. Bush points out that Kris's discussion encompasses three different phenomena: the removal of anticathectic or defensive barriers between the ego and the id, which in turn affects preconscious thought formation; a shift of energy among ego functions that may involve repression to more primitive levels of ego functioning, but that may also involve a shift in priorities among different ego operations that is not necessarily regressive in nature; and the emergence of preconscious (or in some cases unconscious) material into consciousness. In his opinion, other writers do not distinguish sufficiently between the type of regression involved when new ideas emerge into consciousness and the subjective meanings of regression in the creative process. In agreement with Bush, Fine (1967) and Fine and Fine (1977) have also shown that in the creative processes of chess masters and mathematicians secondary-process cognitive facility is a more cogent explanation of the phenomena than regression.

The difficulty appears to arise in the multiple meanings of the term "regression." Arlow and Brenner (1964) point out that the topographical meaning of regression is inconsistent with the structural theory, i.e., that the shifting of an idea or feeling from conscious to unconscious can be explained more parsimoniously and more effectively than by topographic regression. If the defensive meaning of regression is maintained, in accordance with the structural theory, however, the confusion can be avoided. Creativity cannot be classified under a general heading as "regressive" or "progressive"; this smacks of the old idea that an artist is either a madman or a genius. Sometimes the creative individual regresses, sometimes he does not; the distinction can only be made on the basis of a full examination of the ego structure. Fine (1975b) has suggested that a clear distinction between inner and outer creativity would help to clarify the issues involved.

Denial (Disavowal)

Denial was the term used by Freud from 1923 onward[16] to describe the defense in which the subject refuses to recognize reality. Freud used it primarily in the metapsychological description of fetishism and psychosis. Since then it has most often been used in the sense of a denial of reality, of the outer world, as contrasted with repression, which blocks off the inner world.[17] Actually Freud had described the defense as early as his first paper on the defense neuropsychoses in 1894[18] but the term was not used until the 1920s.

In the standard edition, Strachey urged that the term "disavowal" be used instead of denial, and today the two words may be used interchangeably. However his idea has not caught on, and denial is still the more commonly employed word.

Trunnell and Holt (1974) have called attention to the many ambiguities in the use of the term by Freud and other writers.[19] For example, Jacobson (1957) saw denial as the most primitive form of defense, a global maneuver, as contrasted with repression, which is more specific; however, this usage differs from Freud.

Most commonly the term is employed in the description of psychotic behavior, in which external reality is denied; this seems to have been Freud's main thought as well. Hence denial has received most attention from those theoreticians who were primarily concerned with the psychoses. Searles (1963), for instance, explains much of the schizophrenic's apparent sensory deprivation as due to the use of an unconscious denial. He quotes a study by Brodey (1959), who showed that in the upbringing of the child who later develops schizophrenia, only those ingredients of what we call outer reality that are significantly supportive of (or significantly threatening to) the mother's "inner workings" compromise the effective outer reality of the child; evidently the remainder of outer reality, for all practical purposes, simply does not exist for him.[20] Searles also hypothesizes that the schizophrenic's unconscious denial of outer reality has a restitutive aspect to it, in that it provides him with a more or less blank screen upon which a necessary reprojection of pathogenic introjects, an externalization of internal conflicts from the past, can now be effected, akin to the function of the neutral screen atmosphere fostered by the analyst in the treatment of the neurotic individual.[21]

In *The Psychoanalysis of Elation* (1950), Lewin offered a masterful description of the use of denial in the manic states (see chapter 6).

Depersonalization is a special form of denial (Jacobson, 1959). What is denied is the identity of the person, rather than the outside world as such.

Neutralization

Neutralization is a broadening of the sublimation concept and has been explored most intensively by Hartmann (1964b). Following Freud's later formulas on desexualization in *The Ego and the Id,* Hartmann defines neutralization as the change of both libidinal and aggressive energy away from the instinctual and toward a noninstinctual mode. By using "noninstinctual" he attempts to avoid all the ambiguities and conflicts surrounding the term sublimation.

Hartmann postulates that neutralization of energy begins as soon as the ego evolves as a more or less demarcated substructure of personality, which would be a few months after birth. While he ascribes neutralization to both libidinal and aggressive drives, he particularly stresses the neutralization of aggression in that it provides a person with a way out of the dire dilemma of destroying either the objects or himself.[22] He also posits different stages or degrees of neutralization, that is, transitional states between instinctual and fully neutralized energy.[23]

At times Hartmann talks of neutralization as if it were only a transformation of energy; at other times he treats it as if it were a defense mechanism. In this respect he differs from other analytic authors. As he writes,

Neutralization, even where it is used for defense, stands apart from other defensive techniques of the ego in so far as it is specially defined by its energic aspect (among others), which means here, by the change of one mode of energy into another one. That sublimation is not really a "mechanism" in the usual sense, Fenichel (1945) has clearly seen, and this holds good also for neutralization in general. Also, that its relation to countercathexis is different from the one we find in other forms of defense. However, I cannot follow Fenichel when he simply equates sublimation with successful defense.[24]

Although Hartmann opposes the view that sublimation is simply a successful defense, which must be abandoned because of the social implications involved (Hartmann, 1964), he seems to wish to place neutralization in its stead as *the* successful defense, the way in which the ego masters reality. Such a view seems to raise the old argument about sublimation in a new form, since neutralization appears desirable only in cultures in which, like ours, affect expression is discouraged. Despite the weight of Hartmann's authority, which dominated psychoanalytic theorizing for almost 20 years (see chapter 5), his stress on neutralization has been rejected by a number of authors.[25] As a defense mechanism, however, it retains its place among the others.

Apart from the mastery of reality, the two most important applications of neutralization as a defense lie in schizophrenia and psychosomatic illness. In a paper on the metapsychology of schizophrenia (1953), Hartmann stressed that the schizophrenic's capacity for neutralization is damaged. As a result the ego is flooded with nonneutralized libido. Self-cathexis is sexualized, leading to what he calls the "sexual overestimation" of the self, and so is at least part of the ego functions, leading to functional trouble.[26] However, Hartmann does not go on to tie this failure of neutralization to other, better-known aspects of schizophrenic pathology (see chapter 13).

The other significant application of the neutralization concept is in Schur's hypothesis linking resomatization to the prevalence of primary-process thinking and the use of deneutralized energy (1955). He described a case of psychosomatic dermatitis in which a physiological regression took place; the ego regression was not limited to a regressive evaluation of danger, but in its response the ego operated with deneutralized energy, which corresponded to the reemergence of somatic discharge phenomena. Thus he linked somatization and ego regression to the failure to neutralize aggression. So many other factors are at play in the psychosomatic phenomena that this would represent only one aspect of the total pathology (see the discussion on psychosomatic phenomena in chapter 8).

Acting-Out

Acting-out is a defense mechanism first described in detail after World War II, although Freud mentioned it as early as 1914, in his paper on "Remembering, Repeating, and Working-Through." It can best be defined as an action, usually repetitive and compulsive in nature, and often self-destructive, that serves the unconscious purpose of resolving a repressed internal conflict by external means. Such action[27] generally displays an impulsive aspect relatively out of harmony with the subject's usual motivational patterns and fairly easy to isolate from the overall trends of his activity. Acting-out often takes the form of aggressive behavior directed at either the self or at others.

The older term "perversion" has been generally replaced by "acting-out disorders." It has been recognized that a wide variety of behavioral pathology can be subsumed under this rubric.[28]

As Anna Freud pointed out in a 1967 panel discussion,[29] the term has been subject to considerable confusion. Laplanche and Pontalis (1973) also comment that the term enshrines an ambiguity that is intrinsic in Freud's thinking here: he fails to distinguish the elements of actualization in the transference from the resort to motor action, which the transference does not necessarily entail. Fine (1973) carefully reexamined the original sources and showed that the term *agieren,* which is not the ordinary German word for action, was in-differently translated either "acting-out" or "action."

The topic has assumed such importance in contemporary ana-lytic thought that a number of symposia and panel discussions have been devoted to it (Milman and Goldman, 1973; Abt and Weissman, 1965; A. Freud, 1968b; Rexford, 1966). Zeligs (1957) called attention to a variety of acting-out within the analytic situation, which he calls acting-in.

In general, as with the other defenses elaborated since Freud, ac-ting-out has been associated with the psychoses and other more re-gressed psychopathological states. This makes sense because devel-opmentally the infant has no control over its actions, and such control has to be built up as part of ego maturation. However, the dividing line between action and acting-out remains a tenuous one and con-tinues to generate much confusion (Fine, 1973; Schafer, 1976).

Splitting

Splitting is an old psychiatric concept taken over by Freud. In his day the concept of the splitting of consciousness in hysteria was a com-monly accepted description, though explanations varied.

As Lichtenberg and Slap (1973) have shown, Freud in the fur-ther course of his work used the concept in four different ways: as a general organizing principle in psychic development and functioning, the pathological counterpart of synthesis; as a process specifically connected to the organzation of mental contents; as a means of defen-sive functioning; and as a process associated with the formation of coincident contradictory psychic concepts such as those of the fe-tishist. "Splitting" is a broadening of the older concept of "isola-tion," which it replaced.

Subsequent writers have elaborated one or another of these meanings of splitting. Nunberg (1930, 1931) opposed it to synthesiz-ing, stressing the synthetic function of the ego. The more recent dis-cussion has centered particularly on the early development of mental life in the infant, with the splitting of good and bad objects (good and bad mother), and the related investigations of the psychopathology of psychotic splitting were conducted by Melanie Klein (1946) and Fair-bairn (1941, 1954) but were later taken over by many other authors.

Currently, splitting is extensively discussed by Mahler (1975),

Kernberg (1976), and Kohut (1977), as well as by Kleinians, Sulli-
vanians, and others. Both Mahler and Kernberg clarify the older idea
that the earliest infantile experiences give rise to an organization of
two sets of memory traces, based on the primordial quality of plea-
surable-good-rewarding and painful-bad-punishing. Mahler (1968)
states that they exist as ''memory islands which contain imprints of
'pleasurable-good' or 'painful-bad' stimuli . . . not yet allocated either to the self or to the nonself.''[30] Sullivan (1940) stated that ''the
discrimination of the Good Mother pattern of events and the Bad
Mother pattern of events constitutes a primary bifurcation of interpersonal experience, evidences of which persist in most people throughout life.''[31] Kernberg, in a recent work (1975), has an excellent summation of the splitting process:

I am using the term "splitting" in a restricted and limited sense, referring
only to the active process of keeping apart introjections and identifications
of opposite quality. . . . Splitting . . . is a fundamental cause of ego weakness, and as splitting also requires less countercathexis than repression, a
weak ego falls back easily on splitting, and a vicious circle is created by
which ego weakness and splitting reinforce each other. The direct clinical
manifestation of splitting may be the alternative expression of complementary sides of a conflict in certain character disorders, combined with a bland
denial and lack of concern over the contradiction in his behavior and internal experience by the patient. One other direct manifestation of splitting may
be a *selective* "lack of impulse control" in certain areas, manifest in
episodic breakthrough of primitive impulses which are ego-syntonic during
the time of their expression (and splitting is prevalent in impulse neurosis
and addictions). Probably the best known manifestation of splitting is the
division of external objects into "all good" ones and "all bad" ones, with the
concomitant possibility of complete, abrupt shifts of an object from one extreme compartment to the other; that is, sudden and complete reversals of
all feelings and conceptualizations about a particular person. Extreme and
repetitive oscillation between contradictory self-concepts may also be the
result of the mechanism of splitting.[32]

Identification

Identification is an old and obvious idea, and cannot be considered
psychoanalytic per se. Throughout his writings Freud made use of it.
As early as 1897, in a letter to Fliess,[33] he writes in connection with
the multiplicity of psychical personalities (then a most significant
topic) that ''the fact of identification perhaps allows us to take the
phrase *literally.*''

In the post–World War I period, when he began to reflect on the problems of interpersonal relationships, Freud paid increasing attention to the process of identification. Initially, he argued, object-cathexis and identification are indistinguishable.[34] With the onset of the Oedipus complex, the object-cathexes (sexual desire for the parents) have to be given up; they are then replaced by identifications with the parents. Whence comes the formula: object-cathexes regress to identifications. "The authority of the father or the parents is introjected into the ego, and there it forms the nucleus of the superego, which takes over the severity of the father and perpetuates his prohibition against incest, and so secures the ego from the return of the libidinal object-cathexis."[35]

Later, in 1936, Anna Freud described a variation of the defense, *identification with the aggressor*. She sees this as involved in a variety of contexts—in physical aggression, criticism, mother–child relationships, and so on. There is a reversal of roles—the victim turns aggressor. This explains the perpetuation of family patterns, e.g., the daughter, badly treated by her mother, in turn treats her own daughter badly by an identification with the aggressor.

Nunberg (1955) distinguished partial and total identifications and gave the clearest exposition of the entire defense mechanism and its relationship to normal identification:

The conception of identification as a defense mechanism does not exclude its other aspect, the positive one. There is, indeed, also an identification out of love, which has nothing to do with defense. As has been stressed, identification can be ambivalent, and, in the present connection, we see that the negative side of an ambivalent process can be used as a defense against its positive side. As love represses hate, the reverse can also occur: hate represses love. In any case, through identification a union is established between the ego and the object or instinct which is to be warded off. What cannot be warded off from the ego is warded off through assimilation, synthesis. This form of defense has approximately this meaning: "If I cannot conquer the enemy in any other way I will unite with him and by this means render him harmless."[36]

Following the publication of Erikson's book *Childhood and Society* (1950), with its extensive discussion of identity and the identity crisis, as well as the dissemination of Sullivan's ideas after World War II, the interest of analysts increasingly turned to the self-image (identity, narcissism) and interpersonal relations. From the 1950s onward, identification as a pure defense mechanism increasingly merged into the total discussion of self- and object-relationships, and interpersonal growth and development. This whole topic is treated in more detail in chapter 15.

Extensions of the Concept of Defense: Summary Comments on the Defense Mechanisms

The defense concept is incorporated in Freud's first significant analytic statement (1894) that neurosis involves a defense against unbearable ideas. In a very real sense the history of psychoanalysis represents an unfolding and enlargement of this formula. It remains basic to the understanding of both neurotic and normal individuals. Human existence seems inevitably to involve some inner conflict, but whether because of biological necessity or cultural pressure remains debatable.

At first Freud limited himself to repression, although he also described sublimation, reaction formation, and regression. Then he enlarged the list of defenses as time went on. When Anna Freud wrote her key work, *The Ego and the Mechanisms of Defense* (1936), she listed nine and added some of her own, such as identification with the aggressor and denial in fantasy and reality.

Freud explored the neuroses so thoroughly that little has had to be added from a theoretical point of view, except for new concepts such as orality, hostility, and ego structure. In the psychoses he was on less sure ground. The literature subsequent to Freud has placed a heavy stress on the defense mechanisms most prominent in psychosis and borderline conditions, such as regression, denial, splitting, and acting-out.

The official list of defense mechanisms by no means exhausts the ways in which human beings can handle conflict. As seen, Bibring and her associates listed 39. Other authors have also repeatedly described defense mechanisms not contained in the "official" inventory. Greenson wrote of screen hunger and screen defenses (1958). Sachs (1973) depicted crying, weeping, and laughing as defenses against sexual drives. Melanie Klein (1948a, passim) wrote of manic defenses and of creativity as reparation for fantasied harm done to the mother.

Many theoreticians have portrayed the varied reactions to object loss at all stages in life. Spitz (1945) saw marasmus as a wasting away due to lack of maternal love; the same phenomenon has been observe in animals. Bowlby (1953) delineated the sequence of protest-despair-detachment in response to the loss of the mother. Wolfenstein (1976) reported a panel discussion on the effects on adults of object loss in the first five years. The panelists reported depression, schizophrenia, and sexual promiscuity, among other problems. Pinderhughes (1971) explored the social, somatic, and psychic sequelae of loss. He stressed the significance of paranoid mechanisms in persons who suffer a loss. Numerous other papers could be cited.

It has become commonplace to see hostility as a defense against sexuality and to see sexuality as a defense against hostility, schizophrenia as a defense against homosexuality, homosexuality as a defense against schizophrenia, and so on. In other words, the concept of defense has been broadened far beyond its original scope to include virtually any dynamic process in which there is anxiety and a way of warding off the anxiety.

The culturalist school, while verbally at odds with the Freudians, has merely provided a further extension of the defense concept by tying it to cultural and other interpersonal processes. Fromm, for example, saw the "marketing" personality as characteristic of Americans (1947). Later, in conjunction with Maccoby (1970), he integrated interpersonal, cultural, and intrapersonal factors in his description of a Mexican village. Diamond (1974) saw schizophrenia as the characteristic defense and illness of Western civilization. Miller and Swanson (1960) showed that denial was more commonly employed by the poor because of the harsher nature of their social reality. In general, the culture-of-poverty school carries the implication that defense mechanisms are socially as well as individually conditioned. Some have even maintained that poverty may be persisted in for psychological reasons (Allen, 1970). Weinstein (1976) sees presidential assassination as a peculiarly American problem because it has occurred so often.

It may be argued that in this kind of extension the defense, loss of defense, and symptom all become confused with one another. Their exact separation poses such knotty problems, however, given the circular character of personality dynamics (e.g., anxiety leads to homosexuality, then homosexuality leads to anxiety; which comes first?) that most theoreticians throw their hands up in despair. Robbins (1955) sees schizophrenia as both conflict and defense, as do Burnham et al. (1969) with their delineation of schizophrenia as a need-fear dilemma.

The basic principle remains that the human personality can be understood in the light of Freud's formula, using defenses against unbearable ideas. Many typical defenses, personal as well as social, can be described. Many others are possible. Psychoanalytic theory, although it has offered profound insights into the defensive process, has not reached the stage of an exact systematization.

Defense and Illness

From the very beginning, Freud strove to define illness in dynamic terms; his seminal paper of 1894 on the "Defense Neuropsychoses" already introduces this effort. As his theoretical scheme altered, he was concerned at each point to correct the metapsychology of illness (Brenner, 1957). In 1926, in his last important theoretical summation, he tried to link the three major illnesses to which he had devoted most of his life's labors with their typical defenses: thus repression is characteristic of hysteria, whereas reaction formation and regression are characteristic of obsessive-compulsive neurosis.

It soon appeared that what he had done was to describe certain typical constellations but not the entire personality. Fenichel puts it as follows:

In most cases . . . analysis succeeds in showing that a special defensive attitude was forced on the individual directly by a particular historical situation: either it was the most suitable attitude in a given situation, and all later situations are then reacted to as if they were still the pathogenic one, or all other possible attitudes were blocked in a given situation, or the attitude was favored by some model in the child's environment, with whom the child identified himself, or the attitude is exactly opposite to that of a model whom the child did not want to be like. Unusual behavior can very often be traced back to unusual conditions in the childhood environment. And psychoanalyses of character disorders certainly give opportunity to study quite a selection of "unusual childhood environments!"[37]

In subsequent literature two theories relating to defense and illness have existed side by side. One states that the specific neurotic illnesses (including the psychotic) are characterized by specific defenses and specific fixation points. Thus repression, reaction formation, and regression are characteristic for the neuroses, while denial, splitting (earlier called isolation), and projection are characteristic for the psychoses. The fixation point for hysteria is to be found in the phallic phase, for obsessional neurosis in the anal stage, and for schizophrenia and other psychoses in the oral stage.[38]

The alternative position which, paradoxically, also stems from Freud, states that personality is too complex to be forced into such rigid straitjackets, and that each individual must be judged in terms of his or her own particular history. Thus in the paper on "Types of Onset of Neurosis" (1912), after describing various cases, Freud states that "not one of them is a pure example of any of the four types of onset."[39] Then he concludes, "Psychoanalysis has warned us that we must give up the unfruitful contrast between external and internal factors, between experience and constitution, and has taught us that we shall invariably find the cause of the onset of neurotic illness in a particular psychical situation which can be brought about in a variety of ways."[40]

Metapsychology of the Defenses

The questions of why defense mechanisms are necessary at all and what function they serve in the general psychic economy belong to what might be called the metapsychology of defense. A number of topics subsumed under this heading have been considered by various authors.

The Defensive Organization

The contemporary theory of the ego is based on the recognition that organization is as essential a part of the human being as impulse, and the ego is the organizing aspect of the personality. Hoffer (1954) seems to have been the first to use term "defense organization" to refer to the totality of defenses used by the individual. This defense organization is one facet of the ego organization. Its origin and prehistory are obscure but its function can be formulated precisely, namely, the regulation of anxiety, not the total avoidance of anxiety.

He saw a hierarchical structure of the defensive organization which is inevitable in the early struggles of childhood and can only be resolved much later. Freud (*The Problem of Anxiety,* 1926) had already commented that the strength of the defense lies in its tie with the id, that is, the defense also gratifies some impulse. Hoffer now asserts that from an ego viewpoint defense serves both a defensive and a constructive purpose. For instance, introjection helps to construct the ego, projection helps the ego to like itself better and prevents its destruction, sublimation enriches the ego (A. Freud, 1952).

Pine pursued this idea further (1970). He argued that there is a structuralized relationship between drive and defense that becomes part of the order and permanence of the psychic life. This permanence is also related to Waelder's principle of multiple function (1936b), which posits that any specific act is an attempted solution to problems of the ego vis-à-vis the drives, the superego, external reality, and the compulsion to repeat. Pine theorized that specific defensive postures that include opportunities for gratification in ways syntonic with the individual's conscience and with his social milieu can have a high degree of permanence, which can be disrupted only by a significant change in internal or external pressures.

Since organization is an essential part of the ego, the relationship of defense to cognition must be considered. Lichtenberg and Slap (1971) believe that the emergence of individual defense mechanisms is a concomitant of perceptual-cognitive maturation.

Defenses and the Treatment Process

Considerable attention has been devoted to the fate of the defense mechanisms in the course of psychoanalysis. Panels were held on this topic by the International and American Psychoanalytic Associations in 1954, 1966, 1970, and 1972. One school of thought has believed that a successful analysis should result in the disappearance of defenses, whereas another has maintained that analysis results in the modification, not the disappearance, of defenses and that while the neurotic individual is restricted to the use of primarily one defense mechanism in all situations, the analyzed person is free to use a variety of defenses in an adaptive manner (Krent, 1970). The disagreement has persisted, although the latter position tends to be favored. In an empirical study done at the San Francisco Institute, Windholz (Panel, 1972) found that defenses do not disappear but become integrated into the ego as regulatory mechanisms.

Early Prototypes and Precursors of Defenses

Inasmuch as defense mechanisms are ways of warding off anxiety-provoking stimuli, it has frequently been suggested that they must in some way derive from the earliest kinds of infantile experience or early psychic states. In his 1937 paper on "Analysis Terminable and Interminable," Freud had again suggested that there could be constitutional bases for the different types of ego structure. "We have no reason to dispute the existence and importance of original, innate distinguishing characteristics of the ego."[41] Among these presumably constitutionally determined resistances he mentioned adhesiveness of the libido, depletion of the capacity for change, and a particularly mobile libido.

With regard to infantile precursors, Freud had already mentioned projection as a derivative of the first negation, or spitting out, while introjection may be presumed to derive from swallowing. Federn (1929) saw isolation as related to the original touching taboo. Other authors have continued this type of speculation with the concept of "ego nuclei" (Fenichel, 1945; Glover, 1925; Hendrick, 1938) without, however, any theoretical or clinical confirmation.

Spitz (1961) offered the most elaborate discussion of the question of early prototypes of ego defenses. He suggested that repression is related to the early stimulus barrier, and denial may derive from eyelid closing. The two main questions he posed were: What kind of mother–child relations favor and facilitate what kind of defense mechanisms? At what point do the mother–child relations transform the physiological prototype into the beginning of a defense mechanism?

Various suggestions have been made on how the defense mechanisms do arise from early infantile experience (Fine 1975b; Rubinfine, 1962), as in the general question of the relationship of the earliest experiences to later personality and intellectual development, but the questions are still too complex to permit any clear answer (Escalona, 1968; Fries, 1961). About all that can be said from a theoretical point of view is that the infant forms representations of both need satisfaction and need frustration which later structuralize further into inner representations of need-satisfying (good) objects and frustrating (bad) objects (Rubinfine, 1962).

Chapter Twelve

Ego Psychology: Character Structure,
Ego Autonomy, Affects, and
Cognitive Functioning

Character Structure

The psychoanalytic conception of character structure is not well crystallized. Different ideas stemming from different periods have been poorly integrated, e.g., the earlier id formulations and the later ones in terms of the ego.

Freud's first approach to the description of character came in the time of id psychology and thus emphasized its instinctual origin. In *Character and Anal Erotism* (1908) he wrote: "We can . . . lay down a formula for the way in which character in its final shape is formed out of the constituent instincts: the permanent character-traits are either unchanged continuations of the original instincts, or sublimations of those instincts, or reaction-formations against them." [1] In terms of ego psychology this definition is grossly incorrect, yet Freud never bothered to change it. Many authors who quote it today do not realize that it must be totally abandoned in the light of contemporary concepts (Tartakoff, cited in Valenstein, 1958).

In Freud's own work the only character type delineated with any thoroughness is the anal character (1908). He described the traits of orderliness, parsimony, and obstinacy as typical of the anal character and traced their development to the conflicts surrounding the child's early bowel training. Later the connection between anal erotism and obsessional neurosis was brought out by Freud (1913), following a suggestion of Ernest Jones (1913).

Assuming mistakenly that regression in the main stops at the

anal level (Abraham, 1924, in *Selected Papers,* vol. 2),[2] almost all
analytic authors before World War I identified deep pathology with
the anal character and the obsessional neurosis, contrasting it in turn
with hysteria. Once the significance of the oral stage was recognized,
after 1940, such a formulation clearly appeared oversimplified, especially when the roles of hostility, anxiety, ego structure, superego
structure, interpersonal relations, and cultural forces had to be taken
into account.

Historically, another complication arose from the defection of
Adler. Freud could easily have utilized some of Adler's contributions, particularly the concept of the life-style and the "guiding fictions" (later renamed the "defense mechanisms" and given a more
secure footing in the id). But because Alder had defected, Freud was
adamant in rejecting his ideas, one of which was that psychoanalysis
should deal with the total character structure. In the *History of the
Psychoanalytic Movement* (1914), Freud wrote:

Psychoanalysis has never claimed to provide a complete theory of human
mentality in general, but only expected that what it offered should be applied to supplement and correct the knowledge acquired by other means.
Adler's theory, however, goes far beyond this point; it seeks at one stroke to
explain the behavior and character of human beings as well as their neurotic
and psychotic illnesses. It is actually more suited to any other field than that
of neurosis.[3]

While he was taking Adler to task in one paper for trying to define
character, in another paper Freud did the very same thing. In the
paper on "Types of Onset of Neurosis" (1912) he distinguished
four types: frustration; inability to meet reality demands (a developmental process); inhibition in development, fixation; and increase in
quantity of libido. In practice all these are mixed, and pure types are
not found. Furthermore he made the statement, which became the
heart of all psychoanalytic characterology, that the differences are
quantitative rather than qualitative, so that there is a continuum from
health to sickness:

The importance in the causation of illness which must be ascribed to quantity of libido is in satisfactory agreement with two main theses of the theory of
neuroses to which psychoanalysis has led us: first, the thesis that the
neuroses are derived from the conflict between the ego and the libido, and
secondly the discovery that there is no qualitative distinction between the
determinants of health and those of neurosis, and that, on the contrary,

healthy people have to contend with the same tasks of mastering their libido—they have simply succeeded better in them.[4]

In a later paper, "Some Character Types Met With in Psychoanalytic Work" (1916), he began the more modern approach, formulating character in terms of some salient feature of the personality. Three types of character were delineated in that study: the exceptions (those who consider themselves exempt from the ordinary rules of life); those wrecked by success; and criminals from a sense of guilt.

Yet the more systematic analytic description of character types remained in a highly unsatisfactory state. Various classifications were suggested, but none caught on. Fenichel[5] defined character as the habitual mode of bringing into harmony the tasks presented by internal demands and the external world, which is necessarily a function of the constant, organized, and integrating part of the personality that is the ego. The question of character would thus be the question of how and when the ego acquires the qualities by which it habitually adjusts itself to the demands of instinctual drives and of the external world, and later also of the superego. Fenichel described various unsystematic types of character structure; he stated that no systematic approach was possible. He particularly stressed the role of the external environment:

The insufficiency of a theoretical description of mechanisms becomes more evident in character disorders than in the case of symptom neuroses. This insufficiency is of a dual nature. First, the types described are an outcome of external influences on the biological structures and vary, therefore, with the external influences. What is not stressed enough in a mere description of types is the fact that they are types of today's world only. The prevailing character structures are especially characteristic for a given culture, and sometimes for a given stratum for a given culture. Specifically, it is the conflict between the contradictory aims of "active independence" and "passive-receptive longing," both of which are stimulated by present-day social conditions that determine today's pathological character structures. Second, the types never correspond point for point with the individual cases.[6]

A significant advance after Freud was made by Wilhelm Reich in the first part of *Character Analysis* (1933). Reich saw character as a chronic alteration of the ego which one might describe as a rigidity. Its meaning is the protection of the ego against external and internal dangers. It can be called an *armor*. The armoring of the ego takes place as a result of fear of punishment, at the expense of id energies, and contains the prohibitions of early education.

Reich contrasted the genital character with the neurotic character. At that time Otto Rank (1932) offered a similar typology, viewing the artistic personality as the ideal normal and contrasting it with the neurotic in terms of the capacity to make one's will felt. While both of these formulations are suggestive, they could be looked upon today as oversimplifications.

A further step was taken by Kardiner who, in *The Psychological Frontiers of Society* (1945), offered the first comprehensive integration of psychodynamic and anthropological data. Every culture has a basic personality type that is characteristic of it; others must be seen as deviations from that type. The institutions of the culture are designed to perpetuate that type. He described a number of key integrational systems: maternal care; induction of affectivity; early disciplines; institutionalized sibling attitudes; induction into work; puberty; marriage; character of participation in society; factors that keep the society together; projective systems (folklore, religion); reality systems, derived from empirical or projective sources; arts, crafts, and techniques; techniques of production. Kardiner's schema has provided a useful model for multitudinous studies of culture and personality (Levine, 1973).

A total description of any person's character structure would involve an enormous amount of information. Included in it would have to be descriptions of the id, the ego, the superego, anxieties, defenses, conscious and unconscious forces, interpersonal relations, significant features of the life history, interests, attitudes, habits, characteristic patterns of handling the world, symptoms (if any), ideals, goals, and many other features. To avoid such extensive labor, for many years analysts sought short-cuts in briefer, more concise evaluations, similar to trait psychology (selfish, ambitious, etc.).

Thus they isolated certain recurrent themes in the life histories of individuals, drew these themes into a consistent constellation (which may or may not be seen as the core of the person), and tried to tie in these themes with the rest of the individual's functioning. Some of the more important characterological descriptions on this basis that are found in the literature can be briefly enumerated.

The Oral Character

The structure of the oral character centers around the activities of taking and giving. Hence, as Glover (1925) pointed out in a seminal paper, one finds in either positive or negative form the characteristics of omnipotence, ambivalence in object relations, sensitiveness in regard to "getting" and to the maternal function of environment, quick emotional discharge, alternation of mood, and rapid motor reactions, together with character traits associated with viewing, touching, and smelling. The genesis of the oral character is to be sought in the patterns of the mother–child relationship rather than in the persistence of oral-erotic traits as such. Naturally, much depends on whether the child finds satisfaction or frustration with the mother. Freud once commented that a man who has been sure of his mother's love feels that he can master any obstacle.

A strong oral base is found in a great many seemingly normal adults. Optimism, ambition, confidence, to the point of overconfidence or even bragadoccio, drive for leadership, and real achievement arising out of these personal qualities are frequently seen. Often men with these characteristics become leaders, sometimes of great importance in the history of the world. In our century Freud, Churchill, and Roosevelt were all oral characters.

In the pathological form, however, the oral character regresses, often to the point of schizophrenia. Rosen (1953) states that his understanding of schizophrenia did not jell until he realized that orality is to psychosis what the Oedipal situation is to neurosis. Almost literally, the schizophrenic relates to nobody except his mother.

Schizophrenia represents the extreme of oral regression. But many milder forms of regression are found (the "borderline" cases). There is a marked weakness of the ego, low frustration tolerance, alternating episodes of elation and depression, outbursts of rage at the slightest frustration, long periods of inactivity, weakness, and depression, addiction to wild "love" experiences that pass quickly, turning to hatred, and a marked tendency to develop somatic symptoms. High achievement is frequently compatible with this personality structure, as among scientists (Fine and Fine, 1977; Roe, 1953). In his study of the Alorese, Kardiner (1945) showed that the predominant mode of the culture was orally fixated.

The Anal Character

The anal character was the one first described by Freud and by a number of his co-workers before World War I (Abraham, 1921; A. Brill, 1912; Ferenczi, 1914; Jones 1918). At the core of the anal character is the triad of orderliness, parsimony, and stubbornness, which were considered to arise in connection with toilet training. The anal triad can be maintained without symptoms in the adjusted anal character, who displays a high degree of compulsivity, regularity, and obsessional attention to detail in his daily life. Everything must be "just right"; otherwise he becomes upset. Beyond this core constellation, however, many different possibilities exist, depending on the nature of the oral experience, the sexual orientation, and many other factors. Freud saw the essential dynamics as the split between love and hate, in which the repression of the hatred is the core conflict that explains the rest of the psychological makeup.

The Phallic-Narcissistic Character

This character formation was first described by Wilhelm Reich (1933), whose elucidation of it is still outstanding. Even in outward appearance the phallic-narcissistic individual, nearly always a man, shows some distinctive features: self-confidence, often arrogance, elasticity, vigor, and impressiveness. In the behavior toward other people the narcissistic element always dominates over the object-libidinal, and there is always an admixture of more or less disguised sadistic traits.

    Dynamically, analysis reveals an identification of the total ego with the phallus (see Sandler, 1959), also a more or less open display of this ego. For such persons the slang expression "the big prick" is quite apt. The pride in the real or fantasied phallus goes along with a strong phallic aggression. To the unconscious of this man, the penis is not in the service of love but is an instrument of aggression and vengeance. This serves as a defense against a regression to passivity and anality. The infantile history regularly reveals serious disappointments in the object of the other sex, disappointments that occurred precisely at the time when attempts were made to win the object through phallic exhibition.

The Hysterical Character

Following Freud's original formulations, the attempt was made to correlate the various clinical entities with the points of fixation in psychosexual development—primarily, orality with schizophrenia, anality with the obsessional neurosis, and the phallic phase with hysteria. Though statements to this effect are still seen in the literature, it is obvious that they represent a great oversimplification in terms of ego psychology.

Freud's elucidation of the hysterical symptoms in 1908 is still correct as far as it goes, but later work has shown that hysterical symptoms may be found in a variety of personality constellations, including the orally regressed (Marmor, 1953). This realization led analysts to formulate the conception of a *hysterical character,* with varied symptomatology. While the symptoms may change fairly quickly, the underlying character structure does not, any more than any other. Interest then shifts to this character structure, and the emotionality of the hysteric is seen as a defense mechanism (Siegman, 1954). This can also merge with various other kinds of character structure.

The Masochistic Character

As with hysteria, the study of masochism began with examination of the sexual symptom. In order to achieve sexual gratification, some people must first (or simultaneously) experience pain. Originally Freud saw this as a component of the sexual instinct; later, in the period of ego psychology, that concept had to be altered. It was then that he assumed the existence of a primary masochism as a derivative of the death instinct, a road where many refused to follow him.

As analytic experience grew, the sexual perversion of masochism receded into the background, giving way to *moral masochism*—the choice, for whatever reason, of suffering over pleasure. Moral masochism became a topic of intense interest in the 1940s and 1950s, giving rise to numerous significant formulations. A number of these are summarized in Theodor Reik's *Masochism in Modern Man* (1941), as well as in a panel discussion of the American Psychoanalytic Association (Stein, 1956) and in an important paper by Berliner (1958), which gives the essential points.

Reik argues that upon closer examination one of the most striking features of masochism, the reversal of all pleasure values, proves
to be fictitious. The masochist aims at the same pleasure as others do,
but he arrives at it by a detour. Intimidated by threatening anxiety,
inhibited by the idea of punishment and later by unconscious guilt
feeling, he finds his particular way of avoiding anxiety and gaining
pleasure. He submits voluntarily to punishment, suffering, and hu-
miliations, and thus defiantly purchases the right to enjoy the gratification denied before.

The basic formula of the masochist is: victory through defeat.
He does not just accept punishment and humiliation, he fantasizes
about them and anticipates them. He not only demonstrates their impotence to withhold the forbidden pleasure, but he affirms and demonstrates that they helped him to it. This is similar to the religious
conviction that the last shall be first, that according to the anticipating
imagination, ignominy and abuse will be turned into fame and honor.

Berliner (1958) stressed the importance of the interpersonal situation more clearly than had been done before. He saw masochism as
a disturbance of object relations, a pathologic way of loving. Masochism means loving a person who gives hate and ill-treatment. It is
the neurotic solution of an infantile conflict between the need for
being loved and the actual experience of nonlove coming from the
person whose love is needed. (Burnham et al. [1969] later referred to
this as the "need-fear dilemma.") It is also a defensive structure
against this need for love and experience of nonlove (Menaker,
1953). The masochistic attitude is the bid for the affection of a hating
love object. Childhood experiences of this kind result in a character
structure that keeps the original situation alive through transferences.
Masochistic suffering represents in the unconscious the original personal love object that once gave suffering. It may also represent unconscious revenge against that object (Bergler, 1949).

Much of the dynamics of masochism, laboriously worked out in
this period, has been rephrased to apply to the borderline-narcissistic
type of personality, which is considered in chapter 14.

The Neurotic Personality of Our Time

Horney (1937) gave a good description of one type of neurotic personality, frequently seen in our day, especially in analysts' offices.

The neurotics she describes are disturbed in attitudes concerning giving and getting affection, evaluation of the self, self-assertion, aggression, and sexuality. They are excessively dependent on the approval or affection of others. There is a marked contradiction between their wish for affection and their own capacity for feeling or giving it. There is an inner insecurity expressed in this dependence on others. In self-assertion there are definite inhibitions. Disturbances of aggression show themselves in two ways: one is a propensity to be aggressive, domineering, overexacting, be bossy, cheat, or find fault. The other is the opposite set: feeling cheated, dominated, scolded, imposed upon, humiliated. In sex there is either a compulsive need for sexual activities or inhibition toward such activities. Horney does not, however, trace these character traits to any particular childhood constellation.

The Authoritarian Personality

The study of the authoritarian personality grew out of the havoc created by World War II. Adorno et al. (1950) described the results of their extensive testing and interviewing of such persons. Their book has almost created a discussion literature of its own, which is still expanding. This syndrome follows the classical psychoanalytic pattern involving a sadomasochistic resolution of the Oedipus complex. Fromm called it the "sadomasochistic character." External social repression is concomitant with the internal repression of impulses. In order to achieve "internalization" of social control, which never gives as much to the individual as it takes, the individual's attitude toward authority and its psychological agency (the superego) assumes an irrational aspect. The subject achieves his own social adjustment only by taking pleasure in obedience and subordination. This brings into play the sadomasochistic impulse structure both as a condition and as a result of social adjustment.

In our form of society, sadistic as well as masochistic tendencies find gratification. The pattern for the translation of such gratification into character traits is a specific Oedipus-complex resolution that defines the formation of this syndrome. Love for the mother, in its primary form, comes under a severe taboo. Hatred for the father results from this taboo and is transformed by reaction-formation into love. This transformation leads to a particular kind of superego. The transformation of hatred into love, the most difficult task an individual has to perform in his early development, never succeeds completely. Stereotypy tends to become heavily libidinized and plays a large part in the subject's inner household. He develops deep compulsive character traits, partly by retrogression to the anal-sadistic phase of development. Sociologically, in Europe this syndrome used to be highly characteristic of the lower middle class. In the United States it may be expected among people whose actual status differs from the one they aspire to.

The As-If Personality

In 1934 Helene Deutsch described a type of personality that she called the ''as-if''; her paper has had wide repercussions (J. Weiss, 1966). Such people force on the observer the inescapable impression that their whole relationship to life is in some way lacking in genuineness and yet outwardly runs along as if it were complete. They are unaware of their defeat in feeling. They should be distinguished from outwardly cold individuals who conceal powerful and differentiated affects. The ''as-if'' personalities have undergone a loss of object cathexis, and their behavior is simply mimicry, based on very early identification. Their facile capacity for identification is such that they characteristically undergo kaleidoscopic shifts in behavior, reflecting the personalities of the individuals with whom they come in contact. They are devoid of object constancy. They manifest a plastic passivity concealing great hostility, a lack of genuine affective response to objective loss, a defect in moral structure, a labile shifting from one social grouping to another, and an enormous suggestibility.

The basic trauma centers around the patient's failure to find objects for cathexis. The objects that these patients had were devalued because of their real deficiencies or because of traumas that these patients experienced. Their upbringers lacked affect. As a result these patients did not develop beyond the stage of imitativeness to the stage of true identification. They did not acquire the capacity to internalize, and they failed to arrive at adequate superego formation. All objects are kept external. ''As-if'' phases appear in schizophrenia and at puberty, but in pure form ''as-if'' phenomena do not appear suddenly, nor are they transient.

Other Character Structures

Numerous other types of character structures and studies of individuals have appeared in the psychoanalytic literature. Jones (1913) described men whose unconscious contains the idea that they are God (the father). In his study of *Hamlet* (1948), Jones also showed how ubiquitous the Hamlet conflict is. Abraham (1925) described the character of the impostor. Erikson (1958) traced Luther's conversion back to his extremely unhappy childhood in which he was mercilessly beaten. Greenson (1958) described the ''screen'' personality, a person searching for a new identity. Gedo (1972) reported a panel discussion on the methodology of psychoanalytic biography. Gilberg (1974) reported on ascetism and the analysis of a nun. Fine (1967) described the personality of the chess player; Fine and Fine (1977) expanded the thesis to describe the mathematician.

The Ego Functions Profile

From the start, the global descriptions of character structure found in the literature always seemed less than satisfactory. They were too similar to the dubious concepts of psychiatric diagnosis, and too close to questionable popular generalizations (e.g., oral character equals fat person). But before the development of ego psychology the tools for precision were lacking.

Beginning with World War II, clinicians and researchers, now armed with psychological tests and a deeper grasp of the variety of ego functions, increasingly turned to more complete and complex measures of the personality. These too could find their inspiration in Freud, who stated in 1937: ''Every normal person, in fact, is only normal on the average. His ego approximates to that of the psychotic in some part or other and to a greater or lesser extent.'' [7]

Since the ego functions vary in strength and significance, it is a natural next step to measure each of these ego functions singly, and then to integrate them into a total description. Such measurement or assessment could, and did historically, take two different approaches: established psychological tests, and clinical interviews in which relevant ego functions were approached more directly.

Psychodynamic psychological testing began with Jung's studies of word associations and their attendant complexes (*Diagnostische Assoziationsstudien,* 1906). The next momentous step was Rorschach's invention of his extraordinary test in 1921 (*Psychodiagnostics*). Murray's Thematic Apperception Test was published in 1935, and his voluminous methods for the exploration of personality appeared in 1938 (Murray et al., *Explorations in Personality*), combining interview and test methods. Wechsler's intelligence test, which soon replaced the older Binet, was first published in 1939. Bender published her visual-motor Gestalt test in 1938. The use of figure drawings as a measure of personality functioning is a simple application of the early discoveries of the relationship between the artist and his conflicts (Machover, 1949; Rank, *Art and the Artist,* 1932; Sachs, 1942).

During and after World War II these tests became the core of the diagnostic kit of clinical psychologists, who began to appear in steadily increasing numbers. The first and most extensive large-scale application of such a test battery, which stresses all the ego functions rather than merely the diagnostic label, was the work of Rapaport and his colleagues. The first publication of their work was by Rapaport, Gill, and Schafer, *Diagnostic Psychological Testing* (1945–1946). Rapaport's group proposed a variety of correlations between the test materials, including the intelligence tests, and personality functioning. Although all of Rapaport's work has been questioned as statistically inadequate, his approach has remained the dominant one for the analytically oriented clinical psychologist and psychiatrist.

In his revision and updating of Rapaport's work, Holt (1968) takes the position that a diagnosis is not a sufficient classification but is a necessary constituent of personality description. He then goes on to summarize the Rapaportian position in eight propositions:

1. Diagnosis is not classification but construction of a verbal model of a personality in adaptive difficulty, or suffering from some malformation or dilapidation.

2. Such a verbal model must be hierarchically organized, by means of intrapersonal comparisons or quantification of the variables used.

3. Typological concepts, like diagnoses, are useful as reference points to aid the description of personalities by means of interpersonal comparison.

4. The central emphasis of diagnosis is structural, using a typology of ego structures based mainly on defenses; dynamic and genetic considerations are important, but secondary.

5. The diagnostic process begins with the identification and measurement of variables by empathic observation and primary inference directly from clinical data (including tests); the clinician then examines the patterning of these variables, and by reference to empirical knowledge about what goes with what and to relevant theory, he makes secondary inferences of a more constructional kind.

6. The clinical usefulness of a personality description is enhanced if it includes both characterological and symptomatic diagnosis.

7. The diagnostician should strive to assess the degree to which aspects of personality play an adaptive role and are well compensated, as against being maladaptive (decompensated).

8. The ultimate purpose of diagnosis is to facilitate understanding and individualized predictions about the behavior of uniquely organized persons. Since a broad range of possible predictions may be clinically called for, the diagnostic description must cover most of the important aspects of personality.

After Rapaport, diagnostic psychological testing zoomed into a virtually independent discipline. It would take us too far afield to trace the development of each test; even a bare inventory of new tests would occupy many pages (Buros, *Mental Measurements Handbook,* 1975). In the main, testing has proceeded independently of the technical advances in psychoanalysis.

Clinical Approaches

The other pathway to the ego functions, the clinical, has been approached with considerable vigor as well. Here the question immediately arises: What should be included under the ego functions? In his last summary work, *An Outline of Psychoanalysis* (1939), Freud included under the principal characteristics of the ego: self-preservation, becoming aware of and dealing with external stimuli, controlling voluntary movement, and learning to influence the external world to one's own advantage through activity. Other aspects he included are the seeking of pleasure and the avoidance of pain, taking

external circumstances into account in deciding when to satisfy instinctual drives, and transmitting an unexpected increase in unpleasure by an anxiety signal. As part of its core functioning, the ego attempts to avoid overly strong stiumli, has a memory function, and
attempts to reconcile the demands from id, superego, and reality.

Hartmann (1950) offered a somewhat different list, but with the
disclaimer that no analyst had ever attempted a complete list and he
would not attempt to do so either. Following upon and enlarging
upon Freud's initial ideas, others have offered various compilations
of ego functions (Bellak, 1955; Beres, 1956; A. Freud, 1965; Greenspan and Cullender, 1973; Knapp et al., 1960; Mahrer, 1970; Waldhorn, 1967). Apart from the studies mentioned in more detail below,
perhaps the most comprehensive discussion is that by Arlow and
Brenner (1964), who include the following among ego functions:
consciousness; sense perception; perception and expression of affect;
thought; control of motor action; memory; language; defense mechanisms and defense activity in general; control, regulation, and binding of instinctual energy; integration and harmonization; reality testing; inhibition or suspension of the operation of any of these
functions and regression to a primitive level of functioning.

The Menninger Research Project (1954–1972)

Spurred on by the need for a more precise description of ego functions, a number of large-scale research projects were undertaken in
the 1950s and later. The Menninger Clinic Project, under the direction of Otto Kernberg and begun in 1954, was the first. A large team
of experts carefully examined the process and outcome of treatment
of 42 adult hospital patients and outpatients treated at the Menninger
Foundation (Kernberg et al., 1972).

The variables quantitatively assessed were divided into three
groups: patient variables (anxiety and symptoms, ego factors, motivational factors, relationship factors), treatment variables (formal elements of the treatment, the process of treatment), and situational variables (stress, conflict triggers, degree of material support, degree of
interpersonal support, degree of need-congruence, mutability, opportunity). Further experience and factor analysis reduced these to a
small number of marker variables.

1. Patient marker variables
    a. Ego strength
    b. Level of anxiety
    c. Self-directed aggression (internally directed agression)
    d. Externalization
2. Treatment marker variables
    a. Interpretive technique
    b. Skill in this case
    c. Degree of permissiveness
    d. Degree of tenseness
3. Situational marker variables
    a. Interpersonal support
    b. Stress
    c. Mutability
    d. Material support

The major finding from the statistical analysis was that a high level of initial ego strength of the patient is an indication of good prognosis for the entire spectrum of treatments conducted within the framework of psychoanalytic theory, that is, psychoanalysis, expressive psychotherapy, expressive-supportive psychotherapy, and supportive psychotherapy. As a result of factor analysis of the patient variables, ego strength was defined as a combination of three intimately linked characteristics: degree of integration, stability, and flexibility of the intrapsychic structures (including variables such as patterning of defenses and anxiety tolerance and, implicitly, the concepts of impulse control, thought organization, and sublimatory channeling capacity); the degree to which relationships with others are adaptive, deep, and gratifying of normal instinctual needs (corresponding to the variable called Quality of Interpersonal Relationships); the degree to which the malfunctioning of the intrapsychic structures is manifested directly by symptoms (corresponding to the variable called Severity of Symptoms).

The study also concluded that patients with ego weakness (which to them meant mainly borderline patients) require a special modality of treatment that could be described as a modified expressive or expressive-supportive approach. The modifications relate especially to the handling of the transference. Other studies at the

Menninger Foundation suggested that patients with low ego strength require a special modality of treatment, an expressive approach which is neither standard psychoanalysis nor supportive psychotherapy (Kernberg, 1968). In a follow-up to the main study, Horwitz (1974) has shown how a variety of clinical predictions can be made and confirmed by the methods employed.

The Hampstead Index

Around 1953–1954 a group of workers at the Hampstead Child Guidance Clinic, which is headed by Anna Freud, began a project known as the Hampstead Index. The guiding spirit in this project has been Joseph Sandler (1962). One outcome of the research is that the technique of indexing can provide the basis for a method of research in psychoanalysis which fulfills the requirements of a scientific method.

First a pilot group, headed by Dorothy Burlingham, classified the analytic and other material of 50 cases that they had in daily treatment. On the basis of this pilot study, it was possible to draw up a preliminary set of common categories, a common framework of classification that would eventually contain much of the case material. The principle was followed throughout that the therapist should order and classify his material according to those categories which he considered most satisfactory. The data to be classified were located under two headings, general case histories and psychoanalytic material; the latter is by far the larger.

The product of the indexing is a set of typed cards. Each card contains a piece of material—a "unit of observation" and a reference to the appropriate pages in the patient's case notes from where it was extracted, or which it summarizes. One of the major outcomes of the indexing process has been the sharpening of definitions and theoretical formulations.

Sandler (1962) observes that the processes involved in constructing the Index fall into a number of interconnected stages. First was the request that therapists conceptualize and categorize their material in terms of their own knowledge of psychoanalytic theory. Second was the refinement of internal psychoanalytic models so that they accorded more precisely with the observations. And third came the reevaluation of the analytic observations in terms of the revised theoretical formulations. He concludes that the indexing is a "scientific technique of potentially wide application."[8]

A number of studies deriving from the Hampstead Index and Anna Freud's Diagnostic Profile, which is related to it, have appeared in the literature. Most of these use the Index material to refine the conceptual framework of psychoanalysis, either by making the theoretical concept more precise in the light of observational material, or by showing how the observational material is illuminated by the theoretical framework.

In a study of obsessional manifestations, Sandler and Joffe (1965) found that there are a number of different but in some ways very similar clinical pictures normally designated as obsessional, not all of which can be labeled obsessional neurosis. The ego changes that occur in obsessional neurosis are attributable, in part at least, to a functional ego regression which accompanies the drive regression so prominent in this disturbance. The ego regression involves those ego functions which showed their most prominent development during the anal phase—particularly those functions which relate to cognition, to perception, and to control in general. In the classification of superego material, Sandler et al. (1962) found it necessary to consider the reactions of the ego to not only the introjects but also real authority figures in the environment, as well as to externalized representatives of introjected authority figures. Two major divisions of superego functioning are delineated, one emphasizing obedience and the other guidance; both are essential to the child.

In the study of fantasy, Sandler and Nagera (1963) distinguished between the capacity of the ego to organize mental content and the organized form imposed on the mental content. Once formed by the ego, fantasy content that becomes id-cathected content (wish content) may retain all or part of the organized qualities that have been imposed on it. In the study of the representational world, Sandler and Rosenblatt (1962) found on the basis of Index material that the concept of the representational world has made it possible to avoid certain theoretical difficulties in research work, and to define mechanisms such as identification and introjection in a relatively simple way.

It is anticipated that other publications will further demonstrate the usefulness of the Hampstead Index for elucidation of ego functions.

The Bellak Study of Ego Functions in Schizophrenics

In 1973 Bellak and co-workers reported the results of a 5-year study of ego functioning in schizophrenics and, for comparison, in neurotics and normals. Their work was methodically and carefully done, and it has far-reaching implications for ego psychology. In effect they provide a well-researched manual for the study of ego functions which is applicable to any type of population.

Bellak's group examined 12 ego functions: reality testing; judgment; sense of reality of the world and of the self; regulation and control of drives, affects, and impulses; object relations; thought processes; adaptive regression in the service of the ego; defensive functioning; stimulus barrier; autonomous functioning; synthetic-integrative functioning; and mastery-competence. The subjects studied were 50 schizophrenics, 25 normals, and 25 neurotics. Both clinical interviews and a variety of psychological tests, standardized and unstandardized, were used.

From the clinical interviews, material on mastery-competence was insufficient. For the other 11 ego functions, judges agreed on the average within 1.5 scale points.[9] There was a mild tendency for ego function ratings to be correlated with the subject's social class, education, IQ, and age, and the four judges' ratings showed different degrees of relationship with each of these background variables. Raters also differed in the degree of interrelation of their ratings. They prepared a rating manual based on their work. With comparable training on the ego-functioning Rating Manual, graduate psychology students attained a degree of agreement comparable to that of more experienced and more knowledgeable psychologists.

Differences in ego functions were in the predicted directions for the three groups, and were statistically significant for all 11 ego functions rated. The differences were not attributable to any of the background factors or to possible contamination by other factors. In a principal-components factor analysis, four factors were tentatively identified: reality orientation, socialization, adaptive thinking, and integrative capacity.

Concluding Comments

In the three research projects discussed, and others referred to, a total assessment of all ego functions has repeatedly been shown to yield meaningful and statistically reliable results. It thus seems likely that the detailed breakdown of ego functions, and their study by trained researchers, will in time replace the global descriptions of which psychoanalysis has made such extensive use. These studies also show that the careful study of ego functions can lead to a meaningful general psychology embracing all areas of the human being, instead of the extremely restricted range to which a psychology based on learning theory has been limited (Fine, 1977; G. Klein, 1976).

Ego Autonomy

The publication of Heinz Hartmann's book on *Ego Psychology and the Problem of Adaptation* (1939) marks one of the two most significant steps forward in ego psychology since Freud, the other being the recognition of the cultural factor in the formation and pathology of personality. The "autonomy" of the ego refers to its autonomy from the id. "Primary ego autonomy" refers to those ego functions which are inherently independent of the id, particularly the cognitive functions of memory, perception, thinking, and learning. "Secondary autonomy" refers to those functions which were at one time determined by id drives but have since lost contact with them. As Hartmann could show, both forms of ego autonomy play a major role in human experience.

Heinz Hartmann (1894–1970) is generally regarded as the greatest theoretician of the era following World War II. From 1945 until his death, a long series of profound papers contributed to what he thought of as a synchronization of Freud's unsystematized and unevenly developed contributions to ego psychology, and the formulation of psychoanalytic propositions in a manner suitable for establishing psychoanalysis as a general psychology (Schafer, 1970).

Although Hartmann's 1939 book represents a major advance, what he really did was to clear up an ambiguity in Freud's own thinking. At some times Freud wrote as if instincts were the only motivating forces in human beings, whereas at other times he explicitly recognized the "ego instincts" or what today would be called the autonomous cognitive factors. For example, his *Psychopathology of Everyday Life* (1901) deals with id interferences with ego functions, and explicitly recognizes that these ego functions are inherently autonomous, although that was not the language he used at that time.

Yet in his structural formulation, in 1923, suddenly in theory he derived everything from the id, while the superego is an offshoot of the ego. Hence in that formulation, strictly speaking, there is no room for an autonomous ego, except for the defenses that acquire secondary autonomy. Other analysts remained equally confused in this area.

Hartmann's book, which is clear and concise, sets forth the necessary theoretical assumptions that would allow psychoanalysis to expand to all of psychology in a meaningful way. The main points he makes are the following.

1. CONFLICT-FREE SPHERE. It is not necessary to assume that all of mental life involves conflict; there is also a conflict-free sphere. Psychoanalysis encounters the issue of adaptation in three forms: as a problem in its ego psychology, as a therapeutic aim, and as an educational consideration. Psychoanalysis can thus claim to be a general psychology in the broadest sense of the word. Ego psychology is the general meeting ground of psychoanalysis with nonanalytic psychology. However, investigations that are confined to the conflict-free sphere (as are most of those of academic psychology) inevitably overlook basic psychological relationships. Psychoanalysis thus also becomes one of the basic sciences of sociology.

2. ADAPTATION. The function more or less closely related to the mastery of reality is adaptation. The concept of adaptation, though it appears simple, implies (or, more crudely, conceals) a great many problems. Generally speaking, we call people well adapted if their productivity, their ability to enjoy life, and their mental equilibrium are undisturbed. The concept of adaptation has the most varied connotations in biology, and it has no precise definition in psychoanalysis either. Adaptation is primarily a reciprocal relationship between the organism and its environment. Psychoanalysis enables us to discern those processes which, by directly and actively changing either the environment or the person, bring about a state of adaptedness between the individual and his environment, and to investigate the relationship between the preformed means of human adaptation and these adaptation processes. The processes of adaptation are influenced by both constitution and external environment and are more directly determined by the ontogenetic phase of the organism. In primitive societies, they tend to be rigid. The human task of adaptation is present from the beginning of life. Hartmann writes: ''I believe I am in har-

mony with Freud's conception when I stress simultaneously the primary importance of social factors in human development and their biological significance."[10] The question is whether and to what extent a certain course of development can count on average expectable stimulations. There are progressive and regressive adaptations.

3. THE REALITY PRINCIPLE. The relationship of individuals to their environment is disrupted from moment to moment and must again and again be returned to an equilibrium. The equilibrium is not necessarily normal; it may be pathological. We understand that the mental apparatus must search the external world for pleasure possibilities as soon as its needs exceed a certain measure and can no longer be satisfied by fantasy. We cannot consider adaptive a relationship to the world in which we take cognizance of the world only insofar as it causes pain. Relations to reality are determined by a reality principle in the broader and in the narrower sense. Psychoanalysis does not in general have a high opinion of the individual's inborn adaptive abilities as guarantees of successful relationships.

4. EGO AUTONOMY. Certain functions of the ego cannot be derived from the instinctual drives. These we call (with some obvious reservations) autonomous ego development. Strictly speaking, there is no ego before the differentiation of ego and id, but there is no id either, since both are products of differentiation. The ego develops autonomously. Later there is secondary autonomy (similar to Allport's functional autonomy).

In more contemporary language, what Hartmann is saying is that the early analytic emphasis on the exclusive importance of the drives was an error. There is an inborn mental apparatus which develops independently of the id; this is called the autonomous ego. Naturally it is related to the id and interacts with it (Hartmann, 1952) but is not its direct descendant. In any function, somatic or psychic, it is possible to distinguish the contributions of the autonomous ego and of the defensive ego. Theoretically the approach is to discover the autonomous development of the various ego functions, to uncover the psychosexual development with its ego defense mechanisms, and then to combine these two branches of knowledge to explain any particular phenomenon. This approach has dominated psychoanalytic thinking since World War II, in contrast to the earlier almost exclusive emphasis on the drives.

In general, the discovery of the autonomous development of the various ego functions is the province of nonanalytic psychology and physiology. Piaget's work has been regarded by many analysts as particularly fruitful in this regard (discussed later in this section [11]). On the other hand, as Hartmann points out, to limit oneself to the autonomous functions severely restricts our knowledge of the human being. G. Klein (1959) comments that what the academic psychologist discovers is laws relating to a particular state of consciousness, which is not often duplicated in actual life. The functional importance of these laws must be understood in terms of the structure and dominant orientation of that particular state of consciousness.

Hartmann's clarification of ego autonomy has had far-reaching implications for psychoanalytic theory. In fact, since World War II all of psychoanalytic theory has moved in some of the directions to which he pointed. Schafer (1970) summarizes the essentials of his contributions as follows: the assault on dualistic constraints in Freud's thinking; establishing or making clear the legitimacy of different modes of psychoanalytic conceptualizing; laying bare the anatomy of the natural-scientific Freudian metapsychology as a necessary step toward elegant systematization and detailing of that theory; synchronization, refinement, and amplification of Freud's psychoeconomic propositions, especially through the use of neutral and neutralized energy; seeming implicitly to follow or parallel a sociopolitical model of the mind as meaningful and purposive government.

Once the theory of ego autonomy had been elucidated by Hartmann, it required little change. Most of the theoretical papers have dealt with amplifications or applications of his theory. Rapaport (1951, 1959) introduced some minor changes. Holt (1965) traced the development of ego autonomy in Freud's thought. S. Miller (1962) showed how ego autonomy fared under sensory deprivation; contrary to what might have been expected, subjects' autonomy diminished under deprivation rather than increased. Wiemers (1957) attempted an integration of primary ego autonomy with data from other disciplines. Menninger (1954) combined ego autonomy and homeostasis to build a new nosology, or classification of diseases, but had little success with it. Grauer (1958) took the position that there is much less ego autonomy in human life than had been thought, but this remains a minority view.

The most important amplification of Hartmann's theory lies in the ties that have been built up between experimental psychology and psychoanalysis. The topic of the cognitive functions and cognitive control is treated more fully later, but attention must be drawn here to the widespread interest that psychoanalysts have shown in the work of the Swiss psychologist Jean Piaget during the past decades (Decarie, 1965; P. Wolff, 1960).

In 1970 Piaget was invited to address the American Psychoanalytic Association. His talk was printed in the *Journal of the American Psychoanalytic Association* in 1973.

In his talk Piaget described himself as an impertinent heretic who had been through a didactic analysis. He drew many parallels between the cognitive unconscious in which he had done such extensive exploration and the affective unconscious of the psychoanalysts. With regard to structures, the cognitive and affective realms are quite similar: relative consciousness of the results, with little or no consciousness of the mechanisms which produce these results. Although conscious awareness in cognition is easy in most instances, there are cases in which it is opposed by an inhibiting mechanism that can be compared to the Freudian affective repression. He urged a comparative study of the affective and cognitive transformations of memory. Piaget quoted a study by his student Decarie (1965), which showed parallels between the cognitive development of the schema of the permanent object and the evolution of object constancy in psychoanalytic theory. He concluded with a plea for the formulation of a general psychology that would bear simultaneously upon the mechanisms discovered by the psychoanalysts and upon the cognitive processes.

Another consequence of Hartmann's theory has been the increasing concern of psychoanalysts with external reality in all its aspects. Wallerstein (1973) made this the theme of his presidential address to the American Psychoanalytic Association in 1972. He considered the relationship of the new psychoanalytic position on reality to development, psychopathology, spontaneous change, technical implications for therapy, and applications of psychoanalysis. In a later presidential address in 1974, Burness Moore (1976) expounded on what he called the ''Janus'' posture of the American Psychoanalytic Association—looking inward and outward at the same time. Meissner (1976) has also stressed that the altered position on external reality implies a thorough-going revision of psychoanalytic metapsychology. Schafer (1976), with his new restatement of psychoanalytic theory in terms of action, is moving in the same general direction.

Ego Development: Strength and Weakness

Once the full structure of the ego was delineated, with Hartmann's
extension to the autonomous function, the development of the ego
could be traced. Here genetic and dynamic considerations intermesh
to place the stress on *ego strength and/or weakness*. This conceptualization has gradually replaced the older diagnostic categories, in
both theory and practice. An ego is strong (Freud) when it can accept
the id, deal with reality, and confront the superego. It is weak to the
extent that it fails in each of these functions (see the earlier discussion
of the ego functions profile). To the extent that the ego breaks down
in any of these requirements the individual becomes sick, engaging in
repetitive, stereotyped, self-destructive or maladaptive behavior.

At birth, ego and id are undifferentiated (Hartmann). They then
develop in separate directions (Hartmann), although they influence
one another. The weak ego is the one that has not developed. Innumerable studies have attempted to establish the developmental processes in the ego; references to them are scattered throughout this
book at the appropriate points. Since the ego can be, and often is,
strong in one respect and weak in another, global measurements or
descriptions are apt to be misleading. Nevertheless, pathology can
roughly be equated with ego weakness. Essential parts of the personality do not develop, or if developed, regress to an earlier level. From
this matrix of a weak ego, the various forms of psychopathology can
then branch out.

Theory of Affects

The psychoanalytic theory of affects embodies a peculiar paradox, as
Edith Jacobson (1953) has pointed out. Although psychoanalysis
began as an affect theory, emphasizing the strangulation of affect as
the cause of neurosis and the liberation of affect as its cure (Freud in
the 1890s), as soon as psychoanalysis switched to instinct theory,
systematic discussion of affects ceased. Accordingly we find every
author deploring the lack of a consistent psychoanalytic theory of affect (Jacobson, 1971; Green, 1977). Arieti (1970) describes the
theory as being in a "state of utter confusion." At the latest symposium on affects, Rangell again emphasized that we still do not have

a complete psychoanalytic theory of affects, and preferred to call his paper "Toward a Theory of Affects" (Castelnuovo-Tedesco, 1974). The theme of the 1977 meeting of the International in Jerusalem was affect theory. Nevertheless, since psychoanalysis has dealt with affects intimately from the very beginning, much pertinent wisdom can be culled from the psychoanalytic literature. Once more we seem to be faced by the persistent dilemma: while the clinical theory is rich and varied, the metapsychological theory remains confused and disorganized.

Freud never really considered the topic systematically. The idea that affects are ego states comes from the 1926 work on *Inhibitions, Symptoms and Anxiety,* where he states: "Anxiety, then, is in the first place something that is felt. We call it an affective state, although we are also ignorant of what an affect is."[12] Since he shifted his theoretical position on anxiety in that book to make anxiety an ego state rather than an id transformation of libido, analysts have assumed that he wanted to take the same position with regard to all affects, although Freud himself is not clear on this point.

Rapaport (1953) is responsible for the main metapsychological theory of affect in the literature. First he attempts to tease out of Freud's own writings three different approaches to affect, which are associated with three stages in the history of psychoanalysis. In the first stage, according to Rapaport, affect was used synonymously with psychic energy. This was accompanied by the hypothesis that strangulated feeling led to neurosis and that the cure which resulted from the cathartic method lay in the release or abreaction of affect. In the second period, roughly from 1900 to 1915, feeling was seen as the outcome of instinct, in somewhat the same way that McDougall saw it. It was so intimately tied to instinct that its essence lay in the bodily processes that accompany it. At the same time Freud was opposed to the James–Lange theory, since he held that it is not the bodily feelings that arouse the emotion (as William James and Lange held) but the emotion that leads to the bodily feelings. In the third phase, after 1915, feeling was seen as a signal emitted by the ego to indicate some stage of internal or external reality that must be noticed. Generally this feeling was used in the negative sense, particularly with the affect of anxiety.

Although Rapaport's attempt to tease out Freud's approach is interesting, one cannot maintain on the basis of the historical evidence that this is what Freud really believed. Freud did not approach the topic systematically but made a variety of statements about affects, some of which had to be changed in the course of time, while others remained unaltered.

Rapaport (1953) in his turn offered a theory of affects which attempted to integrate three components: inborn discharge channels, discharge thresholds, and drive cathexes. But his concentration on this kind of energic theory has found little follow-up in the literature.

The 1973 symposium (Castelnuovo-Tedesco, 1974) revealed the wide differences in theory still persisting among analysts on this topic. Rangell saw cognition and affect intertwined into one organic human web, maintaining that there is no affect without an idea, no unconscious fantasy without its attached affective response. Modell described two theories of affect—discharge and object-relations—the former emphasizing the release of tension and the latter the communication with other people. Moore defined affect as the subjective, conscious manifestation of internal and external perceptivity and reactivity of the organism with regard to the pleasure-unpleasure status. Valenstein emphasized the developmental context for a general theory of affects and, like Moore, spoke of the need for integrating psychoanalytic data with data from modern neurophysiological research. Castelnuovo-Tedesco underscored the need to sharpen the contact between clinical phenomena and theoretical formulations. He particularly stressed the relationship of affectivity to time and sensory experience. In the discussion, Ross suggested that affect is perhaps an autonomous function and is to be regarded as a precursor of the development of the ego. Kaywin urged that affect is first and foremost a highly personal subjective experience, whose elusive quality prevents us from achieving a more precise statement of its characteristics.

In summing up, Moore pointed out not only that we do not have a comprehensive theory of affects, but that it had been difficult for the panel to approach the subject systematically. Yet the presentations and discussions showed recurrent themes and substantial consensus regarding such topics as the role of affects in object relations, the communicative function of affects, the significance of time, and the function of affects in binding together the present and the past, both phylogenetic and ontogenetic.

We may also note Arieti's (1967, 1972) theory of three orders of emotion. The first-order or "protoemotions" are experiences of inner status which cannot be sharply localized, retain some bodily characteristics, are elicited by the presence or absence of specific stimuli, become important motivational factors, have an almost immediate effect, and require a minimum of cognitive work to be experienced. Second-order emotions are not elicited by a direct or impending attack on the organism or by a threatened immediate change in homeostasis, but by cognitive symbolic processes. With the development of language, the gradual abandonment of preconceptual levels and the development of conceptual levels, third-order emotions occur, such as love, resentment, and jealousy. In conjunction with first- and second-order emotions, these offer to the human being a very complex and diversified emotional repertory.

Because of its undogmatic character, one of the most useful papers in the literature is Schafer's exploration of affects from a clinical point of view (1964). Schafer sorts out eight significant categories of affect manifestations: existence, formation, strength, stimuli, complexity and paradox, location, communication, and history.

Affect Development

It had long been assumed by psychoanalytic theory that affects develop out of an infantile matrix by a complex series of intrapersonal and interpersonal interactions. Spitz in his various studies (see 1959) had already designated the three organizers of the psyche in infancy as smiling (2 months), anxiety (8 months), and language (15 months). Emde et al. (1976), continuing Spitz's work, distinguished three stages of infant affect expressions: the first level is crying, during the first 2 months; at the second level, smiling is added to the crying-quiescence system, and it enhances attachment through a different mode; at the third level is stranger-distress, or fearfulness. After that the complexity of the situation defies simple categorization. "The human enters into the symbolic universe, and what the child can tell us in his own words opens new fields for research."[13]

Special Studies of Various Feelings

Psychoanalysis would agree with G. Stanley Hall's famous aphorism that "the intellect is a speck afloat on a sea of feeling." Since the implication of feeling is ubiquitous, specific reference to feeling may be and often is omitted in the literature, which would account for such a curious misunderstanding as that of Tomkins, who writes (1962, 1964) that psychoanalysis deals very little with feelings. It would also help to explain why, almost from the beginning, psychoanalysis rejected the Kraepelinian classification of psychosis into "thought disorder" and "affect disorder"; from the point of view of psychoanalytic theory, there can be no such entity as a thought disorder without affective involvement. As early as 1908, Abraham had shown that the alleged normality of the manic-depressive in the quiescent periods merely concealed a strong obsessive-compulsive defense.

Affect has always been looked upon as combining tension discharge, interpersonal communication (later reformulated as a "signal"), and physiological reactions. It has also generally been assumed that individuals are characterized by persistent kinds of affect reactions, such as the "guilt-laden," the "sad," and the "happy-go-lucky." A further specific contribution of psychoanalysis has been the overriding emphasis on the unconscious aspects of the emotions, the omission of which vitiates most of the nonanalytic studies of emotion.

In accordance with these theoretical convictions, the analytic literature from the very beginning has contained numerous descriptions of individual feelings or feeling-states. These have as a rule been highly exhaustive, probing the id, ego, and superego, conscious and unconscious aspects, history, and a host of other factors of the kind enumerated by Schafer (1964). I shall discuss some of the most striking ones.

LOVE. Throughout his work, but especially in the early id period, Freud was much concerned with love and all its manifestations. His views can best be summarized under the two headings of normal and neurotic love.

In the elucidation of *neurotic love* Freud was especially concerned with the boy's development. The mother is the boy's first love, and she appears by regression in the person of his beloved, who is chosen according to the "anaclitic" type of object choice. In the alternative or narcissistic type, the love object is chosen after the subject's own image and is a substitute for the ego ideal ("Narcissism," 1914). Men, more often than women, choose their love object according to the anaclitic type, i.e., they seek mother-figures. What makes love passionate is the fact that the unconscious has been tapped and its contents, which are strongly cathected, overflow into consciousness.

The man may remain fixated to his mother or go on normally to sister figures and substitute figures. The type of man who remains fixated selects love objects only on the basis of some aspect that is derived from his mother ("A Special Type of Object Choice in Men," 1910). Such repressed memories account for the phenomenon of "love at first sight." With the mother forbidden, love becomes aim-inhibited sexuality. Defense against an infantile mother fixation accounts for the degradation of the love object, and for the Don Juan's constant seeking out and disappointment. It creates both bachelors and unhappily married men.

Normal love results from the union of tender and sexual feelings toward a person of the opposite sex (*Three Essays,* 1905). Its achievement is marked by genital primacy in sexuality and by object love in human relationships. Because of the cultural taboos, it is not often found (1908). Nevertheless Freud shrank from any attempt at societal reformation (1908). The normal individual is the one who can work and love (1917).

Although the subsequent literature has leaned heavily on Freud's formulations (Fromm, 1956; R. May, 1969), many writers seem to have forgotten what Freud said. For instance, the topic is not mentioned by Laplanche and Pontalis (1973).

As interest in and knowledge of the oral stage grew, the importance of love shifted primarily to the relationship between mother and child. The expression "tender loving care" was made prominent by Margaret Ribble (1943) in her famous book *The Rights of Infants.* In a well-known essay Imre Hermann (1936, recently retranslated) called attention to the phenomenon of clinging alternating with going-in-search, tying them both to the need for the mother, and also relating the phenomenon, for the first time, to similar manifestations in apes.

After World War II the literature on the need for mother love proliferated enormously (see chapters 6 and 16). Harlow (1974) was the first to describe the sequence of love relationships in the rhesus monkey, positing a sequence of affectional relationships—mother for the child, child for mother, peer love, heterosexual, and paternal—

which could serve as a biological model for the human being. It has repeatedly been shown how the deprivation of mother love leads to a variety of ego defects and serious psychopathology. There is a good deal of evidence showing that lack of love, leading to lack of social support, can have dire consequences at every stage in life.

For adult love, many writers from Fenichel (1945) onward have stressed the importance of sharing and mutuality (Fromm, 1956). Balint (1949, 1953) was one of the earliest to emphasize love as primary, thereby correcting a certain ambiguity in Freud's own writings; Freud had also stressed physiology. Kernberg (1974) has traced the development of love in terms of internalized object relations and has also revived the theory of the importance of earlier body-surface erotism for later love experiences. Fine (1975b) has highlighted the central importance of love in the psychoanalytic philosophy of living. Hunt (1959) has shown how the history of Western civilization can be understood in terms of the varying efforts to unite the tender and sensual elements of love. Shorter (1975) has offered the surprising thesis that, beginning with a sexual revolution around 1750, mankind has been moving toward a recognition of the need for more warmth and love in human relationships, a recognition to which Freudian theory makes a significant contribution.

JEALOUSY. Jealousy is such a universal experience that most people naively regard it as "normal." In a classic paper (1922), Freud was able to describe its deeper roots. He enumerated three kinds of jealousy: normal, projected, and delusional. Normal jealousy is compounded of grief, feelings of enmity against the successful rival, and a greater or lesser amount of self-criticism. Projected jealousy is derived in both men and women either from their own actual unfaithfulness or from impulses toward it which have succumbed to repression. Delusional jealousy also has its origin in the repressed impulses toward unfaithfulness, but the object in these cases is of the same sex as the subject. Delusional jealousy is what is left of a homosexuality that has run its course, and it rightly is classified with paranoia.

VENGEANCE. Socarides (1966) offers psychoanalytic perspectives on the emotion of vengeance. Surface manifestations of vengeance achieve almost a classic unvarying pattern. The person is grudgeful, unforgiving, remorseless, ruthless, heartless, implacable, and inflexible. In the act of revenge the wish is for acknowledgement of one's power, superiority, rights, and judgment. The avenger hopes thereby to regain strength and a former sense of identity.

The developmental forerunners of vengeance are found in the earliest object relationships. Initial disturbances due to oral frustrations result in the ego's inability to satisfy the instincts autoerotically and to an incorporation of hateful internal objects. In contrast to love, in which the mode of striving of the ego is toward objects as sources of pleasure, in vengeance the striving of the ego is against these objects as a source of pain to ensure their destruction.

BOREDOM. Greenson (1953) saw boredom as easier to describe than to define. The uniqueness of the feeling of being bored seems to depend on the coexistence of the following components: a state of dissatisfaction and a disinclination to action; a state of longing and an inability to designate what is longed for; a sense of emptiness; a passive, expectant attitude with the hope that the external world will supply the satisfaction; a distorted sense of time in which time seems to stand still (the German word for boredom is *Langeweile,* "long time"). Many analytic authors have touched upon boredom; noteworthy are the papers by Bergler (1945), Fenichel (1934), Ferenczi (1919a), Spitz (1937), and Winterstein (1930).

Boredom, according to Greenson, can occur at any level of libidinal organization. However, the general experience that boredom occurs more frequently in depressed people indicates that those with strong oral fixations are particularly predisposed to boredom. The explanation for this lies in the role played by deprivation in the production of boredom as well as in the related states of apathy and depression. Depressed people feel deprived of love, either from an external object or from an internal object, or both. In apathy, too, traumatic deprivation plays a decisive role, only here the external world is responsible. In boredom there is a self-administered deprivation: the loss of thoughts and fantasies that would lead to satisfaction. Depressed persons are full of fantasies in their struggle to regain the unloving object. Apathetic persons have given up the struggle, and their fantasy life is restricted to factors concerned with the question of survival. In boredom there is a longing for lost satisfactions that is similar to what is seen in the depressions, along with the feeling of emptiness characteristic for apathy.

OTHER STUDIES: CONCLUDING COMMENTS ON AFFECTS. Numerous other studies are devoted to various affects. Some of the most important are on: elation (Lewin, 1950), the nightmare (Jones, 1912), shame and guilt (H. Lewis, 1971; Piers and Singer, 1953), envy (M. Klein, 1957), shyness (D. Kaplan, 1972), friendship

(Rangell, 1963), the uncanny (Freud, 1919); the déjà vu experience (Arlow, 1959), the déjà raconté experience (Freud, 1914); enthusiasm (Greenson, 1962), apathy (Greenson, 1949), querulousness (Schmidenberg, 1946), bitterness (J. Alexander, 1960), bereavement (Parkes, 1972), and hope (Stotland, 1969).

In general, the analytic papers confine themselves to the unconscious dynamic and developmental factors associated with any emotion; the physiological correlates are left to other investigations, not denied. Actually, since all of analysis is concerned with the emotions of the human being, the specific literature of affects comprises only a small part of the total picture.

A comparison with the nonanalytic literature reveals that the emphasis there is mainly on surface description, i.e., disregarding the unconscious (Arnold, 1970), and on physiology and ideation (Tomkins, 1962, 1964). In the nature of things, the elimination of unconscious and developmental considerations limits the value of nonanalytic contributions severely.

The Cognitive Functions

Inasmuch as psychoanalysis is now a total psychology, it must necessarily take some theoretical stance toward the cognitive functions. The historical evolution of this stance moves from an oversimplified identification of the cognitive functions with instinctual drives in the id period, to early clarification of ego mechanisms, particularly cognitive controls, to the current sophisticated image of an interplay of ego and id in all cognitive functioning, which thereby becomes an integral aspect of psychoanalytic scrutiny, like any other human phenomenon.

In the id period (1900–1914), Freud and some of his followers were given to extreme pronouncements that today would be considered merely "vulgar Freudianism." For example, Freud wrote that "thought is after all nothing but a substitute for a hallucinatory wish."[14] Perception subserves the experience of satisfaction,[15] and the aim of the first psychical activity is to produce a "perceptual identity."[16]

With regard to memory, he occasionally took the position that everything is stored in the mind, so that there is no such thing as true forgetting, only repression. Thus in *Civilization and Its Discontents* (1930) he wrote:

Since we overcame the error of supposing that the forgetting we are familiar with signified a destruction of the memory-trace—that is, its annihilation—we have been inclined to take the opposite view, that in mental life nothing which has once been formed can perish—that everything is somehow preserved and that in suitable circumstances (when, for instance, regression goes back far enough) it can once more be brought to light.[17]

In the area of learning, Freud wrote in 1908 (*The Sexual Theories of Children*) that the first intellectual efforts are directed at solving the riddle of sex, while later intellectual efforts reawaken the traces, which have since become unconscious, of the first period of sexual interest.[18] In a typical paper from this id period, Strachey (1930) argued that a coprophagic tendency lies at the root of all reading.[19] "The author excretes his thoughts and embodies them in the printed book; the reader takes them, and, after chewing them over, incorporates them into himself."[20] Melanie Klein at this time also emphasized that the roots of intellectual development lie in the destructive impulses (1948).

At other times Freud wrote about the cognitive functions in a more tempered fashion. In the *Psychopathology of Everyday Life* (1901) he took the common-sense position that "by the side of simple cases where proper names are forgotten there is a type of forgetting which is motivated by repression."[21]

Once Hartmann had formulated his theory of ego autonomy in 1939, all of this earlier id material had to be revised. Since it was never systematically revised, many writers, including even some analysts, tend to assume, erroneously, that the comments are equally applicable today. The earlier analytic observations must be looked upon instead as neurotic distortions of the cognitive functions, not as the essence of cognition per se. From the viewpoint of ego psychology, the cognitive functions are autonomous, independent of the id, though an interaction takes place from the earliest years (Hartmann, 1952).

Eventually it has become clear that intellectual development (cognition, in the broad sense) occurs most favorably in a warm, secure environment, and that the disturbances seen represent id interferences with ego functioning. Beginning with the 1950s it became increasingly clear that ego patterns are structuralized fairly early, leading to a variety of cognitive controls (Witkin et al., 1954). In the larger area of societal structure and interpersonal relations, their earlier equation with id drives has had to be abandoned. Instead, society represents a complex interplay of many forces. Parsons (1964) among sociologists has placed special stress on the superego as a concept unifying individual and social psychological observations.

The expansion of psychoanalytic psychology to all aspects of cognitive functioning has become so broad that no simple summary is possible. Instead, I shall refer to various key books and papers to clarify the directions that the historical growth has taken.

Memory

All his life Freud was concerned with the persistence and recapture of early memories. It was this which led to his theories of repression (Brenner, 1957). Eventually many psychologists attempted to incorporate his findings into general psychological theory (Hilgard and Bower, 1975). This early work was summarized by Rapaport in his influential book *Emotions and Memory* (1942), of which the fifth edition was published in 1971. Rapaport argued that the clinical and experimental material pointed to a lawfulness which he stated as follows.

1. "Emotional factors" whose presence was indicated by the subject, either when rating the memory material in question or when reporting in retrospect the experiences of the course of the memory experiment, had some influence on memory.

2. This influence depended on both the intensity and quality of the "emotional factors."

3. The more intellectualized and conventionalized the nature of the "emotional factor," and the more purely quantitative the method of experimentation employed, the more the intensity of the "emotional factor" was correlated with the influence exerted on memory; the more qualitative the methods and the more genuine the emotional experiences employed, the more obvious was the influence of the *quality* of the "emotional factor."

4. In the experiments employing more genuine emotional factors, the qualitative influence of the emotions on the memory process (such as their influence on the sequence of emergence of memories

and their resulting spotlike forgetting, and slips of tongue as well as distortion of the material) was reported.

In the meantime the older model of a telephone switchboard in the experimental investigation of memory gave way to the newer concept of a computer, with information storage and retrieval as the primary activities. It was also shown that there are major differences between short-term and long-term memory (Anderson and Bower, 1973; Deutsch and Deutsch, 1975). Many investigators have attempted to reevaluate the psychoanalytic material in the light of this shift to a computer model for memory in general. George Klein (1970) summarized some of the salient changes: [22]

1. There are two aspects of the retrieval problem that should be distinguished: the experiential mode in which a memory is retrieved and the state of consciousness that frames the context of retrieval.

2. If remembering is conceived in terms of classes of function (tracemaking or registration, storage or retention, and retrieval) it is clear that forgetting need not be regarded as a unitary process; its behavioral meaning will be different in relation to each phase of the remembering process.

3. With memory viewed as comprising several functions, the effects of repression on memory are now seen to take on various forms according to the function implicated.

4. Memory in its adaptive aspects must be emphasized, as a multiple-sided process combining registration, coding and storage, schema assimilation, and retrieval processes. One implication of this emphasis is that memory functioning may reflect different styles of adaptive strategy, or different styles of secondary-process functioning. This viewpoint attaches importance to individual differences in remembering behaviors and tries to understand them in terms of the generalized modes of control that characterize a person's ego system—his typical ways of processing inner and outer stimuli, and his means of arriving at adaptive solutions to his encounters with stimulation. Two modes of control in memory are importing and skeletonizing.

With regard to the recovery of memories in analysis, psychoanalytic theory has also undergone various shifts. Initially, in the 1890s, Freud relied on the recovery of memories through hypnosis; this was

soon replaced by the recovery through direct association. In this process "screen memories" were discovered—seemingly indifferent
memories that cover up more important events (Freud, 1901). Freud
also thought that some derivatives of instinctual drives never reach
consciousness at all, thus leading to *primal* and *secondary* repression (Freud, 1915). This theory of primary repression seems to
have been gradually discarded by later authors; repression today
would imply that something was once conscious and had been pushed
back into the unconscious because of anxiety. In the early 1900s
Freud was relying on his theory of infantile amnesia and focusing his
therapeutic efforts on the attempt to lift these amnesias, especially
those concerning ages 2 to 4, but also for other ages. Both successes
and failures occurred. Accordingly, in 1914 Freud took the momentous step of assuming that it did not matter whether what was recovered was factually correct. What was not remembered directly (recalled) was repeated in action. The decisive factor was not the
memory but the working through.

A further step was taken by Ernst Kris in 1956 in his paper on
"the personal myth." Kris saw the personal myth as the heart of the
autobiographical self-image. In somewhat more colorful language
Sullivan had made the same point when he spoke of the "personified
person I" (1940). The autobiographical self-image has become heir
to important early fantasies, which it preserves.

A particularly important discovery for analytic work relates to
the recall of dreams (see chapter 9). It has been shown that the REM
patterns characteristic of dreaming sleep are far more common than
actual reports of dreams. Hence a distinction must be drawn between
recallers and nonrecallers, rather than between dreamers and non-
dreamers (Goodenough, 1967).

Perception

Although perception may be the oldest topic in psychology, only
fairly recently has the relationship between personality and perception
come to be appreciated. Unlike memory, which plays a central role in
the psychoanalytic process, perception seems peripheral to the whole
affair. Unless it breaks down entirely, as in schizophrenia, the analyst
is apt to ignore it. Only as knowledge of ego psychology accumulated, and as the patient population was extended more and more to

the normal population, did the interaction between personality and perception come to be recognized.

It was not until the 1940s that any systematic links between perception and personality came under discussion. The classic work that definitely confirmed the close links and created the new and fruitful concept of field dependence versus field independence is *Personality through Perception* (1954), by Witkin and his colleagues. These investigators were able to sort out two main groups of individuals: field dependent and field independent. Field dependent persons tend to be characterized by passivity in dealing with the environment, unfamiliarity with and fear of their own impulses (together with poor control over them), lack of self-esteem, and the possession of a relatively primitive, undifferentiated body-image. Field independent persons are the opposite. Witkin and his associates felt that field dependence indicated some arrest in the development of active coping with the environment and with reality.

Cognitive Controls

The Witkin study led to the search for what are now called "cognitive controls" and "cognitive styles." Apart from field dependence and independence, a number of such controls have been discussed. G. Klein (1959) has mentioned importing, skeletonizing, scanning, and tolerance for unrealistic experiences. Important though it is, this field is still in its infancy.

Perceptual Distortions and Perceptual Bias

Beginning in the 1940s, a series of experiments have been conducted to test the hypothesis that motivation does influence perception. By now the concepts of perceptual defense and perceptual bias have been fairly well established. Full discussion would lead too far afield. It is worth noting, however, that the psychodynamic work on perception, though established with all the rigor required of any scientific work, has been largely ignored by experimental psychologists (Baddeley, 1976). Among the exceptions are Dember (1960) and Bruner (1973).

Thinking

Because of the basic role of free association in the psychoanalytic process, thinking has always been central to psychoanalysis. Some topics, such as free association itself and the fantasy life of mankind, have been explored far more fully by psychodynamically oriented theoreticians than any other topics. Some that play a relatively small part in the therapeutic process, such as problem solving, have been ignored.

Free Association

Free association was specifically adopted to get at the underlying unconscious material. The perceptual apparatus is reduced to a minimum, allowing the fantasies to come to the fore. This was the reason Freud gave for choosing this method to replace hypnosis. In 1924 he wrote:

The choice of free association as a means of investigating the forgotten unconscious material seems so strange that a word in justification of it will not be out of place. Freud was led to it by an expectation that the so-called "free association" would prove in fact to be unfree, since, when all conscious intellectual purposes had been supressed, the ideas that emerged would be seen to be determined by the unconscious material. This expectation was justified by experience.[23]

Little has been added to the theory since Freud. In one of the few papers on the topic, Bellak (1961) maintained that associating as a process is best understood as being predicated upon the oscillating function of the ego, involving first letting controls go and then restoring them. The emphasis is on the relative reduction of cognitive ego function.

Other aspects of fantasy have been reviewed in chapters 9 and 10.

Learning

That learning, like all intellectual functioning, must be strongly influenced by emotional factors seems quite obvious, yet systematic attempts at a theory have not been made. In a symposium on the topic at the American Psychoanalytic Association, Pollock (1972b) expressed the hope for interdisciplinary integration of psychoanalysis and learning theory. He listed some important psychoanalytic concepts that are infrequently represented in learning theory, particularly: the relationship of learning to stages of development; the role of values, goals, and ideals in learning; and the psychodynamics of thinking.

At that symposium Neal Miller emphasized that a unified theory of learning had not yet been constructed. "One cannot predict behavior from laws or theories, but only from knowledge of the animal's experience and the situation it is in."[24] Thus the field remains full of isolated observations, but without any consistent theory or integration. Again the whole topic, if pursued adequately, would have to encompass a large segment of psychology. And again the data, with few exceptions, have been ignored by experimental psychologists.

Experimental Work

From the very beginning, psychoanalysis came under the criticism that its results were not experimentally validated. Reactions to this criticism have been mixed. Freud himself is supposed to have said of it, *"ganz amerikanisch"* ("quite American"); others, however, have taken it seriously and attempted to subject various aspects of psychoanalytic theory to more crucial tests.

In the early 1940s the well-known psychologist Robert Sears was retained by the Social Science Research Council to do a survey of the objective studies of psychoanalytic concepts, where he pulled together most of the work that had been done in the area (Sears, 1943). Some of his findings were positive, others negative. In his review of Sears's book, Heinz Hartmann (1944) welcomed the efforts made in this direction, and commented:

Sears' conclusion that psychoanalysis is, by the criteria of physical sciences, not a "good" science is no doubt true. At any rate he is ready to acknowledge that it deals with many things other sciences had ignored. I should like to add that for many important problems of psychology it is the best method available at present and that the verification by other methods of so many heretofore disbelieved analytical findings should lead to a higher evaluation of analysis itself as a scientific *method.*[25]

A number of other investigators have continued the experimental testing of psychoanalytic concepts and theories, usually with much more sophistication than Sears and his colleagues had shown. Best known are the studies of Fisher and his associates on dreams and REM sleep, begun in the 1950s (Fisher, 1965), after the accidental discovery of REM sleep by Aserinsky and Kleitman in 1953. Since then the study of sleep has mushroomed into a vast field, almost independent in its own right. E. L. Hartmann has published good summaries of this work (1970, 1973).

A number of studies have shown that data can be quantified in a meaningful way. Luborsky and Auerbach (1969) used their symptom-context method to quantify symptom formation in psychotherapy. Silverman (1970) presented drive-related and neutral stimuli to subjects at a subliminal level, observing the effects of each stimulus on ego functioning and symptomatology. Dahl (1972) was able to measure meaning in psychoanalysis by computer analysis of verbal contexts. Freedman and Steingart (1976) have been able to show the close connection between body-focused kinetic behavior and language construction.

It cannot be said, however, that any of these studies have had an appreciable effect on either psychoanalytic theory or clinical practice. In the areas most directly involved in psychoanalytic psychology and research, the basic method must remain integration from many different disciplines rather than experimentation (Fine, 1975b).

Concluding Comments on Ego Psychology

Ego psychology represents the extension of psychoanalysis to a general psychology of human behavior. Through the concept of ego autonomy, it can be extended to include all of what is commonly known as experimental psychology. This chapter has only covered some of the highlights, particularly in their historical development. In reality the entire history of psychoanalysis is also the history of ego psychology.

One point worth noting is that ego psychology provides a meeting ground for the traditional Freudian and the less traditional culturalist schools, since the culturalists have in general confined themselves to ego mechanisms, while the Freudians have tended to limit themselves to the more circumscribed id mechanisms or those ego mechanisms most directly related to the id. Ego psychology also provides the meeting ground for psychoanalysis, experimental psychology, and social science in general. Ego functions that are autonomous have in general been dealt with more thoroughly by nonanalytic schools, while ego functions that are less autonomous have been dealt with most thoroughly by psychoanalysis. For a full integration of the science, such as is now going on, both approaches are necessary.

Special Considerations

From time to time various analysts have taken up other aspects of ego functioning. Perhaps best known is Federn's work (1952) on the ego's feeling of continuity. Bergmann (1963) maintains that Federn's ideas in this area have been continued in the current investigation of self- and object-differentiation. However this may be, Federn's conceptualization of ego boundaries has been solidly incorporated into the psychoanalytic theory of schizophrenia, where it still plays a prominent role.

Holland (1973) offered a theoretical statement of the ego's algebra. Moser and Zeppelin (1969) have proposed a simulation model for the ego's defenses. Suppes and Warren (1975) proposed a new and elaborate method of classification of the ego functions. Apfelbaum (1962) questioned much of the standard theory of the ego altogether. Suggestive though they may be, all of these papers nonetheless stand outside the mainstream of psychoanalytic thought.

Chapter Thirteen

Neurosis: Psychoanalysis and Psychiatry

The role of psychoanalysis in the history of psychiatry has been obscured by the power politics that has been so prominent, especially in the United States. One consequence of this power struggle has been the seemingly deliberate confusion of the terms "psychiatrist" and "psychoanalyst," even though the large majority of psychiatrists (more than 90 percent; Marmor, 1975) have not been fully trained analysts, and many analysts have not been trained psychiatrists. The compromise of 1973 in which analysts equated long-term analysis with long-term psychiatric treatment in order to qualify for national health insurance has already been mentioned.

In the clarification of the history of psychopathology, this confusion must be borne in mind. Some needed historical references have been made in chapter 1. In the further developments of the present century, psychiatry has incorporated somatic and psychological points of view. The somatic point of view stems from medical research, the psychological almost entirely from psychoanalysis. Sharp differences of opinion exist, and have always existed, about the relative merits and contributions of each. In general, Freud and psychoanalysts have placed primary emphasis on the psychological factor, nonanalytic psychiatrists on the organic.

Technically psychiatry and psychoanalysis have developed side by side in the twentieth century. It is well to bear the above distinctions in mind when examining the historical picture.

Clarification of the Technical Problems
of Neurosis: Freud

Freud's practice was devoted very largely to the treatment of neurotics, and it is in this area that he made his most enduring clinical contributions. After a number of false starts in the 1890s, from 1900 to 1914 he virtually resolved the problem of neurosis, which then became an integral part of all psychological and psychiatric theory.

The Nature of Neurosis

The degree to which Freud resolved the technical problems of neurosis is still not well recognized. First, he established that neurosis was a psychological problem worthy of study and not a form of hereditary degeneracy or malingering, as had been hitherto believed. Second, he reformulated the disparate symptoms which his predecessors and colleagues had described, dividing them into two major clinical entities—obsessional neurosis (the term itself stems from Freud) and hysteria. Hysteria was further subdivided into conversion hysteria and anxiety hysteria; both designations were Freud's. Third, in terms of the libido theory, he established what could be regarded as the normal course of development and showed how neurosis could be made intelligible by reference to such normal development. Fourth, he demonstrated that neurosis and normality differ only in degree, not in kind, and thereby restored the neurotic (and even more so, the psychotic) to a place in society. Fifth, he established that these neuroses are amenable to psychoanalysis and that psychoanalysis is the best treatment for them. The analyzability of these patients rests on the fact that they form transferences, which can then be worked through.

Even today, the term "neurosis" is only vaguely defined. When Freud began he wrote of the "neuropsychoses," a designation that would be unthinkable now. As late as 1913 (in "The Disposition to Obsessional Neurosis"), he spoke of schizophrenia as one of the major neuroses. The sharp dividing line between neurosis and psychosis postulated by Kraepelinian psychiatry has not been borne out by more careful research, and today the dividing line remains rather unclear. Even the more recent category of "borderline states" has not resolved the problem. Furthermore, the growth of psychoanalysis in general and ego psychology in particular has led to the recognition that there are many kinds of disturbances that cannot be subsumed under the more traditional categories. Only the historical account makes the situation clear.

First Probings in the 1890s

Naturally Freud's discoveries emerged only slowly, and with many errors on the way. In the beginning, as one might expect, he took over what was accepted practice in his day. This included the electrotherapy of Erb, since entirely discarded, as well as a host of suggestions and "horse sense" which had existed from time immemorial. In addition, Freud used his knowledge of hypnotism from the French school, where he had spent several months in intensive study, especially with Charcot. He also learned from the older Viennese physician Breuer that on occasion a hysterical woman can be treated successfully with hypnotism. There is no doubt that Freud himself muddied the historical picture by giving Breuer too much credit. An examination of Freud's early works (up to about 1910) shows that he repeatedly tried to disclaim great originality for his ideas, evidently fearful that he would be considered too revolutionary. Eventually this attitude disappeared, and he emerged as a fearless iconoclast, but this was only in his old age, after World War I.

After the early probings, Freud made the first momentous discovery that neurosis, then not distinguished from psychosis, involves a defense against unbearable ideas ("The Defense Neuropsychoses," 1894). As has been pointed out, in one sense the whole history of psychoanalysis can be seen as an outgrowth of this first basic formula.

The search for the unbearable idea led Freud at first to sexuality, at that time direct genital sexuality in the usual sense. He developed the theory that ungratified sexuality had a direct biochemical effect, leading to anxiety. This state of anxiety that was created by frustrated sexuality he called the *actual neurosis,* distinguishing it from *psychoneurosis,* which he attributed to psychological traumas in childhood. Under the actual neuroses he included neurasthenia and anxiety neurosis; he even traced neurasthenia to excessive masturbation and anxiety neurosis to an excessive abstinence from sexual activity or heightened tension because of such abstinence. The psychoneuroses he divided into hysteria and obsessional neurosis. He postulated in the

1890s that hysteria is caused by a passive seduction in childhood, while obsessional neurosis results from an active seduction, again in childhood. (That is, the girl is seduced by an older man; the boy seduces a girl.) Both are amenable to psychotherapy; the actual neuroses are not.

Freud tells us in his autobiography (1925) that his early theories collapsed when he learned that the stories of being seduced by their fathers, which his hysterical women patients had told him, were untrue. From this collapse, however, he rescued two cardinal ideas— the importance of fantasy and the importance of childhood.

In the period before 1900, Freud's only book-length work was *Studies in Hysteria,* which he published with Breuer in 1895. It is popularly and erroneously supposed that this book marks the beginning of psychoanalysis; it should be considered only a precursor, since the major psychoanalytic ideas of the first id system (the unconscious, psychosexuality, and transference-resistance) were not really developed until the early 1900s. However, even in the *Studies in Hysteria* he pointed to the vital significance of psychology, which then became increasingly central in his theory:

I have not always been a psychotherapist. Like other neuropathologists, I was trained to apply local diagnoses and electroprognosis, and it still strikes me myself as strange that the case histories I wrote should read like short stories and that, as one might say, they lack the serious stamp of science. I must console myself with the reflection that the nature of the subject is evidently responsible for this, rather than any preference of my own. The fact is that local diagnosis and electrical reactions lead nowhere in the study of hysteria, whereas a detailed description of mental processes such as we are accustomed to find in the works of imaginative writers enables me, with the use of a few psychological formulas, to obtain at least some kind of insight into the course of that affection.[1]

Ten years elapsed between the publication of the *Studies in Hysteria* and the *Three Essays on Sexuality* (1905). It was during this decade that the resolution of the problem of the classical neuroses slowly dawned on Freud. In order to resolve them, however, he had to work out a new system of psychology. We have called this the first psychoanalytic system, or id psychology.

It was through this theory that Freud came to clarify the nature of neurosis. From general pathology he borrowed the observation that every developmental process leaves in its wake certain weak spots, varying from individual to individual, that form the basis for future difficulties or retrogressions. The weak spots he called fixations, and he postulated that in time of stress the neurotic regresses to these fixation points that lie in the world of infantile sexuality, roughly the first five years of life. He considered the Oedipal fixations to be the most important, and he looked upon the Oedipus complex as the core of all neurotic difficulties.

It was always Freud's conviction that the specific neuroses could be differentiated from one another in terms of the different levels of fixation. In trying to apply the theory to Freud's work at that time, however, one faces the difficulty that the final schema of the libidinal stages was only clarified over a period of many years.[2]

Freud's various correlations of neurosis with a particular fixation point should be viewed against the light of this historical background. In his 1913 paper on ''The Disposition to Obsessional Neurosis,'' he enumerated four forms of neurosis—hysteria, obsessional neurosis, paranoia, and dementia praecox—and postulated that the fixation points occur in reverse order: hysteria at the genital stage (the phallic stage had not yet been described); obsessional neurosis at the anal-sadistic; paranoia and dementia praecox somewhere between auto-eroticism and narcissism (the oral stage had only barely been mentioned). Although great theoretical changes have occurred, this schema still is often rather uncritically accepted by many authors. The general idea that the more severe the illness, the earlier the fixation, may be considered to be well established, but specific details remain much more obscure.

At that time the unbearable ideas were equated with infantile sexuality or psychosexual stages of development. This view allowed Freud to give a relatively simple explanation of the symptoms of classical neurosis. Most often the symptom is the unconscious sexual activity of the patient. Or it may be a defense against such sexual activity, or else some compromise formation may result.

Once his experience had grown, Freud offered a new distinction on a therapeutic basis in the paper on ''Narcissism'' (1914). There he divided the neuroses into transference and narcissistic neuroses, depending on the capacity to form a transference in psychotherapy. The transference neuroses are hysteria and obsessional neurosis; the narcissistic neuroses are paranoia and dementia praecox (schizophrenia).

Freud himself could not treat psychosis and made no fundamental contribution to the therapy of the psychoses. Such therapy was offered only after he had ended the major portion of his intellectual work, beginning around the 1930s. It is somewhat paradoxical that the advances which have come since 1930 in the understanding and treatment of the psychoses have all been based on Freudian principles, and particularly on the more thorough understanding of the nature of the transference relationship which the psychotic is able to effect. Experience has shown that, if properly approached, the psychotic does establish some relationship with the therapist and that just as in the analogous case of the neurotic, this relationship can be used to therapeutic advantage. Thus Freud's initial observation of a narcissistic neurosis, in which no transference occurs, was merely one in which he followed his psychiatric colleagues without attempting to probe more deeply into the nature of the observed phenomena. When his own views were adopted later and applied more systematically to the study of psychoses, it turned out that they too could in many cases yield to psychotherapy, although the nature of the therapy had to be different and the outcome was always far more dubious.

A further qualification must be added. The classification of the neuroses along the transference–narcissistic lines, or in terms of the major clinical entities of hysteria, obsessional neurosis, paranoia, and schizophrenia, is a qualitative one. Many psychiatrists have argued and still argue that the presence of one such illness excludes the presence of another; that is, that these are mutually exclusive entities. The contrasting quantitative or continuum point of view holds that a person may be afflicted with any one of these in varying degrees. While Freud seems to speak in a qualitative manner, he also emphatically asserts the significance of the quantitative; he could be said to have always subscribed to a continuum theory. Thus in the paper on "Types of Onset of Neurosis" (1913) he writes:

It remains to say a few words on the relation of these types to the facts of observation. If I survey the set of patients on whose analysis I am now engaged, I must record that not one of them is a pure example of any of the four types of onset. In each of them, rather, I find a portion of frustration operating alongside a portion of incapacity to adapt to the demands of realities; inhibition in development, which coincides, of course, with inflexibility of fixations, has to be reckoned with in all of them, and, as I already said, the importance of quantity of libido must never be neglected. I find, indeed, that in several of these patients their illness has appeared in successive waves, between which there have been healthy intervals, and that each of these waves has been traceable to a different type of precipitating cause. Thus, the erection of these four types cannot lay claims to any high theoretical value; they are merely different ways of establishing a particular pathogenic constellation in the mental economy . . . but this situation . . . does not come as a novelty to mental life and is not created by what is spoken of as a "cause of illness." . . . The importance in the causation of illness which must be ascribed to quantity of libido is in satisfactory agreement with two main theses of the theory of neuroses to which psychoanalysis has led us: first, the thesis that the neuroses are derived from the conflict between the ego and the libido, and secondly, that there is no *qualitative* distinction between the determinants of health and those of neurosis, and that, on the contrary, healthy people have to contend with the same tasks of mastering their libido—they have simply succeeded better in them.[3]

Hysteria

The paper "Hysterical Fantasies and Their Relation to Bisexuality" (1908) contains the most comprehensive discussion of hysteria since the 1890s. Earlier, Freud dealt only with genital sexuality; now he could consider the whole range of infantile sexuality. Although superficially some of his statements are the same as before (e.g., those concerning conversion), they have a different meaning in view of the alteration in the underlying psychological theory.

Around this time Freud suggested the classification of anxiety hysteria to Stekel, who included it in his book on anxiety states. This led to a division of hysteria into two types, anxiety and conversion, which in turn meant that there were now three classical neuroses (the third is obsessional neurosis) instead of the previous two. In the "Hysterical Fantasies" paper, however, Freud confined himself to conversion hysteria, although the only difference between it and anxiety hysteria is that in conversion hysteria the patient develops a somatic symptom, while in anxiety hysteria she reacts with anxiety or a phobia.

Freud summarized his revised views on conversion hysteria in a number of formulas. According to these, hysterical symptoms: are memory symbols of certain operative (traumatic) impressions and experiences; are substitutes, produced by "conversion," for the associative return of these traumatic experiences; like other psychic structures, express the fulfillment of a wish; are the realization of an unconscious fantasy which serves the fulfillment of a wish; serve the purpose of sexual satisfaction and represent a portion of the individual's sexual life (a portion that corresponds to one of the constituents of her sexual instinct); correspond to a return of a mode of sexual satisfaction which was a real one in infantile life and has since been repressed; arise as a compromise between two opposite affective and instinctual impulses, of which one is attempting to bring to expression a component instinct or a constituent of the sexual constitution, and the other is attempting to suppress it; may take over the representation of various unconscious impulses which are not sexual, but they can never be without a real sexual significance; and express on the one hand a masculine unconscious sexual fantasy, and on the other hand a feminine one.

The next year Freud wrote a paper on hysterical attacks. Here he was able to confirm in terms of the new theory what had proved to be true in terms of the old, namely, that acute attacks and chronic symptoms have the same underlying basis. He found he could bring to light many of the unconscious fantasies which are acted out in these attacks.

Obsessional Neurosis

The most complete description of the structure of the obsessional neurosis is found in the theoretical portion of the case history entitled "Notes upon a Case of Obsessional Neurosis" (1909), which has come to be known in the literature as the Rat Man case.

Freud began by saying that in 1896 he had defined obsessional ideas as "transformed self-reproaches which have reemerged from repression and which always relate to some sexual act that was performed with pleasure in childhood." This he now considered to be much too narrow a statement, although the position taken was inherently correct. He went on to describe in much finer detail what is today called the character structure of the obsessional neurotic.

In the obsessional person, repression proceeds by the isolation of the affects from the ideation rather than, as in hysteria, by total amnesia or repression of entire events. Later Freud used the formulation: the obsessional neurotic separates the feeling from the idea, while the hysteric simply represses. When he came to describe defense mechanisms more formally in 1926, he stated that the obsessional uses isolation, while the hysteric uses repression; this was the beginning of the thinking that led eventually to the idea that repression was only one of many defense mechanisms.

The obsessional individual suffers from a deep ambivalence between love and hate. This ambivalence was one of the factors that later led Freud to see the anal-sadistic phase as the fixation point for the obsessional neurotic. The two opposite feelings are split apart in childhood and one, usually the hatred, is suppressed. Such a repression leads to a reaction formation in which the surface feeling is the exact opposite of what lies underneath.

Particularly significant in the psychic makeup of the obsessional neurotic is the retention of infantile masturbatory wishes, dating from the period roughly of ages 3 to 5. These wishes may be generalized to include many forms of touching, a point which Freud elaborated in considerable detail in *Totem and Taboo* (1912–1913). The infantile masturbatory wishes are repressed, but the obsessional act tends to approximate more and more to them.

Obsessional thinking uses a secondary defensive process against the primary obsessional ideas. Freud described many features of this type of thinking. There is a considerable distortion in the use of language, which involves substitutions, abbreviations, distortions, ellipses (omissions and condensations) of all kinds. The obsessional individual tends to be very superstitious, even though he may be of high intelligence. Uncertainty and doubt, which appear together with all-pervading procrastination and indecision, are typical. There is a preoccupation with death and a peculiar attitude toward it.

One explanation of many of these peculiarities of the thinking process in the obsessional neurotic is that there is an ''omnipotence of thought,'' a phrase that Freud ascribed to one of his obsessional patients. The patient treats thoughts as if they were real rather than something in his mind. This leads to many varieties of magical thinking. It was again this omnipotence of thought and the prevalence of magical thinking that led Freud to see many similarities between the patterns of the obsessional neurotic and the prohibitions of primitive societies, including religious rituals and practices.

In obsessional neurotics, feelings are frequently displaced; this shift is related to the process of isolation of the affect from the idea. Regressions of all kinds also occur. Thinking replaces action. An obsessive or compulsive thought is one whose function is to represent an act regressively.

Ego-Psychological Considerations

Freud's theory of neurosis was dependent on his system of psychology. When this changed, or was enlarged, the theory of neurosis was bound to change or be enlarged. Although this happened continually throughout Freud's lifetime, and afterward, it has often escaped notice because it was never explicitly formulated. For historical accuracy it must be brought into the light.

Two questions arise here: What is the difference between the normal person and the neurotic? What is the psychodynamic explanation of "neurosis"? With regard to the first, Freud stated on many occasions that the difference between the normal and the neurotic is only one of degree, quantitative rather than qualitative. For example, in a paper on psychoanalysis in 1913, he wrote:

Recognition of the simultaneous presence of the three factors of "infantilism," "sexuality" and "repression" constitutes the main characteristic of the psychoanalytic theory, and marks its distinction from other views of pathological mental life. At the same time psychoanalysis his demonstrated that there is no fundamental difference, but only one of degree, between the mental life of normal people, of neurotics and of psychotics.[4]

As his view of the ego and the structural theory deepened in the 1920s, Freud extended his theories to include the whole of mankind, especially the "civilized" races whom he encountered directly. By 1930, in *Civilization and Its Discontents* he was quite explicit about the widespread incidence of mental and emotional disturbance: "May we not be justified in reaching the diagnosis that, under the influence of cultural urges, some civilizations, or some epochs of civilization—possibly the whole of mankind—have become 'neurotic'? . . . In spite of all these difficulties, we may expect that one day someone will venture to embark upon a pathology of cultural communities."[5] In the very next line, however, he hedged his criticism with the statement that "for a wide variety of reasons, it is very far from my intention to express an opinion upon the value of human civilization."[6]

Thus, typically, in one breath Freud openly condemned the civilization in which he found himself and in the next breath almost withdrew his critique. This ambivalence lies at the root of many later conflicts in the history of psychoanalysis.

From a technical point of view, with the advent of ego psychology. Freud reformulated his position on neurosis (specifically, hysteria and compulsion neurosis) as a conflict between the ego and the id. In ''Neurosis and Psychosis'' (1924) he wrote: *''neurosis is the result of a conflict between the ego and its id, whereas psychosis is the analogous outcome of a similar disturbance in the relations between the ego and the external world.''* [7]

But then he writes in the next paragraph: ''There are certainly good grounds for being suspicious of such simple solutions of a problem. Moreover, the most that we may expect is that this formula will turn out to be correct in the roughest outline.'' And in the paper on ''The Loss of Reality in Neurosis and Psychosis,'' written a few months later, he specified that there was also a loss of reality in neurosis, thus again making the difference between neurosis and psychosis a relative one.

In 1926 in *The Problem of Anxiety* Freud made a further important distinction with his attempt to classify the three transference neuroses in terms of the major defense mechanisms employed. This led eventually to a reclassification of individuals in terms of defenses employed but did not alter the total underlying problem.

Summary Comments

By the time that his essential work was completed in 1926, Freud left the psychoanalytic world with two conceptions of neurosis, which can be called the narrow or technical one and the broad or cultural picture. The technical conception is that of a conflict between the ego and the id, where the clinical material can be subdivided into hysteria (two types: conversion and anxiety) and obsessive-compulsive neurosis. His exploration of these classical neuroses was so thorough and far-reaching that no substantial alterations need be made in his formulations.

The broader meaning of neurosis, or the cultural one (the pathology of civilized communities), can not be embraced, however, in these technical formulas. Here Freud only laid the foundations, and it has remained for many others to continue his essential ideas. Because of the way in which he wrote, it has often been unclear that Freud held both views, the technical and the cultural images of neurosis, or emotional disturbance. It is from this vantage point that further work in the field must be examined.

Post-Freudian Developments

Developments since Freud have proceeded along the two main lines that he started, relating first to the psychodynamics of neurosis, and second to the difference between the neurotic and the normal. Analysts since Freud have had ample opportunity to confirm and amplify the profound clinical observations that he made. From a purely technical standpoint, in the understanding of hysteria and obsessive-compulsive neurosis little has changed. There has been mainly an addition of new viewpoints stemming from broadening psychological horizons. The enlargement of the concept of neurosis to embrace a major portion of mankind represents the major change since Freud.

Obsessional Neurosis

Nagera (1976) has recently summarized the literature on the classical picture of obsessional neurosis, showing how little later writers have deviated from Freud. Sullivan's insights are essentially the same as Freud's, in other language. The statement of Sullivan's student, Salzman (1968), that "the obsessive-compulsive character type is today's most prevalent character structure"[8] is most certainly incorrect, as is the similar statement by William Menninger (1943) that the influences of the anal period are the most potent forces on character structure in our contemporary culture.

A balanced view is struck by Anna Freud (1966) in her summary of the psychoanalytic views on obsessional neurosis, presented at the Amsterdam Congress of the International in 1965. She divided the discussion into eight topics, summarizing each as follows:

1. THE MATRIX OF OBSESSIONAL NEUROSIS. Today, with much analytic interest concentrated on the first year of life, the anal period as the beginning of pathology seems disappointingly late to many authors. Hence, every effort has been made to antedate the obsessional neuroses. In fact, almost every element of early infantile life was brought forward in this respect and, especially, the events within the early mother–infant relationship were named as relevant pathogenic factors.

2. THE INSTINCTUAL BACKGROUND OF OBSESSIONAL NEUROSIS. Not all the contributors to the topic were ready to accept the classical view that it is the id content of the anal-sadistic phase which

is warded off by means of the obsessional symptomatology; some
rival claims were raised, especially for the tendencies toward oral incorporation of the object and for voyeurism. There was even one attempt to disconnect obsessional neurosis altogether from any specific
instinctual content and to consider its symptomatology instead as
wholly determined by the ego mechanisms that are characteristic for
it.

3. A POSSIBLE LINK BETWEEN MATRIX AND ANAL-SADISM. Links
between failure in object relations and heightened anality may be
more common than we realize. If that should be the case, the repercussions for later defenses against anality may be significant. However that may be, no instance of this type was mentioned at the
congress.

4. THE EGO IN OBSESSIONAL NEUROSIS. According to the trends
of the time, the contributions to this topic were numerous and left
few areas unexplored. One innovation, brought more or less independently by a number of authors, was the notion of a general cognitive
and perceptual style of the ego. No new defense mechanisms were
added to those with which we are familiar.

5. MUTUAL INFLUENCES BETWEEN ID AND EGO IN OBSES-
SIONAL NEUROSIS. A number of possibilities were alluded to
regarding the relation between drive and defense. A number of valuable suggestions, amendments, and additions to existing theory were
brought forward about the relation between drive regression and ego
regression.

6. OBSESSIONAL NEUROSIS VERSUS PHOBIC. Great interest was
expressed (on the basis of a case presentation) in the change of pathology from a phobic to a predominantly obsessional illness.

7. ATTEMPTS AT AVOIDING OBSESSIONAL PATHOLOGY. There
are some defensive attitudes which try to do away with sources of
danger altogether. Where they are successful, the need for further
defense activity is eliminated at the expense of a character or behavior change, and no obsessional neurosis proper is organized.

8. BENEFICIAL AND HARMFUL EFFECTS, SUCCESSES, FAILURES,
AND LIMITS OF OBSESSIONAL NEUROSIS. The beneficial effects of
obsessional neurosis lie in their stabilizing effect. The neurosis also
has a harmful effect on ego activity and the personality as a whole. In
some cases there is a partial failure of the obsessional defense. And
finally, the limits of obsessional neurosis may be clearly outlined.

In sum, as is the case for hysteria as well, obsessional neurosis has gradually come to be seen as a syndrome, whose outlines were clearly and correctly described by Freud, within a larger ego structure, which may show considerable variation.

Hysteria

A panel discussion on hysteria today was held at the meeting of the International Psychoanalytical Association in Paris in 1973. There was general agreement that while the views on hysteria had shown considerable alteration since the early days of Freud, his delineation of the core elements of the personality constellation remained correct. Laplanche (1974) summarized the discussion as follows:

To say that hysteria has changed takes two very different meanings, depending on the speakers. For some of them, it is our conception of hysteria which has changed or which *ought* to change. It is not by chance that the school of Melanie Klein has only scarcely and belatedly dealt with hysteria. For the Kleinians and many of their more distant successors, hysteria can only be defined as a particular method of defense against anxieties which are *early, psychotic* and of a *non-sexual* nature. Thus the evident role of "sexuality in the etiology of neurosis"—the foundation of Freud's discoveries—is disputed in favor of a secondary, artificial, defensive sexualization of conflicts. These conflicts are related to the *survival* of the individual rather than to his *desire*. I would like to state my distrust of the desexualization of psychoanalysis, which can be clearly seen in much of the modern theorizing.

For other participants in the conference, the discussion was situated at a more manageable level nearer to the classical coordinates of Freudian thought: has the clinical picture of hysteria changed? This question is of interest because it forces us to ask what structural constants persist beneath these changes. Some participants particularly stressed the so-called "character" forms . . . ; thus putting the stress on the relational aspects of hysteria. Some participants seemed to admit as an evident fact the fading of conversion hysteria. . . . Are we to say that visual hallucinations and attacks are absent or less frequent, or should we say that today we are above all interested in their *relational*, even their *transferential* aspect? We could then say that it is our understanding of the body more than our understanding of hysteria that has changed. The body now appears to us as the locus for a communication which is potential, implicit, veiled and fixed. . . .

We may ask ourselves whether the specificity of hysteria is to be situated at the *instinctual* level (Oedipal level), in the *defense* mechanisms (repression) or in the way that repression makes its *return* (conversion).[9]

Many authors have decried the loose usage of the term "hysteria." A War Department Bulletin[10] referred to the "etymologically absurd 'hysteria' which has by accretion become endowed with protean false popular and scientific significance until—except in psychoanalysis where it is a clearly defined entity—it has become a term of opprobrium.''

It has been widely held that the dissemination of psychoanalytic theory has led to the disappearance of classical hysteria from ordinary medical practice. In her book on hysteria, Ilsa Veith (1965) writes:

From the above it can be seen that Freud's studies on hysteria, instead of endowing this illness with greater significance, actually divested it of much of the mystical importance it had held for more than two millennia. With much of the Freudian terminology having become part of sophisticated language [and if] . . . hysteria is primarily a means of achieving ego-satisfaction, this lack of attention could easily account for the nearly total disappearance of the illness. Thus it may not be too paradoxical to state that it was the intensified understanding of the cause of hysteria by leading psychiatrists during this century that contributed to the near-disappearance of the disease.[11]

Thus Freud's painstakingly thorough elucidation of the psychology of both hysteria and obsessional neurosis led to an unexpected, paradoxical result: the virtual disappearance of both illnesses in their classical form from the practice of the average psychotherapist. Instead, they have been absorbed as syndromes within a larger picture of disturbance. When they do appear as syndromes, the clarification offered by Freud of the psychodynamics, genesis, and appropriate treatment still may be said to hold.

The Broader Meaning of Neurosis

From a very early stage, Freud sensed the wider significance of psychoanalysis for human affairs. But he was so preoccupied with technical questions that this broader aspect of the field was left to one side. In the postwar writings of the 1920s, he returned to what he called philosophical speculations and repeatedly called attention to the broader meanings of his discoveries. In the paper quoted earlier, he referred to the "pathology of civilized communities." Such pathology, which goes well beyond the technical confines of hysteria and obsessions, can be termed the broad meaning of neurosis, the conflict between the ego and the id being the restricted usage.

Taking off from Freud's definition of normality as the ability to love and work, psychoanalysis has formulated an ideal conception of what mankind might become (Fine, 1971). Gradually the idea has grown up that to fall short of this ideal is to be "neurotic" (Offer and Sabshin, 1974). In both the popular and the professional mind this broader meaning of the term neurosis has gained ascendancy to such an extent that even the term "normal-neurotic" has become everyday currency. The historical growth toward this position after Freud can be briefly traced.

In the 1920s a guarded spirit of optimism could be seen among many intellectuals. With the horrors of World War I behind them, they hoped that a new world could be reconstructed along more socialistic and democratic lines (Dahmer, 1973). In this new world Freud and Marx would be the chief guides. The hope was openly expressed that psychoanalysis could lead to a happier world, perhaps even one in which neurosis had disappeared entirely.

One aspect of this hopefulness was the creation of the Psychoanalytic Movement (see chapter 5). Unfortunately the appearance of the Depression, then Hitler in 1933, put a speedy end to this spirit of hope. But the ideals forged in that period have remained ever since.

One of the most significant voices describing the newer turn of events in psychoanalysis and psychiatry was Ernest Jones, who continued to play a leading role in the international psychoanalytic movement until his death in 1958. In an astonishingly modern paper, delivered at the opening of the Psychiatric Institute in Columbia University in 1929, Jones (1929) argued that America had actually created a new profession, of psychiatry, where none had existed before. With regard to the difference between the neurotic and the normal he wrote:

Fundamental complexes and mechanisms, the effects of which radiate through the whole mind, can be very plainly demonstrated in the psychoneurotic when the same processes can often be only dimly inferred in the normal, and yet anyone who urges the objection that there is a qualitative difference between the two classes is merely displaying his own omission to investigate the relationship between them.[12]

With regard to the technical understanding of neurosis, Jones made three points: psychoanalysis has for the first time offered a real comprehension of the meaning of mental morbidity; the disorder underlying all mental morbidity can be defined as a failure on the part of the ego to deal in any final manner with certain fundamental intrapsychic conflicts that are the inevitable lot of every human being; all mental morbidity signifies an arrest in development.

The Cultural Factor

Once the ubiquity of neurosis was recognized, the next question was: What is wrong with modern man? Understandably this question was heatedly discussed in a world that had just concluded one disastrous war and was in the process of starting another. And the further unsettled state of the world since World War II has intensified the search for an answer to the question.

The most important addition to the early Freudian description of the dynamics of neurosis came from the analysis of culture. This too had been begun by Freud, but he had left it in a relatively undeveloped state. Beginning with the 1920s, anthropologists went out into the field, using much more sophisticated concepts and devices such as the Rorschach and Thematic Apperception Test, provided by psychoanalysis. It soon became clear that the current solution to the basic problems of humanity is only one of many possible solutions, and that in many areas it is by no means the best. Many cultures were discovered where far greater sexual freedom was tolerated, much less anger existed, even at times war was absent. It became apparent that the particular neuroses dealt with by analysts were a product of their times (Fenichel, 1935a) and not absolute invariants of the human condition. With increasing insistence the question came to be posed over and over: What is wrong with our culture?

Horney: The Neurotic Personality of Our Time

In 1937 Karen Horney published *The Neurotic Personality of Our Time,* a book that had wide popular appeal but a mixed reception in the profession. Horney described the basic evil as invariably a lack of genuine warmth and affection. Various actions on the part of the parents arouse this feeling, which she called basic anxiety. The anxiety arouses hostility, which has to be repressed. For this repression of hostility she adduced four reasons: helplessness, fear, love, or guilt. In our culture the sexual sphere is the one in which guilt feelings are most frequently stimulated. There is thus aroused an all-pervading, and insidiously increasing, feeling of being lonely and helpless in a hostile world. Against the basic anxiety there are in our culture four principal ways in which people try to protect themselves: affection, submissiveness, power, and withdrawal.

Although at the end of the book she insisted that her theory was not in principle contradictory to Freud's, Horney's book loosed a multitude of criticisms that she had "deviated" too far from the classical models. In turn she took up the cudgels and a fierce battle developed, pursued by both sides with unswerving fanaticism, which can best be characterized by Santayana's definition of a fanatic as one who redoubles his efforts after he has lost sight of his goal. In reality, Horney was merely calling attention to the broader meaning of neurosis which was implicit in Freud. The reasons why this position led to such a bloody political battle have been discussed in chapters 4 and 5.

Sullivan: The Fusion of Psychiatry and Social Sciences

After Horney's pioneering work, a number of other analysts began to place increasing stress on the cultural milieu in which neurosis came into being and, either explicitly or implicitly, to point to a broader meaning of neurosis than the conflict between the ego and the id. Of all American analysts, Harry Stack Sullivan was probably the most influential. In the last 10 years of his life, both during World War II and after it, he concerned himself with what could best be called the mental health of mankind. In 1947 he wrote:

The call for a world-wide mobilization of psychiatry . . . is now made explicit. . . .

We have to make sense; we, every one of us. We have to make sense not about everything, but about principles that are important in promoting harmonious human relations.

Few indeed are the psychiatrists who have nothing to offer to such an effort, and each and every one of us is called upon to further the achievement of this objective in full measure of his capacity.[13]

Other Studies of Culture and Neurosis

A number of other authors made significant contributions to the notion that neurosis is a product of our culture, and therefore the therapist should not confine his efforts to patients with classical neuroses. Kardiner (1939, 1945) provided the first complete outline for the integration of psychoanalysis and anthropology, showing how the basic personality pattern of any culture can be related to the various institutions in that culture. Fromm in *The Sane Society* (1955) continued Freud's argument about the pathology of civilized communities, but then offered a socialist rather than an analytical solution. Perhaps more important is Fromm and Maccoby's careful study of a Mexican village (1970), showing how the personality pattern interacted with the socioeconomic structure. Ari Kiev in *Magic, Faith and Healing* (1964) assembled data from a number of contemporary societies in which he showed how the definition and treatment of neurosis fitted in with the whole ethos of any specific culture.

This topic is discussed more extensively from a theoretical viewpoint in chapter 17. In terms of clarification of the broad meaning of neurosis, all of this work provided convincing evidence that neurosis, defined in the broad sense as unhappiness, is widespread indeed, and that it can be understood and treated by the procedures of psychoanalysis.

Empirical Data on the Frequency of "Neurosis"

Once the conceptual basis for a broader understanding of neurosis had been established by psychoanalytic theory, the next question was: What percentage of the population can be said to be functioning below their optimal level? The urgent need for a definitive answer to this question was prompted by a number of considerations.

1. In World War II the world was plunged into the worst cataclysm in human history by a dictator, Adolf Hitler, who seemed to all appearances to be quite mad. Among his enemies was another dictator, Josef Stalin, who to all appearances seemed equally mad.

2. With the development of nuclear weapons, the danger arising from the antics of a mad dictator, a danger no longer seen as even improbable, was the literal destruction of the world.

3. The high incidence of rejections of men for army service in all the Western countries, and of breakdowns in combat, directed attention to the mental health of the average person in the democratic countries.

4. In spite of decades of intensive research, science had failed to produce convincing evidence that mental disorder, with a few exceptions, had an organic basis. Instead the evidence became increasingly strong that all mental morbidity was the result of disturbed family relationships in childhood, as Freud and the psychoanalysts had always taught. In their influential textbook on psychiatry, Freedman and Redlich (1966) referred to the neuroses as simply "psychosocial disorders."

5. The spread of therapeutic competence among psychiatrists, psychologists, social workers, and other mental health professionals, as a result of the application of psychoanalytic principles, uncovered more and more persons in need of help and willing to accept it if offered. Whatever the verbal differences it became increasingly clear that a common philosophy of therapy underlay all the psychotherapeutic approaches and that this philosophy was essentially a distillation of psychoanalytic wisdom (Henry, 1971).

Still there was skepticism and a widespread call for more precise numbers on how many "neurotics" there are. The first large-scale intensive study of this kind was undertaken by Rennie and his co-workers in New York during the 1950s. Their book (Rennie et al., 1962) proved to be a landmark in the field. They took a home-survey sample of 1,660 adults in Manhattan, conducting an intensive personal interview with each respondent, in contrast to superficial questionnaire approaches. Their astounding finding in summary was that 81.5 percent of the inhabitants of Manhattan were mentally impaired in some degree. The specific breakdown is shown in the accompanying table.[14]

One reaction to these startling findings was the statement that they were peculiar to New York, where large numbers of emotionally

HOME-SURVEY SAMPLE (AGES 20–59), RESPONDENTS' DISTRIBUTION
ON SYMPTOM-FORMATION CLASSIFICATION OF MENTAL HEALTH

Well	18.5%
Mild symptom formation	36.3
Moderate symptom formation	21.8
Marked symptom formation	13.2
Severe symptom formation	7.5
Incapacitated	2.7
Impaired (Marked, severe, and incapacitated combined)	23.4

disturbed individuals congregated. Accordingly, other parts of the world came under scrutiny. The second large-scale study, of equally far-reaching significance, was that of Leighton and his co-workers in the northeastern part of Canada, where conditions of life were markedly different from those in New York. Leighton et al. (1963) came to remarkably similar conclusions on the basis of a study of 1,010 respondents: 17 percent well, 20 percent impaired, 63 percent moderately disturbed: [15] "Our conclusion from all the available information is that at least half of the adults in Stirling County are *currently* suffering from some psychiatric disorder defined in the APA *Diagnostic and Statistical Manual.*" [16]

Of necessity these findings led to a reevaluation of the concepts of normality and mental health. It could no longer be assumed, as traditional psychiatry had assumed, that the statistically average individual was normal (Offer and Sabshin, 1974). Instead, an ideal image of mental health, dominated by psychoanalytic concepts, came increasingly to the fore (Kubie, 1954; Parsons, 1958). The conviction that neurosis is part of the fabric of our social structure became increasingly prominent among mental health professionals and the community at large. Studies of other societies did not disclose any considerably higher incidence of mental health (Kiev, 1964). Nor did a study of the past reveal anything but a long history of neurotic distortions of life (de Mause, 1974). A succinct statement of this position came from Fillmore Sanford, then executive director of the American Psychological Association, in testimony before Congress in 1965: "Mental health is not exclusively a psychiatric problem, or a psychological problem or a taxpayer's problem, or a legislative problem. It is all of these and more. It is a problem of the whole social fabric." [17]

Summary Comments on Neurosis

When Freud began his work in the 1880s, the concept of neurosis was confused and chaotic. He classified the available material into two major types of neurosis, hysteria and obsessional neurosis (the "classical" neuroses), further subdividing hysteria into conversion and anxiety hysteria. He clarified the genesis, dynamics, and structure of these classical neuroses, and developed classical psychoanalysis as the treatment of choice for them.

Freud's work has been added to but not significantly modified. Instead, what happened was that the classical neuroses virtually disappeared from the clinical picture, to be replaced by vague entities generally known as "character disorders." It was then found that these character disorders were not isolated illnesses but were manifested by large segments of the populace; the two largest studies indicated that some two-thirds of the population was impaired emotionally, to a greater or lesser degree. This finding led to broader meanings of neurosis, normality, and mental health, which has prevailed since the early 1960s.

Within this broader meaning of neurosis, the traditional diagnostic categories have become increasingly meaningless (Menninger, 1959), and a different view of human nature and human potential has come to the fore. Saul and Wenar (1965) put it as follows: "The inevitable and simple conclusion is that if all children were properly reared we would have a world of emotionally mature men and women. What we see instead is not human nature, but a variety of characterological disorders which are so nearly universal that we mistake them for human nature." [18]

Chapter Fourteen

Psychosis and Borderline Conditions:
The Psychoanalytic Theory of Psychosis

Unlike the parallel situation with neurosis, psychosis had been known and studied from the time of the Greeks onward. The Greek notion that psychosis is a "brain illness" had been largely accepted by psychiatry. Further contributions also came from nonanalytic psychiatrists such as Eugen Bleuler, who coined the term schizophrenia and distinguished the primary from the secondary symptoms, and Adolf Meyer, who showed that the schizophrenic reacts catastrophically to various threatening life situations. In this area as well, the advances made by organic psychiatry and other disciplines must be given serious consideration.

The discussion of psychosis has merged more and more with the discussion of schizophrenia. Consequently my treatment of the development of psychoanalytic theory is limited largely to an understanding of schizophrenia; other points are considered separately.

Freud's Contributions

Freud's therapeutic work during most of his life was largely confined to the classical neuroses. He discovered at an early date that schizophrenia was not amenable to systematic psychoanalysis, although he always allowed for the possibility that modifications would be found which would make such patients accessible. Hence his approach to schizophrenia was not nearly as thorough and systematic as his approach to neurosis. Nevertheless, he and some of his early followers did make certain fundamental contributions. These may be summed up as follows.

PSYCHOSIS AS A DEFENSE AGAINST FRUSTRATION. As early as 1894, in his first psychoanalytic paper, Freud discussed several cases of psychosis and showed that the patients took flight from reality as a defense against intolerable ideas:

I have only very few analyses of psychoses of this sort at my disposal. But I think we have to do here with a type of psychical illness which is very frequently employed. For no insane asylum is without what must be regarded as analogous examples—the mother who has fallen ill from the loss of her baby, and now rocks a piece of wood unceasingly in her arms, or the jilted bride who, arrayed in her wedding-dress, has for years been waiting for her bride groom.[1]

THE SYMPTOMS HAVE SOME MEANING. In 1907 Jung published his book on *The Psychology of Dementia Praecox,* the main contribution of which was to show that the dissociated complexes seen in the schizophrenic had some dynamic meaning.

DETACHMENT OF THE LIBIDO. In 1908 Abraham was able to offer the first clear-cut differentiation between hysteria and schizophrenia, then still known as dementia praecox. In schizophrenia the libido is detached from objects; in hysteria it overattaches itself to them. Thus autoeroticism (later renamed narcissism) is one of the major features of schizophrenia.

THE SCHREBER CASE. Freud's major contribution to the whole topic was his book on the Schreber case, published in 1911. Schreber was a German judge who had suffered a psychotic episode, recovered, and written up his experiences. On the basis of this material, Freud was able to show that the meaning of the symptoms is an attempt at restitution of the relationship with objects after the libido has detached itself from these objects. In addition, he demonstrated the close connection between homosexuality and paranoia. In a postscript to his paper, written in 1912, for the first time he drew the well-known parallel among psychosis, dreams, childhood, and primitive man: " 'in dreams and neuroses,' so our thesis has run, 'we come once more upon the *child* and his peculiarities which characterize his modes of thought and his emotional life.' 'And we come upon the *savage* too,' we may now add, 'upon the *primitive* man, as he stands revealed to us in the light of the researches of archaeology and of ethnology.' "[2]

NARCISSISTIC VERSUS TRANSFERENCE NEUROSES. In 1914, in the paper on narcissism, Freud introduced a fundamental diagnostic differentiation that had far-reaching significance, since it was based on the dynamic element of reaction to a therapist rather than the static one of description of symptoms. This was the broad classification into two major types, transference neuroses and narcissistic neuroses, i.e., those patients who form a transference and those who do not.

PRIMARY-PROCESS USE OF WORDS. The following year, in his investigation of schizophrenic language, Freud maintained that the schizophrenic uses words the way other people use things. Thus primary-process material breaks through in the schizophrenic, whereas it is held in check in the neurotic.

THE UNCONSCIOUS ON THE SURFACE. Allied to the preceding point is Freud's schematic representation of what different individuals do with their unconscious: the normal person represses unconscious material, the neurotic converts it into symptoms, while the schizophrenic allows it to break through in the form of primary-process material. Related to this was his old notion that the dream is every person's nightly psychosis.

EGO-PSYCHOLOGICAL DIFFERENTIATION. Following his delineation of ego psychology in 1923 (*The Ego and the Id*), Freud wrote two papers on the ego psychology of the psychoses and neuroses in 1924. In the first he saw neurosis as a conflict between the ego and the id, psychosis as a conflict between the ego and reality, and depression as a conflict between the ego and the superego. In the second paper he showed that the loss of reality in psychosis was a relative one, not an absolute one.

All of these viewpoints were useful in greater or lesser degree, but there was still one vital element lacking, which had been present in the theory of neurosis: Freud retained his conviction that psychosis could not be treated by psychotherapeutic means, and therefore he did not build up any personal experience with its treatment. More than any other factor, the treatment of schizophrenics by later analysts was what led to the elaboration, correction, and revision of Freud's theories.

Post-Freudian Development

The first step in going beyond Freud was to get away from his pessimistic conviction that schizophrenics could not be treated analytically. Jung had reportedly attempted to analyze many psychotics at Burghölzli, but with little success. Among Freud's early followers, however, Paul Federn undertook a modification of psychoanalytic technique which, according to his reports, proved to be quite effective (Federn, 1934, 1943). In 1934 he wrote:

It may sound paradoxical but is nevertheless in accordance with our theoretical knowledge when I assert that it is precisely in the case of the psychotic, whose reason is impaired, that our treatment must address itself to his reason, in such measure as he retains it, and, similarly, that the transference is even more important than in a transference-neurosis. Psychotic patients are accessible to psychoanalysis at all, first, because and in so far as they are still capable of transference; secondly, because and in so far as one part of their ego has insight into their abnormal state and, thirdly, because and in so far as a part of their personality is still directed towards reality. . . . The chief precaution in analyzing a psychotic is not to increase regression.[3]

The general conditions laid down for psychoanalytic treatment by Federn were as follows: establishment of positive transference; interruption of treatment when transference becomes negative; provision of a woman as a helper; lasting psychoanalytical postpsychotic help and supervision; settling of the sexual problem.[4] In severe cases he regarded these conditions as indispensable; in milder cases they shortened the treatment.

A number of other analysts also reported some success with the analytic treatment of schizophrenics. As early as 1911 Bjerre reported the intensive treatment, during 40 interviews, of a patient who suffered from chronic paranoia. Boyer and Giovacchini (1967), reviewing the literature, noted a large number of analysts who had reported a single case and were optimistic about the result. However, "since they contributed but one article, it would seem that their optimism waned."[5]

In the 1920s, reports began to be more optimistic. Kempf, an early American pioneer, had reported a successful case in 1919. It may be noted here that the optimism of the American psychiatric scene in general has played a considerable role in the attitude toward schizophrenia. Waelder (1924) suggested that certain schizophrenic patients might benefit from psychoanalysis without gross modifications, and R. Brunswick (1928) supported this stand. Landauer (1924) wrote of his procedure in treating schizophrenics, stressing the beneficial results of passive techniques.

On the whole, however, in this period psychoanalysts remained dubious about the analytic treatment of psychotics and preferred to avoid it if possible.

Sullivan's Contribution (1924–1931)

The first analyst to report successful results in the treatment of schizophrenics on any extended basis was Harry Stack Sullivan.[6] This material has already been described in chapter 4.

The writer will assume that the concept of schizophrenia has been stripped of an implication of inevitable chronicity and deterioration. He will not accept recovery as "remission" or "arrest," but instead will hold that an individual who has undergone a schizophrenic illness, ceased to show schizophrenic processes, and resumed social living with a gradual expansion of life-interests, has in fact to the limit of the meaning of such terms actually *recovered* from the schizophrenic illness. . . . such recoveries are by no means infrequent.[7]

In the wake of Sullivan's work, a host of analysts in the United States undertook the modified analytic treatment of many schizophrenics: Arieti (1974), Boyer and Giovacchini (1967), Chiland (1977), Fromm-Reichmann (1939), Menninger (1963), Searles (1965), among many others. For the first time in history, some optimism, cautious though it had to be, about the ultimate recovery of many schizophrenic patients began to appear in psychiatry.

A parallel development, curiously independent of the American scene, took place in England at roughly the same time. Under the impact of Melanie Klein's theories, the psychotic was not sharply differentiated from the neurotic. She considered that all persons went through paranoid and depressive phases in infancy, that they were all scarred in varying degrees, and that they were all amenable to treatment. Although she herself published little on the subject, a number of her followers did. Particularly notable is the work of Rosenfeld (1965), Segal (1973), and Bion (1961).

The "Heroic Treatments"

Apart from the routine psychoanalytic treatment of schizophrenics reported by many analysts, particularly followers of Sullivan and Klein, a number of heroic treatment cases have appeared in the literature. Perhaps best known is the self-report by Hannah Green, *I Never Promised You a Rose Garden* (1964); she was treated by Frieda Fromm-Reichmann over a period of many years. Sechehaye (1947) described the intense treatment of a schizophrenic girl over an 8-year period. Marion Milner (*The Hands of the Living God,* 1959) took 20 years to cure her patient. Searles (1965) and Rosenfeld (1965) have both reported numerous cases of such extended heroic efforts which eventually resulted in partial or complete recovery of the patient.

In 1947 John Rosen published his first report on the method of "direct analysis" with schizophrenics more deteriorated than those treated by any other analyst (Rosen, 1953); Sullivan, for instance, had limited himself to early schizophrenics. An ingenious bag of tricks allowed Rosen to make contact with seemingly inaccessible individuals and to bring them to some mode of functioning. Arieti (1974) states that while Rosen suffered from excessive enthusiasm, "it is beyond question that Rosen obtained at least temporary results and that he was able to inject faith into many workers at a time when the prevalent opinion was that psychotherapy with schizophrenics was an impossibility." [8]

While gigantic steps have been made forward since Freud, Arieti concludes that the individual psychotherapy of schizophrenia is still in the pioneering stage. [9]

Theoretical Advances

A number of notable advances in theory, derived in part from the treatment results described above, and in part from the general growth of theoretical knowledge, have helped to explain the baffling manifestations of schizophrenia. Freud's hope that the study of the psychoses would lead to an increased understanding of the ego, and vice versa, has been amply fulfilled.

Ego Weakness

Increasingly the concept of ego weakness has come to be central to the understanding of schizophrenia. Freud had already noted it (*The Problem of Anxiety,* 1926) but ascribed it rather inadequately as due to the distance of the ego from the id: "If the ego remains bound up with the id and indistinguishable from it, then it displays its strength."[10]

A more adequate formulation was offered by Jones in 1929, in his paper on "Psychoanalysis and Psychiatry." Jones offered the continuum position that "all mental morbidity is a state of schizophrenia" and such morbidity results from a failure on the part of the ego to deal adequately with conflicts that occur in every human being. In 1937 Freud noted that the normal ego varies from normal to psychotic in its various functions, thus opening the door to a systematic investigation of the various ego functions (Fenichel, 1945; Nunberg, 1955). This progress was further advanced by Hartmann's fundamental contribution of the autonomous or conflict-free area of the ego, which develops independently of the id. The theoretical positions of Sullivan and Klein in this area were essentially the same, though they were formulated in different language.

Anxiety, Panic, and Defense Mechanisms

Once it became clear that ego strength and weakness were the fundamental concepts, the next step lay in clarifying the development of the ego. This was the work of the 1940s and 1950s (see chapters 4 and 5). The infantile ego is weak, for purely developmental reasons; the schizophrenic ego is weak because it regresses to the infantile (Fenichel, 1945).

Since anxiety and its defenses had been recognized after Freud's 1926 book as the core of personality functioning, the question arose as to how the anxiety of the schizophrenic differed from that of the neurotic. To this question Sullivan offered an arresting answer (1931b): the schizophrenic reaches a situation where he is suffering from panic.[11] Sullivan compared it to that undergone by an individual awakening from a vivid nightmare. If this panic continues, the clinical picture becomes that of catatonia; such a state may go on indefinitely. Or one of three changes may occur: recovery because of integration of the different parts of the personality; a massive transference of blame, leading to a chronic paranoid state; or a dilapidation of the repressed system and a regression to early childhood behavior, customarily called hebephrenic dilapidation.

Developmentally, this panic and the defenses against it correspond to acute anxiety states in infancy, which were well described by Melanie Klein; she eventually created the terms "paranoid position" and "depressive position" for these early anxieties (1948). The defenses used by the infant to ward off these overpowering anxieties are generally seriously disruptive of the personality, and include splitting, denial, and projective identifications.

Following the establishment of these concepts, the attention of investigators was focused in two directions: toward clarification of the defense mechanisms, and toward clarification of infantile experience. The defense mechanisms have already been discussed. The infantile factor must now be considered in more detail.

Oral Regression

Freud's original view that the deeper the pathology the greater the regression had been stymied for a while by the inability to see the oral character of the regression in schizophrenia. Once the dynamics of the oral stage had been elucidated, however, this error was corrected. In the Schreber case (1911) Freud drew an important parallel among psychosis, childhood, dream life, and primitive culture, but he did not tie these parallels specifically to the oral stage and oral regression. This connection was soon drawn, however. Papers on the oral stage began to appear in the 1920s (Glover, 1925), and the connection between oral regression and schizophrenia was soon made (Sullivan, 1931b).

While delusions of persecution had initially been linked with the anal stage (van Ophuijsen, 1920), it soon became apparent that they were primarily oral (Bychowski, 1930). By the 1930s it had become clear that oral regression was an outstanding feature of the dynamics of schizophrenia (Bak, 1939).

At this point a new difficulty arose, which eventually led to the broadening of the concept of schizophrenia, especially in American psychiatry. A number of other disorders were described as emanating from oral regressions as well: addictions (Rado, 1926), alcoholism (Crowley, 1939), psychosomatic disorders (Alexander, various papers), and many other severe conditions, unclassifiable by traditional means, which came to be lumped together in that period as character disorders (Deutsch, 1942; Jones, 1929). In 1942 Helene Deutsch made the following pertinent remarks about patients with such disorders:

Whether the emotional disturbances described in this paper imply a "schiz-ophrenic disposition" or constitute rudimentary symptoms of schizophrenia is not clear to me. These patients represent variants in the series of abnor-mal distorted personalities. They do not belong among the commonly ac-cepted forms of neurosis, and they are too well adjusted to reality to be called psychotic. . . . In so far as they are accessible to analysis, one may be able to learn much in the field of ego psychology, especially with regard to disturbances of affect, and, perhaps, make contributions to the problem of the "schizoid" which is still so obscure.[12]

Thus the problem of the "latent psychosis," or prepsychotic condi-tion, became increasingly important (Bychowski, 1951). Observa-tions of this kind strengthened the position of those who held to the continuum theory of mental illness, which tended to prevail in the United States, whereas European psychiatrists showed more of a ten-dency to maintain the old rigid, Kraepelinian distinctions.

Hostility Stronger than Sexuality

In the wake of Freud's death instinct theory, a gradual shift took place from an emphasis on sexuality to an emphasis on hostility, even though most analysts disagreed with the theory of the death instinct. Gradually the conviction grew that the greater the pathology, the greater the hostility. For example, the common world-destruction fantasy with which many schizophrenic episodes begin came to be seen as a projection of the patient's destructive urges.

Papers stressing the role of hostility (rage, anger, hatred) be-came increasingly numerous. Only a few can be mentioned. In 1924 Abraham published his sketch of the development of the libido, in which he emphasized the oral-sadistic (or oral-cannibalistic) stage, as well as the anal-sadistic. Shortly thereafter Melanie Klein, who was a student of his, began to write of the sadistic fantasies in early in-fancy. In 1929 Jones wrote that "the primary hate is probably the in-stinctive purpose [sic] of the infant, usually in the form of rage, to frustration of its wishes, particularly its libidinal wishes."[13]

Similar positions were put forth by many others (Horney, 1937; Sadger, 1926; Sullivan, 1927). Sullivan (1962) connected early temper tantrums with a later psychotic or prepsychotic development. Whether the hostility was instinctual in its own right or was the reac-tion to frustration is less important than the growing clinical convic-tion that rage was primary in the whole spectrum of psychopathology. Freud's conceptualization of "defusion" of the two instincts was rather confusing (Brenner, 1971); however, the basic observation remained that in psychopathology there is excessive rage.

In 1953 Hartmann suggested further that one of the major sources of pathology in the schizophrenic lies in the failure to neutralize the aggression. As a result of this failure, the schizophrenic's ego is from time to time flooded with either excessive libido or excessive aggression, or both, with consequent damage to the personality. In this area as well, the decisive role of aggression in the psychic economy of the schizophrenic was given due recognition.

The Schizophrenogenic Mother

Once the significance of the oral regression had been established, the next question was, Where does it come from? To this, two answers were given. One postulated the existence of a "schizophrenogenic mother," a mother who created a double bind for her child in which it could find no peace, so that it fled to the world of psychosis. The term "schizophrenogenic mother" was first used by Frieda Fromm-Reichmann (1948), one of Sullivan's most brilliant pupils. She assumed that psychosis resulted from damaging behavior on the part of the mother in earliest infancy.

Perhaps because of the unsatisfactory results of any kind of therapeutic intervention (results always inferior to those in the milder disturbances), the existence of a schizophrenogenic mother has been questioned by other analysts who hold an organic view of the disturbance, separating it sharply from neurosis. Most prominent among those who disagree with the theory of the schizophrenogenic mother is Margaret Mahler (1968), who sees the primary defect in the child's inability to use maternal care; this inability may be either hereditary or acquired very early in life. Opinion continues to be divided on this score.

Family Studies

Going beyond the mother as such, and stimulated by the observations about cultural factors in personality, many investigators began to investigate the nature of the family of the schizophrenic patient. Perhaps the first of the intensive investigations, and the most thorough, was that conducted by Theodore Lidz and his co-workers at Yale. Some of these studies started as early as 1940, but the book summarizing the major results was not published until 1965 (*Schizophrenia and the Family*). In 1973 Lidz summarized his position as follows:

The synthesis presented in this volume brings the various significant findings of the family studies, as the essential clinical features of schizophrenic disorders, into a coherent theory. It evolved from the recognition that the serious disturbances of the family settings derived from the profound egocentricity of one or both parents; that the disturbances of language and thought that form the critical attribute of schizophrenic disorders are largely types of egocentric cognitive regressions to developmental stages described by Piaget and Vygotsky; and that the parents' disturbed styles of communication, which are manifestations of their egocentricities, are essential precursors of the patient's cognitive regression that occurs when he cannot surmount the essential developmental tasks of adolescence.[14]

Cultural Observations

In line with the theory that cultural conditions are conducive to the development of schizophrenic disorder, in the 1930s investigators began to study various cultural factors. The classic study was by Hollingshead and Redlich (1958), who found that the incidence of schizophrenia was 11 times higher in the lowest class than in the highest. Numerous other studies have led to the specialized field of epidemiology of schizophrenia, and of mental disorders in general. Eaton and Weil (1955) found schizophrenia to be almost nonexistent among the Hutterites. According to Arieti (1976), the other-directed type of culture particularly predisposes to schizophrenia.

The Meaning of Schizophrenic Symptoms

From the earliest days, psychoanalysts had sought to decipher the meaning of the apparently absurd symptoms of schizophrenia. In his first paper (1894), Freud offered a dynamic explanation of one type of psychosis, viewing it as a defense against an unbearable idea. Later, in the Schreber case, he amplified this position by hypothesizing that the hallucinatory and delusional symptoms were attempts at restitution after the libido had been withdrawn from objects. In general, he saw a strong parallel between dreams and psychosis, and therefore the psychotic material could be understood in much the same way as dream material.

Following Freud's lead, analysts working with schizophrenics began to make sense of their productions. In general, the same kinds of symbolic transformations and distortions were found that are seen in dreams and other psychic productions, confirming Freud's hunch.

Perhaps the most important single paper in this body of literature interpreting schizophrenic productions was that by Tausk (1918) on the influencing machine in schizophrenia.[15] According to Tausk, the evolution by distortion of the human apparatus into a machine is a projection that corresponds to the development of the pathological process which converts the ego into a diffuse sexual being, or into a genital, a machine independent of the aims of the ego and subordinated to a foreign will. Later Bettelheim (1967) offered a fine clinical description of an autistic child with such a syndrome.

After the work of the early years, in principle the productions of any schizophrenic could be understood by a perceptive inquirer. What schizophrenics do fits into the known structure of symbolism and language formation.

The Organic Factor

In general, analysts have not taken a strong position on the significance of the organic factor in the etiology of schizophrenia. There seems to be some tendency for Freudian analysts to favor an organic hypothesis, with consequent therapeutic pessimism, while culturalists, following Sullivan, have favored an environmentalist position and have been more optimistic therapeutically. However, the matter is probably more individual than anything else, as in psychiatry at large. In 1968 Bellak and Loeb estimated that purely psychogenic factors will be demonstrated to play the primary role in 50 percent of schizophrenic pathology, genetic factors in 25 percent, and various organic factors in the remaining 25 percent. The matter is still one in which wide differences of opinion exist among psychoanalysts. However, since it is quite clear that schizophrenia is not so different from other regressive disorders, such as addictions and psychosomatic disturbances, a generally psychogenic theory is bound to prevail among psychoanalysts. Biological research has still reached no definitive conclusions (Wynne, Cromwell, and Matthysse, 1978).

Developments in Psychiatry and Allied Disciplines

A number of developments in other fields have played a role in shaping the psychoanalytic theory and therapy of psychosis. Until the 1930s, following Kraepelin, schizophrenia was seen by psychiatry as a chronic malignant form of illness of hereditary origin, which offered little hope for improvement. It was thought that, barring some unforeseen spontaneous remission, patients would have to spend the rest of their life in a hospital.

The first person to express a more optimistic view was Adolf Meyer, a Swiss psychiatrist who had emigrated to the United States and who from the early years of this century urged that schizophrenia is one of many types of reaction to the stresses of life. Although Sullivan was among his students, on the whole he influenced only a small segment of American psychiatry, which remained organically oriented and therapeutically pessimistic.

Beginning with the 1930s, various physical modalities of treatment were introduced. First came the shock therapies—convulsive, insulin, and electric shock. Even though the results were questionable and risks were involved, these methods were widely used (Bellak and Loeb, 1968). They had no appreciable effect on the population of the mental hospitals.

A new era began in the middle of the 1950s (Arieti, 1976), encouraged by many different factors. First of all, there were the new tranquilizers, which seemed to have a specific effect on many of the symptoms of schizophrenia. In the mid-1950s Thorazine was introduced. Later many other drugs appeared on the market (Chiland, 1977).

While the tranquilizers are widely used, buttressed by studies such as those of May (1968), more sober evaluations indicate that psychiatric use of them has no clear-cut rationale. Klein and Gittleman-Klein (1975), in their authoritative review of drug treatment, state: "For the practicing clinician no system is yet available, either from empirical research or accumulated clinical experience, to enable matching of particular phenothiazines with particular schizophrenic patients in terms of their symptom profiles."[16]

Other studies, such as those of Bleuler (1970) and Achte and Niskanen (1972), indicate that on a long-term basis it makes little difference whether the drugs are used or not. Tissot (1977), in a very careful and exhaustive review of all the studies available, concludes:

There are countless studies whose results demonstrate either the positive or the negative action or else the absence of action of neuroleptics in psychoses. . . . Should one come to the conclusion then, as many already have, that in the final analysis empirical methods constitute the most valid judgment criteria? Whatever the case may be, the prescription of neuroleptics in psychoses is practically universal.[17]

Arieti (1976) states that although he considers psychotherapy the treatment of choice for schizophrenia, he routinely uses drug therapy in many cases, in addition to psychotherapy. Thus a purely eclectic orientation does seem to prevail in the field.

Together with the widespread use of the drugs has come the development of community psychiatry, community mental health centers, and the "emptying" of the mental hospitals. The consistent decline in the population of mental hospitals since the middle of the 1950s is an established fact, as is the change in attitude toward hospitalization. Bleuler (1970) attributes the improvement to the entire therapeutic activity and nursing conditions, rather than to drugs.

Genetic and biochemical theories of schizophrenia have been advanced for some time but must still be regarded as unproven. The attractive catecholamine hypothesis of schizophrenia has not yet been borne out by careful studies (Arieti, 1976; Kety, 1969). The bulk of the evidence still seems to favor the psychosocial theory.

Within psychology the most important advance has been the growth of behavior therapy, which received an official endorsement from the American Psychiatric Association in 1975. However, there is as yet no convincing evidence of the effectiveness of behavior therapy in schizophrenia. In any case, therapy must be divorced from etiology. Many analysts, while holding to a psychogenic theory of causation, have maintained that real psychoanalysis is not possible with the schizophrenic patient (Eissler, 1963). This topic is discussed further in chapter 18.

Summary Comments

The development of the psychoanalytic theory of schizophrenia runs parallel to the general development of psychoanalytic theories of psychopathology, differing only in the greater significance attributed by some (not all) psychoanalysts to the organic factor. First a symptom complex was described. Conventional psychiatry had no explanation for this complex; it was thought to be primarily the result of "hereditary degeneracy." Freud then offered some dynamic explanations prior to World War I, in line with his theory of id psychology.

In view of these dynamic explanations, the question then arose: What is the difference between the psychotic and the neurotic? (The normal person was absent for the time being from this comparison.) Freud sought the answer in a quantitative factor, offering a continuum theory, which has also been phrased as the deficiency theory, as contrasted with the deficit theory of organic psychiatry.

The dynamic factors in this continuum theory were then applied to the broader population. Analysts working with psychotics in hospitals discovered that their narcissistic fixations were not nearly as impenetrable as Freud had supposed them to be. Since there was no apparent difference in the id, the focus shifted to the ego, and later to the superego, to clarify the dynamics of this new group of patients, as well as the older group. Thus a new dynamic conceptualization arose, and a broadened range of understanding and therapy for the patient population.

Again the question arose: What is the difference between this kind of patient population and others, e.g., addicts or alcoholics, or homosexuals? No significant differences could be pointed to. Hence the concept arose of a broad group of orally regressed individuals, including schizophrenics, other psychotics, alcoholics, addicts, those with psychosomatic disorders, and homosexuals.

The next question was: How did these patients differ from the general run of the population or other patients? Here three factors were assumed to enter the picture: familial background (particularly the schizophrenogenic mother), cultural factors, and constitutional predisposition. This is the situation as it stands today. Research now is focused on disentangling the respective contributions made by each of these three factors.

Borderline States

Kraepelin, with his rigid categories, had postulated a sharp cleavage between the psychotic and the neurotic. His approach has appropriately been labeled "diagnosis by outcome." Thus schizophrenia (in his terms, dementia praecox) had a hopeless prognosis, while manic-depressive psychosis was a "circular" affair, in which lucid intervals alternated with psychotic episodes (for which he could offer no reason other than heredity). From the very beginning Freud challenged such a theoretical approach, insisting on a continuum from normal to psychotic, and quantitative rather than qualitative differences among patients. In such a continuum there must be "borderline" states, where the patient could not be said to have become psychotic yet, but where he was no longer clearly "neurotic."

While Freud himself had nothing to say about these borderline states, others did. Bleuler, in his fundamental work in 1911, had already expressed the opinion that latent schizophrenia was the most frequent form of the disease. He applied the concept to individuals who hardly ever become hospitalized yet show many abnormalities. He wrote: "In this form we can see *in nuce* all the symptoms and the combinations of symptoms which are present in the manifest types of the disease. Irritable, odd, moody, withdrawn and exaggeratedly punctual people arouse, among other things, the suspicion of being schizophrenic." [18]

In this country, Sullivan, who, more than anyone except Freud, was responsible for broadening the narrow concept of mental illness so characteristic of the United States, continually emphasized the gradual deterioration that occurred in schizophrenia. He wrote:

Search for the phenomena actually constituting the onset of schizophrenia has brought several interesting facts to light. As already indicated in the case of delusions of reference, a great deal of the early phenomenology is an accentuation of what can be elicited from almost any mild case of mental disorder. A clear to vague content indicative of [the feeling that other people show] an unfriendly interest in him is general in psychopathological states. A great proportion of all maladjusted individuals believe that they suffer invidious discussion. The "neurotic" tendency to detract in a relatively unwitting effort to reduce others to a lower level than that adjudged to self, is evidenced not only in more direct behavior and thinking, but indirectly by projection as these persecutory trends. With any excuse, this progresses into notions that one is being slighted, annoyed, or definitely wronged. *Were all those who entertained mild delusions of this sort to be assembled in institutions, the state would collapse immediately from depopulation* (italics added).[19]

For many years a variety of terms were used to designate this type of individual: latent schizophrenic, ambulatory, pseudoneurotic, incipient, prepsychotic, chronic undifferentiated, schizo-affective, and the like.[20] In the 1968 *Diagnostic and Statistical Manual (DSM)* of the American Psychiatric Association the classification of "schizophrenia, latent type" was adopted: "This category is for patients having clear symptoms of schizophrenia but no history of a psychotic schizophrenic episode. Disorders sometimes designated as incipient, pre-psychotic, pseudoneurotic, pseudopsychopathic, or borderline schizophrenia are categorized here."[21]

Gradually the concept of the borderline state became more deeply entrenched. The first significant paper in which the term borderline was used for patients of this type appears to be one by Adolph Stern (1938).[22]

It is well known that a large group of patients fit frankly neither into the psychotic group nor into the psychoneurotic group, and that the borderline group of patients is extremely difficult to handle by any psychotherapeutic method. What forced itself on my attention some three or four years ago was the increasing number of these patients who came for treatment.[23]

As the outstanding traits of these patients Stern listed the following: narcissism; psychic bleeding (a constant feeling of being wronged); inordinate hypersensitivity; psychic and body rigidity— "the rigid personality"; negative therapeutic reactions; what look like constitutionally rooted feelings of inferiority, deeply imbedded in the personality of the patient; masochism; what can be described as a state of deep organic insecurity or anxiety; the use of projection mechanisms; difficulties in reality testing, particularly in personal relationships.

In a paper on "borderline states," Knight (1953a) did not recommend the term for diagnosis but stressed the need for a comprehensive psychodynamic and psychoeconomic appraisal of the patient. By 1954 the topic was considered sufficiently important to warrant a panel discussion by the American Psychoanalytic Association (Rangell, 1955). At that panel the continuing uncertainty about the condition was emphasized by a number of speakers. Gregory Zilboorg stated that "we seem to seek we know not yet quite clearly what."[24] At a panel the following year (Robbins, 1956), Rangell pointed out that the increased interest in borderline states came from two opposite directions. These were, first, the gradually increased understanding downwards of the transference neuroses themselves, beyond and below the phase of the Oedipal conflicts, to the deeper pregenital structures, and, second, an upward direction from work with the narcissistic neuroses, which in the meantime had also been found to be accessible.

In 1968 Grinker and his co-workers published a significant long-term study of the borderline syndrome. As the overall characteristics of this syndrome they listed anger as the main or only affect, a defect in affectional relationships, the absence of indications of self-identity, and depressive loneliness. Four subgroups were differentiated.

Following the Grinker book the diagnostic category of "borderline syndrome" became much more popular (Wolberg, 1973). Particularly influential in the popularization of this category has been the work of Otto Kernberg, from 1966 onward. He summarized his views in *Borderline Conditions and Pathological Narcissism* (1975), after publication of the 18-year research study of the Menninger Clinic (Kernberg et al., 1972).

Kernberg emphasizes the following in borderline patients: non-specific manifestations of ego weakness; a shift toward primary-process thinking; specific defensive operations, particularly splitting and the lack of synthesis of contradictory self- and object-images; primitive idealization; early forms of projection, especially projective identification; denial; omnipotence and devaluation; pathological internalized object relations, particularly the persistence of primitive unrealistic self-images. Rather overschematically, Kernberg offers this synthesis:

In an attempt to differentiate psychotic, borderline, and neurotic patients, one might briefly say that psychotic patients have a severe lack of ego development, with mostly undifferentiated self and object images and concomitant lack of ego boundaries; borderline patients have a better integrated ego than psychotics, with differentiation between the self and object images to a major extent and with the development of firm ego boundaries in all but the areas of close interpersonal involvement; they present, typically, the syndrome of identity diffusion; and neurotic patients present a strong ego, with complete separation between self and object images and concomitant delimitation of ego boundaries; they do not present the syndrome of identity diffusion.[25]

Unfortunately there has been, as so often in the history of psychoanalysis, a strong tendency to extend the diagnosis of borderline to virtually all known conditions other than clear-cut psychosis. Thus Masterson (1976) stresses the borderline person's inability to work and to love,[26] which is Freud's classical definition of neurosis.

"Normality": The Cultural Fiction and the Psychoanalytic Reality

The classification of mental and emotional disturbance depends on assumptions, stated or implied, about the nature of normality. In the conceptualization of the "average" or "normal" person, vast changes have occurred during the history of psychoanalysis. These changes have by no means been capricious or arbitrary. Rather, they cut through to the heart of psychoanalytic theory and technique.

Freud always emphasized the close relationship between theory and technique. As a result there has been a continuing reciprocal and spiraling interaction between the concepts of normality and neurosis. Initially, in the 1880s, Freud as a neurologist ("neuropathologist") was confronted with certain symptoms that brought patients to physicians. These symptoms were the traditional ones of severe hysteria, some forms of "neurasthenia," and various manifestations of psychosis; patients with these symptoms were totally incapacitated for life. Therapy involved magical devices such as electrotherapy or suggestion. In general, psychotherapists felt hopeless about helping anybody. Psychotherapists, either medical or lay, were few and were held in low esteem by the general community. The only theories of etiology available were those of hereditary degeneracy, or, a small variant, the harmful effects of masturbation.

In this depressing jungle Freud introduced the first signs of hope. He offered a dynamic explanation of certain forms of neurotic illness, a new kind of psychology, and, for the first time in history, a therapeutic method that made sense and helped many of the patients who came to him. Such was the situation in the first decade of this century.

Once dynamic factors were recognized, there emerged a question that still persists as a key to the whole problem of human affairs: What is the relationship between normality and neurosis? Or, to put it differently, how does the patient in psychoanalysis or psychotherapy differ from the person who is not a patient?

When the focus was on description and symptoms, as in Kraepelinian thinking, the answer was easy: the person with symptoms is "sick," the person without symptoms is healthy. This naive analogy with the medical situation was recognized as an illusion by Freud from a very early stage.

The dynamic considerations forced a continual revision of the psychoanalytic approach to the "normal." For if the neurotic suffers from sexual repression, Oedipal conflicts, frustration, and unresolved aggression, how does he differ from the normal person? It required little discernment to realize that many apparently normal individuals suffered from exactly the same dynamic problems. Why then did some become patients, and others not?

Freud's first concern with this issue, although expressed in different terms, appears in two papers, published in 1907 and 1908. In 1907 a brief paper on "Obsessive Actions and Religious Practices" stressed the parallel between religion and obsessional neurosis: the resemblances lie in the qualms of conscience brought on by the neglect of certain actions, in their complete isolation from other actions, and in the conscientiousness with which they are carried out in every detail.[27] The difference seems to be that religious rituals have a meaning, and those of obsessional neurotics apparently have none. Upon closer analysis, this difference disappears, since psychoanalysis always reveals the unconscious meaning of the obsessional ritual. Thus Freud reaches the famous conclusion that religion is a universal obsessional neurosis:

In view of these similarities and analogies one might venture to regard obsessional neurosis as a pathological counterpart of the formation of a religion, and to describe that neurosis as an individual religiosity and religion as a universal obsessional neurosis. The most essential similarity would reside in the underlying renunciation of the activation of instincts that are constitutionally present; and the chief difference would lie in the nature of those instincts, which in the neurosis are exclusively sexual in their origin, while in religion they spring from egoistic sources.[28]

If religion is a universal obsessional neurosis, why don't religious people come to treatment? To this question there are two answers. First, religion is experienced by most people as egosyntonic, i.e., as creating no conscious anxiety, so that a main motive for coming to therapy is absent. Second, and even more important, after the dissemination of psychoanalytic thought, religious people did begin to come to treatment, and in increasing numbers. Freud, as he himself was ready to admit, was not the first person to point up the inconsistencies, absurdities, hypocrisy, contradictions, and horrors of all organized religions; what he added was the notion that the religious person is merely perpetuating his infantile state by projecting the parents to some less immediate minister or god-figure.

Perhaps the most important religious figure in the early history of psychoanalysis who came to Freud was the Swiss minister Oskar Pfister (1873–1953). Pfister was one of the few who combined both analysis and ministerial duties, though his religious beliefs were badly shaken by his encounter with psychoanalysis. Pfister's life work was summed up in his book *Christianity and Fear* (1944). Like so many kindly men before him, Pfister was dismayed by the horrors inflicted in the name of the religion of love throughout the ages: "Murder, arson and cruelty were practised more savagely than by wild beasts—all this in the name of Him who died for love on the Cross in order to confirm by His death His message of love."[29]

Most of Pfister's book is devoted to a careful historical study of Christianity, to understand why it has so often appeared in such perverted form. The only road to a true Christianity, he finally concluded, lay through the psychoanalysis of Christians. Otherwise, religion degenerates into dogma, and the religion of love becomes a religion of fear. "The neurosis of individuals leads to a neurotic malformation of their Christian faith, and in certain circumstances must do so inevitably; and when this process is applied to the masses it necessarily affects entire Churches, the Protestant as well as the Catholic."[30]

Pfister continued to urge Freud to combine psychoanalysis with what he considered true Christianity, the religion of love. Freud was adamant, however, in his conviction that psychoanalysis would do best without religion. In 1928 he wrote to Pfister:

I do not know if you have detected the secret link between the *Lay Analysis* and the *Illusion.* In the former I wish to protect analysis from the doctors and in the latter from the priests. I should like to hand it over to a profession which does not yet exist, a profession of *lay* curers of souls who need not be doctors and should not be priests.[31]

Eventually large numbers of persons who had sought solace in religion, and failed to find it, turned to psychoanalysis. In the United States, Anton Boisen, a Protestant minister who had recovered from a schizophrenic breakdown and had undergone some analysis with Harry Stack Sullivan, began the movement of pastoral counseling. Boisen described his breakdown and recovery in *The Exploration of the Inner World* (1936).

Religion is but one of many instances where the widening range of psychodynamic interpretation brought large numbers of persons within the purview of psychoanalytic thought and treatment. Another area that aroused considerable interest was sexuality. In the 1890s Freud had formulated a theory of actual neurosis, according to which sexual abstinence or frustration per se induced anxiety via a process of biochemical changes, not further specified. This toxicological theory of anxiety, as it has been called, was maintained until 1926, though its force was considerably weakened by developments even before then. Furthermore, in the early 1900s he saw psychoneurosis as the consequence of the frustrations of infantile sexuality. Thus normal sexuality became a desideratum of the good life. In the paper on " 'Civilized' Sexual Morality and Modern Nervous Illness" (1908) he could still write: "The sexual behavior of a human being often *lays down the pattern* for all his other modes of reacting to life." [32]

At another point in this paper he insisted that a considerable percentage, perhaps a large majority, of the population of that day had been rendered neurotic by the excessive demands of conventional sexual morality:

It may be asserted, however, that the task of mastering such a powerful impulse as that of the sexual instinct by any other means than satisfying it is one which can call for the whole of a man's forces. Mastering it by sublimation, by deflecting the sexual instinctual forces away from their sexual aims to higher cultural aims, can be achieved by a minority and then only intermittently, and least easily during the period of ardent and vigorous youth. Most of the rest become neurotic or are harmed in one way or another. Experience shows that the majority of the people who make up our society are constitutionally unfit to face the task of abstinence. [33]

With such a point of view, it was inevitable that large numbers of persons who were sexually frustrated, but had none of the classical neurotic symptoms, would come to psychoanalysts. Thus again the range of the patient population was broadened by the growth of psychoanalytic theory.

The catastrophe of World War I directed more careful attention to the doctrines of psychoanalysis. It was recognized that no psychological doctrine which failed to take into consideration the power of the instinctual drives could possibly account for the tumultuous wars and revolutions that seemed to be springing up everywhere.

Many observers in the 1920s noted a change in the patient population. Clearly the balance was shifting away from the most severely disturbed segment of the population. Psychoanalysis had created an additional new clientele by the force of its doctrines—persons who realized that they were hampered by inner inhibitions yet were considered culturally normal.

However, these patients did not fit the established categories. The classical neuroses, hysteria and compulsion neurosis, almost seemed to have disappeared. Diagnostic categories such as "prepsychotic" and "borderline" began to come into use. In reality, these diagnoses did nothing to clarify the situation; what had happened was that the growth of psychoanalytic thought was catching up with the social situation.

The theoretical advances of the 1920s and 1930s helped to explain the dynamics of the new patients being seen. Character analysis gradually became the order of the day, replacing the older symptom analysis. Hence the concepts of egosyntonicity, egodystonicity, superego, oral regression, and the like acquired increasing importance.

Again the question was raised, this time in terms of ego psychology, What is the difference between the patient in analysis (the "neurotic") and the person outside? A second group of catastrophes, this time in the 1930s, intervened to make this question even more pressing: fascism, communism, the Great Depression, genocide, and World War II.

The Impact of World War II

Historical events that are within recent memory are notoriously difficult to assess objectively. Nevertheless it can already be stated that among the other enormous changes wrought by the war a psychiatric revolution was one of the most important. In essence, a total change occurred in the training of psychiatrists, in the introduction of other mental health professionals, particularly psychologists and social workers but also those called paraprofessionals, in the attitude toward psychoanalysis, and in the total social climate. This change was spurred by a number of factors. By the time of the Watergate scandal in 1973, even ordinary newspapers routinely discussed the question of whether Nixon was suffering from some psychiatric disturbance that had led him to do what he did.

The Shift in the Patient Population after World War II

As a result of the wholesale upheaval of established values, a large change in the patient population of psychoanalysts and other mental health professionals took place following World War II. Broadly speaking, if World War I shifted the patient population from the psychotic to the neurotic, World War II shifted the patient population from the neurotic to the normal.

The shift to the normal population had already begun between the two wars. Its most notable instance was the increasing recognition, which became standard by about 1930, that a training analysis was necessary for any individual who wanted to practice analysis. The absolute need for such a training analysis was affirmed in the early institutes (Lewin and Ross, 1960) and has been reaffirmed most emphatically by subsequent research (Goodman, 1977).

At first the training analysis was seen as a didactic experience (H. Sachs, 1930), but it soon became apparent that psychiatrists and other candidates needed analysis as much as anybody else (Balint, 1954), perhaps more so. The euphemism of "didactic analysis" was dropped and was replaced by "personal analysis" or simply "analysis."

Yet the psychiatrist is a doctor of medicine, presumably well integrated, functioning at a high level in our culture. Why then should he need analysis? The answer could lie only in the nature of the culture: everybody in our culture seems to require some psychological help to reach the analytic ideal (Fine, 1972).

Epidemiological studies, beginning in the 1950s, confirmed the existence of emotional disturbance on an unbelievable scale (Dohrenwend and Dohrenwend, 1969; Leighton, 1963; Rennie et al., 1962). As a result it became customary for even ordinary individuals with no pressing problems to consult professionals and to seek assistance in handling life's difficulties. The focus shifted from the resolution of neurotic problems to the pursuit of happiness.[34]

However, once the emphasis is shifted from the technical definition of neurosis to the pursuit of happiness, an entirely new situation emerges. First of all, it is recognized that in a culture like ours (and probably in all known cultures up to now) everybody has something or other the matter with him, so exact diagnosis is of secondary importance. Instead, human concerns, such as sexuality, religiosity, marital happiness, and love, move into the foreground. Second, when the problem is defined in these terms—of lack of love, sexual frustration, and the like—an increasing number of people recognize that they could use some professional help. Third, the problem then becomes one of the shortage of trained professionals, not the "incidence of illness." And finally, in this spiraling process psychoanalysis comes to be seen as a form of social reform, in which the stress is on inner change rather than outer (Fine, 1971).

The Nosological Jungle

The diagnostic system in common use stems principally from clinical psychiatrists, steeped in the Kraepelinian tradition, who have from time to time grafted psychoanalytic ideas onto the traditional scheme. This has caused discontent and confusion among psychoanalysts, and, because of the lack of adequate dynamic criteria, it has also led to a constant alteration of diagnostic categories, resulting in a revision of the standard *DSM* about every 10 years since its inception in 1917 (Brill, 1965). The last revision was in 1968, replacing the 1952 classification. Another revision is in preparation (Wynne et al., 1978).

Psychoanalysts have repeatedly objected to the diagnostic system in current usage, sometimes in very strong terms. In 1959 Menninger wrote: "Diagnosis in the sense in which we doctors have used it for many years is not only relatively useless in many cases; it is an inaccurate, misleading, philosophically false predication." [35]

Several panel discussions on diagnosis have come to the same conclusion: the current psychiatric system is quite inadequate, but a better one has yet to be found to take its place (Grinker, 1968). Concerning the panel in 1959, Ross wrote (1960):

With one exception, the participants expressed dissatisfaction with our current nosological pattern, while at the same time they evinced no disposition to discard it entirely. (The latter alternative is not without its protagonists.) For a long time it has been apparent that a classificatory scheme, based phenomenologically on symptom clusters, and dynamically on levels of psychosexual development, is not adequate. There was no inclination to underestimate the complexity of the task of revising and modifying traditional nosological concepts in accordance with the now-recognized intricate interplay between instinctual and ego-developmental levels, but the necessity of doing so was repeatedly emphasized. [36]

Even more devastating to the standard system of nosology was the experience of the Central Fact-Gathering Committee, which had been charged to report the results of psychoanalytic treatment (see chapter 5). When it finally issued its report in 1967, it stated: "Since specifying the diagnostic category had proven, over the years, to be most frustrating to the participating analysts, and probably quite unreliable as well (and the reliability not subject to check), we decided to eliminate the diagnostic categories from further use." [37]

In the light of this universal experience with diagnosis and diagnostic categories, no further attempt is made here to review the history of the innumerable suggestions for strengthening or revising the current diagnostic system. Instead, some historical material is presented on the most important clinical entities described in the literature. Since hysteria, obsessional neurosis, schizophrenia, and borderline states have already been discussed, they are omitted here.

Depression

Depression is such a common manifestation of all psychopathology that it had often come to Freud's attention. Initially he saw it simply as due to sexual frustration (Freud, 1893; Abraham, 1911), accompanied by lack of self-confidence. Abraham (1911, 1916) then stressed the factors of orality and hostility; in depression the person turns his hostility against himself.

A major step forward was taken with Freud's 1917 paper, "Mourning and Melancholia." Here for the first time Freud postulated the internalization of a bad object, against which the reproaches of the melancholic are really directed. This idea was the forerunner of the concept of the superego, which thereafter became central in all discussions of psychopathology (*The Ego and the Id,* 1923). In depression the superego punishes the ego either for forbidden wishes or for not living up to the ego-ideal set by the parents (Deutsch, 1965; Jacobson, 1971; Rado, 1928).

Melanie Klein then postulated a feeling of depression due to loss of the parents' love in the second three months of life (1948b). For some time, depression had been linked up with object loss, as it has since invariably been.

E. Bibring (1953) emphasized the loss of self-esteem in the depressive, which may result from fixation at any level of development. Cohen and her co-workers (1954) provided illuminating clinical material about the childhood background of this loss of self-esteem.

The question of childhood depression was suggested by John Bowlby (1961), and has since been known as the Bowlby controversy. Briefly, Bowlby argued that there is a mourning process in childhood, occasioned by the loss of the mother, which is exactly parallel to that of mourning in the adult. The child reacts with protest, despair, and finally detachment, if the loved object is not restored. The detached state is by far the most pathological and the hardest to reverse. Anna Freud and others have argued that the childhood reaction is not as severe as the adult one (1960).

Engel and his associates have done interesting work on psychosomatic disorders. Engel has stressed what he calls the giving up–given up syndrome, or helplessness–withdrawal, which results from loss of love in early childhood (Engel 1967; Engel and Reichsman, 1956). In one striking case of a 15-month-old infant, he was able to observe a direct correlation between the physiological reactions and the presence or absence of the love object (Engel and Reichsman, 1956).

In summary, depression involves sexual frustration, oral regression, excess of hostility (largely turned inward), superego reproaches, inadequate ego-ideal, a lowering of self-esteem, object loss, and detachment from object loss in varying degrees, and a reaction of helplessness–withdrawal. That some depressives become psychotic, and others suicidal, is a result of quantitative and internal-economic factors (Jacobson, 1971; Kubie, 1964; Shneidman, 1967).

Mania and Hypomania

In Kraepelinian psychiatry the manic-depressive cycle was punctuated by "normality" in the free periods. From a psychoanalytic point of view this seems impossible. The first to point up this impossibility was Abraham (1908), who showed that the so-called symptom-free cycle was really a form of compulsion neurosis. The next important step forward came with the conceptualization of the superego. In 1923 Freud was able to show that in mania there is a fusion of the ego with the superego, so that the individual feels approval for everything that he does.

The classic study of elation is Bertram Lewin's *The Psychoanalysis of Elation* (1950). Lewin postulates an oral triad of "to eat, to be eaten, and to sleep," and shows how the symptomatology of mania can be understood in terms of this oral triad, in addition to the superego functioning pointed out by Freud (see chapter 6).

Alcoholism and Addiction

Although addiction had always been a problem, it first received the attention of psychoanalysts when Ernst Simmel opened a clinic near Berlin for the treatment of drug addicts after World War I. Shortly thereafter, Rado (1926) provided the basic theoretical explanation for addictions, which has not been materially altered since then. They are oral regressive states, in which an alimentary orgasm replaces every other form of gratification. Because of this oral kind of orgasm, the regulation of the personality structure by means of drugs ensues. Both alcoholics and drug addicts have been notoriously resistant to psychotherapy (Chafetz et al., 1974; Nyswander, 1974).

Psychopathy

Although Freud had made some comments about criminality, the first significant discussions in the literature came from Wilhelm Reich (1925), with his conception of the impulse-ridden character, and from August Aichhorn (1925), who did pioneeering work with juvenile delinquents.

Analysis does not bear out the oft-stated assumption that psychopaths have no superego. Their superego functioning is warped in various ways but always present. In the post-World War II literature, the problems of these patients have come to be known as acting-out disorders. Their dynamics can be understood in terms of the relationship of acting out to the total ego structure.

Homosexuality

The first of Freud's three essays in 1905 was devoted to homosexuality, indicating that the topic was an important one for him. There he contributed the fundamental distinction of differentiating aim from object and showed that the homosexual has a deviation with regard to the object but may not have one with regard to the aim. In his essay on Leonardo, Freud also described a possible object choice along narcissistic lines for homosexual men, in that the man chooses another man who is like himself.

Originally the dynamics of homosexuality were seen in terms of the Oedipal struggle. Later, when oral factors were recognized, it became clear that there was a strong oral fixation as well; Jones (1927), reporting on the analyses of five homosexual women, stressed the unusually strong oral eroticism and the intense sadism. Since that time analysts have uniformly placed the greatest emphasis on the oral factor in homosexuality, viewing the homosexual pair as generally a mother–child pair in fantasy.

One of the few large-scale studies in the literature with adequate statistics is the work by Bieber and his associates on male homosexuals (1962). These investigators correlated results of analysis with 106 male homosexuals and 100 male heterosexuals. Of the 72 who began as exclusively homosexual, 14 (or 19 percent) became heterosexual. Of the 30 men who began as bisexual, 15 (50 percent) became heterosexual. These investigators also confirmed the dynamics of the phallic (close-binding, intimate) mother and the distant father as essential to the development of male homosexuality.

Socarides (1978) has provided the most complete description of the dynamics of homosexuality in the literature. He confirmed the over-intense affective relationship to the mother, often with conscious incestuous desires, and an inaccessible father. The sexual wish for the mother leads to anxiety, guilt, and simultaneous, conflicting urges to cling to and to avoid intimate contact with her and later all other women. Other factors stressed are the breast–penis equation, psychic masochism, the erotization of anxiety, isolation and loneliness, and narcissistic identification with the partner.

Other sexual disorders such as fetishism, voyeurism, and pedophilia (Bak, 1965) have all been interpreted in terms of early oral disturbances.

Summary Comments on Nosological Entities

The developments of ego psychology have pushed into the background the specific psychodynamic constellations relating to various clinical entities. It has repeatedly been found that the classical syndromes may be present in some cases but absent in others and that the same bit of behavior may be reached via a number of different routes. In general, the more serious forms of pathology, such as homosexuality, addiction, and psychopathy have been traced to various kinds of oral deprivations. Just why one orally regressed individual turns to homosexuality, another to psychopathy, a third to fetishism, and a fourth to schizophrenia remains one of the great unanswered questions. In specific cases, differing family constellations account for the symptoms in question, but it has not yet been possible to make valid generalizations about the choice of neurosis.

The problem of diagnosis thus needs to be discussed in the light of the larger meaning of psychoanalysis, in chapter 19. It may be noted here, however, that currently the American Psychiatric Association has expressed the opinion that psychodynamics remains the core of psychiatric education,[38] which is in essential agreement with the psychoanalytic attitude.

Chapter Fifteen

Interpersonal Relations (Object Relations),
Drives and Objects,
and the Shift to Interpersonal Theory

It has become commonplace to say that psychoanalysis is a drive theory and that Freud was an instinct theorist. Like so many clichés, this is both true and misleading at the same time. Again historical reconstruction sheds some much-needed light.

When Freud published his astounding sexual theories in *Three Essays on Sexuality* in 1905, he made a number of novel proposals. Most novel was the division of the sexual instinct into an object and an aim, the development of each of which could be traced.

In his original work Freud defined the sexual object as a person: "I shall at this point introduce two technical terms. Let us call the person from whom sexual attraction proceeds the *sexual object* and the act towards which the instinct tends the *sexual aim*." [1] Eventually the term "sexual object" was shortened to "object," and since the word has no immediate interpersonal connotations, many mistakenly assumed that objects could be inanimate as well as animate. Freud further observed, quoting an American psychologist (Bell, 1902), that "the existence of love in childhood stands in no need of discovery." [2]

At that time Freud believed that in the earliest stages the infantile sexual instinct does not need an object. Very quickly, however, component instincts appear which "from the very first involve other people as objects." [3] It is only in puberty that a clear sexual object is found. [4]

As has been seen, in the period of id psychology (1900–1914), Freud's attention was focused primarily on the manifestations of sexuality; object-choice remained in the background. In theory, however, object relations or interpersonal relations were always there.

Freud's first systematic approach to the question of interpersonal relations was the paper on "Narcissism" in 1914. Looked at today, this essay is both confusing and confused. Jones described it as "bewildering."[5] Freud himself, writing to Abraham, said: "The narcissism was a difficult labor and bears all the marks of a corresponding deformation."[6]

The essential new points in Freud's 1914 paper are the following.

1. It describes libido as a quantitatively variable force, whose transformations explain the manifestations of psychosexuality. This is the libido theory proper, which Freud took from the 1914 paper and included under that heading in all later editions of the *Three Essays*.

2. It contains the first systematic description of object choice.

3. It establishes the various meanings of "narcissism," a most useful clinical concept.

4. It offers a new classification of human beings on a therapeutic basis: the division into narcissistic neuroses, in which the patient is unable to make a relationship to the therapist, and transference neuroses, in which he is able to form a relationship. The notion that human beings could be classified in accordance with their *therapeutic* reactions was an idea with extensive implications.

5. It introduces for the first time the concept of an ego-ideal, which was later rechristened the superego, one of the best fruits of Freud's genius.

Post-Freudian Developments

Immediately after World War I, Freud elaborated his tripartite structure of the personality, which from then on occupied the center of the stage. Since narcissism could not be fitted into this structure in its pure form, it remained relatively neglected for many years. When Bing, McLaughlin, and Marburg reviewed its metapsychology in 1959, they could find only three papers after Freud to refer to, none of which were directly concerned with the topic. Since the late 1960's it has experienced a revival through the work of Heinz Kohut (1971, 1977).

Even though the word narcissism played a relatively minor role in psychoanalytic theory until recently, the ideas contained in Freud's paper underwent considerable elaboration in different language. The term derives from the Greek myth about Narcissus, who fell in love with his reflection in a pool, pined away, and died. The Greek myth brings out the elements of self-love, self-involvement, and self-destructiveness.

The concept was first applied to the narcissistic disorders, known with increasing frequency as the psychoses. Then analysts studying the creative individual recognized that he too was basically a narcissistic person.

In the 1930s Sullivan engaged in an extensive analysis of the self-image, especially as it appeared in the psychic structure of schizophrenics and borderline cases. Following his work, Erikson introduced the term "identity" in the 1940s, a concept that has broadened out enormously.

While the psychology of the self had long remained outside the purview of classical Freudian theory, it was brought back with the publication of Edith Jacobson's *The Self and the Object World* (1964). She also attempted to unify Erikson's work on identity with the more classic metapsychological propositions of Hartmann, Kris, and Loewenstein (1946).

Beginning in the 1950s and culminating with *The Psychological Birth of the Human Infant* (Mahler et al., 1975), Margaret Mahler offered a large-scale integration of all her previous work with her conceptualization of the separation-individuation process. In the past 10 years the theme of separation-individuation, with its allied notions such as self–object differentiation, has become a central topic in psychoanalytic theory.

Thus Freud's paper on narcissism has had many repercussions, though often not in the directions that he intended. Perhaps this is what he had in mind when he wrote in his autobiography: "I have made many beginnings and thrown out many suggestions. Something will come of them in the future, though I cannot myself tell whether it will be much or little." [7]

The Libido Theory

Inasmuch as the libido theory in its pure form (libido as a quantitatively variable force manifesting itself at different life stages) has become the most controversial of Freud's theories, its injection into the 1914 paper calls for some explanation. The metapsychological notions of ego libido, object libido, and primary narcissism, which were introduced there, have caused untold difficulties.

At the time he wrote the paper, Freud was furious with Jung and Adler; he was also composing his polemical *History of the Psychoanalytic Movement*. When Freud was angry or upset, he tended to feel nervous about his psychological observations, which were his real contribution, and to fall back on the neurology and physiology of his youth, which he had first given expression to in the 1895 "Project" and then discarded. In 1914, libido is made to behave exactly like the Q of the "Project," explaining the variety of clinical manifestations by its quantitative transformations. Furthermore, libido carries the same ambiguity as Q—is it physical or is it psychological, or is it a bit of both?

Two panels of the American Psychoanalytic Association, in 1954 and in 1955, reexamined the concepts inherent in the libido theory (Reider, 1954; Rangell, 1955). Both proponents and opponents of the theory were given the floor. It is of considerable historical interest that these panels mark the last time that culturalists and Freudians engaged in public dialogues. Shortly thereafter (perhaps as a result of the panels) the American Academy of Psychoanalysis was formed, and each group went its own way.

None of the panelists seemed to be aware of the historical fact that the libido theory was introduced post hoc by Freud in 1914 and was not essential to his psychosexual theories, which he had stated without reference to the libido theory in 1905. Sharp clashes marked both panels.

The most spirited attack on the libido theory came from Herbert Birch in the 1955 panel, who described the libido theory as "an anachronistic relic of the nineteenth century and . . . 'an incorrect biological conceptualization.' "[8] The most vigorous defense of the theory came from Rapaport, who erroneously insisted that Freud's concept of libido was essentially a qualitative one.[9]

The panel was characterized by its polemical nature. Much discussion was on the failure of the genetic component of the libido theory to account for the executive functions of the ego, societal structure and certain metapsychological considerations. . . . On the affirmative side, it could be stated that substantial parts of the presentations dealt with vicissitudes of libidinal drives and their relation to ego functions, the molding effects of culture on drives via the ego, and the relation of the conception of quantity to nosology and dynamics.[10]

Subsequently the lines hardened and the two sides moved off into different organizations. Once the political factor had entered the picture, after 1956, the question of "biological" versus "cultural" became the battle-cry with which the armies engaged one another.

Since the initial battle, a whole generation has passed. In the literature today, the entire question has receded into the background. Little, if any, reference is ever made to the pure libido theory as described by Freud in 1914; the center of interest has shifted elsewhere. What remains is that drives are important in human experience, but exactly how they are to be integrated into the remainder of psychoanalytic theory is still very much in dispute. In this respect, too, there seems to be movement toward a unified science, and a blurring of divisions that once were quite sharp.

The Shift to Interpersonal Theory

If we look at the broad scope of psychoanalytic theory since 1955, we see a decided shift to questions related to interpersonal theory and a considerable decline in questions related to the instincts (see also chapter 8). This is scarcely surprising, since interpersonal relations were just as much a part of Freud's scheme of psychosexual development as were the instinctual drives; he simply postponed consideration of them. Actually, most of Freud's work was completed before the culturalist–Freudian controversy erupted. Without denying instincts, Freud nevertheless ascribed great importance to culture. In a footnote to the *Three Essays,* for example, added in 1910, he wrote:

The most striking distinction between the erotic life of antiquity and our own no doubt lies in the fact that the ancients laid the stress upon the instinct itself, whereas we emphasize the object. The ancients glorified the instinct and were prepared on its account to honor even an inferior object; while we despise the instinctual activity in itself, and find excuses for it only in the merits of the object.[11]

The British Object-Relations School

In the 1930s and 1940s a number of British analysts, most prominent of whom were W. Ronald D. Fairbairn and Harry Guntrip, objected to the excessive emphasis on instincts in what was then classical Freudian theory, and stressed object relations instead. Following a paper by Bibring (1947), the object-relations school also came to be known as the British school or British object-relations school. In 1963 Fairbairn summarized his object-relations theory as follows:[12]

1. An ego is present from birth.
2. Libido is a function of the ego.
3. There is no death instinct, and aggression is a reaction to frustration or deprivation.
4. Since libido is a function of the ego and aggression is a reaction to frustration or deprivation, there is no such thing as an "id."
5. The ego, and therefore libido, is fundamentally object-seeking.
6. The earliest and original form of anxiety, as experienced by the child, is separation anxiety.
7. Internalization of the object is a defensive measure originally adopted by the child to deal with his original object (the mother and her breast) insofar as the object is unsatisfying.
8. Internalization of the object is not just a product of a fantasy of incorporating the object orally, but is a distinct psychological process.
9. Two aspects of the internalized object—its exciting and its frustrating aspects—are split off from the main core of the object and repressed by the ego.
10. Thus there come to be constituted two repressed internal objects, the exciting (or libidinal) object and the rejecting (or antilibidinal) object.
11. The main core of the internalized object, which is not repressed, is described as the ideal object or ego-ideal.
12. Owing to the fact that the exciting (libidinal) and rejecting (antilibidinal) objects are both cathected by the original ego, these

Shift to Interpersonal Theory

objects carry into repression with them parts of the ego by which they are cathected, leaving the central core of the ego (central ego) unrepressed but acting as the agent of repression.

13. The resulting internal situation is one in which the original ego is split into three egos: a central (conscious) ego attached to the ideal object (ego-ideal), a repressed libidinal ego attached to the exciting (or libidinal) object, and a repressed antilibidinal ego attached to the rejecting (antilibidinal) object.

14. This internal situation represents a basic schizoid position that is more fundamental than the depressive position described by Melanie Klein.

15. The antilibidinal ego, in virtue of its attachment to the rejecting (antilibidinal) object, adopts an uncompromisingly hostile attitude to the libidinal ego and thus has the effect of powerfully reinforcing the repression of the libidinal ego by the central ego.

16. What Freud described as the "superego" is really a complex structure comprising the ideal object or ego-ideal, the antilibidinal ego, and the rejecting (or antilibidinal) object.

17. These considerations form the basis of a theory of the personality conceived in terms of object-relations, in contrast to one conceived in terms of instincts and their vicissitudes.

Sullivan's Interpersonal Approach

In the United States the most significant figure in the emphasis on interpersonal theory has been Harry Stack Sullivan. There can be little doubt that he has had far more extensive influence here than has any representative of the British school.

A major difficulty in presenting the historical picture is that Sullivan was a woefully inarticulate individual. In his biography of Sullivan, Chapman (1976) states that he dropped out of college in his first or second year and that even the medical school he attended was little more than a diploma mill (this was before the Flexner report, which established the present high standards for medical education). Sullivan never formulated his theories in as clear and cogent a fashion as Fairbairn did. Only one of his books, *Conceptions of Modern Psychiatry* (1940), was published during his lifetime. For the rest, his lectures were taken down with a transcribing machine, and he left quantities of unedited material at his death. These were edited and published posthumously by his secretary, Helen Swick Perry.

When Sullivan's ideas are examined, they hardly seem startling or deserving of the uproar they have caused in some circles. Much of his theory is a reformulation of Freud. Thus he spoke of satisfaction and security rather than ego and id, of dynamisms and defense mechanisms, of awareness rather than consciousness; and he described the developmental process somewhat differently.

In the introduction to Sullivan's book *The Fusion of Psychiatry and Social Science* (1964), Charles Johnson paid tribute to Sullivan's ability to carry over the rich insights of psychiatry into the actual relations between people, which has made possible a new and expanding attraction for both psychiatry and the social sciences.

Sullivan himself emphasized the directed movement in interpersonal relations toward constructive, loving relationships, or destructive, hating ones. In 1936–1937 he wrote:

It would seem that interpersonal processes free from parataxic elements are either positive-constructive movements toward intimacy, with the securing of satisfactions and the maintenance of ("personal") security, or negative-destructive movements of hostile avoiding, ostracizing, or dominating of persons more or less clearly identified as the sources of insecurity, and thus barriers to the securing of satisfactions. An indeterminate but certainly very great part of the manifest negative-destructive motivation in the world today must be identical in character with the instances that come to the attention of the psychiatrist. The latter include without exception important parataxic elements. In other words there is every apparent justification for questioning the inevitable, necessary character of some great part of the hostile-destructive interpersonal processes that are so conspicuous a feature of current life; and therefore [there is] a notable implication as to the possibility of a social order in which they would at most have a minor role.[13]

Mahler: The Separation-Individuation Process

By far the most convincing integration of much of the postwar work on interpersonal relationships has come from Margaret Mahler's research into the first three years of life. She refers to the earliest stage as the autistic, followed by the symbiotic. Thereafter she delineates four stages in the individuation process: hatching, practicing, rapprochement, and object constancy.

Her concepts of the normal autistic, normal symbiotic, and

separation-individuation phases of personality development are developmental reconstructions, which refer primarily to the development of object relationships. They are complementary to the concepts of the oral, anal, and phallic phases, constructions referring to the theory of drive development. She further summarizes her views as follows.

There is a multiform and complex circular interaction between the shifting and progressive drive development, the maturing ego, and the separation-individuation process, whose result is the differentiation of self- and object-representations. The maturation of the perceptual-conscious system, the core of the ego, paves the way for the emergence of the infant from the normal autistic phase of the first weeks of life (Spitz's objectless stage) toward the symbiotic phase, a twilight stage of still primary narcissism.

The symbiotic phase coincides in time with what Anna Freud (1953) has called the "need-satisfying relationship." Anna Freud (1965b) and Spitz (1965) speak of this phase as a "preobject" and "part-object" phase. It seems that at first a dim sensory impression of the symbiotic object sets up engrams, or memory traces, of some "good mothering principle" or agent within the fused self–object representations. This gives rise to "confident expectation" of forthcoming relief within the omnipotent mother–infant fused and undifferentiated common orbit. In the symbiotic phase the need becomes a wish, or it may also be said that the affect of longing replaces the objectless tension state with the feeling of "craving" which already has psychological meaning.

The danger in the symbiotic phase is the loss of the symbiotic object, which amounts at that stage to loss of an integral part of the ego itself and thus constitutes a threat of self-annihilation (without the mother, the child is lost).

The peak of the symbiotic phase, the third quarter of the first year, coincides with the beginning of differentiation of the self from the symbiotic object, and this marks the onset of the separation-individuation phase. The normal separation-individuation process takes place within the setting of the child's developmental readiness for, and pleasure in, independent separate functioning. The concept of separation, in this sense, means differentiation of the self from the symbiotic object as an intrapsychic process. It takes place, for best emotional development, with optimal emotional availability of the mother.

During the course of the normal separation-individuation process, the predominance of pleasure in separate functioning, in an atmosphere in which the mother is emotionally available, enables the
child to overcome a measure of separation anxiety. This anxiety appears at the point of the separation-individuation phase at which a differentiated object representation separate from the self gradually
enters conscious awareness. Small amounts of separation anxiety are
probably evoked with each new step of separation functioning, and
may be necessary requirements for progressive personality development.

The separation-individuation process implies two distinct, albeit
interdependent, kinds of development. One line is the toddler's rapidly progressing individuation, which is brought about by the evolution and expansion of the autonomous ego functions. These center
around the child's developing self-concept. The parallel line of development is the child's growing awareness of his functioning independently of, and separately from, the hitherto symbiotically fused external part of his ego—the mother. This line centers perhaps more
around the child's developing object representations.

At the stage of object relationship referred to as separation-
individuation, the particular danger is object loss. The specific danger
situation toward the end of the separation-individuation phase, as object constancy is approached, is akin to the danger of loss of the love
of the libidinal object, although there may still remain some form of
object loss as well.

The dangers of loss of love and of object loss are very much
aggravated by the accumulation of aggressive impulses during the
oral-sadistic phases, in which the child must struggle to preserve the
object in the face of his own great ambivalence. By the end of the
second and the beginning of the third year, the fear of loss of love is
compounded by castration anxiety. When the girl reacts to the anatomical sex difference, usually at the height of toilet training and
complicated by anal fears, the ambivalence toward the mother is con-
taminated with anger at the mother for not having given her a penis.

In the later book (Mahler et al., 1975), Mahler refined many of
the points made earlier and added some new ones. The most important addition is the detailed investigation of the *rapprochement crisis*.
In this phase the toddler oscillates between leaving the mother and
going back to her, with considerable mood swinging and emotionally
disturbing reactions:

It seems to be inherent in the human condition that not even the most normally endowed child, with the most optimally available mother, is able to weather the separation-individuation process without crises, come out unscathed by the rapprochement struggle, and enter the oedipal phase without developmental difficulty. . . . In fact . . . the fourth subphase of the separation–individuation process has no single definite terminal point.

One of the main yields of our study was the finding that the infantile neurosis may have its obligatory precursor, if not its first manifestation, in the rapprochement crisis, which we have therefore made a particular focus in our book. It often continues far into the third year and may overlap the phallic-oedipal phase, in which case it interferes with repression and with the successful passing of the Oedipus complex.[14]

The sequence of stages in the separation-individuation process as described by Mahler has been taken as a paradigm for development at later stages of life as well. The detachment from the parents in adolescence, which Freud (1905) had already noted as the primary goal of adolescence, can now be viewed as a recapitulation of the separation-individuation process in the first three years of life (Marcus, 1973). Spiegel (1958) has emphasized, however, that in adolescence the factor which promotes greater individuation is being in love, both hetero- and homosexual. At later periods narcissistic, borderline, and psychotic persons handle aging with difficulty, in part because of loss of a clear sense of self and the threat of loss or breakdown of their feeling of identity. The identity crises described by Erikson are also relevant here (Sternschein, 1973).

Kohut and the Revival of Interest in Narcissism

One of the few theoreticians who has gone against the trend toward interpersonal theory is Heinz Kohut, with his work on narcissism. His first important paper on this topic was "Forms and Transformations of Narcissism" (1966). One of his main points is that narcissism has been neglected because the value judgment of "bad" has been attached to it and the judgment of "good" has been attached to object love. Hence, he argued, therapists try to push their patients toward object love instead of considering the goal of transformed narcissism, which would be appropriate in many cases.

Kohut traces the differentiation of primary narcissism in two directions: the narcissistic self (later renamed the grandiose self) and the idealized parental image. In further elaboration of his main theme, he enumerates five transformations of narcissism: creativity, empathy, transience, humor, and wisdom. A major point is that the developmental lines for narcissism and object relations are independent of one another. He postulates:

two separate and largely independent developmental lines: one which leads from autoerotism via narcissism to object love; another which leads from autoeroticism via narcissism to higher forms and transformations of narcissism. . . . I am inclined to believe that the imputing to a very small child of the capacity for even rudimentary forms of object love (not to be confused, however, with object relations) rests on retrospective falsifications and on adultomorphic errors in empathy.[15]

Critique of Kohut: The Kohut–Kernberg Controversy

Kohut's work has had wide reverberations in the psychoanalytic community; some have even spoken of a "Kohutian revolution." There has also been wide criticism. Hanly and Masson (1976) state that "no single work in psychoanalytic literature on this subject, since Freud, has had a greater impact in the psychoanalytic community."[16] Nevertheless they reject his position, insisting that narcissism cannot be separated from object relations.

The most trenchant critique of Kohut has come from Kernberg (1974, 1975, 1977; Ornstein, 1974), whose work on borderline cases has been widely compared and contrasted with that of Kohut. Kernberg maintains that one cannot divorce the study of normal and pathological narcissism from the vicissitudes of both libidinal and aggressive drive derivatives and from the development of structural derivatives of internalized object relations (Kernberg, 1971, 1972; Volkan, 1976). The essence of his disagreement is the following:

1. The specific narcissistic resistances of patients with narcissistic personalities reflect a pathological narcissism which is different from both the ordinary, adult narcissism and from fixation at, or regression to, normal infantile narcissism. The implication is that narcissistic resistances that develop in the course of interpretation of character defenses in patients other than narcissistic personalities are of a different nature, require a different technique and have a different prognostic implication from narcissistic resistances of patients presenting pathological narcissism.

2. Pathological narcissism can only be understood in terms of the combined analysis of the variations of libidinal and aggressive drive derivatives. Pathological narcissism does not merely reflect libidinal investment in the self in contrast to libidinal investment in objects, but libidinal investment in a pathological self-structure.

3. The structural characteristics of narcissistic personalities cannot be understood simply in terms of fixation at an early level of development, or lack of development in certain psychic structures. They are a consequence of the development of pathological (in contrast to normal) differentiation and integration of ego and superego structures, deriving from pathological (in contrast to normal) object relationships.

Thus Kernberg stays more directly within the mainstream of psychoanalytic thought. The title of his latest book, *Object Relations Theory and Clinical Psychoanalysis* (1976), testifies to his adherence to an interpersonal theory.

Transference

The topic of transference is normally limited to discussions of psychotherapy. However, as Freud had already pointed out, as a concept it is related to the entire range of human behavior. In 1925 he wrote: "Transference is merely uncovered and isolated by analysis. It is a universal phenomenon of the human mind, it decides the success of all medical influence, and in fact dominates the whole of each person's relations to his human environment." [17]

Transference implies that every person's human relations are the outcome of his early familial environment, from which he transfers to the outside world. Thus transference is the decisive factor in all object choice, though the statement is not usually put in that form. Since the early family is the root of all later human relationships, it becomes even more important in the entire theory of psychology.

The Family

In a review of the development of psychoanalytic ideas about the family, two essential facts must be borne in mind: Psychoanalysts have been essentially concerned with the *dynamics* of the family, not its external structure. And while the theoretical significance of the family for human growth has never been questioned, this assumption does not mean that family therapy becomes the treatment of choice. (Problems of technique are taken up in chapter 18.)

Psychoanalytic ideas about the family have evolved through a number of stages. When Freud began his work, the family was being blamed for all neuropathic disturbances; the only cause known was hereditary degeneracy. This term was found occasionally in Freud's early writings, but disappeared as time went on. In his paper on heredity in the etiology of the neuroses (1896), he argued quite rightly that the clinical facts are not sufficiently explained by the assumption of a hereditary taint. His reasoning is still interesting, even though outmoded. He distinguished three causes of neurosis: preconditions, concurrent causes, and specific causes. While admitting heredity as a precondition, he still held that sexual disturbances were the specific causes.

Since the notion of hereditary degeneracy gradually disappeared, Freud was not inclined to probe more deeply into the familial background. For many years his main interest lay in unraveling the specific childhood determinants of his patients' troubles. In this search the family played a secondary role, especially after he discovered that the sexual seduction stories of his hysterical women patients were fantasies. Thereafter fantasy, particularly childhood fantasy, was seen as one of the main causes of neurosis.

One of the fantasies that he elicited was the *family romance* (1909). This term referred to the common wish of children to have different parents, more exalted and generous than the parents they knew. Freud explained this as the child's turning away from the father whom he knows today to the father in whom he believed in the earlier years of his childhood; and his fantasy is no more than regret that those days have gone.

This paper was typical of the attitude toward the family in the days of id psychology. The child had many impulses, of which the prime one was the Oedipal. The family interfered with his gratifications, so he had to repress the impulses. The result was a neurosis. Thus family repression caused neurosis, and so the family spelled trouble. This was the essential theme of the first period of psychoanalysis, embodied, for instance, in Flugel's *Psychoanalytic*

Study of the Family (1921), which focused particularly on the problems connected with family life. The main problem that Flugel pointed to was the need to repress the incestuous wishes connected with the Oedipus complex.

As has already been pointed out, this position remained dominant until the time of ego psychology and the altered views of the oral stage. A. S. Neill's *Summerhill* (1960) was one product of this kind of thinking, which incidentally coincided with the early attempts at destruction of the family in Soviet Russia. The family was an enemy, both politically and sexually.

Once ego psychology and the need for the mother were recognized, beginning with the 1940s, the attitude toward the family changed. In accord with Freud's second theory of 1926, separation anxiety was now seen as more dangerous than castration anxiety, and therefore separation was to be avoided for the child. Experiences with children separated from their parents during World War II were particularly convincing in this respect.

The father is also necessary to maintain the mother, both psychologically and economically. Hence the total family is necessary to give the child a sense of security and stability. Family disruption leads to frustration, depression, and neurosis. This was the position reached in the 1950s, brought out most clearly by Ackerman (1958) and his conceptualizations of family dynamics (see chapter 5). Ackerman stressed the need for security provided by an intact family.

At that time numerous studies were initiated to see whether the characteristics of healthy parents, as distinguished from disturbed ones, could be adequately delineated. A typical study is reported by Sylvia Brody in *Patterns of Mothering* (1956). She used feeding as the main variable but could detect only gross differences between "good" and "bad" mothers. Her general conclusions were:

The typology is a tentative one. It considers only twenty-nine self-selected white mothers between the ages of 20 and 35, and from Lower Lower to Upper-Middle socioeconomic groups. They resided in two adjacent Midwestern communities, lived with their husbands and had normal infants between the ages of 4 and 28 weeks. The diversity of maternal behavior in so small a sample is no surprise to the clinician, and it has seemed to set a sufficient base for a typology. The purpose of the typology, it may be restated, was only to find out whether maternal behavior followed any distinguishable patterns, so that within each pattern the significance of one activity, Feeding, might be measured. As mentioned above, a larger sample of mothers would probably yield a finer typology.[18]

Brody's study was preceded and followed by many other studies of "normal" and "disturbed" mothers. A review of this extensive literature discloses no general trends. This conclusion should not be taken as negative, however. Psychoanalysts have concluded, rather, that the external circumstances of the family are of lesser importance. What counts above all is the internal environment, which is extremely hard to measure. It is to this internal environment that analysis has turned (Benedek and Anthony, 1970; Muensterberger, 1969). Hence interest in the family structure as such has never been strong among analysts. For optimal child-rearing, what seem to count more than anything else are the maturity and emotional health of the parent, and these depend on the inner structure of the family.

Object Constancy and Object Loss

Following the investigations of the oral stage and the first three years, the concept which has emerged as decisive for mental health has been *object constancy,* while the fundamental problem has been seen as *object loss.* These two topics have been central in the analytic literature for the past decade.

The term object constancy was coined by Hartmann, who thereby also unified the observations of experimental and analytic psychology. In 1952 he wrote:

"Object formation" has a somewhat different meaning in analytic and nonanalytic child psychology. Still, I emphasized long ago that what nonanalytic psychologists have carefully described in their experimental work as the evolving of constant and independent objects in the child's world . . . cannot be fully understood without considering the child's object relations in our sense. . . . One may suggest that the element of identity and constancy in what one calls "objects" in the general sense is partly traceable to the element of constancy gradually developing in what we describe as libidinal or aggressive cathexis—though, of course, other factors, too, partly autonomous ones, are involved. The child learns to recognize "things" probably only in the process of forming more or less constant object relationships.[19]

Later he wrote: "The protracted helplessness of the human child causes a situation in which the 'value of the object . . . is enormously enhanced' (Freud, 1926). *One may well say that in man the human objects are by far the most important sector of reality"* (italics added).[20]

The process by which object constancy is attained, in the course of separation-individuation, has already been described. This is now seen as the end point of the process of introjection. Healthy growth would now be seen as the attainment of object constancy, unhealthy growth as ambivalence and instability.

Links with Experimental Psychology; Piaget

The psychic processes of children in the first few years have engaged the attention of many careful researchers, analytic and nonanalytic. Beginning with the 1960s these lines of investigation began to move in the same direction, and in some places to merge, because of two serendipitous discoveries: first, one of the major signs that the good internal object is functioning properly is that the child's cognitive abilities are developing adequately; and second, the attainment of the capacity for object constancy with an inanimate object runs a course roughly similar to that for the attainment of animate object constancy. Many researchers have been at work in both these areas, but the person most responsible for this joining of two lines of thought is the Swiss psychologist Jean Piaget (1896–   ).

At a meeting of the American Psychoanalytic Association in 1970 (Piaget, 1973), Piaget drew extensive parallels between his system and psychoanalysis: "these questions, relating to the area of the cognitive unconscious, are parallel to those that psychoanalysis raises with respect to the affective unconscious."[21] At the end of his talk he envisaged a future general psychology in which both streams of research would be united:

the conclusion of all this is that multiple problems still remain to be resolved, and today is not too soon to start thinking of formulating a general psychology which would bear simultaneously upon the mechanisms discovered by psychoanalysis and upon the cognitive processes; the kinds of comparison which we have made here are but a beginning and appear to be rich with promise.[22]

P. Wolff (1960) showed extensive correspondences between the development of thought processes as seen by Piaget and the views of psychoanalysis. Piaget divides the first 18 months into six stages according to the emergence of qualitatively new interactions between the child and his environment. The entire period from birth to 18 months he calls the sensorimotor period. It culminates in the capacity to keep an object in mind, i.e., object constancy with regard to inanimate objects. The crucial advances that bring the development of sensorimotor intelligence to a close and prepare the way for the next phase are:

1. The conversion of the object, its displacements, and the temporal and cause-effect relationships pertaining to it even when the object cannot be directly perceived (the mental representations).

2. The mental anticipation of new ways of interacting with objects before these interactions have been experienced (the mental inventions).

Spurred on by these ideas, a variety of researchers in the 1960s and 1970s then attempted to draw other parallels and tease out other relationships between affective and cognitive development in the first few years of life (Blatt et al., 1976; Decarie, 1965; Werner, 1948). In general they found that the development of a wide range of cognitive capacities is highly dependent on the mother's interactions with her infant. Spitz had already shown this for highly deprived infants; now it was generalized.

Brody and Axelrod (1978) showed that there are highly consistent findings which indicate that gentle, firm, and close physical contact, distinctive and frequent auditory stimulation, and a high degree of eye contact all have a positive effect on the infant's very early development of cognitive, linguistic, social, and motor capacities, and on the formation of his attachment to and responsiveness to the mother. The amount of stimulation provided by the mother correlated positively with the child's overall cognitive development. In addition, particular forms of maternal stimulation are correlated with the development of specific skills in the infant.

Bell (1970), investigating the relationship between the quality of mother–child interaction and development of object permanence, found confirmation for Piaget's hypothesis that object and person permanence develop in parallel and that person permanence usually precedes object permanence. He found that the development of the concept of the object is closely related to the quality of the mother–child interaction. Infants who developed object permanence before they developed person permanence had mothers who were prone to express disapproval and rejection, often through physical punishment.

Object Loss

Given the central importance of object constancy, object loss becomes all the more significant. Two separate cases can be distinguished: those in which there is a real object loss, or actual separation, and those in which there has been an emotional object loss, or distance of the child from the parents, especially the mother.

Bowlby (1973) has reviewed the development of theories relating to actual separation from the mother. He describes six such theories, in the order in which they have received attention from psychoanalysis.

1. The first, advanced by Freud in the *Three Essays,* is a special case of the general theory of anxiety of that day. Anxiety is transformed libido. Hence when a child is separated from the mother, his libido is unsatisfied and undergoes transformations.

2. Rank's birth-trauma theory (1932) held that the anxiety shown by young children on separation from their mother reproduces the trauma of birth, so that birth anxiety is the prototype of all the separation anxiety subsequently experienced.

3. According to Freud's signal theory of 1926, in the absence of his mother an infant or young child is subject to the risk of a traumatic psychic experience. He therefore develops a safety device which leads to his exhibiting anxiety behavior whenever she leaves him. Such behavior has a function: it may be expected to ensure that he is not parted from her for too long.

4. The next theory was that of depressive anxiety (Melanie Klein, 1935, in Klein, 1948). Separation anxiety results from a young child's believing that when his mother disappears he has eaten her up or otherwise destroyed her, and that in consequence he has lost her forever. This belief arises from the ambivalent feeling that a child has for his mother, an ambivalence made inevitable, in Klein's view, by the existence of the death instinct.

5. Another theory was that of persecutory anxiety (Melanie Klein, 1934, in Klein, 1948). As a result of projecting his aggression, a young child perceives his mother as persecutory, and this leads him to interpret her departure as due to her being angry with him or wishing to punish him. For this reason, whenever his mother leaves him he believes that she will either never return or will return only in a hostile mood, and he therefore experiences anxiety.

6. The modern synthesis (Bowlby) is the theory of frustrated attachment. Initially the anxiety is a primary response not reducible to other terms and due simply to the rupture of a child's attachment to his mother. This is the counterpart of theories that regard a child's pleasure in his mother's presence as being as primary as his pleasure in food and warmth. Bowlby states that a theory of this sort was advanced by William James (1890), Suttie (1935), and Hermann (1936) but has never been given much credence in analytic circles. However, this does seem to have been the prevalent common-sense theory among practicing analysts, especially since the formulation of Freud's second theory of anxiety in 1926.

The observation that humans suffer severely from separation or object loss, especially in infancy, prompted a large number of experiments with animals. In an early paper Hermann (1936) pointed to the alternation of clinging and searching in monkeys. Since then many studies, including Harlow's classic work with rhesus monkeys (1974), have established the pathological reactions of animals to separation. Thus evidence from both human and nonhuman observations and experiments supports the existence of a general motivational system associated with attachment-separation behavior.

The effects of loss are far-reaching. Pinderhughes (1971) attempted to summarize much of this material in a thoughtful paper in which he cited the somatic, psychological, and social sequelae of loss. They had long been known for infancy but were now extended to the entire life-span.

Studies by Wolff et al. (1950), Selye (1956), and many others had shown how various kinds of stress can easily lead to disease. Wolff wrote that, in man, "sickness may ensue and his life may be dramatically shortened in his struggle for issues beyond himself. His aspirations and appetite for adventure may engender ominous conflict yet make possible growth to undefined limits."[23]

By the 1960s it had become known that one of the major causes of stress was loneliness, separation, and isolation. For example, a major risk of suicide occurs in middle-aged men who are living alone and have lost their sense of purpose in life (Shneidman, 1967). More recently Lynch (1977) has adduced a wide body of evidence that a "broken heart" is not just a figure of speech. "The central assumption of this book is that . . . a person's life may be shortened by the lack of human companionship."[24] For instance, the mortality for heart disease among adult Americans who are not married is as much as two to five times as high as for married individuals.[25]

Among older people, separations are especially painful and often fatal. In a study of 870 old people before and after they underwent radical shifts in living arrangements (Lieberman, 1974), death rates for those involved in environmental change were triple the rates of matched controls who did not undergo environmental upheavals.[26]

When the separation is emotional rather than physical, the effects are equally deleterious. However, it is obviously much more difficult to quote comparable statistics. In one sense, the entire body of analytic literature could be cited.

Mourning

In view of the increased significance attached to object loss at any age, the experience of mourning has become increasingly important in psychoanalytic theory and observation. The process of mourning after the death of his father was what led Freud to undergo his self-analysis and uncover a number of profound truths (Anzieu, 1975). Yet the importance of mourning did not occur to Freud for a long time. His first extensive description of it came in the paper on "Mourning and Melancholia" (1917). Here he gave what is still an excellent dynamic account of the mourning process:

In what, now, does the work which mourning performs consist? I do not think there is anything far-fetched in presenting it in the following way. Reality-testing has shown that the loved object no longer exists, and it proceeds to demand that all libido shall be withdrawn from its attachments to that object. This demand arouses understandable opposition—it is a matter of general observation that people never willingly abandon a libidinal position, not even, indeed, when a substitute is already beckoning to them. . . . Normally, respect for reality gains the day. But its orders cannot be obeyed at once. . . . In the meantime the existence of the lost object is psychically prolonged. . . . When the work of mourning is completed the ego becomes free and uninhibited again.[27]

In this paper Freud differentiated mourning from depression; in mourning there is a real object loss, while in depression there is an internalized object loss. Nevertheless, since object loss was not a focus of attention at that time, his observations about mourning received little follow-up.

One of the few analysts who gave weight to the mourning process before World War II was Melanie Klein; with her notion of the depressive position, the mourning process assumes central importance. New feelings occur as a result of loss: mourning and pining for the good object felt as lost and destroyed, and guilt, a characteristic depressive experience. She also stressed artistic creativity as reparation for the guilt, thus part of the mourning experience.

The Bowlby Controversy

Only in the late 1950s did analysts begin to pay more attention to mourning. The spark was provided by John Bowlby, a British analyst, with a paper on "Grief and Mourning in Infancy and Early Childhood" (1959). Bowlby put his central thesis as follows:

In this and the succeeding papers I shall advance the view that grief and mourning occur in infancy whenever the responses mediating attachment are activated and the mother figure continues to be unavailable. It is by now widely recognized that loss of the mother figure in the period between about six months and three or four or more years is an event of high pathogenic potential. The reason for this, I postulated, is that the processes of mourning to which it habitually gives rise all too readily at this age take a course unfavorable to future personality development.[28]

Bowlby went on to describe three phases of the mourning process: protest, despair, and detachment. In adults commonly there is a period of promiscuity between the relinquishment of the lost object and attachment to a new one. However, if the object is not relinquished, the end state is the most pathological of all—detachment from all human relationships. Bowlby also maintained that the processes in children do not differ in any significant respect from those in adults.

In the discussion that followed Bowlby's paper (A. Freud, 1960; Schur, 1960; Spitz, 1960), his thesis was criticized on a number of counts. Anna Freud's main objection was that he paid too little attention to chronological age; she argued that the nearer the child is to object constancy, the longer the duration of grief reactions, with corresponding approximation to the adult internal processes of mourning. Spitz considered that Bowlby was merely restating the earlier observations about depression; Spitz thus regarded the whole question as a problem in semantics. Nevertheless, Bowlby's thesis has been incorporated into psychoanalytic theory and has proved to be of enduring value.

Pollock: Mourning and Adaptation

Beginning in 1961, George Pollock has published a series of papers dealing with mourning from a broader point of view (listed in the References). For him, mourning is an adaptational process having sequential phases and stages, phylogenetically evolved and present as a reaction to loss but not solely to object loss. It is a fundamental and universal process that may be seen as the adaptation to loss and change with an outcome of resolution, gain, creativity, and/or investment of psychic interest in new areas, activities, or objects. In contrast to Freud, he views the mourning process as a universal adaptation, going on throughout the life cycle of the individual, one found in all cultures, and, when ritualized, found throughout man's existence in his religious, social, and cultural practices. In a recent paper (1977) Pollock stressed the significance of mourning for organizations as well as individuals. To be able to mourn, he argued, is to be able to change. To be unable to mourn, to deny change, carries great risks to the individual and to the organization.

Mitscherlich: The Inability to Mourn

Alexander Mitscherlich, the leading German analyst of the postwar era, has published some arresting reflections on the Germans' inability to mourn for the havoc that they wrought on the world while Hitler was in power. He discerned, as a result of this inability to mourn, a high degree of self-alienation within postwar Germany, derived from living in a state of illusion (1969, 1971, 1975).

Summary Comment: The Centrality of the Object

The course of psychoanalytic theory since World War II has emphasized increasingly the central significance of the introject, or internalized object. All human relations are now seen to revolve about the vicissitudes and the fates of this "immortal" object. Consequently, for healthy living, object constancy involving the introjection of a good object is basic, while in psychopathology the introjection of a bad object is the core phenomenon on the basis of which the further clinical observations can be ordered and understood.

Chapter Sixteen

Values, Philosophy, and the Superego

At first, questions of values and philosophy were not seen as germane to psychoanalytic theory. Freud viewed himself as a scientist, a medical researcher seeking to uncover the causes of illnesses whose nature was poorly understood. Throughout his life this attitude of the detached scientist remained an essential part of his makeup, though other factors entered later.

The Sexual Problem: Before World War I

Freud's early theories, especially in the 1890s, immediately brought him into conflict with the world of established values. For he had come to the conclusion that sexual disturbances were the root causes of all neurosis. His earlier views were even harder for him to handle than the later ones. One of his theories was that sexual abstention leads to an "actual" neurosis, by which he meant that the sexual frustration in some unknown manner was biochemically transmuted into the anxiety manifest in the clinical picture. Thus sexual frustration, demanded by society of a large number of its members, created illness.

There was certainly a need for reform of the antiquated sexual code that prevailed at that time. Others, like Havelock Ellis and Magnus Hirschfeld, were willing to take active roles in this reform process. Freud was not a politically minded man, however, and he remained content with pointing to the need.

In a paper on "The Sexual Etiology of the Neuroses" (1898), he summed up his main views. "In matters of sexuality we are at present, every one of us, ill or well, nothing but hypocrites." [1] He urged changes, but in a general way:

We see that it is positively a matter of public interest that *men should enter upon sexual relations with full potency.* In matters of prophylaxis, however, the individual is relatively helpless. The whole community must become interested in the matter and give their assent to the creation of generally acceptable regulations. At present we are still far removed from such a state of affairs which could promise relief, and it is for this reason that we may with justice regard civilization, too, as responsible for the spread of neurasthenia. . . . Above all a place must be created in public opinion for the discussion of the problems of sexual life. . . . And so here, too, there is enough work left to do for the next hundred years—in which our civilization will have to learn to come to terms with the claims of our sexuality. [2]

The discussions in the Vienna Psychoanalytic Society (Nunberg and Federn, 1962–1975) showed that Freud continued to hold this position of the detached scientist who had discovered a social evil which it was up to others to correct. In a discussion of Wittels's paper on female physicians on May 15, 1907, Freud commented: "The ideal of the courtesan has no place in our culture. The sexual problem cannot be settled without regard for the social problem; and if one prefers abstinence to the wretched sexual condition, one is abstinent under protest." [3]

At a later meeting Freud commented that enlightenment could accomplish something, but it was no panacea. [4] Nevertheless tacitly he gave his approval to various measures of enlightenment and reform that others suggested. At the meeting on April 15, 1908, he took an active role in helping Hirschfeld draw up a questionnaire on the sexual instinct. [5] Furthermore, Christian von Ehrenfels, a professor of philosophy at Prague who was openly critical of marriage, was invited by Freud to present his proposals for reform at the meeting of the Vienna Society on December 23, 1908. Von Ehrenfels was pleading for reform on a polygamous basis. [6] Earlier Freud had said of him, rather characteristically; "One does not venture to declare aloud that marriage is not an arrangement calculated to satisfy a man's sexuality, unless one is driven to do so perhaps by the love of truth and eagerness for reform of a Christian von Ehrenfels." [7]

In a published paper in 1908, Freud elaborated on the extensive harm done to modern people by the prevailing sexual mores. Nevertheless, "it is certainly not a physician's business to come forward with proposals for reform." [8]

The closest that Freud came to expressing his own views on how the sexual neurosis should be handled (other than by psychoanalysis) was in the Vienna Society's meeting on December 16, 1908. The meeting was devoted to a presentation of Wittels's book *Die sexuelle Not* (The sexual need), the epigraph of which was: "Man must give free rein to his sexuality, or else he becomes crippled." [9] In the discussion Freud said that he "personally takes no stand with regard to the efforts at reform. . . . We liberate sexuality through our treatment, but not in order that man may from now on be dominated by sexuality, but in order to make a suppression possible—a rejection of the instincts under the guidance of a higher agency." [10]

Social and philosophical questions other than sexuality, though discussed at the meetings, scarcely seemed to interest Freud. When Adler presented a paper on "The Psychology of Marxism" at the meeting on March 10, 1909, Freud's only comment was the rather irrelevant one that culture requires repression, [11] a position which he was to hold all his life. About Marxism itself, already a burning issue in intellectual circles, Freud said nothing.

Putnam and the Problem of Moral Values

The problem of moral values again came up at the insistence of the American psychoanalyst Putnam. James Jackson Putnam (1846–1918) was already one of the leading neurologists of the United States when in 1909, at the age of 63, he became converted to the cause of psychoanalysis. He was the first president of the American Psychoanalytic Association when it was formed in 1911, and remained active analytically until his death. Freud had the highest regard for him, and the two engaged in a lively correspondence (Putnam, 1971).

Though in agreement with Freud on all essentials, Putnam believed firmly that philosophy was important for psychoanalysis. In particular, he held that psychoanalysis must bring about moral improvement. In 1911 he wrote: "I consider that no patient is really cured unless he becomes better and broader morally, and, conversely, I believe that a moral regeneration helps toward a removal of the symptoms." [12]

Freud disagreed, arguing as before that the analyst should concentrate on his scientific work and leave reform to others. However, in response to repeated prodding from Putnam that he take a stand on these moral issues, a question which was also agitating many others with regard to psychoanalysis at that time, Freud argued that moral and philosophical improvement was desirable but could only take place after the psychoanalytic work had been done. In 1911 he wrote: "Sublimation, that is, striving toward higher goals, is of course one of the best means of overcoming the urgency of our drives. But one can consider doing this only after psychoanalytic work has lifted the repressions." [13]

In this passage can be seen the germ of Freud's later theory of the superego. However, although he came to agree with Putnam that psychoanalysis should bring about moral and ethical improvement, he did not want to entrust this task to the psychoanalyst because he did not want psychoanalysis to be confused with any specific moral or philosophical position. Perhaps referring to Jung, he said he was disgusted with "saintly converts." [14] Then he reverted again to the position of the detached scientist: "At the moment psychoanalysis can accommodate itself to any number of different *Weltanschauungen* but has it really said its last word? For me an all-embracing synthesis never has been the important issue. Certainty, rather, always has been worth the sacrifice of everything else." [15]

The Shock of World War I

The views of leading analysts on the moral question were deeply influenced by the shocking events of World War I. In its way the First World War was even more disturbing than the Second, because the notion of civilized good feeling had become so widespread by 1914, only to be dashed to smithereens.

Freud had three sons at the front and, for this as well as other reasons, he was profoundly affected by the war. For several years his scientific productivity was blocked and it was resumed again only when the war ended, with a last great burst of genius.

In the meantime he tried to digest the lessons of the war in two papers, "Thoughts for the Times on War and Death" (1915) and "On Transience" (1916). One of his main points was that the psychoanalytic emphasis on the power of the primitive instinctual strivings in man had been proved correct. In a letter to the Dutch scholar Frederik van Eeden he wrote:

I venture, under the impact of the war, to remind you of two theses which have been put forward by psychoanalysis and which have undoubtedly contributed to its unpopularity. . . . The primitive savage and evil impulses of mankind have not vanished in any of its individual members. . . . Our intellect is a feeble and dependent thing, a plaything and tool of our instincts and affects. . . . You will have to admit that psychoanalysis has been right in both its theses.[16]

The Superego: The Key Concept

Spurred on by these various trends and events, Freud took a giant step forward in his theoretical structure. As described in chapter 15, beginning with the paper on "Narcissism" (1914), his thoughts had been directed toward the process of internalizing objects. In 1923 he developed the idea that the internalization of the parents, following the Oedipal period, led to a structure he called the superego. With this concept he and other analysts were able to approach the problems of philosophy and moral values from an entirely novel angle.

It now appeared that the individual's and society's values are incorporated in the superego. In the individual the superego takes the place of the parents, serving as the regulator of self-esteem after the Oedipal period in the same way that the parents had served as regulators before. For the group and for society, the superego serves as a powerful cohesive force, the dictates of which, no matter how absurd, can only be defied at the expense of severe guilt and often outright punishment.

The Superego: Post-Freudian Developments

The concept of the superego, once formulated, was of such compelling quality that it was elaborated in a number of directions by many authors. The theory of the superego was reasonably complete by about 1960. Thereafter interest shifted to the earlier introject (see chapter 15), the forerunner of the superego.

Clarification of Psychopathology

The superego now allowed for a more elegant resolution of the problem of psychopathology. Freud had schematically clarified neurosis, depression (melancholia), and psychosis on the basis of the tripartite structure (1924): in neurosis there is a conflict between the ego and the id, in depression between the ego and the superego, and in psychosis between the ego and external reality.

It soon appeared that this scheme was overly rigid, and various authors began to modify his formulas. In particular the strange phenomenon of the *need for punishment* called for clarification. Papers by Reik (1941) and Nunberg (1926) and the book by Alexander (1927) on *Psychoanalysis of the Total Personality* were among the works that analyzed various aspects of this need for punishment. Reik linked it with the compulsion to confess, an observation which many had made about certain types of criminal behavior (as in Dostoevsky's *Crime and Punishment*). Alexander offered the notion of the *corruptibility of the superego* to explain the alternation of forbidden pleasure and punishment: if punishment follows, or, in many cases, precedes the instinctual gratification, then pleasure becomes permissible.

In schizophrenia the break with external reality occurs because of the harshness of the superego (Nunberg, 1955). The delusion of persecution can be considered an attempt at freeing oneself from the tormenting conscience.[17] Incidentally, Sullivan's image of the self in the schizophrenic, with its controlling and at times tormenting qualities, makes it remarkably similar to the Freudian superego.

As mentioned earlier, in mania there is a fusion of the ego and the superego, as a result of which the person feels approval for everything that he does (Lewin, 1950). The intensity of the struggle between the ego and the id in neurosis derives from the relatively benign character of the superego; besides, a conflict between ego and id occurs in all personality structures. Once the superego concept was formulated, Freud used it to explain the anxiety or punishment dream more economically than he had done before. Many other extensions of superego punishment or pressure in all forms of psychopathology were studied.

The Genesis of the Superego

Many theoreticians traced the development of the superego from the interaction between the instinctual drives and the parental commands and prohibitions. Jacobson (1954) pointed to the series of disillusionments that the child experiences, as well as the hostility thereby released, which can be used by the ego for the expansion of realistic perceptions of the self and the world.

Sandler (1960), basing his ideas on direct clinical and research experience with the Hampstead Index, traces the origin of the superego to an early organizing activity, which leads the child to make inner models. As object relations develop, the child acquires techniques for restoring the state of union with the mother which is threatened with increasing discrimination between the self and other schemata. Two of these techniques are obedience to and compliance with the demands of the parents, and identification with and imitation of the parents.

There is a preautonomous superego schema. What develops in the mind of the child in the pre-Oedipal years is an organization that reflects the idealized and desirable qualities of the parents and that prompts the child to suitable object-related behavior. It is not yet a structure, but a sort of plan for the later superego. The introjection of parental authority will elevate it to autonomous superego status.

With elevation of the superego schema to autonomous status, and consequent structuralization, what was previously experienced as the threat of parental disapproval becomes guilt, though the affective experience is probably the same in both. An essential component of this affective state is the drop in self-esteem. This differentiates guilt from anxiety and links it with feelings of inferiority and inadequacy as well as with the affect that is experienced in pathological states of depression.

An opposite and equally important affective state is also experienced by the ego, when the ego and superego are functioning together in a smooth and harmonious fashion; that is, when the feeling of being loved is restored by the approval of the superego. This is the counterpart of the affect experienced by the child when his parents show signs of approval and pleasure at his performance, when the earliest state of being at one with the mother is temporarily regained.

Many authors have noted that additions to and changes in the superego occur in later years. Hartmann et al. (1946) stress the importance of cultural conditions for the function of the superego. They state that throughout latency one can watch a gradual adjustment of superego functions. That adjustment is partly due to the growth of intellectual comprehension, and educational or religious indoctrination, but partly also to the fact that the function of the superego is progressively less endangered; therefore it needs less protection. The pubertal changes create new dangers; they reactivate the situation that once led to superego formations. The ensuing polarization of behavior between asceticism and indulgence has often been described (A. Freud, 1936). A new set of ideals is often chosen at this stage. They become part of the adolescent's conscious moral equipment (ego ideal). Throughout latency the child has identified with many models, including the whole set of images made available by his culture. All of these may enter into and modify the superego.

The Superego of Women

Much furor has arisen over Freud's position that the superego of women is weaker than that of men. It was most clearly stated in his 1925 essay on "anatomy is destiny":

for women the level of what is ethically normal is different from what it is in men. Their superego is never so inexorable, so impersonal, so independent of its emotional origins as we require it to be in men. . . . That they show less sense of justice than men, that they are less ready to submit to the great exigencies of life, that they are more often influenced in their judgments by feelings of affection or hostility—all these would be amply accounted for in the modification of the formation of their superego.[18]

A number of recent papers have examined Freud's views on women and found them inadequate. Schafer (1974) concludes "that Freud's estimates of women's morality and objectivity are logically and empirically indefensible."[19] This is another instance where the progress of psychoanalysis requires overcoming Freud's errors.

The Ego Ideal

In his earlier papers Freud used the term ego ideal; for a while he used ego ideal and superego interchangeably. Some authors, notably

Bergler (1949), liked to refer to the superego as the "daemonium," or devil. Horney (1945) referred to the ego ideal as the "idealized image." Most authors, however, have felt that the positive and negative aspects of the superego cannot reasonably be separated from one another. Accordingly, the term ego ideal, if used at all in the contemporary literature, refers to the positive aspects of the superego.

In a thoughtful paper Schafer (1960) has pulled together the material on the loving and beloved superego. This loving aspect represents the loved and admired Oedipal and pre-Oedipal parents who provide love, protection, comfort, and guidance, who embody and transmit certain ideals and moral structures more or less representative of their society, and who, even in their punishing activities, provide needed expressions of parental care, contact, and love.

In principle, then, if the child has loving parents, the superego will be loving and beloved; if the child has punishing, sadistic parents, the superego will be harsh and punitive. While Freud and others have assumed that the superego incorporates the parental superego rather than the parent as such, since the parental superego is harsher than the actual parents, healthy children generally come from warm, tender families, whereas disturbed children come from conflict-ridden, destructive families. Often enough these families are conflict-ridden only with regard to the instinctual impulses, but that is enough.

The Superego and the Social Order: Parsons

Talcott Parsons has been primarily responsible for showing how the superego concept serves to connect individual and social functioning (1953). For him, the place of the superego as part of the structure of personality must be understood in terms of the relation between personality and the total common culture, by virtue of which a stable system of social interaction on the human level becomes possible. Although he feels that the issue of moral standards on which Freud focused is indeed crucial, Parsons feels it is too narrow a focus. Not only moral standards, but all the components of the common culture are internalized as part of the personality structure. Moral standards in this respect cannot be dissociated from the content of the orientation patterns which they regulate.

In a more recent paper Fortes (1977) has indicated that while the central role of parent–child relationships was well appreciated by anthropologists before Freud, what was not realized was the crucial importance of parental authority in the structure of these relationships, i.e., the superego. No culture so far examined has been found to exist without a superego. Furthermore, the superego of one culture may be diametrically opposed to that of another, with regard to dress, or religion, or food, or other patterns. Yet the members of any culture find themselves bound, willy-nilly, by the superego which they take over from their parents, and efforts to break away from this superego are seriously disruptive, both personally and socially.

Shame and Guilt as Superego Affects

Most authors have held that the two affects most closely tied up with the superego are shame and guilt. In an important book, Piers and Singer (1953) tried to establish various dynamic differences between these two and to set up a classification of shame cultures as contrasted with guilt cultures. The main differences they drew between shame and guilt are that: shame arises out of a tension between the ego and the ego ideal, not between ego and superego as in guilt; whereas guilt is generated whenever a boundary (set by the superego) is touched or transgressed, shame occurs when a goal (presented by the ego ideal) is not being reached; the unconscious irrational threat implied in shame anxiety is abandonment whereas in guilt it is mutilation; the law of talion obtains in guilt, but not in shame. However, they felt that the common notion that many primitive cultures are pure shame cultures is a mistake.

Helen Lewis (1971) tried to connect shame and guilt with cognitive controls and styles. For her, shame is experienced more by field-dependent individuals, guilt more by field-independent ones. In addition, she drew basic distinctions in the operations of the self in shame and guilt: in shame, the self is an object of scorn, paralyzed, assailed by noxious body stimuli, childish, focal in awareness, and functioning poorly as an agent or perceiver. In guilt, the self is the source of guilt, intact, adult, occupied with guilty acts or thoughts, and functioning silently. Her conclusions are buttressed by an experimental investigation of patients' proneness to shame or guilt, but the quantification of these two variables certainly requires further confirmation.

The Superego and Treatment

When the concept of the superego was introduced, the goals of treatment altered fundamentally. One of the major goals became to reduce or eliminate the severity of the superego. This topic is discussed more fully in chapter 18, on technique.

Values and Philosophy

Once the psychoanalytic system was fully established with the superego concept, and there was a larger number of patients and practitioners, questions of values and philosophy began to be more insistent. A further reason for this increased interest was the shift in the patient population. When the patients were persons totally incapacitated for ordinary life, merely returning them to a culturally acceptable routine was an achievement. But when, as happened increasingly after World War I, patients were already functioning in society, then the issues of the basic values inherent in psychoanalysis assumed much greater importance.

The Optimism of the 1920s

The immediate aftermath of World War I was of course highly disruptive. Nevertheless, the ensuing recovery created a new spirit of optimism in the world (Gay and Webb, 1973). The treaty of Locarno of 1925 created the "Locarno spirit," a sense of genuine reduction in tension. It was followed in 1928 by another pact in which a number of the leading powers renounced war as an instrument of national policy.[20] Many people were coming to feel that the worst was over.

The Dialogue with Marxism

In the first flush of the Soviet revolution, and smaller ones along the same lines occurring elsewhere, Freud's and Marx's general orientation toward the world appeared somewhat similar. The early socialists had seen social and sexual liberation as going hand in hand. A psychoanalytic movement began to grow in Russia, and societies were formed in several cities. In fact a Soviet analyst, M. Kanabich, appeared on the masthead of the *International Journal of Psychoanalysis* as an advisory editor, and continued to be listed there as late as 1948.[21]

Freud's works were translated into Russian, and for a while he was looked upon with favor. As mentioned before, in Hungary psychoanalysis was in favor with the revolutionary regime.[22] Max Eastman, one of the leading American Marxists, stated in 1926 that Marx and Freud "both contemplate the same facts and their view of these facts is in complete harmony."[23] Although most of the Soviet theoretical psychologists were opposed to what they called "Freudianism," in the early days some of them saw the two approaches as compatible (Dahmer, 1973).

Among analysts outside the Soviet Union, the course of the Revolution had a mixed reception. Freud was largely detached. Adler, a lifelong Marxist, was appalled by its excesses: "We know that this [bolshevik] party . . . pursues goals which are also ours. But the intoxication of power has seduced it."[24] Many other analysts were willing, in that period, to ascribe the excesses to the turmoil of war and revolution; after all, millions had just died in a totally senseless struggle. At the Frankfurt Institute for Social Research, Max Horkheimer was equally critical of the university's mishandling of sociology and its rejection of psychoanalysis. Accordingly he invited a number of prominent analysts, including Karl Landauer, Heinrich Meng, and Erich Fromm, to join the faculty. Horkheimer saw psychoanalysis as an "indispensable auxiliary science" for his critical social theory.[25]

The struggle was seen mainly as the battle between communism (or socialism) and fascism. In 1926 Siegfried Bernfeld led a discussion at the Society of Socialist Physicians in Berlin on the question of "socialism and psychoanalysis." He saw psychoanalysis and Marxism as compatible, but rejected as premature the question of how psychoanalysis could help the proletariat in the class struggle. An Adlerian analyst, Alice Ruehle-Gerstel, argued in 1927 that individual psychology is Marxism applied to the spiritual life, while Marxism is individual psychology applied to social life.[26]

The best known Marxist analyst of that period is Wilhelm Reich, who was already driving his theories to extremes. Reich saw himself as the real heir of Freud, and his Sexpol movement intended to preserve and develop the revolutionary insights of the early period of psychoanalysis. In a paper on "Dialectical Materialism and Psycho-analysis," he argued that the methods and results of psychoanalysis must be dialectic-materialistic (Reich, 1945). He was critical of the psychoanalytic reality principle, which he claimed only leads the patients to an affirmation of capitalistic society. Reich was equally critical of communism, however, especially after a visit to the Soviet Union in 1929, calling the Soviet Union a "besieged fortress." Eventually Reich left the Communist party, devoting the remainder of his life to "orgonomy." Interestingly, even in this Communist period Reich continued to do orthodox analytic work, as O. Spurgeon English, who was in analysis with him from 1929 to 1932, has recently reported.[27]

Of the various Marxist analysts of that period, Erich Fromm is the only one who has maintained a conviction that somehow psychoanalysis and socialism can be made compatible. Perhaps this is one source of his especially strong emphasis on values, and the correspondingly lesser importance attached to technique.[28]

Whatever the psychoanalysts may have wanted, the advent of Stalinism in the Soviet Union[29] soon ended any hopes that the Russians would find something of value in psychoanalysis. In a typical article in 1926 a Stalinist spokesman named Deborin "shattered" psychoanalysis. Shortly thereafter psychoanalysis disappeared from the Soviet Union, never to return.[30]

The antianalytic stance of the Soviet Union has hardened rather than softened over the years. In the 1955 edition of the Soviet *Short Philosophic Dictionary,* Freudism is defined as "a reactionary idealistic trend widespread in bourgeois psychological science . . . now in the service of imperialism which utilizes these 'teachings' for the purpose of justifying and developing the basest and most repellent instinctual tendencies."[31] In more recent years the prostitution of psychiatry to political ends in the Soviet Union has become well known and has aroused widespread indignation.

In the political struggle around Marxism, Freud remained neutral. Hartmann (1933), modifying Freud's views slightly, maintained only that the values pursued by psychoanalysis are health values. Both Freud and Hartmann, however, clearly believed that Marxism, by blaming hostility on the property system, was pursuing an illusion.[32] Freud commented, "One only wonders, with concern, what the Soviets will do after they have wiped out their bourgeois."[33]

By the 1930s almost all analysts had given up hope of reconciling analysis with Marxism. In 1944, Fenichel, perhaps thinking back to his Marxist period, when he was closely allied with Reich, wrote:

The ways of production and distribution, and their contradictions, inflict severe frustrations upon individuals of all classes. . . . Today they arouse especially feelings of being lost and of "not belonging." These feelings have various mental consequences; one of these consequences is a longing to have once more an omnipotent person in the external world to whom one may submit, losing one's helpless individuality in a magnificent oceanic feeling. This longing forms the psychological condition in the masses which meets the influence of Fascism halfway.[34]

The Rejection of Religion

Among the major value systems of Western civilization (and all others hitherto) religion must be given prime importance—in Western culture primarily Christianity. In his 1907 paper on "Obsessive Actions and Religious Practices," Freud had already stated his view that religion represents an obsessional neurosis. This position did not change. In 1927, in *The Future of an Illusion,* he added to this that the hold of religion derives from its perpetuation of the dependency of childhood. Thus even the religious figures are known as father, mother, brother, sister, and so on.

Only a few exceptions to this antireligious or, more properly, unreligious attitude may be found among later analysts. Jung, in accordance with his past (his father was a minister), did emphasize mankind's religious life, but this was one of the reasons why the mainstream of psychoanalytic thought turned against him.

Oskar Pfister, a minister and lay analyst who was a friend of Freud's, tried to refute Freud's thesis, replying to his paper with one called "The Illusion of a Future" (1928). In more recent years Erich Fromm (1950) has also tried to show that true religion is compatible with psychoanalysis.

None of this has had any influence on mainstream psychoanalysis. No prominent analyst today could be said to believe that religion has any real value for mankind.

The Sexual Revolution

A natural outgrowth of Freud's sexual theories of the 1890s was the view that the cure was sexual freedom. Freud was too shy of social experiments, however, to state his position clearly. In the 1900s, when his theories changed to the psychosexual scheme, sexual freedom could not be seen as a panacea even in theory. When one of his would-be disciples in Austria prescribed the sexual regimen for a woman in her forties, Freud described it as "wild analysis."[35] Nevertheless, many people were not aware of the changes in Freud's views, and in the 1920s a movement grew up based on the idea that the mere release of instinct would solve all human problems.

Psychoanalysis was only one of a number of forces that led to the radical change in sexual mores after World War I. Above all, the war and its senseless and seemingly interminable slaughter made many wonder why they should continue to maintain what Ferenczi had aptly described as "sphincter morality." Free love was briefly allowed in the Soviet Union as a counterweight to capitalistic oppression, and prostitution was abolished, at least officially. In the Weimar Republic many of the old sexual taboos were demolished; homosexuality was rampant, and many girls would have considered themselves disgraced to be virgins at 16.[36]

Since Freud had abandoned his actual neurosis theory, analysts no longer held that sexual activity per se was therapeutic; they agreed with Freud's position that the repressions had to be lifted before instinctual gratification could become meaningful. An exception was Wilhelm Reich, who published *The Function of the Orgasm* in 1927.[37] Here he repeated Freud's theory of the 1890s: "there is only one thing wrong with neurotic patients: *the lack of full and repeated sexual satisfaction.*"[38] The "cure" thus lies in orgasm, and he described the orgastic process accurately and in the most detail that any analyst had ever devoted to it.

In addition, Reich, as an avowed Communist (he was a member of the German Communist party), tried to combine free sex with Communist politics in a movement he called sexual politics, or "sexpol" for short. He led this movement from 1927 to 1937.[39] In 1931–1932 the movement was under the protection of the German Communist party, which later violently disapproved of Reich and expelled him.[40] Reich (1945) envisaged a complete harmony of nature and culture.[41] Eventually Reich himself gave up his earlier theories, moving on to a meaningless "orgonomy," which has no serious standing among psychoanalysts. However, the lessons of Reich's attempted sexual revolution proved instructive for the future, for they showed that mere bodily release without preliminary psychic change leads nowhere.

The Psychoanalytic Movement: Psychoanalysis as Social Reform

The most important philosophical development of the 1920s was the growing realization, by Freud and others, of the enormous social meaning of psychoanalysis. Freud himself, though he believed it, wrote little about this because he liked to remain the detached scientist, even when he saw the urgent need for social reform. After the war he did express some of his broader ideas, such as training American social workers, or offering universal analysis as a prophylaxis, or tackling the pathology of civilized communities. But on the whole he remained reticent, spending the last five years of his life on what is certainly one of his worst books, *Moses and Monotheism* (1938). The controversy about whether he actually wrote the Bullitt–Freud book about Wilson is part of this ambivalence.[42]

Many of Freud's followers were more optimistic than their master. In the journal *Die Psychoanalytische Bewegung,* in 1929 the first paper was by Thomas Mann, then considered perhaps the world's leading literary figure. Mann, who reportedly had had some analysis earlier, paid effusive tribute to the genius of Freud. He wrote at one point:

I hold that we shall one day recognize in Freud's life-work the cornerstone for the building of a new . . . dwelling of a wiser and freer humanity. . . . Call this, if you choose, a poet's Utopia, but it is after all not unthinkable that the resolution of our great fear and our great hate . . . may one day be due to the healing effect of this very science.[43]

And later W. H. Auden was to say of Freud:

To us he is no more a person
Now but a whole climate of opinion
Under whom we conduct our differing lives. . . .
He quietly surrounds all our habits of growth;
He extends, till the tired in even

The remotest most miserable duchy
Have felt the change in their bones and are cheered.[44]

It is difficult to document a climate of opinion, but there are many pieces of evidence pointing to the growing realization that psychoanalysis could have a significant role in reshaping the future of mankind. A glance through one of the journals of that period, *The International Journal of Psychoanalysis* for 1925, shows how widespread the interest in psychoanalysis had become. W. L. Northridge's book on the unconscious was reviewed.[45] Northridge concluded: "whatever be the fate of the Freudian theory as it now stands, there can be no doubt that Freud's psychology has enabled us to understand and explain life to an extent that was not previously possible."[46] Bleuler's revised *Textbook,* in which he paid careful attention to Freudian theory, was also mentioned.[47] J. F. Meagher wrote a book seriously discussing masturbation.[48] W. C. Rivers's book on Walt Whitman was discussed; the reviewer stated that a decade previously, in 1913, Rivers had had to work hard to make a case for Whitman's homosexuality; nowadays it caused scarcely a ripple.[49] William Brown, a professor at Oxford, edited a book on *Psychology and the Sciences,* in which a number of Oxford scholars paid careful attention to psychoanalytic theory.[50] H. Goitein was the first to publish a book attempting a psychoanalytic view of the law.[51] J. R. Beltran, an Argentine scholar, used psychoanalysis to understand a murderer.[52] The contrast with nonanalytic scholars was still sharp; thus McDougall, hailed by his publishers as the most distinguished psychologist of that day, wrote a book in which he warned that the blood of the old American stock in the United States would be intermingled with the blood of other races with "dire consequences."[53] The manner in which the intellectual climate of the world has been changed by psychoanalysis is well brought out in these various citations.

The Reaction of the 1930s

The worldwide Depression in 1929, Hitler's rise to power in Germany, Stalin's in Russia, the Japanese incursion into Manchuria, the obvious uselessness of the League of Nations, all combined to create a pessimistic reaction to the optimism of the 1920s, which was reflected in the psychoanalytic movement as well. As the decade wore on, the promise held out by psychoanalysis seemed to fade. The journal *Die Psychoanalytische Bewegung* had to cease publication. Freud, along with many other leading analysts, fled for their lives. Some did not succeed and died in the Holocaust.

In this atmosphere the lively debate about values and philosophy took a different turn. In *Civilization and Its Discontents* (1930) and *Why War?* (1932) Freud expressed his fear that the world would be destroyed by its hostilities. Nonetheless, he preferred to remain aloof. He retreated from his previous hopes, and insisted once more that psychoanalysis had no special *Weltanschauung;* it was part of science. Most analysts, many still fearful for their lives, tended to agree with him. Jung was scorned; Reich was expelled. Analysts preferred to stick to their analysis. Even Franz Alexander, one of the most liberal men of the time, could write in 1938: "psychoanalysis has assumed a more scientific character, and the emphasis on its contributions to a *Weltanschauung* has retreated correspondingly into the background."[54]

After World War II: The Battle with Other Philosophies

After the hiatus of the war, psychoanalysis emerged in a much stronger position. Within 10 years, psychoanalysts in the United States had captured many positions of importance, and all the mental health professions were dominated by psychoanalytic thinking. Soon the question of values and philosophy was reopened all over again.

Psychoanalysis is a long and costly process; its practitioners are few and far between; its tenets are not easy to grasp. Under these circumstances it was only natural that many alternative philosophies would appear on the scene, challenging both the psychoanalytic credo and the psychoanalytic method.

One major difference between the philosophies that emerged after World War II and the situation after World War I soon became apparent. Psychoanalysis was now so appealing and so strong that every new philosophy and every alternative had to begin with an attack against it.

This "attack" literature usually took the following approach. Freudian psychoanalysis, it was argued, has dehumanized and further isolated the person by viewing him as a catalogue of drives and ego functions. Freud made a basic mistake in regarding the ego as passive and not the active principle it really is. Psychoanalysis lacks scientific methodology and has no scientific standing. It fragments the individual.

Existentialism held that the very nature of the analytic process presents the patient as the sum of his parts. For a long time psychoanalysis was accused of avoiding the self and the psychology of the self. Furthermore, its results were said to be poor and easily surpassed by any one of a dozen other therapies.

Existentialism

Perhaps the most attractive alternative to psychoanalysis was existentialism. Rollo May, its leading American exponent, defined existentialism as "the endeavor to understand man by cutting below the cleavage between subject and object that has bedeviled Western thought and science since shortly after the Renaissance."[55] This approach is contrasted with Freud and psychoanalysis, which, he said, could not understand man in personal relations with fellow men and man in relation to himself. May goes on to make the extraordinary statement that "it does not detract, of course, from the genius of Freud to point out that probably almost all of the specific ideas which later appeared in psychoanalysis could be found in Nietzsche in greater breadth and in Kierkegaard in greater depth."[56]

Basing his ideas on this peculiar notion of history, May then goes on to list six contributions of existential psychotherapy: concern with being; anxiety and guilt as being ontological; being-in-the-world; the three modes of the world (biological, fellow-men, self); consideration of time and history; and transcendence of the immediate situation.

It is noteworthy that May, like other existentialists, scraps the entire understanding of mankind that had been so carefully pieced together by Freud and the psychoanalysts. The attempt is made to replace it by a philosophy. This philosophy, which had many European adherents after World War II, probably because of the war's devastation, has been called the philosophy of despair. Coltrera (1962) described it as follows:

Existentialism, in its chosen role as chorus to our age chants a sad litany: we are born into this world alone, live in loneliness, and go out of the world alone. Death is sure and the nothingness beyond it arouses dread. We have

known original sin, and guilt is the condition of our existence. We are separated, each from the other, by the tradition and ways of our present culture
and times. Existentialism tells us that these are the conditions of existence,
and to be aware of existence is to know them.[57]

Franz Alexander attended the fourth International Congress of
Psychiatry in Barcelona in 1958, at which the main topic was the impact of existential philosophy on psychotherapy. Perhaps because of
his battle with the more orthodox Freudian analysts at that time, he
was a little more charitable to the existential position than he would
have been at some other point in his life. He focused on the central
value of existentialism as returning to the traditional question of philosophy: What is the ultimate meaning of human existence? It puts
emphasis not on the how, but on the why, from where, for what, and
where to. He pointed out that this concern coincides with "some of
the most important newer results of psychoanalytic research,"[58] thus
ignoring even material that he had written in earlier years. His main
criticism of existentialism is that it often attempts to describe psychological realities in terms of philosophical generalities. He also
noted the role of charismatic figures like Viktor Frankl who went in
for prophetic preaching, reminiscent of Biblical Jeremiads. Frankl's
speech he calls "a veritable sermon, a blend of philosophical, psychological and crypto-religious orientations."[59]

Like other philosophies, existentialism cannot be properly understood without reference to the superego and other psychoanalytic
theory. Its message is less important than the context in which it is
offered: that of the powerful figure who exhorts, directs, and controls
his or her children. Unlike Freudian analysis, it established a dependent relationship that gratifies and cannot be broken because it is
never brought to analysis. By ignoring the transference, it preserves
the childhood constellation. This also explains why the philosophy of
existentialism, which is historically false (as in May), psychologically misperceived (anxiety and guilt, for example, derive from
childhood experience more than from ontology), and philosophically
depressed does not lend itself to rational discussion.

The Eastern Religions

Wartime contacts with the Far East, and the new ease of travel and
communication, led to the attempt on the part of some thinkers to
combine psychoanalysis and eastern religion. Most popular was Zen

Buddhism. The Zen master Suzuki led a seminar with Erich Fromm on the relationship between psychoanalysis and Zen in 1957; a book was published about the meeting (Suzuki, Fromm, and De Martino, 1960).

It is difficult to get a clear picture of Zen Buddhism from the Zen writings. The emphasis is on incomprehensibility, as in the koans (such as, What is the sound of one hand clapping?). Clearly Zen Buddhists also are attacking what they consider the excessive rationality of Western man. Suzuki, for example, emphasizes that Asians like to work and are apparently satisfied with an "undeveloped" state of civilization. This seems to be the same glorification of the East as the Westerner practices with the West, and is not borne out by more careful observation.

As Suzuki describes it, Zen Buddhism is a kind of mystical approach to life which ends in satori, or oneness with the world. The cardinal virtues of the Zen-man are six: charity, precepts, humility, energy, meditation, and wisdom.

It has been argued that Eastern thought has developed the resources of the inner man, as Western thought has developed the resources of scientific man. This search for the inner world has been the beacon light guiding many young people. The same appeal has been exercised by drugs, which also reached their height of popularity in the 1960s, with Timothy Leary's "Turn on, tune in, drop out." On careful observation, cults such as Leary's seem to be similar to religious systems in many parts of the world. The psychoanalytic critique remains the same: belonging to a cult represents a superego projection; what is essential is merely that there should be a strong figure and some guiding philosophy that creates a new family for the insecure individual. Furthermore, much of their creed serves as an escape from deep psychological problems, as do all religions. Thus Alexander (1931) described some of the Buddhist training as "artificial catatonia."

Sex Therapy

Following the Masters–Johnson work in the 1960s, the old dream of sexual emancipation appeared in a new guise: that of sex therapy. This time, however, no grandiose claims were made for orgasm, as Reich had done in an earlier epoch—just that it was good to have sexual enjoyment.

As usual, the advocacy of sex therapy began with an attack on psychoanalysis, which allegedly fails to be of any value, even though psychoanalysis began as a form of sex therapy and has a vast body of theory and practice with which it approaches sexual problems. Masters and Johnson explicitly downgraded psychoanalysis, claiming that their system was both much simpler and much more effective. They have attempted to set up a new kind of therapist, a sex therapist for specific sexual problems.

Helen Kaplan (1974) who is a trained analyst (unlike Masters and Johnson) has tried to combine active treatment of sexual dysfunctions with psychoanalysis. Both sides have criticized her for the attempt, each for different reasons. The major analytic criticism of behavioral sex therapy is that it fails to touch the deeper emotional problems connected with the sexual difficulties.

Other Philosophies

Any number of other philosophies, as well as therapeutic techniques, can be found on the contemporary scene; in fact, the profusion of new approaches is characteristic of the postwar world. As mentioned, most begin with a vigorous attack on psychoanalysis, then a glorification of the particular method advocated, with scant regard for either psychological theory or a careful sifting of results. While enormously popular, none of these approaches has had any meaningful influence on either psychoanalytic theory or psychoanalytic therapy. To the analyst they seem to function mainly as forms of resistance (Fine, 1973).

Values Inherent in Psychoanalysis, and the Psychoanalytic Philosophy

Inasmuch as a variety of philosophies have been rejected by psychoanalysts as solutions to life's problems, the question still remains: Is there any philosophy or set of values intrinsic to psychoanalysis? A number of answers have been given.

To begin with, a distinction must be drawn between the attitude an analyst takes toward his patient, and his set of values in his private life. On the question of whether the analyst should analyze or indoctrinate his patient, all analysts would agree that the business of the analyst is first and foremost to analyze. Whatever moral condemnation he may experience for the patient's behavior, it is out of place to inject this into the therapeutic situation. There his job is to help the patient understand himself and get better on his own terms.

A second point on which there would be complete agreement is that the adoption of any set of values must be preceded by a thorough-going superego analysis; in Freud's earlier language (with Putnam), the repressions must be lifted. Otherwise any solution, including analysis itself, would merely be a reshuffling of superego commands and prohibitions. On this score, analysis is critical of all philosophical approaches extant.

However, two points still remain: Are there values intrinsic to psychoanalysis and, if so, what are they? Many analysts have addressed themselves to these questions.

If any philosophy is inherent in the early Freudian position, it could be defined as growth toward maturity, or genitality, the ideal of that day. Since analysis dealt only with severely disturbed individuals at that time (before World War I), greater precision was not necessary. As late as 1945 Fenichel could simply sidestep the problem: "The difficulties of exactly defining 'normality' and 'health' from a psychoanalytic point of view have frequently been discussed. . . . Fortunately practice requires less exactness."[60]

Both Adler and Jung had different underlying philosophical outlooks. Adler's was based on social interest; his book *What Life Should Mean to You* (1931) is still a good popularization of psychoanalytic principles. Adler's conception of social interest centered on three general social ties. He wrote in 1933:

At this point Individual Psychology comes into contact with sociology. For a long time now I have been convinced that all the questions of life can be subordinated to the three major problems—the problems of communal life, of work, and of love. These three arise from the inseparable bond that of necessity links men together for association, for the provision of livelihood, and for the care of offspring.

The three ties in which human beings are bound set the three problems of life, but none of these problems can be solved separately. Each of them demands a successful approach to the other two.[61]

For Jung, on the other hand, social interest was secondary. What was essential for him was the *process of individuation,* in which the individual seeks personal wholeness. It is not surprising that with such a goal he felt sympathetic to the eastern religions. Jung expressed this goal of individuation in various ways. In the Tavistock lectures of 1935 (published in 1968), he called it the objectivation of impersonal images:

Its goal is to detach consciousness from the object so that the individual no longer places the guarantee of his happiness, or of his life even, in factors outside himself, but comes to realize that everything depends on whether he holds the treasure or not. . . . To reach such a condition of detachment is the aim of Eastern practices, and it is also the aim of the teachings of the Church. . . . All that we can say rationally about this condition of detachment is to define it as a sort of centre within the psyche of the individual, but not within the ego.[62]

Thus in a sense genital primacy (Freud), social interest (Adler), and inner self-sufficiency (Jung) were the first three philosophical goals posited by psychoanalysis. However, Freud's was posited on previous analysis, while neither Adler's nor Jung's made that presupposition. The absence of analysis as a prelude to philosophy makes a vital difference.

The Reaction of Philosophers

With these questions, psychoanalysis was already treading on the traditional province of philosophy: What is the *summum bonum,* or how shall man find happiness? The answers offered were not especially novel, but their implementation was. Since the answers as such were not new, philosophers tended to ignore the entire psychoanalytic approach. Wollheim (1974) comments that most twentieth-century philosophers have written as if psychoanalysis never existed. An exception is V. J. McGill; in *The Idea of Happiness* (1967), after reviewing the historical past, he frankly states that the problem of happiness has now shifted from philosophy to psychotherapy: "The fact that this conception [of happiness] is logically connected with medical therapy or with objective tests and controlled studies gives it a significance lacking in earlier theories."[63]

In essence McGill is saying that the central problem of philosophy, the nature of happiness, has now been taken over by psychoanalysis. Freud's hesitation in making this explicit derived primarily from his realization that analysis was fundamental, and that *any* philosophical position would be seized upon for the purpose of resistance. The newer concepts of the superego and acting-out make *all* philosophizing without previous analysis dubious.

The Analytic Debate about Moral Values

The debate about whether there are moral values attached to analysis has continued. Many have tried to avoid it, but, as Ishak Ramzy comments, "the self-imposed moratorium against the study of values in psychoanalysis has been with difficulty enforced in practice and theory." [64] The major postwar difference has been that the newer concepts of the superego and acting-out have become indispensable to any discussion of values and philosophy.

Hartmann: Analytic Therapy as Technology

In 1960 Heinz Hartmann devoted the Freud Memorial Lectures to the topic of psychoanalysis and moral values. Although at an earlier, more optimistic period, in 1933, he had been somewhat critical of Freud's attitude of the detached scientist, now he reaffirmed his full agreement with Freud. "Analytic therapy is a kind of technology," he argued. As such its only values must be health values. Science, he claimed, cannot decide on what goals one "ought" to strive for.[65]

Hartmann distinguished three separate aspects of moral values in analysis, which must be kept separate: the genesis and meaning of the patient's imperatives and ideals (his superego); the confrontation of his attitudes with the codes of his family and more generally of the culture in which he lives; and the personal moral valuations of the analyst with respect to the material presented in analysis. Naturally, he held, as all do, that the personal values of the analyst should be subordinated to the health values.[66]

In response to the major question of whether there are moral values inherent in psychoanalysis, Hartmann fell back on Freud's position, sidestepping the intervening arguments: "That there is nothing that could, strictly speaking, be called an 'analytic *Weltanschauung*' does not imply that the analysis could or should have no *Weltanschauung* of his own, nor does it, of course, mean that the analyst will underrate or depreciate the directive significance of '*Weltanschauung*' in the individual or in society." [67]

Social Class and Psychoanalysis

Apart from the theoretical arguments among psychoanalysts, some empirical data about the class origins of analysts and their patients, which began to appear in the 1950s, cast considerable doubt on the image of the analyst as a completely detached scientist. Studies, particularly at Yale (Hollingshead and Redlich, 1958; MacIver and Redlich, 1959; Myers and Bean, 1968; Myers and Roberts, 1959), showed unequivocally that psychoanalytic practice was intimately tied up with the class structure. Only patients of the upper classes received psychoanalytic treatment; no lower-class patient in the original study was in psychoanalysis.

Even more important for the present discussion was the study by MacIver and Redlich (1959) describing a deep split in the ranks of the American psychiatric profession between a group designated as analytic and psychological, or the A-P group, and a group whose orientation is directive and organic, or the D-O group. Eclectics, they found, are rare birds. Both groups belong socially to the upper two classes. The A-P group is more mobile, less tradition bound, admits more ethnic variation, and is further removed from the core of the medical profession.[68] Professionally, the two groups are strikingly different. The D-O group is closer to other physicians, favors organic diagnoses, uses directive, suggestive psychotherapy (as contrasted with nondirective, analytic therapy). Redlich concludes that "social and economic values determine to a significant degree what type of treatment a patient will receive."[69]

Other studies have shown that analysts are largely upward-mobile middle-class individuals who limit their activities to large urban centers. Zinberg (1972) reported that in 1968 over 90 percent of the members of the American Psychoanalytic Association lived within 30 miles of a large urban center; in some 30 states there were then only 13 members practicing. Henry and his colleagues (1971), in a study of 4,000 psychotherapists throughout the country, found that persons from whatever professional specialty who become psychotherapists are highly similar in social and cultural background, and that with increasing time they overcome the manifest goals of their particular training system and become more and more like their colleague psychotherapists in other training systems. Thus he argued that a "fifth profession" has been created, that of the psychotherapist, who may come from medicine, psychology, social work, or psychoanalysis.

Kadushin (1969), in a study of groups of patients, divided them broadly into three groups—the psychiatric, the family-oriented, and the psychoanalytic; the latter go to analysis because of inner dissatisfactions.

Thus there is a good body of empirical evidence that values are inherent in psychoanalysis. The question is: What are they and how should they be formulated?

Psychoanalysis as Integrative Living

Most analysts who have reflected on the subject have seen the core of the psychoanalytic philosophy in two separate directions: a negative one of overcoming neurotic disabilities, and a positive one of living life in a fuller, more integrated manner. Jones (1931) saw fearlessness as the essence of normality, and Chisholm (1946) pleaded for living free from guilt. In 1945 an American analyst, J. J. Michaels, emphasized the need for integration:

In the theory of psychoanalysis, the conception of integration probably finds its most complex expression and elaboration. Although this conception is not expressly stated, it is implicit and inherent in the system as a whole and in its component parts. It seems as if Freud took for granted the conception of integration and built upon it extensively.[70]

In this passage Michaels may be referring to Freud's well-known comment that "what is moral is self-evident." [71] It can be said that this morality is in essential agreement with the democratic humanistic tradition of Western thought that can be traced as far back as the Greeks (see chapter 2).

Some theoreticians have tried to spell out the solution in more detail, others have contented themselves with clarifying the direction. Brierley (1951) in one of the earlier publications, wrote:

Existentialists maintain that life is an experience to be lived, and not a problem for solution. The findings of psychoanalysis support the conception that life is simply for living, but they also show that experience raises a host of problems whose solution is likely to be found only through the fuller use of intelligence and the development of a more trustworthy subjective and objective reality-sense.[72]

Her solution is that after the superego has been sufficiently dissolved, the play of reason on human problems will show the way. Fromm (1947) took a similar position, calling his system "naturalistic ethics." Fine (1971) tried to describe the analytic ideal, starting from Freud's dictum that the normal person is the one who can love and work. Esman (1977), insisting that psychoanalysis has a value system of its own, sees its essentials as the primacy of reason, the acceptance of delayed gratification in the service of future goals, the idea of stable, monogamous, heterosexual bonds, and a commitment to a lifelong career.

Thus a considerable body of opinion among analysts holds that beyond the negative rejection of traditional philosophies, religions, and various forms of acting-out, there is a positive philosophy of living that lies at the heart of psychoanalytic theory and therapy (Fine, 1977).

Chapter Seventeen

The Psychoanalytic Approach to Culture

The clarification of the role of culture in the formation of personality is one of the most important psychoanalytic developments since Freud. It has helped to consolidate ego psychology, thrown fresh light on the problem of instincts, underscored the usefulness of the superego concept, and provided a vantage point from which contemporary cultures can be evaluated. The battles involved in it should not obscure the solid achievement that it represents.

Early Freud: Culture as Repression

With Wilhelm Wundt, psychology began to take an interest in "cultural products." His book on *The Psychology of Peoples* was published in 1900.[1] Like the other psychologists of his day, however, Wundt lacked a dynamic point of view, and his book has had no lasting influence.

Freud's first approach to the question was a rather common-sense one: culture requires instinctual repression. He had already expressed such a view in his preanalytic days. For instance, in a letter written to his fiancée from Paris in 1886 he had said: "The mob give vent to their impulses and we deprive ourselves."[2] Later he came to view this as an inevitable necessity. In an essay on love in 1912 he had written: "we may perhaps be forced to become reconciled to the idea that it is quite impossible to adjust the claims of the sexual instinct to the demands of civilization; that in consequence of its cultural development renunciation and suffering, as well as the danger of extinction in the remotest future, cannot be avoided by the human race."[3]

Totem and Taboo: The Cornerstone of Anthropology

Although Freud's pessimistic views about culture have been widely quoted, from a scientific viewpoint they are much less important than his major work *Totem and Taboo* (1912–1913). Here for the first time he offered, on the basis of the best anthropological fieldwork available at that time, a dynamic picture of the human being that led to and solidified the main analytic thesis of the essential psychic unity of all mankind. It is worth looking at this book in more detail.

The work is divided into four parts or essays. The first, on "The Horror of Incest," demonstrates that incest surprisingly is a stronger taboo among primitive people than among the more civilized, and that this incest taboo extends much further among primitives. It may lead to a system of exogamy, in which a considerable percentage (sometimes as high as 85 percent) of the women in the tribe are out of bounds to the men, who thus are forced to seek their mates in other groups.

The second essay is on "Taboo and Emotional Ambivalence." Here he continued the arguments of his 1907 paper on obsessive acts and religious practices. He was able to point to far-reaching similarities between taboo and obsessional neurosis; in fact, the illness of the modern obsessional neurotic could just as well be called "taboo sickness."

The third essay is on "Animism, Magic and Omnipotence of Thoughts." Here Freud accepted the account which was standard in his day (though now superseded) of the evolution of human views of the universe: first an animistic phase, second a religious, and finally a scientific phase. These three phases he could explain in terms of the vicissitudes of the omnipotence of thoughts.

The fourth essay is "The Return of Totemism in Childhood." This is the historical section containing the famous primal-horde theory, which has usually been the reason for anthropological attacks on the whole book, although it is only one small element in the total thesis (and other analysts have since abandoned it). According to this theory, the sons killed the father, and this murder led to setting up a totem. In this way the murder of the father of the primal horde led to the two main taboos of totemic religions—totemism and exogamy. A corollary of this view is the universality of the Oedipus complex.

However, Freud did not hypothesize that the universality of the Oedipus complex is the only factor in the development of culture; he saw it as one of many and insisted that psychoanalytic explanations must be combined with others (e.g., economic, historical, and sociological) to offer a complete picture.

The major contribution of this revolutionary book was to show that the dynamic picture derived from the study of Westerners was applicable to all cultures. Thus anthropology becomes simply another aspect of psychology (as Wundt had also insisted). The objections of his critics were not so much to this thesis as to Freudian psychology.

The Expansion of the Anthropological Perspective

When the war ended in 1918, psychoanalysis experienced what Malinowski (1927) called "a truly meteoric rise in popular favor." [4] Anthropologists, inspired by Boas to go out into the field and see for themselves, found that the theories of psychoanalysis were among the most fruitful at their disposal. Malinowski himself, perhaps the best known of the early fieldworkers, paid ample tribute to the stimulation derived from Freudian theory and to the confirmation of various Freudian ideas by field research. In 1923 he wrote:

By my analysis, I have established that Freud's theories not only roughly correspond to human psychology, but that they follow closely the modification in human nature brought about by various constitutions of society. In other words, I have established a deep correlation between the type of society and the nuclear complex found there. While there is a notable confirmation of the main tenet of Freudian psychology, it might compel us to modify certain of its details, or rather to make some of the formulae more elastic.[5]

In spite of his praise of Freud and psychoanalysis, and tributes to their stimulation and value, Malinowski came to be widely quoted as having "disproved" the Oedipus complex because for the Trobriand Islanders, among whom he had done his fieldwork, the uncle played the role of the father in our culture. This by no means disproves the Oedipus complex. Furthermore, Roheim (1950) was later able to show, on the basis of a psychodynamic analysis of material similar to Malinowski's, that a more careful search for unconscious determinants among the Trobrianders revealed classical Oedipal conflicts.

Anthropologists collected much other relevant material as well. Since Freud had placed so much stress on dreams, Rivers (1923) reviewed the available material and took issue with Freud on some relatively minor points.[6] It soon became apparent that dreams are a universal human experience and that they have pretty much the same meaning in other cultures that they have in ours (Fromm, 1951; Jones, 1924).

Somewhat later, the two new projective devices of the psychologist, the Rorschach and the TAT, became routine aids for every fieldworker. Considerable data accumulated pointing to cross-cultural validation.

A number of anthropologists also undertook personal analyses. Weston Labarre (1961) reported on a questionnaire survey he had done of all the Fellows of the American Anthropological Association (exact date of the questionnaire is not given). Of 635 persons queried, 331 replied within a month. Of these respondents, 37 (11 percent) stated that they had experience of personal psychoanalysis, ranging from 2 months to 84 months or more, with a median of somewhat over 20 months. Labarre considered this "remarkable." Some, like Kroeber, even became analysts for a while.[7]

The Jones–Malinowski Controversy

In his investigation of the Trobrianders, Malinowski had discovered that they were ignorant of the role of the father in procreation. He then proposed to substitute for the Freudian Oedipus complex what he called a "nuclear family complex" traced to the organization of the matrilineal family. Jones argued in rebuttal that the "ignorance" was really a form of denial, or a defense mechanism which permitted them to escape from the guilt of infantile sexuality, while the deflection onto the maternal uncle of the less amiable qualities of the father image protected father and son from mutual hostility.

Jones's thesis led squarely to the demand that anthropologists should take unconscious forces into account in their attempt to understand other peoples. Jones himself published a number of essays on anthropological topics in which unconscious motives were given full recognition. According to Fortes (1977), it was Jones's advocacy that really brought home to anthropologists the revolutionary importance of psychoanalysis.

Pioneering Syntheses: Roheim and Kardiner

Once it had started, analytically oriented fieldwork grew enormously. Many different cultures were studied, some superificially, some in depth. To make sense of this material, two major syntheses were offered, one by Roheim and the more classical Freudians, the other by Kardiner and the neo-Freudians.

Roheim's expedition to Central Australia in 1928, and his paper on his findings in 1932, have already been mentioned. Although he recognized many differences among cultures, Roheim's concern was to ferret out what is essential to mankind. His final thoughts on the subject were summed up in *Psychoanalysis and Anthropology* (1950). Roheim saw the biological basis of the human psyche in the prolonged period of dependency, longer than for any other species, and the precocious growth of the brain during development. He agreed with Freud's observation that throughout childhood development, the ego is not strong enough for the id, so that special controls are necessary.

From this observation of very prolonged dependency he enumerated six important aspects of human beings: the anti-sex attitude; the search for new objects; regression, ambivalence; the immortality of fathers; and conservatism. By the latter he means that education involves the tendency on the part of adults to perpetuate their own personalities in their descendants.

Kardiner (1939), on the other hand, has argued that while there are certain underlying biological givens in human nature, what is done with them depends on the culture in which the individual is brought up. Hence what psychoanalysis provides is essentially the tools with which to analyze any culture.

As discussed in chapter 5, the battle between these two points of view erupted into a political battle as well. At present, some amalgamation of the two views seems to be taking place. This is understandable, since it is more a question of emphasis than of either–or.

Research indicates, for example, that the Oedipus complex is universal, but its form and intensity vary with the culture (Fortes, 1977).

Total Cultural Analysis

Apart from the elucidation of many problems in both psychology and anthropology, work in the analysis of society has permitted a newer and deeper approach to the total understanding of any culture. Since Ruth Benedict's *Patterns of Culture* (1934), the notion of some one or several character traits as distinctive for a given culture had captured both the professional and the popular imagination. It remained, however, for psychoanalysis to tie these traits to the total life circumstances of the culture. Some representative studies along these lines from differing periods in analytic history can be discussed.

Roheim: The Psychology of the Central Australian Cultural Area (1932)

Roheim's analysis of Central Australia, where he had done his fieldwork (1932), epitomizes the psychoanalytic point of view after World War I. His main points were:

1. THE ID. There is compulsive repetition, the most primitive form of life. With regard to the various libidinal zones, the oral is central. There is oral optimism and oral aggression. An extraordinary peculiarity of the tribe is that even though the mothers never wean the child, and are always giving, they kill every second child and eat it. Thus one child is completely gratified, while its successor is killed and eaten. Toilet training is minimal, and there is no concern with ritual or punctuality or cleanliness. At the Oedipal level, when the child is faced by the rivalry of the father, hate and dread of this rival arise.

Roheim felt that there was no latency period among these people, no period in which they do not make more or less successful attempts at coitus. The difference lies in the ego reaction to the parental castration threat or to the refusal which is interpreted as a castration threat.

In terms of sexuality their sleeping customs are peculiar. The mother lies on her baby son like the male on the female. This infantile trauma becomes repressed and gives rise to the myth of the ''alknarintja'' woman, the unattained goal of the boy's love, the phallic mother of mythology.

3. THE EGO. A major defense is displacement upward. Repression is only skin deep. Ceremonial avoidance is observed. There is an immediate transition of direct genital libido from the parents to their child, to all children of the same age. Projection is very frequent. To his surprise, Roheim discovered that primitive people are fully adapted to their own environment, and no progress in this respect has been made by civilization.

There is much narcissism. Every native is both a real person and a hidden person.

3. THE SUPEREGO. The superego is vindictive and aggressive, but hardly exists before puberty. Men show a marked or even exaggerated maleness, manifested in using violence against women and in developing an exclusively male society.

Roheim concludes: ''With a superego based mainly on deflected phallic strivings, with a phallic and aggressive ego, and a minimum of reaction-formations in character development, the Aranda is a happy man.''[8]

Kardiner and Du Bois: The People of Alor (1945)

In 1944 Cora du Bois, a student of Kardiner's, published her work on the people of Alor, a small island in what is now Indonesia, about 600 miles east of Java. At the time du Bois studied the group, they were still ruled by the Dutch. The raw material was presented in a seminar to Kardiner, who integrated it in accordance with his schema of the basic personality (Kardiner, 1945) (see chapter 12). A novel feature of this work was the accumulation of Rorschach test data, which were then analyzed ''blind'' and independently by Emil Oberholzer.

Kardiner sums up the Alorese personality as follows: Although details may be wrong, the main outline is clear. The combination of influences from birth to adulthood must create a deeply insecure and isolated individual. The personality gets off to a bad start; the Alorese is orally frustrated. More tensions are created than discharge avenues are available; there is a vast predominance of painful tension, which begins so early in life that it prevents the formation of effective action systems. This can be seen especially in the aggression patterns, in which the affect predominates; the capacity to act effectively is very low, however. The individual therefore is in constant dread that this aggression may break its confines. Hence the defenses against anything that will relax this vigilance—the desistance from intoxicants, fear of comatose conditions, etc. Although their war patterns are influenced by external pressures, they show violent, explosive, and indiscriminate aggression, together with the desire to have done with the aggression altogether and to accept token forms of placation. Another consequence of maternal neglect germane to the disorganized aggression patterns is the strangulation of all action systems that pertain to interest in and mastery of the outside world. Hence they cannot construct, systematize, plan, or forestall; have little mechanical ability or interest; fail in aesthetic development; give up enterprise easily; and allow themselves to die without a fight.

This affect strangulation must prevent tender and cooperative relations with others. In their place are deep predatory and exploitive wishes, with all the mutual anxiety thus created, because the predatory trend must be repressed or expressed through financial channels. This is probably why finance becomes the chief emotional vehicle.

In their protective systems (in religion and folklore), we find the remnants of the childhood constellations, with special emphasis on parental hatreds and revenge. The same emotional constellations dominate the relations between the sexes—hence the generally discordant marriages.

The basic personality in Alor is anxious, suspicious, mistrustful, lacking in confidence, with no interest in the outside world. There is no capacity to idealize a parental image or deity. The personality is devoid of enterprise and is filled with repressed hatred and free-floating aggression over which constant vigilance must be exercised. The personality is devoid of high aspirations and has no basis for the internalization of discipline. Individuals so constituted must spend most of their energy protecting themselves against each other's hostility. Cooperation must be at a low level, and a tenuous cohesion can be achieved only by dominance-submission attitudes, not by affection and mutual trust.

Fromm and Maccoby: A Psychoeconomic Study
of a Mexican Village (1970)

In 1957 Erich Fromm, then head of an analytic society in Mexico, initiated a large-scale, intensive study of a small Mexican village, 50 miles south of Mexico City. The study, which used a special questionnaire, projective tests, and other data, continued for more than 10 years. The report was published in 1970. Its most original features are that it attempted a total census of the village's adults and that it tried to link psychological with socioeconomic factors.

Some 95 percent of the adult population (200 men and 206 women) could be included. Traits were scored by frequency and by a factor analysis. Six main traits emerged.

ADULTHOOD VERSUS ADOLESCENCE. The main aspects of adulthood were being married, having children, conditional love, and a tendency toward authoritarianism.

PRODUCTIVENESS VERSUS UNPRODUCTIVENESS. The characteristics of productiveness were love, creativeness, enterprise-energy, traditional authority, and democratic modes of sociopolitical relatedness.

EXPLOITIVENESS VERSUS NONEXPLOITIVENESS. The main traits here were authoritarianism and extreme narcissism.

HOARDING VERSUS RECEPTIVE MODES OF ASSIMILATION. Hoarding is the main finding.

SEX ROLE (MASCULINITY VERSUS FEMININITY). For men, the main values are narcissism and traditionalism. For women, the main values include masochism, submissiveness, and love.

MOTHER-CENTERED VERSUS FATHER-CENTERED ORIENTATIONS. The main origin for the mother-centered orientation is fixation on the mother (the dominant Mexican attitude), and for father-centered, fixation on the father.

Out of these factors three main character types were distilled: the nonproductive-receptive character (the most frequent); the productive-hoarding; the exploitive character. Correlations between character and socioeconomic variables were then computed. These correlations show that the hoarding orientation has been the one best adapted to the economic demands of peasant farming in the village. Furthermore, because his character and his work fit each other, the hoarding peasant is likely to be more productive and energetic, indeed more confident and hopeful, than the receptive peasant who finds himself increasingly out of tune with the world. There is little or no room for a productive-receptive individual in this culturally impoverished village.

The passive-receptive villagers can find work as peons, but they are likely to be exploited by the new entrepreneurs. Those receptive men fortunate enough to be *ejidatarios* (owners of land) may be able to survive with a certain degree of security by planting cane, but their position is precarious. As cultural traditions change, as status is determined by the values of the modern world, they are unable to defend themselves from the new entrepreneurs, and they are likely to feel inferior because they do not earn more money. Many such receptive individuals feel weak, overly dependent, and inferior. They may try to compensate for these feelings by acting tough, by trying to prove they are "men," but this syndrome is likely to lead to alcoholism.

Boyer et al.: Ecology and Personality in the Athabascans (1976)

The harsh climate experienced by the subarctic Athabascans of Alaska (temperatures of −70° F. are not extraordinary) has produced certain personality characteristics that can be traced as far back as 1700 (Boyer, Boyer, and Hippler, 1976). Three main facets of the personality organization were especially adaptive: there was so much hostility in the people that the culture had to provide still other objects on which to project and against which to discharge aggression; emotional distance, which made it possible to lose loved ones without suffering too much; and suspiciousness, which was necessary for self- and group preservation in the hostile surroundings. The authors report these as preliminary observations that need further elaboration.

Summary Comments

Four types of total cultural analysis have been described: Roheim, with his emphasis on sexuality; du Bois and Kardiner, elaborating on his basic personality concept; Fromm and Maccoby, relating the psychological material to economics; and Boyer, Boyer, and Hippler, who see personality as reactive to the environment. Still other types of analysis could be cited. The psychoanalytic approach to a total cultural analysis has proved to be immensely rewarding, but it is not yet unified and still requires much research.

Perspective on American (and European) Culture

Important though the psychoanalytic dissection of different cultures may be, it is far overshadowed by the insights afforded into our own culture. Most of this literature has been written about the American culture, but what has been said applies to the European as well, so that the observations refer in general to "Western" culture. While careful research has indicated that other cultures, though different, are no happier, the prime concern in the modern industrial countries has been the clarification of the world in which we live.

After the technical exploration of the 1890s, all of Freud's theories implied some criticism of the existing social order—if dreams are so important, the inability to relate them impoverishes life; if sexuality and genital primacy are crucial, most men and women are found to be sexual cripples; religion is a universal obsessional neurosis. The list could be extended indefinitely. Yet, for personal reasons, Freud was reluctant to appear as a social critic. He preferred to speak in terms of "neurosis" and "psychopathology." Only toward the end of his life did he openly recognize that he had "society as his patient," as Lawrence Frank said in a famous essay.[9]

In one chapter in *The New Introductory Lectures* in 1932, to let himself go "as a relief from the dry tone of these lectures,"[10] he speculated on the more positive implications of the psychoanalytic philosophy:

The recognition that most of our children pass through a neurotic phase in the course of their development carries with it the germ of a hygienic challenge. The question may be raised whether it would not be expedient to come to a child's help with an analysis even if he shows no signs of a disturbance. . . . Prophylaxis like this against neurotic illness, which would probably be very effective, also presupposes a quite other constitution of society.[11]

Apart from analysis, his prime hope was placed in reason. Later in the same passage he wrote:

Intellect—or let us call it by the name that is familiar to us, reason—is among the powers which we may most expect to exercise a unifying influence on men—on men who are held together with such difficulty and whom it is scarcely possible to rule. . . . Our best hope for the future is that intellect—the scientific spirit, reason—may in process of time establish a dictatorship in the life of man. . . . The common compulsion exercised by such a dominance of reason will prove to be the strongest uniting bond among men and lead the way to further unions. Whatever, like religion's prohibition against thought, opposes such a development, is a danger for the future of mankind.[12]

Thus, as in the earlier period when sexual frustration was seen as the core of human misery, Freud recognized the social disturbance, but for personal reasons he preferred to sit on the sidelines. Many of his followers, however, were eager to play a more aggressive role.

General Critiques of Western Society

Once the ideal and the philosophy of psychoanalysis had been clarified, as it had been (however imperfectly) by Freud, it was only natural to apply this conceptual framework to the culture in which the analysts found themselves. For the first time, scientists had a valid tool or set of tools with which they could appraise their fellow men. The first approach was the technical one to which they were accustomed, so studies began to appear about the widespread incidence of "neurosis."

Two large-scale studies, by Rennie and his co-workers in New York (1962) and Leighton and his group in Canada (1963), have already been discussed. While subsequent studies have offered different percentages, by and large the results pointed to the frequency of emotional disturbances of all kinds, in all classes, in virtually all cultures investigated. These findings, as well as others, led to such an enormous growth in the mental health professions that the initiative was taken out of the hands of the pure psychoanalysts. Psychiatrists, psychologists, social workers, social scientists, literary figures, and even some physical scientists entered the picture. As a result, in what follows much material is included from scholars who are not technically psychoanalysts but who have been strongly influenced by analysis, either because of past training or because of general intellectual sympathies. As discussed earlier and in chapter 19, this process of expanding the ideas of psychoanalysis to other fields has been going on for a long time and has steadily increased in importance.

Particular concern was caused by the almost universal finding of an inverse relationship between socioeconomic status and personality disorder: the rich get richer and the poor become neurotic (Dohrenwend and Dohrenwend, 1969). Since the poor are also the ones who crowd the slums in the center of the cities (Faris and Dunham, 1939), are those least able to afford any kind of remedial help and least able to benefit from help even when it is available (Hollingshead and Redlich, 1958), it was only natural that the government should step in to take some remedial action. In typically American fashion, there ensued a kind of crusade for mental health. A Mental Health Study Act was passed in 1955, a National Institute of Mental Health was formed, and a report was issued, *Action for Mental Health* (Joint Commission on Mental Health, 1961). Recommendations were made with regard to manpower, facilities, and costs. Under the impact of this report and supporting data, the Community Mental Health Centers Act of 1963 was passed by Congress and approved by President Kennedy.[13] The original intent was to establish 2,000 centers to serve the country's entire population. For various reasons, the target date for reaching this goal has been postponed by a number of years.

Statistics, of course, tell only half the story. One goal of the community mental health centers was to do away with the state hospitals, now considered antiquated as a result of consistent criticism from psychoanalytically oriented psychiatrists and others. There was a steady decline in the patient population in state hospitals, but the poor quality of the care received outside them produced considerable disillusionment. On June 5, 1977, the *New York Times* editorialized:

The past decade has brought a revolution in the care of the mentally ill and retarded. In 1970, the population of the nation's mental hospitals stood at 430,000; today it is about 300,000 and still declining. . . . Most of the patients who were released . . . are now adrift in cities or relegated to private nursing homes where care is rudimentary. For some, life has become a revolving door; half of those released from long-term facilities in New York City end up back in hospital receiving wards.[14]

Despite all the efforts expended, when another report was issued by the Joint Commission on the Mental Health of Children in 1969, it was entitled *Crisis in Child Mental Health*. Evidently the crash programs had effected little social change.[15]

Confusion of Diagnosis and Social Criticism

Many observers were quick to note that the terms "neurosis" and "psychosis" were used to cover a variety of sins. "Neurosis" was largely intended in the broad sense (see chapter 13), as equivalent to unhappiness, rather than the more technical meaning of a conflict between ego and id. "Psychosis" was somewhat clearer but still suffered from an essential vagueness, except in the extreme cases.

What had happened was that the ideal of mental health derived from analysis had been applied to the society at large. In a sense it represented a philosophical redirection of the entire culture. As early as 1938 the sociologist Kingsley Davis had pointed this out in an article in *Psychiatry:*

Mental Hygiene hides its adherence to ethical preconceptions behind a scientific façade. . . . The unconscious assumption of the dominant ethic (the philosophy of private initiative, personal responsibility and the individual achievement) together with the psychologistic interpretation has served to obscure the social determinants of mental disease, and especially the effects of invidious relationships.[16]

At a more technical level, much criticism has been directed at the indiscriminate use of the diagnosis of "schizophrenia" and "borderline," with their corollaries of pessimism about psychotherapy and increased reliance on drugs. At a panel of the American Psychoanalytic Association in 1972 (Gunderson, 1974), a sharp clash developed between advocates of a deficit (organic) theory of schizophrenia and a conflict (psychogenic) theory. The title of the panel ("The Influence of Theoretical Models of Schizophrenia on Treatment Practice") indicates that the theoretical model chosen has a powerful effect on treatment practice. Searles, emphasizing the psychoanalytic philosophy of life, issued the strongest statement from the side of the psychogenic theoreticians. The report stated:

The estimated 47% of all mental hospital patients who suffer from schizophrenia are there, many of them for decade after decade, not only because they have written off their fellow human beings as not kin to them, but also because their fellow human beings have come to accept this presumed difference as functionally true. Searles warned that if the psychoanalytic movement takes refuge in what he would regard essentially as a phenothiazine-and-genetics flight from this problem, then the long dark night of the soul will have been ushered in, not only for these vast numbers of schizophrenic patients . . . [but also] for the profession of psychoanalysis generally, and for the patients . . . whom psychoanalysts treat.[17]

Specific Cultural and Individual Conflicts

From Freud onward, a number of theoreticians described a variety of conflicts that were characteristic of Western civilization. A new variety of social critic was launched: analysts who evaluated the existing culture in the light of their own ideals, and found it wanting in certain respects. As time went on, this kind of social criticism acquired increased momentum until today it has become commonplace.

Riesman: The Lonely Crowd (Inner- and Other-Directedness)

In 1950 David Riesman, a sociologist from the University of Chicago, leaning heavily on the formulations of Erich Fromm, published *The Lonely Crowd*. In it he characterized the typical American as lonely and other-directed, and he viewed these traits as the main sources of Americans' neurotic conflicts. The book struck a responsive chord and continues to have wide popular appeal.

Riesman actually distinguished three types: tradition-directed, inner-directed, and other-directed. The tradition-directed person feels the impact of his culture as a unit, but it is nevertheless mediated through the specific, small number of individuals with whom he is in daily contact. These place the stress on proper behavior, and the major social sanction is shame. The inner-directed person has early incorporated a psychic gyroscope which is set going by his parents and can receive signals later on from other authorities who resemble his parents. Getting off course may lead to feelings of guilt. Because of these inner controls, the inner-directed person is capable of great stability.

The other-directed person learns to respond to signals from a far wider circle than is constituted by his parents. The family is no longer a closely knit unit to which he belongs but is merely part of a wider social environment to which he early becomes attentive. In a sense he is at home nowhere and everywhere, capable of a rapid if sometimes superficial intimacy with and response to everyone. A prime psychological characteristic of this type is diffuse anxiety.

Authoritarian and Democratic Personality: The Berkeley Studies

Shortly after World War II, the American Jewish Committee, horrified by the Holocaust and the war, sponsored a study of the kinds of personalities that manifest strong ethnic prejudices, especially anti-Semitism. A number of prominent, analytically oriented social psychologists headed the research group, which also derived some of its inspiration from the earlier work of the Frankfurt school of sociology (Max Horkheimer, Theodor Adorno, and others). Their work was summed up in Adorno et al., *The Authoritarian Personality,* published in 1950. Extensive interviews and projective tests were used. Eventually a total of 2,099 subjects were evaluated, drawn largely from the middle class.

The most crucial result, the authors felt, was the demonstration of two distinctly different types of personalities: democratic and authoritarian, whose attitudes portray a good deal of consistency in many different areas. Thus a basically hierarchical, authoritarian, exploitive parent–child relationship is apt to carry over into a power-oriented, exploitively dependent attitude toward one's sexual partner and one's God and may well culminate in a political philosophy and social outlook that have no room for anything but a desperate clinging to what appears to be strong and a disdainful rejection of whatever is relegated to the bottom. The inherent dramatization likewise extends from the parent–child dichotomy to the dichotomous conception of sex roles and moral values, as well as to a dichotomous handling of social relations as manifested especially in stereotypes, and of ingroup–outgroup cleavages.

The other pattern is characterized chiefly by affectionate, basically equalitarian, and permissive interpersonal relationships. This pattern encompasses attitudes within the family and toward the opposite sex, as well as an internalization of religious and social values. Greater flexibility and the potential for more genuine satisfactions appear as results of this basic attitude.

Of immediate concern to therapists was the observation that the authoritarian personality, with its rigidity, stereotypy, and emotional flatness, is generally opposed to psychotherapy and whatever it stands for. The authors conclude: "If fear and destructiveness are the major emotional sources of fascism, *eros* belongs mainly to democracy." [18]

In psychology proper the work of Horkheimer, Adorno, and their colleagues has also been continued in the concept of the *locus of control,* proposed and measured by Julian Rotter (Lefcourt, 1977). Even though their work has excited considerable dissension and controversy, it has proved to be extremely fruitful.

Other Observations

A large number of other observations and comments have been made about the American and Western personality traits and conflicts. Fromm has written of the American marketing orientation (1947). Rapaport and his co-workers (1945–1946) saw the typical American as schizoid, as did West (1945). Erikson saw the typical American's identity crisis as polarized between aristocracy and mobocracy (1950). McClelland (1961) designated America and other countries "achieving societies," though he sidestepped the question of what this achievement orientation does to the individuals in those societies. Sullivan (1962) saw the paranoid personality as far more common than usually supposed, as had Bleuler (1911) and more recently Pinderhughes (1971). Eissler (1963) identified normality with analyzability, which Reiff (1966) took further and hailed the appearance of "psychological man." The list could be extended indefinitely.

These global descriptions are interesting and provocative, though they remain too general. Equally fruitful is the social-psychological analysis of various aspects of the ideal of mental health set up by psychoanalysis, i.e., the comparison of the statistical average with the analytic ideal.

Psychoanalysis and Community Psychiatry

The need for far-reaching social changes to combat the high incidence of neurosis led to the movement known as community psychiatry. Since community psychiatry tended to focus on superficial treatment of large numbers, rather than intensive treatment of small numbers, its methods and philosophy often led to clashes with more traditional psychoanalysis. Nevertheless, in 1968 the American Psychoanalytic Association appointed a Standing Committee on Community Psychiatry, with Viola Bernard as chairman.[19]

At the meeting of May 1968, the Council passed a resolution that: "the American Psychoanalytic Association expresses its positive support for the aims of community and social psychiatry and encourages its Members and Affiliate Societies to participate appropriately in the development and implementation of research, sound programs, and well-founded principles in this complex and far-reaching field."[20]

This fine-sounding resolution served to cover up what everyone knew was the deep cleavage between the mass methods of community psychiatry and the individual ones of psychoanalysis. On the whole, however, the opposition of community psychiatry to psychoanalysis seems to have been stronger than the other way around. This follows the pattern of preceding any innovation in the field, no matter how worthwhile, with an attack on "Freudianism."

A panel discussion on the topic was held at the meeting of the American Psychoanalytic Association in 1974 (Wadeson, 1975).

Antipsychiatry

As part of the reaction to the analytic dissection of culture, a movement arose in the 1950s, known as antipsychiatry, which held that all of conventional psychiatry should be scrapped because the trouble essentially lay with a society that was in itself schizophrenic. The leaders in this movement were the British psychiatrists R. D. Laing and David G. Cooper; along somewhat different lines, Thomas Szasz in the United States made equally caustic comments about conventional psychiatry.

The first major publication of this group was Laing and Esterson's *Sanity, Madness and the Family* (1964). The book was part of the literature showing that schizophrenics all come from disturbed families. "We believe that we show that the experience and behavior of schizophrenics is much more socially intelligible than has been supposed by most psychiatrists."[21] The authors, while making a valid point, did not seem to be aware that the same point had been made many times by pioneer analysts (see chapter 14). Laing (1971) has been particularly vehement in his denunciations of society, the family, and conventional psychiatry, apparently viewing himself as a "phenomenologist." All of this dramatized him to the lay public but has little to convey to the profession (his books are directed primarily at the public).

A different message is offered by Thomas Szasz, who is a trained analyst and has remained a member of the American Psychoanalytic Association. Szasz attacks the "myth of mental illness" (1961), by which he means what is ordinarily called the medical model. Although his views at times go to extremes, on the whole he has popularized certain psychological points of view about mental illness and nonanalytic psychiatry. Principally he has stressed the need to separate psychological from organic causes, and the confusion which results when that is not done.

Explorations in "Normality"

A good part of the psychoanalytic critique of the culture has been contained in specific analyses of what passes for "normal." Freud made significant comments on the topic, in *The Psychopathology of Everyday Life* (1901) and many other books. He even wrote in 1937 that the normal person is only normal on the average. "His ego approximates to that of the psychotic in some part or other and to a greater or lesser extent."[22]

It remained for others to draw the full conclusions from Freud's findings. It soon became apparent that psychoanalysis envisaged a state of mental health far superior to that found in the average person, that it was in fact an ideal. Thus "normality" developed two meanings: statistical (the average person) and ideal. Two questions then arose: What is the nature of the gap between the statistically average and the ideal, and how is the ideal to be reached?

Paradoxically, it was a technical innovation that provided one of the main sources of support for the analytic theory. As of 1930, all prospective analysts had to undergo a personal analysis as part of their training. It soon appeared that this analysis, once known as a "didactic" experience, was the same as anyone else's analysis. But the candidates were for the most part doctors of medicine or philosophers, or had other substantial credentials, and would not be considered in the slightest degree "neurotic" by the average professional at that time. It turned out, however, that their inner conflicts differed in no essential respect from those encountered in their patients. Freud's continuum theory, that the difference between neurotic and normal is only one of degree, was confirmed.

In a paper published in 1931, Ernest Jones gave the clearest exposition of the analytic image of normality seen up to that time. He argued that a thorough analysis has the effect not only of removing any manifest psychoneurotic symptoms, but also of dealing with the fundamental conflicts and complexes in a way that brings about a considerable freeing and expansion of the personality. In so doing, it leads to changes of a general order in the character and even intellect, notably in the direction of increased tolerance and open-mindedness. Furthermore, it leads to the final stage of maturity, a degree of friendliness and affection, which can only be judged by the internal freedom of such feelings rather than their outward manifestations. He concluded: "In centuries to come, when the social and educational sciences take note of the findings of depth psychology, the knowledge gained by studying this problem [of normality] will be perceived to be of inestimable practical value, and will rank as not the least of the gifts which psychoanalysis has bestowed upon the world." [23]

Then and subsequently, analysts took great pains to investigate all the characteristics of the presumably normal person in our culture, and came up with a wealth of significant findings. Individual analysts, however, could only offer qualitative judgments; it remained for others to translate these into quantitative estimates. We now turn to these psychoanalytically oriented studies to gain further perspectives on our culture.

Sexuality

From the beginning, Freud had held that sexual conflicts were present in a considerable percentage of the population, probably the majority. "Experience shows that the majority of the people who make up our society are constitutionally unfit to face the task of abstinence." [24] For a long time the hypocrisy involved in the standard sexual code was denied or ignored. Then came the Kinsey reports, on men in 1948 and on women in 1953.

THE KINSEY STUDIES. Alfred Kinsey was a professor of zoology at the University of Indiana. Aided by grants from various agencies, particularly the Rockefeller Foundation, he and his associates engaged in extensive interviews of thousands of persons. The publication of their two books had far-reaching consequences in the society at large.

Kinsey was no friend to psychoanalysis. He did not even cite Freud's publications correctly[25] and obviously did not grasp Freud's psychological ideas. Nevertheless his statistics provided a good deal of support for the Freudian hypotheses about our sexually frustrated culture.

One of the major findings was a direct confirmation of Freud's statement that few people can tolerate abstinence: "On a specific calculation of our data, it may be stated that at least 85% of the younger male population could be convicted as sex offenders if law enforcement officials were as efficient as most people expect them to be."[26]

By "sex offenders" he did not mean rapists but persons who engaged in masturbation, extramarital intercourse, childhood sex play, even intercourse with animals, and other forbidden forms of sexual activity which were commonly indulged in by a large percentage of the population. Statistics were subdivided by urban and rural groupings, educational levels, religious groups, and age levels. The fact that the sexual code was so widely flouted made Kinsey into a permissive superego for many (Margolin, 1948).

In his later book Kinsey showed that women could not stick to the official sexual code any more than men. The statistics were even more damning; Kinsey stated that more than 99 percent of the people who violate the sexual laws are never apprehended.[27]

With regard to dynamics, psychoanalysts had found that most people were sexually inadequate in some form, men suffering from premature ejaculation, women frigid, etc. In spite of his denials, Kinsey confirmed the psychoanalytic hypotheses. He found that most males ejaculated very quickly, perhaps 75 percent within 2 minutes, many within less than a minute or after 10 or 20 seconds. Nevertheless, he wrote:

The idea that the male who responds quickly in a sexual relation is neurotic or otherwise pathologically involved is, in most cases, not justified scientifically. . . . Far from being abnormal, the human male who is quick in his sexual response is quite normal among the mammals, and usual in his own species. It is curious that the term "impotence" should have ever been applied to such rapid response. It would be difficult to find another situation in which the individual who was quick and intense in his responses was labeled anything but superior, and that in most instances is exactly what the rapidly ejaculating male probably is, however inconvenient and unfortunate his qualities may be from the standpoint of the wife in the relationship.[28]

This statement is all the more remarkable since it comes from a trained physiologist. After all, the man whose heart beats more rapidly, or who bolts his food, or who is incontinent, is regarded as ill, not superior. Such is the power of the hostile attitude to analysis.

With regard to women, he stigmatized the analytic view of the transfer from the clitoris to the vagina, with vaginal orgasm the goal, as a "biologic impossibility."[29] Some women reported vaginal spasms, but this had nothing to do with maturity. In fact, he says: "The convulsions following orgasm also resemble those which follow an electric shock. This makes it all the more amazing that most persons consider [that] the sexual orgasm with its after-effects may provide one of the most supreme of physical satisfactions."[30]

All in all, the Kinsey reports can only be properly appreciated in the light of the cultural reaction to the psychoanalytic discoveries about sexuality. In spite of their clumsy errors, they seem to have made a positive contribution toward the more permissive sexual atmosphere of the present.

THE MASTERS–JOHNSON REPORT. The second large-scale study of sexuality which has had a profound impact has been the Masters and Johnson report, *Human Sexual Response* (1966). Their investigation was begun at the Washington University School of Medicine in 1954, and since 1964 has continued under the auspices of the Reproductive Biology Research Foundation. Later they developed various therapeutic techniques for the treatment of sexual dysfunction. Their treatment procedures have spread to a variety of clinics and installations all over the country (*Human Sexual Inadequacy*, 1970).

Apart from a number of gynecological details, the major novel contribution of the Masters–Johnson study was the denial of the difference between vaginal and clitoral orgasm. This was discussed in chapter 8, especially in connection with the book by Mary Sherfey. As with the earlier Kinsey reports, no attention is paid to unconscious dynamic factors in the sexual experience. In at least one offshoot of the Masters–Johnson work, *The Hite Report* (1976), clitoral masturbation is regarded as at least as satisfying as intercourse, in which only 30 percent of the respondents reached orgasm.[31]

The analytic criticism of the behavioral therapy employed by Masters and Johnson is that it ignores the newer concepts of the superego and acting-out, as well as the basic knowledge of the unconscious. An ironic situation has been created in which the behavioral therapist à la Masters regards himself as "sexually enlightened," while the analyst is derided or attacked as antisexual.

The whole experience with sexual enlightenment and sex therapy illustrates the problems connected with the growth of psychoanalysis and its critique of the culture. Since the dynamic factors are much harder to grasp, what is seized upon is overt behavior, and all kinds of acting-out are then encouraged, with unknown consequences.

Hatred, Violence, and Anger

It requires no special marshaling of evidence to bring home to modern people the ubiquity of hatred, violence, and anger. The contemporary psychoanalytic attitude toward these topics is not easy to sum up (see chapter 8). In general, it can be said that anger is more easily aroused than love by almost any kind of frustration, that once aroused it maintains its own strong momentum, and that an excess of anger is characteristic of the more infantile and the more disturbed personalities. Furthermore, chronic resentment can have serious physiological consequences, including death. On the other hand, in some cases the release of anger has a positive constructive value.

The psychoanalytic emphasis on love as constructive and hatred as destructive has been a potent force in focusing the attention of various social scientists on the ways in which hatred and violence have been manifested. In previous epochs, violence had been glorified as a sign of the human capacity for adventure and conquest; now it was deplored as an index of psychopathology.

In 1968, after the assassinations of Robert Kennedy and Martin Luther King, President Johnson appointed a commission to study the subject of violence. The commission issued a lengthy and informative report, *The History of Violence in America* (Graham and Gurr, 1969).

One of the conclusions was a reevaluation of the historians' myth that Western civilization has been a peaceful one. Tilly, a professor of sociology at the University of Toronto, wrote:

Historically, collective violence has flowed regularly out of the central political cal processes of Western countries. Men seeking to seize, hold, or realign the levers of power have continually engaged in collective violence as part of their struggles. The oppressed have struck in the name of justice, the privileged in the name of order, those in between in the name of fear.[32]

Various studies have emphasized how widespread violence is and has been. De Mause (1974), in tracing the history of childhood, has shown that until fairly recently infants were subjected to the grossest maltreatment, including infanticide. Gelles (1972) has documented the degree of violence in the contemporary home, especially in regard to physical agression between husbands and wives. Shorter (1975) has offered the surprising thesis that there has been a growth toward love and warmth since about the middle of the eighteeenth century.

A study by the Institute for Social Research of the University of Michigan (Kahn, 1972), stimulated by the murder of King, examined the attitudes of American men which justify violence. They offered a typology in which men were classified as pacifists, vigilantes, warriors, or anarchists. Pacifists and anarchists were more person-oriented and gave greater emphasis to equality, freedom, and human dignity. Vigilantes and warriors were the opposite. (The typology shows some similarity to the authoritarian–democratic one.)

Quantification is necessarily highly complex here. In general, the psychoanalytic theory that hatred is infantile, based on splitting, and tied up with deep psychopathology is beginning to have some far-reaching effects on social theory.

Family Structure and Dynamics

The topic of family structure has already been touched upon at several points. Analytic theory had involved a severe criticism of existing family arrangements, for which it had proposed education and therapy as remedies. In the 1950s this argument took a new turn; many analysts began to point to positive features in the family, while others started to experiment with treatment of the entire family (family therapy).

The major theoretician of the new movement was Nathan Ackerman, although many others soon followed. Trained as a psychoanalyst, Ackerman for many years had specialized in the treatment of children along classical lines. Then both his views and his practice changed, and he came to stress the family as a total system. Beyond classical theory, Ackerman (1958) delineated six social purposes of the modern family: [33]

1. The provision of food, shelter, and other material necessities.
2. The provision of social togetherness, which is the matrix for the affectional bond of family relationships.
3. The opportunity to evolve a personal identity, tied to family identity.
4. The patterning of sexual roles.
5. The training toward integration into social roles and acceptance of social responsibility.
6. The cultivation of learning and the support for individual creativity and initiative.

Ackerman concluded with a statement that has become the rallying cry for both family theorists and family therapists:

Clearly the configuration of family determines the forms of behavior that are required in the roles of husband and wife, father, mother, and child. Mothering and fathering, and the role of the child, acquire specific meaning only within a defined family structure. Thus the family molds the kinds of persons it needs in order to carry out its functions, and in the process each member reconciles his past conditioning with present role expectations. Clearly this process is a continuing one, for the psychological identity of a family changes over a period of time. And within the framework of this process, each member at times conforms and, at other times and within limits, actively alters these role expectations. [34]

Ackerman felt that the contemporary family failed miserably in living up to these expectations. He found that a typical middle-class, urban, white family lacked an adequate psychological identity, was unstable, full of conflict and restitution, and blocked satisfactory role adaptation. Many others agreed with him, in other terms. Grotjahn (1960) wrote of the family neurosis. Jackson (1968) described the mirages of marriage and the "gruesome twosome." Cuber and Harroff (1965), interviewing only the elite of their Ohio environment, found marriage to be mainly a matter of convenience, and the conflict-habituated couple to be the most frequent. What the family theoreticians were discovering, in other words, was that the image of an ideal life envisaged by psychoanalysis was not being provided by the family, as it should have been. At the same time, if the family broke up, serious insecurity and anxiety resulted. Thus people were caught up in a need–fear dilemma (Burnham et al., 1969)—they needed the family, yet were afraid of its harmful influence.

At the same time, family theoreticians like Nathan Ackerman, Helm Stierlin, Don Jackson, Salvador Minuchin, and others turned to family therapy as a solution, on the way castigating individual psychoanalysis and therapy severely. Like all technical innovations, this one has to be considered carefully in the light of what is known about transference, resistance, and other aspects of analysis (see chapter 18). The rosy hopes for family therapy, as for other social interventions, have met serious disillusionment (Rossi and Williams, 1972).

Other theoreticians have, on the basis of various research projects, maintained that there are far more healthy families than is commonly supposed by psychoanalytic theory. Beavers (1977) lists the following as characteristics of optimally functioning families: a systems orientation; boundary issues; contextual clarity; power issues; encouragement of autonomy; affective issues; task efficiency; transcendent values. He fails to observe that all this is part of the analytic image of normality. Beavers concludes: "The underlying thesis is that various schools of psychotherapy will gradually give way to a synthetic, pluralistic, scientific psychotherapy, continuing the strong points of each and eliminating various closed system quirks that have been defended by coercive, intragroup pressures rather than by scientific dialogue and treatment results."[35] One could scarcely take issue with Beavers's conclusion; indeed this whole book is an elaboration of the same thesis. But it is couched in such highly generalized language that it lends itself to myriad interpretations.

Family research in general tends to confirm the analytic criticism of contemporary culture: the family does not provide the security, stability, and identity that it should. How this should be corrected, however, is an entirely different problem.

Class Dynamics

Contrary to popular conception, Freud was well aware of the class-bound character of analysis, though he did not put it that way. Generally he took the position (since shown to be exaggerated) that the poor will not submit to instinctual repression, and hence neurosis is more often found among the middle and upper classes. Over time, he came to see the errors in these ideas. In an address to the International Psychoanalytical Association in 1918, he urged the extension of therapy to all classes.

[But] the necessities of our existence limit our work to the well-to-do classes, who are accustomed to choose their own physicians and whose choice is diverted away from psychoanalysis by all kinds of prejudices. At present we can do nothing for the wider social strata, who suffer extremely seriously. . . . We shall then be faced by the task of adapting our technique to the new conditions. . . . We shall probably discover that the poor are even less ready to part with their neuroses than the rich, because the hard life that awaits them if they recover offers them no attraction, and illness gives them one more claim to social help.[36]

Freud's predictions were to be borne out and, especially after World War II, psychoanalytic therapy of all kinds began to be extended to all the classes, through insurance and government subsidies. However, as the Yale studies cited above showed (Hollingshead and Redlich, 1958), even with everything paid for, psychoanalysis appealed primarily to the more affluent, more sophisticated, better educated segments of the population. In a study at the Boston Psychoanalytic Institute (Knapp et al., 1960), of 100 consecutive cases accepted for low-cost treatment, 72 percent were in the professional and academic fields. Although referrals of persons in work related to psychiatry and psychoanalysis were discouraged, approximately half of the cases were in such work, e.g., social work, psychology, medicine, teaching, and nursing. The four most frequent complaints that brought people to the clinic were depression, difficulties in relationships, excessive anxiety or tension, and work difficulty. None of these problems could be considered serious by the standards of conventional organic psychiatry.[37]

Thus in a real sense Freud's prediction had come true: the more sophisticated elements of the population were going into therapy in increasing numbers, attracted by its novel philosophy that inner conflicts can be overcome, while the poorer classes could not be reached because of their hard reality circumstances. If the reality circumstances were not devastating, cultural differences did not seem to affect the formation of transferences and the usual course of psychoanalysis (Jackson, 1968). In the United States at least, this situation led to extensive concern with the poor and the blacks.

THE CULTURE OF POVERTY. The rise of Marxist regimes after World War II, ruling more than one-third of the world and expanding rapidly, served to focus on the characteristics (psychological, social, and otherwise) of the lower classes. In 1959 the sociologist Oscar Lewis coined the term "the culture of poverty," which soon caught on. He distinguished four characteristics of this culture of poverty: the lack of effective participation and integration of the poor in the major institutions of the larger society; locally, a minimum of organization beyond the level of the nuclear and extended family; on the family level, the absence of a protected childhood, early sexual experience, mother-centered families, lack of privacy, and authoritarian emphasis; strong feelings of helplessness, dependence, and inferiority.[38] The mention of psychological factors like dependence and helplessness was a measure of the influence of psychoanalytic ideas, since more classic studies such as the Lynd and Lynd's *Middletown* (1929) and Warner's *Yankee City* (1963) had failed to give any consideration to them. Later work such as the *Moynihan Report* (Rainwater and Yancey, 1967) and others (Deutsch et al., 1968) have confirmed the widespread incidence of psychological problems among the poor.

Psychoanalysts have at times translated these observations into more dynamic clarifications (Bernard, 1953; Spurlock, 1970; Wadeson, 1975). For example, Coleman (in Wadeson, 1975) saw the functioning character of people living in the ghetto as displaying a broad range of oppositional defensive screening in relation to the world at large, with a spectrum of reactions, overt and covert, ranging from skepticism to rage. "We see more clearly than in any other situation, at least within one culture, the enormous importance for character functioning of 'outside' influences."[39] Linn (in Wadeson, 1975) described a wide variety of superego variants resulting from such depressing conditions. Spurlock (1970) listed a variety of ego distortions in black children who experience deprivation early in life.

Whenever possible, analysts have used their therapeutic skills to help poverty-stricken and black patients. In one report on interracial analysis, Fischer (1971) expresses the feeling that the racial difference between analyst and analysand involves issues of unconscious meaning at many levels, and that there are serious hazards in either overestimating or ignoring the interracial factor. Spurlock (1970), reporting on experiences in a clinic, found that a large number of families maintained an intactness and orderliness in their way of life even though the family unit itself was incomplete or had been disrupted. When this happened, the results of psychotherapy of children and mothers were positive. When it did not, the results were negative.

The identification of psychoanalysis with middle-class values has been widely misinterpreted. First of all, psychoanalysis has not taken over all the middle-class values, such as sexual asceticism, but has chosen what seems beneficial and discarded what seems harmful. Second, these values have been incorporated into a meaningful philosophy of living which has made a profound impression on modern people. It is this point which has helped to elevate psychoanalysis to a unified science of human behavior. This idea is further elaborated in chapter 19.

Identity and Alienation

The concept of identity is indissolubly linked with the name of Erik Erikson (Erikson, 1950; Coles, 1970). Allied to it is the notion of alienation, which has been seen as the hallmark of people in our era. For Erikson, identity represented a combination of individual and cultural observations basic to the understanding and self-esteem of the person and his society.

The earlier discussions about identity had centered largely on sexual identity, and even there particularly on women. This battle is now virtually over, and it is generally recognized that the identity of women, within certain anatomical limits, is essentially culturally determined (Schafer, 1974).

The same holds for masculine identity, which has been much less discussed. It is as though psychoanalysis had fallen prey to the cultural myth that men are too macho to have any problems. In his 1925 paper Freud had said:

we shall, of course, willingly agree that the majority of men are also far behind the masculine ideal and that all human individuals, as a result of their bisexual disposition and of cross-inheritance, combine in themselves both masculine and feminine characteristics, so that pure masculinity and femininity remain theoretical constructions of uncertain content.[40]

What literature exists has generally emphasized the man's failure to live up to the ego-ideal held out for men. The classic paper in this regard is Boehm (1930), "The Femininity Complex in Men," where the homosexual conflict was stressed above all. As with women, later work has referred particularly to the cultural circumstances affecting the man's role (M. Lamb, 1976). In the technical psychoanalytic literature, only recently have any papers appeared on the psychology of the father (Abelin, 1971).

ERIKSON'S CONTRIBUTION. Erikson (1959) began to use the term ego identity (or identity, for short) to denote certain comprehensive gains which the individual, at the end of adolescence, must have derived from all of his preadult experience in order to be ready for the tasks of adulthood. His use of this term, he says, reflects the dilemma of a psychoanalyst who was led to a new concept not by theoretical preoccupation but rather through the expansion of this clinical awareness to other fields, particularly social anthropology and comparative education and through the expectation that such expansion would, in turn, benefit his clinical work. For him, identity is both a psychosocial concept and a legitimate part of the psychoanalytic theory of the ego. Once formulated, the concept received wide acclaim as a profound addition to theory. However, it could not readily be fitted into the classical tripartite structure (Lichtenberg, 1975; Lichtenstein, 1963; Rubinfine, 1958). This was one of the factors that led to the expansion of theory into the exploration of the self and self–object relationships.

GROUP FORMATION AND IDENTITY. Although it is immediately obvious that the identity of any individual depends heavily on the family into which he is born, and the later groups of which he forms a part, the embattled political divisions within psychoanalysis have tended to obscure this simple fact. This is all the more remarkable in that Freud himself, in his pioneering work on the subject, *Group Psychology and the Analysis of the Ego* (1921), made this point: "In the individual's mental life someone else is invariably involved, as a model, as an object, as a helper, as an opponent; and so from the very first individual psychology, in this extended but entirely justifiable sense of the words, is at the same time social psychology as well." [41]

In this work Freud made the further point that the cohesiveness of a group derives from the fact that the individuals in it have a common superego, usually embodied in a leader, though it may also be incorporated in an idea (leader versus leaderless groups). These distinctions have been the basis of a dynamic group psychology ever since (Billig, 1976). Thus Freud saw the identity of any person as coming first from the identifications with family members, and later from identifications with other figures, which are then embodied in the superego.

Much, if not most, of the literature in this field has centered around group analysis or group therapy. Wolf (1949, 1950) attempted to apply the principles of individual psychoanalysis directly to groups. Foulkes (1951) saw the group as a kind of orchestra, in which each member had a distinctive role. Bion (1961) delineated the three alternatives in groups—fight, flight, or pairing-off. Helene Deutsch (1967) oversimplified the situation, seeing the group only as an aggregate of individuals. Durkin (1964) has summarized the various available approaches to groups. Much of the literature, in an attempt to glorify group therapy, has tended to overstress the group at the expense of the individual (Rosenbaum and Berger, 1975; Rosenbaum and Snadowsky, 1976). Some have tried to ascribe an almost mystical healing power to groups (Almond, 1974). Kanter (1976) has aptly called attention to the "romance of community" contained in these theories.

ALIENATION AND IDENTITY DIFFUSION. Increasingly, psychoanalysts and other observers of the human scene have commented on modern people's sense of alienation (Schacht, 1971). This phrase has been used in three different senses: first, the alienation of the person from his "true" self; second, the alienation of the individual from the group; and third, the alienation of minority groups from the larger society of which they are a part. The first two meanings have received considerable attention from psychoanalysts; the third has been seen more as a social problem.

The split between the true self and the false self has been described in many different terminologies. Melanie Klein used the term splitting in her later writings; Sullivan, dissociation; Freud, splitting and repression; Jacobson, neurotic and psychotic identifications; Bergler, leading and misleading identification; Winnicott, the false self; and so on. The idea is essentially the same: the individual presents one self to the world and has another, more private self inside that dominates his actions although he is either in no contact or in poor contact with it. The result is conflict. Roheim (1932) had already shown that such a conflict can be found in the most primitive social group on earth.[42] Thus this split, while accentuated by civilization, must to some extent be a problem in human nature. It could be put as the awareness of the difference between the inner and outer worlds.

Kardiner's concept of the basic personality structure can be used for understanding the alienation of the individual from the group. Another approach is through the feeling of aloneness and loneliness (Fromm-Reichmann, 1959). Mijuskovic (1977) puts the dilemma as follows: "the same principle and paradigm of an isolated human existence, which represents the reflexive psyche, testifies also to an accompanying and corresponding model of individual human freedom. As man has being, or exists, alone, so he wills alone, he chooses in utter solitude." [43]

Work

Since love and work are the two cornerstones of the psychoanalytic philosophy of normality, it was only natural that the work experience should also come under analytic scrutiny. In the extensive literature on this topic, the most profound observations have come out of the motivation-hygiene theory of Frederick Herzberg. The theory is best described in Herzberg's two books, *The Motivation to Work* (Herzberg et al., 1959) and *Work and the Nature of Man* (Herzberg, 1966).

Herzberg's theory is based on extensive studies in depth of the satisfactions and dissatisfactions of various workers. The elements of work that contribute to job satisfaction are those which essentially describe the relationship of the worker to what he or she does, the task or job content as opposed to the job context. The most frequent of these facts are achievement, recognition for achievement, interesting work, responsibility, professional growth, and advancement.

Job dissatisfaction is determined by those aspects of work which essentially describe the environment or surroundings within which one performs one's work tasks. Some of the more familiar environmental factors that are common sources of dissatisfaction include company policies and administrative practices, supervision, interpersonal relationships with supervisors, peers, and subordinates, working conditions, security, status, and salary.

Herzberg links his theory with analytic ideals. The definitive dynamic characterizing mental illness is the use of hygiene for inappropriate purposes, that is, the alleviation of pain to achieve positive satisfaction. The role of psychotherapy must be the reorientation of the individual's motivation to seek satisfaction in its proper source—psychological growth.[44]

Psychiatric Symptomatology

The question of the epidemiology of mental illness has been a thorny and difficult one from the beginning. When Freud started, in the 1880s, it was widely held that there was a large increase in neurosis because of the hectic conditions of modern life (as judged by the standards of that time). Actually, hard data for schizophrenia have been collected, but "neurosis" was first clearly defined by Freud, and so statistics for periods prior to World War I are nonexistent.

Statistics told only a small part of the story, yet they were alarming in their own right. It was usually stated that schizophrenics occupied half the hospital beds in the country, though this number is declining in view of the newer policy of quick release.[45]

Currently, figures for new admissions and chronic care are far higher in the United States than in any other country.[46] Other alarming statistics can also be cited. About seven percent of the adults in this country are alcohol abusers or outright alcoholics.[47] Drug abuse is notoriously common. The three Presidential commissions (in 1968, 1969, and 1970) agreed that "violence in American has risen to alarmingly high levels."[48]

COMPARISON WITH OTHER CULTURES. The figures or the United States have been compared with those for various other cultures. Necessarily the comparisons are incomplete, since adequate statistical evaluations have been difficult or impossible.

In *Magic, Faith and Healing* (1964), Ari Kiev assembled psychiatric data from a number of contemporary cultures. In general the definitions of psychiatric disturbance fitted into the dominant thinking of the particular culture. As in our own society, official figures were generally low, reflecting the fact that superego pressure forces conformity in all cultures, regardless of the differences in prohibitions or ideals. Since then the field of transcultural psychiatry has found psychiatric problems everywhere.

The earlier Rousseauean image of the unspoiled happy native has been shattered. It derived primarily from lack of information. Wittkower and Prince (1974) state that "in the 1930's when Freud's ideas began to make themselves felt . . . [they] opened up whole new areas for exploration not only of psychiatric disorders but also of cultural institutions, such as religions and ceremonial behavior. . . . The result was a major shift in the kind of data collected in the field."[49]

THE REDEFINITION OF PSYCHIATRY. Perhaps the most important result of the close psychoanalytic examination of the various psychiatric syndromes has been a total redefinition of what is meant by psychiatry. Freud saw that he had "all mankind" as his patient. At a more technical level, Sullivan (1962) once commented that more than half of the adult personalities that one encounters have some schizophrenic or preschizophrenic process in their background.[50]

If everybody is "a little schizzy," the term loses meaning, and it becomes more useful to talk in dynamic than diagnostic terms (see chapter 13). One way of putting it is to say that the gap between the statistically normal individual and the analytically normal is tremendous. This growing realization has produced, and is continuing to produce, a cultural revolution of unforeseen and even unforeseeable dimensions.

In the first volume of the *American Handbook of Psychiatry* (1975), the editor, Silvano Arieti, included a chapter that was a general assessment of psychiatry. Rifkin, the author of this chapter, stated: "The question [of the general assessment of psychiatry] reflects a certain uneasiness, a need to clarify the scope of psychiatry, to determine the nature of the problems to which it should address itself, and to study the conceptual and technical tools fashioned for the solution of problems."[51]

The assessment of psychiatry has been approached in two ways. First, psychiatry has been equated with psychoanalysis. In the *American Handbook* Arieti takes such an approach. The trouble with it is that there is a considerable body of professionals, from psychology, sociology, social work, and other disciplines, who object to identification with the "medical model."

The second approach has been to see psychiatry, in the traditional sense of the medical approach to overt mental illness, as a branch of psychoanalysis. In this vein, some have seen the relationship of psychiatry to psychoanalysis as similar to gross anatomy and histology. But the analogy is misleading, since even the gross observations of the behavior of psychotics are incorrect without some reference to their motivations. It is the same fallacy that bedevils the behavioral psychologist.

It seems more appropriate to recognize that psychoanalysis has become an all-encompassing approach to the human being, including psychiatry, psychology, sociology, anthropology, history, and philosophy in its purview. The elaboration of this position, that psychoanalysis has evolved into a unifying science of human behavior and experience, is the subject of chapter 19.

Chapter Eighteen
The Maturation of Technique

The technique of psychoanalysis did not spring full-blown from Freud's head. In fact, it took him almost 30 years from the time he began (1886) to his first clear formulation in terms of transference and resistance, and another quarter of a century (1937) before he formulated his ideas of how technique had to change in the light of ego psychology. It need cause no surprise, then, if analysts since his day take such a long time to learn technique, and if so many fall by the wayside in the attempt

The evolution of Freud's analytic work can be centered on four major ideas: make the unconscious conscious (1886–1905); work through resistances, particularly the transference-resistance (1905–1914); where the id was the ego shall be (1915–1923); and the object of analysis is to create optimal conditions for ego functioning (1923–1939). These dates are only approximate, since there were many backings and fillings as he formulated his ideas. As late as 1904, for example, he treated the musician Bruno Walter by recommending a trip, then with encouragement and suggestion[1] (Pollock, 1975a). On the whole, however, his ideas followed this development, whose details were reviewed in chapter 2.

The Reaction to Freud, and Psychoanalysis as Art and Science

Freud's formulation of the analytic process has remained basic for classical Freudians and revisionists alike. There are arguments about many details, but no longer, as with Jung and Adler or some of the modern "lunatic fringe" therapies, any dispute about the fundamental concepts.[2]

Despite this underlying consensus, there are still wide differences in the interpretation of Freud's formulas. When should interpretations be offered? Kleinians say immediately, others say when the transference is established, still others say only toward the end. How is one to decide what the optimal conditions are for the functioning of the ego? Clearly this question leads to a host of technical and philosophical problems that are still unresolved. Psychoanalysis remains as much of an art as it is a science, and each analytic procedure bears the unmistakable stamp of both the analyst and the analysand. Anna Freud wrote in 1954:

Years ago, in Vienna, we instituted an experimental technical seminar among colleagues of equal seniority and equal theoretical background, treating cases with similar diagnosis and therefore, supposedly, similar structures. We compared techniques and found . . . "that no two analysts would ever give precisely the same interpretation throughout an analysis" and . . . that such uniformity of procedure was never kept up for more than a few days in the beginning of an analysis. After that, the handling of the material would cease to run parallel. . . . Even though the final results may be the same, the roads leading there were widely divergent.[3]

Anna Freud's confidence that the "final results" would be the same has not been shared by others. All clinical experience shows that there is considerable variability. In a significant study, Glover (1955) tabulated the results of a questionnaire sent to the 29 analysts who were members of the British Psychoanalytic Association in 1938. There has seldom, if ever, been a more cohesive group of analysts. All of them had been trained either directly by Ernest Jones or by persons trained by Jones. Notwithstanding this uniformity of background, a wide divergence in various aspects of technique was noted. In the manner of handling resistance, transference, childhood material, interpretation, reassurance, anxiety, even in such finer matters of technique as the handling of fees, broken appointments, or taking notes during sessions, there were great contrasts.

In the 1937 paper, Freud had already made it clear that the image of the perfectly analyzed analyst is a myth; the situation has not changed since. The analyst is a human being who, despite his progress with himself, still has problems, some of them mild, some even severe (Brenner, 1976). Under these circumstances, the notion that the technical procedures adopted are the same (all being guided by the same philosophy) is equally a myth. Analysts are all different. Technically, Freud admonished analysts to undergo repeated analysis, every five years or so, which among other things would clarify their countertransferences.

A number of Freud's patients have written up their experiences with him; also, the daily notes to the Rat Man Case (1909) were found after Freud's death (Blanton, 1971; Grinker, 1940; Kardiner, 1977; Oberndorf, 1953; Wolf Man, 1971). From all of this material, Freud emerges as an engaged, warm, generous person who demonstrated considerable flexibility in the application of psychoanalytic technique. Anyone who wishes to evaluate psychoanalysis must take all these personal factors into account.

The Negative Therapeutic Reaction

Freud was a highly optimistic therapist, and he wrote with great optimism about his techniques. This very optimism becomes misleading, however, because as long as he believed in one technique he claimed marvelous results with it, only to find it severely wanting when he had moved on to something new.[4] It is also obvious that a number of patients did not recover and that others made only partial recoveries.

In the ego psychology period, Freud called this resistance to recovery a "negative therapeutic reaction." He saw it as one of the most powerful obstacles to psychoanalytic success:

In the end we come to see that we are dealing with what may be called a "moral" factor, a sense of guilt, which is finding its satisfaction in the illness and refuses to give up the punishment of suffering. . . . This sense of guilt expresses itself only as a resistance to recovery which it is extremely difficult to overcome. It is also particularly difficult to convince the patient that this motive lies behind his continuing to be ill; he holds fast to the more obvious explanation that treatment by analysis is not the right remedy for his case.[5]

This conception of an unconscious unwillingness to get better has played a powerful role in the subsequent history of psychoanalysis. Freud explained the unwillingness as being due to a harsh superego, but that still does not answer the therapeutic problem. Recently Asch (1976) distinguished three types of intrapsychic conflicts that may give rise to this negative reaction: a masochistic ego; unconscious guilt; ambivalent identification with a depressed and pre-Oedipal maternal love object. Whether one calls it masochism, or narcissism or guilt, or regressive oral identification, it still points to the core problem in psychoanalysis: some patients get better, while others do not. How to explain this theoretically and clinically, and what to do about it, has become in a sense the key problem in technique. Dissatisfaction with therapeutic results has always been what has prompted both experimentation and attempted theoretical clarification.

Ferenczi: Active Technique

After World War I many persons began to experiment with variations on Freud's technique. The most important of that era was Sandor Ferenczi (1873—1933), a member of the Committee who had vowed to spread Freud's teachings, and one of Freud's oldest and closest collaborators. Dissatisfied with some of his therapeutic results, Ferenczi introduced what he called an "active" technique, contrasting this obviously with Freud's "passive" one. Actually Ferenczi's innovations were of two kinds, or rather at two extremes. The first was really further passivity. In the analysis of a case of hysteria (1919), he felt that the patient was making no progress. Noticing that the woman kept her legs crossed as she lay on the couch, he diagnosed this as "larval masturbation" and forbade it. Very soon her orgastic capacity was restored. He wrote: "All abnormal channels of discharge being closed to it, her sexuality found of itself, without any assistance, the way back to its normally indicated genital zone, from which it had been repressed at a certain time in development, as though exiled from its home to foreign countries." [6]

Ferenczi turned to the better-known active technique in the following years. It is difficult to describe precisely what Ferenczi did, since he never put it very clearly in his writings, but the general conclusion is that he permitted his patients to be much more active in their dealings with him, encouraging them in both their aggressive and tender feelings toward him, including the long-tabooed physical contact. He called this technique neorelaxation or neocatharsis, describing it in an address to the International at Oxford in 1929. [7] He urged the adoption of a principle of indulgence, to operate side by side with the principle of abstinence or frustration that Freud had adopted. He urged his colleagues to "train their patients to a greater liberty and a freer expression in behavior of their aggressive feelings towards their physicians."[8] For many cases he urged a "comforting preparatory treatment,"[9] and expressed the feeling that there should be less distinction between the treatment of adults and the treatment of children. "What such neurotics need is really to be adopted and to partake for the first time in their lives of the advantages of a normal nursery."[10]

Ferenczi's active technique created another cleavage in the ranks of the analysts, although the majority stayed with the more classical approach favored by Freud. In 1924, Glover called it a "therapeutic adjuvant, to be used sparingly like the forceps in midwifery."[11] Ferenczi's work is forerunner of the more active approaches, such as those of Alexander, Sullivan, and others who led the revisionist group from the 1950s onward. His technique also pointed to the need for a closer examination of the interaction between analyst and analysand, still a rather neglected topic (Langs, 1976).

On the other hand, Ferenczi's sincerity, his stature in the field, his obvious mastery of therapy, and his long experience contributed to a lively discussion of technique that is still going on. In 1945 Fenichel wrote: "It is meaningless to distinguish an 'orthodox' psychoanalysis from an 'unorthodox' one."[12] The wide areas of disagreement in the field are as important as the wide areas of agreement.

The Concept of Analyzability

By the end of World War I, psychoanalysis had already become a long and expensive procedure. It was only natural that analysts should seek criteria to determine at the outset whether a given patient was likely to succeed at the process or not, i.e., whether he or she was analyzable. In one sense this concept of analyzability is a reflection into analysis of the older concept of hypnotizability from hypnosis. It would theoretically be more proper to speak of the degree of change to be expected from any patient, given a certain therapeutic technique. Perhaps because of that, the concept of analyzability has aroused a great deal of controversy, still unresolved.

Freud had laid down the principle of working through the resistances to strengthen the ego. Yet he had never written a technical paper on resistances, or on working through. Analysts were therefore left somewhat in the dark about when they should give up on a patient or when they should continue. Some continued for many years, almost a lifetime, and others gave up after a short while. In general, however, trained analysts tended to persist, and so the duration of analyses tended to lengthen.

Because analysis requires that a pact be made with the healthy part of the ego (according to Freud), some way to measure ego strength was clearly necessary for an estimate of the likelihood of success. Others, however, particularly the Kleinians and the culturalists, simply analyzed, with the feeling that the outcome of intensive psychotherapy was always useful.

Statistical Evaluations

After World War II a number of statistical studies were undertaken to evaluate the results of therapy and to clarify the image of analyzability. The failure of the American Psychoanalytic Association to come to any clear consensus on either the definition of psychoanalysis or the outcome of therapy was noted in chapter 5.

The most ambitious research project, though with a very small patient population (42), was at the Menninger Foundation and headed by Otto Kernberg. After some 18 years of intensive work, the group published their results in 1972. They attempted to coordinate therapeutic technique with ego strength.[13] The major conclusions were described in chapter 14. These results have formed the statistical background for Kernberg's later papers on the borderline patient.

A more qualitatively oriented study was reported by Lower, Escoll, and Huxter (1972) from the Philadelphia Psychoanalytic Institute and Clinic. These investigators attempted to answer two questions: By what criteria do practicing analysts decide on analyzability, and how do screening analysts and committees differ in their approach to analyzability? Comparing screening analysts with the institute committee on analyzability, they came to the following conclusions after comparing 40 applicants:[14]

1. Screening analysts tended to respond to applicants more favorably than did the analyzability committee. Screening analysts recommended two-thirds of the applicants for analysis, while the committee accepted only one-third.

2. The main favorable qualities in rank order of mention by screening analysts were: psychological-mindedness, motivation, favorable subjective response, ego strength, lack of defensiveness. The main favorable qualities in rank order of mention by the committee were: Oedipal pathology, good social adaptation, good work performance, ego strength, mature motivation.

3. The main unfavorable factors mentioned by screening analysts were: poor ego strength, poor social adaptation, pre-Oedipal pathology, defensiveness. The main unfavorable qualities listed by the committee were: poor ego strength, pre-oedipal pathology, social adaptation, defensiveness.

In both studies the criteria for estimating analyzability remain primarily qualitiative and clinical, the major emphasis being on ego strength, however it is measured or evaluated. How successful these estimates are in predicting the course of an analysis (analyzability) remains an open question.

Qualitative Evaluations

In an early published paper on psychotherapy, Freud had laid down the general requirements for a patient in analysis: a reasonable education, a fairly reliable character, a "normal mental condition," age not over 50, no dangerous symptoms requiring speedy removal.[15] Translated into the language of ego psychology, this has been the general qualitative evaluation ever since.

A number of authors have tried to assess the requirements more closely. Nunberg (1955) stressed the wish for recovery, while Fenichel (1945) placed the greatest weight on the balance between the resistance and the wish for recovery. Glover (1955) followed the traditional nosology, dividing his case list into accessible, moderately accessible, and intractable.

Reporting on the deliberations of a study group at the New York Psychoanalytic Society, Waldhorn (1960) described an elaborate pro-

cedure for assessing analyzability. He emphasized frustration tolerance, the ability to tolerate a passive role, introspective capacity,
self-observation, and the ability to tolerate anxiety without turning it
into panic. Negative factors were severe organic illnesses, intellec-
tualization, and excessive emotionality.

It can be stressed that in each case an effort will be made to appraise an individual ego function or isolated subgroup of ego functions by scrutinizing
certain aspects of the patient's communications and history. Admittedly this
involves a wholly arbitrary separation of component functions, since all of
these ego functions operate simultaneously, along with derivatives from the
rest of the psychic apparatus, and from the side of the external environment.
. . . The combined operation of all of these psychic influences requires that
. . . [we] weigh each detail. . . . Only then will an assessment of analyzability rest on rational grounds.[16]

Stone (1954) expressed the view that there is no absolute barrier
to analysis; it merely becomes more difficult as pathology becomes
greater. In the study by Knapp et al. (1960) predictions about analyzability seemed to be borne out after a year of analysis.

Nevertheless there is little doubt that fewer and fewer patients
are assessed as analyzable by experienced analysts. Feldman (1968)
reported that in California only one patient in eight had been accepted
by the clinic for assignment to a student. Hildebrand and Rayner
(1971) stated that in London only one patient in three referred by
analysts had been accepted for students. Lazar (1976) also substantiated the high rejection rate of candidates for analysis by students: in
1972, of 119 persons interviewed, only 8 were accepted by the Admissions Service, while in 1973, 16 of 156 interviewed were accepted.

It is clear that among analysts a considerable caution has arisen
concerning which patients are analyzable and which are not. This
caution suggests that the image of "analyzability" has become an
ideal fiction that few patients can live up to.

Psychoanalysis and Dynamic Psychotherapy

Since 1945, the field has divided roughly into two camps. One favors
a pure psychoanalysis (however that may be defined) which will
reach a clear-cut conclusion, somewhat along the lines of a medical

model. The other favors the idea that the patient is suffering from difficulties in living which can be ameliorated by psychoanalysis but for which no clear-cut "cure" can be seen. Both of these views are compatible with Freud, who in his 1937 paper specified that clear-cut termination is to be seen only in the cases of traumatic neurosis. Evaluations remain qualitative and clinical, and thus widespread controversy persists.

Transference

Ever since Freud's papers on technique of 1912–1915, it had been recognized that the establishment of a regressive transference neurosis and its working out were the hallmarks of analysis. This did not change in the era of ego psychology. Subsequent developments have expanded and fleshed out Freud's typically sparse comments about the transference.

Freud had enjoined the analyst to be relatively silent and passive, waiting for the transference neurosis to develop. In the majority of cases, this proved to be sufficient.

Blum (1971), reviewing developments since Freud, states that in the transference neurosis the urges and defenses as well as the underlying neurotic symptoms and character reappear in renewed analytic conflicts. It is a neurosis and includes transfer of symptoms in relation to the analyst, and it should be understood in terms of structure and character. It is a new neurotic formation but does not preclude the development of extra-analytic symptoms or pathological behavior.

Calef (1971), synthesizing the views of a panel on the transference neurosis, emphasized the shift of cathexes into a new love toward the analyst, which is then frustrated and reawakens the infantile conflicts. There is then a search for a new solution and the development of new compromise formations. The formation of the transference neurosis requires a certain degree of maturation of the ego, including the capacity to develop a psychoneurosis. While this is a dynamic replay of the same factors that produced the infantile and adult neuroses, it need not be phenomenologically identical to them. Early interpretations of resistances foster the development of the transference neurosis with its concentration on the analyst. This experience includes the recognition of the analyst as a new and different person.

Alexander, fearful that the transference neurosis would make the patient forever helplessly dependent on the analyst (Alexander et al., 1946), recommended manipulation of the transference in order to curtail or avoid this dependency. The Kleinians (Klein, 1952) go to the opposite extreme and welcome every transference manifestation from the very beginning, no matter how intense it may be. In Klein's view, psychotic elements exist in the infantile personality and are reproduced in the transference; this view allowed her to attempt the analysis of psychotics from the very beginning. Some authors prefer to share more of themselves with their patients in order to avoid the extreme rejection which the patient would otherwise feel in the transference neurosis; Freud acted in this way at times.

Transference and Reality

In theory, Freud's effort was to create a kind of pure atmosphere in which the patient's transference communications would unfold solely according to the analysand's inner needs. This is why the analyst was strictly enjoined to avoid social relations with his patients and not to reveal anything about himself to them. He was merely to be a blank screen on which the patient's childhood conflicts would be projected, there to be analyzed and overcome. Greenacre (1954) made this admonition so strong that she even recommended that the analyst refrain from involvement in social or public causes. Any other policy would "contaminate" the transference.

This position has been challenged on three different grounds. First of all Freud, though he urged it, did not behave in that way. When the Rat Man came in and said he was hungry, Freud fed him; when the Wolf Man was economically destitute after the war, Freud helped to support him. Many other instances could be given. Stone (1961), in an important book, also urged that the air of total neutrality was often too hard for patients to take.

A second objection comes from Greenson, who stresses the realistic and genuine relationship between analyst and patient. In more recent years, he has championed the position, paradoxically, that the successful outcome of an analysis depends more on the real relationship than on anything else; this goes together with his concept of the working alliance. Greenson (1971) states that for the full flowering and ultimate resolution of the patient's transference reactions, it is essential in *all* cases to acknowledge, clarify, differentiate, and even nurture the nontransference or relatively transference-free reactions between patient and analyst. The technique of "only analyzing" or "only interpreting" transference phenomena may stifle the development and clarification of the transference neurosis and act as an obstacle to the actualization of the transference-free or "real" reactions of the patient.

There can be no question about the centrality of interpreting the transference, Greenson says, but it is also important to deal with the nontransference interactions between patient and analyst. This may require noninterpretative or nonanalytic interventions, but these approaches are very different from anti-analytic procedures, including such techniques as reassurance, suggestion, or intervention in the patient's life.

A third approach, which has led to questioning of the classical image of the blank screen, is the recognition that somehow the interaction between analyst and analysand plays a role in the transference manifestations. Langs (1976) has codified this material most systematically. Langs places special emphasis on the reality stimuli for transference reactions. He also notes two aspects of the reactions: the perception of the stimulus and the reaction to it.

Langs further distinguishes at least three different types of stimuli for transference fantasies and responses: those based on appropriate and necessary interventions by, or behaviors of, the therapist; those evoked by stimuli in which the therapist's or analyst's countertransferences play a significant role; and those based primarily on the patient's powerful and often unconscious efforts to evoke behaviors in the analyst, or others, that are congruent with his own unconscious fantasies and past pathogenic interactions. Only the second of these, countertransferences and errors, has been given serious consideration by the classical literature.

Aspects of Transference: Empirical Investigations

The numerous ambiguities in the concept of transference led Sandler and his colleagues to investigate the topic through their clinical material in the Hampstead Index. It quickly became clear to them that the clinical and technical usage of the term transference covered a very broad spectrum of phenomena (Sandler et al., 1969). This seemed to be due to some intrinsic difficulty in the definition of transference. Nevertheless, they were able to group the material under a number of headings.

1. All those manifestations that could be understood in terms of the way in which past experiences, impulses, fantasies, and conflicts were revived in the course of the analysis, and that now relate to the person of the analyst in their manifest or latent content.

2. A relationship that corresponds to the transference neurosis as it has been described in adult psychoanalysis also occurs in a considerable number of child analyses. By transference neurosis they mean "the concentration of the child's conflicts, repressed wishes, fantasies etc. on to the person of the analyst, *with the relative diminution of their manifestations elsewhere.*" [17] The changes within the analytic situation were connected with changes in the direction of obtaining a more realistic self-image.

3. Various forms of externalization. It becomes extremely difficult to draw a dividing line between the externalization of the superego as a structure and the externalization of the introjects that form the basis of the superego, in which case there is a revival of a past relationship, which would definitely have to be called a transference. Under the heading of externalization can be included all those forms relating to the externalization of one or another aspect of the patient's own self-representation. The range of possible externalizations is infinite, and it is often extremely difficult to divorce externalization from the types of transference described earlier.

4. Displacements and extensions of other relationships. These may be called "transferences in breadth" as opposed to "transferences in depth."

5. Character transference. This includes reactions, attitudes, and relations manifested toward the therapist which can be considered to be habitual and characteristic for the patient concerned. Such reactions often are seen in the earliest sessions and involve very intense feelings.

6. Certain other aspects of the analytic relationship. Relating to the analyst as a real person, using the analyst as an auxiliary ego, and seeing the analyst as a need-satisfying person, are among them.

7. The therapeutic or working alliance. This is usually contrasted with transference, but there can be little doubt that the success or failure of a treatment alliance depends in part on the existence of a "basic" or "primary" transference (Greenacre, 1954). Thus a form of transference itself appears to be a basic ingredient of the treatment alliance.

8. The whole host of fantasies and expectations which the patient may bring to treatment.

The authors conclude:

If we start, as Freud did, from the view that transference represents the transferring of an impulse directed towards the infantile object, towards a new object—the analyst—in the present, we are limiting ourselves to a very narrow field, and excluding much of what is, in present-day usage, considered to be transference. . . . The problem is basically a conceptual one, but as such it is also a problem in psychoanalytic communication, and consequently an important one in psychoanalytic teaching.[18]

The Working or Therapeutic Alliance

Freud had visualized the analytic situation as dependent on a pact between the analyst and the healthy part of the patient's ego. This pact, he thought, would work well if there was a positive transference, poorly or not at all with a negative transference.

Beginning in the 1950s, a number of theoreticians began to express the feeling that more was involved in a well-functioning analysis. Elizabeth Zetzel (1956b), following Bibring, differentiated between transference as therapeutic alliance and the transference neurosis. She maintained that effective analysis depended on a sound therapeutic alliance. Her idea was further substantiated and elaborated by Greenson (1965), who preferred to use the term working alliance. He defined the working alliance as the relatively nonneurotic, rational rapport the patient has with the analyst. The reliable core of this alliance is the patient's motivation to overcome his illness and his ability to cooperate with the analyst. The alliance is between the patient's reasonable ego and the analyst's analyzing ego, and it is based largely on the patient's partial identification with the analyst's approach. It requires the patient's ability to split off from his experiencing ego a reasonable, observing ego; if he cannot, he will have difficulty in maintaining a working relationship with the analyst.

Greenson (1967) insists that "the working alliance deserves to be considered a full and equal partner to the transference neurosis in the patient–therapist relationship."[19] Although he equates his concept with Zetzel's "therapeutic alliance," Fenichel's "rational transference," and Stone's "mature transference,"[20] he seems to have something more in mind than Freud or these other authors. He implies that there must somehow be a "good fit" between analyst and patient, and that if this does not occur the analysis will not go well. Many analysts agree with him, though they tend to put it in other terms, such as that analysts will generally work better with certain types of patients than with others.

Interpretation of the Transference, or Manipulation

We come now to the basic question that has divided analysts from the very beginning. As is known, Breuer abandoned his patient Anna O. (Freeman, 1972) because he did not have the concept of the transference and accordingly did not know what to do with her love for him (Pollock, 1973). Freud, on the other hand, in the celebrated instance where a woman patient got up at the end of the hour and threw her arms around him, maintained his composure sufficiently to analyze the transference.

In fact, one could look at the whole development of Freud's technique as the insistence on analyzing the transference rather than manipulating it. For him, analysis was identified with transference analysis. When he divided patients in 1914 into those with narcissistic neuroses and those with transference neuroses, he regarded the former as unanalyzable because they did not form any transferences.

The first break with this position was Ferenczi's use of his active technique. He contended that no matter how long you analyzed some patients (and Ferenczi was notorious for the length of his analyses) and no matter how often the transference reactions were pointed out to them, they would not change. Hence something else had to be done, and here his active technique came in.

Between the two wars Ferenczi's position remained the major bone of contention. When rational discourse was reestablished after World War II, the controversy was resumed about analysis or manipulation of the transference. One of the clearest arguments for long-term analysis came in a well-known paper by Greenacre in 1954. She saw the basic or primary transference arising from the early contact between mother and child. Greenacre discussed various possible manipulations of the transference and rejected them all as unsatisfactory because they would lead to contamination. Dependency, guilt, erotic, or hostile feelings—all could be analyzed. "The safeguarding of the transference relationship is of prime importance."[21] In this paper she even made the remarkable statement that sexual relationships between analyst and patient are not as uncommon as one might think, and said that "the carrying through into a relationship in life of the incestuous fantasy of the patient may be more grave in its subsequent distortion of the patient's life than any actual incestuous seduction in childhood."[22]

Greenacre's paper was part of two larger symposia, one on classical technique and its variations, the other on psychoanalysis and psychodynamic psychotherapy. In this discussion Alexander (1954b) presented some of his views and some of his experiences at the Chicago Institute. While he no longer agreed with Ferenczi's views of the 1920s, he recognized their merit as having introduced a healthy experimental spirit into psychoanalytic therapy. "Only actual experimentation and observation of the psychodynamic effect of well-defined and theoretically sound technical measures can lead to an advancement of our therapeutic effectiveness."[23]

Alexander argued that many transference problems retard therapy. Of these the most important is dependency. Transference gratifications consist primarily in the satisfaction of the patient's dependent needs. This dependency can become for many patients an "intractable resistance." They may go on for many years without effecting any change.

To combat the dependency, Alexander suggested various technical measures; less frequent contact and planned interruptions of treatment were the most important. The "corrective emotional experience"[24] will not work unless the dependency is overcome. Edith Weigert (1962), a classical analyst who had been strongly influenced by the culturalist trends, concurred in that position, emphasizing particularly the need for flexibility in technique. Alexander summed up his argument as follows (1954a):

The problem of how to handle the patient's dependent needs is a central issue of psychoanalytic therapy and it will remain in the future one of the most difficult technical issues. In order to cure the patient we have to allow him some regression to an infantile state. We pay for this powerful therapeutic device with the difficulty of terminating the treatment. All this amounts to the fact that the medicine of artificial regression in the transference can be given in overdoses. Like radiation therapy, it is a powerful weapon, but can become the source of new illness.[25]

The question of dependency leading to interminable analyses was central. Neither Greenacre nor any of the other more classical discussants addressed themselves to this problem. Instead they did what Freud had done with Jung and Adler: they declared that what Alexander and his group were doing was psychotherapy, whereas what they were doing was psychoanalysis. Gill, following the standard tradition, insisted that in psychoanalysis the regressive transference neurosis is to be resolved "by techniques of interpretation alone."[26] He did not take up those cases where the transference neurosis could not be resolved, as Alexander had claimed.

Rangell (1954b) likewise drew the distinction between psychoanalysis and psychoanalytic therapy in terms of the resolution of the transference neurosis: psychoanalysis has the potential of resolving it, psychotherapy does not. But then he became quite vague about which was really better and what the optimal conditions were for each: .

The points in common and the crucial differences between psychoanalysis and dynamic psychotherapy have been described. One method is neither better nor worse nor more nor less praiseworthy than the other. There are indications and contraindications for each . . . and each must be applied on rational grounds. There is a spectrum of patients who require one or the other method and a spectrum of therapists able to do both. And there is a borderland of conditions, with great fluidity, which may at times call for a change of the technical approach in either direction.[27]

After this debate the two sides parted company, never again to exchange views in an open panel. Shortly thereafter the Academy of Psychoanalysis was formed (see chapter 5), and each side pursued its own course. To this day the question of the excessively dependent patient remains an unresolved, thorny problem of psychoanalytic technique. Analysts who manipulate the transference (like Alexander) do so on the grounds that they are avoiding excessive dependency; their critics (like Greenacre) often find that the manipulations, such as reduced frequency, make the patient more dependent, not less. The debate goes on. This is another instance where the formation of schools, each with its own labeling system, closed the door to a rational resolution of the problem.

Eissler: The Concept of Parameters

In 1953 Kurt Eissler added a valuable conceptual tool with the notion of the "parameter." A parameter is defined as "the deviation, both quantitative and qualitative, from the basic model technique, that is to say, from a technique which requires interpretation as the exclusive tool."[28] The basic model technique is pure psychoanalysis, requiring only interpretations from the analyst. Everything else is psychotherapy.

Whether parameters should be introduced, and which ones should be used, depends on the structure of the patient's ego. The ideal conditions Eissler set up were: "1) A parameter must be introduced only when it is proved that the basic model technique does not suffice; 2) the parameter must never transgress the unavoidable minimum; 3) a parameter is to be used only when it finally leads to its self-elimination; that is to say the final phase of the treatment must always proceed with a parameter of zero."[29]

Eissler's ingenious suggestion brings some much-needed order into this chaotic area. Parameters (manipulations) are justified when pure analysis does not work; however, they should be eliminated before the end of the therapy, if possible, and the problems finally resolved by pure analysis (interpretation of the transference neurosis).

The Widening Scope of Psychoanalysis

In spite of the disagreements in the field, the scope of psychoanalysis has steadily widened. To the layman it makes little difference whether what he is receiving is called psychoanalysis or psychoanalytic therapy; he comes for help and is satisfied if he gets help. As early as 1954, in a widely discussed paper Leo Stone indicated the enormous extension which psychoanalysis had already experienced. His conclusion was:

The scope of psychoanalytic therapy has widened from the transference psychoneurosis, to include practically all psychogenic nosologic categories. The transference neuroses and character disorders of equivalent degrees of pathology remain the optimum general indication for the classical method. While the difficulties increase and the expectations of success diminish in a general way as the nosological periphery is approached, there is no absolute barrier. . . . Psychoanalysis remains . . . the most powerful of all psychotherapeutic instruments, the "fire and iron," as Freud called it.[30]

Transference Intensity and Pathology

Freud had seen transference as a sign of treatability, regardless of its intensity, in contrast to narcissistic individuals, who formed no transference (see Freud, 1915, on transference love and 1920, on the treatment of a female homosexual). Sometimes he spoke of "elemental passion" or described patients with such strong transferences as "children of nature, . . . [who] are accessible only 'to the logic of soup, with dumplings for arguments.' "[31] Yet, although he felt that he could not succeed with some of these women (it is noteworthy that he did not include men), he concluded: "We shall never be able to do without a strictly regular, undiluted psychoanalysis which is not afraid to handle the most dangerous mental impulses and to obtain mastery over them for the benefit of the patient."[32]

After World War II, the attitude toward the erotic and other powerful transferences began to change. Blitzsten, the pioneering Chicago analyst, was the first to link a highly sexualized attitude toward the analyst and serious pathology,[33] and other authors have followed suit (Greenson, 1967, Rappaport, 1956). Langs (1974, 1976) proposed the term "instinctualized transferences"; others (Blum, 1971, 1973) used the term "erotized transference." Kernberg (1975) viewed such early emotional flooding as part of the borderline syndrome. That all of this may be merely part of analytic folklore can be gleaned from the dry remark of Sandler et al. (1973) that "in the course of time psychoanalysts have not come to expect their patients to fall in love with them so frequently and to such a degree."[34] To specify the point at which the intensity of the transference reaction makes the patient "unanalyzable" requires extraordinary care. In an actual case, considerable controversy would be found within any group of analysts. The whole question thus shades into that of the analysis of psychotics.

Transference and Psychosis

Freud's 1914 view that there are narcissistic individuals who form no transferences has come under increasing criticism over the years. When institutional psychiatrists began to be analysts, they found their patients less narcissistic than had been thought. Subsequently a number of analysts have turned to the treatment of psychotics (see chapter 5) with results which, though not generally as good as those with the less disturbed, are still worth describing.

It is usually agreed that the florid psychotic cannot be treated in the classical manner, with the couch and elicitation of free associations. Some modification of technique is required, and such modifications have been proposed by a number of authors beginning with Federn (1943) and Sullivan (1931 a,b). Notwithstanding the universal use of neuroleptic drugs, many psychiatrists prefer to combine drugs with analysis (Chiland, 1977).

The argument has arisen whether the therapy adopted under these circumstances can be considered "analysis." In 1945 Fenichel could still comment that "everyone who analyzes psychotics is doing pioneer work."[35] This is obviously no longer the case, but the obstacles remain formidable. Nevertheless, many able clinicians have approached and do approach the psychotic with an attempt to understand transference and resistance (see especially, Chiland, 1977; Rosenfeld, 1965; Searles, 1965). Inasmuch as these therapists attempt to work out the transferences and resistances (Boyer and Giovacchini, 1967), they are doing analysis by Freud's definition, even if other parameters are introduced. Whether one calls this psychotherapy or psychoanalysis seems to be a matter of semantics.

Countertransference

Freud saw countertransference as the transference of the analyst to the patient. He came to this concept rather late. His main concern seems to have been to maintain his equanimity and not get overinvolved with his patients.

The correspondence with Jung has shed some new light on the evolution of this attitude. In 1909 Jung "indignantly" reported that a woman patient "whom years ago I pulled out of a sticky neurosis with unstinting effort, has violated my confidence and my friendship in the most mortifying way imaginable. She has kicked up a vile scandal solely because I denied myself the pleasure of giving her a child."[36] Any analyst today would immediately recognize this as a case of erotic transference and unconscious countertransference; Jung was oblivious to both. In 1911 Jones, then living in Toronto, reported involvement in a similar situation, with an ex-patient accusing him of having had sexual intercourse with her. Jones recognized the transference, but nevertheless paid the woman $500 "to avoid a scandal."[37]

Freud urged everybody to keep their composure. "To be slandered and scorched by the love with which we operate—such are the perils of our trade, which we are certainly not going to abandon on their account."[38] He declared that "no psychoanalyst goes further than his own complexes and internal resistances permit."[39] He consistently regarded countertransference as an obstruction, but he was not entirely sure yet that that was so: "We are almost inclined to insist that he [the analyst] shall recognize this countertransference in himself and overcome it." Yet Freud was still recommending self-analysis at the time, and not analysis by another person.[40]

Privately Freud left no doubt that his main concern was overinvolvement. In a letter to Jung on December 31, 1911 he wrote:

Frau C. has told me all sorts of things about you and Pfister, if you can call the hints she drops "telling"; I gather that neither of you has yet acquired the necessary objectivity in your practice, that you still get involved, giving a good deal of yourselves and expecting the patient to give something in return. Permit me, speaking as the worthy old master, to say that this technique is invariably ill-advised and that it is best to remain reserved and purely receptive. We must never let our poor neurotics drive us crazy. I believe an article on "countertransference" is sorely needed; of course we could not publish it, we should have to circulate copies among ourselves.[41]

Thus his main concern at that time was with the protection of the analyst, not the patient. A quarter of a century later, in "Analysis Terminable and Interminable," he made his famous recommendation that the analyst should not be ashamed to return to analysis every five years, to avoid the pitfalls created by countertransference problems.

Post-Freudian Developments

As with transference, the narrower meaning of countertransference envisaged by Freud was broadened in time (Little, 1951). Sandler et al. (1973) list the following main elements or meanings in the current usage:[42]

1. "Resistances" in the analyst due to the activation of inner conflicts in him. These disturb his understanding and conduct of the analysis, producing blind spots.
2. The transferences of the analyst to his patient.

3. The disturbance of communication between analyst and patient due to anxiety aroused in the analyst by the patient–analyst relationship (Cohen, 1952).

4. Personality characteristics of the analyst that are reflected in his work and that may or may not lead to difficulties in his therapeutic work (Balint, 1939, 1949; Kemper, 1966).

5. Specific limitations in the analyst brought out by particular patients; also the specific reaction of the analyst to his patient's transference (Gitelson, 1952).

6. The "appropriate" or "normal" emotional response of the analyst to his patient, which can be an important therapeutic tool and a basis for empathy and understanding (Heimann, 1950; Money-Kyrle, 1956).

Issues in Countertransference

The dynamics of countertransference have been considered by a large number of authors (e.g., Kernberg, 1965; Langs, 1976; Racker, 1957; Sandler et al., 1973). In principle, these psychodynamic factors do not differ from other forms of psychodynamics. The analyst cannot be idealized. Having undergone analysis himself, he should have fewer problems than other people, but the notion that he is completely free of problems has long since been abandoned. These problems then interact with those of the analysand. Basically all analysts agree that these countertransference problems should be handled by further analysis. Nevertheless, even with the utmost refinements of analysis, a certain number of issues remain and have received extensive discussion in the literature.

Is Countertransference Harmful or Helpful?

Following Freud, the classical position was that countertransference consists of a series of errors, which should be overcome; essentially, then, it is harmful to the whole process. Beginning in the 1950s a contrary position was taken by a number of analysts.

Heimann (1950), a member of the Kleinian group, argued that the countertransference is the patient's creation as much as the analyst's. By looking at his own countertransferences, the analyst possesses a most valuable means of checking whether he has understood or failed to understand the patient. Langs (1976) saw such counter-transferences as so ubiquitous that he called for continuous self-scrutiny by the analyst, a recommendation with which all analysts would agree. Many would feel, however, that the notion that the analyst's countertransference is created by the patient is an exaggeration. Barchilon (1958), for example, spoke of "countertransference cures," in which the analyst's blind spots led him to overlook certain problems of the patient.

Is Countertransference Inevitable?

While most analysts have agreed with Freud that countertransference derives from the analyst's pathology and is thus avoidable, many have taken issue with him. A significant paper which took the contrary position was by Tower (1956); in it she urged that one must study the psychoanalyst's unconscious in the treatment situation in order to illuminate that which is defensive and acting out, and that which is scientifically and demonstrably constructive. She stated her major thesis thus:

I doubt that there is any thorough working through of a deep transference neurosis, in the strictest sense, which does not involve some form of emotional upheaval in which *both* patient and analyst are involved. In other words, there is both a transference neurosis and a corresponding "countertransference neurosis" (no matter how small and temporary) which are both analyzed in the treatment situation, with eventual feelings of a substantially new orientation on the part of both persons toward each other.[43]

A subsidiary question is, if countertransference reactions are not inevitable to all patients, are they unavoidable with some? Many have argued in the affirmative. Winnicott (1949), in a widely quoted paper (significantly called "Hate in the Countertransference"), argued that in dealing with psychotics the analyst must necessarily hate and fear them, besides loving them, and should become aware of the hate and fear so that these are not the motives that determine what he does to his patients. He even recommended that the hate for the psychotic should be communicated to the patient for the sake of the therapy (Winnicott, 1949). He also touched upon a point to be discussed later, that in doing psychoanalysis the analyst too will grow: "analysis of psychotics becomes impossible unless the analyst's own hate is extremely well sorted out and conscious."[44]

C. Thompson (1938) noted that the patient's choice of an analyst has unconscious neurotic determinants. If the analyst has a counter-transference problem and blind spot in the area that complements the patient's neurosis, there will be a stalemate. Every analyst, she urged, has specific liabilities in his own personality that can probably never be completely eradicated. Essentially the same point was made by Racker in his series of papers on transference and countertrans-ference (1953, 1957, 1958a,b). Some have even argued that there sometimes seems to be a tacit agreement between the analyst and pa-tient, a secret understanding to keep quiet about a certain topic. J. McLaughlin (1957), tackling a problem that every analyst has faced yet no one wishes to discuss—falling asleep during sessions—attributes it to countertransferences to certain patients. Glover (1955), A. Reich (1960), and Greenson (1967) would argue, however, that these are problems to be worked out in the analyst's analysis.

Revealing Countertransferences to the Patient

Most analysts, even when they are aware of their countertransfer-ences, are reluctant to reveal them to the patient, since they do not see how he can make constructive use of the information. There are some exceptions. An extreme is represented by Tauber (1954) and Tauber and Green (1959), who feel that sharing such feelings is a means of preventing the patient's defensive use of the analyst's re-serve. Langs (1976) warned, however, as had others, that too loose a manipulation of the countertransference could easily induce a variety of syndromes, such as excessive dependency, extreme demands, and abrupt termination of treatment.

The Patient's Gratification in the Analysis

Ever since Ferenczi espoused an active technique, the extent to which an analyst should permit the patient to experience gratification in the analysis has been a problem. While in general adhering to the clas-sical posture of neutrality, Stone (1961) warned against the analyst's excessive adherence to it. Total silence may create the danger of undue regression in the patient and may generate impairments in the unfolding of the transference neurosis. Stone believed that finding the analyst to be human even when revelations reflect technical errors is less detrimental to the analysis than stiff, inconsiderate, unreal attitudes and practices. In advocating acknowledgment of selective facts about the analyst, Stone suggested that the facts serve as a reasonable corrective or measuring rod for distorted information that supports transference resistances rather than the therapeutic alliance.

Analysis or Manipulation of the Countertransference

The question of whether the countertransference should be analyzed or manipulated is the counterpart to the similar question about the transference. Many have argued that Alexander's measures to combat dependency are really nothing more than manipulations of the countertransference. Manipulations might involve bodily contact (including sex), use of the patient in the analyst's personal life, and taking advantage of the patient in various ways. Many of the groups who oppose Freud have come to recommend broad manipulations of the countertransference, always with the allegation that the patient is "inherently unanalyzable." The nonmanipulation of the countertransference (with a few exceptions) remains the hallmark of the analyst.

Countertransference and the Growth of the Analyst

Finally the question can be raised as to whether the analytic situation can be inherently growth-producing for the analyst. If the analyst has to return to analysis every once in a while, as Freud recommended, could he use his countertransference experiences to foster his own growth?

The outstanding advocate of this point of view is Searles. In a paper on Oedipal love in the countertransference (1959a,b), he presented three main points: in the course of a successful analysis, the analyst goes through a phase of reacting to and eventually relinquishing the patient as his Oedipal love object; in normal development the parent reciprocates the child's Oedipal love more intensely than has previously been recognized; and the passing of the Oedipus complex is important in the development of the ego as well as the superego. In a later paper (1975) he asserts that part of the patient's illness is that his therapeutic strivings have been frustrated by his early environment, and that this wish to help the other person can now be worked out in the analysis. The analyst should learn to accept the patient's initiative.

Searles has probably been more open about his countertransference reactions than any other analyst. Although his early work was largely confined to hospitalized schizophrenics, in more recent years he has been working with neurotics, with whom, he claims, he has had essentially similar countertransference experiences.

Some of Greenson's comments in his book on technique (1967) are appropriate here: While it is acceptable for an analyst to talk to his friends about his exhaustion, some analysts are actually embarrassed to admit that they enjoy their work. At the same time some analysts suffer from overwork, apparently an occupational hazard.[45] At another point Greenson remarks on the high percentage of analysts who suffer very much from stage fright.[46] With such problems it is easy to see how the analyst, who necessarily engages in, or should engage in, more self-analysis than other people, could easily profit from reflection on his countertransference experiences. This topic has scarcely been touched, however, in the larger body of the literature.

Resistance

In his 1914 paper on remembering and working through, Freud made the point that the working through of resistances was now the heart of analysis, particularly the transference resistances. Although the topic was crucial, Freud never elaborated on it in any technical paper.

In 1926 in an addendum to *Inhibitions, Symptoms and Anxiety,* he noted briefly that the analyst has to combat no less than five kinds of resistance in the patient, emanating from the ego, the id, and the superego. The three ego-resistances are repression resistance, transference resistance, and the secondary gain from the illness. The fourth kind of resistance emanates from the id, and necessitates working through. The fifth, superego resistance, was the last to be discovered, "though not always the least powerful one."[47] It seems to originate from the sense of guilt or the need for punishment, and it opposes every move toward success, including the patient's own recovery through analysis. Earlier Freud had also referred to this resistance as the negative therapeutic reaction.

Resistance Analysis or Analysis of Resistance

The next step came with Wilhelm Reich, who elaborated what he called *systematic resistance analysis,* described in his book *Character Analysis* (1933). Reich saw every patient as inherently resistive, regardless of surface appearances; thus he saw no possibility of a genuine positive transference in the early stages. Since negativism was always there under the surface, the only technique was systematic resistance analysis, in which only the resistances were tackled. Many cases, he argued, become chaotic in spite of systematic interpretation because of a lack of consistency in the working through of resistances that had already been interpreted.

In every patient there is one major resistance position with which he or she begins. Since the patient is obviously in constant flight and since efforts to satisfy the analyst with substitute productions remain sterile, the task of the analyst is to bring the patient back repeatedly to the first resistance position until he finds the courage to tackle it analytically. Reich urged that one cannot be too early in analyzing resistances and one cannot be too reserved in the interpretation of the unconscious, apart from resistances. From this period and Reich's work emerged the basic rule: interpret resistance before content.

In spite of Reich's fundamental contribution, other analysts felt that he was overly schematic. A reply was soon forthcoming in Anna Freud's book, *The Ego and the Mechanisms of Defense* (1936). She saw his approach as too one-sided, omitting too much of the patient's individuality:

A technique which inclined too far in the other direction, so that the foreground was occupied exclusively by the analysis of the patient's resistances, would also be defective in its results, but on the opposite side. This method would give us a picture of the whole structure of the analysand's ego, but depth and completeness in the analysis of his id would have to be sacrificed.[48]

Thus the lines were drawn between a rigidly schematic resistance analysis à la Reich and a looser analysis of resistances as Freud had originally proposed. Fenichel (1941) observed that Reich's book gives way so extensively to some personal characteristics of the author, especially to his penchant for schematic simplification, that his theory suffers. Eventually a more flexible analysis of resistances won out, although some of Reich's points became solid ingredients of all analytic theory, particularly his observations of body activities, the patient's "character armor," and the admonition to analyze from the surface down.

Apart from this controversy of the 1930s, there have been no significant additions to the theory of resistances. Although some authors take a slightly different point of view, essentially the concept of resistance is a translation into the therapeutic situation of the concept of defense in the personality structure. Changes in the conceptualization of the defense mechanisms (see chapter 11) are thus reflected in changes in the elucidation and management of resistances.

Some authors have maintained that resistances cannot really be worked out and that the proper technique is, at least for some time, to *side with the resistances*. This has been called the *paradigmatic technique* (Nelson, 1969; Spotnitz, 1968). However, like many of the deviant techniques, this moves so far from the basic principles of analysis that it loses its moorings.

Working Through

Since psychoanalysis had no adequate learning theory available with which to explain its results, it had to invent one. This invention led to the peculiar locution of "working through," introduced by Freud in his 1914 paper. Essentially, for Freud, working through meant repetition of the material, and analysis of any new material, until the necessary conviction was acquired by the patient and he had changed:

One must allow the patient time to become more conversant with this resistance that is unknown to him, to *work through it,* to overcome it, by continuing, in defiance of it, the analytic work according to the fundamental rule of analysis. . . . The doctor has nothing else to do than to wait and let things take their course, a course which cannot be avoided nor always hastened. If he holds fast to this conviction he will often be spared the mistake of thinking he has failed when in fact he is conducting the treatment along the right lines.[49]

In this conceptualization, the essential elements are time, the passivity into which the analyst is forced, and, by implication, repetition of the same or similar material, since working through was contrasted with merely pointing out the resistance once. These three elements have remained at the core of the psychoanalytic theory of change, and actually little has been added to the theory since Freud. What has altered is the view of the psychodynamic material offered by the patient; how he works out this material in the analysis remains the same. Some of the later clarifications of Freud may be mentioned.

Alexander: The Metapsychology of Cure

In 1914 the two major psychic parts were the ego and the id (although this word did not yet exist). Once the superego was added, its role in therapy was immediately clear. Alexander (1925b) drew out the implications in a classic paper. The ego (reality) has to take over the functions of the superego (prohibitions). Hence the curative process consists in overcoming the resistances to such a take-over of the superego's functions by the ego. Later Nunberg (1955) put it more succinctly: "the changes which are achieved through treatment in the *ideal case* involve the entire personality and are as follows: the energies of the id become more mobile, the superego becomes more tolerant, the ego is freer from anxiety and the synthetic function is restored."[50]

Strachey: The Mutative Interpretation

Following up on Alexander's notion that the superego must be mollified or destroyed in analysis, in an important paper in 1934 Strachey took up the question of how this is to be done. He began by pointing to the negative cycle in which the infant finds itself by virtue of unmastered strivings. Because of its oral-aggressive strivings (he was writing in the Melanie Klein framework), it projects these strivings onto the object, which it sees as aggressive. This object is then introjected, reinforcing the aggressive threats. The aggression is then further reprojected to the object, which is then reintrojected in aggressive form. A vicious circle is set up, in which the infant bounces back and forth between aggressive threat and aggressive defense.

Strachey then proposes that the same pattern is operating in the analytic situation. The difference is that the analyst can function as an auxiliary superego. And when the aggression is directed at him, he does not have to respond, and in fact he does not respond, in the same way as the mother did when the patient was an infant.

By virtue of his (strictly limited) power as an auxiliary superego, the analyst gives permission for a small quantity of the patient's id-energy to become conscious. This id-energy will then be directed at the analyst. If all goes well, the patient's ego will become aware of the contrast between the aggressive character of his feelings and the real nature of the analyst, who does not behave like the patient's good or bad archaic objects (introjects). As a result the interpretation produces a breach in the circle.

Later Reconsiderations

A panel discussion of the problem of working through was held by the American Psychoanalytic Association in 1964. Windholz (in H. Schmale, 1966) summarized the various views as follows: the panel agreed on working through as a concept for those aspects of a therapeutic process which occur in the course of the analysis of screen memories and screen affects, and that it is necessary for the recovering of traumatic events. The question of whether or not the concept of working through is indispensable remains.

In his most recent work, Brenner (1976) takes the position that working through can never eliminate all conflicts. In individual cases, analytic goals are limited. "Psychic conflicts can never disappear."[51] They can only change so that the resulting compromise formations are clinically normal rather than clinically pathological. However, such changes must not be thought of as minor. On the contrary, they often have great importance and value to a patient. Their importance is all the greater because, when analysis is successful, its beneficial results are always widespread. Thus working through (though he does not use the word) can reduce the severity of many conflicts, but it cannot eliminate them entirely.

Termination

In the literature on termination, Freud's 1937 paper still plays a significant role. A panel reported by Pfeffer (1963a) reviewed the progress made in the quarter of a century since Freud and offered evaluations of his positions by a number of leading analysts.

The authors of the article, reviewing Freud's paper 25 years later, subdivide his argument into eight topics: length of the analysis; termination date; constitutional strength of the drives; activation of latent conflicts; structure of the patient's ego; primary congenital variations of the ego; personality of the analyst; repudiation of femininity.

Length of the Analysis

The length of the average analysis seems to have increased considerably. In spite of this increase, Freud's remark still holds: in the traumatic case (what we would call today the symptomatic case), a short, clear-cut result is feasible; where the goal of the analysis is to change the ego structure, a rapid result is not feasible.

The main reason for the increase in the length of the analysis is that the focus has shifted more and more from the symptoms to the character structure. Although an immediate symptom may have cleared up in short order, the patient has been made aware of the many difficulties in his character structure that should be worked on. Not infrequently, a symptom clears up without any discussion whatsoever, merely as a result of the development of a positive transference. In these cases, the symptomatic improvement serves as a spur to deeper, more extensive analytic work.

The numerous difficulties involved in termination account for the gap between the ideal and the real. Ideally, as Freud says, analysis should continue until a point of diminishing returns, or where further analysis would effect no appreciable change in the patient's personality. Such termination is rarely feasible. In practice, analysis continues until a satisfactory real-life solution is achieved.

The factors that Freud enumerates as most responsible for the length of analysis are the strength of the instincts and the weakness of the ego. To this could now be added the gap between the neurotic culture and the analytic ideal. As time has gone on, in fact, this gap between the reality of the culture and the ideal of analysis looms larger and larger as the main source of the long analysis.

Termination Date

Setting a date for termination was a device used by Freud in the case of the Wolf Man. This patient, a wealthy Russian who was incapacitated by a variety of obsessional conflicts, had gone on in analysis for some five years without effecting the kind of change that Freud considered most desirable. At this point, Freud told him that the analysis would stop in six months, whatever he did.[52] The patient was so alarmed by this threat that he produced a number of childhood memories and made further dramatic and significant changes in his personality. This device has since been known as the end-setting.

Unfortunately this device can no longer be used with its original impact because numerous analysts are now available. When Freud gave his patient the ultimatum in 1914, there was virtually nobody else to turn to. Accordingly, the ultimatum meant to the patient: either get better or get out. It has since been revealed, however, that even the Wolf Man continued to go to analysts all his life, though not with the same intensity with which he saw Freud.[53]

Nowadays, when every large city has a considerable number of analysts, the end-setting is interpreted differently by the patient. It means to him that the analyst is no longer sure that the patient's problems will be resolved, and no longer has a desire to work with him. Accordingly, the patient interprets the end-setting as either a suggestion that he go to another analyst or a suggestion that the mode of treatment be altered. Since this is the way in which the patient is bound to interpret an end-setting to which he has not agreed, it has become more customary to suggest to the patient under these circumstances that if he does not change more within, say, six months or a year, he will be switched to another person. In some cases, this will produce more changes in the desired direction, in others it will not.

Kubie (1968) has championed switching to another analyst for the termination of a seemingly endless analysis. However, it cannot be said that there is any unanimity among analysts on this score, and in some cases it seems desirable to continue even though the therapy seems to have bogged down for a long period of time. As Freud had said, time, repetition, and the forced passivity of the analyst are essential to all working through.

The Constitutional Strength of the Drives

Freud was always impressed by the power of the id, which he sometimes referred to as the tyranny of the drives. But the trend of thinking since his day has been toward the view that the id itself has dynamics (see chapter 8). If the drives have their own dynamics, then the strength displayed in the clinical situation is not due to pure physiology but also has a large psychological component. In the contemporary analytic literature, references to the constitutional strength of the drives are much less frequent than in Freud's time.

The Activation of Latent Conflicts

In his 1937 paper Freud had expressed his conviction that latent conflicts could not be handled. The switch to character analysis changed thinking in this regard. Necessarily, every character analysis activates conflicts that were only dormant before. Hence the question is no longer relevant in the form in which Freud put it. What is relevant is whether the analyst can succeed in getting the patient to face his character problems or whether the achievement will have to be confined to purely symptomatic change.

Ego Structure

It need scarcely be stressed that ego structure is the dominant theme of modern analysis, together with its genesis, composition, and change. The far-reaching alterations in the concept of ego functioning have been documented throughout this book.

The Personality of the Analyst

As time goes on, the analyst's personality has proved to be more and more important in the question of termination. The analyst, as Freud pointed out, cannot bring the patient farther than where he himself is, yet the analysis of the prospective analyst has proved to be a formidable task. The brief encounters of three or four months' duration that Freud tried in the early 1920s (Kardiner, 1977) would be dismissed as preposterous today. Analysis has become longer and longer, yet the same problems remain.

In his 1937 paper Freud remarked that the analysis of the prospective analyst runs up against a special obstacle, inasmuch as the student uses analytic theory for defensive purposes. This statement is even more true now. One result is what Glover has called "training transferences," in which a group of analysts approve of themselves and their students but vehemently disapprove of outside colleagues and their students. The splits and dissensions in the analytic movement that this leads to have already been discussed (chapters 4 and 5).

Nevertheless, there seems to be no alternative to the profound soul-searching that modern analysis has become. The growth process is long and formidable, but as with so much else that takes time and effort, analysts have found it to be indispensable and most valuable.

In this connection there seems to be a strong trend toward reanalysis among analysts, even after graduation from an institute. Goldensohn (1977), in a study of graduates of the William Alanson White Institute in New York, found that 55 percent of the study sample had at one time or another sought further psychoanalytic therapy.[54] There were two patterns among those who entered reanalysis. First, a higher percentage of respondents who graduated more than 10 years ago sought further therapy compared to those who graduated within the past 10 years. Second, the oldest graduates, those more than 20 years away from graduation, returned more often to one-to-one psychoanalysis, whereas the younger graduates moved toward other modalities as well.

Obviously, comparable figures for other institutes are hard to come by. In a symposium held by the New York Center for Psychoanalytic Training in 1976,[55] an informal survey of the participating analysts revealed that some 50 to 75 percent of their patients (nonanalysts) were in reanalysis.

Repudiation of Femininity

Freud's view that penis envy in women and passivity in men provide the psychological bedrock (so to speak) that analysis cannot penetrate further has scarcely stood the test of time. Both are secondary to the crisis of identity that is so characteristic of modern people, and the introjects from where it proceeds. Identity crisis and its concomitant alienation lead to a deeper examination of the culture. It is here, perhaps, that the greatest advances have been made since Freud.

Follow-up Studies and Evaluation of Results

It was always difficult to pin down the results of an analysis in quantitative terms; it is even more difficult now, in the era of ego psychology. Ernest Jones (1936a) defined analytical success as follows: ''analytical success goes beyond the pathological field altogether. It betokens an understanding . . . of the developmental lines of all the subject's main interests in life . . . so that ultimately one can see his whole life as a gradual unfolding of a relatively few primary sources of interest."[56] When the criteria of success are so qualitative, statisticians understandably have a hard time with them. Nevertheless attempts have been made along two different lines.

The first has been tabulation of results in a rather mechanical manner; the pioneer studies of Alexander (1937), Fenichel (1930), and Jones (1936b) set the model for these (see chapter 5). Generally such studies show that one-half to two-thirds of the patients treated show considerable improvement. Other studies have yielded comparable results (F. Feldman, 1968; Hamburg et al., 1967).

These statistics have been questioned by critics, such as Eysenck (1965), who maintain that they are no better than spontaneous recovery. It would take us too far afield to review Eysenck's work in detail, but Meltzoff and Kornreich (1970), reexamining his work, found it hopelessly at fault in its basic data; his "conclusions were based upon a small, unrepresentative sample of the available evidence."[57] The problems posed by statistical studies in this area are notorious (Bergin and Garfield, 1971). Even the simple baseline for spontaneous remission has never been satisfactorily established; in a careful perusal of 216 schizophrenics over a 20-year period, Bleuler (1970) found that a number had stabilized themselves surprisingly well, while Müller (1977) turned up with the astounding finding that schizophrenics tend to improve with age!

Qualitatively, some studies have been reported. The most elaborate is the work undertaken at the New York Psychoanalytic Institute (Pfeffer, 1961, 1963b), where patients who had finished treatment were called back for analytic follow-up interviews. A frequent finding was that in these interviews the earlier symptoms might flare up again, only to be analyzed and disappear very quickly. Thus the patient's ego seemingly had been strengthened to the point where he could handle traumatic situations more effectively, but not to the point where his earlier symptoms would never recur under any circumstances. These findings would fit in well with the general analytic theory of therapy.

Summary Comments on Technique

Using Freud's four basic formulas—making the unconscious conscious, working through the resistances (especially the transference resistance), where the id was the ego shall be, and setting optimal conditions for the functioning of the ego—psychoanalytic technique has matured in all ways. In spite of continual attacks on its basic postulates and methods, it continues to grow and flourish. The focus has shifted, however, from curing symptoms to changing character structure. Because of this increase in complexity, psychoanalysis is even more difficult to evaluate than before.

Chapter Nineteen

The Advance of Psychoanalysis to a Unifying Theory of Human Behavior

There is a wide gap between Freud's public utterances and his privately held beliefs. Nowhere does this gap become more apparent than in his total appraisal of psychoanalysis in relation to the other sciences that deal with mankind. The discovery of his letters to Fliess revealed his youthful hopes and dreams of summing up all the knowledge of mankind, hopes and dreams he never shared with the public. In the same way his letters to Jung, recently published, show plainly his soaring ambitions for the science he had founded, again fantasies which he was loath to display in print.

In a letter to Jung on October 17, 1909, Freud wrote: "I am glad you share my belief that we must conquer the whole field of mythology. Thus far we have only two pioneers: Abraham and Rank. We need men for more far-reaching campaigns. Such men are so rare. We must also take hold of biography." [1]

The military analogies are striking. On November 21, 1909, he quoted to Jung from a letter from Stanley Hall, who had said that psychologists must look to work in the abnormal or borderline field for their chief light. Then on December 19, 1909 he wrote to Jung: "I long for mythologists, linguists, and historians of religions: if they don't come to our help, we shall have to do all that ourselves." [2] On January 2, 1910, he expressed regret that he did not have enough specialists available, with their highly valuable knowledge. Then on July 5, 1910, he stated his greatest hope: "I am becoming more and more convinced of the cultural value of psychoanalysis, and I long for the lucid mind that will draw from it the justified inferences for philosophy and sociology." [3] At that time philosophy was the broad understanding of all human concerns, rather than the specialized field it has become. Thus Freud was hoping for the expansion of psychoanalysis to become a unified science of mankind.

Publicly he confined himself to a rather reserved article for the Italian journal *Scientia,* on "The Claims of Psychoanalysis to Scientific Interest," in 1913. Here he still described psychoanalysis as a medical procedure but called attention to the light it had already cast on other fields. His boldest statement was:

Fundamental changes will have to be introduced into normal psychology if it is to be brought into harmony with these new findings. . . . The number of detailed psychoanalytic findings which cannot fail to be of importance for general psychology is too great for me to enumerate them here. I will only mention two other points: psychoanalysis unhesitatingly ascribes the primacy in mental life to affective processes, and it reveals an unexpected amount of affective disturbance and blinding of the intellect in normal no less than in sick people.[4]

In his later writings he gave some hints about what he thought were the far-reaching effects of psychoanalysis. The strongest theoretical statement came in *The New Introductory Lectures* in 1932, when he said: "Strictly speaking there are only two sciences: psychology, pure and applied, and natural science."[5] By implication he was asserting here that all the social sciences represent applications of psychoanalysis.

Post-Freudian Views

Heinz Hartmann, generally regarded as the leading theoretician of the period from 1945 to 1970, repeatedly and emphatically asserted that psychoanalysis must become a general psychology (Hartmann, 1964b). However, his papers were on the whole more programmatic than integrative. He did stimulate a whole generation of research workers, headed by Rapaport, to broaden psychoanalysis far beyond its clinical base.

The clearest statement in the literature of the image of psychoanalysis as a unified theory of behavior is in a paper by Gardner Murphy (1960). He cautioned that the danger to science today lies not in making too much use of Freud, but in failing to use him as we use Darwin. He shows that Freud did build a systematic theory of human behavior, but that what stands most in the way of appreciating his achievement is his followers' too literal adherence to his verbal formulations. To integrate the theory properly, he urges, we have to have a more generous, glory-sharing conception of human research in which all the human sciences contribute, one to another.

The Scientific Status of Psychoanalysis

From the very beginning, psychoanalysis was attacked as "unscientific," and among wide circles this opprobrium continues in undiluted form. Two questions must now be raised: What is the evidence for this depreciation? How is the scientific status of psychoanalysis to be evaluated today?

Much of the derogation of psychoanalysis was little more than senseless vituperation. For instance, in 1928 John Watson, the father of behaviorism, wrote: "The scientific level of Freud's concept of the unconscious is exactly on a par with the miracles of Jesus."[6] Charges of this kind simply betray the ignorance of the accuser, since the miracles of Jesus are a supposed historical fact, which may or may not be true, whereas the unconscious is a concept, neither true nor false, that may or may not be useful.

Of the more serious evaluations, the best known in the early days was that by Robert Sears (1943), a psychologist who was retained by the Social Science Research Council to do a survey of objective studies of psychoanalytic concepts. Although Sears concluded that psychoanalysis is not a "good" science (i.e., it does not define terms carefully and experiment), he did state that "all the work . . . serves to emphasize the increasing significance attached to psychoanalysis, by nonanalysts, as a guide to the planning of research on personality."[7] Sears made the same logical error as Watson, since he attached truth values to concepts, rather than seeing them as tools with which to approach data.

In 1958 the philosopher Sidney Hook organized a symposium on the topic of scientific method, philosophy, and psychoanalysis, in which a number of philosophers and psychoanalysts took part. Various opinions were expressed pro and con (Hook, 1959). Hook himself reached the core of the problem with his comment that on the question of the necessary and sufficient criteria for a scientific discipline no consensus had been reached by philosophers of science. The book by Thomas Kuhn (1962) had not yet been written; it later showed that what has passed for philosophy of science has only a very tenuous connection with the scientific enterprise. Philipp Frank commented at the symposium that the roots of psychoanalysis and of logical positivism grew up in one and the same soil, the intellectual climate of Vienna before and after the First World War.[8] Both thus had the same or similar intellectual attitudes.

The Fisher-Greenberg Synthesis

Since Sears's book in 1943, a large number of studies on the scientific status of psychoanalysis have appeared. Recently, Fisher and Greenberg (1977) have sifted through almost 2,000 individual works and reached some interesting conclusions. Most surprising is their finding that Freudian theory has been subjected to *more* scientific appraisal than any other theory in psychology:

We have been amused by the fact that while there is the stereotyped conviction widely current that Freud's thinking is not amenable to scientific appraisal, the quantity of research data pertinent to it that has accumulated in the literature grossly exceeds that available for most other personality or developmental theories (for example, Piaget, Witkin, Allport, Eysenck). We have actually not been able to find a single systematic psychological theory that has been as frequently evaluated scientifically as have Freud's concepts. This is a real paradox. But why has the opposite impression become common coinage?[9]

Fisher and Greenberg state that they are impressed with how often the results have borne out Freud's expectations. They mention the following: [10]

1. Important aspects of his developmentally based oral and anal personality typologies have emerged as reasonable propositions.
2. The etiology of homosexuality, phrased by Freud largely in developmental terms, has also stood up well to the known facts.
3. A key idea in Freud's formulation concerning the origin of the paranoid delusion has been moderately well validated.
4. Several aspects of the complex Oedipal theory, primarily as applied to the male, have been partially affirmed.
5. Although major components of Freud's dream theory did not come off well when empirically appraised, his idea that the dream

can provide a vent or outlet for tension and disturbance was moderately supported.

They felt that in the following they had detected faults in Freud's "inventions," as they termed them:

1. His understanding of the nature of dreaming has been contradicted by many scientific observations.
2. It became clear, as they traced his thoughts concerning psychoanalytic therapy, that Freud never specified the necessary and sufficient conditions for achieving a therapeutic effect.
3. Particular segments of Freud's network of Oedipal concepts about the male seem to be untenable in the face of what is now known.
4. A moderately negative picture can be derived from their analysis of Freud's formulations concerning women, i.e., he often was not correct.

In spite of their effort to be scientific, a certain amount of confusion persists in Fisher and Greenberg's evaluations. In particular, they often mix up observations, concepts, and hypotheses. Because they lump these three together, they often find the matter inadequately studied. For instance, they state that "Freud's ideas concerning the relationship between insight and change have not been adequately tested."[11] However, they do show that many of the hypotheses put forward have been tested, and are testable, which may help to put to rest the complaint that "psychoanalysis and science are incompatible."

Some Comments on Science and Psychoanalysis

The mere compilation of empirical studies, impressive though it may be, does not resolve the question of the scientific status of psychoanalysis. The field of inquiry must first be clarified and delimited.

The problem of scientific status is not peculiar to psychoanalysis but is shared with all the social sciences that deal with mankind. The notion that experimental psychology is "scientific," while psychoanalysis is not, has to be discarded once and for all. The assumptions, methods, and conclusions of experimental psychology are open to considerable question, and have been questioned. The textbook notion of scientific method can no longer be considered adequate, since it does not pay sufficient attention to what scientists have actually done (Kuhn, 1962).

Psychoanalysis, as a dynamic system of psychology, has three aspects: a vision of what people are; a vision of what they might become, and a conceptual framework with which to give substance to these ideas. Each of these aspects must be considered separately in an attempt to evaluate how scientific psychoanalysis is.

The vision of what mankind is could be approached in terms of conflict and suffering, which have been emphasized by psychoanalysis from the very beginning. That there is much more conflict and suffering in human beings than had hitherto been believed, or than other theoretical approaches admit, is amply documented by many empirical studies, and could be added to easily enough. Ultimate questions, such as Brenner's recent contention (1976) that there is *always* conflict, may be left for further investigation.

The vision of what mankind could become is part of the philosophical aspect of psychoanalysis, related to therapy. Many analysts, from Freud onward, have held that what is seen in daily life is a mere caricature of what people might be. The frequent success of therapy in changing the course of individuals' lives is evidence that there is some truth to this belief. That other approaches also might change people's lives leads to the empirical question of how the other changes effected compare with those effected by psychoanalysis. Falling back on a conventional image of "neurosis," which cannot be defined, or even "psychosis," which also is vague, becomes an exercise in futility. Empirical investigation is needed. Freud actually once said: "What we lack most is case material. I am never quite satisfied with my own." [12]

Finally, the conceptual framework of psychoanalysis requires no confirmation, any more than does the conceptual framework of any other science (Hanson, *Patterns of Discovery,* 1958). Concepts are either useful or not. Yet without certain concepts the facts of any science may become impossibly obscure. Thus, for example, without the concept of unconscious motives, the motives of a subject in any experimental situation are almost impossible to disentangle. This has vitiated a large body of motivational research.

A further, urgent problem facing psychoanalytic psychology is that its findings are disturbing to people. This dilemma confronts psychoanalysts as well as nonanalysts. Fisher and Greenberg have correctly observed that a unified and consistent treatment approach called "psychoanalysis" does *not* exist.[13] I discussed earlier the political conflicts within the American Psychoanalytic Association and others like it that have led to such a state of affairs. Under these circumstances, empirical observation of what actually happens is called for, not testing of any hypotheses. Inasmuch as psychoanalysis is also a method of therapy, limitations are imposed upon research into it which do not exist in other fields. The simple design of treating one person analytically and using a similar one as a control is unethical. Nevertheless, despite these and other limitations, research has gone on and does go on.

In its essence psychoanalysis represents a dynamic approach to psychology, a grand vision of mankind. As such it is no more or less scientific than any other approach. Much of its material can be handled on an empirical basis, but the empirical research must be guided by some meaningful theory. In spite of all the obstacles put in its path, psychoanalytic science has made considerable progress.

The Structure of Psychoanalytic Theory: Freud and the Alternatives

The structure of psychoanalytic theory has to be inferred from the total corpus of Freud's writings and the writings of all the analysts who have followed him. This is a lengthy but unavoidable procedure. In the present book the attempt has been made to trace these theories historically. In a previous work (Fine, 1975b) I tried to sum up psychoanalytic theory as it stands at present. In no case is it possible to summarize psychoanalytic science in any simple way. Complexity may be annoying, but it is unavoidable.

From time to time various theoreticians, dissatisfied with such a cumbersome approach, have proposed alternatives. Now that the basic historical material has been reviewed, some of these alternatives can be discussed in greater detail.

Sullivan's Interpersonal Theory

Sullivan's interpersonal theory has been hailed by many as a revolutionary advance over Freudian theory. Sullivan himself never maintained that he was proposing a new theory; he merely held that he was offering a better emphasis. But the need for a charismatic figure has distorted the historical sequence.

Reviewing Sullivan's own works, all but one of which were published posthumously from lecture notes, I find no really significant differences from Freudian theory. His language is often different, but the ideas remain the same. His most distinctive idea, that of the self system, has been for many years an integral part of all analytic theory, and has been elaborated much more carefully than he did (see chapter 5).

One of Sullivan's most gifted students, Gerard Chrzanowski, has recently tried to systematize Sullivan's teaching (1977). He states that Sullivan's aim "was to create a sounder epistemological foundation for clinical observations than Freudian metapsychology permitted. In particular, he focused attention on a larger transactional field by including cultural, societal and other environmental components in his developmental, operationally oriented scheme."[14] It is difficult to see how this means more than any contemporary Freudian ego-psychological statement. Chrzanowski seems to overlook the fact that interpersonal, cultural factors have long since been absorbed into standard Freudian theory. Sullivan and members of his group have made and continue to make significant contributions to both analytic theory and practice. But to designate them as a "school" seems very misleading.

Rapaport's Systematization

In 1960 Rapaport, in response to an invitation from Sigmund Koch, published a systematization of psychoanalytic theory. He had little faith in what he was trying: "To my mind it is too early to attempt a systematization of the psychoanalytic theory. A science can be a "good science" without being ready for a systematic presentation: all old sciences were once in this position."[15] Rapaport tried to encompass the structure of the system in 10 points of view: empirical,

Gestalt, organismic, genetic, topographic, dynamic, economic, structural, adaptive, and psychosocial. The system turned out to be too far removed from clinical data and has had no follow-up.

Topography and Systems: Gill, and Arlow and Brenner

Freud never made it clear that his structural system of 1923 was intended to replace the topographic system of 1900 entirely. Gill (1963) and Arlow and Brenner (1964) devoted extensive works to showing that this was indeed the case, so that the topographic was to be considered one point of view, but not a system in the larger sense of a general psychology.

Peterfreund: Information Systems

In a number of communications Emmanuel Peterfreund, a New York analyst, has argued that the traditional formulations of ego psychology and the structural hypotheses are entirely outmoded (Peterfreund, 1971, 1975). For him, metapsychology lacks explanatory power and is primitive in nature. He urged its replacement by an information-processing and systems model that is consistent with neurophysiology.

Klein: More Revolt against Metapsychology

Peterfreund is one of many who have voiced strong objections to Freud's traditional metapsychology, which they consider completely inappropriate to the field. G. Klein (1976) argued for a separation of the clinical from the metapsychological. He urged concentration on the clinical: "My intent . . . is to try to breathe new life into a way of thinking which revolutionized twentieth-century psychology but which has been overgrown with an obscurantist jargon, suffers the dry rot of overconceptualization, and is bedevilled by the intertwining of two incompatible modes of explanation."[16]

Schafer: Action Language

Since 1973 Roy Schafer has been advocating the substitution of an action language for the classical metapsychology (Schafer, 1976).

Unifying Theory of Human Behavior 543

His argument is that metapsychology has evolved into a complex set of rules governing the choice and use of terms and the framing and interrelating of propositions about human development and conflict. Many features and consequences of this set of rules lack clarity, consistency, and necessity or relevance; additionally, many of them are inadequate to do the theoretical jobs for which they have been designed.

Many analysts have agreed with Schafer that metapsychology is needlessly obscure and complicated, but few have followed him into his new pathway of "psychoanalysis without psychodynamics." As with so many other systems (see Gedo and Goldberg, *Models of the Mind,* 1973), criticism of the old is easy, creation of a new substitute is difficult.

Summary Comment: The Battle against Metapsychology

All of the alternative theories to Freud (including Sullivan's) involve jettisoning the metapsychology. The term "metapsychology" is defined by Laplanche and Pontalis (1973) as follows:

a term invented by Freud to refer to the psychology of which he was the founder when viewed in its most theoretical dimension. Metapsychology constructs an ensemble of conceptual models which are more or less far removed from empirical reality. Examples are the fiction of a psychical apparatus divided up into agencies, the theory of the instincts, the hypothetical process of repression, and so on. Metapsychology embraces three approaches, known as the dynamic, the topographical and the economic point of view.[17]

Actually, for Freud metapsychology consisted of two different sets of concepts. One involved ideas such as the id, ego, superego, and repression, which are close to clinical realities and are directly translatable into clinical realities. The other is the more hypothetical ideas such as cathexis, energy, and energy transformations, and psychophysical concepts such as the actual neurosis. It is against the latter set that most criticisms have been directed.

At this point, a knowledge of the historical development becomes highly illuminating. Freud always returned to theoretical metapsychology when he proposed daring new ideas or observed some new clinical material. At such times he seemed to become frightened, for these were all psychological propositions and, in the scientific climate of his youth, psychology divorced from physiology was absolutely taboo. Furthermore, after the early days he felt himself (and actually was) under continual attack by many critics, so he defended himself by resorting to physiology.

This pattern can be traced in a number of instances. The "Project," his first extended neurological explanation of psychology, was undertaken at the beginning of his self-analysis (1895). It was replaced by the immortal *Interpretation of Dreams* (1900), the cornerstone of psychoanalytic theory; he felt so sure of his new ideas that for once he offered no physiological underpinning. When his observations on psychosexual development had ripened to the point of publication in 1905, he buttressed them with the instinct theory current in his day, which has long since been outmoded. In 1914, stung by the defections of Jung and Adler, he published his profound observations on narcissism, but these were supported by a very peculiar libido theory. When he recognized the fundamental significance of aggression in 1920, he used the death instinct as base; this book was written under the impact of the devastation of the war. Finally, in the main work dealing with the structural theory, *The Ego and the Id,* (1923) he introduced his argument with considerations of topography and the unconscious that could just as well have been omitted.

At every stage Freud could have deleted his metapsychological propositions about energy, libido, death instinct, etc., without impairing the value of any of his major theories. With the heavy attacks on metapsychology now coming from all quarters, this seems to be the direction in which psychoanalysis is moving.

Psychoanalysis and the Social Sciences

In his 1913 paper on "The Claims of Psychoanalysis to Scientific Interest" Freud had already drawn attention to the relevance of psychoanalysis for other fields of science. His own hope was that analysis would make a basic contribution to biology; he expected that psychoanalysis would act "as an intermediary between biology and psychology." [18] Darwin was the great hero of his youth, and biology was, like America, the land of unlimited possibilities, as he put it later.

Although numerous intercorrelations have been recorded, psychoanalysis has not made any fundamental contributions to nonhuman biology. In human biology it has made great strides in the explanation of psychosomatic phenomena and psychophysiological interconnections.

The great achievement of psychoanalysis with regard to other fields is actually in the social sciences. Here, despite numerous obstacles and regressions, a veritable revolution has occurred. My thesis is that psychoanalysis integrates, or has the capacity to integrate, all the social sciences into one science of mankind; here again a careful perusal of the historical picture is most illuminating. Chapters 1–2 surveyed the state of the sciences in 1890, when Freud began, and the intervening developments. A comparison of the situation now with what existed then shows how much of the change is due to psychoanalysis.

Psychology

Since Freud always referred to psychoanalysis as a system of psychology, it is natural to begin with that discipline. In summing up any field so large, simplification is unavoidable. "Psychology" will be taken to concern those who view themselves professionally as psychologists, i.e., mainly the membership of the American Psychological Association. While great differences among the members exist and have always existed, certain strong trends are noticeable.

Fanatical Rejection before World War II

Before about 1940, psychoanalysis was almost violently rejected by all the leading figures in the world of psychology. The situation was similar to that in neurology and psychiatry, where, as Rapaport and Shakow comment (1964), the list of those who expressed vehement opposition to Freudian ideas at various times prior to 1910 was almost a "Who's Who" of these fields.[19]

Although there were many individual exceptions, Freud and psychoanalysis remained anathema to the American psychological establishment. Typical among the critics is the long-forgotten Knight Dunlap, who inveighed unceasingly against the unconscious, against the theory of instincts, against the role of emotions, and against everything else of a dynamic nature that psychoanalysis stood for.[20]

The Curious Contradiction

Despite this seemingly relentless opposition, many psychologists went to analysts for their personal troubles. The contradiction was a glaring one, yet they faced it honestly, and a number of them reported on their experiences. In 1940 the *Journal of Abnormal and Social Psychology* organized a symposium on the topic of "Psychoanalysis as Seen by Psychoanalyzed Psychologists," consisting of personal accounts of their analysis by a number of prominent psychologists. The symposium was later published separately by the American Psychological Association (1953). The psychologists represented included Edwin Boring, Austin Wood, Carney Landis, J. F. Brown, Raymond Willoughby, Percival Symonds, Henry Murray, Else Frenkel-Brunswik, David Shakow, and Donald V. McGranahan. A number of the analysts who treated these psychologists are mentioned, and Hanns Sachs and Franz Alexander both contributed perceptive reflections on the topic.

All the participating psychologists reported benefiting from their analysis, in varying degrees. Wood stated that "the understanding of human motivation and behavior which the experience has brought me seems, as nearly as I can judge, to be at least as much as I had acquired in seven years of formal study and an equal number of years of teaching."[21] J. F. Brown asserted that "psychoanalysis is the major contribution made to psychology in our times,"[22] and Raymond Willoughby observed: "It seems clear that if anything should be included in psychology, psychoanalysis should; the study of emotional habits, normal and disturbed, is precisely what is meant by a major fraction of psychology. That academic psychology has kept sedulously away from these major problems must, however, be not only admitted, but deplored as an important reason for its sterility."[23]

Percival Symonds commented: "Time was—and still is—when psychoanalysis was anathema to many psychologists. . . . Now with comparative suddenness psychologists everywhere are ready to embrace psychoanalysis, to put it to rigorous experimental tests, and to determine exactly what it contains of value to be incorporated into psychological theory."[24] Henry Murray remarked: "I can hardly think myself back to the myopia that once so seriously restricted my view of human nature."[25]

Most interesting was the account by Edwin Boring, author of the standard *History of Experimental Psychology* and widely respected as one of the deans of American academic psychology. Four years after his analysis (with Hanns Sachs), Boring could not say whether it had made any important change in him, although he states that he got over an acute emotional crisis. In view of his long emphasis on experimentation, Boring's remarks are quite pertinent:

It seems strange that a psychologist after his psychoanalysis should not have a message for his colleagues, when there has been so much questioning of psychoanalysis by the orthodox psychologists; and yet it is true that four years after my analysis I still cannot assess with assurance the significance of the experience in my life. Since, nevertheless, my hesitation is a datum in itself, I welcome this opportunity to make it in specific detail a matter of record. Apparently psychology is not yet in a position to validate or invalidate psychoanalysis experimentally—with selected groups and carefully chosen controls. Hence we are reduced to the collection of case histories; and critical autobiographical histories by sophisticated, scientifically minded persons ought to be worth more than the enthusiasm of naive persons about an event which has helped them.[26]

Two conclusions emerge from this symposium. First, I am reminded of Heinrich Heine's verses, that in public they preach water, and in private they drink wine. Whatever barbs psychologists might shoot in public, in private whenever they were in trouble they sought out analysts. (The same finding emerged from a study of behavior therapists by Lazarus [1971]; he polled 20 behavior therapists and found that 10 went to psychoanalysts, while none went to behavior therapists.) And second, the symposium bore out a major contention of psychoanalysis through the years, that without some personal experience of the process the doctrine remains essentially incomprehensible to the individual because of his personal complexes. As Alexander commented, the feud between experimental psychology and psychoanalysis has no rational foundation, only an emotional one.[27]

After World War II: The Rise of Clinical Psychology

As noted, the events of World War II sparked a sharp rise in interest in psychoanalysis. In 1945 there were less than 1,000 trained analysts *in the world*. Thus the need for new blood was great. One result was the rise of clinical psychology.

Looking back, the term "clinical psychology" was a kind of compromise to allow the introduction of psychoanalytic ideas and approaches into psychology without permitting the forbidden word "psychoanalysis" to emerge from its taboo. In an illuminating study, Kris et al. (1943) reviewed the treatment of dreams and other topics in American textbooks of elementary psychology. They found that when something became generally accepted, it was considered part of psychology; when it remained dubious, it remained part of psychoanalysis. In this way large areas of psychoanalytic thought were incorporated into psychology, without the use of the word psychoanalysis. This process, which has gone on in other fields as well, has obscured the historical picture. Carl Rogers, for instance, with his client-centered therapy, shows a clear derivation from psychoanalytic thinking, particularly the transference insistence of Otto Rank. Yet in Rogers's writings and those of his followers a vehement opposition to psychoanalysis is expressed; the name of his system seems to have been chosen to imply that while psychoanalysis is therapist-centered, his focuses on the patient.

In any case, once clinical psychology had entered the picture, the rise of psychology was dramatic. From a small group of about 4,000 academicians in 1945, it increased to a total of 44,650 members in 1977, according to the APA *Register of Members;* the largest groupings are now in the clinical division, with 4,313 members, personality and social psychology (heavily involved with psychodynamic theories), with 4,203, and psychotherapy, with 3,356.[28] The clinical psychologist with a doctorate can perform a variety of functions essentially similar to those of a psychiatrist; many even administer drugs under medical supervision. "Freedom of choice" laws increasingly provide that if a patient is covered for psychiatric treatment, the insurance companies have to recognize a licensed (or certified) psychologist as an adequate practitioner.

Psychoanalysis proper and Freud have been taught in diverse departments in the universities, generally not in psychology, often in English, sociology, or philosophy. Nevertheless, an informal survey by one publisher in 1977 showed that there were 898 courses in universities throughout the country where Freud was the only or main subject matter.[29]

The literature, both popular and professional, has expanded tremendously. The journal *Psychology Today,* a literate presentation of psychological discoveries for the general public, claims more than a million readers.

With regard to psychoanalytic training, in 1971 Henry and his co-workers compiled some statistics on the four major psychological professions, which they argued really included a "fifth profession" of psychotherapist. Of the psychiatrists 49 percent considered their formal training completed by the end of the psychiatric residency. Among psychiatrists who do take postresidency training, about 30 percent enter analytic training programs conducted by institutes approved by the American Psychoanalytic Association, 26 percent enter unapproved programs, 20 percent enroll in programs offered by universities, and the remainder receive varied training.[30] Since only 10–30 percent of all psychiatric residents apply for psychoanalytic training,[31] less than 10 percent of the psychiatrists are fully trained analysts, even though analysis plays a central role in their thinking.

Of the psychologists, according to Henry,[32] 35 percent of the clinicians went on to postdoctoral training, most often (51 percent) in analytic institutes. The mean time for postgraduate training for clinical psychologists was 3.9 years. Thus the average time spent by clinical psychologists in postdoctoral programs was less than the average of 5.4 years spent by psychoanalysts in institutes, but slightly more than the 3.3-year average for psychiatrists in postresidency training programs. Henry concludes that "clinical psychologists who elect to take additional training at the postgraduate level receive as much, if not more, training than psychiatrists who do not enter psychoanalytic training."[33]

The Nature of Analytic Influence

It is a herculean if not impossible task to sort out from the vast stream of ideas in twentieth-century thought what is analytic and what is not. However, some summary evaluations may be made. Writing in 1964 on the occasion of Sigmund Koch's total evaluation of psychology as a science, Rapaport and Shakow offer the following picture of the influence of psychoanalysis on psychology up to that time:[34]

1. What is accepted is Freud's new view of mankind and his pioneering in new areas for psychological study. There has been a slow realization that Freud awakened interest in human nature, in in-

fancy and childhood, in the irrational in mankind; that he is the foun-
tainhead of dynamic psychology in general, and of psychology's
present-day conceptions of motivation and of the unconscious in particular.

2. Although there are many striking exceptions, for the most
part his *conception of* these fields of study and his *observations* in
them, not his *concepts and theories* about them, have been accepted.

3. When the theory itself is referred to, it is usually transformed
into some "common-sense" version or is taken at the level of its
clinical referents. In either case psychoanalysis is likely to be criticized. One can even say that until recently no serious efforts were
made to study thoroughly or to define Freud's concepts before either
"testing" them experimentally or rejecting them.

4. The methods by which Freud arrived at his theories have not
been used. Only recently has some effort been made to examine the
psychoanalytic method as a tool for research.

By the mid-1950s the earlier proliferation of schools had ended
and there were now mainly two theoretical approaches in the field:
psychoanalysis, or dynamic psychology, and learning theory. Clinical
psychology was largely a refinement and application of the dynamic
ideas of psychoanalysis, even though the formation of a division of
psychoanalysis within the American Psychological Association had
not yet materialized. If pressed, most psychologists at that time
would no doubt have viewed themselves as eclectic, although the ex-
perimental-behavioristic position still dominated the universities and
the national organization. Nevertheless, considerable discontent
reigned. In 1959, Sigmund Koch, when he came to sum up the
state of the science in his attempted synthesis, had this to say:

It can in summary be said that the results of Study I set up a vast attrition
against virtually all the elements of the Age of Theory [approximately the
1930–1955 period]code. . . . There is a longing, bred on perception of the
limits of recent history and nourished by boredom, for psychology to embrace . . . problems over which it is possible to feel intellectual passion. . . .

For the first time in its history, psychology seems ready—or almost
ready—to assess its goals and instrumentalities with primary reference to its
own indigenous problems.[35]

In the ensuing years numerous battles have raged within the
body psychological about the issues brought up by psychoanalysis.

Some of these may be briefly reviewed, in the framework of the clinical versus experimental approaches.

RELEVANCE VERSUS PRECISION. It is universally admitted that one of the great contributions of psychoanalysis was to focus squarely on issues relevant to the human enterprise. As early as 1920, G. Stanley Hall, in his introduction to the American edition of Freud's *Introductory Lectures,* made precisely this point: that Freud was moving where other psychologists feared to tread. The topics of love, sexuality, emotions, the unconscious, neurosis, psychotherapy, and hostility are but a few of those virtually ignored by psychology before Freud.

As yet, it has not been possible to handle these areas with the precision that is common in the physical sciences. Nevertheless, if the psychologist is not to remain a "rat in a maze," they must be handled; absolute precision seems unattainable, but they should be handled with as much precision as possible. The book by Fisher and Greenberg (1977) cited earlier is in this tradition.

UNCONSCIOUS MOTIVES VERSUS BEHAVIORAL ACTS. A running argument has gone on about whether the psychologist should try to infer unconscious motives from the productions of his subjects (or patients), or whether he should limit himself to what is behaviorally observable. In line with this argument, dynamic clinicians have generally preferred measures of personality assessment that provide clues to underlying unconscious motives, such as the Rorschach and TAT, while behavioral psychologists have preferred direct measures of behavior, such as the California Personality Inventory, or the Minnesota Multiphasic (MMPI). This is a topic on which intense controversy continues, but it is pertinent to quote what one authority, Norman (1967), has said about the MMPI, the most widely used behavioral measure of personality:

[The MMPI's] original clinical criteria are anachronistic; its basic clinical scales are inefficient, redundant, and largely irrelevant for their present purposes; its administrative format and the repertoire of responses elicited are, respectively, inflexible and impoverished; and its methods for combining scale scores and for profile interpretations are unconscionably cumbersome and obtuse.[36]

DYNAMIC VERSUS CONDITIONING APPROACH. A third source of dispute is whether human beings should be seen as the product of the interplay of dynamic forces, as Freud had postulated, or whether they are simply the consequence of conditioning mechanisms, as Pavlov and B. F. Skinner had maintained. Actually, there is no necessary contradiction between these two points of view (Breland and Breland, 1961) but in practice they have been sharply opposed (Skinner, 1971).

What it seems to boil down to is the image of mankind, often put as the Lockean theory of the *tabula rasa* versus the Leibnizian doctrine of internal forces. In the light of what has happened, the sociopolitical implications of each theory cannot be ignored. Dynamic psychology of the Freudian variety has been outlawed in all totalitarian countries, whereas experimental psychology is permitted everywhere. Thus the problem is not the approach but what is revealed about the behavior and suffering of individuals in any given society. It becomes a question of the underlying philosophy of living, which cannot be evaded by recourse to the magic word "science." Alexander's remark is still pertinent, that the conflict between experimental and analytic psychology is an emotional one, not a matter of cool reason.

AFFECTIVE VERSUS COGNITIVE FACTORS. A fourth issue is that of emotion. In the traditional world view of experimental psychology, emotions are emergency reactions, disturbances of what should normally be a state of peace and quiet. In the world view of analytic psychology, the exact opposite is true: emotions are vital, long-standing reactions of the organism. Chronic resentments can and do exist for a lifetime, causing severe distress and even loss of life. This issue touches on previous ones. Emotions cannot be handled experimentally with the same precision as cognition, nor can they really be understood without some reference to the unconscious. It is again the image of mankind that is at stake.

PSYCHOANALYTIC THERAPY VERSUS BRIEFER (SYMPTOMATIC) THERAPIES. A fifth issue is the kind of therapy that should be administered. Psychologists have in the main leaned toward briefer, more eclectic, nonanalytic therapies, although there are many exceptions (Corsini, 1973). Again this raises the question of the degree of suffering that does exist among people, and the image of mankind involved in the psychotherapeutic enterprise. It may also be true that psychologists have reacted in a very human way to their exclusion from the psychoanalytic institutes: if you don't want me, your theory is of no value. As the analytic institutes change, the further incorporation of psychoanalysis and psychoanalytic therapy into the practice of psychologists seem likely.

IS PSYCHOLOGY A CLINICAL OR AN EXPERIMENTAL SCIENCE?
Finally, there is the most basic question of all: how should psychology be pursued, in an experimental or a clinical manner? It is surely noteworthy that the clinical approach deriving from psychoanalysis has made enormous inroads, while the experimental view has either stood still or retreated in many instances.

Again the image of mankind and the underlying philosophy of living are involved. Boring, in his personal statement quoted earlier, saw the clinical approach as unavoidable, pending the development of more rigorous experimental techniques. These more rigorous techniques have not yet been forthcoming, because of the inherent difficulties of the field. The shift in membership affiliations of the American Psychological Association attests to the fact that a considerable percentage of psychologists today prefer to approach the human being from a clinical point of view. This does not rule out experimentation or careful observation where feasible (Rosenthal, 1976) but focuses more squarely on questions of relevance and the basic philosophy of the study of mankind.

Psychiatry

The influence of psychoanalysis on psychiatry has been even more direct and more complete than on psychology or other fields. It has reached the point where the layman today often confuses the term "psychiatrist" with "psychoanalyst." Again the historical development is useful.

Before World War II

Prior to World War II, psychiatry was one of the least rewarding specialties in medicine. For the most part it lacked a theoretical rationale for its endeavors, it had no meaningful therapeutic modalities, and its therapeutic outlook in every area was largely pessimistic.

As noted in chapter 2, psychiatry at the time of Kraepelin had not even caught up to the ancient Greeks. Kraepelin codified a system of psychiatric diagnosis, an assumption of hereditary etiology, and a

pessimistic outlook on therapy that resulted in the severe overcrowd-
ing of large mental hospitals with thousands of cases regarded as
hopeless by everybody involved.

After the French Revolution, psychiatry had put its faith in brain
anatomy research, which would, practitioners were confident, eventually reveal the causes of insanity, and in the asylum or mental hospital, where kindly "moral treatment" would make the insane sufficiently tractable to live in society again. Neither of these hopes was
realized. Brain anatomy research did show that paresis, or general paralysis of the insane, was the last stage of syphilis, and, later, that
there was a characteristic brainwave pattern in the epileptic. Apart
from that, nothing, until the modern era. But the search continued.

In the meantime, the plight of the insane confined to hospitals
went from bad to worse. From the first half of the nineteenth century
to the second half, there was a dramatic decline from reform to a custodial operation (Rothman, 1971). In 1917 Kraepelin could write:

The broad outlines of psychiatry as it existed a century ago have been
revealed by our cursory survey: negligent and brutal treatment of the insane;
improper living conditions and inadequate medical care; beclouded and
false notions concerning the nature and cause of insanity; senseless, haphazard and at times harmful therapeutic measures which aggravated the
plight of those afflicted by mental illness.[37]

But if the treatment of the mentally ill was barbarous and cruel
before Kraepelin, it seems to have worsened with his ideas. Under
the influence of the Kraepelinian diagnostic system (which still prevails in theory), schizophrenics were given shocks, injected almost to
death, castrated, lobotomized, had other parts of the brain removed
or cauterized, had teeth extracted and intestines removed, were bound
hand and foot, beaten mercilessly, and largely neglected in filthy,
poorly kept "mental hospitals," which are now being systematically
dismantled.

In the late 1930s new somatic treatments were introduced: metrazol convulsive therapy, insulin coma therapy, electric shock therapy, lobotomy, and lobectomy. While these were the vogue, psychiatrists swore by them; today they are practically forgotten. In 1974
Milton Greenblatt, former Commissioner of Mental Hygiene of Mas-
sachusetts, evaluated the state of the hospitals more than 50 years
after Kraepelin's statement:

Although it is an indelible blot on the escutcheon, we must admit poverty and deprivation still prevail in most of the large mental institutions in the United States. Poverty is not new in America, but the mentally ill and the mentally retarded are poor many times over. They come from poor backgrounds, they are poor in mental and often physical health, we treat them in poverty-stricken institutions, and then we return them to their poverty-ridden surroundings—often, inevitably, to begin the cycle again.[38]

The Revolution of the Mid-1950s

A dramatic change in psychiatry occurred in the mid-1950s. Sometimes this has been hailed as the drug revolution, but many other forces were also at play—the emptying of the hospitals, the growth of psychoanalytic sophistication leading to a shift in the patient population, the greater availability of all kinds of mental health personnel, the improved training of psychiatrists, and the consistent pursuit of large-scale research studies, especially in the area of community psychiatry.

THE DRUG REVOLUTION. In 1952 a French anesthesiologist discovered the drug chlorpromazine (Thorazine). Soon thereafter it was administered to schizophrenic patients by two French psychiatrists, Delay and Deniker. The patients seemed to be tranquilized and to experience a striking reduction in their psychosis. Thus began the drug revolution. Numerous other drugs have been introduced, and are still being introduced (Klein and Gittelman-Klein, 1976). The practice of psychiatry has been profoundly altered.[39]

Arguments pro and con about the use of drugs for various conditions have raged ever since. One of the most widely-quoted research studies is that headed by Philip May at Camarillo State Hospital in California (May 1968). There 228 schizophrenic patients who had not had significant prior hospital treatment were chosen from male and female first admissions. Five different modes of treatment were tested: antipsychotic drugs alone; individual psychotherapy alone; individual psychotherapy plus antipsychotic drugs; electroshock; and milieu. Various measures of outcome were used, of which release from the hospital was most global. Drug use alone was the most effective treatment, and drugs plus psychotherapy also led to high release rates. Psychotherapy alone had a release rate of 65 percent.[40] May's study is open to many criticisms. One is that the psychological measures used to evaluate outcome were not dynamic (MMPI mostly). Another, voiced by one of the psychologists, Luther Distler, is that the magnitude of the effects may have been due to the high quality of the milieu treatment, which was unusually intense.[41]

In a recent review of the topic, Tissot (1977) concludes that the use of neuroleptics (tranquilizing drugs) for schizophrenia has now become universal, even though the evidence is far from conclusive. The drop in the hospital population certainly has something to do with the use of drugs, but, he argues, it depends on other factors as well, particularly hospital policy. Gurle (1966) showed, for example, that the mere transfer of patients from one hospital to another is followed by a definite increase in the frequency of discharge of patients hospitalized for over two years.

THE EMPTYING OF THE HOSPITALS. Concurrent with the development of the drugs has come the emptying of the hospitals. In 1955 the resident population in public mental hospitals was 558,000; in 1976 it was less than 215,000. Readmission rates ranged from 30 to 60 percent.[42] This change reflects primarily a change of policy, not some underlying improvement. Zwerling (1977) comments, for instance, that in 1970 New York and California had approximately equal populations but disproportionate numbers of patients hospitalized: California had 11,000 patients in mental hospitals; New York, 47,000. California had developed an extensive network of outpatient clinics and filled all available places; New York built a network of gigantic hospitals and filled all the beds.[43]

There have also been increasing numbers of complaints about the state of patients after they have been released from the hospital. H. Lamb (1976), reviewing the problems of community survival for long-term patients, stresses that patients should be treated primarily in the community. Further, he enunciates a series of essentially psychoanalytic principles for such treatment: among them are working with the healthy part of the ego, giving the patient a sense of mastery, use of work therapy, and normalization of the patient's environment.

DRUGS VERSUS PSYCHOTHERAPY. The advent of drugs ushered in a new debate—whether patients should be treated with drugs or with psychotherapy. The May study (1968) has been widely cited as the major basis for stressing drugs with schizophrenics, but other psychiatrists have viewed even those results with some skepticism. Chiland (1977) cites a number of experiments from all over the world, in which the predominant mode of approach is psychotherapeutic, with drugs used as adjuvants. This would appear to be the usual mode of operation today, and so psychoanalytic principles retain their basic role even with the treatment of psychotics.

As far as the treatment of milder disorders is concerned, numerous drugs have become available: Valium, Librium, and meprobamate, among others. Unlike the situation with psychosis, however, no one seriously claims that the use of these drugs eliminates the need for psychotherapy.

Furthermore, a number of studies examining the long-term effects of the drugs have come to less rosy conclusions. Much interest has been aroused by a study by Manfred Bleuler (the son of the great Eugen Bleuler), who followed the life histories of 208 schizophrenics over a period of 23 years, beginning in 1940. Bleuler (1970) emphasized that his 1965 percentages are based on thorough familiarity with his own cohort as published 25 years earlier and with the still earlier studies of his father and of Kraepelin. Bleuler found that catastrophic schizophrenia was dying out; he could not find a single case that began after 1942. Furthermore, a considerable percentage of his cases stabilized themselves after a five-year period, regardless of what treatment was given to them. The long-term results of the drugs do not differ from milieu therapy, and thus the drugs should be regarded as having primarily short-term relief value. Bleuler stated:

Research on the clinical course of the illness confirms what clinicians realized long ago: in the schizophrenic, the healthy human is hidden and remains hidden, even if the psychosis lasts long. The healthy life of schizophrenics is never extinguished. How different such an observation is from what we see in patients with chronic brain diseases![44]

Gralnick (1969), head of High Point Hospital at Rye, New York, in reviewing 500 hospitalized cases where psychotherapy was used, stressed three variables: the selection of patients, the psychotherapeutic community structure, and the conduct of family therapy, as contributing to success.[45]

Serious disillusionment with reliance on drug therapy has already begun. Tardive dyskinesia (the inability to control certain muscles), among other reactions, is a serious side-effect of long-term use of neuroleptics.[46] But even without the physiological side-effects, psychological neglect remains crippling. In reviewing the results of closing the state mental hospitals, Ahmed and Plog (1976) state:

This is a book about a movement—a movement begun by Dorothea Dix that started as the hope of the future for the mentally disturbed, and is now ending with hopes shattered and expectations unmet, under the aegis of judicial scrutiny and with public outcry. The mental hospital as an institution is under fire, not for what it has done for the mentally disturbed and ill, but for what it has not done. . . . [A] new definition of mental hospital is emerging . . . [and] will continue to be reshaped on the basis of judicial adjudication and public scrutiny.[47]

Legal Reaction: The Rights of Patients

The constant criticism of the deplorable conditions in mental hospitals finally led to a change in legal attitudes in the 1960s. A number of court decisions established the right of the mental patient to adequate care and treatment; some have characterized these decisions as judicial atonement for society's neglect of the mentally ill. Judge David Bazilon, in a landmark case in 1966 (*Rouse* v. *Cameron*) gave judicial standing to the concept of the right to treatment for involuntarily committed mental patients. In a later decision in Alabama (*Wyatt* v. *Stickney,* 1970), Judge Frank Johnson specified three principal aspects of an adequate treatment program: an individual treatment plan for each patient; staffing adequate in numbers and training to provide treatment; and a humane physical and psychological environment.[48] These decisions highlight the dramatic shift in psychiatry's public image and responsibilities.

The Shift in the Patient Population

In a sense, the most important factor in the incorporation of psychoanalytic thought into psychiatry has been the shift in the patient population, from the psychotic to the normal. This can be understood by citing what is currently taught in medical-school departments of psychiatry:[49]

1. Normal development and expectable human behavior at various stages of the life cycle.
2. Biological, psychological, and social forces that influence behavioral illness, and the treatment of such illness.
3. Interviewing skills and the complexities of the doctor–patient relationship.

4. Psychopathology, the recognition of abnormal behavior.

5. Clinical psychiatric syndromes.

6. Treatment and management of common behavioral problems seen by the nonpsychiatric physician, including such areas as human crises, marriage counseling, death and dying, and child abuse.

7. Psychiatric and mental health resources, including knowing which patients to refer and the process of referral.

In addition, psychiatry departments emphasize a commitment to continuing self-education for mastery of new knowledge of and treatment techniques for behavioral disturbance. The entire range of human behavior, normal and abnormal, has now been brought within the purview of the psychiatrist.

Improved Training Programs

In 1948 there were 4,700 practicing psychiatrists in the country. In 1977 there were approximately 28,000. This spectacular growth was naturally accompanied by an equal increase in training programs. Constant reviews have been conducted to maintain these programs at a high level. Langsley et al. (1977) found that high-quality programs are characterized by a well-rounded faculty, a psychodynamic orientation, a greater commitment to medical-student education than to resident training, varied teaching methods, enthusiastic student response, and systematic evaluation that produces change in subsequent years.

Theoretical Issues

The expansion of psychiatry to include the entire population has created confusion in the minds of many psychiatrists and renewed the emphasis on a number of profound theoretical issues. The more traditional psychiatrists have complained (e.g., Ludwig, 1975) that psychiatry has become a hodgepodge of unscientific opinions, assorted philosophies and "schools of thought," mixed metaphors, role diffusion, propaganda, and politicking for "mental health" and other esoteric goals. They pray to be embraced by standard organic medicine, and offer to go back to the old image of the psychiatrist as the caretaker of the mentally ill. By contrast, the more sophisticated psychiatrists, mostly analytically trained, insist that the extension of psychiatry to the general population is a natural outgrowth of all the research of this century, that social, psychological, economic, and political forces are just as important in determining who is "mentally ill" as the traditional diagnostic system (for which they generally have little use), and that psychodynamics must be the basic orientation of psychiatry and psychotherapy must be its essential treatment modality, with everything else as an adjuvant.

Engel (1977) has insisted that the crisis of psychiatry in fact pertains to all of medicine. And medicine's crisis derives from adherence to a model of disease that is no longer adequate for the scientific tasks and social responsibilities of either medicine or psychiatry.[50] The formation of a Society for Health and Human Values and a journal of *Medicine and Philosophy* are signs that many physicians are ready to embrace the broader meaning of their field.

Unfortunately, organizations vie for power, and psychiatry is no exception. Holman (1976) has argued that the entire medical establishment "in significant part is engaged in special interest advocacy, pursuing and preserving social power."[51] Within psychiatry proper, instances of this power struggle are seen in the refusal to condemn the Soviet prostitution of psychiatry to political ends, the endorsement of behavior therapy, the bizarre reclassification of homosexuality as a "sexual orientation disturbance," and the determined effort to exclude long-term analysis from national health insurance. In this respect the psychiatrists do not differ from the other mental health organizations, which also pursue their special interests at the expense of the greater good (Halleck, 1971).

Psychiatry and Psychoanalysis

Analysts from Freud onward have felt called upon to write essays on psychoanalysis and psychiatry. When psychiatry was limited to the custodial care of the advanced mentally ill, they called for expansion of the horizons and depth-analytic interpretations of psychosis. Today, the situation is entirely different.

It is practically official policy now that the psychiatrist may be called upon to consult about and treat every human problem that comes up, since a psychological element enters into almost everything. In this sense psychoanalysis has absorbed all of psychiatry, with drugs seen as an auxiliary device. Unfortunately, as Engel (1977) points out, the training of the average psychiatrist often does not equip him properly for such an all-embracing task. Since the older duties and older concepts still hang on, the current scene presents a picture of considerable confusion and uncertainty, usually described as a "crisis" or "psychiatry's identity crisis."

Other Sciences

In all the social sciences, psychoanalysis has made substantial contributions. A few of the highlights can be noted here.

In *history,* a novel element has been introduced by focusing more on the psychology and the psychological motivations of historical figures. Historians always had offered sweeping judgments about the state of mind of any epoch, the normality of actions, the motives for war, revolutions, and so on. But as with academic psychology, their approach was limited to a surface rationality. Since psychoanalysis has made people aware of the deeper irrational strivings, many historians have tried to absorb these ideas into their work. Others, like Jacques Barzun, have pooh-poohed the whole approach, using much the same arguments about the past that academic-experimental psychologists have used about the present. The argument is not about whether psychological forces play a role in history; of course they do. The question is how to determine these forces from the historical record, and which forces to emphasize and look for.

Among the analysts, Lifton (1974) and Erikson (on Luther, 1958; on Gandhi, 1969; on Jefferson, 1974) have been outstanding. Among the historians, Walter Langer, a former president of the American Historical Association, has said: "I more and more came to realize that we historians indulged in very superficial estimates of men and their motives. In time I became completely converted to the notion that historians should explore and exploit the findings of modern psychology. And, eventually, I became a very apostle of this doctrine." [52]

In an article in a recent issue of the *Journal of Psychohistory,* George Kren (1977) presents some interesting data on the teaching of psychohistory in American colleges and universities. According to Kren, 10 years ago only two courses were offered in psychohistory throughout the country, but by 1977 there were 200. There can be no doubt that psychohistory has achieved a secure position within the academic enterprise. Although many different approaches are used, the one element that appears in common is the need to introduce psychoanalytic ideas to students. The problem, says Kren, is conceptual. Students find Freud difficult, find the vocabulary of psychoanalysis strange, and are not really convinced of the whole approach. Since, as a rule, no help is forthcoming from the psychology departments, paradoxically psychohistory serves to introduce students to a kind of psychology which they cannot learn elsewhere.

In *philosophy,* problems of ethics and happiness can no longer be seriously considered without some knowledge of psychology, which means psychoanalysis. Most philosophers have paid little attention to psychoanalysis (Wollheim, 1974). McGill (1967), one philosopher who is au courant of the psychoanalytic revolution, frankly recognizes that the problem of happiness has been shifted from philosophy to psychology:

In this final chapter we shall confine ourselves to the most important current development of the theory of the good life, i.e., the good-enough, the better, and the best or ideal life. The disciplines that are obliged, more than any others, to say what they mean by an improvement of the individual's general condition, and hence what they mean by a satisfactory or ideal life, are personality theory and psychotherapy. Both are concerned with undesirable symptoms and their removal, but their interest often goes beyond this negative result to a positive conception of "mental health" which is close to what we have been discussing under the name of "happiness." The fact that this conception is logically connected with medical therapy or with objective tests and controlled studies gives it a significance lacking in earlier theories.[53]

In the age-old problems of free will and the mind–body relationship, psychoanalysis is also in a position to make some contributions, but these are not as vital to the whole field as is the redefinition of happiness along psychoanalytic lines.

In *anthropology,* the promising beginnings of the 1920s and 1930s have already been discussed. Starting in the 1950s a vigorous attack on the culture–personality school took place (Levine, 1973), which seemed to block the considerable progress that had been made up to that point. Since then the numerous currents and cross-currents in this field have paralleled those in psychology and psychoanalysis itself.

In *sociology* there are a number of classics, including Erich

Fromm's *Escape from Freedom* (1941), Adorno's *The Authoritarian Personality* (1950), John Dollard and Alison Davis's *Children of Bondage* (1940), and Rennie et al.'s *Midtown Study* (1962) and its sequels. Many other excellent psychosocial studies are to be found in the literature. On a theoretical level, Talcott Parsons is noteworthy for his efforts to combine psychoanalysis and sociology. Other sociologists in this country have tended to place psychology in the background in the theoretical formulations, in line with the Durkheimian tradition. Goffman's *Frame Analysis* (1974) is a good example of this subordination of psychology. The Frankfurt school has made a more concerted effort to integrate psychoanalysis into social theory; Jurgen Habermas is the leading contemporary theorist of that school.

In *economics* the main psychoanalytic contribution has come in the area of motivation, and more particularly work motivation. The books of Frederick Herzberg have already been mentioned. John Kenneth Galbraith in his numerous writings has emphasized the orthodox economists' neglect of the motivational factor and has made a number of suggestions, particularly stressing the basic psychological character of the whole economic enterprise (1973, 1976). Harry Levinson, who has been director of the industrial psychology division at the Menninger Foundation, has made many perceptive contributions to industrial health (among them, *Emotional Health in the World of Work,* 1964). Many other industrial psychologists have applied the basic principles of psychoanalysis to industry (see Bray et al., 1974).

In *political science* a large literature exists on the topic of personality influences in political events. Two early classics are Harold Lasswell's *Psychopathology and Politics* (1930), in which the paranoid complexion of the American politician was first depicted, and his *Power and Personality* (1948). Greenstein, in *Personality and Politics* (1969), provides an excellent summary of the literature. The large number of studies of prominent political figures now almost always draw on psychoanalytic principles; for example, Tucker's *Stalinism* (1977) and Stierlin's *Adolf Hitler* (1977). Naturally work in this area soon merges into history, sociology, and straight psychology.

In *law,* applications of psychology, particularly psychoanalytic psychology, are found at every level. The legal reaction to the discovery of the neglect experienced by mental patients has already been mentioned. Slovenko's *Psychiatry and Law* (1973) offers an excellent summary of the leading contemporary trends. An American Academy of Psychiatry and Law, limited to psychiatrists, had a membership of 250 in 1969; a similar organization was founded by psychologists in 1968.[54] The book by Anna Freud, Goldstein, and Solnit, *Beyond the Best Interests of the Child* (1973), has already had an impact on custody decisions in the United States. Slovenko, viewing the trends as a whole, comments that society may end up with two kinds of institutions: mental hospitals for treatment on a voluntary basis, and correctional institutions for the involuntary treatment of those who are bothersome to society.[55]

In *literature and literary criticism,* even a bare listing of works would fill a volume. Many studies of prominent literary figures have appeared, and new ones come out every day. A National Association for Psychoanalytic Criticism has been formed and issues a journal, *Literature and Psychology,* in cooperation with the English department of Fairleigh Dickinson University. Many specialists in literature have taken additional training in psychoanalytic institutes, which have welcomed them from the start. By this time the whole area of literary criticism is a well-established discipline within clinical psychology.

In *education,* too, the influence of psychoanalytic ideas has been enormous. It encompasses the whole field of the dynamic understanding of the child. Since educators are superego figures, their activities frequently clash with those of a therapist, but many proposals have been made for softening the harsh kind of authoritarian discipline sometimes seen in the schools. In this respect Freud and Dewey go hand in hand. For a while a group at Teachers College in New York were actively promoting the introduction of more psychoanalytic material into the standard educational curriculum. Arthur Jersild had recommended that academic credit be given for personal analysis. Jersild and his assistant Lazar (1962) also collected data on the meaning of psychotherapy in teachers' lives and work, reporting that most of the teachers interviewed had found it extremely valuable.

In *religion* the interest of psychoanalysts has been confined largely to elucidation of the various rituals used by different religions. The vast majority of analysts have agreed with Freud's contention that religion is an infantile neurosis.

In summary, even these highlights of the past 30 years bear

witness to the extraordinary degree to which psychoanalytic thought has penetrated all the sciences that deal with mankind. In the present era we hear repeated calls for "interdisciplinary cooperation." A hundred years ago the social sciences were united at least for administrative purposes, under the department of philosophy; the present Ph.D. degree is a relic of that period. All the social sciences found their identity by separating from speculative philosophy. Now they are in the process of finding a new identity by uniting under the new image of mankind offered by psychoanalysis. ✳

Concluding Comments

At the conclusion of a long historical inquiry it is appropriate to look back, see where the field has come from, and to speculate about where it might be going. Coincidentally, such an evaluation comes close to the hundredth anniversary of its birth.

Freud had three goals in mind: to establish a theory of psychology; to develop a technique of psychotherapy; and to found a new profession. The question now is: How well did he and his successors succeed in each of these endeavors?

Psychoanalysis as Theory

The development of psychoanalysis as a theory has moved in two broad directions: first, toward making it a comprehensive psychology, and second, toward establishing a unitary science of mankind.

As a psychology, the main contribution of psychoanalysis lies in its *dynamic* approach, which allows the scientist to tackle questions that have relevance and significance to the human being. The fact that psychoanalytic psychology is tabooed in totalitarian countries is evidence that it makes a marked difference in people's lives, unlike experimental psychology, which, if it so wishes (and it often has), can busy itself with problems peripheral to mankind's main concerns. The political struggles in psychoanalytic psychology show that philosophical questions cannot be sidestepped. The vision of what mankind is is inseparably tied to the vision of what mankind might become.

In terms of the larger issues, two errors have crept into the interpretation of psychoanalysis. One is the parochial image that psychoanalysis is an independent discipline, essentially unconnected to any other field. Because he had to start from scratch in so many areas, Freud sometimes can be read in this way, but he quickly realized that he had the entire domain of human experience and behavior as his true province. The second error is the opposite one, of grandiosity, using psychoanalysis to explain every human manifestation. Usually this has taken the form of picking on some infantile fantasy or experience and applying that to all later behavior. Thus Geoffrey Gorer once tried to explain the Russian character as due to excessive swaddling in infancy. Some "primal scream" devotees try to explain all neurosis as being a result of the repression of feeling expressions in earliest childhood. Such attempts should be rejected as "vulgar Freudianism" by any intelligent person.

Instead, I have suggested that psychoanalysis should be looked upon as a psychology with a philosophical approach attached to it, since it offers a proposal to make people happy. This philosophical approach can start from Freud's famous aphorism that the normal person is the one who can love and work, and go on from there. The various aspects of psychoanalytic psychology, such as love, sexuality, family structure, communication, and psychiatric symptomatology, can all be viewed in this light: their psychological aspects can only be properly evaluated when the philosophical resolution is borne in mind.

THE QUESTION OF "SCHOOLS." Now that the detailed presentation of the historical development is available, the question of schools can again be raised. I have argued that in general the disciples of any school misrepresent the theories of other schools (in particular, Freud) and then go on to build similar theories, or raise other issues that could be resolved if approached in a rational manner. The differences between schools are more emotional than rational. Insistence on the "point of view" blocks serious consideration of issues and leads to arbitrary, authoritarian statements without presentation of evidence. I would again urge that the notion of "schools" be dropped, and all problems faced directly in their own right.

What applies to schools also applies to disciplines. The sciences of mankind must again be united, this time under the aegis of the dynamic psychoanalytic approach. There is always a mixture of objective and emotional factors; the elucidation of the objective factors is supplied by one set of tools, the elucidation of the emotional factors comes ultimately from psychoanalysis. The core of the science of mankind must be seen as psychoanalysis. In one measure or another, all the sciences that deal with mankind have to take this into account.

Psychoanalysis as Technique

Classical analysis, the main outlines of which were laid down by Freud, has been extended and perfected. It seems to be most effective with a highly motivated, articulate, intelligent individual, and in such cases it can virtually create a new kind of individual. It is less effective with deeply troubled persons who are also hampered by realistic life obstacles. There too, however, while analysis can be modified, and has been modified in various ways, the principles of psychoanalysis remain basic to all technical approaches.

Here again the question of schools has obscured the situation badly. Since people respond to suggestion, any kind of authoritative approach will produce some effects in certain types of people. However, these effects can only be properly evaluated in the light of the total understanding of the individual, which must come from psychoanalysis.

Psychoanalysis as a Profession

Freud once said (in a letter to Pfister) that he wanted to turn psychoanalysis over to a new profession who need not be doctors but who should not be priests. From the four physicians who first gathered at his house in 1902, the profession has grown to include some 4,000 members in the International Psychoanalytic Association and perhaps 6,000 fully trained analysts who are not in that body, or 10,000 in all. Most of these are doctors, but a considerable proportion are not. Furthermore, the profession of therapist embraces a large number of other professionals, most of whom are not physicians. Henry has aptly suggested the term "fifth profession" for therapists, all of whom move toward the same basic philosophy and the same basic techniques, regardless of the profession they come from.

Although the names are the same as before, the activities are entirely different. The psychiatrist of today, if well trained, bears no more relationship to the psychiatrist of 100 years ago than the surgeon of today bears to the barber-surgeons who preceded him. Similarly for the psychologist.

So psychoanalysis has in fact created a new profession. Some have proposed to set it off by a doctorate in mental health, others, a doctorate in psychology, others, social work, still others, analysis. But what has been created is a new profession, that of psychoanalytic psychotherapist.

Thus ends the first 100 years of psychoanalysis. What will the next 100 years bring?

Chapter Twenty

Observations, Hopes, and Dreams

Psychoanalysis has had, currently and historically, three separate meanings. First it has been seen as a body of principles of psychology deriving from Freud. Second, it has been viewed as a specialized kind of technique, "classical" psychoanalysis. And finally, it has been separated out from the main body of doctrine as a specialized theory or technique, as contrasted with others—Freudian versus non-Freudian (e.g., Jungian or Sullivanian). Inevitably these three meanings have been intertwined and confused with one another. However, it is essential to untangle them. In what follows, unless otherwise stated, "psychoanalysis" will be used in the broad sense as the body of psychological doctrine deriving from, but going well beyond, Freud.

The Training of the Psychoanalyst

The scheme of training first devised by Eitingon and his brilliant colleagues at Berlin in 1920 has become the standard for all future institutes and has not changed in its essentials. This training involves personal analysis, theoretical courses, and controls (analyses under supervision). A fourth aspect, control of training by the psychoanalytical societies, has played a powerful role in the history of the field but is not, strictly speaking, part of the training of the analyst.

This training process turns out to be long and arduous. In the 1950s Kris spoke of the "formative decade," and it does seem to be rare for an analyst to complete his training in less than 10 years. When these 10 years are added to previous education and experience,

the psychoanalyst is often well into middle age before he is fully independent as a private practitioner. Nevertheless, all attempts to
shorten or circumvent this long training period have failed.

Why should such a long training period be necessary? Freud
even wanted to make it longer (and many have followed his recommendation by having the analyst go back to analysis every five years
or so). Technically the reason given is the countertransference: without the detailed knowledge of his own psyche that derives only from
personal analysis, the analyst will foist his own prejudices and imma-
turities onto his patients, who are not in a position to fight back.

Yet once again, why all the prejudice against analysis? This
brings us back to the observation that psychoanalysis has shifted to
the consideration and treatment of the "normal" person, really for
the first time in history. I have suggested the term "adjustment neurosis" to clarify what we mean by "normal" in any culture. Freud
and his colleagues began with the maladjustment neurosis of the
social outcast. Gradually they shifted to the adjustment neurosis of
the average person in our culture.

It is this shift that has made psychoanalysis so enormously attractive. For analysis offers individuals a philosophy of living, tied to
a meaningful psychology, which will help them to find their way in
the dilemmas of existence. And it is primarily the success or failure
of his personal analysis that determines the degree to which the practitioner will succeed or fail with his own patients. Or, more precisely,
his own degree of mental health and maturity will be the main factor
in helping him guide patients through the usual compromises offered
the individual in our society, and on to a life freer and more gratifying than that known to most.

The Quantum Jump of Psychcanalysis

Historians are trained to look for continuities. Yet while these naturally exist, there are also discontinuities. The invention of the micro-
scope, the telescope, the theory of evolution, the theory of relativity,
all represent discontinuities in the course of intellectual history. What
happened afterward can in no significant sense be compared with
what happened before.

One thesis that emerges from this study is that psychoanalysis

represents another discontinuity in intellectual history. It has created
a whole new world, far different, more exciting, more extensive, and
more meaningful than anything known before. It is precisely this
quantum jump that has made psychoanalysis so hard to evaluate and
integrate into the general body of knowledge.

Psychoanalysis and Psychology

One consequence of this quantum jump is that psychoanalysis represents a wholly new kind of psychology. The relationship between
psychology and psychoanalysis that is usually described is the reverse
of the truth. Psychoanalysis, as a dynamic approach to the human
being, represents the core of *all* psychology and not just a highly
technical, specialized branch.

It is true, of course, that the dynamic factor will be more relevant in some areas than in others. Yet for a full science it can never
really be ignored. For example, the perception of colors depends on
the concatenation of the rods and cones, the structure of the eye, the
optic nerve, the sensory coding system, etc. All of this can be described without reference to dynamics. But once the question arises
of why any person has decided to look at any particular color, dynamics immediately enters in.

In psychoanalytic theory such a presentation of color vision can
be expressed through the concepts of the autonomous and the defensive ego. There are autonomous areas of ego functioning, in the
conflict-free sphere (or spheres), where defensive functions play either no role or a minor role. But once these autonomous factors are
deployed in real life, the defensive ego must necessarily enter the picture to present a rounded image of the human being.

In general, academic psychology and the social sciences have
explored the autonomous areas of human functioning. Because of the
limitations of their methods (and personal biases, it should be added),
they have largely ignored the defensive areas. These latter have been
explored by psychoanalysis. To achieve a complete science, both are
necessary.

Nevertheless, the resistances to dynamic thinking remain emotional rather than rational. In a recent article an anthropologist takes
his fellow-anthropologists to task for neglecting to study the intentions of members of primitive communities. The same has been said

of economists, sociologists, and others—intentions are bypassed because they are too complex to be subjected to "scientific" inquiry. Psychoanalysis is at hand to show how such a scientific inquiry should be conducted.

Psychoanalysis and Psychiatry

Psychoanalysis has been more fully integrated into psychiatry than into any other discipline. Yet even here much remains to be done. Since less than 10 percent of psychiatrists get full psychoanalytic training, it follows that the others often have an incomplete understanding of dynamic material. In addition, the public's confusion about the differences between the "psychiatrist" and the "psychoanalyst" allow the less scrupulous practitioner to trade on the high status accorded the psychoanalyst, to his personal and material advantage.

Today progressive leaders in the field are continually warning that psychiatry is experiencing an "identity crisis." In its dynamic formulations it has incorporated psychoanalytic thinking in toto. Most psychiatric residents who are taught psychodynamic formulations do not realize that they are learning psychoanalytic theory. Perhaps this is one reason why such a small percentage are willing to move on to the more rigorous training demanded by the psychoanalytic institutes.

At the same time, psychiatry incorporates knowledge of somatic functioning. In therapeutics especially, psychiatry is in the midst of the "drug revolution." Although use of drugs has by now become universal, especially with the more disturbed patients, opinion remains divided on their rationale and their ultimate efficacy. Philosophically, the indiscriminate use of drugs, reminiscent of Aldous Huxley's *Brave New World,* derives from a radically different image of mankind than the psychoanalytic view of love and work as the keys to happiness. Searles's warning that the phenothiazine–genetics combination may well usher in the "long dark night of the human soul" should be taken seriously (see chapter 14).

Psychoanalysis and the Social Sciences

With some exceptions, the social sciences have explored the autonomous aspects of ego functioning, again leaving the defensive ones to the psychoanalysts. This has given many of their research studies a peculiar, one-sided slant. Much is known, for instance, about the kinds of persons who marry one another, but little is explored about the happiness that exists or does not exist in marriage.

In essence, the social sciences have two psychologies to choose from: the behaviorist and the psychoanalytic. By and large they have opted for a rational behavioristic point of view because it is so much easier to manage and because of the biases of the investigators.

Throughout this book the opinion has been voiced, quite strongly, that the social sciences and psychology are part and parcel of one science of mankind, the core of which is psychoanalysis. Neurotic man, economic man, sociological man, must be studied with all the means at our disposal. It is the function of psychoanalysis, as the core of a dynamic psychology, to bring meaning and coherence to the social sciences. This process has gone on and is now going on at an uneven rate in the different fields, depending on the training and astuteness of the scholars.

Psychoanalysis and Philosophy

As a form of psychotherapy, psychoanalysis replaces the age-old philosophical quest for happiness by a new kind of search that promises to be more rewarding than anything ever tried before. Here above all, psychoanalysis presents a quantum jump in history, offering a combination of philosophy and psychology that is in its essence completely novel.

The search for a way of living that makes sense is one of the most powerful human motives. The myriad philosophies and religions currently available, each with its own gurus and theology, offer a tremendous temptation. Analytically, the problem is that they merely replace one superego figure by another, without really altering the inner-dynamic structure.

Many psychoanalysts will reject the statement that they are basically philosophers. They prefer to regard themselves as technicians who are above all the value systems offered to them. This is a comforting, extremely widespread illusion.

Rigidity in Psychoanalysis

On the negative side, psychoanalysis has shown a strong tendency to ossify into rigid systems in which no questions may be asked and no changes may occur. The distribution into "schools" has given a powerful impetus to such ossification, in that if any question is raised, the leaders can hide behind the answer that theirs is simply a "different point of view." There is no reason to avoid discussion and argument about the fundamental tenets of psychoanalysis. The evidence is available for all to see, and for all to pursue. Perhaps the frequent stance of the analyst in therapy as an authority figure dealing with dependent patients who worship him contributes to this kind of rigidity.

I hope that careful study of the history of the field, of which many analysts have only the foggiest notions, will help to undo some of this rigidity. Certainly, doctrinaire assertions without evidence, or with very little evidence, have played a significant role in the innumerable splits and dissensions in the field. Among the best people, from Freud onward, the road was always open for criticism and dissent. The rest of us would do well to follow their example. The "freedom from myth" that Hartmann (1956) stressed as one of the goals of psychoanalytic history should do much to further the progress of the field.

The Charismatic Figure

Allied to rigidity is the frequency with which charismatic figures have dominated the field for shorter or longer periods of time. Many of them have had their say and long since disappeared. Others persist, through groups of devoted followers who limit themselves to the works of the master. The whole phenomenon is more reminiscent of religion and philosophy than of science.

Nevertheless the field is and always has been filled with such charismatic figures, and the historian must offer some explanation of the phenomenon. Several explanations seem justified. First, the science is so difficult that it takes years to master, even a lifetime, and many times it is not mastered at all. Under these circumstances, adherence to a guru becomes the easiest way out; he knows the answers, just follow him.

Then there is the frequent need for a fight, which has many different roots. We have seen that Freud himself had the neurotic problem of needing a beloved friend and a hated enemy; one of his greatest blunders was to make Jung the beloved friend and Adler the hated enemy. Many analysts have unconsciously, or perhaps unwittingly, followed his example. In the United States the medical psychiatrist has often been the beloved friend of the medical analyst, the lay analyst the hated enemy; the consequences of this bifurcation have been as detrimental as Freud's choices of Jung and Adler.

And finally there is the practical question, not to be underestimated, of the struggle for patients. The layman is accustomed to choosing charismatic figures; indeed he cannot be expected to master the intricacies of the field. Accordingly he goes after the followers of his idol, and the professional, needy and eager for patients, follows suit.

Psychoanalysis and the Hate Culture

Developed during a rare interlude of peace in the history of Western Europe, psychoanalysis nonetheless has had to contend with the hate culture in which it grew and still grows. The "moral schizophrenia," of which Peter Gay speaks, on the eve of World War I certainly existed in 1880 when Freud began, and still exists today. It is only in the light of this enormous reservoir of hatred that many of the developments in psychoanalysis can be understood.

To begin with, hatred is always rationalized. No one likes to be told that he has hateful feelings; if he is told that, he reacts with "appropriate" rage. Hence the analytic criticism of the culture has always had to be muted. The analyst is caught between the Scylla of the lunatic fringe, like Laing and Wilhelm Reich, and the Charybdis of conservative orthodoxy, in which analysis is regarded as a purely technical device, with no inherent relationship to the culture. A rational critique of the world is difficult but absolutely essential.

From the very beginning Freud saw love as the end product of a long developmental process. In the early years he even proposed setting up an Academy of Love. In the discouragement attending the horrifying events that followed—two World Wars, genocide, and the like—these positive ideals have tended to be forgotten. Yet they remain as ideals, difficult though they may be to reach. Psychoanalysis should be looked upon as theory of love. The psychoanalyst may be defined as a person who teaches others how to love.

Technique versus Philosophy

The analyst's role as a technician is relatively easy to accomodate; his role as philosopher, relatively difficult. Freud was caught all through his life between these two positions, and he only let himself go, with great caution, toward the end. Others have since been caught up in a similar dilemma, though they have attempted to resolve it in different ways.

Yet what the world has mainly reacted to has been the basic philosophical implications in analysis, and less to its technique. Here is a system of psychology that explains both neurosis and normality, that embodies a vision of mankind consistent with the ideals of Western civilization, and that promises a technique that can bring these ideals to fruition.

Looking at these dreams, many current analysts have complained that analysis has been "oversold." It would be more correct to say that it has been undersold. Its vast promise for the future of mankind is only now beginning to be apparent. The analysts who complain of the oversell are those who prefer their comfortable role as well-paid technicians and resent being drawn into the wider world. One prominent analyst, as noted, has even recommended that analysts steer clear of any social or political movement in order to keep the transference "pure." Such "purity" can serve only to sabotage the vast potential for good which analysis holds.

The Broad versus the Narrow Meaning of Psychoanalysis

Throughout the history of the field, analysts have been caught between the broad and the narrow meaning of their discipline. In 1914 Freud criticized Adler for trying to get too much out of analysis, then a few years later turned around and did the same thing himself.

I have stressed the broad meaning of the field throughout this book. Analysis should be looked upon as embodying a central vision of what mankind is, a conceptual framework, and a central vision of what mankind can become. The specific technical problems can only be adequately resolved within this philosophical framework.

Toward a Definition of Psychoanalysis

It comes as a distinct surprise that psychoanalysts, despite years of endeavor, have been unable to define their own field with precision. In part this failing is due to the different meanings attached to the word: technique, theory, or specific subfield of technique or theory. In part, however, it is due to the reluctance to grasp the broader implications.

Simply defined, psychoanalysis is dynamic psychology. No doubt the adequacy of this definition has escaped the field because psychologists as a professional group have been so opposed to psychoanalysis, ridiculed it, and excluded it from their university departments. All of this opposition is understandable in the light of the hate culture in which psychology has had to operate. To face what mankind is really like would have meant, and still would mean, exclusion from the universities. Hence psychology is presented as a discipline with unclear subject matter, varying methodologies, and many different points of view. In this way the professional psychologist can play it safe all around. That the tide is turning may be gauged from the fact that the clinical approach to psychology is steadily gaining ground, to the point where almost half the members of the American Psychological Association are involved in clinical affairs in one way or another.

On the other hand, psychiatrists, eager for their own separate identity, are understandably reluctant to call themselves psychologists. The magic of medicine is too much for modern men and women, who still find it much easier to swallow a pill than to face a bitter truth about themselves. Hence the crazy quilt that makes up the world of mental health today. Doctors of medicine, without being willing to say so, practice psychology, while doctors of psychology pursue meaningless statistics. Fortunately, some clarity seems to be breaking through the mists.

From a scientific point of view, however, it can be stated quite emphatically: psychoanalysis is psychology. Properly pursued, it embraces the whole of the field, since learning theory, the other main branch today, can easily be incorporated into psychoanalytic theory, whereas psychoanalytic theory cannot be reduced to learning without content, as some wish to do.

Psychoanalysis as an Integrative Discipline

As a psychology, psychoanalysis is in a position to integrate everything that is known about mankind into one unified science. The barriers between the disciplines must fall. There is only one science of mankind. Information can be obtained in many different ways. But it must be integrated in accordance with the dynamic conceptualizations of psychoanalysis.

History and Blind Alleys

Inasmuch as the psychologist cannot experiment on human beings, history serves an immediately useful purpose; it presents the past efforts that have failed and thus can help to avoid blind alleys. Here freedom from myth is particularly important. Arthur Janov's primal screaming goes back to the early catharsis, Carl Rogers's nondirectivism comes directly from Rank's image of the transference, Kohut's version of narcissism is similar to Jung's, William Glasser's reality therapy goes back to common-sense psychiatry, and so on. A firm grasp of what has happened in the past can avoid many errors and save much time.

That there is so much repetition should not be taken to imply that all of the problems of psychology have been resolved. Wherever one turns, whether in affect, or the theory of hostility, or creativity, or psychosis, or ego functioning, or character structure, much still remains to be done. The rigidity involved in devotion to charismatic leaders has blocked the course of scientific progress, not facilitated it. Psychology should be seen as a growing science, not a finished one.

Splits and Dissensions

Again one has to come back to the numerous splits and dissensions in the field. Careful and honest study of what led to them should be undertaken more thoroughly in order to avoid future conflicts. The conventional histories now flooding the market, which reveal nothing of the true state of affairs, are of no help.

"Dependent" and "Independent" Patients

Every practicing therapist is well aware that some patients are extremely dependent, and would even prefer to remain dependent on the analyst all their lives, while others are quite independent and flee at the first sign of disagreement. The problems posed by these two types of patients have dominated the field from the beginning.

There is a strong tendency to rename the predominant kind of patient every 20 years or so. In the beginning, they were all hysterics, then obsessionals, then castrates, then masochists, and for the last 15 years or so, borderlines. Comparison of the characteristics of each type of patient would reveal marked similarities all along the line. Patients have not changed; our experience has grown and knowledge has increased.

The diagnostic system is one of the worst burdens the analytic world has had to inherit from psychiatry. As noted, the *DSM* has been changed every 10 years or so since it began in 1917; and another change has been announced for 1979. It is time to recognize that the whole diagnostic system, with its overemphasis on pathology, is grossly incorrect and misleading because it ignores many of the vital attributes of human beings.

The Future of "Classical" Analysis

It is frequently argued that "classical" analysis, in which the patient is seen five or six times a week, lies on a couch, and free associates, is on the way out because there are not enough analysts, there are too many people in need of help, and it does not work anyhow. All of these arguments are fallacious. For certain types of individuals (note that I am avoiding the word "patient"), this classical approach leads to the greatest freeing of the person. It is a liberating experience without equal.

Furthermore, the classical approach serves as a guidepost by which to evaluate other modalities. Many practitioners avoid the classical approach not because it is inadequate but because they have not mastered it. It is not true that psychoanalysis is easier on the therapist than a more active therapy; if anything, the reverse is true.

The alternative therapies should in many cases be looked upon as practical alternatives, useful under certain circumstances, not useful under others. There are also different techniques needed at different stages of the individual's development. Technique still remains more of an art than a science.

Toward Greater Unity

Ideally we should be moving toward one profession, that of psychoanalytic therapist, toward one theory, that of psychoanalytic psychology, and toward one technique, deriving from but not at all limited to classical analysis. This vision belongs under hopes and dreams, yet "we are such stuff as dreams are made on," and it is psychoanalysis that discovered the fundamental significance of dreams for human existence.

The Future of Psychoanalytic Institutes

And finally, what will become of the analytic institutes? They were born of the resistance of the established educational institutions, and nurtured in spite of them. What will happen when the established institutions change their minds and recognize the vital contributions of psychoanalysis, as they are coming to do more and more? In that case, special institutes may still exist, as groups of scholars devoted to specific topics. But psychoanalysis as such will become the department of psychology in the universities.

Notes

Abbreviations used in the Notes:

CP   Collected works of authors other than Freud
IJP   *International Journal of Psychoanalysis*
JAPA   *Journal of the American Psychoanalytic Association*
PQ   *Psychoanalytic Quarterly*
PSC   *Psychoanalytic Study of the Child*
PSM   *Psychosomatic Medicine*
SE   Standard Edition of Freud's works

Chapter 1: The Need for Historical Perspective

1. *JAPA, 24,* 1976, pp. 440–42.
2. Ibid., p. 911.

Chapter 2: The Precursors of Psychoanalysis

1. Gay and Webb, *Modern Europe,* p. 831.
2. Ibid., p. 747. These authors also remark (p. 745) that "no one knew precisely what the war was being fought for."
3. Ibid., p. 929.
4. K. Menninger, *Vital Balance,* p. 456.
5. I. Drabkin, "Remarks on Ancient Psychopathology," p. 229.
6. Ibid., p. 225.
7. Charmides, 150B, quoted in Drabkin, ibid.
8. P. L. Entralgo, *Therapy of the Word in Classical Antiquity,* p. 66.
9. Ibid., p. 13.
10. Ibid., p. 104.
11. See *Encyclopaedia Britannica,* 1963, s.v. "Sophism," which states that the main defect of the Sophists was their "indifference to truth."
12. *SE,* vol. VII, p. 292.
13. I. Veith, *Hysteria,* p. 184.
14. Ibid., p. 192.

15. Ibid., p. 188.
16. *SE,* vol. IV, p. 90.
17. K. Menninger, *Vital Balance,* p. 454.
18. H. Strassman et al., p. 349.
19. G. Murphy, *Historical Introduction to Modern Psychology,* p. 149.
20. "APA Election Ballot 1977," p. 26.
21. Murphy, *Historical Introduction to Modern Psychology,* p. 194.
22. E. Jones, *Life and Work of Sigmund Freud,* vol. 2, p. 57.
23. *Membership Directory,* American Psychological Association, 1976.
24. *Encyclopaedia Britannica,* 1963, s.v. "Sociology."
25. Quoted in M. Harris, *Rise of Modern Anthropological Theory,* p. 168.
26. Ibid., p. 258.
27. *Encyclopaedia Britannica,* 1963, s.v. "History."
28. Ibid., s.v. "Economics."
29. Ibid., s.v. "Biology."
30. *SE,* vol. XXIII, p. 100.

Chapter 3: The Legacy of Freud

1. E. Jones, *Life and Work,* vol. 3, p. 228.
2. H. Ellenberger, *Discovery of the Unconscious,* p. 242.
3. *SE,* vol. I, p. 268.
4. Jones, *Life and Work,* vol. 1, p. 196.
5. *SE,* vol. XX, p. 16.
6. *The Origins of Psychoanalysis,* pp. 119–20.
7. Ibid., p. 162.
8. Ibid., p. 269.
9. The "Project" itself has given rise to a considerable literature. Pribram and Gill (1976) have recently tried to show that it is fully in harmony with the best neurological knowledge, even of our day. However, since Freud never published it, it cannot in any sense be regarded as a major work. It is included in *SE,* vol. I.
10. *SE,* vol. VII, p. 120.
11. Jones, *Life and Work,* vol. 1, p. 320.
12. Ibid., p. 327.
13. Ibid., p. 327.
14. *SE,* vol. XI, p. 145.
15. *SE,* vol. XXIII, p. 234.
16. *SE,* vol. I, p. 271.
17. *SE,* vol. XXIII, p. 234.
18. *SE,* vol. XIV, p. 20.
19. *SE,* vol. IV, p. xxvi.
20. *SE,* vol. XXII, p. 113.
21. *SE,* vol. XIX, p. 142.
22. *SE,* vol. VII, p. 151.
23. *SE,* vol. XIX, p. 141.
24. *SE,* vol. VII, p. 49.
25. *SE,* vol. XIV, p. 44.
26. H. Nunberg and E. Federn, eds., *Minutes,* vol. 3, p. 558.
27. Ibid., p. 564.
28. A. Grinstein, *Sigmund Freud's Dreams,* pp. 247–50.
29. Jones, *Life and Work,* vol. 3.

30. *SE,* vol. XIV, p. 190.
31. *SE,* vol. V, p. 613.
32. *SE,* vol. VII, p. 302.
33. Ibid., p. 229.
34. *SE,* vol. XII, p. 168.
35. *SE,* vol. XVIII, p. 101.
36. *SE,* vol. XI, p. 190.
37. Ellenberger, *Discovery of the Unconscious,* p. 102.
38. *SE,* vol. IX, p. 175.
39. S. Ferenczi, *Sex in Psychoanalysis,* p. 303.
40. K. Abraham, *Selected Papers,* vol. 2, pp. 394–95.
41. *SE,* vol. XIV, p. 16.
42. Jones, *Life and Work,* vol. 2, pp. 185–87.
43. *SE,* vol. XIV, p. 311.
44. Ibid., p. 133.
45. Ibid., p. 58.
46. Jones, *Life and Work,* vol. 3, p. 266.
47. Nunberg and Federn, *Minutes,* vol. 2, p. 417.
48. See also Max Schur, *Freud Living and Dying.*
49. *SE,* vol. XXIII, p. 235.
50. *SE,* vol. XII, pp. 155–56.
51. *SE,* vol. XXIII, p. 250.
52. *SE,* vol. XII, p. 104.
53. *SE,* vol. XIX, p. 34.
54. Ibid., p. 33.
55. Ibid., p. 54.
56. *SE,* vol. XX, p. 59.
57. Ibid., p. 70.
58. Ibid., p. 248.
59. Freud, *Psychoanalysis and Faith,* p. 126.
60. *SE,* vol. XX, pp. 249–50.
61. *SE,* vol. XXI, p. 97.
62. Ibid., p. 83.
63. Ibid., p. 115.
64. Ibid., p. 144.
65. *SE,* vol. XXII.
66. Ibid., p. 146.
67. Ibid., p. 148.

Chapter 4: Organizational Vicissitudes

1. Jones, *Life and Work,* vol. 1, p. 360.
2. Ibid., p. 355.
3. Ellenberger's argument that this isolation was a retrospective falsification by Freud (*Discovery of the Unconscious,* ch. 7) is wholly erroneous.
4. Nunberg and Federn, *Minutes,* vol. 1, pp. xviii–xix.
5. Ibid., p. xix.
6. Ibid., p. xxxvii.
7. Ibid., vol. II, p. 472.
8. Ibid., p. 202.
9. Ibid., p. 47.

10. Ibid., p. 42.
11. *SE,* vol. XIV, p. 25.
12. Ibid., pp. 3–66.
13. Ibid., p. 26.
14. Freud and Jung, *Letters,* pp. 3–4.
15. Jones, *Life and Work,* vol. 2, p. 35.
16. Ibid., p. 40.
17. *SE,* vol. XIV, p. 42.
18. Ibid., p. 43.
19. Ibid., p. 44.
20. J. Millet, in F. Alexander et al., *Psychoanalytic Pioneers,* p. 551.
21. *JAPA, 24,* 1976, p. 262.
22. Ibid., pp. 440–42.
23. Nunberg and Federn, *Minutes,* vol. 3, p. 158.
24. Freud and Jung, *Letters,* p. 387.
25. Ibid., p. 413.
26. Nunberg and Federn, *Minutes,* vol. 3, p. 179.
27. Ellenberger, *Discovery of the Unconscious,* p. 585.
28. H. Ansbacher and R. Ansbacher, *Individual Psychology of Alfred Adler,* p. 45.
29. Ibid., p. 358.
30. Ibid., p. 358.
31. Freud and Jung, *Letters,* p. 421.
32. Jones, *Life and Work,* vol. 3, p. 415.
33. C. G. Jung, *Letters,* vol. 1, 1906–1950. See especially letters to Schultz, p. 124, Allers, p. 131, Bjerre, p. 135, Maeder, p. 136, Bruel, p. 144, Cimbal, p. 145, Van der Hoop, p. 146, Pupato, p. 147, Van der Hoop, p. 149, Heyer, p. 157, among others.
34. Ibid., p. 238.
35. See also ibid., p. 156.
36. In L. Pongratz, ed., *Psychotherapie in Selbstdarstellungen,* p. 291.
37. Brett, *History of Psychology,* p. 730.
38. Jung, *Letters,* pp. 66–67.
39. Jones, *Life and Work,* vol. 2, ch. 6.
40. Ibid., p. 153.
41. Nunberg and Federn, *Minutes,* vol. 4.
42. *IJP, 1,* pp. 211–12.
43. Jones, *Life and Work,* vol. 3, pp. 26–27.
44. C. Oberndorf, *A History of Psychoanalysis in America,* p. 164.
45. *IJP, 6,* 1925, p. 285.
46. See below, pp. 109–11.
47. S. Lorand, Ferenczi, in F. Alexander et al., *Psychoanalytic Pioneers,* p. 24.
48. M. Balint, Obituary of Roheim, *IJP, 35,* 1954, p. 434.
49. *IJP, 7,* 1926, pp. 144ff.
50. *IJP, 20,* 1939, pp. 498ff.
51. J. Millet, in F. Alexander et al., *Psychoanalytic Pioneers,* pp. 557–61.
52. *SE,* vol. XIV, p. 20.
53. Jones, *Life and Work,* vol. 3.
54. B. Lewin and H. Ross, *Psychoanalytic Education in the United States,* p. 28.
55. *IJP, 35,* 1954, p. 158.
56. *Zehn Jahre Berliner Psychoanalytisches Institut,* p. 53.
57. *SE,* vol. XX, p. 252.
58. *Zehn Jahre,* p. 73.

59. D. Schuster et al., *Clinical Supervision of the Psychiatric Resident,* p. 33.

60. *IJP,* 44, 1963, pp. 362–67.

61. Jones, *Life and Work,* vol. 3, p. 298.

62. *IJP, 8,* 1927, p. 248.

63. *IJP, 7,* 1926, p. 142.

64. Oberndorf, *History of Psychoanalysis in America,* p. 122.

65. *IJP, 16,* 1935, p. 245.

66. Schjelderup, *IJP, 20,* 1939, p. 216.

67. Oberndorf, *History of Psychoanalysis in America,* p. 111.

68. In F. Alexander et al., *Psychoanalytic Pioneers,* pp. 333–41.

69. E. Jones, *Collected Papers,* ch. 19.

70. Ibid., p. 368.

71. *IJP, 6,* 1925, p. 106.

72. H. Sullivan, *Schizophrenia as a Human Process,* p. 236.

73. Ibid., p. 238.

74. D. Noble and D. Burnham, *History of the Washington Psychoanalytic Institute,* p. 39.

75. *IJP, 29,* 1948, p. 287.

76. M. J. White, in P. Mullahy, ed., *The Contributions of Harry Stack Sullivan,* p. 118.

77. E. Jones, *Collected Papers,* p. 373.

78. See H. Kohut, *The Restoration of the Self,* p. 192.

79. *IJP, 2,* 1921, p. 372.

80. T. Reik, *Die Psychoanalytische Bewegung, I,* 1929, pp. 115–16.

81. O. Rank, *Art and the Artist,* pp. 430–31.

82. G. Maetze, *Psychoanalyse in Berlin,* p. 82.

83. Ibid., p. 73.

84. *IJP, 13,* 1932, p. 221.

85. Profile in *Journal of the American Academy of Psychoanalysis,* April, 1977, pp. 153–54.

86. Data in this section are drawn from F. Alexander et al., *Psychoanalytic Pioneers.*

87. E. Hitschmann, Ten Years Report of the Vienna Psychoanalytical Clinic, *IJP, 13,* 1932, pp. 245–50.

88. Oberndorf, *History of Psychoanalysis in America,* p. 177.

89. H. Dahmer, *Libido und Gesellschaft,* part II, p. 358.

90. I. Reich, *Biography of Wilhelm Reich,* p. 31.

91. F. Alexander et al., *Psychoanalytic Pioneers,* p. 435.

92. Oberndorf, *History of Psychoanalysis in America,* p. 168.

93. Ibid., ch. 10.

94. Ibid., p. 165.

95. *IJP, 18,* 1937, pp. 346–47.

96. *IJP, 20,* 1939, p. 121.

97. *PQ, 1,* 1932, front page.

98. The story of the Berlin Institute during the war years has been recounted by a number of authors. See Kemper (in Pongratz, 1973), Maetze (1971, 1976), Chrzanowski, Spiegel (1975), et al. Boehm, ''Dokumente zur Geschichte der Psychoanalyse in Deutschland, 1933–1951,'' Deutsche Psychoanalytische Gesellschaft, n.d.

Chapter 5: Organizational Vicissitudes Since World War II

1. *IJP, 30,* 1949, p. 182.

2. Ibid., pp. 191–92.

3. *IJP, 51,* 1970, p. 97.

4. Ibid., pp. 98ff.
5. Ibid., p. 98.
6. Ibid., p. 99.
7. Ibid., p. 99.
8. Ibid., p. 100.
9. *IJP, 49,* 1968, p. 132.
10. Ibid., p. 151.
11. *IJP, 53,* 1972, p. 87.
12. *IJP, 50,* 1969, pp. 417–18.
13. Actually, if it is considered that the main unique element in analytic training is the personal analysis, in this respect the American Psychoanalytic Association has been less exacting than the European institutes, which for the most part retained more intensive and longer training analyses. This is only one of the many paradoxes in the situation.
14. *IJP,* Roster, 1977.
15. *JAPA, 1,* 1953, p. 210.
16. Ibid., p. 215.
17. Ibid., p. 217.
18. Ibid., p. 219.
19. *JAPA, 3,* 1955, p. 589.
20. *JAPA, 12,* 1964, p. 474.
21. *JAPA, 19,* 1971, pp. 3–25.
22. Ibid., p. 8.
23. Ibid., p. 12.
24. Ibid., p. 19.
25. B. Moore, *JAPA, 24,* 1976, pp. 257–83.
26. Ibid., p. 265.
27. Ibid., p. 271.
28. S. Goodman, ed., *Psychoanalytic Education and Research,* p. 347.
29. *Roster 1976–1977,* American Psychoanalytic Association, pp. 10–13.
30. Lewin and Ross, *Psychoanalytic Education in the United States,* p. 73.
31. Goodman, *Psychoanalytic Education and Research,* p. 347.
32. Lewin and Ross, *Psychoanalytic Education in the United States,* p. 158.
33. Ibid., p. 335.
34. Ibid., p. 45.
35. Ibid., p. 175.
36. Goodman, *Psychoanalytic Education and Research,* p. 342.
37. Lewin and Ross, *Psychoanalytic Education in the United States,* p. 192.
38. Ibid., p. 236.
39. Ibid., p. 227.
40. *JAPA, 20,* 1972, pp. 518–609.
41. Ibid., p. 559.
42. R. Ekstein, "Biography of Bernfeld," in F. Alexander et al., *Psychoanalytic Pioneers,* p. 418.
43. *JAPA, 20,* 1972, p. 549.
44. Ibid., p. 559.
45. *JAPA, 23,* 1975.
46. *JAPA, 20,* 1972, p. 549.
47. *By-Laws,* American Psychoanalytic Association, Jan., 1976.
48. *Bulletin of the William Alanson White Institute,* 1976–1977, p. 4.
49. *Bulletin of the American Psychoanalytic Association,* 5 (no. 3), 1949.
50. *By-Laws,* p. 24.

51. G. Kriegman, History of the Virginia Psychoanalytic Institute, 1976. Unpublished manuscript.

52. *Roster,* American Psychoanalytic Association, 1976–1977.

53. Goodman, *Psychoanalytic Education and Research,* p. 333.

54. Ibid., p. 339.

55. *JAPA, 22,* 1974, p. 450.

56. *JAPA, 23,* 1975, p. 876.

57. Goodman, *Psychoanalytic Education and Research,* p. 40.

58. Lewin and Ross, *Psychoanalytic Education in the United States,* p. 110.

59. Goodman, *Psychoanalytic Education and Research,* p. 332.

60. Ibid., p. 332.

61. *JAPA, 18,* 1970, p. 493.

62. Goodman, *Psychoanalytic Education and Research,* p. 341.

63. *JAPA, 23,* 1975, p. 876.

64. *JAPA, 24,* 1976, pp. 918–21.

65. *JAPA, 8,* 1960, p. 733.

66. *JAPA, 9,* 1961, pp. 340–41.

67. *JAPA, 21,* 1973, p. 445.

68. Goodman, *Psychoanalytic Education and Research,* p. 200.

69. *JAPA, 19,* 1971, p. 355.

70. *JAPA, 20,* 1972, p. 751.

71. *JAPA, 18,* 1970, p. 508. Remarks by Van der Leeuw.

72. *JAPA, 2,* 1954, pp. 811–12.

73. Ibid., p. 357.

74. Ibid., p. 362.

75. *JAPA, 3,* 1955, p. 344.

76. *JAPA, 24,* 1976, p. 921.

77. Ibid., p. 911.

78. Quoted in S. Gifford, Psychoanalysis in Boston, p. 26. Unpublished manuscript.

79. *JAPA, 3,* 1955, p. 325.

80. *JAPA, 4,* 1956, p. 699.

81. *JAPA, 5,* 1957, p. 357.

82. Millet, in F. Alexander et al., *Psychoanalytic Pioneers,* p. 571.

83. *JAPA, 2,* 1954, p. 735.

84. *JAPA, 8,* 1960, p. 727.

85. *JAPA, 24,* 1976, p. 451.

86. *IJP, 37,* 1956, p. 120.

87. Oberndorf, History of Psychoanalysis in America, p. 82, describes Freud's strong annoyance with Oberndorf's opposition to lay analysis.

88. *JAPA, 24,* 1976, p. 274.

89. *JAPA, 19,* 1971, p. 840.

90. *JAPA, 20,* 1972, p. 845.

91. *JAPA, 22,* 1974, p. 910.

92. *JAPA, 24,* 1976, pp. 569–86.

93. *JAPA, 20,* 1972, pp. 576, 583.

94. *JAPA, 23,* 1975, p. 433.

95. Ibid., p. 876.

96. Data here are taken from H. Thomä, Some Remarks on Psychoanalysis in Germany, Past and Present, *IJP, 50,* 1969, pp. 683–92.

97. *IJP, 33,* 1952, p. 253.

98. Thomä, Psychoanalysis in Germany, p. 689.

99. G. Maetze, *Psychoanalyse in Deutschland*, p. 1174.

100. J. Pontalis, *IJP, 55*, 1974, pp. 85–87.

101. I. Barande and R. Barande, *Histoire de la Psychanalyse en France*, pp. 10–12.

102. *IJP, 51*, 1970, p. 110.

103. Barande and Barande *Histoire de la Psychanalyse en France*, pp. 96–105.

104. G. Aberastury, *Historia, Ensenanza, y Ejercicio Legal del Psicoanalisis;* see also G. Sanchez Medina, Historic Summary of the Colombian Society and Institute of Psychoanalysis.

105. *JAPA, 20*, 1972, p. 559.

106. A. Kawada, Psychoanalyse und Psychotherapie in Japan, *Psyche, 31*, 1977, pp. 284–85.

107. F. Arnhoff et al., *Manpower for Mental Health*.

108. *Roster, 1976*, American Psychological Association.

109. *JAPA, 24*, 1976, p. 354.

Chapter 6: Extensions and Elaborations: The Oral Stage

1. *SE*, vol. XII, p. 316.

2. *SE*, vol. XXIII, p. 155.

3. Ibid., p. 100.

4. O. Fenichel, *Psychoanalytic Theory of Neurosis*, p. 62.

5. M. Ribble, *Rights of Infants*, p. 14.

6. R. Spitz, *First Year of Life*, p. 280.

7. Ibid., p. 278.

8. Ibid., p. 282.

9. F. Hsu, *Psychological Anthropology*, p. 6.

10. H. Sullivan, *Schizophrenia as a Human Process*, pp. 113–15.

11. L. Bellak and L. Loeb, *Schizophrenia*, p. 779.

12. Originally 1935, reprinted in *PQ, 45*, 1976, pp. 5–36.

13. Quoted in G. Roheim, *Psychoanalysis and Anthropology*, p. 435.

Chapter 7: Extensions and Elaborations: Later Stages

1. E. Erikson, *Identity and the Life Cycle*, pp. 101–2.

2. Ibid., p. 52.

3. Ibid., p. 87.

4. H. Sullivan, *Conceptions of Modern Psychiatry*, pp. 17–19, 34–37.

5. J. Bowlby, *Attachment and Loss*, vol. 1, p. 208.

6. R. Spitz, Authority and Masturbation, *PQ, 21*, 1952, p. 493.

7. Francis and Marcus. *Masturbation from Infancy to Senescence*, p. 42.

8. *JAPA, 21*, 1973, pp. 333–50.

9. *SE*, vol. XXIII, p. 154.

10. R. Stoller, *Sex and Gender*, p. xviii.

11. B. Malinowski, *Sex and Repression in Savage Society*, pp. 223–24.

12. G. Murdock, *Social Structure*, p. 2.

13. M. Temerlin, *Lucy: Growing Up Human*, p. 134.

14. Van Lawick-Goodall, *In the Shadow of Man*, p. 135.

15. E. Mayr, *Populations, Species and Evolution*, p. 135.

16. Fenichel, *Psychoanalytic Theory of Neurosis*, p. 62.

17. *SE*, vol. V, pp. 544, 618.

18. *Adolescent Psychiatry, I*, p. vii.

19. R. Kahana and S. Levin, *Psychodynamic Studies on Aging*, pp. 108–9.

Chapter 8: Instinct Theory

1. Jones, *Life and Work,* vol. 2, pp. 302–3.
2. Fenichel, *Psychoanalytic Theory of Neurosis,* p. 54.
3. M. Schur, *The Id and the Regulatory Principles of Mental Functioning,* p. 29.
4. Quoted in Fletcher, *Instinct in Man,* p. 48.
5. Jones, *Life and Work,* vol. 3, pp. 272–80.
6. Mayr, *Populations, Species, and Evolution,* p. 5.
7. Dobzhansky, *Genetic Diversity and Human Equality,* p. 8.
8. Ibid., p. 418.
9. A. Kardiner, *Individual and His Society,* p. 3.
10. *SE,* vol. XX, p. 37.
11. *IJP, 55,* 1974, p. 467.
12. Jones, *Life and Work,* vol. 3, p. 195.
13. S. Freud and L. Andreas-Salome, *Letters,* p. 174.
14. H. Kohut, *Restoration of the Self,* p. 171.
15. A. Ellis, Is the Vaginal Orgasm a Myth?
16. A. Kinsey et al., *Sexual Behavior in the Human Female,* p. 584.
17. Ibid., p. 125.
18. *JAPA, 16,* 1968, pp. 585–86.
19. Ibid., p. 586.
20. *JAPA, 18,* 1970, p. 316.
21. Ibid., p. 282.
22. In Adelson, *Sexuality and Psychoanalysis,* ch. 13.
23. *SE,* vol. III, p. 278.
24. Jones, *Life and Works,* vol. 3, p. 464.
25. *PQ, 42,* 1973, p. 184.
26. *IJP, 52,* 1971, p. 143.
27. Nunberg and Federn, *Minutes,* vol. 1, pp. 406–10.
28. Fenichel, *Psychoanalytic Theory of Neurosis,* p. 59.
29. *IJP, 29,* pp. 201–23.
30. Ibid., p. 201.
31. *IJP, 30,* 1949, pp. 69–74.
32. *IJP, 31,* 1950, pp. 156–60.
33. *IJP, 32,* 1951, pp. 157–66.
34. *IJP, 33,* 1952, pp. 355–62.
35. *IJP, 34,* 1953, pp. 102–10.
36. *IJP, 35,* 1954, pp. 129–34.
37. Ibid., p. 1.
38. *PSC, 5,* 1949, p. 18.
39. *Essays on Ego Psychology,* p. 227.
40. *Psychosomatic Medicine,* p. 69.
41. Ibid., p. 124.
42. Ibid., p. 133.
43. Ibid., p. 147.
44. Ibid., p. 178.
45. *SE,* vol. XVIII, pp. 258–59.
46. *SE,* vol. XIX, p. 41.
47. *PQ, 42,* 1973, p. 193.
48. Quoted in Montagu, 1976, p. 203.
49. E. Valenstein, *Brain Control,* p. 353.
50. *IJP, 52,* 1971, p. 167.

51. *SE*, vol. I, p. 295.
52. Ibid., p. 289.
53. *SE*, vol. XXIII, pp. 163–64.
54. *SE*, vol. XIV, p. 153.
55. *JAPA, 19*, 1971, pp. 413–14.

Chapter 9: The Unconscious: The Fantasy Life of Mankind

1. C. G. Jung, *Analytical Psychology*, pp. 40–44.
2. Ibid., p. ix.
3. *SE*, vol. V, p. 476.
4. *SE*, vol. V, p. 558.
5. *SE*, vol. IV, p. 396.
6. *SE*, vol. V, p. 385.
7. *IJP, 46*, 1965, p. 436.
8. *IJP, 57*, 1976, p. 315.
9. *SE*, vol. V, p. 580n.
10. In J. Flavell, *Psychology of Piaget*, p. 407n.
11. See also Deschner: *Das Kreuz mit der Kirche*, 1975, for a full presentation of the sexual aberrations in the history of Christianity.
12. O. Rank, *Myth of the Birth of the Hero*, p. 61.
13. G. Devereux, *Study of Abortion in Primitive Societies*, p. vii.

Chapter 10: The Unconscious: Creativity, Language, and Communication

1. The German word *Kunst* has a broader reference than the literal English translation "art."
2. *SE*, vol. I, p. 256.
3. *SE*, vol. IV, p. 266.
4. *SE*, vol. VII, p. 304.
5. Ibid., p. 310.
6. *SE*, vol. IX, pp. 152–53.
7. Ibid., p. 146.
8. Ibid., p. 148.
9. Ibid., p. 152.
10. *SE*, vol. XI, p. 63.
11. It has been noted that Freud's essay was based on a mistranslation of the bird that supposedly put its beak into Leonardo's mouth as an infant. He took it to be a vulture, in accordance with the available translation, while it was really a kite. However, the main thrust of Freud's argument is not affected by this error.
12. *SE*, vol. XI, p. 136.
13. *SE*, vol. XIII p. 233.
14. J. Spector, *Aesthetics of Freud*, p. 104.
15. *SE*, vol. XVI, pp. 375–76.
16. This position is quite similar to that taken by Kohut in *Restoration of the Self*, 1977; cf. ch. 15.
17. H. Segal, Psychoanalytical Approach to Aesthetics. Reprinted in M. Klein et al., *New Directions in Psychoanalysis*, p. 386.
18. See F. Barron, *Artists in the Making*.
19. See L. Terman, *Men of Genius*.

20. *IJP, 53,* 1972, p. 25.
21. M. Klein, *Envy and Gratitude,* p. 5.
22. Ibid., pp. 4–5.
23. *IJP, 18,* 1939, pp. 291–92.
24. This term has in the meantime disappeared from the psychoanalytic literature.
25. M. Mahler et al., *Psychological Birth of the Human Infant,* p. 117.
26. Behavioral genetics, while it embodies many correct scientific observations, neverthe-less continues to incorporate and justify the concept of "innate badness." Cf. Medawar, 1977.
27. E. Jacobson, *Self and the Object World,* pp. 52–54.
28. O. F. Kernberg, *Object Relations Theory and Clinical Psychoanalysis,* p. 73.
29. What traditional logic called the universe of discourse.
30. J. Ruesch, *Values, Communication and Culture,* p. 20.
31. *SE,* vol. XIV, p. 199.
32. *SE,* vol. VIII, o. 143.
33. Nonanalytic authors have scarcely gone beyond Freud's theory; cf. Chapman and Foot, 1976.

Chapter 11: Ego Psychology: An Overview, and Defense Processes

1. *SE,* vol. XIX, p. 25.
2. *SE,* vol. III, p. 60.
3. *SE,* vol. XX, p. 149.
4. A. Freud, *Ego and the Mechanisms of Defense,* p. 47.
5. J. Laplanche and J. Pontalis, *Language of Psychoanalysis,* p. 110.
6. *SE,* vol. VII, pp. 238–39.
7. For a fuller discussion, see chapter 10.
8. H. Segal, *Introduction to the Work of Melanie Klein,* pp. 27–28.
9. *SE,* vol. I, pp. 270–71.
10. *SE,* vol. XVI, pp. 340–41.
11. *SE,* vol. XX, p. 114.
12. *IJP, 17,* p. 285–303.
13. Ibid., p. 290.
14. E. Kris, *Explorations in Art,* pp. 303–18.
15. Quoted in L. Bellak et al., *Ego Functioning,* p. 118.
16. *SE,* vol. XIX, p. 143.
17. Laplanche and Pontalis, 1973, p. 118.
18. *SE,* vol. III, p. 59.
19. *JAPA, 22,* 1974, pp. 769–84.
20. H. Searles, *Collected Papers on Schizophrenia,* p. 632.
21. Ibid., p. 634.
22. H. Hartmann, *Essays in Ego Psychology,* p. xiii.
23. Ibid.
24. Ibid., p. 171.
25. A. Applegarth, Psychic Energy Reconsidered, *JAPA, 24,* 1976, pp. 647–58.
26. Hartmann, *Essays in Ego Psychology,* p. 193.
27. Laplanche and Pontalis, *Language of Psychoanalysis,* p. 4.
28. Panel on Acting Out, *IJP, 47,* 1968, pp. 165–230.
29. Ibid., p. 165.
30. Mahler, *On Human Symbiosis,* p. 44.
31. H. Sullivan, *Conceptions of Modern Psychiatry,* p. 79.
32. O. Kernberg, *Borderline Conditions,* pp. 29–30.

33. *SE*, vol. I, p. 249.
34. *SE*, vol. XIV, p. 29.
35. *SE*, vol. XIX, pp. 176–77.
36. H. Nunberg, *Principles of Psychoanalysis*, p. 216.
37. Fenichel, *Psychoanalytic Theory of Neurosis*, p. 524.
38. See, e.g., M. Drellich, Classical Psychoanalytical School.
39. *SE*, vol. XII, p. 237.
40. Ibid., p. 238.
41. *SE*, vol. XXIII, p. 240.

Chapter 12: Ego Psychology: Character Structure, Ego Autonomy, Affects, and Cognitive Functioning

1. *SE*, vol. IX, p. 175.
2. K. Abraham, *Selected Papers*, vol. 2, pp. 393–95.
3. *SE*, vol. XIV, p. 50.
4. Ibid., pp. 231–37.
5. O. Fenichel, *Psychoanalytic Theory of Neurosis*, p. 462.
6. Ibid., p. 532.
7. *SE*, vol. XXIII, p. 235.
8. *IJP, 43*, 1962, p. 291.
9. Bellak et al., *Ego Functioning*, p. 323.
10. Hartmann, *Ego Psychology and The Problem of Adaptation*, p. 32.
11. Piaget was a member of the Swiss Psychoanalytic Society before World War II. It is not clear when or why he withdrew.
12. *SE*, vol. XX, p. 132.
13. Emde et al., *Emotional Expression in Infancy*. p. 146.
14. *SE*, vol. V, p. 567.
15. Ibid., p. 565.
16. Ibid., p. 566.
17. *SE*, vol. XXI, p. 69.
18. *SE*, vol. IX, p. 224.
19. *IJP, 11*, 1930, pp. 322–31.
20. Ibid., p. 329.
21. *SE*, vol. VI, p. 7.
22. G. Klein, *Perception, Motives and Personality*, pp. 302–7.
23. *SE*, vol. XIX, pp. 195–96.
24. *JAPA, 20*, 1972, p. 624.
25. *PQ, 13*, 1944, p. 102.

Chapter 13: Neurosis: Psychoanalysis and Psychiatry

1. *SE*, vol. II, pp. 160–61.
2. Fine, *Development of Freud's Thought*, p. 66.
3. *SE*, vol. XII, pp. 236–37.
4. Ibid., p. 210.
5. *SE*, vol. XXI, p. 144.
6. Ibid., p. 144.
7. *SE*, vol. XIX, p. 149.
8. L. Salzman, *Obsessional Personality*, p. vii.
9. *IJP, 55*, 1974, pp. 467–68.

10. Quoted in *PQ, 15*, 1946, p. 274.
11. Veith, *Hysteria,* pp. 272–73.
12. Jones, Psychoanalysis and Psychiatry, p. 368.
13. H. Sullivan, *Fusion of Psychiatry and Social Science,* p. 273.
14. T. Rennie et al., *Mental Health in the Metropolis,* p. 138.
15. A. Leighton et al., *Character of Danger,* p. 356.
16. Ibid., p. 356.
17. Quoted in Rennie et al., *Mental Health in the Metropolis,* p. 337.
18. *PQ, 34,* 1965, p. 379.

Chapter 14: Psychosis and Borderline Conditions

1. *Se,* vol. III, p. 160.
2. *SE,* vol. XII, p. 82.
3. *IJP, 15,* 1934, p. 210.
4. P. Federn, *Ego Psychology and the Psychoses,* p. 122.
5. B. Boyer and P. Giovacchini, *Psychoanalytic Treatment of Schizophrenia and Character Disorders,* p. 89.
6. Sullivan's later elaboration of an "interpersonal" theory, which differs but little from Freud except in terminology, was made in a strictly analytic framework.
7. H. Sullivan, *Schizophrenia as a Human Process,* p. 236.
8. S. Arieti, *Interpretation of Schizophrenia,* p. 539.
9. Ibid., p. 531.
10. *SE,* vol. XX, p. 97.
11. Ibid., p. 244.
12. *PQ,* 11, 1942, pp. 320–21.
13. E. Jones, *Collected Papers,* p. 306.
14. T. Lidz, *Origin and Treatment of Schizophrenic Disorders,* pp. ix-x.
15. Originally 1918, reprinted in *PQ, 2,* 1933, pp. 517–56.
16. D. Klein and R. Gittelman-Klein, *Progress in Psychiatric Drug Treatment,* vol. I, p. 374.
17. In C. Chiland, ed., *Long-Term Treatments of Psychotic States,* pp. 114–16.
18. Quoted in G. Bychowski, *Psychotherapy of Psychosis,* p. 284.
19. Ibid., p. 113.
20. *Diagnostic and Statistical Manual,* American Psychiatric Association, 1952.
21. *DSM,* 1968, p. 34.
22. *PQ, 7,* 1938, pp. 467–89.
23. Ibid., p. 467.
24. *JAPA, 3,* 1955, p. 285.
25. O. F. Kernberg, *Borderline Conditions and Pathological Narcissism,* p. 39.
26. J. Masterson, *Treatment of the Borderline Patient,* p. 3.
27. It is noteworthy that the Catholic notion of overscrupulosity seems to be an observation of the obsessional manner in which even accepted religious ritual can be carried to extremes.
28. *SE,* vol. IX, pp. 126–27.
29. O. Pfister, *Christianity and Fear,* p. 22.
30. Ibid., p. 193.
31. *Psychoanalysis and Faith,* p. 126.
32. *SE,* vol. IX, p. 198.
33. Ibid., p. 193.
34. Cf. *U.S. News and World Report,* Aug., 1973.

35. K. Menninger, *Psychiatrist's World*, p. 673.
36. *JAPA, 8,* 1960, p. 535.
37. D. Hamburg et al., Report of Ad Hoc Committee, p. 845.
38. *American Journal of Psychiatry,* March 1977.

Chapter 15: Interpersonal Relations . . . , Drives and Objects, and Shift to Interpersonal Theory

1. *SE,* vol VII, pp. 135–36.
2. Ibid., p. 174n.
3. Ibid., pp. 191–92.
4. Ibid., p. 207.
5. Jones, *Life and Work,* vol. 2, p. 302.
6. Ibid., p. 304.
7. *SE,* vol. XX, p. 70.
8. *JAPA, 4,* 1956, p. 165.
9. *JAPA, 3,* 1955, p. 301.
10. Ibid., p. 308.
11. *SE,* vol. VII, p. 149n.
12. *IJP, 44,* 1963, pp. 224–25.
13. H. Sullivan, *Fusion of Psychiatry and Social Science,* pp. 27–28.
14. M. Mahler et al., *Psychological Birth of the Human Infant,* p. 227.
15. H. Kohut, *Analysis of the Self,* p. 220.
16. *IJP, 57,* 1976, p. 49.
17. *SE,* vol. XX, p. 42.
18. S. Brody, *Patterns of Mothering,* p. 266.
19. H. Hartmann, *Essays in Ego Psychology,* p. 173.
20. Ibid., p. 255.
21. *JAPA, 21,* 1973, p. 250.
22. Ibid., p. 261.
23. H. Wolff et al., *Stress and Disease,* p. 261.
24. J. Lynch, *The Broken Heart,* p. 31.
25. Ibid., p. 35.
26. Quoted in *JAPA, 25,* 1977, p. 27.
27. *SE,* vol. XIV, pp. 244–45.
28. *PSC, 15,* 1960, pp. 9–10.

Chapter 16: Values, Philosophy, and the Superego

1. *SE,* vol. III, p. 266.
2. Ibid., p. 278.
3. Nunberg and Federn, *Minutes,* vol. 1, p. 200.
4. Ibid., p. 274.
5. Ibid., p. 372.
6. Ibid., vol. 2, p. 94.
7. *SE,* vol. VIII, p. 111.
8. *SE,* vol. IX, p. 204.
9. Nunberg and Federn, *Minutes,* vol. 2, p. 82.
10. Ibid., p. 89.
11. Ibid., p. 174.
12. Putnam, *James Jackson Putnam and Psychoanalysis,* p. 118.

13. Ibid., p. 121.

14. Ibid., p. 189.

15. Ibid., p. 190.

16. *SE*, vol. XIV, pp. 301–2.

17. H. Nunberg, *Principles of Psychoanalysis*, p. 140.

18. *SE*, vol. XIX, pp. 257–68.

19. *JAPA, 22*, 1974, p. 468.

20. Gay and Webb, *Modern Europe*, pp. 975–76.

21. *IJP, 27, 1948.*

22. Material in this section is cited from H. Dahmer, *Libido und Gesellschaft.*

23. M. Eastman, *Marx, Lenin and the Science of Revolution*, p. 101.

24. Quoted in Dahmer, *Libido und Gesellschaft*, p. 281n.

25. Ibid., p. 307.

26. Ibid., p. 331.

27. O. S. English, Some Recollections of a Psychoanalysis with Wilhelm Reich, *Journal of the American Academy of Psychoanalysis, 5,* 1977, pp. 239–54.

28. E. Fromm, *The Sane Society* and *Marx's Concept of Man.*

29. R. Tucker, ed., *Stalinism.*

30. Quoted in Dahmer, *Libido und Gesellschaft*, p. 292.

31. Quoted in Jones, *Life and Work*, vol. 3, pp. 345–46.

32. *SE*, vol. XXI, p. 113.

33. Ibid., p. 115.

34. O. Fenichel, *Collected Papers*, vol. 2, pp. 266–67.

35. *SE*, vol. IX, pp. 219–27.

36. Quoted in Gay and Webb, *Modern Europe*, p. 1020.

37. Reich's later work is too absurd to be taken seriously; only his writings before 1933 need be considered.

38. W. Reich, *Function of the Orgasm*, p. 64.

39. Dahmer, *Libido und Gesellschaft*, p. 398.

40. Ibid., pp. 399–400.

41. W. Reich, *The Sexual Revolution*, p. 25.

42. It has been stated, though not authoritatively, that the Freud estate has accepted some royalties from the sale of the book.

43. T. Mann, *Essays of Three Decades*, p. 427.

44. W. H. Auden, *Selected Poetry*, (New York: Random House, 1971), p. 57.

45. *IJP, 5,* 1924, pp. 62–68.

46. Ibid., p. 68.

47. Ibid., p. 82.

48. Ibid., p. 84.

49. Ibid., p. 89.

50. Ibid., pp. 86–87.

51. Ibid., p. 92.

52. Ibid., p. 229.

53. Ibid., p. 517.

54. F. Alexander, *Scope of Psychoanalysis*, p. 526.

55. R. May, *Existence*, p. 10.

56. Ibid., p. 33.

57. *JAPA, 10,* 1962, p. 166.

58. F. Alexander, *Scope of Psychoanalysis*, p. 550.

59. Ibid., p. 554.

60. O. Fenichel, *Psychoanalytic Theory of Neurosis*, p. 581.

61. Quoted in Ansbacher and Ansbacher, *Individual Psychology of Alfred Adler,* p. 131.
62. C. G. Jung, *Analytical Psychology,* pp. 186–87.
63. V. J. McGill, *Idea of Happiness,* p. 322.
64. In S. Post, ed., *Moral Values and the Superego Concept in Psychoanalysis,* p. 224.
65. H. Hartmann, *Psychoanalysis and Moral Values,* pp. 20–21.
66. Ibid., p. 51.
67. Ibid., p. 61.
68. Data here are taken from Redlich, Psychoanalysis and the Problem of Values, *Science and Psychoanalysis, 3,* 84–103.
69. Ibid., p. 89.
70. *Journal of Nervous and Mental Diseases,* 1945, p. 54.
71. Putnam, *James Jackson Putnam and Psychoanalysis,* p. 188.
72. M. Brierley, *Trends in Psychoanalysis,* p. 293.

Chapter 17: The Psychoanalytic Approach to Culture

1. G. Murphy, *Historical Introduction to Modern Psychology,* p. 158.
2. Jones, *Life and Work,* vol. 1, pp. 190–91.
3. *SE,* vol. XI, p. 190.
4. B. Malinowski, *Sex and Repression in Savage Society,* p. vii.
5. Quoted in M. Harris, *Rise of Modern Anthropological Theory,* p. 431.
6. *IJP, 4,* 1923, pp. 499–502.
7. W. Labarre, Psychoanalysis and Anthropology. *Science and Psychoanalysis, 4,* 10–20.
8. *IJP, 13,* 1932, p. 119.
9. L. K. Frank, Society as the Patient, 335–45.
10. *SE,* vol. XXII, p. 136.
11. Ibid., pp. 148–49.
12. Ibid., pp. 171–72.
13. A. I. Levenson, A Review of the Federal Community Mental Health Centers Program, in S. Arieti, ed., *American Handbook of Psychiatry,* vol. 2, pp. 593–604.
14. *New York Times,* June 5, 1977, p. E16.
15. *Crisis in Child Mental Health: Report of the Joint Commission on the Mental Health of Children.*
16. K. Davis, *Psychiatry, 1,* 1938, pp. 55–65.
17. *JAPA, 22,* 1974, p. 94.
18. T. Adorno et al., *The Authoritarian Personality,* p. 976.
19. *JAPA, 17,* 1969, p. 644.
20. *JAPA, 16,* 1968, p. 847.
21. R. Laing and A. Esterson, *Sanity, Madness and the Family,* p. 13.
22. *SE,* vol. XXIII, p. 235.
23. E. Jones, *Collected Papers,* p. 216.
24. *SE,* vol. IX, p. 193.
25. A. Kinsey et al., *Sexual Behavior in the Human Male,* p. 773.
26. Ibid., p. 224.
27. A. Kinsey et al., *Sexual Behavior in the Human Female,* p. 18.
28. Kinsey et al., *Sexual Behavior in the Human Male,* p. 580.
29. Kinsey et al., *Sexual Behavior in the Human Female,* p. 584.
30. Ibid., p. 530.
31. S. Hite, *The Hite Report,* pp. 134–35.
32. Quoted in H. D. Graham and T. R. Gurr, *History of Violence in America,* p. 788.

33. N. Ackerman, *Psychodynamics of Family Life*, p. 19.

34. Ibid.

35. R. W. Beavers, *Psychotherapy and Growth*, p. 250.

36. *SE*, vol. XVII, p. 167.

37. *PQ, 29*, 1960, pp. 459–77.

38. O. Lewis, *Anthropological Essays*, pp. 67–80.

39. *JAPA, 23*, 1975, p. 181.

40. *SE*, vol. XIX, p. 258.

41. *SE*, vol. XVIII, p. 69.

42. *IJP, 13*, 1932, p. 103.

43. *Psychiatry, 40*, 1977, p. 132.

44. *Book Forum, 1*, 1974, pp. 213–21; F. Herzberg, *Work Satisfaction and Motivation-Hygiene Theory*.

45. S. Arieti, *Interpretation of Schizophrenia*, p. 492.

46. Ibid., pp. 492–503.

47. Health, Education, and Welfare Department, *Alcohol and Health*, p. xv.

48. M. Blumenthal et al., *Justifying Violence*, p. 1.

49. E. Wittkower and R. Prince, in S. Arieti, ed., *American Handbook of Psychiatry*, vol. 2, p. 536.

50. H. Sullivan, *Schizophrenia as a Human Process*, p. 185.

51. A. Rifkin, 1974, in S. Arieti, ed., *American Handbook of Psychiatry*, vol. 1, p. 117.

Chapter 18: The Maturation of Technique

1. G. Pollock, *Chicago Institute Annual of Psychoanalysis, 3*, pp. 287–96.

2. Nevertheless, there are still some who first distort Freud beyond recognition, and then come back to him in different words.

3. *JAPA, 2*, 1954, pp. 606–9.

4. E.g., in *Studies in Hysteria, SE*, vol. II, p. 6, he claimed that "each individual hysterical symptom immediately and permanently disappeared." Once he had moved on to psychoanalysis, this claim was forgotten.

5. *SE*, vol. XIX, pp. 49–50.

6. S. Ferenczi, *Further Contributions*, p. 192.

7. S. Ferenczi, *Final Contributions*, pp. 108–25.

8. Ibid., p. 113.

9. Ibid., p. 122.

10. Ibid., p. 124.

11. Quoted in M. Bergmann and F. Hartman, *Evolution of Psychoanalytic Technique*, p. 133.

12. O. Fenichel, *Psychoanalytic Theory of Neurosis*, p. 573.

13. O. Kernberg et al., *Final Report*, pp. 181–95.

14. *JAPA, 20*, 1972, p. 620.

15. *SE*, vol. VII, pp. 263–64.

16. *PQ, 29*, 1960, p. 501.

17. *IJP, 50*, 1969, p. 639.

18. Ibid., p. 642.

19. R. Greenson, *Technique and Practice of Psychoanalysis*, p. 191.

20. Ibid., p. 192.

21. *JAPA, 2*, 1954, p. 680.

22. Ibid., p. 684.

23. Ibid., p. 689.

24. This concept simply presents a reformulation of the working out of the transference neurosis; it has been grossly misunderstood by Alexander's opponents.

25. *JAPA, 2,* 1954, p. 733.

26. Ibid.

27. Ibid., p. 744.

28. *JAPA, 1,* 1953, p. 110.

29. Ibid., p. 111.

30. *JAPA, 2,* 1954, p. 593.

31. *SE,* vol. XII, pp. 166–67.

32. Ibid., p. 171.

33. J. Sandler et al., *Patient and Analyst,* p. 51.

34. Ibid.

35. O. Fenichel, *Psychoanalytic Theory of Neurosis,* p. 451.

36. Freud and Jung, *Letters,* p. 207, letter of Jung dated March 7, 1909.

37. Putnam, *James Jackson Putnam and Psychoanalysis,* pp. 252–53.

38. Freud and Jung, *Letters,* p. 210, letter of Freud dated March 9, 1909, in reply to Jung's letter.

39. *SE,* vol. XI, pp. 144–45.

40. Ibid.

41. Freud and Jung, *Letters,* pp. 475–76.

42. J. Sandler et al., *Patient and Analyst,* pp. 67–68.

43. *JAPA, 4,* 1956, pp. 249–50.

44. *IJP, 30,* 1949, p. 69.

45. R. Greenson, *Technique and Practice of Psychoanalysis,* p. 336.

46. Ibid., p. 400.

47. *SE,* vol. XX, p. 160.

48. A. Freud, *Ego and the Mechanisms of Defense,* p. 28. At the time it was widely believed that her views echoed her father's reaction to Reich.

49. *SE,* vol. XII, p. 155.

50. H. Nunberg, *Principles of Psychoanalysis,* p. 360.

51. C. Brenner, *Psychoanalytic Technique and Psychic Conflict,* p. 199.

52. *SE,* vol. XVII, p. 11.

53. *JAPA, 11,* 1963, p. 139 (Muriel Gardner).

54. Goldensohn, Evaluation of Psychoanalytic Training, p. 56.

55. Personal communication, symposium arranged by Reuben Fine.

56. E. Jones, Criteria of Success in Treatment, p. 381.

57. J. Meltzoff and M. Kornreich, *Research in Psychotherapy,* p. 74.

Chapter 19: The Advance of Psychoanalysis to a Unifying Theory of Human Behavior

1. Freud and Jung, *Letters,* p. 255.

2. Ibid., p. 276.

3. Ibid., p. 340.

4. *SE,* vol. XIII, pp. 171–75.

5. Ibid., p. 179.

6. Quoted in S. Hook, ed., *Psychoanalysis, Scientific Method and Philosophy,* p. 212.

7. *PQ, 13,* 1944, pp. 101–2.

8. S. Hook, Psychoanalysis, Scientific Method and Philosophy, p. 309.

9. S. Fisher and R. Greenberg, *Scientific Credibility of Freud's Theories,* p. 396.

10. Ibid., pp. 393–95.

11. Ibid., p. 361.

12. Freud and Jung *Letters*, p. 166.

13. *Scientific Credibility of Freud's Theories*, p. 285.

14. G. Chrzanowski, *Interpersonal Approach to Psychoanalysis*, p. 1.

15. D. Rapaport, *Structure of Psychoanalytic Theory*, p. 9.

16. G. Klein, *Psychoanalytic Theory*, pp. 12–13.

17. Laplanche and Pontalis, *Language of Psychoanalysis*, p. 249.

18. *SE*, vol. XIII, p. 182.

19. D. Rapaport and D. Shakow, *Influence of Freud on American Psychology*, p. 20.

20. Ibid., pp. 111–12.

21. Quoted in American Psychological Association, *Psychoanalysis as Seen by Psychoanalyzed Psychologists*, p. 90.

22. Ibid., p. 44.

23. Ibid., p. 53.

24. Ibid., p. 149.

25. Ibid., p. 160.

26. Ibid., p. 4.

27. Ibid., p. 323.

28. Numbers are taken from American Psychological Association's *Register of Members*, 1977, p. vi.

29. Avery Publishing Co., personal communication, 1978.

30. W. Henry et al., *Fifth Profession*, p. 141.

31. S. Goodman, ed., *Psychoanalytic Education*, p. 200.

32. Henry et al., *Fifth Profession*, pp. 143–44.

33. Ibid., p. 144.

34. D. Rapaport and D. Shakow, *Influence of Freud*, p. 10.

35. Ibid., p. 198.

36. In J. Butcher, ed., *Objective Personality Assessment*, p. 64.

37. E. Kraepelin, *One Hundred Years of Psychiatry*, p. 99.

38. M. Greenblatt, Psychopolitics. *American Journal of Psychiatry, 131,* 1974, pp. 1200–1201.

39. J. Davis and J. O. Cole, Antipsychotic Drugs, in S. Arieti, ed., *American Handbook of Psychiatry*, vol. 5, ch. 22.

40. P. May, *Treatment of Schizophrenia*, p. 136.

41. Ibid., p. 297.

42. H. Lamb, *Community Survival for Long-Term Patients*, p. viii.

43. C. Chiland, ed., *Long-Term Treatment of Psychotic States*, p. 635.

44. M. Bleuler, Some Results of Research in Schizophrenia, *Schizophrenic Syndrome, 1,* 1971, p. 7.

45. A. Gralnick, *Psychiatric Hospital*, p. 65.

46. *American Journal of Psychiatry, 134,* 1977, special section on tardive dyskinesia, pp. 756–89.

47. P. Ahmed and S. Plog, *State Mental Hospitals*, p. 3.

48. *American Journal of Psychiatry, 134,* 1977, pp. 354–55, Position Statement on the Right to Adequate Care and Treatment for the Mentally Ill and the Mentally Retarded.

49. American Psychiatric Education: A Review. *American Journal of Psychiatry*, special suppl., *134,* 1977, p. 16.

50. G. Engel, The Need for a New Medical Model: A Challenge for Biomedicine, *Science, 196,* 1977, pp. 129–36.

51. H. R. Holman, *Hospital Practice, 11,* 1976, p. 11.
52. W. Langer, *Mind of Adolf Hitler,* p. vi.
53. V. McGill, Idea of Happiness, p. 322.
54. R. Slovenko, *Psychiatry and Law,* p. ix.
55. Ibid.

Bibliography

Abbreviations used in the Bibliography:

CP	Collected works of authors other than Freud
IJP	*International Journal of Psychoanalysis*
JAPA	*Journal of the American Psychoanalytic Association*
PQ	*Psychoanalytic Quarterly*
PSC	*Psychoanalytic Study of the Child*
PSM	*Psychosomatic Medicine*
SE	Standard Edition of Freud's works

Abelin, E. 1975. Some Further Comments and Observations on The Earliest Role of the Father. *IJP, 56*, 293–302.

Aberastury, G. 1960. *Historia, Enseñanza, y Ejercicio Legal del Psicoanalisis*. Buenos Aires: Bibliografia Omega.

Abraham, K. 1908. The Psychosexual Differences between Hysteria and Dementia Praecox. *CP, 1,* 64–79.

Abraham, K. 1911. Notes on the Psychoanalytic Investigation and Treatment of Manic-Depressive Insanity and Allied Conditions. *CP,* vol. 1, 137–56.

Abraham, K. 1916. The First Pregenital Stage of the Libido. *CP,* vol. 1, 248–79.

Abraham, K. 1920. Manifestations of the Female Castration Complex. *CP,* vol. 1, 338–69.

Abraham, K. 1921. Contributions to the Theory of the Anal Character. *CP,* vol. 1, 370–92.

Abraham, K. 1924. A Short History of the Development of the Libido. *CP,* vol. 1, 418–501.

Abraham, K. 1925. The History of an Impostor. *CP,* vol. 2, 291–305.

Abraham, K. 1927–1955. *Selected Papers*. 2 vols. New York: Basic Books. Cited above as *CP*.

Abt, L. E., and Weissman, S. L., eds. 1965. *Acting Out: Theoretical and Clinical Aspects*. New York: Grune & Stratton.

Achte, K. A., and Niskanen, O. P. 1972. *The Course and Prognosis of Psychoses in Helsinki*. Monographs from the Psychiatric Clinic of the Helsinki University Central Hospital. Helsinki.

Ackerman, N. W. 1958. *The Psychodynamics of Family Life*. New York: Basic Books.

Adelson, E., ed. 1975. *Sexuality and Psychoanalysis*. New York: Brunner/Mazel.

Adler, A. 1908. Sadism in Life and in Neurosis. In H. Nunberg and E. Federn, eds., *Minutes of the Vienna Psychoanalytic Society*, vol. II, pp. 406–10.

Adler, A. 1929. *Individual Psychology*. New York: Humanities Press.

Adler, A. 1931. *What Life Should Mean to You*. Boston: Little, Brown.

Adler, G., ed. 1974. *Success and Failure in Analysis: Proceedings*. New York: G. P. Putnam's.

Adorno, T., et al. 1950. *The Authoritarian Personality*. New York: Harper.

Ahmed, P. I., and Plog, S. C., eds. 1976. *State Mental Hospitals: What Happens When They Close*. New York: Plenum.

Aichhorn, A. 1925. *Wayward Youth*. New York: Viking Press, 1935.

Alanen, Y. O. 1958. *The Mothers of Schizophrenic Patients. Acta Psychiatrica et Neurologica Scandinavica*, suppl. 24.

Alanen, Y. O. 1966. The Family in the Pathogenesis of Schizophrenic and Neurotic Disorders. *Acta Psychiatrica Scandinavica 42, suppl. 189.*

Alexander, F. 1925a. Dreams in Pairs or Series. *IJP, 6,* 446–52.

Alexander, F. 1925b. A Metapsychological Description of the Process of Cure. *IJP, 6,* 13–34.

Alexander, F. 1930. *The Psychoanalysis of the Total Personality*. New York: Nervous and Mental Diseases Publishing Co.

Alexander, F. 1931. Buddhistic Training as an Artificial Catatonia. *Psychoanalytic Review, 18,* 129–45.

Alexander, F. 1937. *Five Year Report of the Chicago Institute for Psychoanalysis*. Chicago: Chicago Institute for Psychoanalysis.

Alexander, F. 1938. Psychoanalysis Comes of Age. *PQ, 7,* 299–306.

Alexander, F. 1950. *Psychosomatic Medicine*. New York: Norton.

Alexander, F. 1954a. Psychoanalysis and Psychotherapy. *JAPA, 2,* 722–33.

Alexander, F. 1954b. Some Quantitative Aspects of Psychoanalytic Technique. *JAPA, 2,* 685–701.

Alexander, F. 1959. Impressions from the Fourth International Congress of Psychotherapy. In F. Alexander, *The Scope of Psychoanalysis*, pp. 548–57.

Alexander, F. 1961. *The Scope of Psychoanalysis*. New York: Basic Books.

Alexander, F., and French, T. M. 1948. *Studies in Psychosomatic Medicine*. New York: Ronald Press.

Alexander, F., and Wilson, G. W. 1935. Quantitative Dream Studies. *PQ, 7,* 299–306.

Alexander, F., et al. 1946. *Psychoanalytic Therapy*. New York: Ronald Press.

Alexander, F., Selesnick, S., and Grotjahn, M. 1966. *Psychoanalytic Pioneers*. New York: Basic Books.

Alexander, J. 1960. The Psychology of Bitterness. *IJP, 14,* 514–20.

Allen, V., ed. 1970. *Psychological Factors in Poverty*. Chicago: Markham.

Almond, R. 1974. *The Healing Community*. New York: Jason Aronson.

Altman, L. L. 1977. Some Vicissitudes of Love. *JAPA, 25,* 35–52.

Altman, L. L. 1969. *The Dream in Psychoanalysis.* New York: International Univs. Press.

Amacher, P. 1965. *Freud's Neurological Education and Its Influence on Psychoanalytic Theory.* Psychological Issues Monograph 16. New York: International Univs. Press.

American Psychiatric Association 1952. *Diagnostic and Statistical Manual: DSM-1.* Washington, D.C.

American Psychiatric Association 1968. *Diagnostic and Statistical Manual: DSM-2.* Washington, D.C.

American Psychiatric Association 1974. *Behavior Therapy in Psychiatry.* New York: Jason Aronson.

American Psychological Association 1953. *Psychoanalysis as Seen by Psychoanalyzed Psychologists.* Washington, D.C.

American Psychological Association 1977. *Register of Members.* Washington, D.C.

Anderson, J. A., and Bower, G. H. 1973. *Human Associative Memory.* New York: Wiley.

Ansbacher, H., and Ansbacher, R. 1956. *The Individual Psychology of Alfred Adler.* New York: Basic Books.

Antrobus, J. S., Dement, W. C., and Fisher, C. 1964. Patterns of Dreaming and Dream Recall. *J. Abnormal Social Psychology, 69,* 341–44.

Anzieu, D. 1975. *L'Auto-analyse de Freud et la découverte de la psychoanalyse.* rev., enlarged ed. Paris: Presses Universitaires de France. (1st ed., 1959.)

Apfelbaum, B. 1962. Some Problems in Contemporary Ego Psychology. *JAPA, 10,* 526–37.

Applegarth, A. 1971. Comments on Aspects of the Theory of Psychic Energy. *JAPA, 19,* 379–416.

Applegarth, A. 1976. Psychic Energy Reconsidered (Panel). *JAPA, 24,* 647–58.

Arieti, S. 1967. *The Intrapsychic Self.* New York: Basic Books.

Arieti, S. 1972. *The Will To Be Human.* New York: Quadrangle.

Arieti, S. 1974. *Interpretation of Schizophrenia.* New York: Basic Books.

Arieti, S., ed. 1974–1975. *The American Handbook of Psychiatry.* 6 vols. New York: Basic Books.

Arieti, S. 1976. *Creativity: The Magic Synthesis.* New York: Basic Books.

Arlow, J. A. 1959. The Structure of the Déjà Vu Experience. *JAPA, 7,* 611–31.

Arlow, J. A. 1972. Ten Years of COPE: Perspectives in Psychoanalytic Education. *JAPA, 20,* 556–66.

Arlow, J. A. 1973. Perspectives on Aggression in Human Adaptation. *PQ, 42,* 178–84.

Arlow, J. A., and Brenner, C. 1964. *Psychoanalytical Concepts and the Structural Theory.* New York: International Univs. Press.

Arnold, M. B. 1970. *Emotion and Personality.* New York: Columbia Univ. Press.

Asch, S. S. 1976. Varieties of Negative Therapeutic Reaction and Problems of Technique. *JAPA, 24,* 383–408.

Aserinsky, E., and Kleitman, N. 1953. Regularly Occurring Periods of Eye Motility and Concomitant Phenomena during Sleep. *Science, 118,* 273–74.

Aserinsky, E., and Kleitman, N. 1955a. A Motility Cycle in Sleeping Infants as

Manifested by Ocular and Gross Bodily Activity. *Journal of Applied Physiology, 8,* 11– 18.

Aserinsky, E., and Kleitman, N. 1955b. Two Types of Ocular Activity Occurring in Sleep. *Journal of Applied Physiology, 8,* 1–10.

Axelrad, S., and Brody, S. 1970. *Anxiety and Ego Formation.* New York: International Univs. Press.

Babcock, C. G. 1966. The Manifest Content of the Dream (Panel). *JAPA, 14,* 154–71.

Baddeley, A. D. 1976. *The Psychology of Memory.* New York: Basic Books.

Bak, R. C. 1939. Regression of Ego Orientation and Libido in Schizophrenia. *IJP, 20,* 64–71.

Bak, R. C. 1954. The Schizophrenic Defence against Aggression. *IJP, 35,* 129–34.

Bak, R. C. 1965. Comments on Object Relations in Schizophrenia and Perversions. *PQ, 34,* 473–75.

Bak, R. C. 1973. Being in Love and Object Loss. *IJP, 54,* 1–8.

Balint, M. 1948. On the Psychoanalytic Training System. *IJP, 29,* 163–73.

Balint, M. 1949. Early Developmental Stages of the Ego: Primary Object Love. *IJP, 30,* 265–73.

Balint, M. 1952. On Love and Hate. *IJP, 33,* 355–62.

Balint, M. 1953. *Primary Love and Psychoanalytic Technique.* New York: Liveright.

Balint, M. 1954. Analytic Training and Training Analysis. *IJP, 35,* 157–62.

Balint, M. 1968. *The Basic Fault.* London: Tavistock.

Balint, M., and Balint, A. 1939. On Transference and Countertransference. *IJP, 20,* 223–30.

Bandura, A. 1973. *Aggression.* Englewood Cliffs, N.J.: Prentice-Hall.

Bandura, A. 1977. *Social Learning Theory.* Englewood Cliffs, N.J.: Prentice-Hall.

Barande, I., and Barande, R. 1975. *Histoire de la psychanalyse en France.* Paris: Privat.

Barchilon, J. 1958. On Countertransference "Cures." *JAPA, 6,* 222–36.

Barker, W. 1968. Female Sexuality (Panel). *JAPA, 16,* 123–45.

Barron, F. 1972. *Artists in the Making.* New York: Seminar Press.

Beach, F. A., ed. 1977. *Human Sexuality in Four Perspectives.* Baltimore: John Hopkins Univ. Press.

Beavers, R. W. 1977. *Psychotherapy and Growth: A Family Systems Perspective.* New York: Brunner/Mazel.

Bell, A. 1965. The Significance of the Scrotal Sac and Testicles for the Prepuberty Male. *PQ, 34,* 182–206.

Bell, S. 1902. A Preliminary Study of the Emotion of Love between the Sexes. *American Journal of Psychology, 13,* 341.

Bell, S. 1970. The Development of a Concept of Object as Related to Infant-Mother Attachment. *Child Development, 41,* 291–311.

Bellak, L. 1954. *The TAT and CAT in Clinical Use.* New York: Grune & Stratton.

Bellak, L. 1955. An Ego-Psychological Theory of Hypnosis. *IJP, 36,* 375–78.

Bellak, L. 1961. Free Association. *IJP, 42,* 9–20.

Bellak, L., ed. 1964. *A Handbook of Community Mental Health.* New York: Grune & Stratton.

Bellak, L., and Loeb, L. 1968. *The Schizophrenic Syndrome*. New York: Grune & Stratton.

Bellak, L., Hurvich, M., and Gediman, H. 1973. *Ego Functioning in Schizophrenics, Neurotics and Normals*. New York: Wiley.

Bender, L. 1938. *A Visual Motor Gestalt Test and Its Clinical Use*. American Orthopsychiatric Association Research Monograph no. 3. New York.

Bendix, R. 1960. *Max Weber*. Garden City, N.Y.: Doubleday.

Benedek, T. 1959. Parenthood as a Developmental Phase. *JAPA, 7*, 389–417.

Benedek, T. 1973. *Psychoanalytic Investigations*. New York: Quadrangle.

Benedek, T. 1977. Ambivalence, Passion and Love. *JAPA, 25*, 53–80.

Benedek, T., and Anthony, E. J., eds. 1970. *Parenthood*. Boston: Little, Brown.

Benedict, R. 1934. *Patterns of Culture*. Boston: Houghton Mifflin.

Beres, D. 1956. Ego Deviation and the Concept of Schizophrenia. *PQ, 25*, 460–62.

Bergin, A. E., and Garfield, S. L., eds. 1971. *Handbook of Psychotherapy and Behavior Change*. New York: Wiley.

Bergler, E. 1945. On the Disease Entity Boredom ("Alyosis") and its Psychopathology. *PQ, 19*, 38–51.

Bergler, E. 1949. *The Basic Neurosis: Oral Regression and Psychic Masochism*. New York: Grune & Stratton.

Bergler, E. 1954. *The Writer and Psychoanalysis*. New York: Brunner.

Bergmann, M. S. 1963. The Place of Paul Federn's Ego Psychology in Psychoanalytic Metapsychology. *JAPA, 11*, 97–116.

Bergmann, M. J., and Hartman, F. 1977. *The Evolution of Psychoanalytic Technique*. New York: Basic Books.

Berliner, B. 1958. The Role of Object Relations in Moral Masochism. *PQ, 27*, 38–56.

Bernard, V. 1953. Psychoanalysis and Members of Minority Groups. *JAPA, 1*, 256–67.

Bernfeld, S. 1922. Some Remarks on Sublimation. *IJP, 3*, 134–35.

Bernfeld, S. 1931. Zur Sublimierungstheorie. *Imago, 17*, 399–403.

Bernfeld, S. 1952. On Psychoanalytic Training. *PQ, 31*, 453–82.

Bettelheim, B. 1954. *Symbolic Wounds*. Glencoe, Ill.: Free Press.

Bettelheim, B. 1967. *The Empty Fortress*. New York: Free Press.

Bibring, E. 1947. The So-Called English School of Psychoanalysis. *PQ, 16*, 69–93.

Bibring, E. 1953. The Mechanism of Depression. In P. Greenacre, ed., *Affective Disorders*, 13–48.

Bibring, E. 1954. Psychoanalysis and the Dynamic Psychotherapies. *JAPA, 2*, 745–70.

Bibring, G. 1959. Some Considerations of the Psychological Processes in Pregnancy. *PSC, 14*, 113–21.

Bibring, G. L. 1964. Some Considerations Regarding the Ego Ideal in the Psychoanalytic Process. *JAPA, 12*, 517–21.

Bibring, G., et al. 1961. A Study of the Psychological Processes in Pregnancy and the Earliest Mother–Child Relationship. *PSC, 16*, 9–72.

Bieber, I., et al. 1962. *Homosexuality*. New York: Basic Books.

Billig, M. 1976. *Social Psychology and Intergroup Relations*. New York: Academic Press.

Bing, J. F., McLaughlin, F., and Marburg, R. 1959. The Metapsychology of Narcissism. *PSC, 14,* 9–28.

Bion, W. R. 1961. *Experiences in Groups.* New York: Basic Books.

Birdwhistell, R. 1970. *Kinesis and Context.* Philadelphia: Univ. of Pennsylvania Press.

Bjerre, P. C. 1911. Zur Radikalbehandlung der chronischen Paranoia. *Jahrbuch fuer psychoanalytische und psychopathische Forschung, 3,* 795–847.

Blanton, S. 1971. *Diary of My Analysis with Freud.* New York: Hawthorn Books.

Blatt, S. J., et al. 1976. Disturbances of Object Relationships in Schizophrenia. *Psychoanalysis and Contemporary Science, 4,* 235–88.

Bleuler, E. 1911. *Dementia Praecox oder Gruppe der Schizophrenen.* Leipzig and Vienna: Deuticke.

Bleuler, M. 1970. Some Results of Research in Schizophrenia. *Schizophrenic Syndrome, 1,* 3–16.

Blos, P. 1962. *On Adolescence.* New York: Free Press.

Blum, H. P. 1971. Transference and Structure: On the Conception and Development of the Transference Neurosis. *JAPA, 19,* 41–53.

Blum, H. P. 1973. The Concept of Erotized Transference. *JAPA, 21,* 61–76.

Blum, H. P. 1976. The Changing Use of Dreams in Psychoanalytic Practice. *IJP, 57,* 315–24.

Blum, H. P., ed. 1977. *Female Psychology.* New York: International Univers. Press.

Blumenthal, M. D., et al. 1972. *Justifying Violence.* Ann Arbor, Mich.: Institute for Social Research.

Boas, F. 1908. The History of Anthropology. *Science, 20,* 513–24.

Boehm, F. 1930. The Femininity Complex in Men. *IJP, 11,* 444–69.

Boisen, A. T. 1936. *The Exploration of the Inner World.* New York: Harper.

Bonaparte, M. 1947. A Lion Hunter's Dreams. *PQ, 16,* 1–10.

Bonime, W. 1962. *The Clinical Use of Drams.* New York: Basic Books.

Bornstein, B. 1945. Clinical Notes on Child Analysis.

Bornstein, B. 1951. On Latency. *PSC, 6,* 279–85.

Bornstein, B. 1953. Masturbation in the Latency Period.

Boss, M. 1938. Psychopathologie des Traumes bei Schizophrenen und organischen Psychosen. *Zeitschrift Gesamte Neurologie und Psychiatrie, 162,* 459–94.

Bowlby, J. 1951. *Maternal Care and Mental Health.* New York: Schocken Books.

Bowlby, J. 1953. Some Pathological Processes Set in Train by Early Mother-Child Separation. *Journal of Mental Sciences, 99,* 265–72.

Bowlby, J. 1960. Grief and Mourning in Infancy and Early Childhood. *PSC, 15,* 9–52.

Bowlby, J. 1961. Processes of Mourning. *IJP, 42,* 317–40.

Bowlby, J. 1969. *Attachment and Loss,* vol. 1: *Attachment.* New York: Basic Books.

Bowlby, J. 1973. *Attachment and Loss,* vol. 2: *Separation.* New York: Basic Books.

Boyer, L. B., Boyer, R. M., and Hippler, A. E. 1976. The Subarctic Athabascans of Alaska. *Psychoanalytic Study of Society, 7,* 293–330.

Boyer, L. B., and Giovacchini, P. L. 1967. *Psychoanalytic Treatment of Characterological and Schizophrenic Disorders*. New York: Science House.

Bradlow, P. A. 1971. Murder in the Initial Dream in Psychoanalysis. *Bulletin of the Philadelphia Association for Psychoanalysis, 21,* 70–81.

Bradlow, P. A., and Coen, S. S. 1975. The Analyst Undisguised in the Initial Dream in Psychoanalysis. *IJP, 56,* 415–25.

Bray, D. W., Campbell, R. J., and Grant, D. L. 1974. *Formative Years in Business*. New York: Wiley.

Breger, L., Hunter, I., and Lane, R. W. 1971. *The Effect of Stress on Dreams*. Psychological Issues Monograph 27. New York: International Univs. Press.

Breland, K., and Breland, M. 1966. *Animal Behavior*. New York: Macmillan.

Breland, K., and Breland, M. 1961. The Misbehavior of Organisms. *American Psychologist, 16,* 681–84.

Brenman, M., and Gill, M. M. 1947. Alterations in the State of The Ego in Hypnosis. *Bulletin of the Menninger Clinic, 11,* 60–66.

Brenman, M., and Gill, M. 1961. *Hypnosis and Related States*. New York: International Univs. Press.

Brenner, C. 1956. Reevaluation of the Libido Theory (Panel). *JAPA, 4,* 162–69.

Brenner, C. 1957. The Nature and Development of the Concept of Repression in Freud's Writings. *PSC, 12,* 19–46.

Brenner, C. 1971. The Psychoanalytic Concept of Aggression. *IJP, 52,* 137–44.

Brenner, C. 1976. *Psychoanalytic Technique and Psychic Conflict*. New York: International Univs. Press.

Brett, G. S. 1914–1921. *A History of Psychology*. London: Routledge and Kegan Paul.

Brett, G. S. 1965. *A History of Psychology*, abridged ed. by R. S. Peters. Cambridge, Mass.: M.I.T. Press.

Briehl, W. 1966. Biography of Wilhelm Reich. In F. Alexander, et al., *Psychoanalytic Pioneers*, pp. 430–38.

Brierley, M. 1947. Psychoanalysis and Integrative Living. *IJP, 28,* 57–105.

Brierley, M. 1951. *Trends in Psychoanalysis*. London: Hogarth Press.

Brill, A. A. 1912. Anal Eroticism and Character. *Journal of Abnormal Psychology, 7,* 196–203.

Brill, H. 1965. Psychiatric Diagnosis, Nomenclature and Classification. In B. Wolman, ed., *Handbook of Clinical Psychology*, Chap. 24. New York: McGraw-Hill.

British Psychoanalytical Society 1963. *Fiftieth Anniversary*. London.

Brodey, W. M. 1959. Some Family Operations and Schizophrenia. *Archives of General Psychiatry, 1,* 379–402.

Brody, S. 1956. *Patterns of Mothering*. New York: International Univs. Press.

Brody, S., and Axelrad, S. 1978. *Mothers, Fathers and Children*. New York: International Univs. Press.

Bromberg, W. 1954. *The Mind of Man: A History of Psychotherapy and Psychoanalysis*. New York: Harper.

Bruner, J. 1973. *Beyond the Information Given*. New York: Norton.

Bruner, J., et al. 1966. *Studies in Cognitive Growth*. New York: Wiley.

Bruner, J., et al. 1976. *Play.* New York: Basic Books.

Brunswick, D. 1954. A Revision of the Classification of Instincts or Drives. *IJP,* 35, 224–28.

Brunswick, R. M. 1928. A Supplement to Freud's "A History of an Infantile Neurosis." *IJP, 9,* 439–76.

Buber, M. 1970. *I and Thou.* New York: Scribner's.

Bullitt, W. C., and Freud, S. 1967. *Thomas Woodrow Wilson: A Psychological Study.* Boston: Houghton Mifflin.

Bunker, H. A. 1953. A Dream of an Inhibited Writer. *PQ, 22,* 519–24.

Burnham, D. L., Gladstone, A. I., and Gibson, W. 1969. *Schizophrenia and the Need–Fear Dilemma.* New York: International Univs. Press.

Buros, O. K. 1975. *Mental Measurements Yearbook.* Rutgers, N.J.: Gryphon Press.

Burr, A. R. 1909. *The Autobiography.* Boston: Houghton Mifflin.

Burrow, T. 1958. *A Search for Man's Sanity.* New York: Oxford Univs. Press.

Bursten, B., and D'Esppo, R. 1965. The Obligation to Remain Sick. *Archives of General Psychiatry,* 12, 402–7.

Busch, F. 1974. Dimensions of the First Transitional Object. *PSC, 29,* 215–30.

Bush, M. 1969. Psychoanalysis and Scientific Creativity, with Special Reference to Regression in the Service of the Ego. *JAPA, 17,* 136–90.

Butcher, J. N., ed. 1967. *Objective Personality Assessment.* New York: Academic Press.

Butler, R. 1967. The Destiny of Creativity in Later Life: Studies of Creative People and the Creative Process. In R. J. Kahana, and S. Levin, eds., *Psychodynamic Studies on Aging,* pp. 20–63.

Butler, R. 1968. Toward a Psychiatry of the Life Cycle. *Psychiatric Research Reports, 23,* 233–48.

Bychowski, G. 1930. A Case of Oral Delusions of Persecution. *IJP, 11,* 332–37.

Bychowski, G. 1951. Remarks on some Defense Mechanisms and Reaction Patterns of the Schizophrenic Ego. *Bulletin of the American Psychoanalytic Association, 7,* 141–43.

Bychowski, G. 1952. *Psychotherapy of Psychosis.* New York: Grune & Stratton.

Bychowski, G. 1964. Freud and Jung: An Encounter. *Israel Annals of Psychiatry and Related Disciplines, 2,* 129–43.

Calef, V. 1954. Training and Therapeutic Analysis (Panel). *JAPA, 2,* 175–78.

Calef, V. 1971. On the Current Concept of the Transference Neurosis (Panel). *JAPA, 19,* 22–25, 89–97.

Calef, V., and Weinshel, E. 1973. Reporting, Nonreporting and Assessment of the Training Analysis. *JAPA, 21,* 714–26.

Campbell, J. 1949. *The Hero with a Thousand Faces.* New York: Meridian Books.

Cannon, W. B. 1929. *Bodily Changes in Pain, Hunger, Fear and Rage.* Boston: Branford.

Carlson, E. T., and Quen, J. M., eds. 1978. *American Psychoanalysis: Origins and Development.* New York: Brunner/Mazel.

Castelnuovo-Tedesco, P. 1974. Toward a Theory of Affects (Panel). *JAPA, 22,* 612–25.

Chafetz, M. E., et al. 1974. Alcoholism: A Positive View. In S. Arieti, ed., *The American Handbook of Psychiatry,* vol. 3, pp. 367–92.

Chapman, A. 1976. *Harry Stack Sullivan: The Man and His World*. New York: Putnam.

Chapman, T., and Foot, H. 1976. *Humor and Laughter*. New York: Wiley.

Chasseguet-Smirgel, J., et al. 1970. *Female Sexuality*. Ann Arbor, Mich.: Univ. of Michigan Press.

Chess, S., and Thomas, A. 1977. *Temperament and Development*. New York: Brunner/Mazel.

Chiland, C., ed. 1977. *Long-Term Treatment of Psychotic States*. New York: Human Sciences Press.

Chin, R., and Chin, S. 1969. *Psychological Research in Communist China*. Cambridge, Mass.: MIT Press.

Chisholm, G. B. 1946. The Psychiatry of Enduring Peace and Social Progress. *Psychiatry, 9,* 3–20.

Christensen, H. 1939. Report on the Dano-Norwegian Psychoanalytical Society. *IJP, 20,* 216–217.

Chrzanowski, G. 1977. *Interpersonal Approach to Psychoanalysis*. New York: Wiley.

Clarke-Stewart, K. A. 1973. Interactions between Mothers and their Young Children. *Monographs of the Society for Research in Child Development, 38* (6–7, serial no. 153).

Cohen, M. B. 1952. Countertransference and Anxiety. *Psychiatry, 15,* 231–43.

Cohen, M. B., et al. 1954. An Intensive Study of Twelve Cases of Manic-Depressive Psychosis. *Psychiatry, 17,* 103–37.

Cohen, Y. 1966. *The Transition from Childhood to Adolescence*. Chicago: Aldine.

Coles, R. C. 1970. *Erik Erikson*. Boston: Little, Brown.

Collingwood, R. G. 1946. *The Idea of History*. New York: Oxford Univ. Press.

Coltrera, J. 1962. Psychoanalysis and Existentialism. *JAPA, 10,* 166–215.

Coltrera, J. 1965. On the Creation of Beauty and Thought. *JAPA, 13,* 634–703.

Compton, A. 1972. A Study of the Psychoanalytic Theory of Anxiety. *JAPA, 20,* 3–44.

Corsini, R., ed. 1973. *Current Psychotherapies*. Itasca, Ill.: F. S. Peacock.

Crowley, R. 1939. Psychoanalytic Literature on Drug Addiction and Alcoholism. *Psychoanalytic Review, 26,* 39–54.

Cuber, J., and Harroff, P. 1965. *The Significant Americans*. New York: Appleton.

Cushing, J. G. N. 1952. Report of the Committee on Definition of Psychoanalysis. *Bulletin of the American Psychoanalytic Association, 8,* 44–50.

Dahl, H. 1972. A Quantitative Study of a Psychoanalysis. *Psychoanalysis and Contemporary Science, 1,* 237–57.

Dahmer, H. 1973. *Libido und Gesellschaft*. Frankfurt a/M: Suhrkamp.

D'Amore, A. 1976. *William Alanson White: The Washington Years*. Washington, D.C.: Department of Health, Education, and Welfare.

D'Amore, A. 1978. *Historical Reflections on Psychoanalysis: 1920–1970. The Organizational History of Psychoanalysis in America*. New York: Brunner/Mazel, in press.

Davis, A., and Dollard, J. 1940. *Children of Bondage*. Garden City, N.Y.: Doubleday.

Davis, G. A. 1973. *Psychology of Problem Solving*. New York: Basic Books.

Davis, K. 1938. Mental Hygiene and the Class Structure. *Psychiatry, 1,* 55–65.

Decarie, T. 1965. *Intelligence and Affectivity in Early Childhood: An Experimental Study of Jean Piaget's Object Concept and Object Relations.* New York: International Univs. Press.

Decker, H. S. 1978. *Freud in Germany.* Psychological Issues Monograph 41. New York: International Univs. Press.

De Mause, L., ed. 1974. *The History of Childhood.* New York: Psychohistory Press.

Dember, W. N. 1960. *Psychology of Perception.* New York: Holt.

Dement, W. C. 1955. Dream Recall and Eye Movements during Sleep in Schizophrenics and Normals. *Journal of Nervous and Mental Diseases, 122,* 263–69.

Dement, W. C. 1958. The Occurrence of Low Voltage, Fast EEG Patterns During Behavioral Sleep in the Cat. *EEG Clinical Neurophysiology, 10,* 291–95.

Dement, W. C. 1960. The Effect of Dream Deprivation. *Science, 131,* 1705–07.

Dement, W. C. 1965. An Essay on Dreams. In W. Edwards et al., *New Directions in Psychology.* New York: Holt.

Dement, W. C., and Fisher, C. 1963. Experimental Interference with the Dream Cycle. *Canadian Psychiatric Association Journal, 8,* 400–405.

Dement, W. C., and Kleitman, N. 1957. The Relation of Eye Movements during Sleep to Dream Activity. *Journal of Experimental Psychology, 53,* 339–46.

Dement, W. C., and Wolpert, E. A. 1958. The Relation of Eye Movements, Body Motility and External Stimuli to Dream Content. *Journal of Experimental Psychology, 55,* 543–53.

De Rivera, J. 1977. *A Structural Theory of the Emotions.* Psychological Issues Monograph 40. New York: International Univs. Press.

Deschner, K. 1974. *Das Kreuz mit der Kirche.* Dusseldorf: Econ Verlag.

Deutsch, D., and Deutsch, J. A., eds. 1975. *Short-Term Memory.* New York: Academic Press.

Deutsch, F. 1952. Analytic Posturology. *PQ, 20,* 196–214.

Deutsch, H. 1930. Melancholic and Depressive States. Reprinted in H. Deutsch, *Neurosis and Character Types,* pp. 145–56.

Deutsch, H. 1934. Ueber einen Typus der Pseudoaffektivitaet ("als ob"). *Zeitschrift fuer Psychoanalyse, 20,* 323–35.

Deutsch, H. 1942. Some Forms of Emotional Disturbance and their Relationship to Schizophrenia. *PQ, 11,* 301–21.

Deutsch, H. 1945. *The Psychology of Women.* 2 vols. New York: Grune & Stratton.

Deutsch, H. 1961. Frigidity in Women. *JAPA, 9,* 571–84.

Deutsch, H. 1965. *Neurosis and Character Types.* New York: International Univs. Press.

Deutsch, H. 1967. *Selected Problems of Adolescence.* New York: International Univs. Press.

Deutsch, H. 1973. *Confrontations with Myself.* New York: Norton.

Deutsch, M., et al. 1968. *Social Class, Race and Psychological Development.* New York: Holt.

Deutsche Psychoanalytische Gesellschaft 1951. *Dokumente zur Geschichte der Psychoanalyse in Deutschland 1933–1951.* Report by F. Boehm.

Devereux, G. 1951. *Reality and Dream.* New York: International Univs. Press.

Devereux, G. 1955. *A Study of Abortion in Primitive Societies.* New York: Julian Press.

Diamond, S. 1974. *In Search of the Primitive.* New Brunswick, N.J.: Transaction.

Dickes, R. 1975. Technical Considerations of the Therapeutic and Working Alliances. *JAPA, 15,* 508–33.

Dobzhansky, T. 1973. *Genetic Diversity and Human Equality.* New York: Basic Books.

Dohrenwend, B. P. and Dohrenwend, B. S. 1969. *Social Stress and Psychological Disorder.* New York: Wiley.

Dollard, J. 1937. *Caste and Class in a Southern Town.* New York: Harper.

Dollard, J., Miller, N., et al. 1939. *Frustration and Aggression.* New Haven: Yale Univ. Press.

Drabkin, I. E. 1954. Remarks on Ancient Psychopathology. Paper read at a meeting of the History of Science Society, New York, Dec. 29, 1954.

Drellich, M. 1974. Classical Psychoanalytic School. In S. Arieti, ed., *The American Handbook of Psychiatry,* vol. 1, pp. 737–64.

Drucker, J. 1975. Toddler Play. *Psychoanalysis and Contemporary Science, 4,* 479–527.

Du Bois, C. 1944. *The People of Alor.* Minneapolis: Minnesota Univ. Press.

Dührssen, A. 1971. Zum 25 Jährigen Bestehen des Instituts fuer Psychogene Erkrankungen. Special number of *Zeitschrift fuer Psychosomatische Medizin und Psychoanalyse.* Göttingen: Vandenhoek und Ruprecht.

Dunbar, F. 1935. *Emotions and Bodily Changes.* New York: Columbia Univ. Press.

Duncan, O. D., et al. 1972. *Socioeconomic Background and Achievement.* New York: Seminar Press.

Dunkell, S. 1977. *Sleep Positions.* New York: Morrow.

Durkheim, E. 1895. *The Rules of Sociological Method.* Reprint ed., New York: Free Press, 1966.

Durkin, H. E. 1964. *The Group in Depth.* New York: International Univs. Press.

Eastman, M. 1926. *Marx, Lenin and the Science of Revolution.* London.

Eaton, J. W., and Weil, R. J. 1955. *Culture and Mental Disorders: A Comparative Study of the Hutterites and Other Populations.* Glencoe, Ill.: Free Press.

Edelheit, H. 1969. Speech and Psychic Structure. *JAPA, 17,* 381–412.

Edelson, M. 1972. Language and Dreams. *PSC, 27,* 203–82.

Egbert, D. 1970. *Social Radicalism and the Arts.* New York: Knopf.

Ehrenwald, J. 1958. History of Psychoanalysis. In J. S. Masserman, ed., *Science and Psychoanalysis,* vol. 1, pp. 145–51.

Ehrenwald, J. 1976. *The History of Psychotherapy.* New York: Jason Aronson.

Eibl-Eibesfeldt, I. 1972. *Love and Hate.* New York: Holt.

Eibl-Eibesfeldt, I. 1977. Evolution of Destructive Aggression. *Aggressive Behavior, 3,* 127–44.

Eissler, K. R. 1953. The Effect of the Structure of the Ego on Psychoanalytic Technique. *JAPA, 1,* 104–43.

Eissler, K. R. 1955. *The Psychiatrist and the Dying Patient.* New York: International Univs. Press.

Eissler, K. R. 1960. The Efficient Soldier. *Psychoanalytic Study of Society, 1,* 39–97.

Eissler, K. R. 1963. Notes on the Psychoanalytic Concept of Cure. *PSC, 18,* 424–63.

Eitingon, M. 1928. Ansprache bei der Einweihung der Neuen Institutsraüme. In *Zehn Jahre Berliner Psychoanakytisches Institut,* pp. 71–74.

Ekstein, R. 1955. Termination of the Training Analysis within the Framework of Present-Day Institutes. *JAPA, 3,* 600–613.

Ekstein, R. 1966. Biography of S. Bernfeld. In F. Alexander, et al., *Psychoanalytic Pioneers,* 415–29.

Ekstein, R. 1965. Historical Notes Concerning Psychoanalysis and Early Language Development. *JAPA, 13,* 707–31.

Ekstein, R., and Caruth, E. 1967. Distancing and Distance: Devices in Childhood Schizophrenia and Borderline States: Revised Concepts and New Directions in Research. *Psychological Reports,* 20, 109–10.

Ellenberger, H. F. 1970. *The Discovery of the Unconscious.* New York: Basic Books.

Ellis, A. 1953. Is the Vaginal Orgasm a Myth? In A. D. Pillay and A. Ellis, *Sex, Society and the Individual. International Journal of Sexology* (Bombay), 155–62.

Ember, M. 1975. On the Origin and Extension of the Incest Taboo. *Behavior Science Research, 10,* 249–81.

Emde, R. N., et al. 1976. *Emotional Expression in Infancy.* Psychological Issues Monograph 37. New York: International Univs. Press.

Engel, G. L. 1955. Studies of Ulcerative Colitis. *American Journal of Medicine, 19,* 231–56.

Engel, G. 1967. Psychoanalytic Theory of Somatic Disorder. *JAPA, 15,* 344–65.

Engel, G. L. 1977. The Need for a New Medical Model: A Challenge for Biomedicine. *Science, 196,* no. 4286, 129–36.

Engel, G. L., and Reichsman, F. 1956. Spontaneous and Experimentally Induced Depressions in an Infant with a Gastric Fistula. A Contribution to the Problem of Depression. *JAPA, 4,* 428–52.

English, O. S. 1977. Some Recollections of a Psychoanalysis with Wilhelm Reich: Sept. 1929–April 1932. *Journal of the American Academy of Psychoanalysis, 5,* 239–54.

Entralgo, P. L. 1970. *The Therapy of the Word in Classical Antiquity.* New Haven: Yale Univ. Press.

Erikson, E. 1950. *Childhood and Society.* New York: Norton.

Erikson, E. 1954. The Dream Specimen of Psychoanalysis. *JAPA, 2,* 5–56.

Erikson, E. 1958. *Young Man Luther.* New York: Norton.

Erikson, E. 1959. *Identity and the Life Cycle.* Psychological Issues Monograph 1. New York: International Univs. Press.

Erikson, E. 1969. *Gandhi's Truth.* New York: Norton.

Erikson, E. 1974. *Dimensions of a New Identity.* New York: Norton.

Escalona, S. 1963. Patterns of Infantile Experience and the Developmental Process. *PSC, 18,* 197–244.

Escalona, S. 1968. *The Roots of Individuality.* Chicago: Aldine.

Escalona, S., and Heider, G. M. 1959. *Prediction and Outcome.* New York: Basic Books.

Esman, A. 1975. *The Psychology of Adolescence.* New York: International Univs. Press.

Esman, A. 1977. Changing Values: Their Implications for Adolescent Development and Psychoanalytic Ideas. In S. Feinstein, et al., eds., *Adolescent Psychiatry,* vol. 5, pp. 18–34.

Ewing, J. A., et al. 1961. Concurrent Group Psychotherapy of Alcoholic Patients and Their Wives. *International Journal of Group Psychotherapy, 11,* 329–38.

Eysenck, H. J. 1965. The Effects of Psychotherapy. *International Journal of Psychiatry, 1,* 97–143.

Fairbairn, W. R. D. 1941. A Revised Psychopathology of the Psychoses and Psychoneuroses. *IJP, 22,* 250–79.

Fairbairn, W. R. D. 1954. *An Object Relations Theory of the Personality.* New York: Basic Books.

Fairbairn, W. R. D. 1963. An Object Relations Theory of the Personality. *IJP, 44,* 224–25.

Faris, R. E. L., and Dunham, H. W. 1939. *Mental Disorder in Urban Areas.* Chicago: Univ. of Chicago Press.

Federn, P. 1928. Narcissism in the Structure of the Ego. *IJP, 9,* 401–19.

Federn, P. 1929. The Ego as Subject and Object in Narcissism. *Internationale Zeitschrift fuer Psychoanalyse, 15,* 393–425. Reprinted in P. Federn, *Ego Psychology and the Psychoses,* pp. 283–322.

Federn, P. 1934. The Analysis of Psychotics. *IJP, 15,* 209–14.

Federn, P. 1943. Psychoanalysis of Psychoses. *Psychiatric Quarterly, 17,* 3–19.

Federn, P. 1952. *Ego Psychology and the Psychoses.* New York: Basic Books.

Feinstein, S. C., Giovacchini, P., and Miller, A. A. 1971–1977. *Adolescent Psychiatry,* vols. 1–5. New York: Basic Books.

Feldman, F. 1968. Results of Psychoanalysis in Clinic Case Assignments. *JAPA, 16,* 274–300.

Feldman, S. S. 1943. Interpretation of a Typical Dream: Finding Money. *Psychiatric Quarterly, 17,* 423–25.

Feldman, S. S. 1945. Interpretation of a Typical and Stereotyped Dream Met with Only During Psychoanalysis. *PQ, 14,* 511–15.

Feldman, S. S. 1959. *Mannerisms of Speech and Gestures in Everyday Life.* New York: International Univs. Press.

Fenichel, O. 1930. Statistischer Bericht ueber die Therapeutische Taetigkeit. In *Zehn Jahre Berliner Psychoanalytisches Institut,* pp. 13–19.

Fenichel, O. 1934. On the Psychology of Boredom. *CP,* vol. 1, pp. 292–302.

Fenichel, O. 1935a. Concerning Psychoanalysis, War and Peace. *Internationaler Aerztliche Bulletin, 2,* 30–40, 77.

Fenichel, O. 1935b. Concerning the Theory of Psychoanalytic Technique. *CP,* vol. 2, pp. 332–57.

Fenichel, O. 1938. The Drive to Amass Wealth. *PQ, 7,* 69–95.

Fenichel, O. 1941. *Problems of Psychoanalytic Technique*. New York: Psychoanalytic Quarterly.

Fenichel, O. 1944. Psychoanalytic Remarks on Fromm's Book "Escape from Freedom." *Psychoanalytic Review*, *31*, 133–52.

Fenichel, O. 1945. *The Psychoanalytic Theory of Neurosis*. New York: Norton.

Fenichel, O. 1954. *Collected Papers*. 2 vols. New York: Norton. Cited above as *CP*.

Ferenczi, S. 1914. Obsessional Neurosis and Piety. *CP*, vol. 2, p. 450.

Ferenczi, S. 1916. *Collected Papers*, vol. 1: *Sex in Psychoanalysis*. Boston: Richard G. Badger, Gorham Press.

Ferenczi, S. 1919a. Sunday Neuroses. *CP*, vol. 2, pp. 174–77.

Ferenczi, S. 1919b. Technical Difficulties in the Analysis of a Case of Hysteria. *CP*, vol. 2, pp. 189–97.

Ferenczi, S. 1926. *Collected Papers*, vol. 2: *Further Contributions*. London: Hogarth.

Ferenczi, S. 1930. The Principles of Relaxation and Neocatharsis. *IJP*, *11*, 428–32.

Ferenczi, S. 1955. *Collected Papers*, vol. 3: *Final Contributions*. New York: Basic Books.

Ferreira, A. J. 1960. The "Double-Bind" and Delinquent Behavior. *Archives of General Psychiatry*, *16*, 659–67.

Fine, B. D. and Moore, B. E. 1967. *A Glossary of Psychoanalytic Terms and Concepts*. New York: Amer. Psychoanalytic Ass'n.

Fine, B. D., et al. 1969. *The Manifest Content of the Dream*. Kris Study Group Monograph III, pp. 58–113. New York: International Univs. Press.

Fine, R. 1967. *The Psychology of the Chess Player*. New York: Dover.

Fine, R. 1969. On the Nature of Scientific Method in Psychology. *Psychological Reports*, *24*, 519–40.

Fine, R. 1971. *The Healing of the Mind*. New York: McKay.

Fine, R. 1972. The Age of Awareness. *Psychoanalytic Review*, *60*, 55–71.

Fine, R. 1973. *The Development of Freud's Thought*. New York: Aronson.

Fine, R. 1974. Freud and Jung. *Book Forum*, *1*, 369–74.

Fine, R. 1975a. The Bankruptcy of Behaviorism. *Psychoanalytic Review*, *63*, 437–51.

Fine, R. 1975b. *Psychoanalytic Psychology*. New York: Aronson.

Fine, R. 1977. Psychoanalysis as a Philosophical System. *Journal of Psychohistory*, *4*, 1–66.

Fine, R., and Fine, B. 1977. The Mathematician as a Healthy Narcissist. In M. Coleman, ed., *The Narcissistic Condition*, pp. 213–47. New York: Behavioral Sciences Press.

Firestein, S. K. 1974. Termination of Psychoanalysis of Adults: A Review of the Literature. *JAPA*, *22*, 873–94.

Firestein, S. 1978. *Termination in Psychoanalysis*. New York: International Univs. Press.

Fischer, N. 1971. An Interracial Analysis: Transference and Countertransference Significance. *JAPA*, *19*, 736–45.

Fisher, C. 1953. Studies on the Nature of Suggestion. *JAPA*, *1*, 222–55, 406–37.

Fisher, C. 1954. Dreams and Perception. *JAPA*, *2*, 389–445.

Fisher, C. 1956. Dreams, Images and Perception. *JAPA, 4,* 5–48.

Fisher, C. 1957. A Study of the Preliminary Stages of the Construction of Dreams and Images. *JAPA, 5,* 5–60.

Fisher, C. 1959. Subliminal and Supraliminal Influences on Dreams. *American Journal of Psychiatry, 116,* 1009–17.

Fisher, C. 1965. Psychoanalytic Implications of Recent Research on Sleep and Dreaming. *JAPA, 13,* 197–303.

Fisher, C. 1966. Dreaming and Sexuality. In M. Schur et al., eds., *Essays in Honor of Heinz Hartmann's Seventieth Birthday,* pp. 537–69.

Fisher, C., and Dement, W. C. 1961. Dreaming and Psychosis. *Bulletin, Philadelphia Association for Psychoanalysis, 11,* 130.

Fisher, C., and Dement, W. C. 1963. Studies on the Psychopathology of Sleep and Dreams. *American Journal of Psychiatry, 119,* 1160.

Fisher, C., and Paul, I. H. 1959. Subliminal Visual Stimulation and Dreams. *JAPA, 7,* 35–83.

Fisher, C., Gross, J., and Zuch, J. 1965. A Cycle of Penile Erection Synchronous with Dreaming (REM) Sleep. *Archives of General Psychiatry, 12,* 29–45.

Fisher, C., et al. 1970. A Psychophysiological Study of Nightmares. *JAPA, 18,* 747–82.

Fisher, S., and Greenberg, R. P. 1977. *The Scientific Credibility of Freud's Theories and Therapy.* New York: Basic Books.

Flavell, J. H. 1963. *The Developmental Psychology of Jean Piaget.* Princeton, N.J.: Van Nostrand.

Fleming, J. 1972. The Birth of COPE as Viewed in 1971. *JAPA, 20,* 546–55.

Fleming, J. 1976. Report of Ad Hoc Committee. *JAPA, 24,* 910–15.

Fletcher, R. 1966. *Instinct in Man.* New York: International Univs. Press.

Fliegel, Z. O. 1973. Feminine Psychosexual Development in Freudian Theory: A Historical Reconstruction. *PQ, 42,* 385–408.

Flugel, J. C. 1921. *The Psychoanalytic Study of the Family.* London: Hogarth Press.

Fortes, M. 1969. *Kinship and the Social Order.* Chicago: Aldine.

Fortes, M. 1977. Custom and Conscience in Anthropological Perspective. *International Review of Psychoanalysis, 4,* 127–54.

Foulkes, S. 1951. Concerning Leadership in Group-Analytic Psychotherapy. *International Journal of Group Psychotherapy, 1,* 319–29.

Foulkes, S. 1964. *Therapeutic Group Analysis.* New York: International Univs. Press.

Francis, J. J., and Marcus, I. M. 1975. *Masturbation from Infancy to Senescence.* New York: International Univs. Press.

Frank, L. K. 1936. Society as the Patient. *American Journal of Sociology,* 335–45.

Freedman, D. X., and Redlich, F. C. 1966. *The Theory and Practice of Psychiatry.* New York: Basic Books.

Freedman, N., and Steingart, I. 1975. Kinesic Internalization and Language Construction. *Psychoanalysis and Contemporary Science, 4,* 331–54.

Freeman, L. 1972. *The Story of Anna O.* New York: Walker Press.

Freud, A. 1928. *Introduction to the Technique of Child Analysis.* New York: Nervous and Mental Diseases Publishing Co.

Freud, A. 1936. *The Ego and the Mechanisms of Defense*. New York: International Univs. Press.

Freud, A. 1952. Some Remarks on Infant Observation. *CP*, vol. 4, pp. 509–85.

Freud, A. 1953. Instinctual Drives and their Bearing on Human Behavior. *CP*, vol. 4, 498–527.

Freud, A. 1954. The Widening Scope of Indications for Psychoanalysis: Discussion. *JAPA, 2*, 607–20.

Freud, A. 1960. Discussion of Dr. John Bowlby's Paper. *PSC, 15*, 53–62.

Freud, A. 1963. The Concept of Developmental Lines. *PSC, 18*, 245–65.

Freud, A. 1965a. Diagnostic Skills and Their Growth in Psychoanalysis. *IJP, 46*, 31–38.

Freud, A. 1965b. *Normality and Pathology in Childhood: Assessment of Development. CP*, vol. 6.

Freud, A. 1966. Obsessional Neurosis: A Summary of Psychoanalytic Views. *IJP, 47*, 116–22.

Freud, A. 1968a. *The Writings of Anna Freud*. 8 vols. to date. New York: International Univs. Press. Cited above as *CP*.

Freud, A. 1968b. Acting Out. *IJP, 49*, 165–230.

Freud, A., Goldstein, J., and Solnit, A. 1973. *Beyond the Best Interests of the Child*. New York: Free Press.

Freud, S. 1953–1974. *The Standard Edition of the Complete Psychological Works of Sigmund Freud,* edited by J. Strachey. London: Hogarth Press and Institute for Psychoanalysis. 24 vols. All references, unless otherwise noted, are to the Standard Edition, abbreviated *SE*.

Freud, S. 1954. *The Origins of Psychoanalysis: Letters to Fliess*. New York: Basic Books.

Freud, S., and Andreas-Salomé, L. 1972. *Letters*. New York: Harcourt.

Freud, S., and Jung, C. G. 1974. *Letters*. Princeton: Princeton Univ. Press.

Freud, S., and Pfister, O. 1963. *Psychoanalysis and Faith: The Letters of Sigmund Freud and Oskar Pfister*. New York: Basic Books.

Fried, E., et al. 1964. *Artistic Productivity and Mental Health*. Springfield, Ill.: C. C. Thomas.

Friedman, N. 1967. *The Social Nature of Psychological Research*. New York: Basic Books.

Fries, M. E. 1961. Some Factors in the Development and Significance of Early Object Relationships. *JAPA, 9*, 669–83.

Fries, M. E. 1977. Longitudinal Study: Prenatal Period to Parenthood. *JAPA, 25*, 115–32.

Fromm, E. 1939. Selfishness and Self-love. *Psychiatry, 2*, 507–23.

Fromm, E. 1941. *Escape from Freedom*. New York: Farrar and Rinehart.

Fromm, E. 1947. *Man for Himself*. New York: Rinehart.

Fromm, E. 1950. *Psychoanalysis and Religion*. New Haven: Yale Univ. Press.

Fromm, E. 1951. *The Forgotten Language*. New York: Rinehart.

Fromm, E. 1955. *The Sane Society*. New York: Rinehart.

Fromm, E. 1956. *The Art of Loving*. New York: Harper and Row.

Fromm, E. 1961. *Marx's Conception of Man*. New York: Frederick Ungar.

Fromm, E. 1973. *The Anatomy of Human Destructiveness.* New York: Norton.

Fromm, E., and Maccoby, M. 1970. *Social Character in a Mexican Village.* Englewood Cliffs, N.J.: Prentice-Hall.

Fromm-Reichmann, F. 1939. Transference Problems in Schizophrenia. *PQ, 8,* 412–26.

Fromm-Reichmann, F. 1948. Notes on the Development of the Treatment of Schizophrenics by Psychoanalytic Therapy. *Psychiatry, 11,* 263–73.

Fromm-Reichmann, F. 1950. *Principles of Intensive Psychotherapy.* Chicago: Univ. of Chicago Press.

Fromm-Reichmann, F. 1954. Psychoanalytic and General Dynamic Conceptions of Theory and of Therapy. *JAPA, 2,* 711–21.

Fromm-Reichmann, F. 1959. Loneliness. *Psychiatry, 22,* 1–16.

Frosch, J. 1976. Psychoanalytic Contributions to the Relationship between Dreams and Psychosis: A Critical Survey. *International Journal of Psychoanalytic Psychotherapy, 5,* 39–64.

Fuchs, S. H. 1937. On Introjection. *IJP, 18,* 269–93.

Galbraith, J. K. 1973. *The New Industrial State.* Boston: Houghton Mifflin.

Galbraith, J. K. 1976. *Economics and the Public Purpose.* Boston: Houghton Mifflin.

Garma, A. 1953. The Internalized Mother as Harmful Food in Peptic Ulcer Patients. *IJP, 34,* 102–10.

Garma, A. 1971. Within the Realm of the Death Instinct. *IJP, 52,* 145–54.

Gay, P., and Cavanagh, G. 1972. *Historians at Work.* New York: Harper.

Gay, P., and Webb, R. K. 1973. *Modern Europe.* New York: Harper.

Gedo, J. 1972. The Methodology of Psychoanalytic Biography. *JAPA, 20,* 638–49.

Gedo, J. 1975. Review of G. Blanck and R. Blanck: Ego Psychology. *JAPA, 23,* 265–66.

Gedo, J., and Goldberg, A. 1973. *Models of the Mind.* Chicago: Univ. of Chicago Press.

Geleerd, E. R. 1964. Child Analysis: Research, Treatment and Prophylaxis. *JAPA, 12,* 242–58.

Gelles, R. J. 1972. *The Violent Home.* Beverly Hills, Cal.: Sage Foundation.

Gifford, S. 1973. *Psychoanalysis in Boston.* Unpublished paper.

Gilberg, A. L. 1974. Asceticism and the Analysis of a Nun. *JAPA, 22,* 381–93.

Gill, M. M. 1963. *Topography and Systems in Psychoanalytic Theory.* Psychological Issues Monograph 10. New York: International Univs. Press.

Giovacchini, P., ed. 1972, 1975. *Tactics and Techniques in Psychoanalytic Therapy.* Vol. 1, 1972; Vol. 2, 1975. New York: Jason Aronson.

Gitelson, M. 1952. The Emotional Position of the Analyst in the Psychoanalytic Situation. *IJP, 33,* 1–10.

Gitelson, M. 1964. On the Identity Crisis in American Psychoanalysis. *JAPA, 12,* 451–76.

Globus, G. G., Maxwell, G., and Savodnik, I. 1976. *Consciousness and the Brain.* New York: Plenum Press.

Glover, E. 1925. Notes on Oral Character Formation. *IJP, 6,* 131–54.

Glover, E. 1943. The Concept of Dissociation. *IJP, 24,* 7–13.

Glover, E. 1945. Examination of the Klein System of Child Psychology. *PSC, 1*, 75–118.

Glover, E. 1955. *The Technique of Psychoanalysis*. New York: International Univs. Press.

Glover, E. 1956a. *Freud or Jung?* New York: Meridian Books.

Glover, E. 1956b. *On the Early Development of Mind*. New York: International Univs. Press.

Glover, E. 1966. Psychoanalysis in England. In F. Alexander et al., *Psychoanalytic Pioneers*, 535–45.

Goffman, E. 1974. *Frame Analysis*. New York: Harper.

Goldberg, A., ed. 1978. *The Psychology of the Self: A Casebook*. New York: International Univs. Press.

Goldberg, M., and Mudd, E. 1968. The Effects of Suicidal Behavior upon Marriage and the Family. In H. L. Resnick, ed., *Suicidal Behaviors*. Boston: Little, Brown.

Goldensohn, S. 1977. Evaluation of Psychoanalytic Training. *Journal of the American Academy of Psychoanalysis, 5*, 57–64.

Goldstein, K. 1944. The Mental Changes due to Frontal Lobe Damage. *Journal of Psychology, 17*, 187–208.

Goodenough, D. R. 1967. Some Recent Studies of Dream Recall. In H. Lewis and H. Witkin, eds., *Experimental Studies of Dreaming*, pp. 138–47.

Goodman, S., ed. 1977. *Psychoanalytic Education and Research*. New York: International Univs. Press.

Gorer, G., and Rickman, J. 1949. *The People of Great Russia*. London: Cresset Press.

Gould, R. 1972. *Child Studies Through Fantasy*. New York: Quadrangle.

Graff, H., and Luborsky, L. 1977. Long-Term Trends in Transference and Resistance: A Report on a Quantitative-Analytic Method Applied to Four Psychoanalyses. *JAPA, 25*, 471–90.

Graham, H. D., and Gurr, T. R. 1969. *The History of Violence in America*. New York: New York Times.

Gralnick, A. 1969. *The Psychiatric Hospital as a Therapeutic Instrument*. New York: Brunner/Mazel.

Grand, H. G. 1973. The Masochistic Defense of the "Double Mask." *IJP, 54*, 445–54.

Grauer, D. 1958. How Autonomous is the Ego? *JAPA, 6*, 502–18.

Green, A. 1977. Conceptions of Affect. *IJP, 58*, 129–56.

Green, H. 1964. *I Never Promised You a Rose Garden*. New York: Holt.

Green, R. 1974. *Sexual Identity Conflict in Children and Adults*. New York: Basic Books.

Green, R., and Money, J., eds. 1969. *Transsexualism and Sex Reassignment*. Baltimore: Johns Hopkins Univ. Press.

Greenacre, P. 1953. *Affective Disorders*. New York: International.

Greenacre, P. 1954. The Role of Transference. *JAPA, 2*, 671–84.

Greenacre, P. 1957. The Childhood of the Artist. *PSC, 12*, 47–72.

Greenacre, P. 1958. The Family Romance of the Artist. *PSC, 13*, 9–36.

Greenblatt, M. 1974. Psychopolitics. *American Journal of Psychiatry, 131,* 1200–1201.

Greene, E. L., et al. 1973. Some Methods of Evaluating Behavioral Variations in Children Six to Eighteen. *Journal of the American Academy of Child Psychiatry, 12,* 531–53.

Greenson, R. R. 1949. The Psychology of Apathy. *PQ, 18,* 290–302.

Greenson, R. R. 1953. On Boredom, *JAPA, 1,* 7–21.

Greenson, R. R. 1958. On Screen Defenses, Screen Hunger and Screen Identity. *JAPA, 6,* 242–62.

Greenson, R. R. 1962. On Enthusiasm. *JAPA, 10,* 3–21.

Greenson, R. R. 1965. The Working Alliance and the Transference Neurosis. *PQ, 34,* 155–81.

Greenson, R. R. 1967. *The Technique and Practice of Psychoanalysis.* New York: International Univs. Press.

Greenson, R. R. 1971. The Real Relationship between the Patient and the Psychoanalyst. In M. Kanzer, ed., *The Unconscious Today,* pp. 213–32. New York: International Univs. Press.

Greenspan, S. I., and Cullander, C. H. 1973. A Systematic Metapsychological Assessment of the Person: Its Application to the Problem of Analyzability. *JAPA, 21,* 303–27.

Greenstein, F. I. 1969. *Personality and Politics.* Chicago: Markham.

Grigg, K. A. 1973. "All Roads Lead to Rome": The Role of the Nursemaid in Freud's Dreams. *JAPA, 21,* 108–26.

Grinberg, L. 1963. Relations between Psychoanalysts. *IJP, 44,* 263–80.

Grinberg, L., et al. 1972. Panel on "Creativity." *IJP, 53,* 21–30.

Grinberg, L., et al. 1977. *Introduction to the Work of Bion.* New York: Jason Aronson.

Grinker, R. R. 1940. Reminiscences of a Personal Contact with Freud. *American Journal of Orthopsychiatry, 10,* 850–55.

Grinker, R. R. 1964. Psychiatry Rides Madly in all Directions. *Archives of General Psychiatry, 10,* 228–37.

Grinker, R. R., and McLean, H. V. 1940. The Course of a Depression Treated by Psychotherapy and Metrazol. *PSM, 2,* 119–38.

Grinker, R. R., et al. 1968. *The Borderline Syndrome.* New York: Basic Books.

Grinstein, A. 1968. *On Sigmund Freud's Dreams.* Detroit: Wayne State Univ. Press.

Grinstein, A. 1971. *The Index of Psychoanalytic Writings.* 14 vols. New York: International Univs. Press.

Groddeck, G. 1923. *The Book of the It.* Reprinted, New York: Funk and Wagnalls, 1950.

Gross, A. 1949. Sense of Time in Dreams. *PQ, 18,* 466–70.

Grotjahn, M. 1957. *Beyond Laughter.* New York: McGraw-Hill.

Grotjahn, M. 1960. *Psychoanalysis and the Family Neurosis.* New York: Norton.

Grunebaum, M. G., et al. 1962. Fathers of Sons with Primary Learning Inhibitions. *American Journal of Orthopsychiatry, 32,* 462–72.

Gunderson, J. G. 1974. The Influence of Theoretical Models of Schizophrenia on Treatment Practice (Panel). *JAPA, 22,* 182–99.

Gurle, L. 1966. Community Stay in Chronic Schizophrenia. *American Journal of Psychiatry, 122,* 892–99.

Gutheil, E. 1960. *The Handbook of Dream Analysis.* New York: Grove Press.

Guthrie, R. D. 1970. Evolution of Human Threat Display Organs. In T. Dobzhansky, et al., eds., *Evolutionary Biology,* vol. 4, pp. 257–302. New York: Meredith.

Haas, A. 1963. Management of the Geriatric Psychiatric Patient in a Mental Hospital. *Journal of the American Geriatrics Society, 11,* 259–65.

Hacker, F. 1972. Sublimation Revisited. *IJP, 53,* 219–23.

Hale, N. G. 1971. *Freud and the Americans.* New York: Oxford Univ. Press.

Haley, J. 1959. The Family of the Schizophrenic: A Model System. *Journal of Nervous and Mental Diseases, 129,* 357–74.

Hall, C. S. 1963. *Dreams of American College Students.* Lawrence: Univ. of Kansas Press.

Hall, C. S. 1966. *The Meaning of Dreams.* New York: McGraw-Hill.

Hall, C. S. and Castle, R. L. 1966. *The Content Analysis of Dreams.* New York: Appleton.

Halleck, S. 1971. *The Politics of Psychotherapy.* New York: Harper.

Hamburg, D. 1973. An Evolutionary and Developmental Approach to Human Aggressiveness. *PQ, 42,* 185–96.

Hamburg, D., et al. 1967. Report of Ad Hoc Committee on Central Fact-Gathering Data of the American Psychoanalytic Association. *JAPA, 15,* 841–61.

Hanly, C., and Masson, J. 1976. A Critical Examination of the New Narcissism. *IJP, 57,* 49–66.

Hanson, N. R. 1958. *Patterns of Discovery.* Cambridge: Cambridge Univ. Press.

Harlow, H. 1974. *Learning to Love.* New York: Jason Aronson.

Harris, I. D. 1960a. Typical Anxiety Dreams and Object Relations. *IJP, 41,* 604–11.

Harris, I. D. 1960b. Unconscious Factors Common to Parents and Analysts. *IJP, 41,* 123–29.

Harris, I. D. 1962. Dreams about the Analyst. *IJP, 43,* 151–58.

Harris, M. 1968. *The Rise of Anthropological Theory.* New York: Thomas Y. Crowell.

Hart, H. 1948. Sublimation and Aggression. *Psychiatric Quarterly, 22,* 389–412.

Hartmann, H. 1933. Psychoanalyse und Weltanschauung. *Psychoanalytische Bewegung, 5,* 416–29.

Hartmann, H. 1939. *Ego Psychology and the Problem of Adaptation.* New York: International Univs. Press.

Hartmann, H. 1944. Review of Sears' "Objective Studies of Psychoanalytic Concepts." *PQ, 13,* 102–3.

Hartmann, H. 1948. Comments on the Psychoanalytic Theory of Instinctual Drives. *PQ, 17,* 368–87.

Hartmann, H. 1949. Comments on the Psychoanalytic Theory of the Ego. *PSC, 3–4,* 75–96.

Hartmann, H. 1951. Technical Implications of Ego Psychology. *PQ, 20,* 31–43.

Hartmann, H. 1952. The Mutual Influences in the Development of Ego and Id. *PSC, 7,* 9–30.

Hartmann, H. 1953. Contributions to the Metapsychology of Schizophrenia. In *Essays in Ego Psychology*, pp. 182–206.

Hartmann, H. 1956. Presidential Address. *IJP, 37,* 118–20.

Hartmann, H. 1960. *Psychoanalysis and Moral Values.* New York: International Univs. Press.

Hartmann, H. 1964. *Essays in Ego Psychology.* New York: International Univs. Press.

Hartmann, H., Kris, E., and Loewenstein, R. M. 1946. Comments on the Formation of Psychic Structure. *PSC, 2,* 11–38.

Hartmann, H., Kris, E., and Loewenstein, R. M. 1949. Notes on the Theory of Aggression. *PSC, 3–4,* 1–18.

H. D. [Hilda Doolittle] 1974. *Tribute to Freud.* Boston: David R. Godine.

Head, H. 1923. *Aphasia and Kindred Disorders of Speech.* New York: Macmillan.

Health, Education, and Welfare Department. n.d. *Alcohol and Health.* New York: Scribner's.

Heilbroner, R. 1972. *The Worldly Philosophers.* New York: Simon & Schuster.

Heimann, P. 1950. On Countertransference. *IJP, 31,* 81–84.

Hendrick, I. 1938. The Ego and the Defense Mechanisms. *Psychoanalytic Review, 25,* 476–97.

Hendrick, I. 1955. Professional Standards of the American Psychoanalytic Association. *JAPA, 3,* 561–99.

Henry, W., et al. 1971. *The Fifth Profession.* San Francisco: Jossey-Bass.

Henry, W., et al. 1973. *The Public and Private Lives of Psychotherapists.* San Francisco: Jossey-Bass.

Hermann, I. 1936. Clinging–Going-in-Search: A Contrasting Pair of Instincts and Their Relation to Sadism and Masochism. Reprinted, *PQ, 45* (1976), 5–36.

Herzberg, F. 1966. *Work and the Nature of Man.* New York: World.

Herzberg, F. 1974. Work Satisfaction and Motivation-Hygiene Theory. *Book Forum, 1,* 213–21.

Herzberg, F., et al. 1959. *The Motivation to Work.* New York: Wiley.

Hildebrand, H., and Rayner, E. 1971. *The Choice of the First Analytic Patient.* Paper read at the International Psychoanalytic Congress, Vienna, 1971.

Hilgard, E. R. 1965. *Hypnotic Susceptibility.* New York: Harcourt.

Hilgard, E. R., and Bower, G. H. 1975. *Theories of Learning.* Englewood Cliffs, N.J.: Prentice-Hall.

Hill, B., ed. 1967. *Such Stuff as Dreams.* London: Hart-Davis.

Hite, S. 1976. *The Hite Report.* New York: Macmillan.

Hitschmann, E. 1932. A Ten Years Report of the Vienna Psychoanalytical Clinic. *IJP, 13,* 245–55.

Hoedemaker, F., et al. 1964. Dream Deprivation: An Experimental Reappraisal. *Nature, 204,* 1337–78.

Hoffer, W. 1950. Oral Aggressiveness and Ego Development. *IJP, 31,* 156–60.

Hoffer, W. 1954. Defensive Process and Defensive Organization: Their Place in Psychoanalytic Technique. *IJP, 35,* 194–98.

Holland, N. N. 1966. *Psychoanalysis and Shakespeare.* New York: McGraw-Hill.

Holland, N. N. 1973. Defense, Displacement and the Ego's Algebra. *IJP, 54,* 247–57.

Hollingshead, A. B., and Redlich, F. C. 1958. *Social Class and Mental Illness*. New York: Wiley.

Holloway, R. L., ed. 1974. *Primate Aggression, Territoriality and Xenophobia*. New York: Academic.

Holman, H. R. 1976. *Hospital Practice, 11*, 11.

Holt, R. R. 1962. A Critical Examination of Freud's Concept of Bound vs. Free Cathexis. *JAPA, 10*, 475–525.

Holt, R. R. 1965. Ego Autonomy Reevaluated. *IJP, 46*, 151–67.

Holt, R. R. 1968. Editor's Foreword to D. Rapaport, M. Gill, and R. Schafer: *Diagnostic Psychological Testing*. New York: International Univs. Press.

Holt, R. R., and Luborsky, L. 1958. *Personality Patterns of Psychiatrists*. New York: Basic Books.

Hook, S., ed. 1959. *Psychoanalysis, Scientific Method and Philosophy*. New York: Grove Press.

Horney, K. 1937. *The Neurotic Personality of Our Time*. New York: Norton.

Horney, K. 1939. *New Ways in Psychoanalysis*. New York: Norton.

Horney, K. 1945. *Our Inner Conflicts*. New York: Norton.

Horney, K. 1950. *Neurosis and Human Growth*, New York: Norton.

Hornick, E. 1975. Sexuality in Adolescents: A Plea for Celibacy. In E. Adelson, ed. *Sexuality and Psychoanalysis*, 238–41.

Horwitz, L. 1974. *Clinical Prediction in Psychotherapy*. New York: Jason Aronson.

Hsu, F., ed. 1971. *Kinship and Culture*. Chicago: Aldine.

Hug-Hellmuth, H. von. 1912. Analyse eines Traumes eines Funfeinhalbjährigen Knaben. *Zentralblatt fuer Psychoanalyse und Psychotherapie, 2*, 122–27.

Hug-Hellmuth, H. von. 1921. On the Technique of Child Analysis. *IJP, 2*, 287–305.

Hunt, M. 1959. *The Natural History of Love*. New York: Knopf.

Indian Psychoanalytical Society. 1964. *Bose–Freud Correspondence*. Previously published in part in *Samiksa, 10*, nos. 2 and 3, 1938.

Isakower, O. 1938. A Contribution to the Pathopsychology of Falling Asleep. *IJP, 19*, 331–45.

Jackson, D., and Lederer, W. 1968. *The Mirages of Marriage*. New York: Norton.

Jackson, S. W. 1968. Aspects of Culture in Psychoanalytic Theory and Practise. *JAPA, 16*, 651–70.

Jacobson, E. 1953. The Affects and Their Pleasure-Unpleasure Qualities in Relation to Psychic Discharge Processes. In R. Loewenstein, ed., *Drives, Affects, Behavior*, pp. 38–66.

Jacobson, E. 1954. Contribution to the Metapsychology of Psychotic Identifications. *JAPA, 2*, 239–62.

Jacobson, E. 1955. Sullivan's Interpersonal Theory of Psychiatry. *JAPA, 3*, 149–56.

Jacobson, E. 1957. Denial and Repression. *JAPA, 5*, 61–92.

Jacobson, E. 1959. Depersonalization. *JAPA, 7*, 581–610.

Jacobson, E. 1964. *The Self and the Object World*. New York: International Univs. Press.

Jacobson, E. 1971. *Depression*. New York: International Univs. Press.

James, M. 1973. Review of H. Kohut "The Analysis of the Self." *IJP, 54*, 363–68.

James, W. 1890. *The Principles of Psychology*. New York: Holt.

Jersild, A., and Lazar, E. A. 1962. *The Meaning of Psychotherapy in the Teacher's Life and Work*. New York: Teachers College Press.

Joffe, W., and Sandler, J. 1968. Comments on the Psychoanalytic Psychology of Adaptation. *IJP, 49*, 445–53.

Joint Commission on Mental Illness and Health. 1961. *Action for Mental Health*. New York: Basic Books.

Joint Commission on the Mental Health of Children. 1969. *Crisis in Child Mental Health*. New York: Harper.

Jones, E. 1912. *On the Nightmare*. Reprint ed., London: Hogarth Press, 1931.

Jones, E. 1913a. The God Complex. Reprinted in *Essays in Applied Psychoanalysis*, vol. 2, pp. 244–65.

Jones, E. 1913b. Hate and Erotism in the Obsessional Neurosis. *Collected Papers*, 3d ed., pp. 553–61.

Jones, E. 1916. The Theory of Symbolism. *CP*, 87–144.

Jones, E. 1918. Anal-Erotic Character Traits. *CP*, 438–51.

Jones, E. 1924. Psychoanalysis and Anthropology. Reprinted in *Essays in Applied Psychoanalysis*, vol. 2, pp. 114–44.

Jones, E. 1927. The Early Development of Female Sexuality. *IJP, 8*, 459–72.

Jones, E. 1929. Psychoanalysis and Psychiatry. *CP*, 365–78.

Jones, E. 1931. The Concept of a Normal Mind. *CP*, 201–16.

Jones, E. 1936a. The Criteria of Success in Treatment. *CP*, 379–83.

Jones, E. 1936b. *Report of the Clinic Work, 1926–1936*. London: London Clinic of Psychoanalysis.

Jones, E. 1939. Presidential Address. *IJP, 20*, 121–25.

Jones, E. 1943. Obituary of Max Eitingon. *IJP, 24*, 190–92.

Jones, E. 1948a. The Death of Hamlet's Father. *IJP, 29*, 174–76.

Jones, E. 1948b. *Collected Papers on Psychoanalysis*, 5th ed. London: Bailliere, Tindall and Cox. Cited above as *CP*.

Jones, E. 1949. Presidential Address. *IJP, 30*, 178–90.

Jones, E. 1951. *Essays in Applied Psychoanalysis*. 2 vols. London: Hogarth Press.

Jones, E. 1953–1957. *The Life and Work of Sigmund Freud*. 3 vols. New York: Basic Books.

Jung, C. G. 1906. *Diagnostische Assoziationsstudien*. Leipzig: J. A. Barth.

Jung, C. G. 1907. *Ueber die Psychologie der Dementia Praecox*. Halle: Marhold.

Jung, C. G. 1910. The Association Method. *American Journal of Psychology, 21*, 216–69.

Jung, C. G. 1912. *Wandlungen und Symbole der Libido*. Leipzig and Vienna: Deuticke.

Jung, C. G. 1916. *Psychology of the Unconscious*. London: Routledge and Kegan Paul.

Jung, C. G. 1923. *Psychological Types*. London: Routledge and Kegan Paul.

Jung, C. G. 1938. *The Basic Writings*. New York: Random House, Modern Library.

Jung, C. G. 1945. On the Nature of Dreams. In *Basic Writings*, pp. 363–79.

Jung, C. G. 1958. *Psyche and Symbol*. Garden City, N.Y.: Doubleday.

Jung, C. G., ed. 1964. *Man and His Symbols*. London: Aldus Books.

Jung, C. G. 1968. *Analytical Psychology. Lectures at Tavistock Clinic, 1935*. New York: Pantheon Books.

Jung, C. G. 1973. *Letters.* 2 vols. Bollingen Series, no. 95. Princeton, N.J.: Princeton Univ. Press.

Jung, C. G. 1976. *Abstracts of the Collected Works of C. G. Jung.* Rockville, Md.: Information Planning Associates.

Kadushin, C. 1969. *Why People Go to Psychiatrists.* New York: Atherton Press.

Kahana, R., and Levin, S., eds. 1967. *Psychodynamic Studies on Aging: Creativity, Reminiscing and Dying.* New York: International Univs. Press.

Kahn, R. L. 1972. The Justification of Violence. *Journal of Social Issues, 28,* 155–76.

Kant, D. 1952. Dreams of Schizophrenic Patients. *Journal of Nervous and Mental Diseases, 95,* 335–47.

Kanter, R. M. 1976. The Romance of Community. In M. Rosenbaum and A. Snadowsky, eds., *The Intensive Group Experience,* pp. 146–85.

Kanzer, M. 1955. The Communicative Function of the Dream. *IJP, 36,* 260–66.

Kaplan, A. H. 1975. History of Psychoanalysis in St. Louis. Unpublished manuscript.

Kaplan, D. 1972. On Shyness. *IJP, 53,* 439–53.

Kaplan, H. S. 1974. *The New Sex Therapy.* New York: Brunner/Mazel.

Kardiner, A. 1939. *The Individual and His Society.* New York: Columbia Univ. Press.

Kardiner, A. 1945. *The Psychological Frontiers of Society.* New York: Columbia Univ. Press.

Kardiner, A. 1977. *My Analysis with Freud.* New York: Norton.

Kardiner, A., and Preble, E. 1965. *They Studied Man.* New York: World.

Kardiner, A., Karush, A., and Ovesey, L. 1959. A Methodological Study of Freudian Theory. *Journal of Nervous and Mental Diseases, 129,* 11–19, 133–43, 207–21, 341–56.

Kaufman, C. I. 1960. Some Ethological Studies of Social Relationships and Conflict Situations. *JAPA, 8,* 671–85.

Kawada, A. 1977. Die Psychoanalyse in Japan. *Psyche, 31,* 272–85.

Kemper, W. W. 1966. Transference and Countertransference as a Functional Unit. *Official Report on Panamerican Congress for Psychoanalysis, 1966.*

Kempf, E. J. 1919. The Psychoanalytic Treatment of a Case of Schizophrenia. *Psychoanalytic Review, 6,* 15–58.

Kernberg, O. F. 1965. Notes on Countertransference. *JAPA, 13,* 38–56.

Kernberg, O. F. 1968. The Treatment of Patients with Borderline Personality Organization. *IJP, 49,* 600–19.

Kernberg, O. F. 1969. A Contribution to the Ego-Psychological Critique of the Kleinian School. *IJP, 50,* 317–33.

Kernberg, O. F. 1971. Prognostic Considerations Regarding Borderline Personality Organization. *JAPA, 19,* 595–635.

Kernberg, O. F. 1972. Early Ego Integration and Object Relations. *Annals of the New York Academy of Sciences, 193,* 233–47.

Kernberg, O. F. 1974. Barriers to Falling and Remaining in Love. *JAPA, 22,* 486–511.

Kernberg, O. F. 1975. *Borderline Conditions and Pathological Narcissism.* New York: Jason Aronson.

Kernberg, O. F. 1976. *Object Relations Theory and Clinical Psychoanalysis.* New York: Jason Aronson.

Kernberg, O. F. 1977. Boundaries and Structures in Love Relations. *JAPA, 25,* 81–114.

Kernberg, O. F., et al. 1972. Psychotherapy and Psychoanalysis: Final Report. *Bulletin of the Menninger Clinic, 36,* nos. 1 and 2.

Kestenberg, J. 1967. Phases of Adolescence with Suggestions for a Correlation of Psychic and Hormonal Organizations. *Journal of the American Academy of Child Psychiatry, 6,* 577–612.

Kestenberg, J. 1971. Development of the Young Child as Expressed Through Bodily Movement. *JAPA, 19,* 746–64.

Kety, S. 1969. Biochemical Hypotheses and Studies. In L. Bellak and L. Loeb, eds., *The Schizophrenic Syndrome,* pp. 155–71.

Keynes, J. M. 1935. *The General Theory of Employment, Interest and Money.* New York: Harcourt.

Khan, M. M. R. 1962. Dream Psychology and the Evolution of the Psychoanalytic Situation. In M. Khan, *The Privacy of the Self.*

Khan, M. M. R. 1972. The Use and Abuse of Dreams in Psychic Experience. In M. Khan, *The Privacy of the Self.*

Khan, M. M. R. 1974. *The Privacy of the Self.* London: Hogarth Press.

Khan, M. M. R. 1976. In Search of the Dreaming Experience. *IJP, 57,* 325–30.

Kiev, A., ed. 1964. *Magic, Faith and Healing.* New York: Free Press.

Kinsey, A. C., et al. 1948. *Sexual Behavior in the Human Male.* Philadelphia: Saunders.

Kinsey, A. C., et al. 1953. *Sexual Behavior in the Human Female.* Philadephia: Saunders.

Kintsch, W. 1977. *Memory and Cognition.* New York: Wiley.

Klein, D., and Gittelman-Klein, R. 1975, 1976. *Progress in Psychiatric Drug Treatment,* vols. 1 and 2. New York: Brunner/Mazel.

Klein, G. S. 1959. Consciousness in Psychoanalytic Theory. *JAPA, 7,* 5–34.

Klein, G. S. 1970. *Perception, Motives and Personality.* New York: Knopf.

Klein, G. S. 1976. *Psychoanalytic Theory.* New York: International Univs. Press.

Klein, H. 1965. *Psychoanalysts in Training.* New York: Columbia Univ. Press.

Klein, M. 1929. Infantile Anxiety Situations Reflected in a Work of Art and in the Creative Impulse. *IJP, 10,* 436–43.

Klein, M. 1931. A Contribution to the Theory of Intellectual Inhibition. Reprinted in M. Klein, *Contributions to Psychoanalysis, 1921–1945,* pp. 254–66.

Klein, M. 1946. Notes on Some Schizoid Mechanisms. Reprinted in M. Klein et al., eds., *Developments in Psychoanalysis,* pp. 292–320.

Klein, M. 1948a. *Contributions to Psychoanalysis, 1921–1945.* London: Hogarth Press.

Klein, M. 1948b. A Contribution to the Theory of Anxiety and Guilt. *IJP, 29,* 114–23.

Klein, M. 1949. *The Psychoanalysis of Children.* London: Hogarth Press.

Klein, M. 1952. The Origins of Transference. *IJP, 33,* 433–38.

Klein, M. 1957. *Envy and Gratitude.* New York: Basic Books.

Klein, M., et al., eds. 1952. *Developments in Psychoanalysis.* London: Hogarth Press.

Klein, M., et al., eds. 1953. *New Directions in Psychoanalysis.* New York: Basic Books.

Kligerman, C. 1970. The Dream of Charles Dickens. *JAPA, 18,* 783–99.

Kluckhohn, C. 1959. Recurrent Themes in Myths and Mythmaking. *Daedalus, 88,* 268–79.

Knapp, P. H., et al. 1960. Suitability for Psychoanalysis: A Review of One Hundred Supervised Cases. *PQ, 29,* 459–77.

Knight, F., and Baumol, W. 1963. Economics. *Encyclopedia Britannica, 7,* 936–43. Chicago: William Benton.

Knight, R. P. 1953a. Management and Psychotherapy of the Borderline Schizophrenic Patient. In R. P. Knight and C. R. Friedman, *Psychoanalytic Psychiatry and Psychology,* pp. 110–22.

Knight, R. P. 1953b. The Present Status of Organized Psychoanalysis in the U.S. *JAPA, 1,* 197–221.

Knight, R. P., and Friedman, C. R., eds. 1954. *Psychoanalytic Psychiatry and Psychology.* New York: International Univs. Press.

Koff, R. H. 1961. A Definition of Identification: A Review of the Literature. *IJP, 42,* 362–70.

Kohn, M. 1977. *Social Competence, Symptoms and Underachievement in Childhood.* New York: Wiley.

Kohut, H. 1966. Forms and Transformations of Narcissism. *JAPA, 14,* 243–72.

Kohut, H. 1971. *The Analysis of the Self.* New York: International Univs. Press.

Kohut, H. 1977. *The Restoration of the Self.* New York: International Univs. Press.

Kraepelin, E. 1906. *Lectures on Clinical Psychiatry.* London: Bailliere, Tindall and Cox.

Kraepelin, E. 1917. *One Hundred Years of Psychiatry.* New York: Citadel Press.

Kren, G. 1977. Psychohistory in the University. *Journal of Psychohistory, 4,* 339–50.

Krent, J. 1970. The Fate of the Defenses in the Psychoanalytic Process (Panel). *JAPA, 18,* 177–94.

Kriegman, G. 1977. History of the Virginia Psychoanalytic Society. Unpublished manuscript.

Kris, E. 1936. The Psychology of Caricature. *IJP, 17,* 285–303.

Kris, E. 1952. *Psychoanalytic Explorations in Art.* New York: International Univs. Press.

Kris, E. 1956. The Personal Myth. *JAPA, 4,* 653–81.

Kris, E., Herma, H., and Shor, J. 1943. Freud's Theory of the Dream in American Textbooks. *Journal of Abnormal and Social Psychology, 38,* 319–34.

Kroeber, A. L. 1948. *Race, Language, Culture, Psychology, Prehistory.* New York: Harcourt.

Kubie, L. 1954. The Fundamental Nature of the Distinction between Normality and Neurosis. *PQ, 23,* 167–204.

Kubie, L 1958. *Neurotic Distortion of the Creative Process.* Lawrence: Univ. of Kansas Press.

Kubie, L. 1962. The Fallacious Misuse of the Concept of Sublimation. *PQ, 31,* 73–79.

Kubie, L. 1964. Multiple Determinants of Suicidal Efforts. *Journal of Nervous and Mental Diseases, 138,* 3–8.

Kubie, L. 1968. Unsolved Problems in the Resolution of the Transference. *PQ, 37,* 331–52.

Kuhn, T. S. 1962. *The Structure of Scientific Revolutions.* Chicago: Univ. of Chicago Press.

Labarre, W. 1961. Psychoanalysis in Anthropology. *Science and Psychoanalysis, 4,* 10–20.

Labarre, W. 1966. Biography of Geza Roheim. In F. Alexander et al., *Psychoanalytic Pioneers,* pp. 272–81.

Lacan, J. 1977. *Ecrits.* New York: Norton.

Laffal, J. 1965. *Pathological and Normal Language.* New York: Atherton Press.

Laing, R. D. 1971. *The Politics of the Family.* New York: Pantheon Books.

Laing, R. D., and Esterson, A. 1964. *Sanity, Madness and the Family.* New York: Basic Books.

Lamb, H. R. 1976. *Community Survival for Long-Term Patients.* San Francisco: Jossey-Bass.

Lamb, M. E. 1976. *The Role of the Father in Child Development.* New York: Wiley.

Landauer, K. 1924. "Passive" Technik. Zur Analyse narzissistischer Erkrankungen. *Internationale Zeitschrift fuer Aerztliche Psychoanalyse, 10,* 415–22.

Langer, W. 1972. *The Mind of Adolf Hitler.* New York: Basic Books.

Langs, R. 1974. *The Technique of Psychoanalytic Psychotherapy.* 2 vols. New York: Jason Aronson.

Langs, R. 1976. *The Therapeutic Interaction.* New York: Jason Aronson.

Langsley, D. G., et al. 1977. Medical Student Education in Psychiatry. *American Journal of Psychiatry, 134,* 15–19.

Laplanche, J. 1974. Panel on "Hysteria Today." *IJP, 55,* 459–69.

Laplanche, J., and Pontalis, J.-B. 1973. *The Language of Psychoanalysis.* New York: Norton.

Lapouse, R., and Monk, M. A. 1964. Behavioral Deviations in a Representative Sample of Children. *American Journal of Orthopsychiatry, 29,* 803–18.

Lasswell, H. D. 1930. *Psychopathology and Politics.* New York: Viking.

Lasswell, H. D. 1948. *Power and Personality.* New York: Viking.

Laughlin, H. P. 1970. *The Ego Defenses.* New York: Appleton.

Lazar, N. D. 1973. Nature and Signifiance of Changes in Patients in a Psychoanalytic Clinic. *PQ, 42,* 579–600.

Lazar, N. D. 1976. Some Problems in Faculty Selection of Patients for Supervised Psychoanalysis. *PQ, 45,* 416–29.

Lazarus, A. A. 1971. Where do Behavior Therapists Take Their Troubles? *Psychological Reports, 28,* 349–50.

Leavy, S. 1977. The Significance of Jacques Lacan. *PQ, 46,* 201–19.

Lefcourt, H. M. 1977. *Locus of Control*. New York: Wiley.

Lehman, H. 1953. *Age and Achievement*. Philadelphia: American Philosophical Society.

Lehmann, H. E. 1971. The Impact of the Therapeutic Revolution in Nosology. *Schizophrenic Syndrome, 1,* 136–153.

Leighton, A. H. 1963. *The Character of Danger*. New York: Basic Books.

Levey, H. B. 1938. Poetry Production as a Supplemental Emergency Defense against Anxiety. *PQ, 7,* 232–42.

Levey, H. B. 1939. A Critique of the Theory of Sublimation. *Psychiatry, 2,* 239–70.

Levine, R. A.1973. *Culture, Behavior and Personality*. Chicago: Aldine.

Levinson, H. 1964. *Emotional Health in the World of Work*. New York: Harper.

Levy, D. 1943. *Maternal Overprotection*. New York: Norton.

Lewin, B. 1946. Sleep, The Mouth and the Dream Screen. *PQ, 15,* 419–34.

Lewin, B. 1950. *The Psychoanalysis of Elation*. New York: Norton.

Lewin, B., and Ross, H. 1960. *Psychoanalytic Education in the U.S.* New York: Norton.

Lewis, H. 1958. Over-Differentiation and Under-Individuation of the Self. *Psychoanalysis and the Psychoanalytic Review, 46,* 21–35.

Lewis, H. 1971. *Shame and Guilt in Neurosis*. New York: International Univs. Press.

Lewis, J. M., et al. 1976. *No Single Thread: Psychological Health in Family Systems*. New York: Brunner/Mazel.

Lewis, O. 1966. The Culture of Poverty. In O. Lewis, *Anthropological Essays,* pp. 67–80. New York: Random House.

Lichtenberg, J. D. 1975. The Development of the Sense of Self. *JAPA, 23,* 453–84.

Lichtenberg, J. D. and Slap, J. W. 1971. On the Defensive Organization. *IJP, 52,* 451–58.

Lichtenberg, J. D., and Slap, J. W. 1973. Notes on the Concept of Splitting and the Defense Mechanism of the Splitting of Representations. *JAPA, 21,* 772–87.

Lichtenstein, H. 1963. The Dilemma of Human Identity. *JAPA, 11,* 173–223.

Lichtenstein, H. 1970. Changing Implications of the Concept of Psychosexual Development: An Inquiry Concerning the Validity of Classical Psychoanalytic Assumptions Concerning Sexuality. *JAPA, 18,* 300–318.

Lidz, T. 1973. *The Origin and Treatment of Schiozphrenic Disorders*. New York: Basic Books.

Lidz, T., et al. 1950. Life Situations, Emotions and Graves' Disease. *PSM, 12,* 184–86.

Lidz, T., Fleck, S., and Cornelison, A. 1965. *Schizophrenia and the Family*. New York: International Univs. Press.

Lieberman, M. A. 1974. Adaptive Processes in Later Life. Quoted in Pollock, 1977.

Lifschutz, J. 1976. A Critique of Reporting and Assessment in the Training Analysis. *JAPA, 24,* 43–60.

Lifton, R. 1969. *Thought Reform and the Psychology of Totalism*. New York: Norton.

Lifton, R., ed. 1974. *Explorations in Psychohistory*. New York: Simon and Schuster.

Lipowski, Z. J., et al. 1977. *Psychosomatic Medicine*. New York: Oxford Univ. Press.

Litowitz, B. E. 1975. Language: Waking and Sleeping. *Psychoanalysis and Contemporary Science, 4,* 291–330.

Little, M. 1951. Countertransference and the Patient's Response to It. *IJP, 32,* 32–40.

Loevinger, J. 1976. *Ego Development*. San Francisco: Jossey-Bass.

Loewenstein, R. M. 1949. A Posttraumatic Dream. *PQ, 18,* 449–54.

Loewenstein, R. M., ed. 1953. *Drives, Affects, Behavior*. New York: International Univs. Press.

Loomie, L. 1970. Report for Committee on Membership. *JAPA, 21,* 492–93.

Lorenz, K. 1963. *On Aggression*. New York: Harcourt.

Loveland, R. 1947. Review of W. Sachs: Black Anger. *PQ, 16,* 576–77.

Lower, R. B., Escoll, P. J., and Huxter, H. K. 1972. Bases for Judgments of Analyzability. *JAPA, 20,* 610–21.

Lowry, R., and Rankin, R. 1970. *Sociology*. New York: Scribner's.

Luborsky, L., and Auerbach, A. H. 1969. The Symptom-Context Method. *JAPA, 17,* 68–99.

Ludwig, A. M. 1975. *J. Amer. Med. Ass'n., 234,* 603.

Luminet, D. 1962. A Short History of Psychoanalysis in Belgium. Unpublished.

Luzes, P. 1973. A Criacao da Sociedade Portuguesa de Psicanalise. *O Medico, 56,* no. 1125, 873–74.

Luzes, P. 1976. History of Psychoanalysis in Portugal. Unpublished manuscript.

Luzes, P., et al. 1972. Quatro Cartas Ineditas de Freud Dirigidas a Um Portugues. *Revista Brasileira de Psicanalise, 6,* nos. 3–4.

Lynch, W. H. 1977. *The Broken Heart*. New York: Basic Books.

Lynd, R., and Lynd. H. 1929. *Middletown*. New York: Harcourt.

McClelland, D. 1961. *The Achieving Society*. Princeton, N.J.: Van Nostrand.

Maccoby, M. 1977. *The Gamesman*. New York: Simon and Schuster.

Maccoby, E. M., and Jacklin, C. N. 1974. *The Psychology of Sex Differences*. Stanford, Cal.: Stanford Univ. Press.

McDevitt, J. B., and Settlage, C. F., eds. 1971. *Separation-Individuation*. New York: International Univs. Press.

McDougall, W. 1948a. *The Energies of Men*. 7th ed. London: Methuen.

McDougall, W. 1948b. *An Introduction to Social Psychology*. 29th ed. London: Methuen.

McFarlane, J. W., et al. 1962. *A Developmental Study of the Behavior Problems of Normal Children 21 mos. to 14 Years*. Berkeley: Univ. of California Press.

McGill, V. J. 1967. *The Idea of Happiness*. New York: Praeger.

Machover, K. 1949. *Personality Projection in the Drawing of the Human Figure*. Springfield, Ill.: C. C. Thomas.

MacIver, J., and Redlich, F. C. 1959. Patterns of Psychiatric Practice. *American Journal of Psychiatry, 115,* 692–97.

McLaughlin, F. 1959. Problems of Reanalysis (Panel). *JAPA, 7,* 537–47.

McLaughlin, J. 1973. The Nonreporting Training Analyst, The Analysis and the Institute. *JAPA, 21,* 697–712.

McLaughlin, J. 1975. The Sleepy Analyst. *JAPA, 23*, 363–82.

Maetze, G. 1971. *Psychoanalyse in Berlin*. Meisenheim Am Glan: Verlag Anton Hain.

Maetze, G. 1976. Psychoanalyse in Deutschland. In *Die Psychologie des 20. Jahrhunderts*, Vol. 2. Kindler Verlag.

Mahler, M. 1968. *On Human Symbiosis and the Vicissitudes of Individuation*. New York: International Univs. Press.

Mahler, M., et al. 1975. *The Psychological Birth of the Human Infant*. New York: Basic Books.

Mahrer, A., ed. 1970. *New Approaches to Personality Classification*. New York: Columbia Univ. Press.

Malinowski, B. 1927. *Sex and Repression in Savage Society*. New York: Harcourt.

Mann, T. 1947. *Essays of Three Decades*. New York: Knopf.

Marcus, I. 1973. The Experience of Separation-Individuation In Infancy and Its Reverberations Through the Course of Life: 2. Adolescence and Maturity (Panel). *JAPA, 21*, 157–66.

Margolin, S. 1948. Review of Kinsey. *PQ, 17*, 265–72.

Mark, V. H., and Ervin, F. R. 1970. *Violence and the Brain*. New York: Harper.

Marmor, J. 1953. Orality in the Hysterical Personality. *JAPA, 1*, 656–71.

Marmor, J. 1955. Validation of Psychoanalytic Techniques. *JAPA, 3*, 496–505.

Marmor, J. 1975. *Psychiatrists and Their Patients*. Washington, D.C.: American Psychiatric Association and National Association for Mental Health.

Mason, J. W. 1969. Organization of Psychoendocrine Mechanisms. *PSM, 30*, 565–608.

Mason, J. W. 1975. Clinical Psychophysiology: Psychoendocrine Mechanisms. In S. Arieti, ed. *American Handbook of Psychiatry*, vol. 5, pp. 553–82.

Masterson, J. 1976. *Treatment of the Borderline Patient*. New York: Jason Aronson.

Masters, W., and Johnson, V. 1966. *Human Sexual Response*. Boston: Little, Brown.

Masters, W., and Johnson, V. 1970. *Human Sexual Inadequacy*. Boston: Little, Brown.

May, P. R. 1968. *Treatment of Schizophrenia*. New York: Science House.

May, R. 1969. *Love and Will*. New York: Norton.

May, R., et al., eds. 1958. *Experience*. New York: Simon and Schuster.

Mayr, E. 1970. *Populations, Species and Evolution*. Cambridge, Mass.: Harvard Univ. Press.

Mead, M. 1949. *Male and Female*. New York: Morrow.

Mead, M., and Wolfenstein, M., eds. 1955. *Childhood in Contemporary Culture*. Chicago: Univ. of Chicago Press.

Medawar, P. B. 1977. Are IQ's Nonsense? *N.Y. Review of Books, 24*, 13–18.

Meiselman, K. C. 1978. *Incest*. San Francisco: Jossey-Bass.

Meissner, W. W. 1966. Family Dynamics and Psychosomatic Processes. *Family Process, 5*, 142–61.

Meissner, W. W. 1973. Identification and Learning. *JAPA, 21*, 788–816.

Meissner, W. W. 1974. The Role of Imitative Social Learning in Identificatory Processes. *JAPA, 22*, 512–36.

Meissner, W. W. 1976. New Horizons in Metapsychology. *JAPA, 24,* 161–80.

Meltzoff, J., and Kornreich, M. 1970. *Research in Psychotherapy.* New York: Atherton.

Menaker, E. 1953. Masochism: A Defense Reaction of the Ego. *PQ, 22,* 205–20.

Mendelson, W. B., et al. 1977. *Human Sleep and Its Disorders.* New York: Plenum Press.

Menninger, K. 1954. Psychological Aspects of the Organism Under Stress. *JAPA, 2,* 67–106, 208–310.

Menninger, K. 1959. *A Psychiatrist's World.* New York: Viking.

Menninger, K., et al. 1963. *The Vital Balance.* New York: Viking Press.

Menninger, W. C. 1943. Characterologic and Symptomatic Expressions Related to the Anal Phase of Psychosexual Development. *PQ, 12,* 161–93.

Meyer, B. 1964. Psychoanalytic Studies on Joseph Conrad. *JAPA, 12,* 32–58, 357–91.

Michaels, J. J. 1945. The Concept of Integration in Psychoanalysis. *Journal of Nervous and Mental Diseases, 102,* 54–64.

Mijuskovic, B. 1977. Loneliness: An Interdisciplinary Approach. *Psychiatry, 40,* 113–32.

Miller, D. R., and Swanson, G. E. 1960. *Inner Conflict and Defense.* New York: Holt.

Miller, M. L. 1948. Ego Functioning in Two Types of Dreams. *PQ, 17,* 346–55.

Miller, S. C. 1962. Ego Autonomy in Sensory Deprivation, Isolation and Stress. *IJP, 43,* 1–20.

Millet, J. 1966. Psychoanalysis in the U.S. In F. Alexander et al., *Psychoanalytic Pioneers,* pp. 546–96.

Milman, D. S., and Goldman, G. D., eds. 1973. *Acting Out: The Neurosis of Our Time.* Springfield, Ill.: C. C. Thomas.

Milner, M. 1969. *The Hands of the Living God.* New York: International Univs. Press.

Minar, D. W., and Greer, S., eds. 1969. *The Concept of Community.* Chicago: Aldine.

Mirsky, I. A., et al. 1950. Pepsinogen Excretion (Uropepsin) as an Index of the Influence of Various Life Situations on Gastric Secretion. In H. Wolff et al., eds., *Life Stress and Bodily Disease,* pp. 628–46.

Mitscherlich, A. 1969. *Society without the Father.* New York: Harcourt.

Mitscherlich, A. 1971. Psychoanalysis and the Aggression of Large Groups. *IJP, 52,* 161–68.

Mitscherlich, A., and Mitscherlich, M. 1975. *The Inability to Mourn.* New York: Grove Press.

Mittelman, B. 1954. Motility in Infants, Children and Adults. *PSC, 9,* 142–77.

Mittelman, B. 1955. Motor Patterns and Genital Behavior: Fetishism. *PSC, 10,* 241–63.

Mittelman, B. 1960. Intrauterine and Early Infant Motility. *PSC, 15,* 104–27.

Mitzman, A. 1973. *Sociology and Estrangement.* New York: Knopf.

Modell, A. H. 1963. The Concept of Psychic Energy (Panel). *JAPA, 11,* 605–18.

Modell, A. H. 1968. *Object Love and Reality*. New York: International Univs. Press.

Modell, A. H. 1975. A Narcissistic Defense against Affects. *IJP, 56*, 275–82.

Moloney, J. 1945. Psychiatric Observations in Okinawa Shima. *Psychiatry, 8*, 391–401.

Money, J., and Ehrhardt, A. A. 1972. *Man and Woman, Boy and Girl*. Baltimore: Johns Hopkins Univ. Press.

Money-Kyrle, R. E. 1956. Normal Countertransference and Some of Its Deviations. *IJP, 37*, 360–66.

Montagu, A. 1963. *Anthropology and Human Nature*. New York: McGraw-Hill.

Montagu, A. 1974a. Aggression and the Evolution of Man. In R. E. Whalen, ed., *The Neuropsychology of Aggression*, pp. 1–32.

Montagu, A., ed. 1974b. *Culture and Human Development*. Englewood Cliffs, N.J.: Prentice-Hall.

Montagu, A. 1976. *The Nature of Human Aggression*. New York: Oxford Univ. Press.

Moore, B. 1961. Frigidity in Women. *JAPA, 9*, 571–84.

Moore, B. 1968. Psychoanalytic Reflections on the Implications of Recent Physiological Studies of Female Orgasm. *JAPA, 16*, 569–87.

Moore, B. 1976. The American Psychoanalytic Association: Its Janus Posture. *JAPA, 24*, 257–83.

Moos, R. H., and Van Dort, B. 1977. Physical and Emotional Symptoms and Campus Health Center Utilization. *Social Psychiatry, 12*, 107–15.

Morris, G. O., et al. 1960. Misperception and Disorientation During Sleep Deprivation. *Archives of General Psychiatry, 2*, 247–54.

Morrison, C. C. 1968. *Freud and the Critic*. Chapel Hill. Univ. of North Carolina Press.

Moser, T. 1977. *Years of Apprenticeship on the Couch*. New York: Urizen Books.

Moser, U., and Zeppelin, I. von. 1969. Computer Simulation of a Model of Neurotic Defense Processes. *IJP, 50*, 53–64.

Moss, C. S. 1967. *The Hypnotic Investigation of Dreams*. New York: Wiley.

Muensterberger, W. 1969. Psyche and Environment. *PQ, 38*, 191–216.

Mullahy, P., ed. 1952. *The Contributions of Harry Stack Sullivan*. New York: Hermitage House.

Müller, C. 1977. Aging in Psychotics. In C. Chiland, ed., *Long-Term Treatments of Psychotic States*, pp. 583–96.

Murdock, G. P. 1949. *Social Structure*. New York: Macmillan.

Murphy, G. 1960. Psychoanalysis as a Unified Theory of Social Behavior. *Science and Psychoanalysis, 3*, 140–49.

Murphy, G. 1972. *Historical Introduction to Modern Psychology*. New York: Harcourt.

Murray, H. A. 1951. Uses of the Thematic Apperception Test. *American Journal of Psychiatry, 107*, 577–81.

Murray, H. A., ed. 1960. *Myth and Mythmaking*. Boston: Beacon Press.

Murray, H. A., et al. 1938. *Explorations in Personality*. New York: Oxford Univ. Press.

Myers, J. K., and Bean, L. L. 1968. *A Decade Later*. New York: Wiley.

Myers, J. K., and Roberts, B. H. 1959. *Family and Class Dynamics in Mental Illness*. New York: Wiley.

Nacht, S. 1948. Clinical Manifestations of Aggression and Their Role in Psychoanalytic Treatment. *IJP, 29*, 201–23.

Nagera, H. 1967. *Vincent van Gogh*. London: George Allen and Unwin.

Nagera, H. 1976. *The Obsessional Neurosis*. New York: Jason Aronson.

National Commission on the Causes and Prevention of Violence. 1969. *The History of Violence in America*. New York: Bantam Books.

Neel, A. F. 1977. *Theories of Psychology: A Handbook*. New York: Wiley.

Neill, A. S. 1960. *Summerhill*. New York: Hart Publishers.

Nelson, M. C. 1967. The Therapeutic Redirection of Energy and Affects. *IJP, 48*, 1–15.

Neubauer, P., and Flapan, D. 1975. *Assessment of Early Child Development*. New York: Jason Aronson.

Niederland, W. 1965. Memory and Repression (Panel). *JAPA, 13*, 619–33.

Niederland, W. 1974. *The Schreber Case*. New York: Quadrangle.

Niederland, W. 1976. Psychoanalytic Approaches to Creativity. *PQ, 45*, 185–212.

Noble, D. 1950–51. A Study of Dreams in Schizophrenia and Allied States. *American Journal of Psychiatry, 107*, 612–16.

Noble, D., and Burnham, D. 1969. *History of the Washington Psychoanalytic Society*. Np.

Noy, P. 1969. A Revision of the Psychoanalytic Theory of the Primary Process. *IJP, 50*, 155–78.

Nunberg, H. 1926. The Sense of Guilt and the Need for Punishment. *IJP, 7*, 420–33.

Nunberg, H. 1931. The Synthetic Function of the Ego. *IJP, 12*, 123–40.

Nunberg, H. 1932. Psychoanalyse des Schamgefuehls. *Psychoanalytische Bewegung, 4*, 505–7.

Nunberg, H. 1938. Psychological Interrelationships between Physician and Patient. *Psychoanalytic Review, 25*, 297–308.

Nunberg, H. 1948. *Practice and Theory of Psychoanalysis*. New York: Nervous and Mental Diseases Publishing Co.

Nunberg, H. 1955. *Principles of Psychoanalysis*. New York: International Univs. Press.

Nunberg, H., and Federn, E., eds. 1962–1975. *Minutes of the Vienna Psychoanalytic Society*. 4 vols. New York: International Univs. Press.

Nyswander, M. 1974. Drug Addiction. In S. Arieti, ed., *American Handbook of Psychiatry*, vol. 3, 393–403.

Oberndorf, C. P. 1953. *A History of Psychoanalysis in America*. New York: Grune & Stratton.

Oden, M. H. 1968. The Fulfillment of Promise. *Genetic Psychology Monographs, 77*, 3–93.

Odier, C. *Anxiety and Magic Thinking*. New York: International Univs. Press.

Offer, D., and Sabshin, M. 1974. *Normality*. New York: Basic Books

Opler, M. K., ed. 1959. *Culture and Mental Health*. New York: Macmillan.

Oremland, J. D. 1973. A Specific Dream during the Termination Phase of Successful Psychoanalyses. *JAPA, 21,* 285–302.

Ornstein, P. H. 1974. A Discussion of the Paper by Otto F. Kernberg. *IJP, 55,* 241–47.

Ostow, M. 1960. Psychoanalysis and Ethology (Panel). *JAPA, 8,* 526–34.

Parens, H. 1975. Parenthood as a Developmental Phase (Panel). *JAPA, 23,* 154–65.

Parkes, C. M. 1965. Bereavement and Mental Illness. *British Journal of Medical Psychology, 38,* 1.

Parkes, C. M. 1971. The First Year of Bereavement. *Psychiatry, 33,* 444.

Parkes, C. M. 1972. *Bereavement.* New York: International Univs. Press.

Parsons, T. 1953. The Superego and the Theory of Social Systems. In T. Parsons et al., *Working Papers in the Theory of Action,* pp. 13–28. Clencoe, Ill.: Free Press.

Parsons, T. 1958. The Definitions of Health and Illness in the Light of American Values and Social Structure. In E. G. Jaco, ed., *Patients, Physicians and Illness.* Glencoe, Ill.: Free Press.

Parsons, T. 1961. The Contribution of Psychoanalysis to Social Science. *Science and Psychoanalysis, 4,* 28–38.

Parsons, T. 1964. *Social Structure and Personality. New York: Free Press.*

Paz, C. A. 1971. *Analizabilidad.* Buenos Aires: Paidos.

Peller, L. F. 1954. Libidinal Phases, Ego Development and Play. *PSC, 9,* 178–98.

Peterfreund, E. 1971. *Information Systems and Psychoanalysis.* Psychological Issues Monograph 25/26. New York: International Univs. Press.

Peterfreund, E. 1975. The Need for a New Theoretical Frame of Reference for Psychoanalysis. *PQ, 44,* 534–49.

Peters, R. J. 1961. Immortality and the Artist. *Psychoanalysis and the Psychoanalytic Review, 48,* 126–37.

Pfeffer, A. 1961. Follow-up Study of a Satisfactory Analysis. *JAPA, 9,* 698–718.

Pfeffer, A. 1963a. Analysis Terminable and Interminable 25 Years Later (Panel). *JAPA, 11,* 131–42.

Pfeffer, A. 1963b. The Meaning of the Analyst after Analysis. *JAPA, 11,* 229–44.

Pfister, O. 1928. Die Illusion einer Zukunft. *Imago, 14,* 149–84.

Pfister, O. 1944. *Christianity and Fear.* London: Allen and Unwin.

Pfister, O. 1963. *Psychoanalysis and Faith.* New York: Basic Books.

Phillips, W., ed. 1957. *Art and Psychoanalysis.* New York: Criterion Books.

Piaget, J. 1973. The Affective Unconscious and the Cognitive Unconscious. *JAPA, 21,* 249–61.

Piers, G., and Singer, M. 1953. *Shame and Guilt.* Springfield, Ill.: C. C. Thomas.

Pinderhughes, C. A. 1971. Somatic, Psychic and Social Sequelae of Loss. *JAPA, 19,* 670–96.

Pine, F. 1970. On the Structuralization of Drive-Defense Relationships. *PQ, 39,* 17–37.

Pine, F., and Holt, R. R. 1960. Creativity and Primary Process: A Study of Adaptive Regression. *Journal of Abnormal Social Psychology, 61,* 370–79.

Ping-Nie, P. 1979. *Schizophrenic Illness: Theory and Treatment.* New York: International Univs. Press.

Plotnik, R. 1974. Brain Stimulation and Aggression. In R. Holloway, ed., *Primate Agression, Territoriality and Xenophobia*, pp. 389–415.

Pollock, G. H. 1961. Mourning and Adaptation. *IJP, 42*, 341–61.

Pollock, G. H. 1962. Childhood Parent and Sibling Loss in Adult Patients. *Archives of General Psychiatry, 7*, 295–305.

Pollock, G. H. 1970. Anniversary Reactions, Trauma and Mourning. *Psychiatric Quarterly, 39*, 347–71.

Pollock, G. H. 1972a. Bertha Pappenheim's Pathological Mourning. *JAPA, 20*, 476–93.

Pollock, G. H. 1972b. Ten Years of COPE: Perspectives in Psychoanalytic Education. *JAPA, 20*, 574–90.

Pollock, G. H. 1973. Bertha Pappenheim: Addenda to Her Case History. *JAPA, 21*, 328–32.

Pollock, G. H. 1975a. On Freud's Psychotherapy of Bruno Walter. *Annual of Psychoanalysis* (Chicago Institute), *3*, 287–95.

Pollock, G. H. 1975b. Mourning and Memorialization through Music. *Annual of Psychoanalysis* (Chicago Institute), *3*, 423–36.

Pollock, G. H. 1975c. On Mourning, Immortality and Utopia. *JAPA, 23*, 334–62.

Pollock, G. H. 1976. *The Chicago Institute for Psychoanalysis: From 1932 to the Present* (in press).

Pollock, G. H. 1977. The Mourning Process and Creative Organizational Change. *JAPA, 25*, 3–34.

Pollock, G. H., et al. 1976. Chicago Selection Research. *Annual of Psychoanalysis* (Chicago Institute), *4*, 307–82.

Pomer, S. 1966. Biography of Max Eitingon. In F. Alexander et al., *Psychoanalytic Pioneers*, pp. 51–62.

Pongrätz, L. J., ed. 1973. *Psychotherapie in Selbstdarstellungen*. Bern: Hans Huber.

Pontalis, J. 1974a. The Dream as an Object. *International Review of Psychoanalysis, 1*, 125–33.

Pontalis, J. 1974b. Freud in Paris (Inaugural Address). *IJP, 55*, 455–58.

Post, S., ed. 1972. *Moral Values and the Superego Concept in Psychoanalysis*. New York: International Univs. Press.

Pribram, K. H., and Gill, M. M. 1976. *Freud's 'Project' Reassessed*. New York: Basic Books.

Provence, S., and Lipton, R. 1962. *Infants in Institutions*. New York: International Univs. Press.

Provence, S., et al. 1977. *The Challenge of Daycare*. New Haven: Yale Univ. Press.

Putnam, J. J. 1971. *James Jackson Putnam and Psychoanalysis: Letters*. Cambridge, Mass: Harvard Univ. Press.

Racker, H. 1953. A Contribution to the Problem of Countertransference. *IJP, 34*, 313–24.

Racker, H. 1957. The Meaning and Uses of Countertransference. *PQ, 26*, 303–57.

Racker, H. 1958a. Countertransference and Interpretation. *JAPA, 6*, 215–21.

Racker, H. 1958b. Psychoanalytic Technique and the Analyst's Unconscious Masochism. *PQ, 27*, 555–62.

Racker, H. 1968. *Transference and Countertransference*. New York: International Univs. Press.

Rado, S. 1926. The Psychic Effects of Intoxication. *IJP, 7,* 396–413.

Rado, S. 1928. The Psychic Effects of Intoxication. *IJP, 9,* 301–17.

Rado, S. 1933. The Psychoanalysis of Pharmacothymia (Drug Addiction). *PQ, 2,* 1–23.

Rado, S. 1969. *Adaptational Psychodynamics*. New York: Science House.

Raglan, Lord. 1956. *The Hero: A Study in Tradition, Myth and Drama*. New York: Knopf.

Rainwater, L., and Yancey, W. L. 1967. *The Moynihan Report and the Politics of Controversy*. Cambridge, Mass.: MIT Press.

Rakoff, V. M., et al. 1977. *Psychiatric Diagnosis*. New York: Brunner/Mazel.

Rangell, L. 1952. The Analysis of a Doll Phobia. *IJP, 33,* 43–53.

Rangell, L. 1954a. The Psychology of Poise. *IJP, 35,* 313–32.

Rangell, L. 1954b. Similarities and Differences between Psychoanalysis and Dynamic Psychotherapy. *JAPA, 2,* 734–44.

Rangell, L. 1954c. Reporter: Psychoanalysis and Dynamic Psychotherapy. *JAPA, 2,* 152–66.

Rangell, L. 1955. The Borderline Case (Panel). *JAPA, 3,* 285–95.

Rangell, L. 1959. The Nature of Conversion. *JAPA, 7,* 632–62.

Rangell, L. 1963. On Friendship. *JAPA, 11,* 3–54.

Rangell, L. 1968. A Further Attempt to Resolve the "Problem of Anxiety." *JAPA, 16,* 371–404.

Rank, O. 1909. *The Myth of the Birth of the Hero*. Reprinted ed., New York: Brunner, 1952.

Rank, O. 1932. *Art and the Artist: Creative Urge and Personality Development*. New York: Tudor.

Rankin, R. P., and Lowry, R. P. 1969. *Sociology: The Science of Society*. New York: Scribner's.

Rapaport, D. 1942. *Emotions and Memory*. New York: International Univs. Press.

Rapaport, D. 1951. The Autonomy of the Ego. *Bulletin of the Menninger Clinic, 15,* 113–23.

Rapaport, D. 1953. On the Psychoanalytic Theory of Affects. *IJP, 34,* 177–98.

Rapaport, D. 1958. The Theory of Ego Autonomy: A Generalization. *Bulletin of the Menninger Clinic, 22,* 13–35.

Rapaport, D. 1959. A Historical Survey of Psychoanalytic Ego Psychology. In *Psychological Issues Monograph 1*, pp. 5–17. New York: International Univs. Press.

Rapaport, D. 1960. *The Structure of Psychoanalytic Theory*. Psychological Issues Monograph 6. New York: International Univs. Press.

Rapaport, D. 1967. *Collected Papers*. New York: Basic Books.

Rapaport, D., and Shakow, D. 1964. *The Influence of Freud on American Psychology*. Psychological Issues Monograph 13. New York: International Universities Press.

Rapaport, D., Gill, M. M., and Schafer, R. 1945–1946. *Diagnostic Psychological Testing*. 2 vols. Chicago: Yearbook Publ.

Rappaport, E. A. 1956. The Management of an Erotized Transference. *PQ, 25,* 15–29.

Rappaport, E. A. 1959. The First Dream in an Erotized Transference. *IJP, 40,* 240–45.

Redlich, F. C. 1960. Psychoanalysis and the Problem of Values. *Science and Psychoanalysis, 3,* 84–103.

Reich, A. 1960. Further Remarks on Countertransference. *IJP, 41,* 389–95.

Reich, I. O. 1969. *Wilhelm Reich.* New York: St. Martin's Press.

Reich, W. 1922. Zwei Narzisstische Typen. *Internationale Zeitschrift fuer Psychoanalyse, 8,* 456–62.

Reich, W. 1925. Der Triebhafte Charakter. *Neue Arbeiten zuer Aerztliche Psychoanalyse, 4.*

Reich, W. 1927. *The Function of the Orgasm.* New York: Orgone Institute Press.

Reich, W. 1933. *Character Analysis.* New York: Orgone Institute Press.

Reich, W. 1945. *The Sexual Revolution.* New York: Farrar, Straus and Rinehart.

Reider, N. 1955. Reporter. Reevaluation of the Libido Theory. *JAPA, 3,* 299–308.

Reiff, P. 1959. *Freud: The Mind of the Moralist.* New York: Viking.

Reik, T. 1925. *The Compulsion to Confess and the Need for Punishment.* Leipzig: Internationaler Psychoanalytischer Verlag.

Reik, T. 1941. *Masochism in Modern Man.* New York: Farrar, Straus.

Reiser, M..1975. Changing Theoretical Concepts in Psychosomatic Medicine. In S. Arieti, ed., *American Handbook of Psychiatry,* vol. 4, 477–500.

Rennie, T., et al. 1962. *Mental Health in the Metropolis.* New York: McGraw-Hill.

Rexford, E. N. 1966. *A Developmental Approach to Problems of Acting Out: A Symposium.* New York: International Univs. Press.

Ribble, M. A. 1943. *The Rights of Infants: Early Psychological Needs and Their Satisfactions.* New York: Columbia Univ. Press.

Richardson, G. A., and Moore, R. A. 1963. On the Manifest Dream in Schizophrenia. *JAPA, 11,* 281–302.

Richter, C. 1959. The Phenomenon of Unexplained Sudden Death in Animals and Man. In H. Feifel, ed., *The Meaning of Death,* pp. 302–16. New York: McGraw-Hill.

Rickman, J. 1940. On the Nature of Ugliness and the Creative Impulse. *IJP, 21,* 294–313.

Ricoeur, P. 1970. *Freud and Philosophy.* New Haven: Yale Univ. Press.

Riesman, D. 1950. *The Lonely Crowd.* New Haven: Yale Univ. Press.

Rifkin, A. H. 1974. A General Assessment of Psychiatry. In S. Arieti, ed., *American Handbook of Psychiatry,* vol. 1, pp. 117–30.

Ritvo, S. 1971. Psychoanalysis as Science and Profession. *JAPA, 19,* 3–25.

Rivers, W. H. R. 1923. *Conflict and Dream.* New York: Harcourt.

Riviere, J. 1955. The Unconscious Phantasy of an Inner World Reflected in Examples from Literature. In M. Klein et al., *New Directions in Psychoanalysis,* pp. 370–83.

Robbins, L. L. 1956. The Borderline Case (Panel). *JAPA, 4,* 550–62.

Robbins, W. S. 1975. Termination: Problems and Techniques. *JAPA, 23,* 166–76.

Roe, A. 1953. *The Making of a Scientist.* New York: Dodd, Mead.

Roheim, G. 1932. Psychoanalysis of Primitive Cultural Types. *IJP, 13,* 1–224.

Roheim, G. 1950. *Psychoanalysis and Anthropology.* New York: International Univs. Press.

Roheim, G. 1952b. *The Gates of the Dream.* New York: International Univs. Press.

Roheim, G. 1952a. The Anthropological Evidence and the Oedipus Complex. *PQ, 21,* 537–42.

Roiphe, H. 1968. On an Early Genital Phase. *PSC, 23,* 348–65.

Roiphe, H., and Galenson, E. 1971. The Impact of Early Sexual Discovery on Mood, Defensive Organization and Symbolization. *PSC, 26,* 195–216.

Roiphe, H., and Galenson, E. 1972. Early Genital Activity and the Castration Complex. *PQ, 41,* 334–47.

Roiphe, H., and Galenson, E. 1973. *Some Observations on Transitional Object and Infantile Fetish.* Paper presented to the New York Psychoanalytic Society March 27, 1973.

Rorschach, H. 1921. *Psychodiagnostics: A Diagnostic Test Based on Perception.* New York: Grune & Stratton.

Rosen, J. 1953. *Direct Analysis.* New York: Grune & Stratton.

Rosen, S. 1973. *The Conscious Brain.* New York: Knopf.

Rosen, V. H. 1967. Disorders of Communication in Psychoanalysis. *JAPA, 15,* 467–90.

Rosen, V. H. 1975. Some Aspects of Freud's Theory of Schizophrenic Language Disturbance. *Psychoanalysis and Contemporary Science, 4,* 405–22.

Rosen, V. H. 1977. *Style, Character and Language.* New York: Jason Aronson.

Rosenbaum, M. 1965. Dreams in Which the Analyst Appears Undisguised. *IJP, 46,* 429–37.

Rosenbaum, M., and Berger, M., eds. 1975. *Group Psychotherapy and Group Function.* New York: Basic Books.

Rosenbaum, M., and Snadowsky, A., eds. 1976. *The Intensive Group Experience.* New York: Free Press.

Rosenfeld, H. 1965. *Psychotic States.* London: Hogarth Press.

Rosenthal, R. R. 1976. *Experimenter Effects in Behavioral Research.* New York: Wiley.

Ross, N. 1960. An Examination of Nosology According to Psychoanalytic Concepts (Panel). *JAPA, 8,* 535–51.

Ross, N. 1970. The Primacy of Genitality in the Light of Ego Psychology: Introductory Remarks. *JAPA, 18,* 267–84.

Rossi, P. H., and Williams, W. 1972. *Evaluating Social Interventions.* New York: Seminar Press.

Rothenberg, A. 1969. The Iceman Changeth: Toward an Empirical Approach to Creativity. *JAPA, 17,* 549–607.

Rothenberg, A., and Hausman, C. R., eds. 1976. *The Creativity Question.* Durham, N.C.: Duke Univ. Press.

Rothman, D. J. 1971. *The Discovery of the Asylum.* Boston: Little, Brown.

Rubinfine, D. L. 1958. Problems of Identity (Panel). *JAPA, 6,* 131–42.

Rubinfine, D. L. 1962. Maternal Stimulation, Psychic Structure and Early Object

Bibliography 639

Relations with Special Reference to Aggression and Denial. *PSC, 17,* 265–85.

Rubins, J. 1978. *Karen Horney.* New York: Dial Press.

Ruesch, J. 1957. *Disturbed Communication.* New York: Norton.

Ruesch, J. 1961. *Therapeutic Communication.* New York: Norton.

Ruesch, J., and Bateson, G. 1951. *Communication: The Social Matrix of Psychiatry.* New York: Norton.

Sachs, H. 1930. Die Lehranalyse. In *Zehn Jahre Berliner Psychoanalytisches Institut,* 53–54.

Sachs, H. 1942. *The Creative Unconscious.* Cambridge, Mass: Sci-Art Publishing Co.

Sachs, L. J. 1973. On Crying, Weeping and Laughing as Defences against Sexual Drives. *IJP, 54,* 477–84.

Sachs, W. 1947. *Black Anger.* Boston: Little, Brown.

Sadger, I. 1926. A Contribution to the Understanding of Sado-Masochism. *IJP, 7,* 484–91.

Salzman, L. 1968. *The Obsessive Personality.* New York: Science House.

Sanchez Medina, G. 1975. Historic Summary of the Colombian Society and Institute of Psychoanalysis. Unpublished manuscript.

Sandler, J. 1959. The Body as Phallus: A Patient's Fear of Erection. *IJP, 40,* 191–98.

Sandler, J. 1960. On the Concept of Superego. *PSC, 15,* 128-62.

Sandler, J. 1962. The Hampstead Index as an Instrument of Psychoanalytic Research. *IJP, 43,* 287–91.

Sandler, J., and Joffe, W. 1965. Notes on Obsessional Manifestations in Children. *PQ, 20,* 425–38.

Sandler, J., and Joffe, W. 1966. On Skill and Sublimation. *JAPA, 14,* 335–55.

Sandler, J., and Joffe, W. 1969. Towards a Basic Psychoanalytic Model. *IJP, 50,* 79–90.

Sandler, J., and Nagera, H. 1963. Aspects of the Metapsychology of Fantasy. *PSC, 18,* 159–96.

Sandler, J., and Rosenblatt, B. 1962. The Concept of the Representational World. *PSC, 17,* 128–45.

Sandler, J., et al. 1962. The Classification of Superego Material in the Hampstead Index. *PSC, 17,* 107–27.

Sandler, J., et. al. 1965. *The Hampstead Psychoanalytic Index.* New York: International Univs. Press.

Sandler, J., et al. 1969. Notes on some Theoretical and Clinical Aspects of Transference. *IJP, 50,* 633–45.

Sandler, J., Dare, C., and Holder, D. 1973. *The Patient and the Analyst.* New York: International Univs. Press.

Sarnoff, C. 1976. *Latency.* New York: Jason Aronson.

Saul, L. 1940. Utilization of Early Current Dreams in Formulating Psychoanalytic Cases. *PQ, 9,* 453–69.

Saul, L., and Wenar, I. 1965. Early Influences on Development and Disorders of Personality. *PQ, 34,* 327–89.

Schacht, R. 1971. *Alienation*. Garden City, N.Y.: Doubleday.

Schafer, R. 1958. Regression in the Service of the Ego. In G. Lindzey, ed., *Assessment of Human Motives*, pp. 119–48. New York: Rinehart.

Schafer, R. 1960. The Loving and Beloved Superego in Freud's Structural Theory. *PSC, 15,* 163–88.

Schafer, R. 1964. The Clinical Analysis of Affects. *JAPA, 12,* 275–99.

Schafer, R. 1965. Contributions of Longitudinal Studies to Psychoanalytic Theory (Panel). *JAPA, 13,* 605–18.

Schafer, R. 1967. Ego Autonomy and the Return of Repression. *International Journal of Psychiatry, 3,* 515–18.

Schafer, R. 1968. *Aspects of Internalization*. New York: International Univs. Press.

Schafer, R. 1970. An Overview of Heinz Hartmann's Contributions to Psychoanalysis. *IJP, 51,* 425–46.

Schafer, R. 1974. Problems in Freud's Psychology of Women. *JAPA, 22,* 459–85.

Schafer, R. 1976. *A New Language for Psychoanalysis*. New Haven: Yale Univ. Press.

Schecter, M., Toussieng, P., and Sternlof, R. 1972. Normal Development in Adolescence. In B. Wolman, ed., *Manual of Child Psychotherapy*. pp. 22–45. New York: McGraw-Hill.

Scheff, T. J. 1977. The Distancing of Emotion in Ritual. *Current Anthropology, 18,* 483–505.

Schilder, P. 1935. *The Image and Appearance of the Human Body*. Reprint ed., New York: International Univs. Press, 1950.

Schjelderup, H. K. 1939. Report to International Psychoanalytical Association. *IJP, 20,* 216–17.

Schlesinger, N. 1974. Assessment and Follow-Up in Psychoanalysis. *JAPA, 22,* 542–67.

Schmale, A. H. 1962. Needs, Gratifications and the Vicissitudes of the Self Representation. *Psychoanalytic Study of Society, 2,* 9–41.

Schmale, A. H. 1964. A Genetic View of Affects. *PSC, 19,* 287–310.

Schmale, H. T. 1966. Working Through (Panel). *JAPA, 14,* 172–82.

Schmidenberg, M. 1946. On Querulance. *PQ, 15,* 472–501.

Schneider, D. E. 1950. *The Psychoanalyst and the Artist*. New York: Mentor Books.

Schnier, J. 1951. The Symbol of the Ship in Art, Myth and Dreams. *Psychoanalytic Review, 38,* 53–65.

Schur, M. 1955. Comments on the Metapsychology of Somatization. *PSC, 10,* 119–64.

Schur, M. 1960. Discussion of Dr. John Bowlby's Paper. *PSC, 15,* 63–84.

Schur, M., ed. 1965. *Drives, Affects, Behavior*. New York: International Univs. Press.

Schur, M. 1966. *The Id and the Regulatory Principles of Mental Functioning*. New York: International Univs. Press.

Schur, M. 1972. *Freud: Living and Dying*. New York: International Univs. Press.

Schur, M., et. al. 1966. *Essays in Honor of Heinz Hartmann's Seventieth Birthday*. New York: International Univs. Press.

Schuster, D. B., et al. 1972. *Clinical Supervision of the Psychiatric Resident.* New York: Brunner/Mazel.

Schwartz, F., and Schiller, P. H. 1970. *A Psychoanalytic Model of Attention and Learning.* Psychological Issues Monograph 23. New York: International Univs. Press.

Scott, J. P. 1962. Critical Periods in Behavioral Development. *Science, 138,* 949–58.

Scott, J. P., and Senay, E. C. 1973. *Separation and Depression.* Washington, D.C.: American Association for the Advancement of Science.

Scott, W. C. M. 1963. Psychoanalysis in Canada. Unpublished manuscript.

Searles, H. F. 1959a. The Effort to Drive the Other Person Crazy. *CP,* 254–83.

Searles, H. F. 1959b. Oedipal Love in the Countertransference. *IJP, 40,* 180–90.

Searles, H. F. 1961. Schizophrenic Communication. *Psychoanalysis and the Psychoanalytic Review, 48,* 3–50.

Searles, H. F. 1963. The Place of Neutral Therapist Responses in Psychotherapy with the Schizophrenic Patient. *IJP, 44,* 42–56.

Searles, H. F. 1965. *Collected Papers on Schizophrenia and Related Subjects.* New York: International Univs. Press.

Searles, H. F. 1975. The Patient as Therapist to the Analyst. In P. L. Giovacchini, ed., *Tactics and Techniques in Psychoanalytic Therapy,* vol. 2, pp. 95–151.

Sears, R. R. 1943. *Survey of Objective Studies of Psychoanalytic Concepts. Bulletin 51.* New York: Social Science Research Council.

Sears, R. R. 1951. *Survey of Objective Studies of Psychoanalytic Concepts.* Ann Arbor, Mich.: Edwards Bros.

Sechehaye, M. 1947. *Symbolic Realization.* New York: International Univs. Press.

Sechehaye, M. A. 1951. *Symbolic Realization.* New York: International Univs. Press.

Segal, H. 1952. A Psychoanalytic Approach to Aesthetics. *IJP, 33,* 196–207.

Segal, H. 1973. *Introduction to the Work of Melanie Klein.* New York: Basic Books.

Segel, N. P. 1961. The Psychoanalytic Theory of the Symbolic Process, *JAPA, 9,* 146–57.

Selye, H. 1956. *The Stress of Life.* New York: McGraw-Hill.

Shapiro, S., and Sachs, D. 1976. On Parallel Processes in Therapy and Teaching. *PQ, 45,* 394–415.

Shapiro, T. 1975. Childhood Neurosis: The Past 75 Years. *Psychoanalysis and Contemporary Science, 4,* 453–477.

Sharpe, E. 1935. Similar and Divergent Unconscious Determinants Underlying the Sublimations of Pure Art and Pure Science. *IJP, 16,* 186–202.

Sharpe, E. 1937. *Dream Analysis.* London: Hogarth Press.

Sharpe, E. 1950. *Collected Papers.* London: Hogarth Press.

Sherfey, M. J. 1966. The Evolution and Nature of Female Sexuality in Relation to Psychoanalytic Theory, *JAPA, 14,* 28–128.

Sherfey, M. J. 1972. *The Nature and Evolution of Female Sexuality.* New York: Random House.

Shneidman, E. A., ed. 1967. *Essays on Self-Destruction.* New York: Science House.

Shorter, E. 1975. *The Making of the Modern Family*. New York: Basic Books.

Siegal, E. V. 1973. Movement Therapy as a Psychotherapeutic Tool. *JAPA, 21,* 333–43.

Siegman, A. 1954. Emotionality: A Hysterical Character Defense. *PQ, 23,* 339–54.

Silverman, L. H. 1967. An Experimental Approach to the Study of Dynamic Propositions in Psychoanalysis. *JAPA, 15,* 376–403.

Silverman, L. H. 1970. Further Experimental Studies. *JAPA, 18,* 102–24.

Simon, B. 1978. *Mind and Madness in Ancient Greece*. Ithaca, N.Y.: Cornell Univ. Press.

Singer, J. L. 1975. *The Inner World of Daydreaming*. New York: Harper.

Singer, M. T., and Wynne, L. L. 1965. Thought Disorder and Family Relations of Schizophrenics. *Archives of General Psychiatry, 12,* 187–212.

Sinha, T. 1966. Development of Psychoanalysis of India. *IJP, 47,* 427–39.

Skinner, B. F. 1971. *Beyond Freedom and Dignity*. New York: Knopf.

Slovenko, R. 1973. *Psychiatry and Law*. Boston: Little, Brown.

Synder, F. 1966. Toward an Evolutionary Theory of Dreaming. *American Journal of Psychiatry, 2,* 121–36.

Socarides, C. 1966. On Vengeance: The Desire to "Get Even." *JAPA, 14,* 356–75.

Socarides, C. 1968. *The Overt Homosexual*. New York: Grune & Stratton.

Socarides, C. 1974. The Sexual Unreason. *Book Forun, 1,* 172–85.

Socarides, C. 1976. *Beyond the Sexual Revolution*. New York: Quadrangle.

Socarides, C., ed. 1977. *The World of Emotions*. New York: International Univs. Press.

Socarides, C. 1978. *Homosexuality*. New York: Jason Aronson.

Spector, J. 1972. *The Aesthetics of Freud*. New York: Praeger.

Sperling, M. 1946. Psychoanalytic Study of Ulcerative Colitis in Children. *PQ, 15,* 302–29.

Sperling, M. 1973. Conversion Hysteria and Conversion Symptoms: A Revision of Classification and Concepts. *JAPA, 21,* 745–71.

Sperling, M. 1974. *The Major Neuroses and Behavior Disorders in Children*. New York: Jason Aronson.

Sperry, R. W. 1977. Forebrain Commissurotomy and Conscious Awareness, *Journal of Medicine and Philosophy, 2,* 101–26.

Spiegel, L. 1954. Acting Out and Defensive Instinctual Gratification, *JAPA, 2,* 107–19.

Spiegel, L. 1958. Comments on the Psychoanalytic Psychology of Adolescence. *PSC, 13,* 296–308.

Spiegel, R. 1959. Specific Problems of Communication. In S. Arieti, ed., *American Handbook of Psychiatry*, pp. 909–49.

Spiegel, R., et al. 1975. On Psychoanalysis in the Third Reich. *Contemporary Psychoanalysis, 11,* 477–510.

Spielberger, C. D., and Zuckerman, M., eds. 1976. *Emotions and Anxiety*. New York: Wiley.

Spitz, R. 1937. Wiederholung, Rhythmus, Langeweile. *Imago, 23,* 171–96.

Spitz, R. 1945. Hospitalism: An Inquiry into the Genesis of Psychiatric Conditions in Early Childhood. *PSC, 1*, 53–74.

Spitz, R. 1952. Authority and Masturbation: Some Remarks on a Bibliographic Investigation. *PQ, 21*, 490–527.

Spitz, R. 1957. *No and Yes*. New York: International Univs. Press.

Spitz, R. 1959. *A Genetic Field Theory of Ego Formation: Its Implications for Pathology*. New York: International Univs. Press.

Spitz, R. 1960. Discussion of Dr. John Bowlby's Paper. *PSC, 15*, 85–94.

Spitz, R. 1961. Some Early Prototypes of Ego Defenses. *JAPA, 9*, 626–51.

Spitz, R. 1964. The Derailment of Dialogue. *JAPA, 12*, 752–775.

Spitz, R. 1965. *The First Year of Life*. New York: International Univs. Press.

Spotnitz, H. 1969. *Modern Psychoanalysis of the Schizophrenic Patient*. New York: Grune & Stratton.

Spurlock, J. 1970. Social Deprivation in Childhood and Character Formation (Panel). *JAPA, 18*, 622–30.

Staercke, A. 1921. Psychoanalysis and Psychiatry. *IJP, 2*, 361–415.

Stein, M. H. 1956. The Problem of Masochism in the Theory and Technique of Psychoanalysis. *JAPA, 4*, 526–38.

Sterba, R. 1953. Clinical and Therapeutic Aspects of Character Resistance. *PQ, 22*, 1–20.

Stern, A. 1938. Psychoanalytic Investigation of and Therapy in the Borderline Neuroses. *PQ, 7*, 467–89.

Stern, J. T. 1970. The Meaning of "Adaptation" and Its Relation to the Phenomenon of Natural Selection. In T. Dobzhansky, ed., *Evolutionary Biology*, vol. 4, pp. 38–66. New York: Meredith Corp.

Sternschein, I. 1973. The Experience of Separation-Individuation and its Reverberations through the Course of Life: Maturity, Senescence and Sociological Implications. *JAPA, 21*, 633–45.

Stewart, K. 1953–1954. Culture and Personality in Two Primitive Groups. *Complex, 9*, 3–23.

Stewart, P. L., and Cantor, M. G., eds. 1974. *Varieties of Work Experience*. New York: Wiley.

Stierlin, H. 1977. *Adolf Hitler*. New York: Psychohistory Press.

Stierlin, H. 1972. *Separating Parents and Adolescents*. New York: Quadrangle.

Stoller, R. J. 1968. *Sex and Gender*. New York: Science House.

Stone, L. 1954. The Widening Scope of Indications for Psychoanalysis. *JAPA, 2*, 567–94.

Stone, L. 1961. *The Psychoanalytic Situation*. New York: International Univs. Press.

Stotland, E. 1969. *The Psychology of Hope*. San Francisco: Jossey-Bass.

Strachey, J. 1930. Some Unconscious Factors in Reading. *IJP, 11*, 322–31.

Strachey, J. 1934. On the Nature of the Therapeutic Action of Psychoanalysis. *IJP, 15*, 127–59. Reprinted in *IJP, 50*, 275–92.

Strachey, J., ed. 1953–1974. *Standard Edition of Freud's Works*. London: Hogarth Press.

Strassman, H., et al. 1976. The Impact of Psychiatric Residency on Choice of Analytic Training. *JAPA, 24,* 347–55.

Strean, H. 1967. A Family Therapist Looks at "Little Hans." *Family Process, 6,* 227–34.

Strean, H., and Aull, G. 1967. The Analyst's Silence. *Psychoanalytic Forum, 2,* 72–80, 86–87.

Sullivan, H. S. 1925. The Oral Complex. *Psychoanalytic Review, 12,* 30–38.

Sullivan, H. S. 1927. The Onset of Schizophrenia. *American Journal of Psychiatry, 7,* 105–34.

Sullivan, H. S. 1931a. The Modified Psychoanalytic Treatment of Schizophrenia. *American Journal of Psychiatry, 11,* 519–40.

Sullivan, H. S. 1931b. The Relation of Onset to Outcome in Schizophrenia. In *Schizophrenia as a Human Process,* pp. 233–55.

Sullivan, H. S. 1940. *Conceptions of Modern Psychiatry.* New York: Norton.

Sullivan, H. S. 1944. The Language of Schizophrenia. In J. S. Kasanin, ed., *Language and Thought in Schizophrenia.* Berkeley, Cal.: Univ. of California Press.

Sullivan, H. S. 1953. *The Interpersonal Theory of Psychiatry.* New York: Norton.

Sullivan, H. S. 1956. *Clinical Studies in Psychiatry.* New York: Norton.

Sullivan, H. S. 1962. *Schizophrenia as a Human Process.* New York: Norton.

Sullivan, H. S. 1964. *The Fusion of Psychiatry and Social Science.* New York: Norton.

Sullivan, H. S. 1972. *Personal Psychopathology.* New York: Norton.

Suppes, P., and Warren, H. 1975. On the Generation and Classification of the Defence Mechanisms. *IJP, 56,* 405–14.

Suttie, I. D. 1935. *The Origins of Love and Hate.* New York: Julian Press.

Suzuki, D. T., Fromm, E., and De Martino, R. 1960. *Zen Buddhism and Psychoanalysis.* New York: Grove Press.

Szasz, T. S. 1961. *The Myth of Mental Illness.* New York: Harper.

Tanner, J. M. 1972. Sequence, Tempo, and Individual Variation in Growth and Development of Boys and Girls Age 12–16. In J. Kagan and R. Coles, eds., *12 to 16: Early Adolescence,* pp. 1–24. New York: Norton.

Tauber, E. S. 1954. Exploring the Therapeutic Use of Countertransference Data. *Psychiatry, 17,* 331–36.

Tauber, E. S., and Green, M. R. 1959. *Prelogical Experience.* New York: Basic Books.

Tausk, V. 1919. On the Origin of the "Influencing Machine" in Schizophrenia. *PQ, 2,* 519–56, 1933.

Tax, S., ed. 1964. *Horizons of Anthropology.* Chicago: Aldine.

Temerlin, M. K. 1975. *Lucy: Growing up Human.* Palo Alto, Cal.: Science and Behavior Books.

Theobald, D. 1966. *The Concept of Energy.* London: E. and F. Spon.

Thomä, H. 1969. Some Remarks on Psychoanalysis in Germany, Past and Present. *IJP, 50,* 683–92.

Thompson, C. 1938. Notes on the Psychoanalytic Significance of the Choice of Analyst. *Psychiatry, 1,* 205–16.

Thompson, C. 1941. The Role of Women in This Culture. *Psychiatry, 4,* 1–8.

Thompson, C. 1942. Cultural Pressures in the Psychology of Women. *Psychiatry, 5,* 331–39.

Thompson, C. 1943. Penis Envy in Women. *Psychiatry, 6,* 123–25.

Thompson, C. 1950. *Psychoanalysis: Its Evolution and Development.* New York: Hermitage House.

Thompson C. 1958. A Study of the Emotional Climate of Psychoanalytic Institutes. *Psychiatry, 21,* 45–51.

Thompson, R. 1977. *Election Ballot.* Washington, D.C.: American Psychological Association.

Tissot, R. 1977. Long-Term Drug Therapy in Psychoses. In C. Chiland, ed., *Long-Term Treatments of Psychotic States,* pp. 89–171.

Tomkins, S. S. 1962, 1964. *Affect, Imagery, Consciousness.* Vol. 1, 1962; vol. 2, 1964. New York: Springer.

Tower, L. E. 1956. Countertransference. *JAPA, 4,* 224–55.

Trapp, C., and Lyons, R. 1936. Dream Studies in Hallucinated Patients. *Psychiatric Quarterly, 11,* 252–66.

Trunnell, E. E., and Holt, W. E. 1974. The Concept of Denial or Disavowal. *JAPA, 22,* 769–84.

Tucker, R. C. 1973. *Stalin.* New York: Norton.

Tucker, R. C., ed. 1977. *Stalinism.* New York: Norton.

Tulving, E., and Donaldson, W. 1972. *Organization of Memory.* New York: Academic Press.

Turkle, S. 1978. *Psychoanalytic Politics.* New York: Basic Books.

Turner, V. 1967. *The Forest of Symbols.* Ithaca, N.Y.: Cornell Univ. Press.

Ullman, M. 1966a. Dreams: An Introduction. In *Science and Psychoanalysis, 9,* 160.

Ullman, M. 1966b. An Experimental Approach to Dream and Telepathy. *Archives of General Psychiatry, 14,* 605–13.

Usdin, G., ed. 1973. *Sleep Research and Clinical Practice.* New York: Brunner/Mazel.

Valenstein, A. F. 1958. The Psychoanalytic Concept of Character. *JAPA, 6,* 567–75.

Valenstein, E. 1973. *Brain Control.* New York: Wiley.

Vangaard, T. 1972. *Phallos.* New York: International Univs. Press.

Van Lawick-Goodall, J. 1971. *In the Shadow of Man.* Boston: Houghton Mifflin.

Van Lawick-Goodall, J. 1973. The Behavior of Chimpanzees in Their Natural Habitat. *American Journal of Psychiatry, 130,* 1–11.

Van Ophuijsen, J. H. W. 1920. On the Origin of the Feeling of Persecution. *IJP, 1,* 235–39.

Varendonck, J. 1921. *The Psychology of Daydreams.* New York: Macmillan.

Veith, I. 1965. *Hysteria: The History of a Disease.* Chicago: Univ. of Chicago Press.

Volkan, V. D. 1976. *Primitive Internalized Object Relations.* New York: International Univs. Press.

Wadeson, R. W. 1975. Psychoanalysis in Community Psychiatry (Panel). *JAPA, 23,* 177–89.

Waelder, R. 1924. The Psychoses: Their Mechanisms and Accessibility to Influence. *IJP, 6,* 254–81.

Waelder, R. 1936a. On Erotization of Urological Treatment. *PQ, 5,* 491.

Waelder, R. 1936b. The Principle of Multiple Function: Observations of Overdetermination. *PQ, 5,* 45–62.

Waelder, R. 1960. *The Basic Theory of Psychoanalysis.* New York: International Univs. Press.

Waldhorn, H. 1960. Assessment of Analyzability. *PQ, 29,* 478–506.

Waldhorn, H. 1967. *The Place of the Dream in Clinical Psychoanalysis.* Kris Study Group Monograph 2, pp. 52–106. New York: International Univs. Press.

Waldhorn, H., and Fine, B. D. 1974. *Trauma and Symbolism.* Kris Study Group Monograph 5. New York: International Univs. Press.

Wallace, A. F. C. 1970. *Culture and Personality.* New York: Random House.

Wallerstein, R. 1973. Psychoanalytic Perspectives on the Problem of Reality. *JAPA, 21,* 5–33.

Wallerstein, R., and Smelser, N. 1969. Psychoanalysis and Sociology. *IJP, 50,* 693–710.

Walter, B. 1946. *Theme and Variations.* New York: Knopf.

Wangh, M. 1957. The Scope of the Contribution of Psychoanalysis to the Biography of the Artist. *JAPA, 5,* 564–75.

Warner, W. L. 1963. *Yankee City.* New Haven: Yale Univ. Press.

Wechsler, D. 1939. *The Measurement and Appraisal of Adult Intelligence.* Baltimore: Williams and Wilkins.

Weigert, E. 1962. The Function of Sympathy in the Psychotherapeutic Process. *Psychiatry, 22,* 3–14.

Weinstein, E. A. 1976. Presidential Assassination: An American Problem. *Psychiatry, 39,* 291–93.

Weisman, A. D. 1972. *On Dying and Denying.* New York: Behavioral Publications.

Weisman, A. D., and Hackett, T. P. 1967. Denial as a Social Act. In R. Kahana and S. Levin, eds. *Psychodynamic Studies on Aging,* pp. 79–110.

Weisman, A. D., and Kastenbaum, R. 1968. *The Psychological Autopsy.* Community Mental Health Monographs No. 4. New York.

Weiss, E., and English, O. 1957. *Psychosomatic Medicine.* Philadelphia: Saunders.

Weiss, J. 1966. Clinical and Theoretical Aspects of "As If" Characters (Panel). *JAPA, 14,* 569–90.

Weiss, J. 1972. Continuing Research Toward a Psychoanalytic Developmental Psychology (Panel). *JAPA, 20,* 177–98.

Weisskopf, W. 1955. *The Psychology of Economics.* Chicago: Univ. of Chicago Press.

Weisskopf, W. 1971. *Alienation and Economics.* New York: Dutton.

Weissman, P. 1961. Development and Creativity in the Actor and Playwright. *PQ, 30,* 549–67.

Weissman, P. 1968. Psychological Concomitants of Ego Functioning in Creativity. *IJP, 49,* 464–69.

Weissman, P. 1969. Creative Fantasies and Beyond the Reality Principle. *PQ, 38,* 110–23.

Werner, H. 1940. *Comparative Psychology of Mental Development*. New York: International Univs. Press.

Werner, H., and Kaplan, B. 1963. *Symbol Formation*. New York: Wiley.

Werry, J. S., and Quay, H. C. 1971. The Prevalence of Behavior Symptoms in Younger Elementary School Children. *American Journal of Orthopsychiatry*, *41*, 136–46.

West, J. 1945. Plainville U.S.A. In A. Kardiner, *The Psychological Frontiers of Society*, pp. 259–412.

West, L. J. 1962. *Hallucinations*. New York: Grune and Stratton.

West, L. J., et al. 1962. The Psychosis of Sleep Deprivation. *Annals of the New York Academy of Sciences*, *96*, 1.

Wexler, M. 1951. The Structural Problem in Schizophrenia. Therapeutic Implications. *IJP*, *32*, 157–66.

Whalen, R. E., ed. 1974. *The Neuropsychology of Aggression*. New York: Plenum Press.

Whiting, B., ed. 1963. *Six Cultures*. New York: Wiley.

Whyte, W. H. 1956. *The Organization Man*. New York: Simon and Schuster.

Wickler, W. 1972. *The Sexual Code*. New York: Doubleday.

Wiemers, I. 1957. The Autonomy of the Ego: History of the Concept. *Provo Papers*, *1*, 61–77.

Wild, C. 1965. Creativity and Adaptive Regression. *Journal of Personality*, *2*, 161–69.

Wilkes, P. 1973. *These Priests Stay*. New York: Simon and Schuster.

Williams, H. L., et al. 1962. Illusions, Hallucinations and Sleep Loss. In J. L. West, ed., *Hallucinations*.

Windholz, E. 1972. Ten Years of COPE: Perspectives in Psychoanalytic Education. *JAPA*, *20*, 567–73.

Winnicott, D. W. 1949. Hate in the Countertransference. *IJP*, *30*, 69–74.

Winnicott, D. W. 1953. Transitional Objects and Transitional Phenomena. *IJP*, *34*, 89–97.

Winnicott, D. W. 1971. *Playing and Reality*. New York: Basic Books.

Winnicott, D. W. 1975. *Through Pediatrics to Psychoanalysis*. New York: Basic Books.

Winterstein, R. F. 1930. Fear of the New, Curiosity and Boredom. *Psychoanalytische Bewegung*, *2*, 540–54.

Witkin, H., and Lewis, H., eds. 1967. *Experimental Studies of Dreaming*. New York: Random House.

Witkin, H., et al. 1954. *Personality through Perception*. New York: Harper.

Wittkower, E. D., and Prince, R. 1974. A Review of Transcultural Psychiatry. In S. Arieti, ed., *American Handbook of Psychiatry*, vol. 2, pp. 535–50.

Wolberg, A. R. 1973. *The Borderline Patient*. New York: Intercontinental Medical Book Corp.

Wolf, A. 1949, 1950. The Psychoanalysis of Groups. *American Journal of Psychotherapy*, *3*, 16–50; *4*, 525–58.

Wolfenstein, M. 1953. Trends in Infant Care. *American Journal of Orthopsychiatry*, *23*, 120–30.

Wolfenstein, M. 1954. *Children's Humor: A Psychological Analysis*. Glencoe, Ill.: Free Press.

Wolfenstein, M. 1976. Effects on Adults of Object Loss in the First Five Years (Panel). *JAPA, 24,* 659–68.

Wolff, H., and Wolf, S. 1947. *Human Gastric Function*. London: Oxford Univ. Press.

Wolff, H., et al., eds. 1950. *Life Stress and Bodily Disease*. Baltimore: Williams and Wilkins.

Wolff, H., et al. 1968. *Stress and Disease*. 2d ed., rev. Springfield, Ill.: C. C. Thomas.

Wolff, P. H. 1960. *The Developmental Psychologies of Jean Piaget and Psychoanalysis*. Psychological Issues Monograph 2. New York: International Univs. Press.

Wolff, P. H. 1967. *Cognitive Considerations for a Psychoanalytic Theory of Language Acquisition*. Psychological Issues Monograph 17. New York: International Univs. Press.

Wolff, P. H. 1969. The Natural History of Crying and Other Vocalizations in Early Infancy. In B. M. Foss, ed., *Determinants of Infant Behavior,* vol. 4, pp. 81–109. London: Methuen.

Wolf Man 1971. *The Wolf Man*. New York: Basic Books.

Wollheim, R., ed. 1974. *Philosophers on Freud*. New York: Jason Aronson.

Wolpert, E. A. 1972. Two Classes of Factors Affecting Dream Recall. *JAPA, 20,* 45–58.

Woods, R. L., and Greenhouse, H. B., eds. 1974. *The New World of Dreams*. New York: Macmillan.

Wortis, J. 1940. *Fragments of an Analysis with Freud*. New York: Simon and Schuster, 1954.

Wynne, L. 1970. Communication Disorders and the Quest for Relatedness in Families of Schizophrenics. *Annual Review of the Schizophrenic Syndrome, 2,* 395–414.

Wynne, L. C., Cromwell, R. L., and Matthysse, S. 1978. *The Nature of Schizophrenia*. New York: Wiley.

Wyss, D. 1966. *Depth Psychology: A Critical History: Development, Problems, Crises*. New York: Norton.

Yazmajian, R. V. 1964. First Dreams Directly Representing the Analyst. *PQ, 33,* 536–51.

Zehn Jahre Berliner Psychoanalytisches Institut. 1930. Reprint ed., Berlin: Berliner Psychoanalytisches Institut, 1970.

Zeligs, M. A. 1957. Acting In: A Contribution to the Meaning of Some Postural Attitudes Observed during Analysis. *JAPA, 5,* 685–706.

Zetzel, E. 1954. Defense Mechanisms and Psychoanalytic Technique (Panel). *JAPA, 2,* 318–26.

Zetzel, E. 1956a. An Approach to the Relation between Concept and Content in Psychoanalytic Theory, with Special Reference to the Work of Melanie Klein and Her Followers. *PSC, 11,* 99–121.

Zetzel, E. 1956b. Current Concepts of Transference. *IJP, 37,* 369–76.

Zetzel, E. 1966. An Obsessional Neurotic. *IJP, 47,* 123–29.

Zinberg, N. 1972. Value Conflict and the Psychoanalyst's Role. In S. Post, ed., *Moral Values and the Superego Concept in Psychoanalysis,* pp. 169–96.

Zwerling, I. 1955. The Favorite Joke in Diagnostic and Therapeutic Interviews. PQ, 24, 104–14.

Zwerling, I. 1977. Community-Based Treatment of Chronic Psychotic Patients. In C. Chiland, ed., *Long-Term Treatments of Psychotic States,* pp. 631–48.

Index

Abraham, Karl, 51, 76, 83, 88, 92, 346, 413, 534; character structure, 329; depression, 407; headed International Psychoanalytic Association, 77; hostility, 390; mania, 408; oral stage, 151; paranoia, 162; schizophrenia, 383; "Short Study of the Development of the Libido, A," 199; symbols, 256, 260

Abreaction, 24

Abstinence, sexual, 49, 436, 483, 484

Academy of Love, 575

Academy of Psychoanalysis, 514; split from American Psychoanalytic Association, 136, 138–40

Achte, K. A.: treatment of schizophrenia, 394

Ackerman, Nathan, 139, 188; family, 426, 488, 489; *Psychodynamics of Family Life, The,* 187

Acting-in, 309

Acting-out, 46, 209, 308–9; disorders, 409

Action for Mental Health, 476

Adaptation, 338–39; concept of, 202; mourning and, 434

Addiction, 187, 220, 389, 409

Adelphi University Post-Doctoral Program, 144

Adelson, E., 214

Adler, Alfred, 73, 79–81, 87, 499; aggressive drive, 56, 58, 217; defection of, 55, 77, 87, 90, 320, 544; defense mechanisms, 295; did not grasp first psychoanalytic system, 78, 83; ego, 293; followers, 81; Freud's "hated enemy," 79, 80, 575; Marxist, 447; at

meetings of Vienna Psychoanalytic Society, 74, 75; organized Society for Free Psychoanalytic Investigation, 81; philosophy, 458; "Psychology of Marxism, The," 438; superficiality of, 81; unconscious, 238; *What Life Should Mean to You,* 458

Adolescence, 176, 177, 192–95, 422; masturbation in, 182; superego in, 443

Adolescent Psychiatry, 195

Adolf Hitler (Stierlin), 563

Adorno, T., 327; *Authoritarian Personality, The,* 479–80, 563

Adulthood, psychosocial states of, 176–77

Aesthetics of Freud, The (Spector), 278

Affect development, 345

Affectional systems, 164

Affects, 294, 552; theory of, 342–50; writings on various, 349–50

Aggression, 58, 200, 215–30, 417, 544; explanations of, 220; in infants, 151–52; of large groups, 229; neutralization of, 221–22, 307; in schizophrenia, 391; social learning theory of, 228; theory of, 202

Aggressive drive, 56, 58

Aging, 197–98, 422; and separation, 432

Ahmed, P. I., 557–58

Aichhorn, August, 107; delinquency, 409

Aim, 221; sexual, 45–47, 192, 412

Alcoholism, 389, 409, 496

Alexander, Franz, 92, 97, 139, 204, 206, 224, 453, 552, 546, 547; analytic success, 532; clinic in Chicago, 105; curative process, 526; dreams, 253; emi-